# Fodor's 06

# COSTA RICA

Where to Stay and Eat
for All Budgets

Must-See Sights
and Local Secrets

Ratings You Can Trust

Fodor's Travel Publications   New York, Toronto, London, Sydney, Auckland
**www.fodors.com**

W9-CPW-871

**FODOR'S COSTA RICA 2006**
**Editor:** Shannon M. Kelly

**Editorial Production:** Linda K. Schmidt
**Editorial Contributors:** Yolanda Hernandez, Dorothy MacKinnon, Joy Rothke, Ryan Sarsfield, Suzanna Starcevic, Jeffrey Van Fleet
**Maps:** David Lindroth, *cartographer;* Bob Blake and Rebecca Baer, *map editors;* additional cartography provided by Henry Colomb, Mark Stroud, and Ali Baird, Moon Street Cartography
**Design:** Fabrizio La Rocca, *creative director*, Chie Ushio, Guido Caroti, Siobhan O'Hare, Tina Malaney, Brian Ponto
**Photography:** Melanie Marin, *senior picture editor*
**Production/Manufacturing:** Angela L. McLean
**Cover Photo** (red-eyed tree frog): ©Turco

**COPYRIGHT**
Copyright © 2006 by Fodors LLC

Fodor's is a registered trademark of Random House, Inc.

All rights reserved under International and Pan-American Copyright Conventions. Published in the United States by Fodor's Travel Publications, a unit of Fodors LLC, a subsidiary of Random House, Inc., and simultaneously in Canada by Random House of Canada Limited, Toronto. Distributed by Random House, Inc., New York.

*No maps, illustrations, or other portions of this book may be reproduced in any form without written permission from the publisher.*

ISBN 1-4000-1551-0

ISSN 1522-6131

**SPECIAL SALES**
This book is available for special discounts for bulk purchases for sales promotions or premiums. Special editions, including personalized covers, excerpts of existing books, and corporate imprints, can be created in large quantities for special needs. For more information, write to Special Markets/ Premium Sales, 1745 Broadway, MD 6-2, New York, New York 10019, or e-mail specialmarkets@ randomhouse.com.

**AN IMPORTANT TIP & AN INVITATION**
Although all prices, opening times, and other details in this book are based on information supplied to us at press time, changes occur all the time in the travel world, and Fodor's cannot accept responsibility for facts that become outdated or for inadvertent errors or omissions. So **always confirm information when it matters,** especially if you're making a detour to visit a specific place. Your experiences—positive and negative—matter to us. If we have missed or misstated something, **please write to us.** We follow up on all suggestions. Contact the Costa Rica editor at editors@fodors. com or c/o Fodor's at 1745 Broadway, New York, NY 10019.

PRINTED IN THE UNITED STATES OF AMERICA

10 9 8 7 6 5 4 3 2 1

# Be a Fodor's Correspondent

Your opinion matters. It matters to us. It matters to your fellow Fodor's travelers, too. And we'd like to hear it. In fact, we *need* to hear it.

When you share your experiences and opinions, you become an active member of the Fodor's community. That means we'll not only use your feedback to make our books better, but we'll publish your names and comments whenever possible. Throughout our guides, look for "Word of Mouth," excerpts of your unvarnished feedback.

Here's how you can help improve Fodor's for all of us.

**Tell us when we're right.** We rely on local writers to give you an insider's perspective. But our writers and staff editors—who are the best in the business—depend on you. Your positive feedback is a vote to renew our recommendations for the next edition.

**Tell us when we're wrong.** We're proud that we update most of our guides every year. But we're not perfect. Things change. Hotels cut services. Museums change hours. Charming cafés lose charm. If our writer didn't quite capture the essence of a place, tell us how you'd do it differently. If any of our descriptions are inaccurate or inadequate, we'll incorporate your changes in the next edition and will correct factual errors at fodors.com *immediately*.

**Tell us what to include.** You probably have had fantastic travel experiences that aren't yet in Fodor's. Why not share them with a community of like-minded travelers? Maybe you chanced upon a beach or bistro or B&B that you don't want to keep to yourself. Tell us why we should include it. And share your discoveries and experiences with everyone directly at fodors.com. Your input may lead us to add a new listing or highlight a place we cover with a "Highly Recommended" star or with our highest rating, "Fodor's Choice."

Give us your opinion instantly at our feedback center at www.fodors.com/feedback. You may also e-mail editors@fodors.com with the subject line "Costa Rica Editor." Or send your nominations, comments, and complaints by mail to Costa Rica Editor, Fodor's, 1745 Broadway, New York, NY 10019.

You and travelers like you are the heart of the Fodor's community. Make our community richer by sharing your experiences. Be a Fodor's correspondent.

Happy traveling!

Tim Jarrell, Publisher

# CONTENTS

# HOW TO USE THIS BOOK

## Our Ratings

Sometimes you find terrific travel experiences and sometimes they just find you. But usually the burden is on you to select the right combination of experiences. That's where our ratings come in.

As travelers we've all discovered a place so wonderful that its worthiness is obvious. And sometimes that place is so experiential that superlatives don't do it justice: you just have to be there to know. These sights, properties, and experiences get our highest rating, **Fodor's Choice**, indicated by orange stars throughout this book.

Black stars highlight sights and properties we deem **Highly Recommended**, places that our writers, editors, and readers praise again and again for consistency and excellence.

By default, there's another category: any place we include in this book is by definition worth your time, unless we say otherwise. And we will.

Disagree with any of our choices? Care to nominate a place or suggest that we rate one more highly? Visit our feedback center at www.fodors.com/feedback.

## Budget Well

Hotel and restaurant price categories from ¢ to $$$$ are defined in the opening pages of each chapter. For attractions, we always give standard adult admission fees; reductions are usually available for children, students, and senior citizens. Want to pay with plastic? **AE, D, DC, MC, V** following restaurant and hotel listings indicate whether American Express, Discover, Diner's Club, MasterCard, and Visa are accepted.

## Restaurants

Unless we state otherwise, restaurants are open for lunch and dinner daily. We mention dress only when there's a specific requirement and reservations only when they're essential or not accepted—it's always best to book ahead.

## Hotels

Hotels have private bath, phone, TV, and air-conditioning and operate on the European Plan (aka EP, meaning without meals), unless we specify that they use the Continental Plan (CP, with a Continental breakfast), Breakfast Plan (BP, with a full breakfast), or Modified American Plan (MAP, with breakfast and dinner) or are all-inclusive (AI, including all meals and most activities). We always list facilities but not whether you'll be charged an extra fee to use them, so when pricing accommodations, find out what's included.

## Many Listings

| | |
|---|---|
| ★ | Fodor's Choice |
| ★ | Highly recommended |
| ⊠ | Physical address |
| ✛ | Directions |
| ⌂ | Mailing address |
| ☎ | Telephone |
| 🖷 | Fax |
| ⊕ | On the Web |
| ✉ | E-mail |
| 🖃 | Admission fee |
| ☉ | Open/closed times |
| ► | Start of walk/itinerary |
| Ⓜ | Metro stations |
| ▭ | Credit cards |

## Hotels & Restaurants

| | |
|---|---|
| 🏨 | Hotel |
| 🛏 | Number of rooms |
| ⚐ | Facilities |
| ⑩ | Meal plans |
| ✕ | Restaurant |
| ⚏ | Reservations |
| 👔 | Dress code |
| ✕🏨 | Hotel with restaurant that warrants a visit |

## Other

| | |
|---|---|
| ☺ | Family-friendly |
| ⚠ | Camping |
| 🔗 | Contact information |
| ⇨ | See also |
| ⊠ | Branch address |
| ☞ | Take note |

| | |
|---|---|
| **SAN JOSÉ** | |
|  | This is not the Costa Rica of the postcards and travel brochures, and you should not sacrifice precious rain-forest and beach days for time in the sprawling, congested capital of San José. It is the political, economic and cultural center of the country, the font from which all things emanate and hub to which all roads lead. To liken the city to New York or London is grossly unfair; it can't compare. But to the Costa Rican out in the provinces it is their Big Apple . . . well, maybe "Big Pineapple." San José is also an amazingly friendly city and, while you should keep your wits about you, it is safer than many other Latin American capitals. No place in Costa Rica can top the city for restaurants, culture, and nightlife, and after a week of slogging through the rain forest your body may crave a dose of civilization. |
| **THE CENTRAL VALLEY** | |
|  | San José is smack dab in the center of this tidy, prosperous mountain valley with numerous day-trip possibilities. The valley's many beautiful inns are alternatives to staying in the capital on your first and last nights in Costa Rica. And in fact, the international airport is not in San José, but in the Central Valley, in Alajuela. The metro area's urban sprawl is spreading to the Central Valley in some spots, as is evidenced by the shopping-malled, office-towered, fast-food-ed highway entrances to Escazú and Santa Ana, but a few kilometers away, oxcarts bearing sugarcane bound for the local mill or coffee beans destined for the local processor trundle down gravel roads. Three provincial capitals—Alajuela, Cartago, and Heredia—pinpoint the valley; all are quieter versions of what San José once was and never will be again. Farther afield lie the country's two most accessible active volcanoes (Poás and Irazú), the historic Orosi Valley, and the agricultural community of Turrialba, fast becoming Costa Rica's white-water capital. |
| **THE NORTHERN PLAINS** | |
|  | It's tough to pigeonhole the vast region that Costa Ricans call the Zona Norte (Northern Zone). Suffice it to say, if you can't find something in the Northern Plains that interests you, you should consider turning in your passport. Monteverde Cloud Forest, a cooler tropical forest, is the place to fly through the forest on a canopy tour—this is the region that gave birth to |

the concept of zipping along cables (while securely harnessed) between treetop platforms. Nearby, Lake Arenal beckons windsurfers, and Arenal Volcano, the world's third most active, spits fire and warms the waters of the Tabacón Hot Springs. Two overlooked and underrated destinations with eco-appeal are the Sarapiquí region, whose many eco-lodges deserve more popularity, and the wetland Caño Negro Reserve near the Nicaraguan border.

**THE NORTH PACIFIC**

Guanacaste Province, the country's most touristed region, manages to combine beaches and bovines without missing a beat. The dry, grassland interior of the Nicoya Peninsula remains the domain of cowboys and cattle, the folkloric image most associated with Costa Rica, although the rest of the country has happily embraced it as its own. A chain of enormously popular beaches lines the coast, and this is the North Pacific of the tourist brochures. Each beach has traits that confer on it a unique personality: Flamingo's quiet refinement is a respite for the well to do; Tamarindo's nightlife is legendary; Avellanas's strong swells draw the surfers; Ostional's nesting sea turtles continue a millennia-old cycle of life; and the Papagayo Peninsula's all-inclusive resorts envelop you in creature comforts. And here's a region with its own small-but-growing international airport, in Liberia. So if your travels are concentrated here, there's no reason to fly in and out of San José at all.

**THE CENTRAL PACIFIC**

Costa Rica's Central Pacific coast mixes sophistication and funkiness, sometimes right down the street from each other. The port city of Puntarenas, once the country's favorite beach destination (but no longer), anchors the region. The beaches south of there are some of the nearest to San José, hours closer than those on the North Pacific coast, and undeniably popular because of their easy access. This is Costa Rica's "party hearty" region, with funky surf towns Jacó and Malpaís and somewhat more refined, but still lively, twin communities Quepos and Manuel Antonio. You need not be a 19-year-old "spring breaker" to enjoy the Central Pacific. Plenty of grown-up and family-friendly activities are available between the dens of revelry, and we've found the best selection of restaurants outside San José on this section of the coast. Some of the

| | |
|---|---|
| THE SOUTH PACIFIC | strands of beach get downright isolated—just you, the macaws, and the monkeys. And calmer beach towns like New-Agey Montezuma are just a ferry ride away, across the gulf on Nicoya Peninsula's southern tip. |
|  | The South rarely sees first-time visitors. In fact, many second- and third-timers have never ventured south of Cartago. But inevitably, once they do, they kick themselves for waiting so long. Terms get bandied about to describe the region: "the Amazon of Costa Rica" or "the most biodiverse place on the planet." Clichéd though they sound, they're true. Corcovado National Park conjures up the Tarzan-movie jungle images you've seen. Lodges in its Osa Peninsula accommodate those who wish to bond with nature but don't wish to sleep *directly* in it. But not all is jungle down here: the region takes in Chirripó, Costa Rica's highest peak, a long hike of moderate difficulty. And Dominical, Zancudo, and Pavones, three of our favorite beach towns, ones rarely mentioned in the fun-in-the-sun pantheon, are here in the South Pacific. Access (or lack thereof) means everything here, and roads can be atrocious even by Costa Rican standards, making it essential to travel by 4WD vehicle or fly. |
| THE CARIBBEAN | |
|  | Despite its name, Costa Rica's Caribbean is no St. Lucia. It doesn't have miles of white-sand beaches or crystal-blue waters. There is a similar English-speaking, Afro-Caribbean population here, but mixed with indigenous, Asian, and the dominant Latino cultures. What this version of the Caribbean (also called "the Atlantic") *does* have is nature galore, with dense forests, coral reefs, and lumbering turtles engaging in age-old nesting rituals. Long the province of European backpackers, the region is less known in North American circles. Many Costa Ricans write it off as all reggae, rain, and robbery. Yes to the first. Mostly yes to the second: it does rain more here than elsewhere in the country, which is why it's so green. But no to the third: crime is no more prevalent here than anywhere else in the country. If you seek luxury resorts, look elsewhere. Instead, the Caribbean has a wide price range in everything from backpackers' digs to trendy bed-and-breakfasts at a fraction of Pacific-coast prices. |

Peñas Blancas

La Cruz

*Gulf of Santa Elena*

Cuajiniquil

SANTA ROSA NATIONAL PARK

*Gulf of Papagayo*

Culebra Bay

El Coro

Flamingo

LAS BAULAS MARINE NATIONAL PARK

Tamarindo

OSTIONAL NATIONAL WILDLIFE RESERVE

Nosara

Sámara

Carrillo

Punta Islita

Mal País

CABO BLANCO STRICT NATURE RESERVE

Montezuma

*Cabo Blanco*

*Lake Nicaragua*

Los Chiles

NIC.

Caño Negro

GUANACASTE NATIONAL PARK

RINCON DE LA VIEJA NATIONAL PARK

Upala

4

6

CAÑO NEGRO NATIONAL WILDLIFE REFUGE

35

4

Carretera Interamericana

CA1

Liberia

Comunidad

PAN-AMERICAN HWY.

Bagaces

LOMAS BARBUDAL BIOLOGICAL RESERVE

Belén

*Tempisque*

Sta. Cruz

Huacas

Filadelfia

BARRA HONDA NATIONAL PARK

21

Nicoya

Nicoya Peninsula

Carmona

Jicaral

Cañas

Santa Elena

PALO VERDE NATIONAL PARK

*Isla Chira*

*Gulf of Nicoya*

Puntarenas

Caldera

Orotina

*Lake Arenal*

**Volcán Arenal**

La Fortuna

Ciudad Quesada (San Carlos)

Tilarán

CORDILLERA DE TILARÁN

MONTEVERDE CLOUD FOREST BIOLOGICAL RESERVE

CA1

JUAN CASTRO BLANCO N.P.

Zarcero

San Ramón

Atenas

Escazú

San Migu

VOLCÁ POÁ NATION PAR

Paquera

Tambor

Cobano

CURÚ NATIONAL WILDLIFE RESERVE

Tárcoles

Jacó

CARARA NATIONAL PARK

PACIFIC OCEAN

TO ISLA DEL COCO

0        30 miles

0        45 km

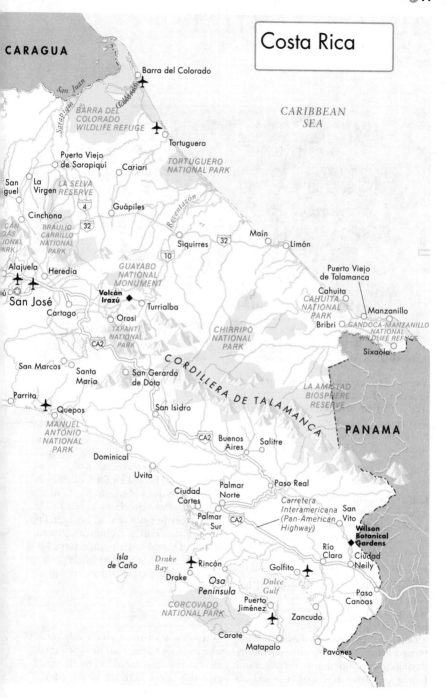

# Costa Rica

CARAGUA

*San Juan*

Barra del Colorado

CARIBBEAN
SEA

*Río Colorado*

*BARRA DEL
COLORADO
WILDLIFE REFUGE*

*Sarapiquí*

Tortuguero

Puerto Viejo
de Sarapiquí

Cariari

*TORTUGUERO
NATIONAL PARK*

San
guel

La
Virgen

*LA SELVA
RESERVE*

4

Guápiles

*Reventazón*

Cinchona

*CAN
GÁS
IONAL
ARK*

*BRAULIO
CARRILLO
NATIONAL
PARK*

32

Moín

Limón

Siquirres

32

10

Alajuela

Heredia

*GUAYABO
NATIONAL
MONUMENT*

Puerto Viejo
de Talamanca

ú

San José

**Volcán
Irazú** ◆

Turrialba

Cahuita
*CAHUITA
NATIONAL
PARK*

Manzanillo

Cartago

Orosi

Bribri

*GANDOCA-MANZANILLO
NATIONAL
WILDLIFE REFUGE*

*TAPANTÍ
NATIONAL
PARK*

*CHIRRIPÓ
NATIONAL
PARK*

Sixaola

CA2

San Marcos

Santa
María

San Gerardo
de Dota

*C O R D I L L E R A   D E   T A L A M A N C A*

*LA AMISTAD
BIOSPHERE
RESERVE*

**PANAMA**

Parrita

Quepos

San Isidro

*MANUEL
ANTONIO
NATIONAL
PARK*

Dominical

Buenos
Aires

Salitre

CA2

Uvita

Palmar
Norte

Paso Real

Ciudad
Cortés

*Carretera
Interamericana
(Pan-American
Highway)*

San
Vito

Palmar
Sur

CA2

**Wilson
Botanical
Gardens** ◆

Río
Claro

*Isla
de Caño*

*Drake
Bay*

Rincón

Golfito

Ciudad
Neily

Drake

*Osa
Peninsula*

*Dulce
Gulf*

Paso
Canoas

*CORCOVADO
NATIONAL PARK*

Puerto
Jiménez

Zancudo

Carate

Matapalo

Pavones

# QUINTESSENTIAL COSTA RICA

You need to scratch below the surface to experience Tico culture—it doesn't hit you like a ton of bricks the way nearby Guatemala's does. The rituals of daily life are quiet, subdued, and peaceful. Costa Ricans wouldn't have it any other way.

## Coffee

Call any Costa Rican business office to speak to someone around 3 PM and you'll probably be told "Está tomando café." (She or he is on a coffee break.) Here in Costa Rica there's no shame in confessing that coffee takes priority over your call.

If nearby Honduras was the original "Banana Republic," 19th-century Costa Rica was a "Coffee Republic," with coffee barons holding enormous sway over the era's affairs. Coffee remains inexorably entwined with the country, with economists paying close attention to world prices and kids in rural areas still taking class time off

to help with the harvest. Costa Rica takes its coffee drinking seriously, and even very young children partake.

The irony is that it's hard to get a decent cup of the stuff here. True to economic realities of developing countries, the quality product gets exported, with the inferior coffee staying behind for the local market. (The same is true of bananas, Costa Rica's other signature agricultural product.) The best places to get a cup of high-quality Costa Rican coffee are upscale restaurants and hotels. Owners understand foreign tastes and have export-quality coffee on hand. Gift shops sell the superior product as well.

## Festivals

Every day is a patron saint's day somewhere in Costa Rica, and unless you spend all your time ensconced in a resort, you'll probably see a sign for some commu-

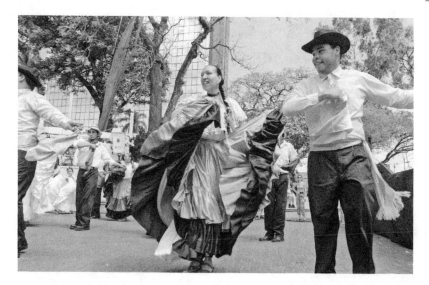

nity's annual *festejo patronale* (patron-saint festival), in homage to its namesake and protector. A loud firecracker explosion rouses participants at dawn to kick off the festivities.

The festivals mirror Costa Rica: devoutly Catholic but increasingly secularized, with bingo games, rickety carnival rides—a certain amount of luck and prayer is in order there—horse parades, and amateurish bullfights. (The bull is not killed in Costa Rica.) The Imperial—Costa Rica's most popular brand of beer—flows copiously. But it is still a religious tradition, and an important part of the day is a mass and parade where the saint's figure is carried through the streets. Visitors are always welcome: "¡Venga!" you'll be told if you stand tentatively at the edge of crowd. "Come, join us!"

## Celebrating Smallness

In a bigger-is-better world it's refreshing to find a country that revels in its smallness. The ostentatious monuments glittering with gold common elsewhere in Latin America are nowhere to be found here. A nation whose first settlers were not conquistadors but hard-working farmers would have none of that. Streets and sidewalks seem a little narrower in Costa Rica, and beds and doorways are a little shorter too. Even the name Costa Ricans give to themselves, Ticos, comes from their peculiar way of forming the diminutive of nouns. Other Spanish speakers add the suffix *-ito* to denote something small (*un momentito*), but Costa Ricans say *un momentico*. (Whether or not it will be just a little moment is another story.) And no phrase brings a sparkle to a Costa Rican's eye like "*Mi país muy chiquitico*" (My very tiny little country).

## Oxcarts

The oxcart is the folkloric symbol of Costa Rica and a common subject for local artisans. The western Central Valley town of Sarchí is the best place to buy these souvenirs, which can take the form of objects as small as paper-clip holders, ashtrays, and earrings, larger items like salad bowls and planters, or full-size oxcarts–turned–coffee tables. (The larger works can be disassembled and shipped home.) Oxcarts do still lumber along rural roads ferrying coffee and sugarcane (and sometimes passengers) to and fro. But in the 21st century they more likely do parade duty; San José holds a large oxcart festival the last weekend in November. The brightly painted carts look anything but utilitarian, with wheels rotating in kaleidoscopic colors.

## Mom & Pop Places

Some 75 percent of the properties in Costa Rica are small, independently owned lodgings with fewer than 30 rooms, even in San José. An individual style imprints each of those lodgings, from scruffy hostels to fashionable inns. What these places lack in a concierge and business center they more than make up for in style and memorable experience. The chain hotels are beginning to take hold in Costa Rica, especially on the North Pacific coast. But the fly-'em-in, fly-'em-out mass tourism fine-tuned in Mexico and the Caribbean Islands remains in its infancy here. That can make a visit to Costa Rica a bit pricier, since you are usually purchasing your lodging, airfare, transportation, and tours à la carte. But it also keeps tourism here more small-scale and exclusive.

Costa Rica has an astounding number of microclimates, dictated by its many forests and changes in altitude, so the weather varies dramatically for such a small country. For information about specific regions, *see* "When to Go" at the front of each chapter.

The sunniest, driest season in most of the country occurs from roughly mid-December through April, which is the busiest tourist season. For you, that means more advance planning, some flexibility in choosing a hotel, and higher prices. Afternoon showers kick in by May and last through November most everywhere, with a brief dry season in June and July. The Caribbean coast flies in the face of these norms with rains spread out fairly evenly throughout the year, with brief *drier* seasons February through April and September through October. Costa Rica promotes the rainy season as the "green season," touting lush vegetation, smaller crowds, and lower prices. Showers interrupt your afternoon beach time and remote roads can be washed out during the worst of the rains.

Temperatures generally range between 70°F (20°C) and 85°F (30°C). It's the humidity, not the heat, that causes you discomfort, especially in the dense forest of the Caribbean coast, the northern lowlands, and the Osa Peninsula. The arid North Pacific is Costa Rica's hottest region, with temperatures frequently exceeding 90°F (33°C) in the dry season.

One final point: We typically hear: "I didn't realize the rain forest would be so . . . *rainy.*" Well, you heard it here: it rains often and heartily in the rain forest. The dense foliage and elaborate root systems rely on frequent showers year-round.

## Climate

⑦ Forecasts **Weather Channel Connection** ☎ 900/932–8437 95¢ per minute from a Touch-Tone phone ⊕ www.weather.com.

San José's average temperatures are typical of other highland towns; and Golfito's are similar to those of most coastal and lowland towns.

# IF YOU LIKE . . .

## Beaches

Costa Rica has 1,278 km (767 mi) of coastline to choose from, most of it lined with beaches, which are, by law, all public. Most are not the picture-postcard white strands of the Caribbean Islands or Mexico; the dark sand here is of volcanic origin and waters tend to be rough, not crystal-blue. Limited access tends to make for more scenic beaches. The following are some of our favorites.

- **Dominical, South Pacific.** A town's flavor does enhance the experience, and in that regard we recommend this great beach in a great beach town.

- **Malpaís, Central Pacific.** Accessed via a steep gravel road, Malpaís is a quiet strand ripe for beachcombing and sunning.

- **Playa Flamingo, North Pacific.** Though not very isolated, Flamingo is an example of how environmentally conscious communities can make their beaches sparkle.

- **Playa Grande, North Pacific.** Conservationists have kept this beach pristine for nesting leatherback turtles.

- **Playa Pavones, South Pacific.** The surfing is good at remote Pavones, a stunning combination of black sand, tropical forest, and glistening waters.

- **Punta Uva, Caribbean.** The farthest from town of the Puerto Viejo de Talamanca beaches, and the most pristine.

- **Tortuguero, Caribbean.** The turtle population here makes this isolated beach one of the world's top naturalist draws.

## Bird-Watching

As part of the narrow isthmus connecting the Americas, Costa Rica is a natural biological melting pot. With less than 0.03% of the planet's surface it is home to 876 bird species, more than the United States and Canada combined. Some stay year-round; others come and go with winter migration.

- **Caño Negro, Northern Plains.** Waterfowl, such as jabiru and snail kites, are abundant.

- **Carara National Park, Central Pacific.** Scarlet macaws are reliable sightings, as are great egrets, boat-billed herons, anhingas, and trogons.

- **Cerro de La Muerte, South Pacific.** This is probably the best place in the country to spot a resplendent quetzal.

- **Corcovado National Park, South Pacific.** The largest population of (endangered) scarlet macaws in the country lives here.

- **La Selva Biological Station, Northern Plains.** If you're interested in (but totally clueless about) bird-watching, sign up in advance for the Birdwatching 101 course. Scientists have tallied nearly 500 species here.

- **Monteverde Cloud Forest, Northern Plains.** The resplendent quetzal, the blue-crowned motmot, the orange-bellied trogon, and the emerald toucanet are just some of the 400 species that have been logged here.

- **Tortuguero National Park, Caribbean.** The bare-throated tiger heron, the sungrebe, and the agami heron are some of Torgutuero's many waterfowl species.

## Rain Forests

Costa Rica has set aside some 15 percent of its territory for national parks and reserves. Yet deforestation takes place at an alarming rate, its old-growth forests falling victim to illegal logging, aided by a scarcity of resources to enforce environmental laws and the pressures of development. That said, Costa Rica's existing rain forests thrive. A typical hectare (2½ acres) of forest might be home to nearly 100 species of trees. (Contrast that with a mere 30 in the richest forests of North America.) Go with a guide, both for your safety and the information they can provide. We forever marvel at their ability to spot a sloth at a hundred paces.

- **Braulio Carrillo National Park, Northern Plains.** Though it's the closest rain forest to San José, this primary swath of jungle is difficult to access, with dense flora and tough trails. But determination yields impressive mammals, birds, and plants.

- **Corcovado National Park, South Pacific.** If you don't mind the mud, you'll love the wild and wooly primary forests here.

- **La Selva Biological Station, Northern Plains.** One of the best opportunities to see lots of wildlife without roughing it.

- **Manuel Antonio National Park, Central Pacific.** Even a quick jaunt along the trails lets you see squirrel monkeys, white-faced coatis, and iguanas.

- **Monteverde Cloud Forest Reserve, Northern Plains.** The most famous of Costa Rica's cloud-forest reserves.

## Surfing

Deliciously warm water, year-round waves, and two coasts add up to one of the world's best-known surfing destinations. There's even better news: that popularity hasn't yet translated into overcrowding. Most surfers bring their own boards, as evidenced by the crowds that get off the plane and make a beeline for the oversize luggage carousel, but you'll find plenty of places to rent equipment if you're not quite that hardcore.

- **Jacó, Central Pacific.** Easily accessible Jacó draws the many surfers who come here as much for the partying as the waves.

- **Pavones, South Pacific.** It's a long trip here, but your reward is one of the world's longest left-breaking waves.

- **Puerto Viejo de Talamanca, Caribbean.** One of the world's best (and toughest) waves, Salsa Brava, laps right offshore in town.

- **Tamarindo, North Pacific.** The north coast's consummate surfing town and a good place for beginners; the stretch of shoreline north to Playa Grande and south to Playa Negra satisfies experts.

## Volcanoes

Of Costa Rica's 300 or so volcanoes, 5 are active (listed below), 60 have been labeled "dormant"—projected to spring back to life at some undetermined future date—and the rest are extinct. Volcán Irazú got its second wind in 1963 after 30 years of inactivity. No one was more surprised than John F. Kennedy, who was here on a visit at the time and was sprinkled with ash like everyone else. Over four decades later, prediction is still an imprecise science.

- **Arenal, Northern Plains.** The most famous volcano in Costa Rica, Arenal has a classic cone that forms an iconic backdrop to the town of La Fortuna. On clear nights you can see red-hot lava spitting from its summit.

- **Irazú, Central Valley.** A cinch to visit as a day trip from San José, here you can walk right up to the edge of steaming craters.

- **Poás, Northern Plains.** Like Irazú, at Poás you can get close the crater, and it is also close to San José. We find Poás, with its beautiful crater lake, a bit more impressive.

- **Rincón de la Vieja, North Pacific.** This moonlike landscape of steaming craters and fizzing fumaroles is worth the rugged drive and rough hike.

- **Turrialba, Central Valley.** The least-visited of the active volcanoes, Turrialba rises 3,320 m (10,900) feet above sea level. You can see the Pacific on a clear day.

## White-Water Rafting or Kayaking

There's a reason why half a dozen Olympic kayaking teams spend the winter on the wild rivers of Costa Rica: steep hills and heavy rainfall make the country a mecca for whitewater sports, and there's a level of ease or difficulty to match anyone's expertise (or lack thereof). Have fun, but be brutally frank with yourself about your abilities and fears before setting out on any rafting or kayaking excursion. (*See* the CloseUp box "White-Water Thrills" *in* chapter 2 for more guidelines.) Base yourself in these places to find white-water outfitters.

- **La Fortuna, Northern Plains.** Trips on the Toro, Balsa, San Carlos, and Sarapiquí rivers are offered out of La Fortuna.

- **Puerto Viejo de Sarapiquí, Northern Plains.** Outfitters based here can take you on similar excursions to those offered from La Fortuna.

- **Quepos, Central Pacific.** Head here for action on the Savegre and Naranjo rivers.

- **San José.** You might not guess it, but San José is a major rafting center; the Reventazón and Pacuare rivers are close enough that you can be back in time for dinner. The Pacuare, El General and Corobicí rivers lend themselves to overnight or multiday trips.

- **Turrialba, Central Valley.** Many outfitters congregate in Turrialba, arguably the country's white-water capital, and close to the action.

## BEACHES, RAIN FORESTS, AND VOLCANOES

### Day 1: Arrival

Arrive in San José (most arrivals are in the evening) and head straight to one of the small luxury hotels north of the city in the Central Valley. A favorite of ours is Finca Rosa Blanca, a fairy-tale retreat overlooking miles of coffee farms.

**Logistics:** Brace yourself for long lines at immigration if you arrive in the evening along with all the other large flights from North America. Try to get a seat near the front of the plane and don't dawdle when disembarking.

### Day 2: Poás Volcano and Tabacón Hot Springs

Volcán Poás, where you can peer over the edge of a crater, lies nearby. Fortify yourself with the fruits, jellies, and chocolates sold by vendors on the road up to the summit. A scenic drive takes you to the La Fortuna/Arenal Volcano area. Drop your luggage at one of many fantastic hotels (Montaña de Fuego is our pick for fabulous volcano views), and go directly to Tabacón Hot Springs & Resort. Take a zip-line or hanging bridges tour through the forest canopy and then pamper yourself with a spa treatment. Finish the day by sinking into a volcanically heated mineral bath with a cocktail at your side as the sun sets behind fiery Arenal.

**Logistics:** Get an early start to get the best views of Poás. Shuttle vans ( ⇨ Bus Travel *in* Smart Travel Tips A to Z) can get you to Arenal and have hotel-to-hotel service.

### Day 3: Caño Negro Wildlife Refuge

Spend your entire day in the Caño Negro Wildlife Refuge, a lowland forest reserve replete with waterfowl near the Nicaraguan border.

**Logistics:** Book your trip the night before; tour operators in La Fortuna keep evening hours for exactly that reason. All transport will be included.

### Day 4: Scenic Drive to the Central Pacific

Today's a traveling day—a chance to really see the country's famous landscape and infamous roads. (Believe us, they get a lot worse than this route.) A few hours' drive from Arenal takes you to fabled Manuel Antonio on the Central Pacific coast. Beyond-beautiful hotels are the norm here, and you have your choice of seaside villas or tree-shrouded jungle lodges. We like the hillside La Mariposa, which has commanding views.

**Logistics:** Hotel-to-hotel shuttle-van services ( ⇨ Bus Travel *in* Smart Travel Tips A to Z) can get you to Manuel Antonio. If you drive instead, start out as early as possible. You'll pass through two mountainous stretches (between La Fortuna and San Ramón, and between Atenas and the coast) that fog over by mid-afternoon.

### Day 5: Manuel Antonio National Park

Manuel Antonio is Costa Rica's most famous national park for a reason: it has beaches, lush rain forest, mangrove swamps, and rocky coves with abundant marine life. You can—and should—spend an entire day exploring the park, home to capuchin monkeys, sloths, agoutis, and 200 species of birds. It's also one of two locales in the country where you'll see squirrel monkeys.

**Logistics:** Almost all Manuel Antonio hotels have transport to the park. If yours doesn't, taxis are plentiful and cheap.

### Day 6: Beach Yourself

Days 1 through 5 were "on the go" days. Reward yourself today with lots of relaxation. Manuel Antonio means beaches, and there are several to choose from. Manuel Antonio and neighboring Quepos mean restaurants, too, the best selection of any beach community in the country.

**Logistics:** Most everything you need here strings along the 5-km (3-mi) road between Quepos and Manuel Antonio National Park. It's practically impossible to get lost.

### Day 7: San José

A morning drive back to San José gives you time to spend the afternoon in the city. We like the cozy, classy Hotel Le Bergerac. Visit the Teatro Nacional, the capital's must-see sight, and save time for late-afternoon shopping. An evening dinner caps off your trip before you turn in early to get ready for tomorrow morning's departure.

**Logistics:** As the number of visitors to Costa Rica grows, so does the number of passengers using Juan Santamaría Airport. We recommend you check in three hours before your flight. Better safe than sorry.

## TIPS

1. Other than Day 2, it's entirely possible to do this route without a car.

2. Hotels in the Central Valley and San José are used to booking visitors for their first and last nights in the country, and may allow you to leave items so you don't have to lug them around.

3. Arenal lies equidistant between Liberia and San José, but we suggest flying into San José for this itinerary because road access to Arenal and from Manuel Antonio is better.

4. Cloud cover makes volcano viewing the luck of the draw, and no one can negotiate with Mother Nature. Early mornings and dry season give you the best chances for seeing Arenal and Poás in action.

5. Get as early a start as possible if you're driving. The mountain roads between San José and La Fortuna and between Manuel Antonio and San José can fog over by mid-afternoon.

# MORE BEACHES, RAIN FORESTS, AND VOLCANOES

### Day 1: Arrival

Most arrivals to Liberia, Costa Rica's second international airport, are in early afternoon. You can't go wrong with any North Pacific beach, but we like Playa Hermosa for its pivotal location, one that lets you use it as a base for visiting area attractions. Check out small, personal, breezy Hotel Playa Hermosa/Bosque del Mar, the perfect antidote to the mega-resorts that lie not too far away.

**Logistics:** The big all-inclusives up here have their own minivans to whisk you in air-conditioned comfort from airport to resort. Smaller lodgings such as Hotel Playa Hermosa/Bosque del Mar can arrange to have transport waiting, with advance notice.

### Day 2: Playa Hermosa

Morning is a great time to laze on the beach in this part of Costa Rica. The breezes are refreshingly cool and the sun hasn't started to beat down. After lunch, explore Playa Hermosa's metropolis, the small town of Playas del Coco. Quite frankly Coco is our least favorite beach up here. But we like the town for its little souvenir shops, restaurants, and local color.

**Logistics:** Taxis are the easiest way to travel between Playa Hermosa and Coco, about 10 minutes away. Have your hotel call one, and flag one down on the street in town when it's time to return.

### Day 3: Rincón de la Vieja Volcano

The top of Rincón de la Vieja Volcano with its steaming, bubbling, oozing fumaroles lies about 90 minutes from Hermosa. Lather on the sunscreen and head for the Hacienda Guachipelín and its volcano-viewing hikes, canopy tours, rappelling, horse riding, mountain biking, and river tubing. Cap off the day with a spa treatment, complete with thermal mud bath.

**Logistics:** If you don't have a rental car, book a private driver for the day, which can usually be arranged through your hotel.

### Day 4: Golf or Diving

Golf is big up here. The 18-hole Garra de León course at the Paradisus Playa Conchal resort is about 45 minutes from Hermosa. The other popular, slightly pricey, sport here is scuba diving. Dive operators are based in nearby Playas del Coco or Playa Panamá. A daylong course gives you a taste of the deep.

**Logistics:** The resort will arrange transport to and from the golf course, and dive operators will pick you up from and return you to your hotel.

### Day 5: Palo Verde National Park

We like the morning guided tours at Palo Verde National Park, one of the last remaining dry tropical forests in Central America. The Organization for Tropical Studies, which operates the biological station there, has terrific guides. Spend the afternoon observing nature in a more relaxed fashion with a float down the nearby Río Corobicí. (These are *not* screaming rapids so famed in white-water circles.)

**Logistics:** This excursion is a bit roundabout, so this is the day that your own vehicle would come in handiest. But you can also hire a private driver (arranged through your hotel). Bring water to drink: it gets hot here.

## Day 6: Sailing

Make your final day a relaxing one with a few hours on the waves. Many sailboats operate out from this section of coast. Our choice is the 52-foot *Samonique III* ( ⇨chapter 4) which sails out of Playa Flamingo most afternoons at 2. A four-hour excursion includes sandwiches, appetizers, and an open bar. Legendary Pacific sunsets are tossed in at no extra charge.

**Logistics:** The *Samonique III* folks can arrange transport from hotel to boat and back again.

## Day 7: Departure

Grab a last dip in the ocean this morning, because your flight departs from Liberia in the early afternoon.

**Logistics:** The advent of international flights to Liberia has fueled this region's meteoric rise to fame, but the airport's size has not kept pace with the number of passengers. Expansion is eventually on the way, but presently lines can be long. Allow yourself plenty of time for check-in.

### TIPS

❶ Fly into Liberia. While it's logical to think "San José" when planning flights to Costa Rica, it makes no sense if you plan to spend your entire time in the North Pacific.

❷ A car is ideal for this itinerary, yet many area attractions and tour operators provide transport to and from area lodging if you aren't too far afield. (One of the reasons we like Playa Hermosa.)

❸ All-inclusive resorts do a good job of organizing local excursions with local operators, so if you're staying at one, take advantage of them.

❹ Beach to beach often requires travel back inland. There is no real (i.e. navigable) coastal road.

❺ If ever there were a case for an off-season vacation, this is it. This driest, hottest part of the country gets very dry and hot from January through April. The rains green everything up, and frankly, we prefer the region during the low season.

# SMART TRAVEL TIPS

*Consult the A to Z sections that end each chapter for information as it relates to specific regions.*

## ADDRESSES

In Costa Rica, addresses are usually given in terms of how many meters the place is from a landmark. Street names and building numbers are not commonly used. Churches, stores, even large trees that no longer exist—almost anything can be a landmark, as long as everyone knows where it is, or where it used to be. A typical address in San José is *100 metros este y 100 metros sur de Más X Menos* (100 meters east and 100 meters south from the Más X Menos supermarket).

■ TIP→→ In towns and cities in Costa Rica, each block is assumed to be 100 meters, although some blocks may be much longer and some may be shorter. So if someone tells you to head down the road 500 meters, they mean 5 blocks. Ticos, as Costa Ricans call themselves, are generally happy to help lost visitors, and they spend a lot of time describing where things are. But be warned—even if they don't know where something is, Ticos will often give uncertain or even wrong information rather than seem unhelpful; triangulated direction-asking is a must. Ask at least two, if not three, people in quick succession to avoid getting hopelessly lost. Key direction terms are: *lugar* (place), *calle* (street), *avenida* (avenue), *puente* (bridge), *piso* (floor), *edificio* (building), *cruce* (intersection), *semáforo* (traffic light), *rotonda* (traffic circle) and *cuadro* (block).

## AIR TRAVEL

### ARRIVING & DEPARTING

If you are visiting several regions of the country, flying into San José's Juan Santamaria Airport, in the center of the country, is the best option. Flying into Liberia's Daniel Oduber Airport makes sense if you are planning to spend your vacation in Guanacaste. Bus travel time between the Liberia airport and most of the resorts is less than two hours.

Most travelers fly into the larger San José airport, the transportation hub to nearly every point in the country. Rarely does an international flight get into San José early enough to make a domestic connection, as the weather for flying is typically clear until about noon only. So you'll likely end up spending your first night in or near the city, and leave for your domestic destination the next morning out of the SANSA terminal next to the international airport or via NatureAir out of tiny Tobias Bolaños Airport.

Heavy rains in the afternoons and evenings during the May-to-November rainy season sometimes cause flights coming into San José to be rerouted to Panama City, where you may be forced to spend the night. ■ TIP➜➜ In the rainy season, always book a flight with the earliest arrival time available.

Once in Costa Rica, some airlines recommend calling the San José office about three days before your return flight to reconfirm; others, such as TACA, explicitly say it's not necessary. It's always a good idea to call the local office the day before you are scheduled to return home to make sure your flight time hasn't changed.

**From the United States:** Miami has the highest number of direct flights, but nonstop flights are also available from New York, Houston, Miami, Dallas, Atlanta, Chicago, Phoenix, Washington, D.C., Charlotte, and Los Angeles. Continental, American, America West, Delta, US Airways, and United are the major U.S. carriers with nonstop service to Costa Rica. Martinair has nonstop flights from Orlando and Miami. From New York, flights to San José are 5½ hours nonstop or 6 to 7 hours via Miami. From Los Angeles, flights are about 6 to 7 hours nonstop or 8½ hours via Mexico; from Houston, 3½ hours nonstop; from Miami, 3 hours; from Charlotte, 4 hours; and from Chicago, 5½ hours. In general, nonstop flights aren't that much more expensive.

Other than obvious considerations such as price and scheduling, a regional airline like Mexicana and TACA (a Central American airline) is a good choice if you're visiting more than one Central American country;

major U.S. airlines don't serve routes such as Costa Rica–Honduras.

**From Canada:** Flights from central and eastern Canada usually connect through Chicago, Miami, or New York, though Air Canada has nonstop flights from Toronto. The best routes from Vancouver usually go through Houston or Dallas, although it's possible to fly through L.A. Flight times vary widely, but direct from Toronto is usually about 6 hours; flights from Vancouver are generally about 9 to 11 hours, including the layover. If you're flying from western Canada, ask travel agents about Skyservice charters—they are the only direct (no plane change, but a stop in Calgary) access from Vancouver. Flying from Seattle is much cheaper than flying from Vancouver—usually as much as half the price, and the Quick Shuttle company provides convenient and excellent service between Vancouver and Sea-Tac airport (about 4 hours) for less than $40; the timing works best for the overnight to San José. The total return trip, including the shuttle, takes about as long as the San José–Vancouver flight.

**From the U.K.:** Flights from London usually stop in Madrid, Miami, Washington, D.C., Dallas, or Mexico City. Flying times to San José from London vary widely, depending on the routing and the number of connections, but the shortest travel time you should expect is about 15½ hours through Houston. American Airlines, United, and Iberia fly from the U.K.

**From Australia or New Zealand:** Consult a travel agent, who will probably send you first to Los Angeles and then on to Costa Rica. Flying times to San José from Sydney and Auckland vary widely, depending on the routing and the number of connections, but the shortest travel time you should expect is about 21 hours. Generally it's faster to stop both in Los Angeles and Miami than wait for a direct flight to Costa Rica from Los Angeles.

**From Nicaragua or Panama:** International flights to Costa Rica tend to be cheaper than those to Nicaragua or Panama, so if you're doing two or three countries, it makes sense, budget-wise, to start in Costa Rica. Copa, TACA, and Lacsa fly between

Panama City and San José and between Managua, Nicaragua, and San José. NatureAir flies between Granada, Nicaragua, and Liberia or San José, and between Bocas del Toro, Panama, and San José. In May 2006 NatureAir plans to begin flights between Bocas del Toro and Limón.

**✈ Major Airlines Air Canada** ☎ 888/247-2262 in Canada, 888/422-7533 or 506/243-1860 in Costa Rica ⊕ www.aircanada.com. **American Airlines** ☎ 800/433-7300 in U.S., 0207/365-0777 in U.K., 300/650-747 in Australia, 0800/887-997 in New Zealand, 506/257-1266 in Costa Rica ⊕ www.aa. com. **America West** ☎ 800/327-7810 in U.S., Costa Rica, inquiries by e-mail only ⊕ www. americawest.com. **Continental** ☎ 800/231-0856 in U.S. 0800/044-0005 in Costa Rica ⊕ www. continental.com. **Delta** ☎ 800/241-4141 in U.S., 506/257-4141 in Costa Rica ⊕ www.delta.com. **Iberia** ☎ 0845/850-9000 in U.K., 506/257-8266 in Costa Rica ⊕ www.iberia.com. **MartinAir** ☎ 800/627-8462 in U.S., 506/232-3246 in Costa Rica

⊕ www.martinairusa.com. **United Airlines** ☎ 800/241-6522 in U.S., 0845/844-4777 in U.K., 0800/052-1243 in Costa Rica. **US Airways** ☎ 800/622-1015 in U.S. and Canada, 430-6690 in Costa Rica ⊕ www. usair.com.

**✈ Regional Airlines Copa** ☎ 800/359-2672 in U.S., 506/223-2672 in Costa Rica ⊕ www.copaair. com. **Mexicana** ☎ 800/531-7921 in U.S., 866/281-3049 in Canada, 506/295-6969 in Costa Rica ⊕ www.mexicana.com. **TACA** ☎ 800/400-8222 in U.S., 800/722-8222 in Canada, 506/296-9353 in Costa Rica, ⊕ www.grupotaca.com.

## GETTING AROUND

Given Costa Rica's often difficult driving conditions, distances that appear short on a map can represent hours of driving on dirt roads pocked with craters; buses can be a slow and uncomfortable way to travel. Domestic flights are a desirable and practical option. And because 4WD rental rates can be steep, flying is often cheaper than driving. Most major destinations are served by daily domestic flights.

The informality of domestic air service— "airports" outside of Liberia and San José usually consist of simply an airstrip with no central building at which to buy tickets—means you might want to purchase your domestic airplane tickets in advance (by phone or online), although you can buy them at the San José or Liberia airports or at travel agencies once you're in the country. In theory, you can purchase tickets up to two hours before the flight is set to go. This is a potentially viable option in the May–October low season, but we recommend grabbing a seat as soon as you know your itinerary.

There are three domestic commercial airlines: SANSA, NatureAir, and Macaw Air. Most NatureAir and SANSA flights leave from the San José area (⇨ Airports). Commercial planes are small—holding between 6 and 19 passengers. Macaw Air flies its six-passenger Cessna 206 out of Liberia, allowing you to bypass San José altogether. Domestic flights are nonstop, with the exception of some flights to the far south, where you might stop in Drake Bay first, then continue on to Puerto Jiménez, for example. You can buy SANSA and NatureAir tickets online, over the phone, and at most travel agencies in Costa Rica. Buy Macaw Air tickets online or by phone. ■ TIP➜➜ SANSA air passes— $199 for one week and $249 for two weeks— can be a good deal.

Charter flights within Costa Rica are not as expensive as one might think, and can be an especially good deal if you are traveling with a group of four to eight people. If a group this size charters a small plane, the price per person will be only slightly more than taking a regularly scheduled domestic flight, and you can set your own departure time. The country has dozens of airstrips that are accessible only by charter planes. The charter companies listed here do not have English-speaking staff, though some allow online booking. Charter planes are most often booked through tour operators, travel agents, or remote lodges.

Most charter planes are smaller than domestic commercial planes—you might even end up on a tiny four-seat supply plane with no copilot.

⚠ Don't book a domestic flight on the day you arrive in or leave Costa Rica; connections will be extremely tight, if possible at all, and you'll be at the mercy of tempermental weather and delays.

🛪 Domestic & Charter Airlines Aerobell Air Charter ☎ 506/290-0000 ⊕ www.aerobell.com. Macaw Air ☎ 506/653-1362 ⊕ www.macawair. com. NatureAir ☎ 800/235-9272 in the U.S. or Canada, 506/299-6000 in Costa Rica ⊕ www. natureair.com. SANSA ☎ 506/221-9414 or 506/441-8035 ⊕ www.flysansa.com.

## BAGGAGE ALLOWANCES

The tiny, domestic passenger planes in Costa Rica require that you pack light. A luggage weight limit of 25 pounds (11.3 kilograms) is imposed by all airlines. Weight restrictions include carry-ons. On some flights extra luggage is allowed, but is charged about 50¢–55¢ per pound. Heavy packers can leave their surplus for free in a locked area at NatureAir's terminal. SANSA flyers can pay to have their extra luggage stored in a locked warehouse ($5/day for large bags, $3/day for small).

## LOST LUGGAGE

If you arrive in Costa Rica and your baggage doesn't, the first thing you should do is go to the baggage claims counter and file an official report with your specific contact information. Then call your airline to find out if they can track it and how long you have to wait—generally bags are located within two days. Continue on your trip as you can; bags can be sent to you just about anywhere in the country. Don't expect too much from local officials; try to get updates from the airline directly.

If your bag has been searched and contents are missing or damaged, file a claim with the TSA Consumer Response Center as soon as possible. If your bags arrive damaged or fail to arrive at all, file a written report with the airline before leaving the airport.

# DOMESTIC FLIGHTS FROM INTERNATIONAL AIRPORTS

*Flight times and prices are accurate at this writing, but are subject to change.*
*SANSA flights leave from a terminal near Juan Santamaría International Airport;*
*NatureAir flights leave from Tobías Bolaños Airport, in the San José suburb of Pavas.*

| DESTINATION (from San José) | DOMESTIC AIRLINES | DAILY DEPARTURE TIMES | DURATION OF FLIGHT | ROUND-TRIP PRICE ($US) *one-way price is half of RT price |
|---|---|---|---|---|
| Barra del Colorado | NatureAir | 6:15 am | 30 min | $142 |
| Barra del Colorado | SANSA | 6 am | 50 min | $124 |
| Drake Bay | NatureAir | 8:45 am; 2 pm | 45 min | $170 |
| Drake Bay | SANSA | 9:30 am; 2:05 pm | 50 min | $146 |
| Golfito | NatureAir | 6, 8 am | 1 hr 10 min | $168 |
| Golfito | SANSA | 6, 10:30 am; 2:15 pm | 1 hr | $142 |
| La Fortuna | NatureAir | noon | 30 min | $130 |
| Liberia | NatureAir | 11 am; 3 pm | 1 hr 15 min | $160 |
| Liberia | SANSA | 11:35 am | 1 hr | $132 |
| Nosara | NatureAir | 9:15 am; 1 pm | 50 min | $160 |
| Nosara | SANSA | 7:50 am | 40 min | $142 |
| Puerto Jiménez | NatureAir | 8:30, 10:45 am; 2 pm | 1 hr 10 min | $168 |
| Puerto Jiménez | SANSA | 6, 9:30 am; 2:05 pm | 50 min | $142 |
| Punta Islita | NatureAir | 7, 9 am; 1:30 pm | 25 min | $160 |
| Punta Islita | SANSA | 7 am | 40 min | $142 |
| Quepos | NatureAir | 7:35, 9, 11 am; 4:30 pm | 30 min | $100 |
| Quepos | SANSA | 7:45, 8:50, 11 am; 12:50, 2:40, 4:25 pm | 30 min | $95 |
| Sámara (Carrillo) | SANSA | 7:50 am | 1 hr | $142 |
| Tamarindo | NatureAir | 11 am; 4 pm | 50 min | $160 |
| Tamarindo | SANSA | 6:10, 9:30 am; 12:30, 2:25, 3:25 pm | 1 hr | $142 |
| Tambor | NatureAir | 9:15 am; 1:30 pm | 30 min | $132 |
| Tambor | SANSA | 7, 10:25, 11:45 am; 4:25 pm | 30 min | $116 |
| Tortuguero | NatureAir | 6:15 am | 50 min | $142 |
| Tortuguero | SANSA | 6 am | 40 min | $124 |
| **FROM LIBERIA** | | | | |
| Nosara | Macaw Air | 7 am | 40 min | $150 |
| Quepos | Macaw Air | 7 am | 1 hr 45 min | $270 |
| Tambor | Macaw Air | 7 am | 1 hr 10 min | $170 |
| Tamarindo | Macaw Air | 7 am | 15 min | $100 |

**NatureAir** *also has flights between Quepos and Palmar Sur (near Drake Bay), and Quepos and Puerto Jiménez.*
**Macaw Air** *also has flights between Tamarindo and Nosara, Tambor, and Quepos.*

## HOW TO COMPLAIN

If your baggage goes astray or your flight goes awry, complain right away. Most carriers require that you **file a claim immediately.** The Aviation Consumer Protection Division of the Department of Transportation publishes *Fly-Rights,* which discusses airlines and consumer issues and is available online. You can also find articles and information on mytravelrights.com, the Web site of the nonprofit Consumer Travel Rights Center.

➶ Airline Complaints **Aviation Consumer Protection Division** ☎ 202/366-2220 ⊕ airconsumer.ost.dot.gov. **Federal Aviation Administration Consumer Hotline** ☎ 800/322-7873 ⊕ www.faa.gov. **Transportation Security Administration** ☎ 866/289-9673 ⊕ www.tsa.gov.

## RECONFIRMING

Once in Costa Rica, reconfirming is not necessary, but you may feel better if you do it. Call the local number three days before departure to confirm.

## CUTTING COSTS

• Start looking as early as possible.

• You can usually get the best deals from May to November, the rainy season in most of Costa Rica.

• Look for departures on Tuesdays, Wednesdays, and Thursdays, typically the cheapest days to travel.

• Don't limit yourself to online consolidators like Priceline.com; tickets directly from the airline are often the best deal.

• Check for departures at different times of the day and from various airports.

• Repeatedly check online travel sites and the airline's Web site for deals.

• When you find a good price, buy immediately. Waiting even 20 minutes might mean paying more.

• If after buying a ticket you find that the price has dropped considerably, request a voucher for the difference from the airline. Most will comply, but will subtract a standard ticket reissue fee.

• Depending on the time of year and what airline specials are available, the cheapest way to arrive may be to combine a round-trip ticket from Miami with a separate round-trip ticket from your departure city. Check these deals carefully, as the cheapest "Miami"–Costa Rica carrier is generally US Airways, which flies from Fort Lauderdale. The hassle and costs of transfer between airports may outweigh the benefits.

• Remember that what you get is as important as what you save. A cheaper flight might have a long layover rather than being nonstop, or it might land at a secondary airport where your ground transportation costs are high.

• When buying from an online consolidator like Priceline, carefully read the fine print detailing penalties for changes and cancellations. Also, be sure to confirm your reservation.

➶ U.S. & Canada Consolidators **Cheap Tickets** ⊕ www.cheaptickets.com. **Expedia** ⊕ www.expedia.com. **Hotwire** ⊕ www.hotwire.com. **Onetravel.com** ⊕ www.onetravel.com. **Orbitz** ⊕ www.orbitz.com. **Priceline.com** ⊕ www.priceline.com. **Travelocity** ⊕ www.travelocity.com.

➶ U.K. Consolidators **cheapestflights** ⊕ www.cheapestflights.co.uk. **Dial-A-Flight** ⊕ www.dialaflight.com. **lastminute.com** ⊕ www.lastminute.com.

➶ Australia Consolidators **lastminute.com** ⊕ www.lastminute.com. **travel.com.au** ⊕ www3.travel.com.au. **Zuji** ⊕ www.zuji.com.au.

➶ New Zealand Consolidator **Travelonline** ⊕ www.travelonline.co.nz.

## AIRPORTS

Costa Rica has two international airports. Juan Santamaría International Airport (SJO) is the country's main airport. It's about 24 km (15 mi), or 30 minutes by car, north of downtown San José, just outside the city of Alajuela. The SANSA terminal for domestic flights is here. The country's other international airport is Daniel Oduber International Airport (LIR), a small airport near Liberia, in the North Pacific, the hub for domestic airline Macaw Air. Only five airlines fly to Liberia: United Airlines, from Chicago; American Airlines, from Miami; Delta, from Atlanta; Continental, from Houston; and US Airways, from Charlotte, NC. The tiny Tobias Bolaños airport, in the San José suburb of Pavas (west of the city), serves domestic airline NatureAir, domestic charter companies, and a handful of private planes.

Other places where planes land in Costa Rica aren't exactly airports. They more resemble a carport with a landing strip, at which an airline representative arrives just minutes before a plane is due to land or take off.

Prepare yourself for long waits at immigration and customs, and for check-in and security checkpoints, especially at Juan Santamaría, where you need to get to the airport three hours before your flight. Most North American flights arrive at this airport in the evening and depart early in the morning, which are the busiest times.

Liberia is a tiny airport, so check-in times are usually shorter. However, infrastructure hasn't quite caught up to the exponential increase in flights, so we recommend that you arrive at least two hours before international departures.

Juan Santamaría is a full-service airport with many arrivals and departures each day, so if you miss your flight or have some other unexpected mishap, you're better off there. Fares are usually lower to San José than to Liberia.

### GROUND TRANSPORTATION FROM JUAN SANTAMARÍA AIRPORT

You exit the airport into a fume-filled parking area flanked by hordes of taxis and tour vans. If you're with a tour, you need only look for a representative of your tour company with a sign that bears your name. If you need a taxi, first buy a voucher at one of two kiosks, then present it to the driver of one of the orange Taxis Unidos cabs (no other taxis are allowed in the arrival area). Rates are standardized to the various parts of town; most areas of San José are $12–$15. Avoid *collectivos,* or minivans—they're almost the same price as a taxi, but the van is often crammed with other passengers, and you'll have to make stops at their hotels, making your transfer another journey in itself.

### DEPARTURE TAXES

When you fly out of Costa Rica, you'll have to pay a $26 airport departure tax in

colones or with a Visa credit card. You can pay the tax upon arrival or departure at the Bancrédito counter in the airport, or at any Bancrédito or Banco de Costa Rica branch in Costa Rica during your trip. Lines are long, so don't leave it until the last minute. At this writing, the Four Seasons is piloting a system in which the cost is added to your hotel bill, but there are no signs yet of this catching on at other hotels.

### DUTY-FREE SHOPPING

■ TIP→→ San José's Juan Santamaría International Airport is a good place to buy souvenirs, including Costa Rican coffee, wood and leather crafts, bottled sauces for cooking, and T-shirts. Prices in the airport are higher than at other souvenir shops, but the extra money may be worth it to avoid carrying souvenirs around during your vacation. Unlike many Latin American countries, Costa Rica does not have a large artisan community and doesn't produce spectacular crafts. The types and quality of souvenirs you find in the airport are generally the same as the products you find elsewhere in the country.

✈ Airport Information **Aeropuerto Internacional Daniel Oduber (LIR)** ✉ 17 km/11 mi west of Liberia ☎ 506/668-1010. **Aeropuerto Internacional Juan Santamaría (SJO)** ✉ 16 km/10 mi northwest of downtown San José, just outside Alajuela ☎ 506/443-2622 or 506/443-2942. **Aeropuerto Internacional Tobías Bolaños** ✉ 3 km/2 mi west of San José, Pavas ☎ 506/232-2820.

## BUS TRAVEL

### ARRIVING & DEPARTING

Tica Bus has daily runs between Costa Rica and Panama or Nicaragua; Transnica has daily service between Costa Rica and Granada and Managua. We recommend choosing Tica Bus if at all possible, but Transnica is acceptable in a pinch. Tica Bus offers an "executive" service on its Managua–Costa Rica run, which means for about $3 more you'll get breakfast. Both companies have comfortable, air-conditioned coaches with videos and on-board toilets, and make it easy to cross the border. For border-crossing details, *see* Chapters 3, 6, and 7.

⊞ Bus Companies **Tica Bus** ⊠ C. 9 and Avda. 4, San José ☎ 221-8954. **Transnica** ⊠ C. 22, between Avdas. 3 and 5, San José ☎ 223-4242 ⊠ Hotel Guanacaste, Liberia ☎ 666-0085.

## GETTING AROUND

All Costa Rican towns are connected by regular bus service. Bus service in Costa Rica is reliable, comprehensive, and inexpensive; fares for long-distance routes are usually $3–$10 one-way. Buses between major cities are modern and air-conditioned, but once you get into the rural areas you may get a converted school bus without a/c. The kind of bus you get is the luck of the draw (no upgrades here). Bus travel in Costa Rica is formal, meaning no pigs or chickens inside and no people or luggage on the roof. On longer routes, buses stop midway at modest restaurants. Near the ends of their runs many nonexpress buses turn into large taxis, dropping passengers off one by one at their destinations; to save time, take a *directo* (express) bus. Be prepared for bus-company employees and bus drivers to speak Spanish only.

The main inconvenience of buses is that you usually have to return to San José to travel between outlying regions and that long-distance service is much slower than flying. For example, a bus from San José to the Osa Peninsula is 9 hours or more, whereas the flight is 1 hour. Shorter distances are more negligible—the bus to Quepos is 3½ hours and the flight 30 minutes—and in those cases the huge price difference might be worth the extra hour of travel. There is no main bus station in San José; buses leave from a variety of departure points.

⚠ Don't put your belongings in the overhead bin unless you have to, and if you do, keep your eye on them. If anyone—even someone who looks like a bus employee—offers to put your luggage on the bus or in the luggage compartment underneath for you, politely decline. If you must put your luggage underneath the bus, get off quickly when you arrive to retrieve it.

Many visitors take the more convenient (but more expensive) alternative of booking a private shuttle van (⇨ Shuttle Van Services, *below*) or hiring a private driver (⇨ Car Travel). Both options are still cheaper than flying in most cases.

## FARES & SCHEDULES

Bus companies don't have printed bus schedules to give out, although departure times may be printed on a sign at the bus company's office and ticket window. Bus-line phones are usually busy or go unanswered. The schedules and prices we list are accurate at this writing, but can change frequently. ■ TIP➜➜ For up-to-date information, go to the bus station a day before your departure, or get a schedule from an ICT tourist office (⇨ Visitor Information). Hotel employees can usually give you the information you need.

Buses usually depart and arrive on time; they may even leave a few minutes before the scheduled departure time.

## TICKETS & RESERVATIONS

Tickets are sold at bus stations and on the buses themselves; reservations aren't accepted, and you must pay in person with cash. If you pay on the bus, be sure to have loose change handy, though the driver will accept bills of 1000 colones. Buses to popular beach and mountain destinations often sell out on weekends and the days before and after a holiday. It's also difficult to get tickets back to San José on Sunday afternoon. Some companies won't sell you a return ticket from the departure point; especially during the peak season, make sure the first thing you do upon arrival is buy your ticket back. Sometimes tickets include seat numbers, which are usually printed on the tops of the chairs. Smoking is not permitted on buses.

## SHUTTLE VAN SERVICES

Two private bus companies, Gray Line Tours Fantasy Bus and Interbus, travel to the most popular tourist destinations in modern, air-conditioned vans. Interbus vans seat 8 to 16 people; Gray Line vans seat 14 to 28 people. This service costs about $15–$55 one-way, but can take hours off your trip. Hotel-to-hotel service is offered as long as your lodging is on the route; if you're heading off the beaten track, it's a hotel-to-nearest-hotel service.

🚐 Shuttle Van Companies **Gray Line Tourist Bus** ☎ 232-3681 or 220-2126 ⊕ www.graylinecostarica.com. **Interbus** ☎ 283-5573 ⊕ www.interbusonline.com.

## CAMERAS & FILM

The best all-round film to bring is 400 ISO, although you may want to take along a couple of rolls of 100 ISO for the bright beach. If you're hoping to bring home shots of wildlife, you may consider investing in a telephoto lens—one that ranges from 70 mm to 300 mm is best. Humidity and rain are the biggest problems facing photographers in Costa Rica, so take plenty of resealable plastic bags for lenses and other camera equipment, and consider buying a dry bag, sold in outdoors stores, for your camera.

Don't pack unprocessed film, single-use cameras, or cameras with film inside in checked luggage. X-ray machines used to view checked luggage are extremely powerful and therefore likely to ruin your film. Lower-intensity X-rays for carry-ons usually will not harm your film (unless it's repeatedly exposed), but play it safe and ask for hand inspection. Keep videotapes and computer disks away from metal detectors. Lead-lined bags can protect film from X-ray scans to some extent. There are no security machines that are known to harm digital cameras. Always keep film, tape, and computer disks out of the sun. Carry an extra supply of batteries, and be prepared to turn on your camera, camcorder, or laptop to prove to airport security personnel that the device is real.

Although travelers are technically allowed to bring only six rolls of film into Costa Rica, customs agents almost never check. Kodak, Fuji, Mitsubishi, and AGFA film is widely available, but most film costs at least 20% more here than in the United States and can be expired, so bring enough film for your trip. Consider waiting until you get home to develop film. Plenty of shops in San José do developing, usually the same day, but they tend to change the chemicals less often than they should, so you risk getting prints of poor quality. If

you can't wait, one of the many Fuji shops would be your best bet; steer clear of Quick Photo shops.

🎞 Photo Help **Kodak Information Center** ☎ 800/242-2424 ⊕ www.kodak.com.

## CAR TRAVEL

■ TIP➔➔ If you're planning to go to only one or two major areas, taking a shuttle van or a domestic flight is usually a better and cheaper option than driving. Renting is a good choice if you're destination hopping, staying at a hotel that's a trek to town, or going well off the beaten path. Car trips to northern Guanacaste from San José can take an entire day, so flying is probably better if you don't have long to spend in the country. Flying is definitely better than driving for visiting the South Pacific.

Many travelers shy away from renting a car in Costa Rica, if only for fear of the road conditions. Indeed, this is not an ideal place to drive: in San José traffic is bad and car theft is rampant (look for guarded parking lots or hotels with lots); in rural areas roads are often unpaved or potholed—and tires aren't usually covered by the insurance. And Ticos are reckless drivers—with an accident rate that's the second highest in the world. But while driving can be a challenge, it's a great way to explore certain regions, especially Guanacaste, the Northern Plains, and the Caribbean coast (apart from Tortuguero and Barra del Colorado). Keep in mind that mountains and poor road conditions make most trips longer than you'd normally expect.

A standard vehicle is fine for most destinations, but a *doble-tracción* (4WD) is often essential to reach the more remote parts of the country, especially during the rainy season. Even in the dry season, you must have a 4WD vehicle to reach Monteverde and some destinations in Guanacaste. The big 4WD vehicles can cost roughly twice as much as an economy car, but compact 4WDs, such as the Daihatsu Terios, are more reasonable, and should be booked well in advance. Agencies may try to bump you up a category—stay firm. Most cars in Costa Rica have manual transmissions.

■ TIP➔➔ Specify when making the reservation if you want an automatic transmission; it usually costs about $5 more per day. Economy Rent a Car in San José ( ⇨ *below*) has reasonably priced automatic KIA Sportage vehicles. Larger, more expensive automatic Jeep and Sorrento models are also available. If you plan to rent any kind of vehicle between December 15 and January 3, or during Holy Week (the week leading up to Easter)—when most Costa Ricans are on vacation—reserve several months ahead of time.

Costa Rica has around 30 car-rental firms. Most local firms are affiliated with international car-rental chains and offer the same guarantees and services as their branches abroad. At least a dozen rental offices line San José's Paseo Colón; most large hotels and Juan Santamaría Airport have representatives. Renting in or near San José is by far the easiest way to go. It's feasible to rent in Liberia, Manuel Antonio, and Tamarindo. In most other places across the country it's either impossible or very difficult and expensive to rent a car.

### EMERGENCIES

Costa Rica has no highway emergency service organization. In Costa Rica 911 is the nationwide number for accidents. Traffic police are scattered around the country, but Costa Ricans are very good about stopping for people with car trouble. Whatever happens, don't move the car after an accident, even if a monstrous traffic jam ensues. Call 911 first if the accident is serious (nearly everyone has a cell phone here and it's almost a given that someone will offer to help). Also be sure to call the emergency number your car-rental agency has given you. For fender benders, contact the Traffic Police, who will try to locate a person to assist you in English—but don't count on it. If you don't speak Spanish, you may want to contact the rental agency before trying the police.

🗐 Emergency Services **Ambulance** ☎ 128. **Police** ☎ 117, 127 outside major cities. **Traffic Police** ☎ 222-9245.

### GASOLINE

There is no self-service gas in Costa Rica; 24-hour stations are generally available only in San José or on the Pan-American Highway. Most other stations are open from about 7 to 7, some until midnight. Try to fill your tank in cities—gas is more expensive in rural areas, and gas stations can be few and far between. Major credit cards are widely accepted. Ask the attendant if you want a *factura* (receipt). Regular unleaded gasoline is called *regular* and high-octane unleaded is called *super*. Gas is sold by the liter. The cost at this writing is 76¢ per liter ($2.90 per gallon) for regular and 80¢ per liter ($3.04 per gallon) for super.

### HIRING A DRIVER

Hiring a car with a driver makes the most sense for sightseeing in and or around San José. You can also usually hire a taxi driver to ferry you around for about $10 an hour. At $50–75 per day plus the driver's food, hiring a driver for areas outside the San José area costs almost the same as renting a 4WD, but is more expensive for multiday trips, when you'll also have to pay for the driver's room. Some drivers are also knowledgeable guides; others just drive. Unless they're driving large passenger vans for established companies, it's doubtful that drivers have any special training or licensing. Hotels can usually direct you to trusted drivers; but the *Tico Times,* available at supermarkets, souvenir shops, bookstores, and hotels, also has ads for drivers. Alternatively, both Alamo and Avis ( ⇨ *below*) provide professional car-and-driver services for minimum three-day rentals. At Alamo you pay $60 on top of the rental fee, plus the driver's food and lodging, or a flat $100 that includes the driver's expenses. At Avis you pay $50 on top of the rental fee, and are responsible for the driver's expenses.

### INSURANCE

If you have a major credit card or auto insurance at home, you may not have to pay the mandatory collision insurance ($10–25 per day, depending on the agency and the kind of car). Before you rent, see what coverage you already have. Deductibles are usually $1,000–$2,000. Third-party injury insurance is generally not covered by credit cards; it costs about $10 per day in addition to the collision insurance, with a 20% deductible; some agencies provide additional insurance to eliminate the deductible.

## INTERNATIONAL DRIVING PERMITS

International driving permits (IDPs) are not necessary in Costa Rica. Your own driver's license is good for the length of your initial tourist visa. You must carry your passport, showing that you entered the country less than 90 days ago.

## RATES

High-season rates in San José begin at $45 a day and $300 a week for an economy car with air-conditioning, manual transmission, unlimited mileage, and obligatory insurance; but rates fluctuate considerably according to demand, season, and company. Rates for a 4WD vehicle during high season are $70–$90 a day and $450–$550 per week. Often companies will also require a $1,000 deposit, payable by credit card. A vehicle with automatic transmission costs about $5 more per day; reserve well in advance and know that options are more limited.

Cars picked up at or returned to Juan Santamaría Airport incur a 12% surcharge. You can't pick up cars directly at the Liberia airport, but a range of firms have offices nearby and transport you from the airport free of charge—and with no surcharge to rent. Check cars thoroughly for damage before you sign the rental contract. Even tough-looking 4WD vehicles should be coddled. ⚠ The charges levied by rental companies for damage—no matter how minor—are outrageous even by U.S. or European standards.

One-way service surcharges are $50–$150, depending on the drop-off point; some companies, such as Hertz and Avis, don't offer this service. To avoid a hefty refueling fee, fill the tank just before you turn in the car, but be aware that gas stations near the rental outlet may overcharge. It's almost never a deal to buy the tank of gas that's in the car when you rent it; the understanding is that you'll return it empty, but some fuel usually remains. Car seats cost about $5 per day. Additional drivers

are about $5–$10 per day if there is any charge at all. Almost all agencies have cell-phone rental; prices range between $2 and $6 per day, with national per-minute costs between 70¢ and $2.

## REQUIREMENTS & RESTRICTIONS

Car seats are compulsory for children under four years old, and can be rented for about $5 per day; reserve in advance. Rental cars may not be driven across borders to Nicaragua and Panama. Seat-belt use is compulsory in the front seat. To rent a car you need a driver's license, a valid passport, and a credit card. The minimum renter age varies; agencies such as Budget and Alamo rent to anyone over 21, Avis sets the limit at 23, and at Hertz it's 25. Though it's rare, some agencies have a maximum age limit.

## ROAD CONDITIONS

San José is terribly congested during weekday morning and afternoon rush hours (7–9 AM and 4–6 PM). Avoid returning to the city on Sunday evening, when traffic to San José from the Pacific coast beaches backs up for hours. Look out for potholes, even in the smoothest sections of the best roads, whether you're in San José or in the countryside. Also watch for unmarked speed bumps where you'd least expect them, particularly on rural main thoroughfares. During the rainy season, roads are in much worse shape. Check with your destination before setting out; roads, especially in Limón Province, are prone to wash-outs and landslides.

San José has many one-way streets and traffic circles. Streets in the capital are narrow. Pedestrians are supposed to have the right of way but do not in reality, so be alert when walking. The local driving style is erratic and aggressive but not fast, because road conditions don't permit too much speed. Frequent fender benders tie up traffic. Keep your windows rolled up in the center of the city, because thieves will reach into your car at stoplights and snatch your purse, jewelry, and so on.

Outside of San José you'll run into long stretches of unpaved road. Frequent hazards in the countryside are potholes, landslides during the rainy season, and cattle on the roads. Drunk drivers are a hazard throughout the country on weekend nights. Driving at night is not recommended anyway, since roads are poorly lighted and many don't have painted center lines or shoulder lines.

## ROAD MAPS

Local road maps are available at gas stations and tourist information offices; local versions run about $3, a snazzier foreign one costs $10. Bookstores in San José that sell maps include Librería Internacional, Librería Lehmann, and Seventh Street Books (⇨ Shopping *in* chapter 1.)

## RULES OF THE ROAD

Driving is on the right side of the road in Costa Rica. The highway speed limit is usually 90 kph (54 mph), which drops to 60 kph (36 mph) in residential areas. In towns limits range from 30 to 50 kph (18 to 31 mph). Speed limits are rigorously enforced in all regions of the country. Seat belts are required, and an awareness campaign has increased enforcement. *Alto* means "stop" and *ceda* means "yield." Right turns on red are permitted except where signs indicate otherwise, but in San José this is usually not possible because of one-way streets and pedestrian crossings.

Signage is notoriously bad, but improving. Watch carefully for *No Hay Paso* (Do Not Enter) signs; one-way streets are common, both in small towns as well as in San José, and it's not unusual for a street to transform from a two-way to a one-way, forcing a not-so-obvious turn. Streetlights are often out of service and key signs missing or knocked down because of accidents.

Local drunk driving laws are strict. You'll get nailed with a 10,000-colón fine if you're caught driving in a "predrunk" state (blood alcohol levels of 0.049–0.099%). If your level is higher than that, you'll pay 20,000 colones; the car will be confiscated and your license taken away. Policemen who stop drivers for speeding and drunk driving are often looking for payment on the spot—essentially a bribe. Whether you're guilty or not, you'll get a ticket if you don't give in.

Asking for a ticket instead of paying the bribe discourages corruption and does not compromise your safety. You can generally pay the ticket at your car-rental company; it will remit it on your behalf.

Car seats are required for children ages four and under, but car-seat laws are not rigorously enforced. Many Tico babies and children ride on their parents' laps. Children are allowed in the front seat. Drivers are prohibited from using hand-held cell phones, but this is almost never enforced, and distracted chatters are the rule.

⚠ There are plenty of questionable drivers on Costa Rican highways; be prepared for harebrained passing on blind corners, tailgating, and failing to signal. Watch, too, for two-lane roads that feed into one-lane bridges with specified rights-of-way. There's not always a method to the driving madness, but locals use two tactics that are surprisingly effective. Stick your left hand out the window and wave slightly if you want to merge left (get your passenger to do it to maneuver to the right), and flick your lights if you want oncoming traffic to slow down so you can turn left. Hone your reflexes: drivers behind you will honk at you a millisecond before the light turns green. Green traffic lights flash just before turning to yellow; always look carefully, as drivers regularly speed through lights that have long since turned red.

🚗 **Major Agencies Alamo** ☎ 800/462-5266 worldwide, 800/011-0214 Costa Rica office, 506/233-7733 ⊕ www.alamocostarica.com. **Avis** ☎ 800/230-4898 in U.S., 800/272-7733 in Canada, 0870/606-0100 in U.K., 300/137-498 in Australia, 0800/655111 in New Zealand, 506/232-9922 in Costa Rica ⊕ www.avis.co.cr. **Budget** ☎ 800/527-0700, 866/693-6666 in Canada, 0870/156-5656 in the U.K., 300/794-344 in Australia, 0800/283-438 in New Zealand, 506/436-2000 in Costa Rica ⊕ www.budget.co.cr. **Dollar** ☎ 866/746-7765 in the U.S., 0800/085-4578 in the U.K., 506/257-0671 in Costa Rica ⊕ www.dollarcostarica.com. **Economy** ☎ 877/326-7368 in the U.S., 506/231-5410 in Costa Rica ⊕ www.economyrentacar.com. **Hertz** ☎ 800/654-3001, 800/263-0600 in Canada, 0870/844-8844 in the U.K., 02/9669-2444 in Australia, 09/256-8690 in New Zealand, 506/221-1818 in Costa Rica ⊕ www.hertz.com. **National Car Rental** ☎ 800/227-7368 in the U.S. and Canada, 0870/600-6666 in the U.K., 07/3854-1499 in Australia, 0800/800-115 in New Zealand, 506/290-8787 in Costa Rica ⊕ www.natcar.com.

## CHILDREN IN COSTA RICA

Thanks to high safety and health standards, Costa Rica is popular with traveling families. Most of the health problems you might associate with the tropics, such as malaria or cholera, are rare or nonexistent in Costa Rica (though they do exist in neighboring Nicaragua), and the country's most popular destinations have plenty to offer kids.

For general advice about traveling with children, consult *Fodor's FYI: Travel with Your Baby* (available in bookstores everywhere).

### ATTRACTIONS

The *Tico Times,* published (in English) on Friday, lists activities for children in the "Weekend" section. The daily Spanish-language newspaper *La Nación* publishes a daily features section called "Viva" that contains ads and articles for events; its Friday "Tiempo Libre" ("Free Time") calendar provides a comprehensive listing of events and activities for families.

Check adventure-tour (canopies, white-water rafting) policies before getting kids' hopes up; many have size or age limits (usually 12).

Sights and attractions listed in this book that are especially appealing to children are indicated by a rubber-duckie icon (🦆) in the margin.

### FOOD & DRINK

If your kids balk at the choices on the menu, ask for plain grilled chicken, fish, or beef: *"Pollo/pescado/carne sencillo para niños"* ("Grilled chicken/fish/meat for children.") Most restaurants are willing to accommodate with options and portion size.

Natural juices, called *frescos,* come with teeth-shattering amounts of sugar. If you're watching your child's intake, request one with only a little sugar (*con poco azucar*); chances are it will be sweet enough, but you can always top it up if need be. Water is generally safe to drink (especially around San José), but quality can vary; to be safe, give kids bottled water.

Pack snacks on drives, as there are few places to stop between cities and towns.

### LODGING

Most hotels in Costa Rica allow children under a certain age to stay in their parents' room at no extra charge, but others charge for them as extra adults; be sure to find out the cutoff age for children's discounts. The Punta Leona Beach Resort has a playground, beach umbrellas, a children's pool, and high chairs and cribs. It's less than two hours' driving time from San José and has tranquil, shallow waters and a wide sandy beach. The high-end Marriott, Meliá, and Barceló hotel chains have cots, cribs, and children's discounts. These hotels and those listed below are our top choices for kid-friendly hotels.

🏅 **Best Choices Barceló Tambor Beach** ⊠ Tambor ☎ 506/683-0303 ⊕ www.barcelo.com. **Best Western Jacó Beach Resort** ⊠ Playa Jacó ☎ 506/643-1000 ⊕ www.bestwestern.com. **Corcovado Lodge Tent Camp** ⊠ Corcovado National Park ☎ 506/222-0333 ⊕ www.costaricaexpeditions.com **Hotel Grano de Oro** ⊠ San José ☎ 506/255-3322 ⊕ www.hotelgranodeoro.com. **Hotel Punta Leona** ⊠ Punta Leona ☎ 506/231-3131 ⊕ www.hotelpuntaleona.com. **Hotel El Sapo Dorado** ⊠ Monteverde ☎ 506/645-5010 ⊕ www.sapodorado.com. **Hotel Sí Como No** ⊠ Manuel Antonio ☎ 506/777-0777 ⊕ www.sicomono.com. **Marriott Costa Rica Hotel** ⊠ San Antonio de Belén ☎ 506/298-0000, 800/228-9290 in U.S. ⊕ www.marriott.com. **Mawamba Lodge** ⊠ Tortuguero ☎ 506/293-8181 ⊕ www.grupomawamba.com. **Meliá Conchal** ⊠ Playa Conchal ☎ 506/654-4123, 800/336-3542 in U.S. **Selva Verde Lodge** ⊠ Puerto Viejo de Sarapiquí ☎ 506/776-6800 ⊕ www.selvaverde.com.

### PACKING & SUPPLIES

Baby formula and disposable diapers are widely available in supermarkets and pharmacies around the country. Buy liquid or lactose-free formula in San José (or bring it from home); it may not be available in outerlying areas. Major U.S. brands of disposable diapers are sold. Prices are about the same as or slightly higher than in the United States. Baby aspirin and other medications for children may not be available; be sure to pack what you might need.

Packing the following items may make for a smoother trip: wet wipes, lightweight and easily collapsible umbrella stroller, disposable cameras so kids can take their own pictures, favorite foods for picky eaters, zip-off pants, and reversible clothing.

The drive to Manuel Antonio is particularly curvy; pack ample motion-sickness medication.

Shipping your luggage in advance can be a great way to cut down on what you have to carry—especially if your packing list includes strollers and car seats.

### SAFETY & PRECAUTIONS

• If you are renting a car, don't forget to arrange for a car seat in advance.

• Riptides are a force to be reckoned with. Ask locals to point out safe places to swim and never let a child swim unattended in the ocean or go deeper than his or her waist.

• Sunburn and dehydration can be serious in Costa Rica. Slather on the sunscreen and make sure kids swim in T-shirts and wear hats. (Even waterproof sunscreen can wear off quickly.) Give kids lots of water or juice. If you're taking bus trips, which can be extremely hot, schedule them for early in the morning or late afternoon.

• Kids are more prone to stomach problems from contaminated water, so avoid tap water and ice.

• Wild animals aren't pets; explain how harmful it is to feed the monkeys, no matter how cute and tame they seem.

• On hikes, make sure a nature-aware adult walks in front of children to watch for camouflaged snakes or fire-ant burrows.

### CUSTOMS & DUTIES

When shopping in Costa Rica, keep receipts for all purchases. Be ready to show customs officials what you've bought. Pack purchases together in an easily accessible place. If you think a duty is incorrect, appeal the assessment. If you object to the

way your clearance was handled, note the inspector's badge number. In either case, first ask to see a supervisor. If the problem isn't resolved, write to the appropriate authorities, beginning with the port director at your point of entry. It usually takes about 10–30 minutes to clear customs when arriving in Costa Rica.

### IN AUSTRALIA

Australian residents who are 18 or older may bring home A$900 worth of souvenirs and gifts (including jewelry), 250 cigarettes or 250 grams of cigars or other tobacco products, and 2.25 liters of alcohol (including wine, beer, and spirits). Residents under 18 may bring back A$450 worth of goods. If limits are exceeded, duty and tax are charged on the entire amount. Members of the same family traveling together and living at the same residence may pool their allowances. Prohibited items include meat products. Seeds, plants, and fruits need to be declared upon arrival.

🚩 **Australian Customs Service** ☎ 02/6275-6666 or 300/363263, 02/8334-7444 or 800/020-504 quarantine-inquiry line ⊕ www.customs.gov.au.

### IN CANADA

Canadian residents who have been out of Canada for at least seven days may bring in C$750 worth of goods duty-free. If you've been away fewer than seven days but more than 48 hours, the duty-free allowance drops to C$200. If your trip lasts 24 to 48 hours, the allowance is C$50; if the goods are worth more than C$50, you must pay full duty on all of the goods. You may not pool allowances with family members. Goods claimed under the C$750 exemption may follow you by mail; those claimed under the lesser exemptions must accompany you. Alcohol and tobacco products may be included in the seven-day and 48-hour exemptions but not in the 24-hour exemption. If you meet the age requirements of the province or territory through which you reenter Canada, you may bring in, duty-free, 1.5 liters of wine *or* 1.14 liters (40 imperial ounces) of liquor *or* 24 12-ounce cans or bottles of beer or ale. Also, if you meet the local age requirement for tobacco products, you may bring in, duty-free, 200 cigarettes, 50 cigars or cigarillos, and 200 grams of tobacco. You may have to pay a minimum duty on tobacco products, regardless of whether or not you exceed your personal exemption. Check ahead of time with the Canada Border Services Agency or the Department of Agriculture for policies regarding meat products, seeds, plants, and fruits.

You may send an unlimited number of gifts (only one gift per recipient, however) worth up to C$60 each duty-free to Canada. Label the package UNSOLICITED GIFT—VALUE UNDER $60. Alcohol and tobacco are excluded.

📋 **Canada Border Services Agency** ☎ 800/461-9999 in Canada, 204/983-3500, 506/636-5064 ⊕ www.ccra.gc.ca.

### IN COSTA RICA
Visitors entering Costa Rica may bring in 500 grams of tobacco, 5 liters of wine or spirits, 2 kilograms of sweets and chocolates, and the equivalent of $500 worth of merchandise. One camera and one video camera, six rolls of film, binoculars, and electrical items for personal use only are also allowed. Customs officials at San José's international airport rarely examine tourists' luggage, but if you enter by land, they'll probably look through your bags. Officers at the airport generally speak English.

### IN NEW ZEALAND
All homeward-bound residents may bring back NZ$700 worth of souvenirs and gifts; passengers may not pool their allowances, and children can claim only the concession on goods intended for their own use. For those 17 or older, the duty-free allowance also includes 4.5 liters of wine or beer; one 1,125-ml bottle of spirits; and either 200 cigarettes, 250 grams of tobacco, 50 cigars, *or* a combination of the three up to 250 grams. Meat products, seeds, plants, and fruits must be declared upon arrival to the Agricultural Services Department.

📋 **New Zealand Customs** ☎ 09/300-5399 or 0800/428-786 ⊕ www.customs.govt.nz.

### IN THE U.K.
From countries outside the European Union, including Costa Rica, you may bring home, duty-free, 200 cigarettes, 50 cigars, 100 cigarillos, or 250 grams of tobacco; 1 liter of spirits or 2 liters of fortified or sparkling wine or liqueurs; 2 liters of still table wine; 60 ml of perfume; 250 ml of toilet water; plus £145 worth of other goods, including gifts and souvenirs. Prohibited items include meat and dairy products, seeds, plants, and fruits.

📋 **HM Customs and Excise** ☎ 0845/010-9000 or 0208/929-0152 advice service ⊕ www.hmce.gov.uk.

### IN THE U.S.
U.S. residents 21 and older may bring back 2 liters of alcohol duty-free, as long as one of the liters was produced in a CBI country. In addition, regardless of your age, you are allowed 200 cigarettes and 100 non-Cuban cigars. Antiques, which U.S. Customs and Border Protection defines as objects more than 100 years old, enter duty-free, as do original works of art done entirely by hand, including paintings, drawings, and sculptures. This doesn't apply to folk art or handicrafts, which are in general dutiable. You may also send packages home duty-free, with a limit of one parcel per addressee per day (except alcohol or tobacco products or perfume worth more than $5). You can mail up to $200 worth of goods for personal use; label the package PERSONAL USE and attach a list of its contents and their retail value. If the package contains your used personal belongings, mark it PERSONAL GOODS RETURNED to avoid paying duties. You may send up to $100 worth of goods as a gift; mark the package UNSOLICITED GIFT. Mailed items do not affect your duty-free allowance on your return.

📋 **U.S. Customs and Border Protection** ☎ 877/227-5551 or 202/354-1000 ⊕ www.cbp.gov.

## DISABILITIES & ACCESSIBILITY
The best way for people with disabilities to see Costa Rica is to go with a tour company. Despite a law requiring all buildings to be accessible by 2008, accessibility in Costa Rica is extremely limited. Wheelchair ramps are practically nonexistent, and streets are often unpaved outside

major cities, making wheelchair travel difficult. Exploring most attractions involves traversing uneven streets, steep trails, or muddy paths. There is some growing awareness of the needs of people with disabilities, and some hotels and attractions have made the necessary provisions.

The Society for Accessible Travel & Hospitality (SATH) has general information about travel for people with disabilities.
🛈 Resource **Society for Accessible Travel & Hospitality (SATH)** ☎ 212/447-7284 in the U.S. ⊕ www.sath.org.

## TRANSPORTATION
The U.S. Department of Transportation Aviation Consumer Protection Division's online publication *New Horizons: Information for the Air Traveler with a Disability* offers advice for travelers with a disability, and outlines basic rights. Visit DisabilityInfo.gov for general information.
🛈 **U.S. Department of Transportation Hotline** ☎ for disability-related air-travel problems, 800/778-4838 or 800/455-9880 TTY.

## TOURS & TRAVEL AGENTS
Vaya con Silla de Ruedas (Go With Wheelchairs) is a Costa Rica-based tour company for people in wheelchairs. The Instituto Internacional de Desarrollo Creativo, also based in Costa Rica, not only plans accessible trips, but trains local tourism personnel in providing more accessible service. Wheels Up!, Flying Wheels Travel, and Accessible Journeys are travel agencies exclusively for wheelchair-bound travelers.
🛈 **Accessible Journeys** ☎ 800/846-4537 or 610/521-0339 in the U.S. ⊕ www.disabilitytravel.com **Flying Wheels Travel** ☎ 507/451-5005 in the U.S. ⊕ www.flyingwheelstravel.com. **Instituto Internacional de Desarrollo Creativo** ☎ 506/771-7482 ⊕ www.empowermentaccess.com. **Vaya con Silla de Ruedas** ☎ 506/454-2810 in Costa Rica ⊕ www.gowithwheelchairs.com. **Wheels Up!** ☎ 888/389-4335 in the U.S. ⊕ www.wheelsup.com.

## EATING & DRINKING
In San José and surrounding cities, *sodas* (informal eateries) are usually open daily 7 AM to 7 or 9 PM, though some close on Sunday. Other restaurants are usually open

11 AM–9 PM. In rural areas restaurants are usually closed on Sunday, except around resorts. In resort areas some restaurants may be open late. Most all-night restaurants are in downtown San José casinos. However, Nuestra Tierra and Manolos are both good 24-hour options, and for late-night cravings the doors at Denny's at the Best Western Irazú just north of San José are always open. Normal dining hours in Costa Rica are noon–3 and 6–9. **Unless otherwise noted, the restaurants listed in this guide are open daily for lunch and dinner.** *Desayuno* (breakfast) is served at most sodas and hotels.

Except for those in hotels, most restaurants close between Christmas and New Year's Day and during Holy Week (Palm Sunday to Easter Sunday). Call before heading out. Those that do stay open may not sell alcohol between Holy Thursday and Easter Sunday. Even if you keep your base in San José, consider venturing to the Central Valley towns for a meal or two.

| WHAT IT COSTS | AT DINNER |
|---|---|
| $$$$ | over $25 |
| $$$ | $20–$25 |
| $$ | $10–$20 |
| $ | $5–$10 |
| ¢ | under $5 |

*Prices are per-person for a main course, excluding 13% tax and 10% service fee.*

The restaurants we list are the cream of the crop in each price category. Properties indicated by an ✕◻ are lodging establishments whose restaurant warrants a special trip.

## PAYING
■ TIP→→ Credit cards are not accepted at most restaurants in rural areas. Always ask before you order to find out if your credit card will be accepted. Visa and MasterCard are the most commonly accepted cards; American Express and Diners Club are less widely accepted. ■ TIP→→ Remember that 23% is added to all menu prices: 13% for tax and 10% for service. Because a gratuity is included, there's no need to tip, but if your service is good, it's nice to add a little money to the obligatory 10%.

## RESERVATIONS & DRESS

Reservations are always a good idea; we mention them only when they're essential or not accepted. Book as far ahead as you can, and reconfirm as soon as you arrive. (Large parties should always call ahead to check the reservations policy.)

Costa Ricans generally dress more formally than North Americans. For dinner, long pants and closed-toed shoes are standard for men except for beach locations, and women tend to wear dressy clothes that show off their figures, with high heels. Shorts, flip-flops, and tank tops are not acceptable, except at inexpensive restaurants in beach towns.

## ECOTOURISM

With tourism in Costa Rica reaching 19.7% of export income in 2003 (the latest figure available), gone are the simplistic days of ecotourism. Over the past 10 years this buzzword has been used in so many ways it's almost been diluted beyond usefulness. On the plus side, many tour companies have incorporated a high level of environmental awareness into their business practices; on the minus, crafty marketers are quick to slap an ecotourism label on any place or tour that takes place in nature.

That said, Costa Rica does have many operators and hotels that shine; you just have to do some research to sniff them out ($\Rightarrow$ Guidelines for Sustainable Travel, *below*). The International Ecotourism Society lists agencies around the world, including Costa Rica, that adhere to its definition of ecotourism. **For our tour-operator recommendations, see Ecotours in Tours & Packages.**

**⊿ Conservation and Ecotourism Groups ACTUAR** ☎ 506/228-5695 ⊕ www.actuarcostarica.com. **ANAI** ☎ 828/524-8369 in the U.S., 506/224-3570 in Costa Rica ⊕ www.anaicr.org. **APREFLOFAS** ☎ 506/240-6087 ⊕ www.natour.co.cr. **COOPRENA** ☎ 506/248-2538 ⊕ www.turismoruralcr.com. **The International Ecotourism Society** ☎ 202/387-7915 in the U.S. ⊕ www.ecotourism.org. **Monteverde Institute** ☎ 506/645-5053. **Neotropica Foundation** ☎ 506/253-2130 ⊕ www.neotropica.org.

## ECO-LODGES

The official government rating system for eco-lodges is the Costa Rican Tourism Board's Certification for Sustainable Tourism (CSR). It rates tourism companies and lodges in four categories: interaction with the surrounding habitat; policies and steps taken to be more sustainable; actions taken to encourage clients to participate in the company's sustainability policy; and interaction with the local community. At this writing, only two hotels have received five leaves (the highest rating): Lapa Ríos (near Puerto Jiménez) and Finca Rosa Blanca Country Inn (near Heredia); four have recieved four leaves. The CSR Web site has a complete list of hotels that have been evaluated, and a detailed list of the grades hotels received. However, many people think that the program is politicized and that certain hotels do not deserve such high ratings. For example, several Barceló hotels were rated highly despite the chain's many past violations of environmental laws.

In our opinion, some of the best eco-lodges in the country are Laguna del Lagarto Lodge (Ciudad Quesada), Lake Coter Eco-Lodge (La Fortuna), La Selva Biological Station, Savegre Hotel de Montaña (San Gerardo de Dota), Playa Nicuesa Rainforest Lodge (Golfito), Tiskita Lodge (Playa Pavones), El Remanso (Cabo Matopalo), Bosque del Cabo (Cabo Matopalo), Lapa Ríos (near Puerto Jiménez), Corcovado Lodge Tent Camp (Carate), Evergreen Lodge (Tortuguero), and Almonds & Corals Tent Lodge Camp (Gandoca-Manzanillo Refuge).

**⊿ Resource Certification for Sustainable Tourism (CSR)** ⊕ www.turismo-sostenible.co.cr.

## GUIDELINES FOR SUSTAINABLE TRAVEL

● Use local guides or services, eat in local restaurants, and buy local crafts or produce to make your visit beneficial to those who live near protected areas.

● Do some research to find out whether or not your prospective tour company actually has "eco-friendly" policies, such as: hiring and training locals as guides, drivers, managers, and office workers; making a serious commitment to educating visitors about plant and animal life, geography, and history; controlling the numbers of people allowed daily onto a given site; restoring watersheds and anything else damaged by trail building, foot traffic, or overuse; and discouraging wildlife feeding or any other disruptive behavior (such as making loud noises that scare birds into flight).

- Donate to local conservation groups that aid ecological efforts in Costa Rica.

- Buy souvenirs from groups such as ANAI, who raise money by selling beautiful locally made items.

- Don't remove plants, rocks, shells, or animals from their natural environment. ⚠ It's illegal to take anything, alive or dead, out of a national park or any other protected area.

- To see turtles nesting, go with a guide. If you go on your own, you will disrupt them.

- Pack out your trash when doing backcountry camping.

- Do not feed wildlife, even when animals appear tame—for their health and your safety.

- Do not stray from the trails for any reason.

## ELECTRICITY

North American appliances are compatible with Costa Rica's electrical system (110 volts) and outlets (parallel two-prong). Australian and European appliances require a two-prong adapter and a 220-volt to 110-volt transformer. Most laptops operate equally well on 110 and 220 volts and so require only an adapter, but you should bring a surge protector for your computer. Never use an outlet that specifically warns against using higher-voltage appliances without a transformer. Dual-voltage appliances (which are usually designed especially for travel) need only a two-prong adapter.

## EMERGENCIES

**Dial ☎ 911 for an ambulance, the fire department, or the police.** Costa Ricans are usually quick to respond to emergencies.

In a hotel or restaurant, the staff will usually offer immediate assistance, and in a public area passersby can be counted on to stop and help.

For emergencies ranging from health problems to lost passports, contact your embassy. (Citizens of Australia and New Zealand should contact the British Embassy.)

🔢 **Emergency Contacts Ambulance (Cruz Roja)** ☎ 128. **Fire** ☎ 118. **Police** ☎ 117, 127 outside major cities. **Traffic Police** ☎ 222-9330.

🔢 **Foreign Embassies British Embassy (Embajada Británica)** ✉ 11th fl., Centro Colón, between Cs. 38 and 40, Paseo Colón, San José ☎ 506/258-2025 🌐 www.embajadabritanica.com. **Canadian Embassy (Embajada Canadiense)** ✉ Sabana Sur, Oficentro Ejecutivo La Sabana, Torre No. 5, 3rd fl., behind the Controlaría building, San José ☎ 506/242-4400 🌐 www.dfait-maeci.gc.ca. **United States Embassy (Embajada de los Estados Unidos)** ✉ C. 120 and Avda. 0, Pavas, San José ☎ 506/519-2000 or 506/220-3939 for after-hours emergencies 🌐 www.usembassy.or.cr.

## ETIQUETTE & BEHAVIOR

If invited to someone's home, take a hostess gift such as flowers or a bottle of wine, or some trinket from your home country. If offered food at someone's home, accept it and eat it even if you aren't hungry. You will be offered coffee and should accept, although it's not necessary to finish the whole cup. Know that Costa Ricans don't like to say no, and will often avoid answering a question or simply say *gracias* when they really mean no.

On the whole, Costa Ricans are extremely polite, quick to shake hands and place a kiss on the right cheek (meaning you need to bear left when going in for the peck). Ticos tend to use formal Spanish, preferring, for example, *con mucho gusto* (with much pleasure) instead of *de nada* for "you're welcome." At the same time, a large number of Costa Rican men make a habit of ogling or making gratuitous comments when young women pass on the street. Women should wear a bra at all times. Family is very important in Costa Rica. It is considered polite to ask about one's marital status and family—don't confuse this with prying.

As you would anywhere, dress and behave respectfully when visiting churches. In churches men and women should not wear shorts, sleeveless shirts, or sandals; women should wear skirts below the knee.

## GAY & LESBIAN TRAVEL

Although outright harassment of gays and lesbians is infrequent in Costa Rica, alternative lifestyles are in no way openly accepted. Public displays of affection may be greeted with hostility, and discretion is advised outside of noted gay-friendly areas. Same-sex couples won't have problems at hotel check-in desks unless they engage in public displays of affection. Ticos, for whom religion and family are very important, tend simply to assume that everyone is straight. Although the country has had some instances of intolerance in the recent past—a gay and lesbian festival was canceled in 1998, and religious protesters have blocked the arrival of gay and lesbian tour groups—the official government position seems to be one of tolerance.

Relative to most other Latin American countries, Costa Rica is quite tolerant, and has consequently attracted many gay people from other Latin American nations and has a large gay community that is becoming more and more active. In 2003 a lawyer launched a constitutional challenge to the ban on gay marriage, and an annual gay-pride parade was recently launched. There are no explicitly antigay laws.

### GAY-FRIENDLY DESTINATIONS

San José and Manuel Antonio are the most gay-friendly towns, and they have several gay and lesbian bars and hangouts. Playita, a beach at the northern end of Playa Espadilla in Manuel Antonio National Park, is a small, secluded cove known to be a gay nude beach. It's a 90-minute walk along the coastline to the beach—check tide schedules before heading out, or you may get stuck.

Two notably gay-and-lesbian-friendly hotels are the Hotel Kekoldi in Barrio Amón, secluded yet close to downtown San José; it also has a sister hotel (with the same name) near Manuel Antonio. The Arco Iris Spanish School, in the San José suburb of Rohrmoser, is exclusively gay and lesbian. It runs the upscale all-gay Colours Oasis Resort, where Spanish students receive a 50% discount. Hotel Villa Roca in Manuel Antonio is exclusively for gays and lesbians, close to beaches, restaurants, bars, and Manuel Antonio National Park. Big Ruby's Plantation in Manuel Antonio organizes social events. Nightlife hotspots in San José include Avispa, a great mixed-crowd dance club, and Deja Vú, which caters to the younger electronic-music crowd.

▣ **Best Choices Arco Iris Spanish School** ☎ 506/686-6948 ⊕ www.arcoiriscostarica.com. **Avispa** ✉ C. 1, Avda. 8/10, Barrio La Soledad, San José ☎ 506/223-5343 ⊕ www.laavispa.co.cr. **Big Ruby's Plantation** ✉ Manuel Antonio ☎ 506/777-1332, 800/477-7829 in the U.S. and Canada ⊕ www.bigrubys.com. **Colours Oasis Resort** ✉ Blvd. Rohrmoser, northwest corner of The Triangle, Rohrmoser, San José ☎ 506/296-1880 ⊕ www.coloursoasis.com. **Deja Vú** ✉ C 2, between Avda 14/16, Barrio La Soledad, San José ☎ 506/256-6332. **Hotel Villa Roca** ✉ Manuel Antonio ☎ 506/777-1349 ⊕ www.villaroca.com. **Kekoldi Garden Hotel** ✉ Avda. 9, between C. 5 and 7, Barrio Amón, San José ☎ 786/221-9011 in the U.S., 506/248-0767 in Costa Rica ✉ Main road to Manuel Antonio, National Park, Quepos ☎ 786/221-9011 in the U.S., 506/248-0767 in Costa Rica ⊕ www.kekoldi.com.

### GAY & LESBIAN RESOURCES IN COSTA RICA

San José's 1@10 Café Internet serves as a gay and lesbian resource center. Its Web page is a wealth of information on whom to contact and where to go. *Gente 10* magazine is a bimonthly Costa Rican magazine that has bilingual, LGBT-friendly tour and hotel listings. You can find it, and the community paper, *Gayness,* in gay-friendly hotels, bars, and bookshops. The informal online Gay and Lesbian Guide to Costa Rica has some good travel information, including hotels that are listed with the Costa Rican Gay Business Association. GayCostaRica.com is a Web site with information on gay-friendly hotels, tour agencies, pharmacies, wedding planners, and real-estate companies. Pick up a copy of the free monthly *Playita* in gay-friendly establishments in Manuel Antonio.

1@10 Café Internet Uno@Diez ✉ C. 3 and Avda. 7, Barrio Amón, San José ☎ 506/258-4561 ⊕ www.1en10.com. GayCostaRica.com ⊕ www.gaycostarica.com. Gay and Lesbian Guide to Costa Rica ⊕ www.hometown.aol.com/gaycrica/guide.html.

## TOUR COMPANIES & TRAVEL AGENCIES

Tiquicia Travel is a well-known Costa Rica-based agency that caters to gays and lesbians. Costa Rican Charm is a local planner that deals mainly with day trips, Kennedy Travel is a big agency that has good links to several gay-friendly vacation planners, but is light on the Costa Rica specialty. Now, Voyager specializes in cruise travel, but works with Canadian-based Footprints travel for smaller Costa Rica nature trips.

Costa Rican Charm ⊕ www.costaricancharm.com. Footprints Travel ✉ 506 Church St., Ste 200, Toronto, ON, Canada M4Y 2C8 ☎ 888/962-6211 in Canada ⊕ www.footprintstravel.com. Gay-Costa Rica.com ✉ 30 Woodland St., Ste. 11-JK, Hartford, CT 06105 United States ☎ 877/987-8482 in the U.S., 860/246-7777 elsewhere ⊕ www.gay-costarica.com. Kennedy Travel ✉ 130 W. 42nd St., Suite 401, New York, NY 10036 ☎ 212/840-8659, 800/237-7433 ⊕ www.kennedytravel.com. Now, Voyager ✉ 4406 18th St., San Francisco, CA 94114 ☎ 415/626-1169 or 800/255-6951 ⊕ www.nowvoyager.com. Tiquicia Travel ✉ 733 C. 3 bis, between Avdas. 7 and 9, Barrio Amón, San José ☎ 506/256-6429 ⊕ www.tiquiciatravel.com.

## HEALTH

Malaria is not a problem in Costa Rica except in some remote northern Caribbean areas near the Nicaraguan border. Poisonous snakes, scorpions, and other pests pose a small (often overrated) threat. The CDC marks Costa Rica as an area infested by the *Aedes aegypti* (dengue-carrier) mosquito, but not as an epidemic region. A few thousand cases in locals are recorded each year, but the numbers have been dropping, and cases of fatal hemorrhagic dengue are rare. The highest-risk area is the Caribbean, and the rainy season is peak dengue season elsewhere. You're unlikely to be felled by this disease, but you can't take its prevention too seriously: *Repelente* (insect repellent spray) and *espirales* (mosquito coils) are sold in supermarkets and small country stores. U.S. insect repellent brands with DEET are sold in pharmacies and supermarkets.

Mosquito nets are available in some remote lodges; you can buy them in camping stores in San José. ■ TIP→→ Mild insect repellents, like the ones in some skin softeners, are no match for the intense mosquito activity in the hot, humid regions of the Caribbean, Osa Peninsula, and Southern Pacific. Repellents made with DEET or picaridin are most effective. Perfume, aftershave, and other lotions and potions can actually attract mosquitoes.

While it's unlikely you will contract malaria or dengue, if you start suffering from high fever, the shakes, or joint pain, make sure you ask to be tested for these diseases when you go to the local clinic. On the off chance you do have them, it's more likely doctors here will be able to provide an accurate diagnosis and treatment. Your embassy can provide you with a list of recommended doctors and dentists.

Government facilities—the so-called "Caja" hospitals (short for Caja Costarricense de Seguro Social, or Costa Rican Social Security System)—and clinics are of acceptable quality, but notoriously overburdened, a common complaint in socialized-medicine systems anywhere. Private hospitals are more accustomed to serving foreigners. They include Hospital CIMA, Clínica Bíblica, and Clínica Católica, which all have 24-hour pharmacies. The long-established and ubiquitous Fischel pharmacies are great places for your prescription needs. Antibiotics and psychotropic medications (for sleep, anxiety, or pain) require prescriptions in Costa Rica. Little else does. But plan ahead and bring an adequate supply with you from home; matches may not be exact.

For specific clinic, hospital, and pharmacy listings, *see* chapters 1 through 7.

Health Warnings National Centers for Disease Control and Prevention (CDC) ☎ 877/394-8747 international travelers' health line, 800/311-3435 other inquiries, 404/498-1600 Division of Quarantine and international health information ☎ 888/232-3299 🌐 www.cdc.gov/travel. **Travel Health Online** 🌐 trip-prep.com. **World Health Organization** (WHO) 🌐 www.who.int.

## DIVERS' ALERT
**Do not fly within 24 hours of scuba diving.**

## FOOD & DRINK
Most food and water is sanitary in Costa Rica. In rural areas you run a mild risk of encountering drinking water, fresh fruit, and vegetables contaminated by fecal matter, which in most cases causes a bit of *turista* (traveler's diarrhea) but can cause leptospirosis (can be treated by antibiotics if detected early). Although it may not be necessary, you can stay on the safe side by avoiding uncooked food, unpasteurized milk (including milk products), and ice—ask for drinks *sin hielo* (without ice)—and by drinking bottled water. Mild cases of turista may respond to Imodium (known generically as loperamide) or Pepto-Bismol (not as strong), both of which can be purchased over the counter. Drink plenty of purified water or tea; chamomile (*manzanilla* in Spanish) is a good folk remedy. In severe cases, rehydrate yourself with a salt-sugar solution (½ teaspoon salt and 4 tablespoons sugar per quart of water).

*Ceviche,* raw fish cured in lemon juice—a favorite appetizer, especially at seaside resorts—is generally safe to eat.

■ TIP➔➔ Buy organic foods whenever possible; chemicals, many of which have been banned elsewhere, are sprayed freely here without regulation.

## OTHER HAZARDS
Heat stroke and dehydration are real dangers, especially for hikers, so drink lots of water. Take at least 1 liter per person for every hour you plan to be on the trail. Sunburn is the most common traveler's health problem. Use sunscreen with SPF 30 or higher. Most pharmacies and supermarkets carry sunscreen in a wide range of SPFs, though it is relatively pricey.

The greatest danger to your person actually lies off Costa Rica's popular beaches—riptides are common wherever there are waves, and several tourists drown in them every year. If you see waves, ask the locals where it's safe to swim; and if you're uncertain, don't go in deeper than your waist. If you get caught in a rip current, swim parallel to the beach until you're free of it, and then swim back to shore. ⚠ Avoid swimming where a town's main river opens up to the sea. Septic tanks aren't common.

## SHOTS & MEDICATIONS
Most travelers to Costa Rica do not get any vaccinations or take any special medications. However, according to the U.S. Centers for Disease Control, travel to Costa Rica poses some risk of malaria, hepatitis A and B, dengue fever, typhoid fever, rabies, Chagas' disease, and *E. coli.* The CDC recommends getting vaccines for hepatitis A and typhoid fever, especially if you are going to be in remote areas or plan to stay for more than six weeks.

Check with the CDC for detailed health advisories and recommended vaccinations. In areas with malaria and dengue, both of which are carried by mosquitoes, bring mosquito nets, wear clothing that covers your body, and apply repellent containing DEET in living and sleeping areas. There are some pockets of malaria near the Nicaraguan border on the Caribbean coast. You probably won't need to take malaria pills before your trip unless you are staying for a prolonged period in the north, camping on northern coasts, or crossing the border into Nicaragua or Panama. You should discuss the option with your doctor. Children traveling to Central America should have current inoculations against measles, mumps, rubella, and polio.

## PHARMACIES
*Farmacia* is Spanish for "pharmacy," and the names for common drugs *aspirina,* Tylenol, and *ibuprofen* are basically the same as they are in English. Pepto-Bismol is widely available. Many drugs for which you need a prescription back home are sold over the counter in Costa Rica. Pharmacies throughout the country are generally open from 8 to 8, though it's best to consult with your hotel's staff to be sure.

Some pharmacies in San José affiliated with clinics stay open 24 hours.

## MEDICAL PLANS

No one plans to get sick while traveling, but it happens, so consider signing up with a medical-assistance company that gives short-term medical assistance. Members get doctor referrals, emergency evacuation or repatriation, hotlines for medical consultation, cash for emergencies, and other assistance. SOS Assistance is one such company. Prices are around $60 to $80 per person for a one- or two-week trip.

⚡ Medical-Assistance Companies **International SOS Assistance** ☎ 215/942-8000 or 800/523-6586 in the U.S., 905/940-2444 in Canada, 20/8762-8000 in the U.K., 02/9372-2400 in Australia, 09/359-1640 in New Zealand ⊕ www.internationalsos.com.

## HOLIDAYS

| | |
|---|---|
| January 1: | First day of the year |
| April 11: | Juan Santamaría Day, a national hero |
| Easter Week: | Thursday and Good Friday, religious activities |
| May 1: | International Labor Day |
| July 25: | Anniversary of the Annexation of Guanacaste Province |
| September 15: | Independence Day |
| August 2: | Day of the Virgin of Los Angeles (patron saint of Costa Rica) |
| August 15: | Mothers' Day |
| December 25: | Christmas Day |

## INSURANCE FOR YOUR TRIP

The most useful travel-insurance plan is a comprehensive policy that includes coverage for trip cancellation and interruption, default, trip delay, and medical expenses (with a waiver for preexisting conditions).

Without insurance you'll lose all or most of your money if you cancel your trip, regardless of the reason. Default insurance covers you if your tour operator, airline, or cruise line goes out of business. Trip-delay covers expenses that arise because of bad weather or mechanical delays. Study the fine print when comparing policies.

If you're traveling internationally, a key component of travel insurance is coverage for medical bills incurred if you get sick on the road. Such expenses aren't generally covered by Medicare or private policies. U.K. residents can buy a travel-insurance policy valid for most vacations taken during the year in which it's purchased (but check preexisting-condition coverage). British and Australian citizens need extra medical coverage when traveling overseas. Check the policy carefully, and make sure it covers the adventure sports, such as canopies or white-water rafting, that you'll be engaging in in Costa Rica.

Always buy travel policies directly from the insurance company; if you buy them from a cruise line, airline, or tour operator that goes out of business you probably won't be covered for the agency or operator's default, a major risk. Before making any purchase, review your existing health and homeowner's policies to find what they cover away from home.

⚡ Insurers In the U.S.: **Access America** ☎ 800/284-8300 ⊕ www.accessamerica.com. **Travel Guard International** ☎ 800/826-1300 or 715/345-1041 ⊕ www.travelguard.com. In the U.K.: **Association of British Insurers** ☎ 020/7600-3333 ⊕ www.abi.org.uk. In Canada: **RBC Insurance** ☎ 800/387-4357 ⊕ www.rbcinsurance.com. In Australia: **Insurance Council of Australia** ☎ 1300/363683 or 02/9251-4456 ⊕ http://app01.ica.com.au. In New Zealand: **Insurance Council of New Zealand** ☎ 04/472-5230 ⊕ www.icnz.org.nz.

## INTERNET

Downtown San José is full of Internet cafés with high-speed connections; prices are usually less than $1 per hour. As you move away from the capital, prices rise to $2–$4 per hour and connections become slower and more unreliable. Wildly expensive satellite Internet is available at some remote, exclusive hotels. Cafés are generally good places to make international Internet calls, but expect echoes and a mediocre connection. Most major hotels geared to business travelers have free wireless access. Dial-up access is spotty and frustrating, but if you're desperate and have access to a telephone line, you can buy one of RACSA's prepaid Internet cards in three amounts: 1,800 colones (5 hours), 3,550 colones (10 hours), and 5,300 colones (15 hours). Cards are sold at Fischel and Catedral pharmacies, as well as at the Banco Nacional. The cards come with the access numbers, and a help line that has helpful English-speaking operators.

## LANGUAGE

Spanish is the official language, although many tour guides and locals in heavily touristed areas speak English. You'll have a better time if you learn some basic Spanish before you go and bring a phrase book with you. At the very least, learn the rudiments of polite conversation—niceties such as *por favor* (please) and *gracias* (thank you) will be warmly appreciated. For more words and phrases, *see* the Spanish glossary *in* the Understanding Costa Rica chapter.

In the Caribbean province of Limón a creole English called Mekatelyu is widely spoken by older generations. English is understood by most everyone in these parts.

## LODGING

A number of Web sites help you through the lodging search. **Budget** options can be found through Costa Rican Hostelling International ( ⇨ Student Travel, *below*). **Low-end** alternatives are often referred to as *cabinas* whether they offer a cement cigar-box motel or free-standing rustic rooms. Most have private rooms, cold-water cement showers, fans instead of air-conditioning, limited—if any—secure parking or storage, and may share bathrooms. Owners tend to be Costa Rican. Often without Web sites, e-mail, or links to major agencies, these hotels tend to follow a first-come, first-served booking policy. They may have room during peak seasons when mid- or upper-end options are booked solid.

**Mid-range** options include boutique hotels, tasteful bungalows, bed-and-breakfasts, and downtown casino hotels. Those in the hotter beach areas may not have hot-water showers. Many have pools, Internet access, and meal options. They tend to be foreign-owned and, with the exception of the casinos, have personalized service. Because they're generally small, you may have to book one or two months ahead, and up to six months in the high season. Booking through an association or agency can significantly reduce the time you spend scanning the Internet, but you can often get a better deal and negotiate longer-stay or low-season discounts. Costa Rica Innkeepers is a good resource.

**High-end** accommodations can be found almost everywhere. They range from luxury tents to exquisite hotels and villa rentals, and are often more secluded. You'll find all the amenities you expect at such areas, with one notable exception: the roads and routes to even five-star villas can be atrocious. This category is sometimes booked up to a year in advance for Christmas, and during this season you may only be able to book through agents or central reservations offices. **Resorts** are generally one of two options: luxurious privileged gateways to the best of the country (such as Punta Islita) or generic budget all-inclusives (such as the Barceló) that probably run counter to what you're coming to Costa Rica for. General local consensus is that the Four Seasons hotel is in a category unto itself, unmatched in pomp and price anywhere in the country.

Several **chain hotels** have franchises in Costa Rica, leaning toward generic and all-inclusive ( ⇨ Chain Hotels, *below*). The upside is that they are rarely booked solid, so you can always fall back on one in a worst-case scenario, and they often have member discounts.

**Nature lodges** and hotels in the South Pacific (where restaurants aren't an option) may be less expensive than they initially appear, as the price of a room usually includes three hearty meals a day, and sometimes guided hikes. These, and other remote accommodations, may not have daily Internet access even though they have a Web site: be patient if you're attempting to book directly. Since many of the hotels are remote and have an eco-friendly approach (even to luxury), and air-conditioning, in-room telephones, and TVs are exceptions to the rule. Consider how isolated you want to be; some rural and eco-lodges are miles from neighbors and other services and have few rainy-day diversions.

⚠ Most hotels, especially those in San José, require that you reconfirm your reservation 24 to 48 hours before you arrive. If you don't reconfirm, you may find yourself without a room. Travel Web Costa Rica and the ICT both provide hotel lists, searchable by star category.

The lodgings we list are Costa Rica's cream of the crop in each price category. We always list the facilities that are available, but we don't specify whether they cost extra; when pricing accommodations, always ask what's included and what costs extra. Properties are assigned price categories based on the range from the least-expensive standard double room at high season (excluding holidays) to the most expensive. **Keep in mind that hotel prices we list exclude 16.4% service and tax.**

| WHAT IT COSTS | FOR 2 PEOPLE |
|---|---|
| $$$$ | over $200 |
| $$$ | $125–$200 |
| $$ | $75–$125 |
| $ | $35–$75 |
| ¢ | under $35 |

*Prices are for two people in a standard double room in high season, excluding service and tax (16.4%).*

🔏 Lodging Resources **Costa Rican Hotel Association** ☎ 506/248-0990 ⊕ www.costaricahotels.com. **Costa Rica Innkeepers** ☎ 506/441-1157 ⊕ www.costaricainnkeepers.com. **Instituto Costarricense de Turismo (ICT)** ☎ 866/267-8274 in the U.S. and Canada, 506/299-5800 in Costa Rica ⊕ www.visitcostarica.com. **Travel Web Costa Rica** ☎ 800/788-7857 in the U.S., 506/256-3222 in Costa Rica ⊕ www.crica.com.

## RESERVATIONS

At Costa Rica's popular beach and mountain resorts reserve well in advance for the dry season (mid-December–April everywhere except the Caribbean, which has a short September–October "dry" season). During the rainy season (May–mid-December except on the Caribbean coast, where it's almost always rainy) most ho-

tels drop their rates considerably, which sometimes sends them into a lower price category than the one we indicate.

■ TIP→→ If you're having trouble finding a hotel that isn't completely booked, consider contacting a tour operator who can arrange your entire trip (⇨ Tours & Packages). Since they reserve blocks of rooms far in advance, you might have better luck.

## APARTMENT, CONDO & VILLA RENTALS

Furnished rentals accommodate a crowd or a family, often for less and at a higher comfort level. Knowledgable Costa Rican Vacations handles bookings for upscale condos and villas in Manuel Antonio, Dominical, and several hotspots in Guanacaste. Nosara Home Page lists apartments and villas on the Nicoya Peninsula; Villas International has an extensive list of properties in Quepos and Tamarindo. The House of Rentals, a Century 21 affiliate, arranges houses and condos in the Flamingo area.

🔏 **Costa Rican Vacations** ☎ 800/247-1351 in the U.S. and Canada, 506/296-7715 in Costa Rica ⊕ www.vacationscostarica.com. **Century 21/House of Rentals** ☎ 506/654-5161. **Nosara Home Page** ⊕ www.nosara.com. **Villas and Apartments Abroad** ☎ 212/213-6435 or 800/433-3020 ⊕ www.vaanyc.com. **Villas International** ☎ 415/499-9490 or 800/221-2260 ⊕ www.villasintl.com.

## CAMPING

One of the cheapest ways to spend the night in this region is to camp; as long as you have your own tent, it's easy to set up house almost anywhere. Most official campgrounds are cement swaths crammed with cranked stereos; the exceptions, and the only camping we would highly recommend, are the national-park camping areas. It's illegal and somewhat dicey to camp outside of campgrounds, but many landowners in rural areas will allow you to camp on their land. Do not pitch your tent without getting permission first. Don't ever leave your belongings or a campfire unattended.

## CHAIN HOTELS

Outside San José, rooms are in great demand between the week after Christmas and the week before Easter; reserve one to three months in advance for those times. Most hotels drop their rates during the "green season" (May to mid-December), and during this time—barring July—it's quite feasible to show up without reservations and haggle over rates, a process that can bring your hotel budget down to nearly half what it might be in the high season.

🎋 **Chain Hotels Aurola Holiday Inn** ☎ 506/222-2424 Downtown San José ✍ aurola@racsa.co.cr. **Barceló** ☎ 800/227-2356 anywhere in the world, 506/220-2034 north of San José, 506/296-5062 Sabana Sur, 506/290-5060 Sabana Norte, 506/653-0363 Playa Langosta, 506/683-0303 Playa Tambor, ⊕ www.barcelo.com. **Best Western** ☎ 0800/011-0063 anywhere in the world, 506/255-4766 Downtown San José, 506/232-4811 north of San José, 506/643-1000 Jacó, 506/654-4070 Flamingo, 506/777-0811 Quepos, 506/666-0144 Liberia, 506/653-0114 Tamarindo ⊕ www.bestwesterninternational.com. **Hampton Inn & Suites** ☎ 800/426-7867 international, 506/442-3320 Alajuela ⊕ www.grupomarta.com. **Marriott** ☎ 506/298-0000 La Ribera de Belén, 506/208-3000 Escazú, 506/630-9000 Jacó ⊕ www.marriotthotels.com. **Meliá** ☎ 506/239-0022 Cariari, 506/232-8122 Sabana Norte ⊕ www.solmelia.com. **Paradisus** ☎ 506/654-4123 Conchal ⊕ www.paradisus-playa-conchal-info.com. **Occidental** ☎ 506/690-9900 [Allegro Papagayo] Papagayo Peninsula, 506/672-0193 [Grand Papagayo], Papagayo Peninsula, 506/460-6000 Alajuela, 506/222-5266 San José ⊕ www.occidental-hoteles.com. **Radisson Europa** ☎ 800/333-3333 international, 506/257-3257 Barrio Tournón ✍ hotelradisson@radisson.co.cr. **Real InterContinental** ☎ 506/289-7000, Guachepelín ✍ www.gruporeal.com.

## HOME EXCHANGES

A handful of home exchanges are available; this involves an initial small registration fee and you'll have to plan farther ahead. It's an excellent way to immerse yourself in true Costa Rica, particularly if you've been here before and aren't relying so heavily on tourism support that hotels can offer. Drawbacks include restricted options and dates. Many companies list home exchanges, but we've found Home-Link International, which lists a handful of jazzy houses in Costa Rica, and Intervac, which as of this writing only listed one

house, to be the most reliable.

🎋 **Exchange Clubs HomeLink International** ☎ 813/975-9825 or 800/638-3841 ⊕ www.homelink.org, $115 yearly for a listing, online access, and catalog, $75 without catalog. **Intervac U.S.** ☎ 800/756-4663 ⊕ www.intervacus.com, $130 yearly for a listing, online access, and a catalog, $70 without catalog.

## MEAL PLANS

In every hotel review, we specify whether a meal plan is included in the base price of a room by using the following acronyms:

**EP:** European Plan (no meals)

**CP:** Continental Plan (Continental breakfast)

**BP:** Breakfast Plan (full breakfast)

**MAP:** Modified American Plan (breakfast and dinner)

**FAP:** Full American Plan (breakfast, lunch, and dinner)

**AI:** All Inclusive (all meals, drinks, and most activities)

## CUTTING COSTS

• When buying from an online consolidator like Hotels.com, carefully read the fine print detailing penalties for changes and cancellations. Also, be sure to confirm your reservation.

• Start looking as early as possible.

• Sign up for free membership programs with chain hotels; you may getting a "signing bonus" of a room upgrade.

• If you're not sure of your dates but you want to book anyway, make sure you're aware of the hotel's cancellation policy so you don't get nailed with a fat fee.

• Don't dismiss nature lodges as overly expensive; they often include three meals and guided tours and can be some of the best deals.

• Try booking directly with mid-range hotels; you may be able to get a better deal.

🎋 **Online Resources Hotels.com** ☎ 214/369-1246, 800/246-8357 in U.S. ⊕ www.hotels.com. **lastminute.com** ⊕ www.lastminute.com. **Zuji** ⊕ www.zuji.com.au.

## MAIL & SHIPPING

The Spanish word for post office is *correos*. Mail from the United States, Canada, or Europe can take two to three weeks to arrive in Costa Rica, a couple of weeks more from Australia or New Zealand (occasionally it never arrives at all). Within the country, mail service is even less reliable. Outgoing mail is marginally quicker, with delivery to North America in five to ten days, to Europe in two weeks, and to Australia and New Zealand about three weeks, especially when sent from San José. Always use airmail for overseas cards and letters. Mail theft is a chronic problem, so do not mail checks, cash, or anything else of value.

Letters from Costa Rica to the United States and Canada cost the equivalent of U.S. 26¢, postcards to the United States 23¢; to the United Kingdom, letters cost 31¢, postcards 23¢; and to Australia or New Zealand, letters cost 40¢, postcards 33¢.

You can have mail sent poste restante (*lista de correos*) to any Costa Rican post office. In written addresses, *apartado*, abbreviated *apdo.*, indicates a post office box. The American Express office in San José does not hold mail, even for those with AE cards or traveller's checks.

Post offices are generally open weekdays 8–5:30, and on Saturdays 8–noon. Stamps can be purchased at post offices and some souvenir shops. These vendors will also accept the mail you wish to send; mailboxes do not exist in Costa Rica. Always check with your hotel, which may sell stamps and post your letters for you.

### EXPRESS SERVICES

UPS has offices in San José, Tamarindo, Jacó, Sarchí, Arenal, and Limón. DHL has dropoffs in San José (Rohrmoser, Paseo Colón), Curridabat, Heredia, Liberia, Limón, Ciudad Quesada, Jacó, Quepos, and San Isidro. Both have central information numbers with English-speaking staff to direct you to the nearest office. FedEx has offices in San José only. Prices are about 10 times what you'd pay at the post office, but packages arrive in a matter of days. ("Overnight" is usually a misnomer—shipments to most North American cities take two days,

to Britain three, and to Australia and New Zealand four or five.)

⚏ **Express-Service Main Offices DHL** ✉ 600 meters northeast of the Real Cariari Mall, La Aurora, Heredia ☎ 506/209-6000 ☞ Call for other locations. **Federal Express** ✉ Zona Franca Metropolitana, Ciudad Barreal de Heredia, Local 1B, Heredia ✉ Centro de Servicio Mundial, Paseo Colón, 100 m east of León Cortés statue, San José ☎ 0800/052-1090. **United Parcel Service** (UPS) ✉ 50 meters east of Pizza Hut, Paseo Colón, San José ☎ 506/290-2828 ☞ Call for other locations.

## SHIPPING PACKAGES

Shipping parcels through the post office is not for those in a hurry, because packages to the United States and Canada can take weeks; to the United Kingdom, Australia, and New Zealand, months. Also, packages may be pilfered. However, post-office shipping is the cheapest way to go, with rates at $6–$12 per kilogram.

Some stores offer shipping, but it is usually quite expensive. If you can, carry your packages home with you.

## MONEY MATTERS

In general, Costa Rica is cheaper than North America or Europe, but travelers looking for dirt-cheap developing-nation deals may find it's more expensive than they bargained for—and prices are rising as more foreigners visit and relocate here. Food in modest restaurants and public transportation are inexpensive. A 1-mi taxi ride costs about $1. Here are some sample prices to give you an idea of the cost of living in Costa Rica: 2-liter bottle of Coca-Cola, $1.40–$1.60; cup of coffee, 50¢–95¢; bottle of beer, $1–$1.50; sandwich, $2–$3.

**All prices in this book are quoted in U.S. dollars.** The Costa Rican currency, the colón (plural: colones), is subject to continual, small devaluations. At this writing, the colón is 470 to the U.S. dollar, 610 to the Euro, 381 to the Canadian dollar, 889 to the pound sterling, 364 to the Australian dollar, and 339 to the New Zealand dollar.

**Prices throughout this guide are given for adults.** Substantially reduced fees are almost always available for children and students.

## ATMS & BANKS

Lines at San José banks would try the patience of a saint; instead, get your spending money at a *cajero automático* (ATM). If you do use the bank, remember that Mondays, Fridays, and the first and last days of the month are the busiest days.

Although they are springing up at a healthy rate, don't count on using an ATM outside of San José. While not exhaustive, the A Todas Horas (ATH) company Web site lists locations of its cash machines, and notes which ones offer colones, dollars, or both; click on *búsqueda de cajeros* to see the lists by region.

All ATMs are 24-hour; in addition to banks, you'll find them in major grocery stores, some hotels, gas stations, and even a few McDonald's. ATH, Red Total, and Scotiabank machines supposedly accept both Cirrus (a partner with MasterCard) and Plus (a partner with Visa) cards, but often don't. If you'll be spending time away from major tourist centers, particularly in the Caribbean, get most or all of the cash you need in San José and carry a few U.S. dollars in case you run out of colones. It's helpful to have both a Visa and a MasterCard—even in San José—as many machines accept only one or the other.

ATMs are sometimes out of order and sometimes run out of cash on weekends. ■ TIP→→ PIN numbers with more than four digits are not recognized at some ATMs in Costa Rica, such as those at Banco Nacional or Banco de Costa Rica. If you have a five-digit PIN, change it with your bank before you travel, or use only cash machines marked ATH.

In San José the main Banco Popular, which accepts Plus cards, is at Avda. 2 and C. 1, near the National Theater. The Credomatic office, on C. Central between Avdas. 3 and 5, is the local representative for most major credit cards; get cash advances there, or at the Banco de San José across the street.

Most state banks are open weekdays 9–3, and some are open Saturday morning. Several branches of Banco Nacional are open until 6. Private banks—Scotiabank, Banco Banex, and Banco de San José—tend to keep longer hours and are usually the best places to change U.S. dollars and traveler's checks. The Banco de San José in Juan Santamaría International Airport is open every day 5 AM–10 PM.

Though it might seem counterintuitive, ■ TIP→→ whenever possible, use ATMs only during bank business hours. ATMs here have been known to "eat" cards, and are frequently out of cash. When the bank is open, you can go in to retrieve your card or get cash from a teller. As a safety precaution, look for a machine in a bank with a guard nearby.

🗂 Resources **A Todas Horas** (ATH) ⊕ www.ath.fi.cr.

## CREDIT CARDS

All major credit cards (except Discover) are accepted at most major hotels and restaurants in this book. As the phone system improves and expands, many budget hotels, restaurants, and other properties have begun to accept plastic; but plenty of properties still require payment in cash. ■ TIP→→ Don't count on using your credit card outside of San José. Carry enough cash to patronize the many businesses without credit-card capability. Note that some hotels, restaurants, tour companies, and other businesses add a surcharge (around 5%) to the bill if you pay with a credit card, or give you a 5%–10% discount if you pay in cash. It's always a good idea to pay for large purchase with a major credit card if possible, so you can cancel payment or get reimbursed if there's a problem.

At this writing, Costa Rica does not have the technology to accept the prepaid American Express card.

Throughout this guide, the following abbreviations are used: **AE,** American Express; **DC,** Diners Club; **MC,** MasterCard; and **V,** Visa.

## CURRENCY EXCHANGE

All non-U.S. currency must be exchanged in banks; Australian and New Zealand dollars cannot be exchanged anywhere, even in banks.

Although ATM transaction fees may be higher here than at home, ATM rates are excellent because they're based on wholesale rates offered only by major banks. You won't do as well at exchange booths in airports, in hotels, in restaurants, or in stores.

Costa Rican colones are sold abroad at terrible rates, so you should wait until you arrive in Costa Rica to get local currency. Residents of Australia, Canada, New Zealand, and the U.K. should bring U.S. dollars to exchange. Private banks—Scotiabank, Banco Banex, and Banco de San José—are the best places to change U.S. dollars and traveler's checks. There is a branch of the Banco de San José in the airport (open daily 5 AM–10 PM) where you can exchange money when you arrive. Taxi and van drivers who pick up at the airport accept U.S. dollars.

Avoid people on the city streets who offer to change money. San José's outdoor money changers are notorious for short-changing people and passing counterfeit bills. The guys who change money at the airport aren't quite as shady, but they might not be above shortchanging you, and they don't offer great rates in any case.

📅 Exchange Services **International Currency Express** ✉ 427 N. Camden Dr., Suite F, Beverly Hills, CA 90210 ☎ 888/278-6628 orders 🖷 310/278-6410 🌐 www.foreignmoney.com. **Travel Ex Currency Services** 🖷 800/287-7362 orders and retail locations 🌐 www.travelex.com.

## TAXES

All Costa Rican businesses charge a 13% sales tax. Hotels charge a 16.4% fee covering service and tax. Restaurants add 13% tax and 10% service fee to meals. Tourists are not refunded for taxes paid in Costa Rica.

## TIPPING

Costa Rica doesn't have a tipping culture, but positive reinforcement goes a long way to fostering a culture of good service, which is hit and miss. Tip only for good service. Taxi drivers aren't tipped, but it's common courtesy to leave an extra 200–300 colones if they've helped you navigate a complicated set of directions. ■ TIP→→ Do not use U.S. coins to tip, because there is no way for locals to exchange them.

Chambermaids get 1,000–1,500 colones per day; for great service try to leave up to 10% of your room bill. Concierges are usually not tipped. Room-service waiters should be tipped about 500 colones, as should bellhops (more in the most expensive hotels).

Restaurant bills include a 13% tax and 10% service charge—sometimes these amounts are included in prices on the menu, and sometimes they aren't. If the menu doesn't indicate whether service is included, ask. An additional gratuity is not expected, especially in cheap restaurants, but people often leave something extra when service is good. Leave a tip of about 200 colones per drink for bartenders, too.

At some point on a trip, most visitors to Costa Rica are in the care of a naturalist guide, who can show them the sloths and special hiking trails they'd never find on your own. Give $10 (or 5,000 colones) per day per person to guides if they've transported and guided you individually or in small groups, and about 10% of the rental to a hired driver of a small car. Give less to guides or drivers on bigger tours. For tour guides, it's okay to pay with U.S. dollars.

## TRAVELER'S CHECKS

Vendors and tour operators are becoming more familiar with traveler's checks, and usually accept them; for security, it's a good idea to bring some money in this form. If you have an American Express card and can draw on a U.S. checking account, you can buy U.S.-dollar traveler's checks at the American Express office in San José for a 1% service charge.

## PACKING

Travel light, and make sure you can carry your luggage without assistance. Even if you're planning to stay only in luxury resorts, odds are at least once you'll have to haul your stuff a distance from bus stops, shuttle drop-off, or the airport. Another incentive to pack light: domestic airlines have tight weight restrictions (at this writing 25 pounds [11.3 kilograms]) and not all buses have luggage compartments.

It's a good idea to ■ TIP→→ pack essentials in one bag and extras in another, so you can leave one bag at your hotel in San José (most hotels allow this if you are staying with them again before your departure flight) or with SANSA or NatureAir (⇨ Air Travel) if you exceed weight restrictions. Frameless backpacks and duffel bags can be squeezed into tight spaces and are less conspicuous than fancier luggage. To avoid having your checked luggage chosen for hand inspection, don't cram bags full. The U.S. Transportation Security Administration suggests packing shoes on top and placing personal items you don't want touched in clear plastic bags.

Bring comfortable, hand-washable clothing. T-shirts and shorts are acceptable near the beach and in tourist areas; long-sleeve shirts and pants protect your skin from ferocious sun and, in some regions, mosquitoes. Leave your jeans behind—they take forever to dry and can't be worn out in the evenings. Pack a waterproof, lightweight jacket and a light sweater for cool nights, early mornings, and trips up volcanoes; you'll need even warmer clothes for trips to Chirripó National Park or Volcán Baru and overnight stays in San Gerardo de Dota or La Providencia Lodge. Bring at least one good (and wrinkle-free) outfit for going out at night.

Women might have a tough time finding tampons, so bring your own. For almost all toiletries, including contact lens supplies, a pharmacy is your best bet. Don't forget sunblock, and expect to sweat it off and reapply regularly in the high humidity. Definitely bring sufficient film and batteries, since they're extremely expensive here.

Snorkelers staying at budget hotels should consider bringing their own equipment; otherwise, you can rent gear at most beach resorts.

In your carry-on luggage, pack an extra pair of eyeglasses or contact lenses and enough of any medication you take to last a few days longer than the entire trip. You may also ask your doctor to write a spare prescription using the drug's generic name, as brand names may vary from country to country. ⚠ Never pack prescription drugs, valuables, or undeveloped film in checked baggage. To avoid customs and security delays, carry medications in their original packaging.

Check *Fodor's How to Pack* (available at online retailers and bookstores everywhere) for more tips.

## PACKING FOR ADVENTURE

You have to get down and dirty—well, more like wet and muddy—to see many of the country's natural wonders. This packing list is not comprehensive; instead, it's a guide to some of the things you might not think to bring. For your main piece of luggage, a sturdy internal-frame backpack is great, but a duffel bag works too. You can get by with a rolling suitcase, but then bring a smaller backpack as well.

- Quick-drying synthetic-fiber shirts and socks

- Hiking boots or shoes that can get muddy and wet

- Waterproof sport sandals (especially in the Osa Peninsula, where most transportation is by boat, and often there are no docks)

- Knee-high socks for the rubber boots that are supplied at many lodges

- A pair of lightweight pants (fire ants, mosquitoes, and other pests make covering yourself a necessity on deep-forest hikes)

- Pants for horseback riding (if that's on your itinerary)

- Waterproof, lightweight jacket, windbreaker, or poncho

- Day pack for hikes

- Sweater for cool nights and early mornings

- Swimsuit

- Insect repellant (with DEET, for forested areas and especially on the Caribbean coast, where there are pockets of malaria)

- Flashlight with spare batteries (for occasional power outages or inadequately lighted walkways at lodges)

- Sunscreen with a minimum of SPF 30 (waterproof sunscreens are best; even if you're not swimming, you might be swimming in perspiration)

- Large, portable water bottle

- Hat and/or bandanas (not only do they provide shade, but they prevent perspiration from dripping down your face)
- Binoculars (with carrying strap)
- Camera (waterproof, or with a waterproof case or dry bag, sold in outdoor shops)
- Film (film in Costa Rica can be expired and is expensive)
- Imodium and Pepto-Bismol (tablet form is best)
- Swiss Army knife (and remember to pack it in your *checked* luggage, never your carry-on—even on domestic flights in Costa Rica)
- Zip-lock bags (they always come in handy)
- Travel alarm clock or watch with an alarm (don't count on wake-up calls)
- Nonelectric shaving utensils
- Toilet paper (rarely provided in public bathrooms)

## PASSPORTS & VISAS

Canadians, U.S. citizens, and citizens of the U.K. need only a passport to enter Costa Rica for stays of up to 90 days. Make sure it's up-to-date—you'll be refused entry if the passport is due to expire in less than six months. Citizens of Australia and New Zealand need only a valid passport to enter Costa Rica for stays of up to 30 days. You are presented with a 30-day tourist visa when you arrive. Once you're here, you can go to the *Migración* office in La Uruca and extend the visa to 90 days. In practice, dealing with local immigration is frustrating and time-consuming. It's easier and more fun to spend a weekend in Nicaragua or Panama—but don't expect to do that undetected more than a couple of times.

The least-busy time to apply for a passport or to renew is in fall and winter. Before any trip, check your passport's expiration date, and if necessary, renew it as soon as possible. If you are traveling with children under age 14, contact your nearest Costa Rican embassy or consulate for guidelines.

When traveling internationally, carry your passport even if you don't need one (it's always the best form of I.D.) and make two photocopies of the data page (one for someone at home and another for you, carried separately from your passport).

Due to high rates of passport theft, travelers in Costa Rica are no longer required to carry their original documents with them at all times, although you must have easy access to them. Photocopies of the data page and your entry stamp are sufficient.

■ TIP→→ For easy retrieval in the event of a lost or stolen passport, before you leave scan your passport into a portable storage device (like an iPod) that you're carrying with you or e-mail the scanned image to yourself.

## LOST PASSPORTS

If your passport is lost or stolen, first call the police—having the police report can make replacement easier—and then call your embassy (⇨ Emergencies, *above*). Australians and New Zealanders can get assistance at the U.K. embassy; the Canadian embassy is also an option for Australians. You'll get a temporary Emergency Travel Document that will need to be replaced once you return home. Fees vary according to how fast you need the passport; in some cases the fee covers your permanent replacement as well. The new document will not have your entry stamps; ask if your embassy takes care of this, or whether it's your responsibility to get the necessary immigration authorization.

## RESTROOMS

Toilet paper is not discarded into the toilet in Costa Rica, but rather in a trash bin beside it. Septic systems are delicate and the paper will clog the toilet. At some public restrooms you might have to pay 50¢ or so for a few sheets of toilet paper. At others, there may not be any toilet paper. It's always a good idea to have some tissues at the ready.

## SAFETY

Violent crime is not a serious problem in Costa Rica, but thieves can easily prey on tourists, so be alert. Crimes against property are rife in San José. In rural areas theft is on the rise. For many English-speaking tourists, standing out like a sore thumb can't be avoided in Costa Rica. But there are some precautions you can take:

- Don't bring anything you can't stand to lose.
- Don't wear expensive jewelry or watches.
- In cities, don't carry expensive cameras or lots of cash.
- Carry backpacks on your front; thieves can slit your backpack and run away with its contents before you notice.
- Don't wear a waist pack, because thieves can cut the strap.
- Distribute your cash and any valuables (including credit cards and passport) among a deep front pocket, an inside jacket or vest pocket, and a hidden money belt. (If you use a money belt, carry some cash in your purse or wallet so you don't have to reach for the hidden pouch in public.)
- Keep your hand on your wallet if you are in a crowd or on a crowded bus.
- Don't let your purse just dangle from your shoulder; always hold on to it with your hand for added security. If you cross the strap over your body, you run the risk of being dragged with your bag if you're mugged.
- Keep car windows rolled up and car doors locked at all times in cities; elsewhere, roll up windows and lock doors whenever you leave your car.
- Park in designated parking lots, or if that's not possible, accept the offer of the *guachimán* (a term adopted from English, pronounced "watchie man")—men or boys who watch your car while you're gone. Give them the equivalent of a dollar per hour when you return.
- Never leave valuables visible in a car, even in an attended parking lot: take them inside with you whenever possible, or lock them in the trunk.
- Padlock your luggage.
- Talk with locals or your hotel staff about crime in the area. They will be able to tell you if it's safe to walk around after dark and what to avoid.

- Never walk in a narrow space between a building and a car parked on the street close to it; a prime hiding spot for thieves.
- Do not walk in parks at night.
- Men should be suspicious of overly friendly or sexually aggressive females. At best they are probably prostitutes; at worst they have targeted you for a scam.
- Never leave a drink unattended in a club or bar: scams involving date-rape drugs have been reported in the past few years, targeting both men and women.
- Never leave your belongings unattended anywhere, including at the beach or in a tent.
- If your hotel room has a safe, use it, even if it's an extra charge. If your room doesn't have one, ask the manager to put your valuables in the hotel safe and ask him or her to sign a list of what you are storing there.
- If you are involved in an altercation with a mugger, immediately surrender your possessions and walk away quickly.

If the worst happens, at the risk of sounding cynical, we wouldn't recommend making a police report, unless your passport was stolen. You'll wait hours for an English-speaking officer, hours to give your statement, and probably the rest of your life to ever see justice done. Call your credit-card company using the numbers we provide ( ⇨ Credit Cards *in* Money Matters).

## LOCAL SCAMS

Scams are common in San José, where a drug addict may tell tales of having recently been robbed, then ask you for donations; a distraction artist might squirt you with something, or spill something on you, then try to clean you off while his partner steals your backpack; pickpockets and bag slashers work buses and crowds; and street money changers pass off counterfeit bills. To top it all off, car theft is rampant. Beware of anyone who seems overly friendly, aggressively helpful, or disrespectful of your personal space.

Don't believe taxi drivers when they say the hotel is closed, unless you've personally gotten out and checked it yourself. Many want to take you somewhere else to earn a commission. If a taxi driver says he does not have change and the amount is substantial, ask him to drive to a store or gas station where you can get change. This might be enough to prompt him to suddenly "find" the difference to give you. Avoid paying with large bills to prevent this.

A number of tourists have been hit with the slashed-tire scam: someone punctures the tires of your rental car (often right at the airport, when you arrive) and then comes to your "aid" when you pull off to the side of the road and robs you blind. Forget about the rims: always drive to the nearest open gas station or service center if you get a flat.

### TIPS FOR WOMEN TRAVELERS

Lone women travelers will get a fair amount of attention from men, but in general should be safe. Women should not hitchhike alone or in pairs. Blondes and redheads will get more grief than brunettes. To avoid hassles, avoid wearing short shorts, short skirts, or sleeveless tops. On the bus, try to take a seat next to a woman. Women should not walk alone in San José at night or venture into dangerous areas of the city at all. Ask at your hotel which neighborhoods to avoid. Ignore unwanted comments. If you are being harassed on a bus, at a restaurant, or in some other public place, tell the manager. In taxis, sit in the back seat. If you want to fend off an earnest but decent admirer in a bar, you can politely say *"Por favor, necesito un tiempo a solas."* (I'd like some time on my own, please.) Stronger is *"Por favor, no moleste."* (Please stop bothering me.), and for real pests the simple *"Vayase!"* (Go away!) is usually effective. Costa Rican men often fancy themselves Latin lovers and profess adoration before the first drink has even arrived; they lean toward machismo and can be persistent, even overaggressive.

### SENIOR-CITIZEN TRAVEL

Older travelers flock to Costa Rica, and many businesses are making an effort to cater to this demographic. Some seniors may encounter more challenges to mobility than they do at home—especially on those muddy jungle trails—but should otherwise find Costa Rica most hospitable.

Specify that you're a senior when you're making your travel reservations (for airplane tickets, hotel rooms, etc.) and keep your identification handy. However, the Costa Rican tourism industry isn't distinguished for its senior-citizen discounts. If you're over 65 and want to get a prescription filled here, though, you're likely to get a good deal. When renting a car, ask about promotional car-rental discounts, which can be cheaper than senior-citizen rates. Note that some rental companies won't rent to people over a certain age (with Budget, for example, drivers must be younger than 75); ask before you book.

### COMPANIES SPECIALIZING IN TRAVEL FOR SENIORS

The American Association of Retired Persons offers its members discounts on travel packages, hotels, airfares, and car rentals in exchange for a $12.50 annual fee. Elderhostel is a not-for-profit organization that organizes study programs for people 55 and over.

**The American Association of Retired Persons** (AARP) ☎ 888/687-2277 in the U.S. ⊕ www.aarp. org. **Elderhostel** ☎ 877/426-8056 in the U.S., 978/ 323-4141 international callers, 877/426-2167 TTY ⊟ 877/426-2166 ⊕ www.elderhostel.org. **Interhostel** ☎ 603/862-1147, 800/733-9753 in the U.S. ⊕ www.learn.unh.edu.

### SHOPPING

Shopping is not a major reason to visit Costa Rica, but some high-quality wooden and leather handicrafts are available. San José has the best shopping opportunities, in small gift stores in the city center, an outdoor market near the Museo Nacional, and a neighborhood called Moravia in the northern part of the city, which has whole streets devoted to souvenir stores. Bargaining is possible in outdoor markets, where you should expect to pay about 80% of the first price the vendor gives. Souvenir stores usually give discounts if you pay cash.

Haggling can be done almost everywhere. Even clothing, shoe, and record stores in the mall are usually willing to give discounts of 5%–10% for cash or multiple purchases. It's always worth it to ask politely—no offense will be taken.

Be prepared to be shadowed closely in stores—so close that when you stop to look at something the salesperson might bump into you. This is business as usual; take it as earnest friendliness (and of course, diligent protection against shoplifting). An indication that you need no help (*"No necesito ayuda, gracias."*) buys you a few feet of personal space.

## KEY DESTINATIONS

The town of Sarchí in the Central Valley, the Moravia neighborhood in San José, and Hotel Don Carlos and La Casona artisan's market in Central San José are good places to shop. Also, there is an outdoor handicraft market in the Plaza de la Democracia, contiguous to the Museo Nacional. All offer the same types of leather and wooden handicrafts, including miniature oxcarts, which are the unofficial national symbol of Costa Rica.

Plaza Esmeralda near the U.S. Embassy in Pavas provides artisans with a place to work and sell crafts; it's well worth a stop. The Green Turtle Souvenir Outlet, north of the Hampton Inn and Suites, supports indigenous artisan work, and is one of the best last-minute stops.

🗐 Best Choices **Green Turtle Souvenir Outlet** ✉ Across from the Hampton Inn, near Juan Santamaría Airport, Alajuela ☎ 506/430-0211 ⊕ www. greenturtlesouvenirs.com. **Plaza Esmeralda** ✉ 800 m west of Jacks, Pavas, San José ☎ 506/296-0312 or 506/232-7949 ⊕ www.plaza-esmeralda.com.

## SMART SOUVENIRS

Attractive souvenirs from Costa Rica include wooden bowls and boxes, wooden mobiles, and wood and leather rocking chairs. All of these can be found at souvenir shops in San José, in crafts stores in the town of Sarchí, and at gift shops in larger hotels. Prices vary depending on the size of the bowls and boxes. The rocking chairs, which fold for shipping, cost about $100. The mobiles cost $15–$20 and also fold for shipping. Oxcarts, shaped into planters, ashtrays, and trinkets, are a uniquely Costa Rican craft and a traditional symbol of the hardworking Tico farmer—a point of national pride.

Artisans in Guaitil and Santa Cruz (near Playa Hermosa) preserve the pre-Columbian pottery techniques practiced by the Chorotega tribe, using local clays, natural dyes, and wood-burning ovens. Buy the simple, beautiful work in these towns, or in San José–area art galleries and gift shops. Hotel Grano de Oro and Hotel Don Carlos in San José, the Marriott in San Antonio de Belén, and Hotel Bougainvillea in Heredia have good gift shops.

Coffee is a good souvenir, and if you choose a high-quality Costa Rican brand with no sugar added, there's no need to pay inflated prices for export brands marketed to foreigners. Local brands Cafe Volio and Cafe Rey sold at ordinary grocery stores and neighborhood shops (*pulperias*) are good. Other popular food items that make great souvenirs include Salsa Alfaro (formerly Salsa Lizano, as it is still commonly known), a tangy cooking sauce used to season beans, meat, and chicken, and Cafe Britt's chocolate-covered coffee beans, macadamias, and other sweets. Buy them at grocery or souvenir stores. Local conservation groups often sell beautiful locally made souvenirs (⇨ Ecotourism).

## WATCH OUT

Cuban cigars are available in Costa Rica but won't be allowed in the country if you take them back to the United States. Don't buy products made of animal skins or tortoiseshell. Indian pottery that is sold on the street as authentic is not.

## STUDENTS IN COSTA RICA

Although prices are on the rise, you can still travel on $25–$30 a day if you put your mind to it. An international student ID card, available from STA, gets you discounts on hotels, park entrance fees, and plane tickets, and provides health insurance. Travel CUTS members (U.S. and Canada only) get many of the same benefits. OTEC, a Costa Rica–based travel agency, is affiliated with Travel Cuts; it specializes in student travel and sells international student ID cards.

**IDs & Services OTEC** ☎ 506/256-0633 in Costa Rica ⊕ www.otecviajes.com. **STA Travel** ☎ 800/781-4040 in the U.S., 888/427-5639 in Canada, 0870/1600599 in the U.K., 0508/782-872 in New Zealand, 300/733-035 in Australia ⊕ www.statravel.com. **Travel CUTS** ☎ 800/592-2887 or 866/246-9762 in Canada, 416/979-2406 international callers 🖷 416/979-8167 ⊕ www.travelcuts.com.

## HOSTELS

There are youth hostels and hotels affiliated with Hostelling International all over Costa Rica. The local Hostelling International Web site lists 18 affiliated members; most are tantamount to inexpensive hotels. Hostal Toruma, the HI center, is an exception, as is Hostel Playa Tamarindo; both offer dorms as well as private rooms, and the latter has surf racks as well. Not on the official list, but with established "backpacker" hostel ambiance, are Tranquilo Backpackers, Gaudy's Backpackers, and Travotel Albergue Costa Linda.

**Costa Rica Hostels Gaudy's Backpackers** ⊠ Avda. 5, between Cs. 36 and 38, Sabana Norte, San José ☎ 506/258-2937 ⊕ www.backpacker.co.cr. **Hostal Toruma** ⊠ Avda. Central, between Cs. 29 and 31, Barrio La California, San José ☎ 506/234-8186 ⊕ www.toruma.com. **Hostel Playa Tamarindo** ⊠ Next to Hotel Pasatiempo, Tamarindo ☎ 506/653-0944 ✐ hostelplayatamarindo@yahoo.com. **Tranquilo Backpackers** ⊠ C. 7, between Avdas. 9 and 11, Barrio Amón, San José ☎ 506/653-0944 ✐ hostelplayatamarindo@yahoo.com. **Travotel Albergue Costa Linda** ⊠ 100 m before the traffic circle, Manuel Antonio ☎ 506/777-0304.

**Hostel Organizations Hostelling International–USA** ☎ 301/495-1240 ⊕ www.hiayh.org. **Hostelling International–Canada** ☎ 613/237-7884 or 800/663-5777 ⊕ www.hihostels.ca. **Hostelling International–Costa Rica** ☎ 506/234-8186 ⊕ www.hicr.org. **YHA England and Wales** ☎ 0870/770-8868 ⊕ www.yha.org.uk. **YHA Australia** ☎ 02/9261-1111 ⊕ www.yha.com.au. **YHA New Zealand** ☎ 03/379-9970 or 0800/278-299 ⊕ www.yha.org.nz.

## TAXIS

Your hotel can usually call you a reputable taxi or private car service, and when you're out to dinner or on the town the restaurant or disco can just as easily call you a cab—it's much easier than trying to hail one on the street in the wee hours, and safer, too.

■ TIP→→ Taxi drivers are infamous for "not having change." If it's just a few hundred colones, it's probably not worth your time. If it's a lot, ask them to drive to a store or gas station where you can make change. They'll often miraculously come up with the difference, or wait patiently while you get it. To avoid this situation, never use a 10,000-colón bill in a taxi, and avoid paying with 5,000-colón bills unless you've run up almost that much in fares.

It's illegal, but taxis charge up to double for hotel pickups or fares that take them out of the province (such as San José to Alajuela or vice versa). Ask the manager at your hotel about the going rate for the destination to which you're heading. Drivers have a fairly standard list of legal fares.

## TELEPHONES

Local telephone numbers have seven digits. The Costa Rican phone system is very good by the standards of other developing countries. However, phone numbers change often and are handed out willy-nilly.

All domestic and international calls from public phones (aside from calls to an operator) require phone cards ( ⇨ *below*).

## CALLING WITHIN COSTA RICA

You can make local calls from any phone with a domestic calling card ( ⇨ Phone Cards, *below*). First dial 197, then the PIN on the back of your card (revealed after scratching off a protective coating), then the phone number. Some phones have a card reader on the right-hand side; swiping the card through once you've dialed 197 saves tedious keying, but the readers are hit-and-miss. There are no area codes in Costa Rica, so you only need dial a seven-digit number; without the 506 country code. Fewer and farther between are the gray coin-operated phones; posted on each are the coins accepted (it varies from phone to phone).

Dial ☎ 113 for domestic directory inquiries and ☎ 110 for domestic collect calls, your only option if you don't have a phone card.

## CALLING OUTSIDE COSTA RICA

The cheapest way to call internationally is to either call from a pay phone using an international phone card ( ⇨ Phone Cards, *below*); call from a pay phone using your own long-distance calling card; or call from a telephone office. Dialing directly from a hotel room is very expensive, as is recruiting an international operator to connect you. ⚠ Watch out for pay phones marked CALL USA/CANADA WITH A CREDIT CARD. They are *wildly* expensive.

To call overseas directly, dial 00, then the country code, the area code, and the number. You can make international calls from almost any phone with an international calling card purchased in Costa Rica. First dial 199, then the PIN on the back of your card (revealed after scratching off a protective coating), then dial the phone number as you would a direct call.

When requesting a calling card from your phone provider, ask specifically about calls from Costa Rica. Most 800-number cards don't work in Costa Rica. Callingcards. com is a great resource for prepaid international calling cards. At this writing, it lists at least one calling-card company with rates of 1¢ per minute for calls to the U.S.

You may find the local access number blocked in many hotel rooms. First ask the hotel operator to connect you. If the hotel operator balks, ask for an international operator, or dial the international operator yourself. To reach an English-speaking operator, you'll have more luck dialing the international operator (☎ 175 or 116). One way to improve your odds of getting connected to your long-distance carrier is to sign up with more than one company: a hotel may block Sprint, for example, but not MCI. If all else fails, call from a pay phone.

AT&T, MCI, and Sprint access codes make calling long-distance relatively convenient but can be very expensive.

To make a collect call from any phone, dial 09 (instead of 00 for a regular call), the country code for the country you're calling, and then the number.

Calls to the United States and Canada are 31¢ per minute; calls to the United Kingdom, Australia, and New Zealand are 59¢) per minute.

The country code for the United States and Canada is 001, Australia 61, New Zealand 64, and the United Kingdom 44.
**Access Codes AT&T Direct** ☎ 0800/011-4114. **British Telecom** ☎ 0800/044-1044. **Canada Direct** ☎ 0800/015-1161. **MCI WorldPhone** ☎ 0800/012-2222. **Sprint International Access** ☎ 0800/013-0123. **Telephone Resources Callingcards.com** ⊕ www.callingcards.com. **International information** ☎ 124. **International operator** ☎ 175.

## CELL PHONES

If your cell phone or pager company has service to Costa Rica, you theoretically can use it here, but expect reception to be impossible in many areas of this mountainous country.

Most car-rental agencies have good deals on cell phones, often better than the companies that specialize in cell-phone rental. If you're not renting a car, a number of companies will rent TDMA or GSM phones; remember, coverage is spotty. Rates range from $6–$9 per day, plus varying rates for local or international coverage and minimum usage charges. You'll need your ID, a credit card, and a deposit of $350–$400; some rent only to those over 21. The deposit then drops significantly with companies that can hook you up with a local chip for your own phone.

Professional but brusque, Cell Phones Costa Rica will get you hooked up. Cellular Telephone Rentals Costa Rica has higher daily rates but free local calls.
**Cellular Phone Rentals Cell Phones Costa Rica** ☎ 866/865-1062 in the U.S. and Canada, 506/293-5892 in Costa Rica ⊕ www.cellularphonescr.com. **Cellular Telephone Rentals Costa Rica** ☎ 800/769-1737 in the U.S., 506/231-3205 in Costa Rica ⊕ www.cellulartelephonerentals.com.

## PHONE CARDS

Most public phones require phone cards (for local or international calls), but phone cards can also be used from any nonrotary telephone in Costa Rica, including residential phones, cell phones, and hotel phones. It's rare to be charged a per-minute rate for the mere use of the phone in a hotel.

Phone cards are sold in an array of shops, including Más X Menos supermarkets, post offices, offices of the Costa Rican Electricity Institute (ICE), and at any business displaying the gold-and-blue TARJETAS TELEFÓNICAS sign. International cards tend to be easier to find in downtown San José and in tourism areas.

With *tarjetas para llamadas nacionales* (domestic calling cards), cards are available in denominations of 500 colones and 1,000 colones. Phone-card rates are standard throughout the country, about 2¢ per minute; a 500-colón card provides about 50 minutes of landline calls. This decreases sharply if calling a cell phone; rates vary. *Tarjetas para llamadas internacionales* (international calling cards) are sold in $10, $20, 3,000-colón, and 10,000-colón amounts (denominations are inexplicably split between dollars and colones). It's harder to find the 10,000-colón cards; your best bet is to try a Fischel pharmacy or an ICE office.

Some public phones accept *tarjetas chip* ("chip" cards), which record what you spend, though they're a dying breed.

■ TIP→→ Avoid buying chip cards: they malfunction, you can use them only at the few-and-far-between chip phones, and they are sold in small denominations that are not sufficient for international calls.

## TIME
Costa Rica does not observe daylight saving time, so in summer it's six hours behind GMT, the equivalent of Central Time in the U.S. (one hour behind New York). In winter Costa Rica is seven hours behind GMT, the equivalent of Mountain Time in the U.S. (two hours behind New York).

## TOURS & PACKAGES
As Costa Rica's tourism community becomes more Web-savvy, more and more travelers to the country are booking their own trips. But getting a package tour—some of which can be custom-organized to fit what you want to do and can be private, with just you and your companions—is an easier, quicker way to go. You can also benefit from the experience of the tour company, which (theoretically) knows

the best local guides, hotels, and outfitters, and provides one convenient point person to answer all of your questions. Travel agents are another quick and easy option (⇨ Travel Agencies).

The best Costa Rican packages are with companies that combine sun and sand with nature and adventure, and do it all responsibly. For tips on choosing a sustainable eco-vacation, *see* Ecotourism. Several major international and specialty-tour package companies sell Costa Rica all-inclusive and custom itineraries direct.

■ TIP→→ Some of the best general package-tour companies are ecotour specialists. For information on these companies, *see* Ecotours, *below*. Costa Rica Expeditions has built a rock-solid reputation for adventure tours, and books Abercrombie & Kent packages for travelers from the U.S. Horizontes is an industry leader known for its excellent service and sophisticated educational, hiking-pace nature immersions; it handles the U.K. and Australian Abercrombie & Kent bookings. Swiss Travel works primarily with cruise ships, and is the best equipped for large groups. TAM Travel is another long-time Costa Rican agency that organizes excellent independent traveler vacations. Lava Tours is a well-established local company.

Conservationists, particularly those into bird-watching, should check out Costa Rica Sun Tours: the founding Aspinall family is renowned in Costa Rica for long-term efforts to preserve the country's wild spaces. U.S.-based companies include Nature Expeditions International, which runs upscale trips to Costa Rica year-round, with flexible dates and itineraries. Austin-Lehman Adventures provides mid- to upscale adventure and family packages focused on sustainable tourism; its Costa Rica Family Adventure is designed for families with children ages 5 and up. Canada-based Butterfield & Robinson flies you to the most luxurious hotels on its high-end nature package tour.

Unless they are specifically marked as private tours, you will be included in a larger group. Ideally you won't want to be sharing the rain forest with more than 12 people at a time.

⬛ Recommended Package-Tour Companies **Abercrombie & Kent** ☎ 800/554-7094 in the U.S. and Canada ⊕ www.abercrombiekent.com. **Austin-Lehman Adventures** ☎ 800/575-1540 in the U.S. and Canada, 406/655-4591 worldwide ⊕ www.austinlehman.com. **Butterfield & Robinson** ☎ 800/678-1147 in North America or 416/864-1354 ⊕ www.butterfield.com. **Caravan** ☎ 800/227-2826 or 312/321-9800 in the U.S. ⊕ www.caravantours.com. **Costa Rica Expeditions** ☎ 506/257-0766 ⊕ www.costaricaexpeditions.com. **Costa Rica Sun Tours** ☎ 506/296-7757 in Costa Rica ⊕ www.crsuntours.com. **Lava Tours** ☎ 278-2558, 888/862-2424 in the U.S. 🖷 413/410-2583 in U.S. ⊕ www.lava-tours.com. **Nature Expeditions International** ☎ 800/869-0639 in the U.S. or 954/693-8852 ⊕ www.naturexp.com. **Swiss Travel** ☎ 506/282-4898 ⊕ www.swisstravelcr.com. **TAM Travel** ☎ 506/256-0203 ⊕ www.tamtravel.com.

## BUYER BEWARE

Each year consumers are stranded or lose their money when tour operators—even large ones with excellent reputations—go out of business. So check out the operator. Ask several travel agents about its reputation, check with the Better Business Bureau, and try to book with a company that has a consumer-protection program. (Look for information in the company's brochure or on its Web site.) In the United States, members of the United States Tour Operators Association are required to set aside funds (up to $1 million) to help eligible customers cover payments and travel arrangements in the event that the company defaults. It's also a good idea to choose a company that participates in the American Society of Travel Agents' Tour Operator Program; ASTA will act as mediator in any disputes between you and your tour operator. Most Costa Rican–based operators won't be members of these organizations, but they are vetted well by reputable tour operators.

Remember that the more your package or tour includes, the better you can predict the ultimate cost of your vacation. Make sure you know exactly what is covered, and beware of hidden costs. Are taxes,

tips, and transfers included? Entertainment and excursions? These can add up.

⬛ Tour-Operator Recommendations **American Society of Travel Agents** ☎ 800/965-2782 in the U.S., 703/739-2782 worldwide ⊕ www.astanet.com. **Council of Better Business Bureaus** ☎ 703/276-0100 ⊕ www.bbb.org. **The National Tour Association** (NTA) ☎ 800/682-8886 in the U.S., 859/226-4444 worldwide ⊕ www.crosssphere.com. **United States Tour Operators Association** (USTOA) ☎ 212/599-6599 ⊕ www.ustoa.com.

## BIKING TOURS

Costa Rica is mountainous and rough around the edges. It's a rare bird that attempts a road-biking tour here. But the payoff for the ungroomed, tire-munching terrain is uncrowded, wildly beautiful off-road routes. Operators generally provide top-notch equipment, including bikes, helmets, water bottles, and so forth, but welcome serious bikers who bring their own ride. Leave the hybrids at home—this is mountain-biking territory. Operators usually meet you at the airport and take care of all logistics. All companies can design custom tours for extreme cyclists if requested.

⬛ TIP➜➜ Check with individual airlines about packing requirements and blackouts—more than one eager tour participant has been turned away because of high-season bike bans.

⬛ Operators **BiCosta Rica** ☎ 506/446-7585 ⊕ www.bruncas.com/bicostarica.html. **Coast to Coast Adventures** ☎ 506/280-8054 ⊕ www.ctocadventures.com. **Jungle Man Adventures** ☎ 506/225-8186 ⊕ www.adventurerace.com. **Lava Tours** ☎ 506/278-2558, 888/862-2424 in the U.S. ⊕ www.lava-tours.com. **Norman List** ☎ 506/692-2062 ✉ info@rockriverlodge.com.

⬛ Bike Maps **Lehmann** ✉ Avda. Central, between Cs. 1 and 3, San José ☎ 223-1212.

## BIRD-WATCHING TOURS

You will almost definitely get more out of your time in Costa Rica by taking a tour rather than trying to find birds on your own. Bring your own binoculars but don't worry about a spotting scope; if you go with a tour company that specializes in birding tours, your guide will have one. Expect to see about 300 species during a weeklong tour. Many U.S. travel companies that offer bird-watching tours subcontract with the Costa Rican tour operators listed below. By arranging your tour directly with the Costa Rican companies, you avoid the middleman and save money. Avian Adventures, out of the U.K., uses local guides.

**Operators Avian Adventures** ☎ 01384/372013 ⊕ www.avianadventures.com. **Birdwatch Costa Rica** ☎ 506/228–4768 ⊕ www.birdwatchcostarica.com. **Costa Rica Expeditions** ☎ 506/222–0333. **Horizontes** ☎ 506/222–2022.

## DIVING TOURS

Costa Rica's Cocos Island—one of the best dive spots in the world—can be visited only on a 10-day scuba safari on the *Okeanos Aggressor* or *Undersea Hunter.* But Guanacaste, the South Pacific, and to a lesser extent, the Caribbean, offer some respectable underwater adventures. Bill Beard's Costa Rica in the Gulf of Papagayo, Guanacaste, is a diving-tour pioneer and has country-wide options. Diving Safaris, in Playa Hermosa, has trips to dive sites in Guanacaste. In the South Pacific, Costa Rica Adventure Divers in Drake Bay arranges five-day trips. In this same area Caño Island is a good alternative if you can't afford the money or time for Cocos Island, particularly in the rainy season, when dive sites closer to shore are clouded by river runoff.

**Bill Beard's Costa Rica** ☎ 954/453–5044, 877/853–0538 in the U.S. ⊕ www.billbeardcostarica.com. **Costa Rica Adventure Divers** ☎ 506/236–5637, 800/317–0333 in the U.S. ⊕ www.costaricadiving.com. **Diving Safaris** ☎ 506/672–0012 ⊕ www.costaricadiving.net. *Okeanos Aggressor* ☎ 506/257–8686, 866/653–2667 in the U.S. and Canada ⊕ www.agressor.com. *Undersea Hunter* ☎ 506/228–6613 ⊕ www.underseahunter.com.

## ECOTOURS

If you park yourself at an all-inclusive hotel, you'll miss Costa Rica's number-one attraction: nature. To get the most out of your trip, pair up with a professional bilingual nature guide who knows the country's diverse landscapes, birds, animals, and where you'll see them. Costa Rica Expeditions, known for its commitment to

conservation, has high-quality tours led by knowledgeable, professional guides. Horizontes is also a top-notch natural-history tour operator with some of the country's best guides. Aventuras Naturales runs terrific adventure tours (including whitewater rafting) either as a one-day trip or multiday package. Sun Tours trips are well organized, and guides are informative and friendly; they do a superb job of planning trips that hit all the country's highlights. There are many tour companies and guides out there (and many lodges staff their own naturalist).

"Soft adventure" travelers are well catered to aboard the 185-foot M.V. *Pacific Explorer,* run by Cruise West, with multiday natural-history cruises along the southern Pacific coast. Lindblad Expeditions runs cruises aboard the larger *Sea Voyager.*

**Aventuras Naturales** ☎ 506/225–3939, 800/514–0411 in North America ⊕ www.toenjoynature.com. **Costa Rica Expeditions** ☎ 506/222–0333 ⊕ www.costaricaexpeditions.com. **Horizontes** ☎ 506/222–2022 ⊕ www.horizontes.com. **Lindblad Expeditions** ☎ 212/765–7740, 800/397–3348 in North America ⊕ www.lindblad.com. **Sun Tours** ☎ 506/296–7757 ⊕ www.crsuntours.com. **Cruise West** ☎ 800/203–8306 ⊕ www.cruisewest.com.

## FISHING TOURS

If fishing is your primary objective in Costa Rica, you are better off booking a package. During peak season you may not even be able to find a hotel room in the hot fishing area, let alone one of the top boats and skippers. The major fish populations move along the Pacific coast through the year, and tarpon and snook fishing on the Caribbean is subject to the vagaries of seasonal wind and weather. San-José-based Costa Rica Outdoors has 10 years of experience arranging fishing packages and is one of the best bets for full service and honest advice about where to go, and works with the widest range of operators around the country. More than 100 outfits have high-quality, regionally based services. Anglers in the know recommend Kingfisher Sportfishing in Playa Carrillo, Guanacaste; J.P. Sportfishing Tours in Quepos; Roy's Zancudo Lodge near Golfito; and Río Colorado Lodge on the northern Caribbean coast. While fishing is hit or miss, when booking a holiday, get it on record from your tour operator that it's the traditional season for the type of fishing you'd like to do.

🔲 **Blue Fin Sport Fishing** ☎ 506/777-1676 ⊕ www.bluefinsportfishing.com. **Costa Rica Outdoors** ☎ 506/282-6743, 800/308-3394 in the U.S. ⊕ www.costaricaoutdoors.com. **J.P. Sportfishing Tours** ☎ 506/244-6361, 866/620-4188 in the U.S. ⊕ www.jpsportfishing.com. **Kingfisher Sportfishing** ☎ 506/656-0091 ⊕ www.costaricabillfishing. com. **Río Colorado Lodge** ☎ 506/232-4063, 800/ 243-4063 in the U.S. and Canada ⊕ www. riocoloradolodge.com. **Roy's Zancudo Lodge** ☎ 506/776-0008, 877/529-6980 in the U.S. ⊕ www.royszancudo.com.

## FLIGHTSEEING

San José–based pilot Jenner Rojas will take you anywhere in Costa Rica for flightseeing and picture taking. The rate is $290 (for up to three people) per hour, with discounts for longer trips. Skyline Nature Ultralight Flying Tours, based in Bahía Ballena on the South Pacific, gives bird's-eye ultralight tours of the area's mangroves and national park; one passenger limit. Rides are $150 per hour, but you can also do a $65 20-minute pass over the mangroves. Macaw Air sends people into the North Pacific sunset for $50 each, and has picture-taking trips on the Pacific Coast.

🔲 **Jenner Rojas** ☎ 506/385-5425 ✎ bluebird@costarricense.com. **Macaw Air** ☎ 506/653-1362 ⊕ www.macawair.com. **Skyline Nature Ultralight Flying Tours** ☎ 506/743-8037 ⊕ www.fly-ultralight.com.

## HIKING TOURS

Most nature tour companies include hiking as part of their itineraries, but these hikes may be short and not strenuous enough for serious hikers. Let the tour operator know what you expect from a hike. Ask a lot of questions about hike lengths and difficulty levels before booking the tour or you may be disappointed with the amount of time you get to spend on the trails. The following companies cater to both moderate and serious hikers.

🔲 **Gap Adventures** ☎ 800/465-5600 in the U.S. and Canada, 0870/080-1756 in the U.K. ⊕ www.

gapadventures.com. **Serendipity Adventures** ☎ 877/507-1358 in the U.S. and Canada ⊕ www. serendipityadventures.com. **The Walking Connection** ☎ 602/978-1887, 800/295-9255 in the U.S. and Canada ⊕ www.walkingconnection.com.

## TRAVEL AGENCIES

Percentage-wise, in Costa Rica do-it-yourselfers are gaining on travel agents in terms of airline-ticket purchases and hotel bookings. But if you want someone else to do the heavy lifting of finding a hotel, arranging reservations with tour operators, etc., consider using a travel agent. Travel agents and planners can often hook you up with guides and operators that know the area inside out, and will help get you to the right place at the right time to see a quetzal or rural cultural event. They also give you a person to call if things go wrong.

▇ **TIP→** Travel agents are excellent resources, and if you run into trouble with hotels or operators, you stand a much better chance of getting the situation resolved. It is otherwise very difficult to hold people accountable in Costa Rica. Some local agents confirm at least three times after definitively booking a hotel for a client; legwork that you may not be aware is necessary and probably something you'd rather leave to someone else.

Beware of some bigger agents, who may steer you to tour companies and large hotels that reward them for volume sales. This is less of a concern in smaller, independent agencies. If you have a special interest, find an agent with expertise in that area. While the American Society of Travel Agents (ASTA) has a database of specialists worldwide, most "specialists" list almost every country and kind of tourism available; those who are clearly specialists in Latin America are your best bet. Log on to the group's Web site to find an ASTA travel agent in your neighborhood.

Make sure your travel agent knows the accommodations and other services of the place being recommended—easier said than done in Costa Rica, where even the most renowned hotels can be notoriously inconsistent with their info. Ask about the hotel's location, room size, beds, and whether it has a pool, room service, or programs for children, if important. Has your agent been there in person or sent others whom you can contact? Improved Internet access has nurtured the growth of reputable online, Costa Rica–based tour agencies. Not only are they truly experts in Costa Rica, but they provide welcome in-country assistance should glitches pop up.

Do some homework on your own, too: local rural tourism organizations ( ⇨ Eco-tourism) can provide information about lesser-known and small-niche operators, some of which may sell only direct. Confirm that the agency belongs to a professional trade organization, like ASTA. For more information on precautions to take when choosing a travel agent, *see* Buyer Beware *in* Tours & Packages.

**🔊 Costa Rica Travel Agents Lynch Travel** ☎ 506/777-1262 or 506/777-2052 ⊕ www.lynchtravel.com. **Travel Store** ☎ 506/279-8927 ⊕ www.allcostaricatravel.com. **Intertur** ☎ 253-7503 ⊕ www.interturcr.com.

**🔊 General Travel Agent Resources American Society of Travel Agents** ☎ 703/739-2782 or 800/965-2782 24-hr hotline ⊕ www.astanet.com. **Association of British Travel Agents** ☎ 0207/307-1907 ⊕ www.abtanet.com. **Association of Canadian Travel Agents** ☎ 613/237-3657 ⊕ www.acta.ca. **Australian Federation of Travel Agents** ☎ 02/9264-3299 ⊕ www.afta.com.au. **Travel Agents' Association of New Zealand** ☎ 04/499-0104 ⊕ www.taanz.org.nz.

## VISITOR INFORMATION

The official tourism board, the Instituto Costarricense de Turismo (ICT), has free maps, bus schedules, and brochures. However, these folks could do better with the information they provide. Arrive armed with specific questions and know that they will not recommend hotels. Visitor information is provided by the Costa Rica Tourist Board in Canada and the United States

**🔊 Tourist Information Costa Rican Embassy in the U.K.** ⊠ Flat 1, 14 Lancaster Gate, London W2 3LH ☎ 020/7706-8844 ⊕ http://costarica.embassyhomepage.com. **Instituto Costarricense de Turismo (ICT)** ☎ 866/267-8274 in the U.S. and Canada, 506/299-5800 in Costa Rica ⊕ www.

visitcostarica.com ⊠ Central Post Office, C. 2, between Avdas 1 and 3 ☎ 506/258-8762 ⊠ Plaza de la Cultura, C. 5, between Avdas. Central and 2 ☎ 506/222-1090 ⊠ Juan Santamaría Airport ☎ 506/443-1535.

**🔊 Government Advisories U.S. Department of State** ☎ 202/647-5225 interactive hotline or 888/407-4747 ⊕ www.travel.state.gov **Consular Affairs Bureau of Canada** ☎ 613/944-6788 or 800/267-6788 ⊕ www.voyage.gc.ca. **U.K. Foreign and Commonwealth Office** ☎ 08/7060-60290 ⊕ www.fco.gov.uk/travel. **Australian Department of Foreign Affairs and Trade** ☎ 02/6261-1299 Consular Travel Advice Faxback Service ⊕ www.smartraveller.gov.au or www.dfat.gov.au. **New Zealand Ministry of Foreign Affairs and Trade** ☎ 04/439-8000 ⊕ www.mft.govt.nz.

## VOLUNTEER & EDUCATIONAL TRAVEL

Costa Rica has an abundance of volunteer opportunities for diverse interests. You can tag sea turtles as part of a research project, build trails in a national park, or volunteer at an orphanage. Many of the organizations require at least rudimentary Spanish. Most of the programs for volunteers who don't speak Spanish charge a daily fee for room and board. The Institute for Central American Development Studies (ICADS) is a nonprofit social justice institute that runs a language school and arranges internships and field study (college credit is available); some programs are available only to college students. ICADS places you with local social service organizations, environmental groups, and other organizations, depending on your interests. The Costa Rica Rainforest Outward Bound School offers two adult programs that combine self-exploration with a truly rural learning experience. Mesoamerica, a nonprofit organization devoted to peace and social justice, has three- and six-month newswriting internships for young journalists.

**🔊 Costa Rica Rainforest Outward Bound School** ☎ 506/278-6058, 800/676-2018 in the U.S. ⊕ www.crrobs.org. **Costa Rican Humanitarian Foundation** ☎ 506/390-4192 or 506/837-5205 ✉ gnystrom@racsa.co.cr. **Institute for Central American Development Studies (ICADS)** ☎ 506/225-0508 ⊕ www.icadscr.com. **Mesoamerica** ☎ 506/253-3195 ⊕ www.mesoamericaonline.net.

## SPANISH-LANGUAGE PROGRAMS

Thousands of people travel to Costa Rica every year to study Spanish. Dozens of schools in and around San José offer professional instruction and home stays, and there are several smaller schools outside the capital. Conversa has schools off Paseo Colón, and in Santa Ana, west of the capital; the latter offers only the company's "Super Intense" program (seven hours per day). On the east side of town, ILISA provides cultural immersion in San Pedro. Mesoamerica is a low-cost language school that is part of a nonprofit organization devoted to peace and social justice. La Escuela D'Amore is in beautiful Manuel Antonio. Arco Iris Spanish School (⇨ Gay & Lesbian Travel) is a unique gay-friendly option. Language programs at the Institute for Central American Development Studies include optional academic seminars in English about Central America's political, social, and economic conditions.

🖪 **Conversa** ☎ 506/221-7649, 800/354-5036 in North America ⊕ www.conversa.net. **ILISA** ☎ 506/280-0700, 800/280-0700 in the U.S. ⊕ www.ilisa.com. **Institute for Central American Development Studies** (ICADS) ☎ 506/225-0508 ⊕ www.icadscr.com. **La Escuela D'Amore** ☎ 506/777-1143, 310/435-9897 in the U.S. ⊕ www.escueladamore.com. **Mesoamerica** ☎ 506/253-3195 ⊕ www.mesoamericaonline.net.

## VOLUNTEER PROGRAMS

In recent years more and more Costa Ricans have realized the need to preserve their country's precious biodiversity. Both Ticos and far-flung environmentalists have founded volunteer and educational concerns to this end.

Caribbean Conservation Corporation (CCC) is devoted to the preservation of sea turtles. Earthwatch Institute leads science-based trips studying octopi, turtles, or the rain forest. The Talamancan Association of Ecotourism and Conservation (ATEC), as well as designing short group and individual outings centered on Costa Rican wildlife and indigenous culture, keeps an updated list of up to 30 local organizations that welcome volunteers. Beach cleanups, recycling, and some wildlife projects don't require proficiency in Spanish.

🖪 **Caribbean Conservation Corporation** ☎ 506/297-5510, 352/373-6441 in the U.S. ⊕ www.cccturtle.org. **Earthwatch Institute** ☎ 978/461-0081, 800/776-0188 in the U.S., 44/01865-318838 in the U.K., 61/03-9682-6828 in Australia ⊕ www.earthwatch.org. **Talamancan Association of Ecotourism and Conservation** (ATEC) ☎ 506/750-0191 ⊕ http://greencoast.com/atec.htm.

## WEB SITES WE LIKE

• We wouldn't be doing our job if we didn't mention Fodors.com (⊕ www.fodors.com), a complete travel-planning site. In addition to researching prices and booking plane tickets, hotel rooms, rental cars, and vacation packages, you can post your pressing questions on the Talk forum and read hotel, restaurant, and sights ratings by fellow travelers. Other planning tools include a currency converter and weather reports, and there are loads of links to travel resources.

• Info Costa Rica (⊕ www.infocostarica.com) has a Web site with maps, photos, news articles, links to local artist sites, and chat rooms.

• For tide info, real estate, news, and travel information, Costa Rica.com (⊕ www.costarica.com) is a good bet.

• For current events, check out the English-language newspaper *Tico Times* (⊕ www.ticotimes.net).

• Horizontes (⊕ www.horizontes.com) is a tour operator that offers nature vacations but also has extensive general information on its Web site.

• Similar, but slightly less user friendly, is the site by competing nature tour company Costa Rica Expeditions (⊕ www.expeditions.co.cr), which offers ecologically minded trips.

• The U.S. Embassy's comprehensive site (⊕ www.usembassy.or.cr) has health information, travel warnings, links to great sites, and much more.

• The Boomers Abroad Costa Rica page (⊕ www.boomersabroad.com/costarica.html) has links to just about everything you'd want to know about the region.

## WOMEN TRAVELERS

If you're looking for a travel partner before you leave, try your local outdoors store notice board or try the Fodors.com Talk forum. Women can register at Hermail.net to connect up with other female travelers to the same destination. Online magazine *Journeywoman* is a good resource for women travelers. Signing up for a women's surf camp, such as Viva Costa Rica Surf Adventures in Playa Hermosa ( ⇨ chapter 5), is a great way to bond before heading out on further adventures. Women traveling solo should follow common sense rules for everyone; for safety information specific to women, *see* Tips for Women *in* Safety or pick up *Solo Traveler: Savvy Tips for Great Trips* at a bookstore.

■ TIP➜➜ Tampons are not widely available. Automercado is your best bet, but to be safe, bring your own.

🛂 Resources **Hermail.net** ⊕ www.hermail.net. **Journeywoman** ⊕ www.journeywoman.com.

## WOMEN-ONLY TOURS

Adventure Women is a company that runs tours for women over 30. Gutsy Women Travel has package tours for groups of up to 20. Adventure Associates' tours focus on ecology. Mariah Wilderness Expeditions plans custom tours and specializes in adventure travel. Women Traveling Together offers many tours throughout the year, though trips to Costa Rica are offered every two to three years. Canyon Calling tours limit groups to 12 members.
🛂 **Adventure Associates** ☎ 206/932-8352, 888/532-8352 in the U.S. ⊕ www.adventureassociates.net. **Adventure Women** ☎ 406/587-3883, 800/804-8686 in the U.S. ⊕ www.adventurewomen.com. **Canyon Calling** ☎ 928/282-0916 ⊕ www.canyoncalling.com. **Del Mar Surf Camp** ☎ 506/385-8535 ⊕ www.costaricasurfingchicas.com. **Gutsy Women Travel** ☎ 866/464-8879 in the U.S. ⊕ www.gutsywomentravel.com. **Mariah Wilderness Expeditions** ☎ 530/626-6946, 800/462-7424 in the U.S. ⊕ www.mariahwe.com. **Women Traveling Together** ☎ 410/956-5250 ⊕ www.women-traveling.com

View of Arenal Volcano on a clear day.

*(above)* Manuel Antonio National Park coastline. *(opposite page, top)* Tica dancer performs at a cultural festival in San José. *(opposite page, bottom)* White-faced capuchins are the most commonly seen monkeys in Costa Rica.

*(top)* Digging into Class-IV rapids on the Pacuáre River. *(bottom)* Sky Walk's hanging-bridge hike in Monteverde Cloud Forest. *(opposite page)* A scarlet macaw and blue-and-gold macaw get chummy.

*(top)* Sun-seekers at Espadilla Beach, in Manuel Antonio National Park. *(bottom)* Black river turtles hang out in Tortuguero, Costa Rica's slowpoke central.

*(top)* Coffee beans must be hand-picked, because they don't all ripen at the same time. *(bottom)* Painted oxcarts are one of Costa Rica's signature crafts.

*(top)* The clear-blue crater lake at Poás Volcano. *(bottom left)* All that glitters is gold at San José's Pre-Columbian Gold Museum. *(bottom right)* The heliconia is found in abundance throughout Costa Rica.

# San José

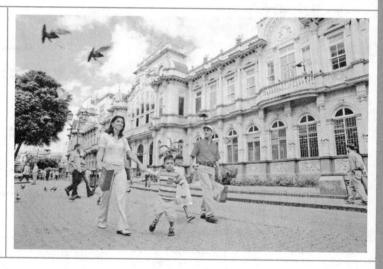

Post Office, San José

## WORD OF MOUTH

"Are you interested in San Jose? Some people would say 'Don't do it—there's nothing there,' but we have found it interesting to walk around town, see the Gold Museum, the Jade Museum, the Teatro Nacional, the Plaza de la Cultura, the Mercado Central."

—shillmac

# WELCOME TO SAN JOSÉ

City view

## TOP 5
## Reasons to Go

1. **Historic Barrios Amón and Otoya:** quiet tree-lined streets and century-old houses turned trendy hotels and restaurants.

2. **Gold and Jade museums:** They're not the Louvre or the Smithsonian, but still fascinating and worth a visit.

3. **Eating out:** the only place in Costa Rica with such a variety of cuisines.

4. **Nightlife:** the hottest scene in the country for dance clubs, bars, and chilled-out late-night cafés.

5. **Location, location, location:** From the capital's pivotal position you can be on a coffee tour, at the base of a giant volcano, or riding river rapids in just 30 minutes.

The primarily residential neighborhoods West of Downtown are anchored by large La Sabana Park. Also here are the recreated historic village Pueblo Antiguo and the Museum of Costa Rican Art.

Spices at Mercado Central     Parque Central

# Getting Oriented

In a high valley, 3,809 feet above sea level, San José lies just 9 degrees north of the equator, but the altitude keeps things refreshingly temperate year round. The metropolitan area holds more than 1 million residents, but the city proper is small, with some 300,000 people living in its 44 square km (17 square mi). Most of the sights are concentrated in three downtown neighborhoods, La Soledad, La Merced, and El Carmen, named for their anchor churches. The borders of the city are fuzzy: San José melts into its suburbs with nary a sign to denote where one community ends and another begins.

Historic barrios Amón and Otoya, the Children's Museum, and the University of Costa Rica are a few of the attractions North of Downtown.

**Downtown** holds San José's historic and commercial districts and most of its tourist attractions, including the Jade and Gold museums, the Mercado Central, and the Teatro Nacional, the city's most impressive building.

**East of Downtown,** a number of good restaurants and hotels are ensconced in the suburb of San Pedro.

Teatro Nacional

# SAN JOSÉ PLANNER

## When to Go

San José is pleasant year-round, with highs of 26–28°C (79–83°F) and lows of 17–19°C (65–68°F). December and February are the coolest months. In March and April the heat picks up noticeably. May–November, the pattern is usually: sunny mornings, brief afternoon showers, and clear brisk evenings. September and October are waterlogged, and it can rain nonstop for days at a time.

## The Kindness of Strangers

In a 2003 *Scientific American* study called "Simple Acts of Kindness" (a take on the famous Blanche DuBois line in Tennessee Williams's play *A Streetcar Named Desire*), Costa Rica's capital was rated the second friendliest city among 58 worldwide. Here the kindness of strangers doesn't stop at giving you directions; locals will often lead you to where you want to go.

## Do It in a Day

If you have only a day in the city, the must-see stops are the National Theater and the Gold Museum, both on the same block. We recommend the guided tour of the theater. If you have more time, take in the Museo del Jade (Jade Museum) and Museo Nacional (National Museum) as well. Or pay a visit to the Museo para la Paz (Peace Museum). The Museo de Niños (Children's Museum), north of downtown, is a popular kid-pleaser. Our Good Walk (⇨ p. 12) takes you past the top sights, giving you a taste of the city in just an hour.

■ TIP→→ Within San José, taxis are inexpensive and much faster than city buses

## Play It Safe

San José is safer than most other Latin American capitals; the biggest problem is theft. But standard precautions apply:

■ Exchange money only at banks.

■ Select ATMs in well-lighted areas, and conceal cash immediately.

■ Use only licensed taxis, with yellow triangles on the front doors.

■ Park in guarded, well-lighted lots.

■ Never leave anything in sight in your parked vehicle.

## City Tours

**Grayline Tours Costa Rica** (☎ 220-2126 ⊕ www.graylinecostarica.com) operates a half-day sightseeing-and-shopping tour.

The **Instituto Costarricense de Turismo** (⇨ San José Essentials, *below*) gives out a brochure outlining a self-guided historical walk through downtown.

**Real Town Tour** (☎ 221-5443 or 396-3033) gives two-hour English-language tours of typical neighborhoods southeast of downtown.

**Tren Tico** (Tico Train; ☎ 226-1346), really a truck pulling a string of wagons, picks you up at the Gran Hotel Costa Rica for a 25-minute city tour without commentary, from 10 to 4 on Sunday and holidays.

## Day Trips from the Capital

Some of these attractions provide pickup service in San José. Alternatively, tour operators include many of these attractions on their itineraries. (⇨ *Central Valley Planner* in Chapter 2 and *Northern Plains Planner* in Chapter 3 for tour-operator contacts.)

| DESTINATION | FROM SAN JOSÉ (BY CAR) | |
|---|---|---|
| Butterfly Farm | 45 min west | ⇨ p. 67 |
| Café Britt | 30 min north | ⇨ p. 75 |
| Carara Biological Reserve | 2 hrs southwest | ⇨ p. 265 |
| Doka Estate | 1 hr west | ⇨ p. 67 |
| Guayabo National Monument | 2 hrs southeast 4WD necessary | ⇨ p. 89 |
| INBioparque | 10 min north | ⇨ p. 73 |
| Irazú Volcano | 60 min east | ⇨ p. 79 |
| La Paz Waterfall Gardens | 2 hrs north | ⇨ p. 140 |
| Orosi Valley | 60 min southeast | ⇨ p. 81 |
| Poás Volcano | 60 min northwest | ⇨ p. 138 |
| Rain Forest Aerial Tram | 45 min north | ⇨ p. 385 |
| River Rafting | 2–2½ hrs | ⇨ p. 88 |
| Sarchí | 60 min northwest 30 min by car from Poás | ⇨ p. 101 |
| Tortuga Island | 3 hrs west | ⇨ p. 253 |

■ TIP➜➜ When you head back to town from a day trip, browse the souvenir shops that congregate around Parque Morazán or in the northeastern suburb of Moravia.

## Prices

| WHAT IT COSTS in Dollars | | | | | |
|---|---|---|---|---|---|
| | **$$$$** | **$$$** | **$$** | **$** | **¢** |
| **Restaurants** | over $25 | $15–$25 | $10–$15 | $5–$10 | under $5 |
| **Hotels** | over $250 | $150–$250 | $75–$150 | $50–$75 | under $50 |

Restaurant prices are per-person for a main course at dinner. Hotel prices are for two people in a standard double room in high season, excluding service and tax (16.4%).

# EXPLORING SAN JOSÉ

## Downtown

By Jeffrey
Van Fleet

It's a trend seen the world over: businesses and residents flee city centers for the ample space, blissful quiet, and lower-priced real estate of the suburbs. Costa Rica's burgeoning capital is no exception to that rule, but downtown San José still remains the historic and vibrant (if noisy and congested) heart of the city. Government offices have largely stayed put downtown—actually, the presidency is the only public institution to have moved its headquarters to the 'burbs—as have the majority of tourist attractions. If you spend any time here sightseeing, you'll find yourself in the center of San José.

Make no mistake: the city's traffic is overwhelming, and the narrow downtown streets, laid out in the days of the oxcart, barely handle the daily influx of vehicles. Pedestrians have the right of way here, but no driver seems to know or care about that little annoyance in Costa Rican traffic law. You can take refuge

> **CAUTION**
>
> Don't drive in the city if you can avoid it. The streets are narrow and congested, and many drivers treat traffic regulations as suggestions rather than laws.

along the several blocks of Avenida Central and Calles 2 and 17 that have been converted into pedestrian malls, and take heart that more of those traffic-free streets are on city planners' drawing boards.

### What to See

**⑭ Catedral Metropolitana** (Metropolitan Cathedral). Built in 1871, and completely refurbished in the late 1990s to repair earthquake damage, this neoclassic structure east of the park with a corrugated tin dome is not terribly interesting outside, but inside are patterned floor tiles, stained-glass windows depicting various saints and apostles, and framed polychrome bas-reliefs illustrating the 14 Stations of the Cross. The renovation did away with one small time-honored tradition: rather than purchase and light a votive candle, the faithful now deposit a 50-colón coin illuminating a bulb in a row of tiny electric candles. The interior of the small Capilla del Santísimo (Chapel of the Host) on the cathedral's north side evokes ornate old Catholicism, much more so than the cathedral itself, and is a place for quiet reflection and prayer. Masses are held throughout the day on Sunday starting at 7 AM, with one in English each Saturday at 4 PM. ⊠ *C. Central, between Avdas. 2 and 4, Barrio La Merced* ☎ *221–3820* ⊙ *Weekdays 6–6, Sun. 6 AM–9 PM.*

**❼ Centro Nacional de la Cultura** (National Cultural Center). Costa Rica cherishes its state enterprises. Here the government is your light and water utility, your phone company, your Internet service provider, your bank, your insurance agent, and your hospital. It is also your distillery, and this complex served as the headquarters of the Fábrica Nacional de Licores (FANAL, or National Liquor Factory) until 1981, when it moved to a modern facility west of Alajuela. In a heartwarming exception to the usual "tear it down" mentality so prevalent in San José, the Ministry of Culture converted the sloped-surface, double-block 1853 factory into a 14,000-square-meter center of its own offices, two theaters, and a museum. The metal **Teatro FANAL** (☎ 222–2974), once the fermentation area, now hosts frequent theater and music performances. The clay-brick **Teatro 1887** (☎ 222–2974) served as the factory's personnel office, and today dedicates itself to performances by the National Dance Company. What is now the theater's lobby was once the chemical testing lab. The stone-block storage depot next to the water towers at the southeast side of the complex became the **Museo de Arte y Diseño Contemporáneo** (⇨ below). A stone gate and sun clock grace the entrance nearest the museum. ✉ *C. 13 between Avdas. 3 and 5, Barrio Otoya* ☎ *257–5524* ☉ *Weekdays 8–5, Sat. 10–5.*

**⑰ Correos de Costa Rica** (Central Post Office). The handsome, carved sea-green exterior of the post office, dating from 1917, is hard to miss among the bland buildings surrounding it. Stamp collectors should stop at the **Museo Filatélico** (Philatelic Museum; ☎ 223–6918), to the left as you face the stamp windows, for its display of first-day stamp issues. Early-20th-century telegraphs and telephones are also on display. The museum is open weekdays 8–5; admission is free. From the second-floor balcony you can see the loading of *apartados* (post-office boxes) going on below: Ticos (which is what Costa Ricans call themselves) covet these hard-to-get boxes, as the city's lack of street addresses makes mail delivery a challenge. The large building behind the Correos is the headquarters of the state-run Banco Nacional. ✉ *C. 2, between Avdas. 1 and 3, Barrio La Merced* ☉ *Weekdays 7:30–6, Sat. 7:30–noon.*

**⑲ Mercado Central** (Central Market). This block-long melting pot is a warren of dark, narrow passages flanked by stalls packed with spices (some purported to have medicinal value), fish, fruit, flowers, pets, and wood and leather crafts. But the 1880 structure is a kinder, gentler introduction to a Central American market; there are no pigs or chickens or their accompanying smells to be found here. A few stands selling tourist souvenirs congregate near the entrances, but this is primarily a place where the average Costa Rican comes to shop. There are also dozens of cheap restaurants and

> ### WORD OF MOUTH
>
> "We really enjoyed walking through the Mercado Central. There are lots of places to eat. We ate at a small soda inside the market but it had an open outside wall, so we were able to view the street. The market is a maze with tons of stalls selling everything you can imagine, such as fresh fruit, vegetables, fish, meat, spices, flowers, birds, clothes, pocketbooks; you name it they've got it!"
>
> –Kwoo

snack stalls, including the country's first ice-cream vendor. Be warned: the concentration of shoppers makes this a hot spot for pickpockets, purse snatchers, and backpack slitters. Enter and exit at the southeast corner of the building (Avda. Central at C. 6). The green-and-white SAL-IDA signs direct you to other exits, but they spill onto slightly less safe streets. Use the image of the Sacred Heart of Jesus, the market's patron and protector, near the center of the building, as your guide; it faces that safer corner by which you should exit. (Things probably weren't planned that way.) ☒ *Bordered by Avdas. Central and 1 and Cs. 6 and 8, Barrio La Merced* ☯ *Mon.–Sat. 6–6.*

**need a break?**

**Pop's.** Here's the place to get the crème de la crème of locally made Costa Rican ice cream. Mango is a favorite flavor. After a long walk on crowded sidewalks, it may just save your sanity. This prolific chain is everywhere, and you'll find three outlets downtown. ☒ *Avda. Central, between Cs. 1 and 3* ☒ *Avda. Central, between Cs. 7 and 9* ☒ *Calle 4, between Avdas. Central and 1.*

**❽ Museo de Arte y Diseño Contemporáneo** (Museum of Contemporary Art and Design). This wonderfully minimalist space is perfect for serving as the country's premier modern-art venue. The MADC, as it is known around town, hosts changing exhibits of work by artists and designers from all over Latin America. You can arrange for a guided visit with a couple of days' advance notice. ☒ *C. 15, between Avdas. 3 and 5, Barrio Otoya* ☎ *257-7202* ⊕ *www.madc.ac.cr* 🔖 *$1* ☯ *Tues.–Sat. 10–5.*

**☝ ❿ Museo de Formas, Espacios y Sonidos** (Museum of Forms, Spaces and Sounds). The 1871 Atlantic Railway Station, which once bustled with passengers leaving and arriving on trains to and from Limón, has been converted into an interactive sound and space museum. Exhibits are labeled in Spanish; you wouldn't get much out of them without a knowledge of the language. In back are a couple of former trains that once served the Caribbean route. A bust outside honors Tomás Guardia, one of the few dictators in this peaceful country's history. He launched construction of the railroad. ☒ *Avda. 3, between Cs. 19 and 21, Barrio La California* ☎ *223-4173* 🔖 *$1* ☯ *Jan. and Feb., Tues.–Sat. 9:30–3; Mar.–Dec., weekdays 9:30–3.*

**★ ❻ Museo del Jade** (Jade Museum). This is the world's largest collection of American jade—that's "American" in the hemispheric sense. Nearly all the items on display were produced in pre-Columbian times, and most of the jade (pronounced *hah*-day in Spanish) dates from 300 BC to AD 700. In the spectacular Jade Room, pieces are illuminated from behind so you can appreciate their translucency. A series of drawings explains how this extremely hard stone was cut using string saws with quartz-and-sand abrasive. Jade was sometimes used in jewelry designs, but it was most often carved into oblong pendants. The museum also has other pre-Columbian artifacts, such as polychrome vases and three-legged *metates* (small stone tables for grinding corn), and a gallery of modern art. The final room on the tour has a startling display of ceramic fertility symbols. A photo-filled, glossy guide to the museum in English sells for $17; the Spanish ver-

> **CAUTION**
>
> The ubiquitous TOURIST INFORMATION signs you see around downtown are really private travel agencies looking to sell you tours rather than provide unbiased information. The ICT (⇨ San José Essentials) is the official tourist office.

sion is only $4. ⊠ *INS building, Avda. 7, between Cs. 9 and 11, 11th fl., Barrio El Carmen* ☎ *287–6034* 🖃 *$2* ⊙ *Weekdays 8:30–3:30.*

⓫ **Museo Nacional** (National Museum). In the whitewashed Bellavista Fortress, which dates from 1870, the National Museum gives you a quick and insightful lesson in English and Spanish on Costa Rican culture from pre-Columbian times to the present. Glass cases display pre-Columbian artifacts, period dress, colonial furniture, religious art, and photographs. Some of the country's foremost ethnographers and anthropologists are on the museum's staff. Outside are a veranda and a pleasant, manicured courtyard garden. A former army headquarters, this now-tranquil building saw fierce fighting during a 1931 army mutiny and during the 1948 revolution, as the bullet holes pocking its turrets attest. But it was also here that three-time president José "Don Pepe" Figueres abolished the country's military in 1949. ⊠ *C. 17, between Avdas. Central and 2, Barrio La Soledad* ☎ *257–1433* 🖃 *$4* ⊙ *Tues.–Fri. 8:30–4:30, weekends 9–4:30.*

★ ❸ **Museo del Oro Precolombino** (Pre-Columbian Gold Museum). The dazzling, modern museum of gold, in a three-story underground structure beneath the Plaza de la Cultura, contains the largest collection of pre-Columbian gold jewelry in Central America—20,000 troy ounces in more than 1,600 individual pieces—all owned by the Banco Central, and displayed attractively in low-lit, bilingual exhibits. Many pieces are in the form of frogs and eagles, two animals perceived by the region's pre-Columbian cultures to have great spiritual significance. Most spectacular are the varied shaman figurines, which represent the human connection to animal deities. One of the halls houses the **Museo Numismática** (Coin Museum; admission included with Gold Museum), a repository of historic coins and bills and other objects used as monetary units throughout the country's history. Rotating art exhibitions live on another level of the complex. ⊠ *Eastern end of Plaza de la Cultura, C. 5, between Avdas. Central and 2, Barrio La Soledad* ☎ *243–4202* ⊕ *www.museosdelbancocentral.org* 🖃 *$5* ⊙ *Daily 10–4:30.*

⓭ **Museo para la Paz** (Peace Museum). Former president Oscar Arias won the 1987 Nobel Peace Prize for his tireless efforts to bring reconciliation to a war-torn Central America, and today he remains a vocal force for international peace and social justice. His Arias Foundation operates this museum, with bilingual exhibits documenting the isthmus's turbulent history and promoting the cause for peace. Messages from other Nobel laureates—the Dalai Lama, Lech Walesa, Rigoberta Menchú, Jimmy Carter, and Henry Kissinger among them—adorn one room. Begin your visit in the auditorium watching a 12-minute video in English, *The Dividends of Peace*. There's also an hour-long video that delves into the topic if you have the time. The museum is a work in progress, expected to double in size and be completed by mid-2006. It may not appear to be open when you walk by. Knock on the gate or, better yet, call and let the attendant know you're coming. ⊠ *Avda. 2 and C. 13, Barrio La Soledad* ☎ *223–4664* 🖃 *Free* ⊙ *Weekdays 8–noon and 1:30–4:30.*

⓯ **Parque Central** (Central Park). At the city's nucleus, this simple tree-planted square—it's more a plaza than a park—has a gurgling fountain and con-

Downtown
San José

crete benches, and a life-size bronze statue of a street sweeper cleaning up some bronze litter. In the center of the park is a spiderlike, mango-color gazebo donated by former Nicaraguan dictator Anastasio Somoza. Several years ago a referendum was held to decide whether to demolish the despot's gift, but Ticos voted to preserve the bandstand for posterity. The city's cathedral fronts the square on Calle 2 to the east, and nondescript stores and office buildings are across Calle 4 to the west and Avenida 4 to the south. The Teatro Popular Melico Salazar stands across the street on Avenida 2. The Burger King and KFC restaurants next door were once the Palace movie theater and, on the outside at least, maintain that film-house-of-yesteryear appearance. ⊠ *Bordered by Avdas. 2 and 4 and Cs. 2 and Central, Barrio La Merced.*

**❺ Parque España.** One of our favorite spots in the capital is this shady little park. A bronze statue of Costa Rica's Spanish founder, Juan Vásquez de Coronado, overlooks an elevated fountain on its southwest corner; the opposite corner has a lovely tiled guardhouse. A bust of Queen Isabella of Castile stares at the yellow compound to the east of the park, the Centro Nacional de la Cultura (National Center of Culture). Just west of the park is a two-story, metal-sided school made in Belgium and shipped to Costa Rica in pieces more than a century ago. Local lore holds that the intended destination was really Chile, but that Costa Rica decided to keep the mistakenly shipped building components. The yellow colonial-style building to the east of the modern INS building is the 1912 **Casa Amarilla** (☎ 223–7555), home of Costa Rica's Foreign Ministry. The massive ceiba tree in front, planted by John F. Kennedy and the presidents of all the Central American nations in 1963, gives you an idea of how quickly things grow in the tropics. The building is rarely open to the public. A garden around the corner on Calle 13 contains a 2-meter-wide section of the Berlin Wall donated by Germany's Foreign Ministry after reunification. Ask the guard to let you into the garden if you want a closer look. A few doors east is the elegant Mexican Embassy, once a private home and the site of the signing of the truce ending Costa Rica's brief 1948 civil war. ⊠ *Bordered by Avdas. 7 and 3 and Cs. 11 and 17, Barrio El Carmen* ☎ *257–7202.*

**❹ Parque Morazán.** Anchored by the 1920 Templo de Música (Temple of Music), a neoclassic bandstand that has become the symbol of the city,

## A GOOD WALK

**A**ll visitors manage to find their way to the **Plaza de la Cultura** ❶, a favorite meeting spot in the heart of the city, and it makes a good kick-off point for a walk. The ornate **Teatro Nacional** ❷ sits on the south side of the plaza. Pop in and buy a ticket for an evening performance and/or grab a cup of coffee at the lobby café. The **Museo del Oro Precolombino** ❸ lies under the plaza. The gold collection could easily captivate for an hour or two. From here, head two blocks north on Calle 5 to **Parque Morazán** ❹, whose centerpiece Tem-

plo de Música is the symbol of the city. Traffic is particularly dangerous here, so take heed. The Edificio Metállico, a metal building that serves as a school, fronts the park's north side. Continue just east of the park on Avenida 3 to the small **Parque España** ❺, one of the city's most pleasant green spaces. The ornate building on the park's north side is the Andrew Carnegie–funded Casa Amarilla. At Avenida 7 is the modern Instituto Nacional de Segoros (INS) building, whose 11th-floor **Museo de Jade** ❻ has an extensive American jade collection and great city views. The

1

the largest park in downtown San José is somewhat barren, though the Pink and Golden Trumpet trees on its northwest corner brighten things up when they bloom in the dry months. The park is named for Honduran general Francisco Morazán, whose dream for a united Central America failed in the 1830s. The general's bust near the north entrance to the park is easy to miss. Much more prominent here are monuments to South American liberators Simón Bolívar and Bernardo O'Higgins, and 1970s Costa Rican president Daniel Oduber. Avoid the park late at night, when a rough crowd and occasional muggers appear. Along the southern edge are a public school and two lovely old mansions, both with beautiful facades—one is a casino, the other a prostitute pickup bar. There's a park annex with a large fountain to the northeast, across busy Avenida 3, in front of the metal school building. ⊠ *Avda. 3, between Cs. 5 and 9, Barrio El Carmen.*

⓫ **Parque Nacional** (National Park). A bronze monument commemorating Central America's battles against American invader William Walker in 1856 forms the centerpiece of this large and leafy park. Five Amazons, representing the five nations of the isthmus, attack Walker, who shields his face from the onslaught. Costa Rica maintains the lead and shelters a veiled Nicaragua, the country most devastated by the war. Guatemala, Honduras, and El Salvador might dispute this version of events, but this is how Costa Rica chose to commission the work by French sculptor Louis Carrier Belleuse, a student of Rodin's, in 1895. Bas-relief murals on the monument's pedestal depict key battles in the war against the Americans. The park paths are made of cobblestone rescued from downtown streets, and tall trees shading concrete benches often hide colorful parakeets in their branches. The modern pink building west of the park houses the Registro Civil (Civil Registry) and the Tribunal Supremo de Elecciones (Supreme Electoral Tribunal), which keep track of voters—as well as their births, marriages, divorces, deaths, and *cédulas* (the national identity cards carried by all citizens)—and oversee elections. The park is best avoided at night, despite ample lighting and security patrols. ⊠ *Bordered by Avdas. 1 and 3 and Cs. 15 and 19, Barrio El Carmen.*

❶ **Plaza de la Cultura.** The crowds of people, vendors, and street entertainers at the Plaza de la Cultura—it's a favored spot for local marimba bands,

---

Ministry of Culture complex, the **Centro Nacional de la Cultura** ➐ fronts the park's east side. From Parque España, walk one long block east to the **Parque Nacional** ➑. Two blocks south on Calle 17 is a pleasant pedestrian mall. Pass the Asamblea Legislativa, where Costa Rica's congress meets, and come to the **Museo Nacional** ➒. Loop around to the museum's west side to one of the higher levels on the Plaza de la Democracia, a great vantage point for sunsets—but otherwise just an expanse of concrete. Avenida Central fronts the plaza's north side. Head back downhill, into the hus-

tle and bustle of the city center. The avenue becomes a lively pedestrian mall at Calle 9, and two blocks later you return to the Plaza de la Cultura. ⏱ TIMING TIPS➙➙ **The walk takes about an hour at a stroll. If you take a more leisurely approach, lingering at the parks or museums, the walk could take hours.**

clowns, jugglers, and colorfully dressed South Americans playing Andean music—hide the fact that the expanse is really just a mass of concrete. The ornate Teatro Nacional, one of San José's signature buildings, dominates the plaza's southern half. Pop in and buy a ticket for an evening performance—the prices are amazingly reasonable. The Museo de Oro Precolombino, with its highly visited exhibits of gold, lies under the plaza. The plaza's western edge is defined by the Gran Hotel Costa Rica, with its 24-hour Café 1930. ⊠ *Bordered by Avdas. Central and 2 and Cs. 3 and 5, Barrio La Soledad.*

⓬ **Plaza de la Democracia.** President Oscar Arias built this terraced open space west of the Museo Nacional to mark 100 years of democracy and to receive dignitaries during the 1989 hemispheric summit. The view west toward the dark-green Cerros de Escazú is nice in the morning and fabulous at sunset. The plaza is dominated by a statue of José "Don Pepe" Figueres, three-time president and leader of the 1948 revolution. Jewelry, T-shirts, and crafts from Costa Rica, Guatemala, and South America are sold in a string of stalls along the western edge. ⊠ *Bordered by Avdas. Central and 2 and Cs. 13 and 15, Barrio La Soledad.*

**need a break?**

Duck into the **Café del Teatro Nacional** (⊠ Plaza de la Cultura, Barrio La Soledad ☎ 221–3262), beside the theater to sit at a marble table, sipping a hazelnut mocha beneath frescoed ceilings. The frescoes are part of an allegory of seminude figures celebrating the 1897 opening of the theater. Coffees run from $1 to $2, depending on how much alcohol or ice cream is added. Sandwiches and cakes are $3 to $4. The place follows standard practice of having a TV on at all times, albeit softly in this case. The café keeps the same hours as the theater, but is open until curtain time on performance nights, and during intermission.

⓲ **Plaza del Banco Central** (Central Bank). An extension of Avenida Central, the plaza is popular with hawkers, money changers, and retired men and can be a good place to get a shoe shine and listen to street musicians. Outside the western end of Costa Rica's modern federal reserve bank building, don't miss Fernando Calvo's *Presentes,* 10 sculpted, smaller-than-life figures of bedraggled *campesinos* (peasants). A bronze 500-kg (1,100-lb) statue by Manuel Vargas of a buxom rural woman took up residence in 2004 at sidewalk level on the small, shady plaza south of the bank. It's public art at its best. Beware: the money changers here are notorious for circulating counterfeit bills and using doctored calculators to shortchange unwitting tourists. Instead, change money at banks or through cash machines, where you get the best rate. In fact, you can stop by a money-exchange kiosk right here operated by Banco Nacional, one of the state banks, and open seven days a week. ⊠ *Bordered by Avdas. Central and 1 and Cs. 2 and 4, Barrio La Merced.*

⓰ **Teatro Popular Melico Salazar** (Melico Salazar Theater). Across Avenida 2 on the north side of Parque Central stands San José's second major performance hall (after the Teatro Nacional). The 1928 building is on the site of a former 19th-century military barracks felled by an earthquake. The venue was later named for Costa Rican operatic tenor Manuel "Melico" Salazar (1887–1950). It was constructed specifically to provide a less highbrow alternative to the Teatro Nacional. But these days the Melico is plenty cultured and provides the capital with a steady diet of music and dance performances. ⊠ *Avda. 2 and C. 2, Barrio La Merced* ☎ *221–4952.*

## West of Downtown

Paseo Colón, one of San José's major boulevards, heads due west from downtown and leads to the vast La Sabana park, the largest parcel of green space in the city. La Sabana anchors the vast west side of the city. A block or two off its exhaust-ridden avenues are quiet residential streets, and you'll find the U.S., Canadian, and British embassies here.

### What to See

**⓴ Museo de Arte Costarricense** (Museum of Costa Rican Art). A splendid collection of 19th- and 20th-century Costa Rican art, labeled in Spanish and English, is housed in 12 exhibition halls here. Be sure to visit the top-floor Salón Dorado to see the stucco, bronze-plated bas-relief mural depicting Costa Rican history, created by French sculptor Louis Feron. Wander the sculpture garden in back and take in Jorge Jiménez's seven-meter-tall *Imagen Cósmica,* which depicts pre-Columbian traditions. ⊠ *C. 42 and Paseo Colón, Paseo Colón* ☎ *222–7155* ⊕ *www. musarco.go.cr* ⊠ *$1, free Sun.* ☉ *Tues.–Sun. 10–5.*

**㉑ Parque Metropolitano La Sabana.** Though it isn't centrally located, La Sabana (the savannah) comes the closest of San José's green spaces to achieving the same function and spirit as New York's Central Park. A statue of 1930s president León Cortes greets you at the park's principal entrance at the west end of Paseo Colón. Behind the statue a 5-meter-tall menorah serves as a gathering place for San José's small Jewish community during Hanukkah. La Sabana was once San José's airport, and the whitewashed Museo de Arte Costarricense, just south of the Cortes statue, served as terminal and control tower. The round Gimnasio Nacional (National Gymnasium) sits at the southeast corner of the park and hosts sporting events and the occasional concert. The Estadio Nacional (National Stadium) near the park's northwest corner is the site of important soccer matches, and is one of the country's major outdoor concert venues. The unattractive headquarters of the Instituto Costarricense de Electricidad, the state electricity and telecommunications monopoly, fronts the park's north side. In between are acres of space for soccer, basketball, tennis, swimming, jogging, picnicking, and kite flying. The park hums with activity on weekend days. You're welcome to join in the early-morning, outdoor aerobics classes on Saturday and Sunday. Like most of San José's green spaces, La Sabana should be avoided at night. ⊠ *Bordered by C. 42, Avda. de las Américas, and Autopista Próspero Fernández, Paseo Colón.*

**㉒ Pueblo Antiguo.** A Tico version of Colonial Williamsburg west of the city depicts Costa Rica between 1880 and 1930. Actors in period costumes staff a turn-of-the-20th-century general store, sugar and coffee mill, and stores, all arranged around a central park with requisite church and bandstand. All the buildings were constructed in the late 20th century. *Típico*

CLOSE UP

# Teatro Nacional

**★ Fodor's Choice** THE NATIONAL THEATER is easily the most enchanting building in Costa Rica, and San José's don't-miss sight. Chagrined that touring prima donna Adelina Patti bypassed San José in 1890, wealthy coffee merchants raised import taxes to hire Belgian architects to design this building, lavish with cast iron and Italian marble. The theater was inaugurated in 1897 with a performance of Gounod's *Faust*, featuring an international cast. The sandstone exterior is marked by Italianate arched windows, marble columns with bronze capitals, and statues of strange bedfellows Ludwig van Beethoven (1770–1827) and 17th-century Spanish golden-age playwright Pedro Calderón de la Barca (1600–1681). The Muses of Dance, Music, and Fame are silhouetted in front of an iron cupola. Given the provenance of the building funds, it's not surprising that frescoes on the stairway inside depict coffee and banana production. Note Italian painter Aleardo Villa's famous ceiling mural *Alegoría del Café y Banano* (*Allegory of Coffee and Bananas*), a joyful harvest scene that appeared on Costa Rica's old five-colón note. (The now-defunct bill is prized by collectors and by tourists as a souvenir, and is often sold by vendors in the plaza between the theater and the Gran Hotel Costa Rica next door. The sumptuous neo-Baroque interior sparkles thanks to an ongoing restoration project. And what's an old theater without its resident ghost? Patrons have claimed to see moving figures in the second-floor paintings in the Teatro Nacional.

The best way to see the theater's interior is to attend one of the performances, which take place several nights a week; intermission gives you a chance to nose around. Stop at the *boletería* (box office) in the lobby and see what strikes your fancy. (Don't worry if you left your tuxedo or evening gown back home; as long as you don't show up for a performance wearing shorts, jeans, or a T-shirt, no one will care.) Alternatively, a nominal admission fee gets you in beyond the lobby for an informative guided daytime visit. Tours in English are available. The theater is sometimes closed for rehearsals, so call before you go. ⊠ *Plaza de la Cultura, Barrio La Soledad* ☎ *221-1329* 🎟 *$3* ⊙ *Mon.–Sat. 9–4.*

restaurants dish up hearty Costa Rican food. Ticket prices include admission to the adjoining Parque de Diversiones amusement park. Noches Costarricenses (Costa Rican Nights) performances take place on Friday and Saturday nights from 6:30 to 9:30, with dinner and music and dance performances. The $40 tour price includes transportation to and from San José hotels and English-speaking guides. ⊠ *2 km (1½ mi) west of Hospital México, La Uruca* ☎ *231–2001* ⊕ *www.parquediversiones. com* 🎟 *$7* ⊙ *Mon.–Thurs. 9–5, Fri.–Sun. 9–7.*

## North and East of Downtown

Immediately northeast of downtown lie the splendid historic neighborhoods of Barrio Amón and Barrio Otoya. Both are repositories of historic houses that have escaped the wrecking ball, and many now serve as hotels, restaurants, and offices. (And a few actually are private residences as well.) Barrio Escalante, to the east, is not quite as gentrified, but fast becoming a fashionable address.

The sprawling suburb of San Pedro begins several blocks east of downtown San José. The area is home to the University of Costa Rica and all the intellect and cheap eats and nightlife that a student or student-wannabe could desire. But away from the heart of the university, San Pedro is also awash in the consumerism of shopping malls, fast-food restaurants, and car dealerships, but also manages to mix in stately districts such as the stylish Los Yoses for good measure. To get to San Pedro, walk a few miles east along Avenida Central's strip of shops and bars or take a $2 taxi ride from downtown and get off in front of Banco Nacional, just beyond the rotunda with the fountain at its center.

## What to See

**㉕ Centro Comercial El Pueblo** (El Pueblo Shopping Center). This shopping center was built to resemble the kind of colonial village that Costa Rica lacks. *Pueblo* means "town, " and the cobbled passages, adobe walls, and tiny plazas are surprisingly convincing. Most of the commercial spaces are occupied by bars, restaurants, and discos that attract a twentysomething crowd. El Pueblo gets very busy at night, especially on weekends—but there are a few shops worth checking out during the day. (And several of those shops keep evening hours if you wish to buy souvenirs in between bar rounds.) ✉ *Avda. 0, Barrio Tournón* ☎ *221–9434* ☉ *Daily 8 AM–3 AM.*

★ ☺ **㉖ Jardín de Mariposas Spyrogyra** (Spyrogyra Butterfly Garden). An hour or two at this magical garden is entertaining and educational for nature lovers of all ages. Self-guided tours enlighten you on butterfly ecology and give you a chance to see the winged creatures close up. After an 18-minute video introduction, you're free to wander screened-in gardens along a numbered trail. Some 30 species of colorful butterflies flutter about, accompanied by 6 types of hummingbirds. Try to come when it's sunny, as butterflies are most active then. A small, moderately priced café borders the garden and serves sandwiches and Tico fare. Spyrogyra abuts the northern edge of Parque Zoológico Simón Bolívar, but you enter on the outskirts of Barrio Tournón, near El Pueblo Shopping Center. ✉ *50 m east and 150 m south of main entrance to El Pueblo, Barrio Tournón* ☎ *222–2937* ✆ *$6* ☉ *Daily 8–4.*

★ ☺ **㉔ Mundo Salvaje** (Wild World). Some of the snakes once exhibited at the now-defunct Serpentario—there are 150 specimens in all—are now displayed here in much more spacious quarters just north of town, along with scorpians, frogs, toads, and butterflies. Admission includes a two-hour guided tour with a bilingual guide who gives tips on identifying poisonous snakes and tells you what to do in case of an encounter in the wild. Snake handler–wannabes may be able to hold the resident nonpoisonous, 9-meter (29-foot) Burmese python. Night tours are available with advance reservations. A minimum of two people is all that's required. ✉ *Carretera a Guápiles, 600 m north of La República, Barrio Tournón* ☎ *241–5656* ⊕ *www.mundosalvaje.com* ✆ *$11* ☉ *Daily 8–6.*

☺ ❷ **Museo de los Niños.** San José's Children's Museum is housed in a former jail, and big kids may want to check it out just to marvel at the castlelike architecture and the old cells that have been preserved in an exhibit about prison life. Three halls in the complex are filled with eye-catching seasonal exhibits for kids, ranging in subject from local ecology to outer space. The exhibits are annotated in Spanish, but most are interactive, so language shouldn't be much of a problem. The museum's most popular resident is the Egyptian exhibit's sarcophagus; the mummy draws the "oohs" and

> **RAINY DAY TIPS**
>
> ■ Do outdoor sightseeing in the morning, before the afternoon rains arrive.
> ■ Duck into museums—our top choices are the Gold and Jade museums.
> ■ Do as Costa Ricans do and *tomar café* (take a coffee break).
> ■ Don't wait until the evening rush hour (5–7 PM) to get a cab—they're nearly nonexistent when it rains.

"ewws." Officially, the complex is called the Centro Costarricense de Ciencia y Cultura (Costa Rican Center of Science and Culture), and that will be the sign that greets you on the front of the building. The **Galería Nacional,** adjoining the main building, is more popular with adults; it usually shows fine art by Costa Rican artists free of charge. Also adjoining the museum is the classical music venue **Auditorio Nacional.** ⊠ *North end of C. 4, Barrio El Carmen* ☎ *258–4929* ⊕ *www.museocr. com* ☞ *$2* ☉ *Tues.–Fri. 8–4:30, weekends 9:30–5.*

☺ ❷ **Parque Zoológico Simón Bolívar.** Considering Costa Rica's mind-boggling diversity of wildlife, San José's zoo is rather modest in scope, and gets mixed reviews for some of its cramped exhibition spaces. It does, however, provide an introduction to some of the animals you might see in the jungle. The park is set in a forested ravine in historical Barrio Amón, offering soothing green space in the heart of the city. ⊠ *Avda. 11 and C. 11, Barrio Amón* ☎ *233–6701* ☞ *$2* ☉ *Weekdays 8–3:30, weekends 9–4:30.*

**need a break?**
We have to admit that Costa Rican baked goods tend toward the dry-as-dust end of the spectrum. But Italian-style bakery **Giacomin** (⊠ Next to Automercado, Los Yoses, San Pedro ☎ 234–2551 ⊠ C. 2, between Avdas. 3 and 5, Barrio La Merced ☎ 221–5652), near the University of Costa Rica, is an exception—it seems that a touch of liqueur added to the batter makes all the difference. Stand, European-style, at the downstairs espresso bar, or take your goodies to the tables and chairs on the upstairs balcony. Both branches close from noon to 2.

❸ **Museo de Insectos.** Scurry on over to the agronomy department at the University of Costa Rica to get a good look at dead insects in re-created habitats. Find information (in English and Spanish) on everything from insect sex to the diseases these little buggers cause. ⊠ *Universidad de Costa Rica, north of Bellas Artes, in the basement of the Artes*

## Are You Ready for Some *Fútbol*?

**1**

**SPORTS MEAN ONE THING IN** San José: soccer. Very young boys (and a slowly increasing number of girls) kick around a ball–or some other object if no ball is available–in street pickup games, and grow into fans passionate about their local team. Everyone puts aside regional differences when Costa Rica's reputation is on the line on the world stage, as it was during its 2002 World Cup appearance.

Consult the Spanish-language daily *La Nación* or ask at your hotel for details on upcoming games–you simply buy

a ticket at the stadium box office. Prices range from $2 to $12. *Sombra numerado* (shaded seats) are the most expensive.

Professional soccer matches are usually played on Sunday morning or Wednesday night in either of two San José stadiums, one of which is the Estadio Nacional (Western end of La Sabana park). The Estadio Ricardo Saprissa (Next to the Clínica Interada de Tibás) hosts professional soccer matches and is in the northern suburb of Tibás.

*Musicales building, San Pedro* ☎ *207–5318* ⊕ *www.insectos.ucr.ac.cr* ✉ *$2* ⊙ *Weekdays 1–4:45.*

🖑 **㉙ Planetario de San José** (San José Planetarium). Catch a falling star and put it in your pocket at one of the city's newest attractions, a joint venture between the University of Costa Rica and the government of Japan. At this writing, the planetarium is set to open in late 2005. ⊠ *500 m north of church of San Pedro, San Pedro* ☎ *207–4000 (University of Costa Rica).*

**㉛ Universidad de Costa Rica.** The University of Costa Rica, or "La U, " is a great place to hang out and meet people, especially if your Spanish is pretty good. Oxford or Harvard with their ivy-covered buildings this is not. Most of the boxy structures date from the 1940s–1950s and are painted in a riot of tropical pastels: the library is sea green; General Studies, orange; Social Science, beige; Medicine is red, yellow, and blue. On campus are the **Museo de Insectos**(⇨ above) and the **Planetario de San José** (⇨ above). Aficionados of Spanish literature should browse around the many off-campus bookstores. Anyone who appreciates cheap grub can revel in the vast selection of inexpensive lunch places around the university. Weeknights at the university are mellow, but nearby bars are packed with students and intellectuals on weekends. ⊠ *Avda. Central and C. Central, San Pedro* ⊕ *www.ucr.ac.cr.*

## WHERE TO EAT

Wherever you eat in San José, be it a small *soda* (informal eatery) or a sophisticated restaurant, dress is casual. Meals tend to be taken earlier than in other Latin American countries; few restaurants serve past 10 PM. Local cafés usually open for breakfast at 7 AM and remain open until 7 or 9 in the evening. Restaurants serving international cuisine are usu-

CLOSE UP

## Missing History

**BLAME IT ON THE EARTHQUAKES.** Costa Ricans are quick to attribute the scarcity of historic architecture in San José and around the country to a history of earth tremors. Indeed, major earthquakes have struck various locales around Costa Rica 10 times since the mid-18th century (6 times in the 20th century), felling untold historical structures.

But blame it on the wrecking ball, too, says architect Gabriela Sáenz, who works with the Ministry of Culture's Center for Research and Conservation of Cultural Patrimony. The tear-it-down approach really began to take its toll in the 1970s, an era when boxy, concrete buildings were in vogue around the world, Sáenz says. Costa Rica didn't establish its first school of architecture until 1972, staffed by faculty from Mexico, England, and Brazil. "It was hard for a real Costa Rican tradition to take hold, " she explains. Mix that with a lack of government regulation and what Sáenz calls a typical Tico do-your-own-thing penchant, and the result is

the San José, chock-full of squat buildings, you see today.

The tide began to turn in 1995 with the passage of the Law of Historic and Architectural Patrimony. Over 300 historic structures in the country are presently protected under the legislation, and new buildings are added to the registry each year. But legal protection is no guarantee of funding necessary to actually restore a historic landmark.

You need to look hard, but San José really does have several diamonds in the rough. The National Theater and Post Office remain the two most visited examples of historic architecture in the capital. But the National Museum the Museum of Forms, Spaces and Sounds, the National Center of Culture, and several small hostelries and restaurants around town—especially in Barrios Amón and Otoya—all are modern transformations and restorations of structures with past histories.

ally open from 11 AM to 9 PM. Some cafés that serve mainly San José office workers are closed Sunday. Restaurants that do open on Sunday do a brisk business: it's the traditional family day out (and the maid's day off). Casino restaurants in downtown San José are open 24 hours.

### San José

AMERICAN    ✕ **JR Ribs.** Frederic Remington meets Barrio Amón in this restaurant made
$-$$    to look like an Old West saloon that happens to butt up against a ravine near the zoo entrance. Texas-style ribs are still enough of a novelty cuisine in Costa Rica that the diners have fun here—there always seems to be someone's birthday lunch or dinner going on here—even if they haven't mastered the art of not getting the tangy barbecue sauce on their ties and blouses and all over the plastic faux-rawhide tablecloths. For the less adventurous, an upstairs dining room serves Costa Rican food buffet-style weekdays for lunch. Stay downstairs; it's much more entertaining. ✉ *Avda. 11 and C. 11, Barrio Amón* ☎ *223–0523* ▭ *AE, DC, MC, V* ☺ *No dinner Sun.*

1

**$–$$** ╳**News Café.** Pounce on one of the six streetside tables if they're free when you enter. The passing parade on Avenida Central is yours for the price of a cup of coffee. (They probably won't be available: a regular expat crowd holds court here.) Breakfast and dinner fare is hearty, but the café is most popular at lunchtime and cocktail hour. You can get a Caesar salad and other American dishes here. Inside, the wrought-iron chairs, wood beams, and brick walls give the place an old-town tavern feel— framed newspaper front pages hang on the wall trumpeting D-Day, Pearl Harbor, and John Glenn's first space mission. The café is on the first floor of the 1960s landmark Hotel Presidente. ⊠ *Avda. Central and C. 7, Barrio La Soledad* ☎ *222–3022* ▭ *AE, DC, MC, V* ☉ *Breakfast served.*

CAFÉS ╳**Café Mundo.** You could easily walk by this corner restaurant without
**$–$$** noticing its tiny sign behind the foliage. The upstairs café serves meals
Fodor'sChoice on the porch, on a garden patio, or in two dining rooms. The soup of
★ the day and fresh-baked bread start you out; main courses include shrimp in a vegetable cream sauce or *lomito en salsa de vino tinto* (tenderloin in a red-wine sauce). Save room for the best chocolate cake in town, drizzled with homemade blackberry sauce. Café Mundo is a popular, low-key gay hangout that draws a mixed gay-straight clientele. This is one of the few center-city restaurants with its own parking lot. ⊠ *C. 15 and Avda. 9, Barrio Otoya* ☎ *222–6190* ▭ *AE, MC, V* ☉ *Closed Sun. No lunch Sat.*

★ **$–$$** ╳**Kafé Ko.** Glass tables, wrought-iron chairs, and lots of candles fill this cozy, upscale restaurant two blocks east of Museo Nacional. Choose from sandwiches, quiches, pastas, and nachos. Top off your meal with a tiramisu or a dessert crepe. The café serves a full range of coffees and teas. The television is going, but unlike the TV in most Costa Rican restaurants, here it might be an *I Love Lucy* episode or an Indian Bollywood video, and the sound will be off, with soft jazzy music playing in the background. You'll be treated to live Indian music each Wednesday evening, and a DJ spins tunes upstairs after 10 on Friday and Saturday nights. Despite all the action, the place remains quiet and laid-back, and is one of the city's most enjoyable places to while away an evening. ⊠ *C. 21, 25 m south of Primavera gas station, Barrio La California* ☎ *258–7483* ▭ *No credit cards* ☉ *Closed Sun.*

**¢–$** ╳**Café de la Posada.** The lack of alfresco dining in this tropical city is disappointing, but this café's terrace with six tables fronting the Calle 17 pedestrian mall is a pleasant exception. The owners of this small café come from Argentina, and they know how to make a great cappuccino. Salads, quiches, and empanadas are the food specialties. The best bargains are the four rotating *platos del día* (daily specials), with entrée, salad, beverage, and dessert for $4. If you opt for dinner, make it an early one: the place closes at 7 on weeknights. ⊠ *C. 17, between Avdas. 2 and 4, Barrio La Soledad* ☎ *258–1027* ▭ *AE, DC, MC, V* ☉ *No dinner Sat. and Sun.*

**¢** ╳**Café Hanna.** Coffee, tea, sandwiches, quiches, croissants, lasagnas, and empanadas are the draws at this quiet café in an irregularly laid-out building on a rounded street corner near Parque España. (There are a scant seven tables here; one on the outdoor patio.) Or you can opt for a buf-

Where to Stay
& Eat in San José

TOURNÓN

SAN FRANCISCO

Parque Zoológico
Simón Bolívar

Avenida 9

Avenida 11

OTOYA

AMÓN

ARANJUEZ

TO GUADALUPE

Avenida 5

Parque Morazán

Avenida 7

Correos de
Costa Rica

Avenida 3

Galería Nacional de
Arte Contemporánea

Avenida 3

Parque Nacional

Avenida 1

CUESTA
DE MORAS

Teatro
Nacional

Catedral
Metropolitana

Plaza de
la Cultura

Museo
Nacional

see inset

SOLEDAD

Avenida 6

TO LOS YOSES,
SAN PEDRO,
ESCALANTE

Avenida 8

TO CURRIDABAT

0          300 yards

0          300 meters

**KEY**

● Restaurants
④ Hotels
↔ Rail Lines
   Pedestrian Zone

fet lunch and top it off with desserts. The café closes at 7 PM. ⊠ *C. 13, between Avdas. 7 and 9, Barrio Otoya* ☎ *222–9593* ▭ *AE, DC, MC, V* ☺ *Closed Sun., no dinner Sat. Breakfast served.*

CHINESE
**$–$$**
✕ **Don Wang.** In a country where "Chinese cuisine" often means rice and vegetables bearing a suspicious resemblance to *gallo pinto* ("spotted rooster, " a typical Costa Rican dish of black beans and rice), Don Wang's authenticity comes as a real treat. Cantonese cuisine is the mainstay here— the owner comes from that region of China—but these folks will Szechuan it up a bit if you ask. Mornings give way to the immensely popular dim sum, called *desayuno chino*, literally "Chinese breakfast." You can order dim sum all day, but the $5 specials last only until 11 AM. The dining area is built around a stone garden and small waterfall. There's no television blaring here, a refreshing change from many Costa Rican restaurants. ⊠ *C. 11, between Avdas. 6 and 8, Barrio La Soledad* ☎ *233–6484 or 223–5925* ▭ *AE, DC, MC, V* ☺ *Breakfast served.*

COSTA RICAN
★ **$–$$**
✕ **La Cocina de Leña.** The name translates literally as "firewood kitchen," and it evokes the age-old Tico style of cooking. Indeed, you'll see bundles of wood as well as old tools and straw bags hung on walls to make you feel like you're down on the farm, but rustic this place is not. Popular Tico dishes such as black-bean soup, ceviche, tamales, oxtail with cassava, and plantains are served, and the restaurant has live marimba music several nights a week during high season. Although the kitchen closes at 11, you're welcome to stay as long as the band keeps playing. It is one of the few places that doesn't close during Holy Week. ⊠ *Centro Comercial El Pueblo, Avda. 0, Barrio Tournón* ☎ *223–3704* ▭ *AE, DC, MC, V.*

¢–$
✕ **La Criollita.** Kick off your day with breakfast at this emerald-green restaurant. Mornings are the perfect time to snag one of the precious tables in the back garden, an unexpected refuge from the noise and traffic of the city. Choose from the *americano*, with pancakes and toast; the *tico*, with bread, fried bananas, and *natilla* (sour cream); or the huge *criollita*, with ham or pork chops; all have eggs on the side. Workers from nearby government office buildings begin to pour in late in the morning, and the lunchtime decibel level increases appreciably. (This is the one time of day we recommend avoiding the place.) They filter out about 2 PM and once again you have a quiet place for coffee and dessert. ⊠ *Avda. 7, between Cs. 7 and 9 Barrio Amón* ☎ *256–6511* ▭ *AE, DC, MC, V* ☺ *Closed Sun. No dinner Sat. Breakfast served.*

¢–$
✕ **Mama's Place.** Mama's is a Costa Rican restaurant with a difference: the owners are Italian, so in addition to corvina *al ajillo* (sautéed with garlic) and other staple Tico fare, they serve homemade seafood chowder, traditional Italian pastas, and meat dishes with delicate wine sauces. The brightly decorated coffee shop opens onto busy Avenida 1; the more subdued dining room upstairs accommodates the overflow crowd. (You'll see former Chicago Bears football coach Mike Ditka's autographed picture up there.) At lunchtime, it's usually packed with business types drawn to the delicious and inexpensive daily specials— choose from the rotating *platos del día* (daily specials) with pasta, meat, fish, or poultry—all to the acompaniment of ample focaccia.

Mama's closes at 7 PM on weeknights. ⊠ *Avda. 1, between Cs. Central and 2, Barrio El Carmen* ☏ *223–2270 or 256–5601* ▭ *AE, DC, MC, V* ⊘ *Closed Sun. No dinner Sat.*

¢–$   ✕ **Manolo's.** For any San José dweller, a mention of Manolo's brings their signature menu item *churros con chocolate* (fried dough with hot fudge sauce) to mind. But this 24-hour eatery is also known for its great sandwiches and espressos. Its location on the bustling Avenida Central pedestrian thoroughfare and its outdoor tables allow for some of the city's best people-watching. Inside, however, the place feels more like a diner than a café, down to its plastic-coated menu and its promise of breakfast food at any hour. The owner always prepares a few Spanish favorites in addition to the typical Tico fare, such as *tortilla española* (a thick potato-and-onion omelet). ⊠ *Avda. Central, between Cs. Central and 2, Barrio La Merced* ☏ *221–2041* ▭ *AE, DC, MC, V* ⊘ *Breakfast served.*

¢–$   ✕ **Nuestra Tierra.** But for the traffic zipping by on one of San José's busiest thoroughfares—and on that note, opt for a table on the side facing less busy Calle 15—you might think you're out in rural Santa Ana. Bunches of onions and peppers dangle from the ceiling, recalling a provincial Tico ranch. The generous homemade meals are delicious, and the incredibly friendly wait staff, who epitomize Costa Rican hospitality and dress in traditional folkloric clothing, prepare your coffee filtered through the traditional cloth *chorreador*. The place is open 24 hours, just in case *gallo pinto* pangs hit at 3 AM. Some disparage the place as "too touristy." Perhaps it is, but it's also fun. ⊠ *Avda. 2 and C. 15, Barrio La Soledad* ☏ *258–6500* ▭ *No credit cards* ⊘ *Breakfast served.*

ECLECTIC   ✕ **Jürgen's.** Jürgen's is a common haunt for *politicos*, and San José's elites
$$–$$$   meet to eat here. Decorated in gold and terra-cotta with leather and wood accents, the dining room of this contemporary restaurant feels more like a lounge than a fine restaurant. In fact, the classy bar, with a large selection of good wine and good cigars, is a prominent feature. The inventive menu, with such delicacies as medallions of roast duck and tuna fillet encrusted with sesame seeds, sets this place apart from the city's more traditional venues. ⊠ *250 m north of the Subaru dealership, on Blvd. Barrio Dent, Barrio Dent* ☏ *283–2239* ▭ *AE, DC, MC, V* ⊘ *Closed Sun. No lunch Sat.*

$–$$   ✕ **Bakea.** Trendy, right down to its small art gallery and whimsical rest-
FodorśChoice   rooms, this restaurant in a restored Barrio Amón mansion is the place
★   to see and be seen, and is one of the few upscale places in town to grab a very late night bite. The term "fusion cuisine" really does apply here: Le Cordon Bleu–trained chef Camille Ratton-Pérez takes French and Costa Rican cuisine and spices it with Thai and Middle Eastern influences. Top off your meal with a *Cahuita caramelo*, a scrumptious chocolate-banana-butterscotch concoction or *tarte tatin* (carmelized apple tart). If you can't decide, go for the *paleta Bakea*, a dessert sampler platter. ⊠ *C. 7 and Avda. 11, Barrio Amón* ☏ *248–0303* ▭ *AE, DC, MC, V* ⊘ *Closed Sun. No dinner Mon. No lunch Sat.*

$–$$   ✕ **Morazán Café.** Within the four walls here lie (from west to east) a casual bar, a slightly more formal café, and a dark, lovey-dovey restaurant. You order from the same menu no matter where you sit. Pastas and fish lead off the eclectic menu. The impeccably groomed staff, all decked out in black, scurry around quickly. You never have to wait too long, even on a night when the place is packed. This brick building dates from 1897 and fronts the east side of Parque Morazán. It lies very close to downtown, yet we recommend taking a taxi here at night. ⊠ *Avda. 3 and C. 9, Barrio El Carmen* ☎ *221–9527* ▤ *AE, DC, MC, V.*

FRENCH    ✕ **Le Chandelier.** San José does not get classier than this restaurant,
**$$–$$$$**   where formal service and traditional sauce-heavy French dishes are part of the experience. The dining room is elegant, with wicker chairs, a tile floor, and original paintings. The Swiss chef, Claude Dubuis, might start you off with saffron ravioli stuffed with ricotta cheese and walnuts. His main courses include such unique dishes as corvina in a *pejibaye* (peach palm) sauce, hearts of palm and veal chops glazed in a sweet port-wine sauce, and the more familiar *pato a la naranja* (duck à l'o-range), or for a tropical twist on that classic dish, try Dubuis's *pato a la maracuyá* (duck in passion fruit). ⊠ *50 m west and 100 m south of ICE building, San Pedro* ☎ *225–3980 or 253–3241* ▤ *AE, DC, MC, V* ⊗ *Closed Sun. No lunch Sat.*

**$$**    ✕ **L'Ile de France.** Long one of San José's most popular restaurants, L'Ile
Fodor'sChoice   de France, in the Bergerac hotel, has dining in a tropical garden court-
★   yard. The fairly traditional French menu has some interesting innova-tions. Start with the classic onion soup or with *pâté de lapin* (rabbit liver pâté); then sink your teeth into a pepper steak, broiled lamb with sea-soned potatoes, or corvina in a spinach sauce. Save room for the prof-iteroles filled with vanilla ice cream and smothered in chocolate sauce. L'Ile de France blends exactly the right level of intimacy, grace, and style, giving it an edge over the sophisticated Chandelier. ⊠ *Hotel Le Berg-erac, C. 35, between Avdas. Central and 2, first Los Yoses entrance, San Pedro* ☎ *283–5812* ⚐ *Reservations essential* ▤ *AE, DC, MC, V* ⊗ *Closed Sun. No lunch.*

ITALIAN    ✕ **Balcón de Franco.** With old sepia photos and a strolling guitarist who
**$–$$**   seems to have been working the room for years, Balcón de Franco trans-ports you to the year of its inception, 1909. Pasta specialties such as the *plato mixto* (mixed plate with lasagna, tortellini, and ravioli) are so pop-ular that they haven't changed much either. (Why tamper with success?) For something lighter, try the scrumptious heart-of-palm salad or sautéed corvina. Grab a table away from the door (i.e., from the noise of the bus stop across the street). FYI, the sign out front reads BALCÓN DE EU-ROPA. ⊠ *Avda. Central and C. 9, Barrio La Soledad* ☎ *221–4841* ▤ *AE, DC, MC, V* ⊗ *Closed Sat.*

**$**    ✕ **La Trattoria.** The green and gold here might make a Green Bay Pack-ers fan feel right at home, but it's the excellent, reasonably priced home-made pasta dishes that make this popular lunch spot worth the stop. Begin your meal with fresh bread and any number of excellent an-tipasti, continuing on with your favorite pasta dish. And for dessert, who can resist tiramisu? ⊠ *Behind Automercado, Barrio Dent, San Pedro* ☎ *224–7065* ▤ *AE, DC, MC, V* ⊗ *No dinner Sun.*

**$**    ✕ **Pane e Vino.** Look closely at the extensive menu here: there are 40 varieties of the capital's best thin-crust pizza, and no one will rush you if you spend too much time pondering what you want. This lively two-level restaurant—it's a small chain, but this was the first location—rounds out its offerings with a complete selection of pastas. You can dine until midnight daily, expect on Sunday, when you'll have to finish dinner by 10 PM. The Pizza Allessandre, topped with prosciutto, mozzarella, and olives, is the most popular dish, and for good reason. ⊠ *50 m west and 15 m south of Más X Menos , San Pedro* ☎ *280–2869* ▭ *AE, DC, MC, V.*

JAPANESE ✕ **Matsuri.** It's a bit off the beaten tourist path and it's in a shopping
★ **$–$$** center, but this is one of the capital's best sushi joints. The chefs here have created 48 recipes for original rolls, sushi, and sashimi, using high-quality imported ingredients. Bento boxes serve as the weekday lunch specials. The oohing and aahing you hear upstairs is for the chefs performing at the teppanyaki grills to the delight and applause of patrons. ⊠ *Plaza Cristal, 600 m south of Pop's ice-cream shop, Curridabat* ☎ *280–5522* ▭ *AE, DC, MC, V.*

MEDITERRANEAN ✕ **Pub Olio.** Although this combination pub and restaurant serves the
**$** full contingent of Mediterranean cuisine, we like to visit the place for drinks and Spanish-style *tapas* (appetizers). The century-old redbrick house with stained-glass windows draws everybody from tie-clad businessmen to unviersity students who have money to spend on something more upscale than run-of-the-mill campus-area bars. Groups liven up the large front room—the quieter, smaller back rooms maintain a bit more romance—and the staff hauls umbrella-covered tables out to the sidewalk on warm evenings. ⊠ *200 m north of Bagelmen's, Barrio Escalante* ☎ *281–0541* ▭ *AE, DC, MC, V* ☉ *Closed Sun; no lunch Sat.*

MIDDLE EASTERN ✕ **Lubnan.** Negotiate the quirky wrought-iron-and-burlap revolving
**$–$$** door at the entrance, and you've made it into one of San José's few Middle Eastern restaurants. The Lebanese owners serve a wide variety of dishes from their native region, so if you can't decide, the *mezza* serves two people and gives you a little bit of everything. For your own individual dish, try the juicy shish kebab *de cordero* (of lamb), or if you're feeling especially adventurous, the raw ground-meat *kebbe naye* (with wheat meal) and *kafta naye* (without wheat meal). A hip bar in the back serves the same menu, but definitely eat out in the front restaurant Thursday nights for the belly dancing show. ⊠ *Paseo Colón, between Cs. 22 and 24, Paseo Colón* ☎ *257–6071* ▭ *AE, DC, MC, V* ☉ *Closed Mon. No dinner Sun.*

PAN-ASIAN ✕ **Tin Jo.** The colorful dining rooms at this converted house just south-
**$–$$** east of downtown evoke Japan, India, China, Indonesia, or Thailand.
Fodor'sChoice In the Thai room an 11-meter (39-foot) mural depicts a Buddhist tem-
★ ple. You can also select from all those cuisines here, with menus to match its varied dining areas. Start with a powerful Singapore sling (brandy and fruit juices) before trying such treats as *kaeng* (Thai shrimp and pineapple curry in coconut milk), *mu shu* (a beef, chicken, or veggie stir-fry with crepes), samosas (stuffed Indian pastries), and sushi rolls. The vegetarian menu is extensive, too. Tin Jo stands out with always exceptional food, attention to detail, and attentive service that make it, hands down,

CLOSE UP

## Where the Streets Have No Name

ADMITTEDLY, SOME OF THE streets in San José do have names, but no one seems to know or use them. Streets in the center of the capital are laid out in a grid, with *avenidas* (avenues) running east and west, and *calles* (streets), north and south. Odd-numbered avenues increase in number north of Avenida Central; even-numbered avenues, south. Streets east of Calle Central have odd numbers; those to the west are even. The farther you get from downtown, the more scarce street signs become. Costa Ricans rely instead on a charming and exasperating system of designating addresses by distance from well-known landmarks, as in "100 meters north and 50 meters west of the school." Another quirk: "100 meters" alway refers to one city block, regardless of how long it actually is. Likewise, "200 meters" is two blocks, and so on. Historically, the reference point was the church, but these days it might be anything from a bar to a Burger King, or even a landmark that no longer exists: the eastern suburb of San Pedro uses the *higuerón*, a fig tree that was felled long ago, but lives on in the hearts of Costa Ricans. It's no wonder that those who can afford it opt to have their mail delivered to a post-office box. Your best bet is to follow the time-honored practice and *ir y preguntar*: keep walking and keep asking.

---

the country's top Asian restaurant. ⊠ *C. 11, between Avdas. 6 and 8, Barrio La Soledad* ☎ *257–3622 or 221–7605* ▤ *AE, DC, MC, V.*

PERUVIAN
★ $–$$

✕ **Machu Picchu.** A few travel posters and a fishnet holding crab and lobster shells are the only props used to evoke Peru, but no matter: the food is anything but plain, and the seafood is excellent at both the east- and west-side branches of this mainstay. The *pique especial de mariscos* (special seafood platter), big enough for two, presents you with shrimp, conch, and squid cooked four ways. The ceviche here is quite different from and better than that served in the rest of the country. A blazing Peruvian hot sauce served on the side adds zip to any dish, but be careful—apply it by the drop. Oh, and one more warning: the pisco sours go down very easily. ⊠ *C. 32, 130 m north of KFC, Paseo Colón* ☎ *222–7384* ⊠ *150 m south of Ferretería El Mar, San Pedro* ☎ *283–3679* ▤ *AE, DC, MC, V* ☉ *Paseo Colón location closed Sun.*

SODAS
¢

✕ **Mercado Central.** A slew of unnamed sodas populate the heart of the central market. Grab a quick bite while you shop, and you just might find yourself rubbing elbows with the president. (He's been known to dine here.) ⊠ *Bordered by Avdas. Central and 1 and Cs. 6 and 8, Barrio La Merced* ☎ *No phone* ▤ *No credit cards* ☉ *No dinner; closed Sun.*

¢

✕ **Soda Argey.** It's really a bit too upscale to qualify as a typical soda, but you'll find standard Costa Rican fare here and a rotating selection of casados. And these folks even deliver. ⊠ *200 m south and 100 m west of Automercado, Los Yoses, San Pedro* ☎ *280–1183* ▤ *No credit cards* ☉ *Closed Sun. No dinner Sat.*

¢  ✕ **Soda La Vasconia.** Hundreds of sports photos plaster the wall here in what the owner calls his *museo futbolístico* (soccer museum), and the place draws crowds for that reason as well as the hearty food. It's one of the few downtown San José sodas to keep late-night hours. ⊠ *Avda. 1, between Cs. 3 and 5, Barrio El Carmen* ☎ 223–4857 ▭ *No credit cards.*

¢  ✕ **Soda Tapia.** One of San José's most popular restaurants fronts the east side of La Sabana park. You can dine outdoors here, but you'll contend with the traffic noise and the sight of the guard flagging cars in and out of the tiny parking lot. The place stays open until 2 AM, and around the clock on weekends. ⊠ *Sabana Este* ☎ 222–6734 ▭ *AE, DC, MC, V* ☉ *Breakfast served.*

SPANISH  ✕ **La Masía.** You can get by without reservations at most San José restau-
**$$–$$$**  rants, but not at this small, traditional, and very formal west-side Span-
ish restaurant. The dining room follows the Spanish theme with a tile floor, wood beams, white tablecloths, leather-and-wood Castilian-style chairs, and red, green, and yellow walls. *Champiñones al ajillo* (mush-rooms sautéed with garlic and parsley) make a fine appetizer; *camarones Catalana* (shrimp in a tomato-and-garlic cream sauce) is a standout en-trée. You'll find one of the city's most extensive wine lists here, strongest in varieties from France and Spain. ⊠ *100 m east and 130 m north of ICE, Sabana Norte* ☎ 296–3528 ⌂ *Reservations essential* ▭ *AE, DC, MC, V* ☉ *Closed Sun.*

★ **$–$$**  ✕ **Casa Luisa.** A big open window looking into the kitchen—where chef María Luisa Esparducer and her staff proudly show off their trade—is the first thing you encounter as you're shown to your table in this homey, upscale Catalan restaurant. The place is eclectic, with wood floors, arresting artwork, soft lighting, and flamenco music in the background. Start the meal with gazpacho or eggplant pâté, accompanied by a glass of top Spanish wine. The excellent main dishes include rosemary lamb chops, suckling pig, and grilled lobster. Finish with a platter of nuts, dates, and figs drizzled with a wine sauce or the decadent *crema catalana* with a *brûlée* glaze. Though La Masía is wonderfully elegant, we give Casa Luisa the nod in the Spanish-restaurant stakes for its combination of style and coziness. ⊠ *400 m south and 40 m east of the Contraloría, Sabana Sur* ☎ 296–1917 ▭ *AE, DC, MC, V* ☉ *Closed Sun.*

VEGETARIAN  ✕ **Shakti.** The baskets of fruit and vegetables at the entrance and the wall
**¢–$**  of herbal teas, health-food books, and fresh herbs for sale by the regis-
ter tell you you're in a vegetarian-friendly joint. The bright and airy restau-
rant—much homier than Vishnu, its major veggie competition—serves breakfast, lunch, and an early dinner, closing at 7 PM each day. Home-made bread, soy burgers, pita sandwiches (veggie or, for carnivorous dining companions, chicken), macrobiotic fruit shakes, and a hearty *plato del día* that comes with soup, green salad, and a fruit beverage fill out the menu. The *ensalada mixta* is a meal in itself, packed with root veg-etables native to Costa Rica. ⊠ *Avda. 8 and C. 13, Barrio La Soledad* ☎ 222–4475 ⌂ *Reservations not accepted* ▭ *AE, DC, MC, V* ☉ *Closed Sun. Breakfast served.*

¢ ✕ **Vishnu.** HACIENDO UN NUEVO MUNDO proudly proclaims the sign at the door. "Making a new world" might be a bit ambitious for a restaurant goal, but Vishnu takes its vegetarian offerings seriously. The dining area looks institutional—you'll sit at a sterile booth with Formica tables and gaze at posters of fruit on the walls—but the attraction is the inexpensive food. A yummy, good-value bet is usually the plato del día, which includes soup, beverage, and dessert, but the menu also includes soy burgers, salads, fresh fruit juices, and a yogurt smoothie called *morir soñando* (literally, "to die dreaming"). ⊠ *Avda. 1, west of C. 3, Barrio El Carmen* ☎ *233–9976* ⌂ *Reservations not accepted* ☐ *AE, DC, MC, V* ☯ *Breakfast served.*

# WHERE TO STAY

San José has a mix of historic houses with traditional architecture that have been converted into either small lodgings or chain hotels. (Best Western, Holiday Inn, Radisson, Quality Inn, Clarion, and Barceló are all here.) The historic houses are usually without concierge or pool and are found mainly in barrios Amón and Otoya, and in the eastern suburb of San Pedro. The city also has a lower tier of lodgings with the simplicity (and prices) beloved of backpackers. Most smaller hotels do not have air-conditioning, but it rarely gets warm enough at this altitude to warrant it. Many lodgings operate at near full occupancy during the high season from December through April. Reconfirm all reservations 24 hours in advance. If you're flying out early in the morning, and prefer lodging near the airport, consider staying near Alajuela or San Antonio de Belén ( ⇨ chapter 2).

## Downtown

Staying in the downtown area allows you to travel around the city as most Ticos do: on foot. Stroll the city's parks, museums, and shops, and then retire to one of many small or historic hotels that have plenty in the way of character.

$$$ 🏨 **Aurola Holiday Inn.** The upper floors of this veritable skyscraper in a city of low-lying buildings give you commanding vistas of the surrounding mountains—day views are the best, since San José doesn't glitter quite like New York at night. The good restaurant and casino are also on the top floor, making full use of their vantage points. Inside, however, you could just as well be in Ohio, as the interior decoration betrays no local influence. The high-ceiling lobby is modern and airy, with lots of shiny marble, and the place has all the facilities a business traveler's heart could desire. ■ TIP➜➜ You'll get the hotel's best rates—a 30-percent discount—by walking in or reserving in advance via the local Costa Rican number. ⊠ *Avda. 5 and C. 5, Barrio El Carmen* ✆ *Apdo. 7802–1000, San José* ☎ *222–2424, 800/465–4329 in U.S.* ☐ *255–1171* ⊕ *www.aurola-holidayinn.com* ⇥ *188 rooms, 12 suites* ⌂ *2 restaurants, a/c, in-room safes, cable TV, indoor pool, hot tub, gym, sauna, spa, bar, casino, laundry service, concierge, in-room data ports, Internet, business services, meeting rooms, airport shuttle, car rental, free parking; no-smoking floors* ☐ *AE, DC, MC, V* ❍| *BP.*

$$ 🏨 **Hotel Balmoral.** You're just as likely to hear Japanese spoken in the Balmoral's lobby as you are Spanish and English; the place is quite popular with Asian visitors. As in the Presidente across the street, you'll find all the standard amenities of a medium-priced business-class hotel here, and like the Presidente, the Balmoral draws a huge number of leisure travelers too. But we prefer the dark wood and plush, older feel here that's lacking across the street. ⊠ *Avda. Central and C. 7, Barrio La Soledad* ☎ *222–5022, 800/691–4865 in U.S.* 🖷 *221–7826* ⊕ *www. balmoral.co.cr* ⇆ *102 rooms, 10 suites* ⌂ *Restaurant, a/c, fans, in-room safes, gym, massage, sauna, cable TV, bar, casino, laundry service, Internet, business center, meeting rooms, free parking* ☰ *AE, DC, MC, V* *EP.*

★ $$ 🏨 **Hotel Fleur de Lys.** We walked by this three-floor Victorian house with the hot-pink-and-lavender exterior dozens of times without ever peeking inside, assuming that a place so brassy on the outside couldn't offer anything of interest beyond its front doors. How wrong we were. A quiet elegance that you'd never imagine lies inside this 80-year-old home with garden restaurant and art gallery on a block-long street that gets little traffic. Unsurprisingly, given the name of the place, rooms are tagged with names of flowers rather than numbers. We like the suites with raised bathtubs—two of them have whirlpool tubs as well—and their dramatic glassed-in balcony entrances. ⊠ *C. 13 between Avdas. 2 and 6, Barrio La Soledad* ⊕ *Apdo. 10736–1000, San José* ☎ *223–1206 or 257–2621* 🖷 *257–3637* ⊕ *www.hotelfleurdelys.com* ⇆ *31 rooms, 5 suites* ⌂ *Restaurant, fans, in-room safes, cable TV, bar, Internet, meeting room, free parking, no smoking rooms ; no a/c* ☰ *AE, DC, MC, V* *EP.*

$$ 🏨 **Hotel Presidente.** The *presidente* referred to here is John F. Kennedy, who walked by during his 1963 visit as the hotel was under construction. You're looking at standard, medium-priced, business-class accommodation here. Each of the comfortable rooms has one double and one single bed. The hotel draws a large contingent of business and leisure-travel guests. The rooftop terrace with hot tub has one of those secret great views of the city that no one knows about. ⊠ *Avda. Central and C. 7, Barrio La Soledad* ⊕ *Apdo. 2922-1000, San José* ☎ *222–3022* 🖷 *221–1205* ⊕ *www.hotel-presidente.com* ⇆ *88 rooms, 12 suites* ⌂ *Restaurant, room service, a/c, fans, cable TV, hot tub, sauna, bar, casino, laundry service, Internet, business services, free parking* ☰*AE, DC, MC, V* *BP.*

$ 🏨 **Gran Hotel Costa Rica.** The one-time grande dame of San José hotels is reclaiming that "Gran" title once again. A major remodeling, redecorating, and retooling of this center-city landmark have moved its clanging, jangling lobby casino and

> ### ¿DONDE ESTA EL HO-JO?
>
> Don't play it safe at a chain hotel, other than the few we recommend. They're all here in the city, but most provide you with the exact sameness you'd find in Cleveland. Smaller hotels and their Tico hospitality (although many are owned by foreigners) are quintessentially Costa Rica.

bar to a less-prominent location on a lower-level mezzanine—in its place are a formal dining room and grand piano that evoke the hotel's

1930s heyday—and have eliminated entirely its thumping top-floor disco. Rooms are large with small windows and tubs in the tiled baths, and are undergoing a brightening and renovation at this writing. The place is a good deal for the money and a first choice of travelers who want to be where the action is. Even if you don't stay here, the arcaded Café 1930 that fronts the hotel is a pleasant stop for a bite any time of the day or night—it's open 24 hours. ⊠ *Avda. 2 and C. 3, Barrio La Soledad* ⟟ *Apdo. 527–1000, San José* ☎ *221–4000, 800/949–0592 in U.S.* 🖷 *255–0139* ⊕ *www.grandhotelcostarica.com* ⥱ *110 rooms, 1 suite* ⚘ *3 restaurants, room service, fans, in-room safes, refrigerators, cable TV, gym, bar, casino, babysitting, laundry service, Internet, business center, meeting rooms, no-smoking floors; no a/c* ⊟ *AE, MC, V* ❑ *CP.*

$ 🖬 **Posada del Museo.** This green Victorian wooden 1928 house is a great place to stay if you're bound for San José's museums, hence the name. It sits diagonally across the street from the Museo Nacional. The friendly Argentine owners live on-site. Each room is different. In the restoration, the owners have maintained the original tiles, wooden double doors, and artfully painted ceilings. The hallway on the second floor overlooks the two-story lobby from what the owners call their "Romeo and Juliet balcony." The Internet-ready data ports in each rooom are a rarity in a lodging of this size. ⊠ *Avda. 2 and C. 17, Barrio La Soledad* ☎ *258–1027* 🖷 *257–9414* ⊕ *www.hotelposadadelmuseo.com* ⥱ *8 rooms, 2 suites* ⚘ *Restaurant, fans, cable TV, laundry service, in-room data ports, free parking; no a/c* ⊟ *AE, DC, MC, V* ❑ *BP.*

¢–$ 🖬 **Hotel Aranjuez.** Several 1940s-era houses with extensive gardens and lively common areas with visitors swapping travel advice constitute this family-run B&B. Each room is different; some have private gardens or small sitting rooms. The Aranjuez is a short walk from most San José attractions and has discount tour services. The complimentary breakfast buffet is an amazing spread of eggs, pastries, tropical fruit, good Costa Rican coffee, and more, served on a marvelous, palm-shaded garden patio. And, a rarity in the heart of the city, this place walks the eco-walk too, with solar-heating panels for hot water, composted gardens, and recycling. Luxurious it is not, but this is deservedly one of San José's most popular budget lodgings; reserve well in advance during the high season. ⚠ Be sure to confirm your reservation 48 hours before you arrive, and, if possible, on the day of your arrival, giving an estimated arrival time. If you don't, you might find yourself without a room when you arrive, despite your reservation. ⊠ *C. 19, between Avdas. 11 and 13, Barrio Aranjuez* ☎ *256–1825, 877/898–8663 in U.S.* 🖷 *223–3528* ⊕ *www.hotelaranjuez. com* ⥱ *33 rooms, 27 with bath* ⚘ *Dining room, fans, in-room safes, cable TV, babysitting, laundry service, Internet, free parking ; no a/c, no smoking rooms* ⊟ *MC, V* ❑ *BP.*

¢ 🖬 **Casa Ridgway.** If you prefer lodgings with a social conscience, this is the place for you. (And even if you don't, it's a great budget find.) Affiliated with the Quaker Peace Center next door, Casa Ridgway draws travelers concerned about peace, the environment, and social issues, and the knowledgeable staff can give you the scoop on what's going on in those areas. In an old house on a quiet street, the bright premises in-

## The Making of a Capital

**1**

SETTLERS MIGRATING FROM then provincial capital Cartago founded San José in 1737. (You'd never know the city is that old, however, from its complete absence of colonial architecture.) After independence in 1821, struggles and a brief civil war ensued with fellow Central Valley cities Cartago, Alajuela, and Heredia, but San José cemented its position as the new nation's capital. Revenues from the coffee and banana industries financed the construction of stately homes, theaters, and a trolley system that was later abandoned and lives on only in old sepia photographs. As recently as the mid-1900s San José was no larger than the present-day downtown area; old-timers remember the vast coffee and sugar cane plantations that extended beyond its borders. The capital began to mushroom after World War II, when old buildings were razed to make room for cement monstrosities, and it eventually sprawled to the point of connecting with nearby cities.

clude a planted terrace, a lending reference library, and a kitchen where you can cook your own food. Rooms are pretty basic and offer the option of bunk, single, or double beds. The dorm-style rooms sleep four, six, or eight. ⊠ *Avda. 6 Bis and C. 15, Barrio La Soledad* ✆ *Apdo. 1507–1000* ☎ *222–1400* ☎☎ *233–6168* ⊕ *www.amigosparalapaz. org* ⊅ *8 dorm-style rooms with shared bath, 1 double room* ♢ *Fans, laundry service, Internet, meeting room, free parking; no a/c, no room phones, no room TVs* ⊟ *No credit cards* ⊠*⊡ BP.*

★ ¢ ⊞ **Kap's Place.** This lodging literally sprawls around the neighborhood: one of the three annexes is almost two blocks away from the main building. (And if you drive by too quickly, you'll likely miss that main building with its unassuming sign and white metal door.) Inside are bright, tropical rooms with lots of tile and wood; coffee and tea are brewing all the time in the reception area, and you can use the shared kitchen. You'll be asked to sign a two-page agreement when you register attesting that you'll keep the noise down and won't bring unregistered guests to your room. The owners are anxious to maintain a family atmosphere here. ⊠ *C. 19, between Avdas. 11 and 13, 200 m west, 50 m north of Shell station, Barrio Aranjuez* ☎ *221–1169 or 257–0432* ☎ *256–4850* ⊕ *www.kapsplace.com* ⊅ *22 rooms, 20 with bath* ♢ *Fans, Internet; no a/c, no TV in some rooms, no smoking rooms* ⊟ *AE, DC, MC, V* ⊠*⊡ EP.*

### Barrios Amón and Otoya

Just north of downtown, old homes converted into small lodgings populate Barrios Amón and Otoya, two of the capital's most historic neighborhoods. While we generally eschew the big hotel franchises, our favorite San José chain lodging is here.

$$$ ⊞ **Clarion Amón Plaza.** The pink Amón Plaza achieves everything we like
Fodor'sChoice in a business-class hotel. It transcends its chain status and provides you
★ with all the services and amenities you need without being a cookie-cut-

ter high-rise. Though large for a Barrio Amón lodging, the low-rise hotel doesn't overpower the surrounding neighborhood, and takes pride in the fact that each of its 80-plus rooms is slightly different. (One common feature: there's nothing mini about the minibars.) The price of the suites (but not the double rooms) includes all international calls and shuttle transport to anywhere in the metro area. Friday night sees cocktails and a buffet dinner at the hotel's open-air Cafetal de la Luz to the accompaniment of light music, but the café makes for a pleasant stop any time, any day, whether you stay here or not. ⊠ *Avda. 11 and C. 3 Bis, Barrio Amón* ☎ *257–0191, 257–8686, 800/575–1253 in U.S., 866/845–3763 in Canada* 🖶 *257–0284* ⊕ *www.choicehotels.com* 🖘 *60 rooms, 27 suites* ♨ *2 restaurants, room service, a/c, fans, in-room safes, some refrigerators, gym, hot tub, massage, sauna, spa, bar, casino, dry cleaning, laundry service, Wi-Fi, meeting rooms, airport shuttle, free parking, no-smoking rooms* ⊟ *AE, DC, MC, V* ⦿ *BP.*

**$$** 🖼 **Hotel Britannia.** This mango-colored home is the largest and most luxurious of the old Barrio Amón houses that now serve as lodgings. Technically, the Britannia is two houses in one: a stately old building with tile porch that has changed little since its construction in 1910, except for the conversion of the old wine cellar into an intimate international restaurant; and a newer addition with slightly smaller, carpeted rooms. We like the deluxe rooms and junior suites in the original house: they're spacious, with high ceilings and windows on the street side, and are worth the extra money but are close enough to the street that noise might be a problem if you're a light sleeper. ⊠ *C. 3 and Avda. 11, Barrio Amón* 🖃 *Apdo. 3742–1000, San José* ☎ *223–6667, 800/263–2618 in U.S.* 🖶 *223–6411* ⊕ *www.hotelbritanniacostarica.com* 🖘 *19 rooms, 5 suites* ♨ *Restaurant, room service, fans, in-room safes, cable TV, bar, dry cleaning, laundry service, Internet free parking; no a/c in some rooms, no smoking rooms* ⊟ *AE, DC, MC, V* ⦿ *EP.*

★ **$–$$** 🖼 **Hotel Don Carlos.** One of the city's first guesthouses (technically it's three different houses), the Don Carlos has been in the same family for four generations. But the spirit of Carlos Bálser, the hotel's Liechtenstein-born founder—painter, geologist, archaeologist, and general jack-of-all-trades—lives on. Most rooms in the rambling old coffee-baron house have ceiling fans and big windows. Those in the Colonial Wing have a bit more personality, and several newer rooms on the third floor have views of the Irazú and Barva volcanoes. Orchids and pre-Columbian statues adorn the abundant public areas, and the 272-tile mural in the lobby depicts the history of San José. Even if you don't stay here, the Don Carlos has arguably the best hotel gift shop in the country, well worth a stop. ⊠ *C. 9 and Avda. 9, Barrio Amón* 🖃 *Box 025216, Dept. 1686, Miami, FL 33102-5216* ☎ *221–6707, 866/675–9259 in North America* 🖶 *255–0828* ⊕ *www.doncarloshotel.com* 🖘 *33 rooms* ♨ *Restaurant, room service, fans, in-room safes, cable TV, outdoor hot tub, dry cleaning, laundry service, Internet, airport shuttle, free parking; no a/c in some rooms* ⊟ *AE, MC, V* ⦿ *BP.*

★ **$–$$** 🖼 **Hotel Santo Tomás.** Don't be put off by the fact that the front of this century-old former coffee-plantation house butts up against the sidewalk on a busy street; close the front door behind you and you'll find the lobby and rooms are set back away from the traffic noise. On the fringe of Barrio Amón, the hotel has spacious rooms with wood or tile floors and lots of deep, varnished-wood furnishings. Some of the tiled bathrooms have skylights. A bright breakfast room adjoins an interior patio, and if you keep traveling back into the interior of the building, you'll find a small outdoor pool, a rarity in a hotel of this size in the capital. Rates include 30 minutes of free Internet access per day, and the especially friendly, helpful staff makes this a real find. ⊠ *Avda. 7, between Cs. 3 and 5, Barrio Amón* ☎ *255–0448* 🖷 *222–3950* ⊕ *www.hotelsantotomas. com* ☜ *20 rooms* ⚭ *Restaurant, fans, cable TV, pool, hot tub, gym, bar, Internet, parking (fee); no a/c* ▤ *AE, MC, V* ❙◯❙ *CP.*

$ 🏨 **Hotel Dunn Inn.** Adjoining 1926 and 1933 houses fuse to create the cozy Barrio Amón experience at bargain prices, so the Dunn Inn is justifiably immensely popular. (Reserve well in advance.) Pinewood dominates in one section; brick in the other. Sun-filled rooms bear indigenous Bribri names. One room has a balcony, and a few do not have street-facing windows but look onto an interior courtyard. All have terra-cotta floors and little touches such as fresh flowers. The delightful, skylight-covered central patio serves as a bar and breakfast room. ⊠ *Avda. 11 at C. 5, Barrio Amón* ☎ *222–3232 or 222–3426* 🖷 *221–4596* ⊕ *www. hoteldunninn.com* ☜ *24 rooms* ⚭ *Restaurant, fans, cable TV, bar, Internet, parking (fee); no a/c* ▤ *V* ❙◯❙ *BP.*

$ 🏨 **Hotel Inca Real.** The Ecuadorian owners have constructed a modern Spanish colonial–style hotel that evokes South, rather than Central, America. Rooms congregate around a bright, skylight-covered, plant-filled central patio with wrought-iron gates around the second- and third-floor passageways. All rooms are ample in size. Those on the first floor are tiled; those on the second and third floors are carpeted. Some rooms have three beds, and all have back-friendly orthopedic mattresses. ⊠ *Avda. 11, between Cs. 3 and 5, Barrio Amón* ☎ *223–8883 or 223–8991* 🖷 *221–1356* ⊕ *www.hotelincareal.com* ☜ *33 rooms* ⚭ *Fans, in-room safes, cable TV, bar, laundry service, Internet, car rental, free parking; no a/c* ▤ *V* ❙◯❙ *CP.*

$ 🏨 **Hotel Kekoldi.** You'd think you were in Miami Beach with all the pastels, but the art-deco, pink-and-white Kekoldi sits right in the heart of Barrio Amón. The secluded interior garden with umbrella-covered tables is a pleasant respite from the hustle and bustle of the city. The enormous, so-called "master queen" room overlooks that garden. The drapes, spreads, and pillows in all rooms echo the bright tropical prints throughout the hotel. Rooms contain in-room safes with a rental cost of $3 per night. Parking here is a scant two spaces, making this place a better option if you don't have a vehicle. ⊠ *Avda. 9, between Cs. 5 and 7, Barrio Amón* ☎ *248–0804* 🖷 *248–0767* ⊕ *www.kekoldi.com* ☜ *10 rooms* ⚭ *Fans, in-room safes, cable TV, laundry service, free parking; no a/c* ▤ *AE, MC, V* ❙◯❙ *BP.*

$ 🏨 **Hotel Rincón de San José.** Never mind that the interior looks more European than Latin American. (It was once called the Hotel Edelweiss, and everyone still refers to it by its old name.) This elegant little inn has comfortable rooms in a charming area near the Parque España. Rooms have carved doors, custom-made furniture, and small bathrooms. Most have hardwood window frames and floors; several have bathtubs. Complimentary breakfast is served in the garden courtyard, which doubles as a bar. ⊠ *Avda. 9 and C. 15, Barrio Otoya* ☎ *221–9702* ⊟ *222–1241* ⊕ *www.hotelrincondesanjose.com* ⇨ *27 rooms* ⌂ *Fans, in-room safes, bar, Internet, parking (fee); no a/c, no TV in some rooms.* ⊟ *AE, MC, V* ⁑ *CP.*

★ ¢–$   🖻 **Cinco Hormigas Rojas.** The name of this whimsical little lodge translates as "five red ants." Behind the wall of vines that obscures it from the street is a wild garden—it's an unexpected urban bird-watching venue—leading to an interior space filled with original artwork. The largest, newest room (the Hoja Dansante, or Dancing Leaf) overlooks the minijungle that is the front entrance. Color abounds, from the bright hues on the walls right down to the toilet seats. Sure enough, the resident owner is an artist—Mayra Güell turned the 80-year-old house she inherited from her grandmother into San José's most original B&B–cum–art gallery. She tosses in thoughtful touches such as a healthful boxed breakfast if you're heading out on an early-morning excursion, and coffee and tea 24/7. If you cherish the sameness and predictability of a chain hotel, look elsewhere, but if there's an artistic bent to your personality, this is your place. ⊠ *C. 15, between Avdas. 9 and 11, Barrio Otoya* ☎ *255–3412 or 357–8872* ⊟ *257–8581* ⊕ *www.crtimes. com/tourism/cincohormigasrojas/maincinco.htm* ⇨ *6 rooms, 1 with bath* ⌂ *Fans, laundry service, parking (fee); no a/c, no room phones, no TV in some rooms* ⊟ *AE, MC, V* ⁑ *BP.*

## West of Downtown

San José's vast west side contains only a smattering of lodgings, but you'll find one of the city's best here.

$$   🖻 **Hotel Grano de Oro.** Two wooden

Fodor'sChoice houses on San José's west side—one

★ dates from the turn of the 20th century, and the other from the 1950s—have been melded together and converted into one of the city's most charming inns, decorated throughout with old photos of the capital and paintings by local artists. Each room in the place is different, and although you can't go wrong with any of them, the older house's rooms are the nicest, especially the Garden Suite, with hardwood floors, high ceilings, and private garden. A modest restaurant, run by a French-

**WORD OF MOUTH**

"We stayed (and ate) at the Hotel Grano de Oro in San José. We had wonderful meals there. It's not big, but they have a quaint dining area, great menu, great service and an outdoor garden patio . . . Dinner for two of us with salad, wine and meal and dessert, tax/tip ran under $50 (expensive by CR standards, but not by our Boston, MA standards). And very good."

–april0404

trained chef, is surrounded by a lovely indoor patio and bromeliad-filled gardens. The hotel's sundeck has a view of both the city and the far-off volcanoes. ⊠ *C. 30, between Avdas. 2 and 4, Paseo Colón* ⌖ *1701 N. W. 97th Ave., SJO 36, Box 025216, Miami, FL 33102-5216* ☎ *255–3322* ⊟ *221–2782* ⊕ *www.hotelgranodeoro.com* ⇨ *32 rooms, 3 suites* ⌂ *Restaurant, room service, fans, in-room safes, cable TV, outdoor hot tub, laundry service, Internet, free parking; no a/c, no smoking rooms* ▭ *AE, MC, V* ⦿❘ *EP.*

## East of Downtown

The small properties beyond downtown, toward the university, offer personalized service and lots of peace and quiet. Plenty of restaurants and bars are within easy reach, and downtown San José is just a 10-minute cab ride away.

**$–$$** 🏨 **Hotel Le Bergerac.** Any other lodging of this caliber would be content to live off its reputation, and we'd never begrudge Le Bergerac if it did rest on its well-established laurels as one of San José's great hotels. But these folks are always tweaking and remodeling, and each time you return you'll likely discover something new. (What doesn't change much is the rates; they've kept pretty constant over time.) The hotel occupies two former private homes and is furnished with antiques. All rooms have custom-made wood-and-stone dressers and writing tables; deluxe rooms have two beds, private garden terraces or balconies, and large bathrooms. The location on a steep hill might disorient you; you could walk upstairs to your room, fling open the terrace doors, expecting to walk out onto a balcony, and find instead a ground-level patio and mountain view. The hotel's restaurant, L'Ile de France ( ⇨ Where to Eat), is one of the city's best, so dinner reservations are essential, even for guests. Breakfast is served on a garden patio. Le Bergerac remains the cream of a crop of small, upscale San José hotels. There are many of them, but the service, attention to detail, and ample gardens set this place apart. Hands down, this is our favorite lodging in the city. ⊠ *C. 35, between Avdas. Central and 2, first entrance to Los Yoses, San Pedro* ⬦ *Apdo. 1107–1002, San José* ☏ *234–7850 B 225–9103* ⊕ *www.bergerachotel.com* 🛏 *26 rooms* ⚑ *Restaurant, fans, in-room safes, cable TV, bar, dry cleaning, laundry service, in-room data ports, Internet, meeting room, airport shuttle, free parking; no a/c, no smoking rooms* ▭ *AE, DC, MC, V* ⦿❘ *BP.*

**$** 🏨 **Hotel Don Fadrique.** This tranquil, family-run B&B on the outskirts of San José was named after Fadrique Guttiérez, an illustrious greatuncle of the owners who constructed the Fortín in Heredia. A collection of original Costa Rican art decorates the lobby and rooms, most of which have hardwood floors, peach walls, and pastel bedspreads. Several carpeted rooms downstairs open onto lots of lush garden space. There are also an enclosed garden patio and an adjoining small art gallery where meals are served. Parking is free, but on the street, with a guard present 24/7. ⊠ *C. 37 at Avda. 8, Los Yoses, San Pedro* ⬦ *Apdo. 1754-2050, San Pedro* ☏ *225–8186 or 225–7050* 🖷 *224–9746* ⊕ *www.hoteldonfadrique.com* 🛏 *20 rooms* ⚑ *Restaurant, fans, in-room safes, cable TV, laundry service, Internet, car rental, free parking; no a/c* ▭ *AE, MC, V* ⦿❘ *BP.*

**$** 🏨 **Hotel Milvia.** Apply the principles of feng shui to an old militia arms depository, and you get a charming B&B on a San Pedro backstreet. Manager Florencia Urbina belongs to a local art consortium called Bocaracá, whose motto is "Art in Society." She takes that maxim seriously: the group's lush tropical paintings adorn the lobby, breakfast salon, small bar, and common areas. Your room will be decorated with lovely hand-painted tiles and classic Tico furniture, and you pass through a Zen meditation garden each time you enter and exit the building. The Milvia is a great value, and makes for a charming, artsy respite from the noise of the city. Julia Roberts and Susan Sarandon are a couple of celebrities who have stayed here. ⊠ *100 m east, 100 m north, and 100 m east of Centro Comercial Muñoz y Nanne, San Pedro* ⊕ *Apdo. 1660–2050, San Pedro* ☎ *225–4543 or 283–9548* ☐ *225–7801* ⊕ *www.hotelmilvia. com* ⌨ *9 rooms* ⟡ *Fans, in-room safes, cable TV, bar, library, laundry service, Internet, free parking, no-smoking rooms; no a/c* ⊟ *AE, DC, MC, V* ⊙| *BP.*

¢ ⊞ **Hostal Toruma.** The headquarters of RECAJ, Costa Rica's active Hostelling International network, is housed in a colonial-style bungalow, built around 1900, several blocks east of downtown. Backpackers from around the world hang out and exchange travel tales in the bright tiled lobby and veranda. The on-site information center offers discounted tours. Beds on the ground floor are in small compartments with doors; rooms on the second floor have standard bunks. There are also three private rooms for couples. HI cardholders receive a 20-percent discount. ⊠ *Avda. Central, between Cs. 29 and 31, Barrio La California* ⊕ *Apdo. 1355–1002, San José* ☎ *234–8186* ☐☐ *224–4085* ⊕ *www. hicr.org* ⌨ *80 beds in 17 dormitory rooms with shared baths, 3 private rooms without bath* ⟡ *Fans, Internet, free parking; no a/c, no room phones, no room TVs* ⊟ *MC, V* ⊙| *CP.*

# NIGHTLIFE & THE ARTS

## The Arts

San José might be a small capital of a small Latin American country, but events pack its cultural calendar most of the year, and ticket prices pale in comparison to what you'd pay back home. There's one downside: the selection of theater and art offerings becomes almost nonexistent during school vacations—from Christmas until early February—which coincides with prime tourist season.

The best source for theater, dance, film, and arts information is the "Viva" entertainment section of the Spanish-language daily *La Nación*. The paper also publishes the "Tiempo Libre" section each Friday, highlighting what's going on over the weekend. *San José Volando* is a free monthly magazine found in many upscale hotels and restaurants, and publishes features about what's going on around town. Listings in both publications are in Spanish, but are easy to decipher. The "Weekend" section of the English-language weekly *Tico Times* lists information about arts and culture, much of it events of interest to the expatriate community. The paper comes out each Friday.

### Art Galleries

San José's art galleries, public or private, museum or bohemian, keep daytime hours only, but all kick off a new show with an evening exhibit opening. They're free and open to the public, and offer a chance to rub elbows with Costa Rica's art community (and to sip wine and munch on appetizers). Listings appear in *La Nación*'s "Viva" section. Your time in the capital might coincide with one of these by happenstance. (They're rarely announced in the paper more than a day or two in advance.) Look for the term *inauguración* (opening).

## Theater & Music

Broadway or the West End it isn't, but San José has an active theater scene. More than a dozen theater groups (many of which perform slapstick comedies) hold forth in smaller theaters around town. If your Spanish is up to it, call for a reservation. The curtain rises at 8 PM, Friday through Sunday, with some companies staging performances on Thursday nights too.

There are frequent dance performances and concerts in the **Teatro FANAL** and **Teatro 1887**, both in the **Centro Nacional de la Cultura** (⊠ C. 13, between Avdas. 3 and 5, Barrio Otoya ☎ 257–5524). The **Eugene O'Neill Theater** (⊠ Centro Cultural Costarricense–Norteamericano, Avda. 1 and C. 37, Barrio Dent, San Pedro ☎ 207–7554) has chamber concerts and plays most weekend evenings. The cultural center is a great place to meet expatriate North Americans.

The **Teatro La Aduana** (⊠ C. 25, Avda. 3, Barrio La California ☎ 257–8305) holds frequent dance and stage performances, and is home to the Compañía Nacional de Teatro (National Theater Company). The baroque **Teatro Nacional** (⊠ Plaza de la Cultura, Barrio La Soledad ☎ 221–1329) is the home of the excellent National Symphony Orchestra, which performs on Friday evenings and Sunday mornings between April and November. The theater also hosts visiting musical groups and dance companies. Tickets are $4–$40. San José's second-most popular theater, the **Teatro Popular Melico Salazar** (⊠ Avda. 2, between Cs. Central and 2, Barrio La Merced ☎ 221–4952) has a full calendar of music and dance, as well as a few offbeat productions. Something goes on nearly every night of the week; tickets are $2–$20. Café Bohemia, off the lobby, is a quiet place to stop for a pre- or post-performance drink.

# Nightlife

Nightlife abounds in various neighborhoods around the city. A few gems really do populate the downtown area, but several bars there double as prostitute pickup joints or are just boozy places where patrons go to pick fights. (If you're in the center city at night, stick to a drink in your hotel or to the places we recommend, and don't wander directly south or west of Parque Central on foot.)

Barrios Amón and Otoya have little in the way of nightlife outside the occasional hotel bar—and most of the hotels there are too small and intimate to have a bar. But those that do offer quiet places to while away the evening.

Bars and discos congregate in the Centro Comercial El Pueblo, an entertainment and shopping complex north of downtown. Several bars there have live music on weekends; it's best to wander around and see what sounds good, but most of the dance places attract a decidedly under-25 clientele. Few people actually know the names of any individual businesses in El Pueblo; they simply refer to any and all of them as "El Pueblo."

The young and the restless hang out in the student-oriented places around the University of Costa Rica in the eastern suburb of San Pedro. The Calle de la Amargura (Street of Bitterness), named for the route Jesus took to the crucifixion, is much more secular than its name suggests and rocks loudly each night. But don't write off every place around the university as rowdy. A few are actually quiet bars and cafés where you can carry on a real conversation.

Barrios La California and Escalante, an area anchored by the Santa Teresita church, amorphously connect central San José with San Pedro, and house some of the city's trendiest nightspots.

## Bars

No one could accuse San José of having too few watering holes, but outside hotels there aren't many places to have a quiet drink, especially downtown—Tico bars tend to be on the lively side.

There's nothing wrong with your eyes; it's the low pinkish lighting when you walk into the ultratrendy **Bajarse al Moro** (⊠ 650 m east of church of Santa Teresita, Barrio Escalante ☎ 234–9814). The African drumbeats are a bit louder than you might need. It's much quieter in the back. Intensely and proudly bohemian **Café Expresivo** (⊠ 350 m east of church of Santa Teresita, Barrio Escalante ☎ 224–1202) hosts poetry readings and acoustic guitar concerts and serves light pastas and sandwiches. You'd think you were in a department store from the blinding fluorescent lighting inside 24-hour **Chelles** (⊠ Avda. Central and C. 9, Barrio La Soledad ☎ 221–1369), a downtown bar that serves monster sandwiches.

**El Cuartel de la Boca del Monte** (⊠ Avda. 1, between Cs. 21 and 23, Barrio La California ☎ 221–0327) is a large bar where young artists and professionals gather to sip cocktails and share plates of tasty bocas (snacks). It has live music Monday night, the busiest evening of the week, but becomes oddly subdued on weekends. **El Observatorio** (⊠ C. 23, across from Cine Magaly Barrio La California ☎ 223–0725) strikes an unusual balance between casual and formal: it's the kind of place where an over-30 crowd goes to watch a soccer game on TV, but wears a tie or dress to do so. The cap-

### DANCE FEVER

Step into a San José nightclub and you might think Costa Ricans are born dancing. They aren't, but most learn to merengue, rumba (bolero here), mambo, cha-cha, and swing as children. Play catch-up at dance school Merecumbe (☎ 224–3531), which has ten branches around the city. With a few days' notice you can arrange a private lesson with an English-speaking instructor and get the basics of merengue and bolero. Other steps are projects for longer stays—or for continuing back home.

★ ital's best live-music venue, hands-down, is the New York–style **Jazz Café** (⊠ Avda. Central next to Banco Popular, San Pedro ☎ 253–8933), which draws big crowds, especially for live jazz on Tuesday and Wednesday nights.

Costa Rica's only microbrewery, **K & S Brewery** (⊠ Centro Comercial Cristal, 600 m south of Pop's ice-cream shop, Curridabat ☎ 283–7583) serves its own pilsners and lagers—they're a refreshing change from the ubiquitous Imperial brand drunk by the masses—in an "oom-pah-pah" German-style bar and restaurant.

Regulars hold court on weekends at **Karaoke 88** (⊠ 300 m north of church of San Pedro, San Pedro ☎ 225–0601), part bar, part student cafeteria. Weeknights you'll likely have the place to yourself and will feel less self-conscious about belting out your rendition of "You Light Up My Life."

A refreshing change from the ultrayoung, ultrahip El Pueblo venues, **Los Balcones** (⊠ Centro Comercial El Pueblo, Avda. 0, Barrio Tournón ☎ 256–9494) specializes in *nueva trova* music, a folk genre that grew out of Latin American protest movements. (Think Joan Baez transported to the 21st century and singing in Spanish.) Trendy **Luna Roja** (⊠ C. 3, between Avdas. 9 and 11, Barrio Amón ☎ 222–5944) doubles as restaurant and dance floor with occasional live music. The quiet upstairs café draws diners of all ages. The early-to-mid-20s crowd downstairs gets much louder. An older expat crowd hangs out at **Mac's Bar** (⊠ South side of La Sabana Park, next to the Tennis Club, Sabana Sur ☎ 234–3145), which gets our nod for serving the city's best burgers and usually has a sporting event playing on the television.

The dressy **Meridiano al Este** (⊠ Across from La Primavera gas station, Avda. Central and C. 21, Barrio La California ☎ 221–0650) is a mixed bag with everything from rock to nueva trova. Call first to see if the evening matches your tastes.

Fill up on Spanish-style tapas at Mediterranean bar and restaurant **Pub Olio** (⊠ 200 m north of Bagelmen's, Barrio Escalante ☎ 281–0541). It draws a mix of professionals and older college students. San José's large Argentine community packs the smoky **Rincón del Tango Che Molinari** (⊠ Centro Comercial El Pueblo, Barrio Tournón) after 9 PM Friday and Saturday nights to belt out their favorite tangos to the accompaniment of the mournful accordionlike *bandoleón*. Videos from the '60s, 70's, and '80s provide the backdrop at **Vyrus** (⊠ 100 m west of Spoon, San Pedro ☎ 280–5890). Inside is dark, couply, and kissy; the outdoor balcony is much more conducive to singing along with that Duran Duran song you haven't heard in ages.

## Cafés and Restaurants

In a country so economically dependent on coffee, and one that takes its afternoon coffee breaks at home or work religiously, the European-style café concept is only beginning to catch on. Many restaurants do double café-and-bar duty in the evening, and are quiet places to linger over dinner or a drink.

Classy, hip, trendy **Bakea** (⊠ C. 7 and Avda. 11, Barrio Amón ☎ 248–0303) is one of the few upscale and very late night places to grab a bite. **Café 1930** (⊠ Avda. 2 and C. 3, Barrio La Soledad ☎ 221–4011), under the arcades at the entrance to the Gran Hotel Costa Rica, pulls 24-hour duty as a pleasant place for a drink or coffee in the evening.

The highly recommended restaurant **Café Mundo** (✉ C. 15 and Avda. 9, Barrio Otoya ☎ 222–6190) is also quiet spot for a drink frequented by gay and bohemian crowds. Partake of 26 varieties of crepes, with or without rum, with or without Grand Marnier, on the front patio of **Co-corrico Verde** (✉ 75 m south of former Banco Popular, San Pedro). It's a stone's throw, but a world away, from the commotion of the campus nightlife. **Denny's** (✉ Autopista General Cañas, La Uruca ☎ 231–3500) holds court here, for those late-night, predawn, after-bar munchies.

Near the university, **Fezcafé** (✉ C. de la Amargura, San Pedro ☎ 280–6982) is a quiet alternative to the noisy bars nearby, at least until 8 PM on weeknights. Restaurant **Kafé Ko** (✉ C. 21, 25 m south of La Primavera gas station, Barrio La California) morphs into central San José's only true late-night coffee spot. It's a quiet place for conversation, with soft, jazzy music playing. Walk by **Manolo's** (✉ Avda. Central between Cs. Central and 2, Barrio La Merced ☎ 280–6982) any hour of the night and a lively crowd is sure to be conversing over coffee and *churros con chocolate* (fried dough covered with chocolate sauce). Smack-dab in the center of the campus nightlife, **Omar Khayyam** (✉ C. de la Amargura, San Pedro ☎ 253–8455) is a blissfully quiet refuge from the noise of the nearby bars. Share a jug of wine and falafel or hummus with fried yuca on the covered patio. **Saudade** (✉ C. 17, between Avdas. 2 and 6, Barrio La Soledad ☎ 233-2134) holds poetry readings many Wednesday evenings, and has live music on Fridays, all to the accompaniment of desserts and quiches.

## Casinos

Ask about casino rules before you dive in and play: there are a few Costa Rican variations—for example, you don't get a bonus for blackjack, but you do for three of a kind or straights under local rules—and yet some places proudly boast that they play exactly like they do in Las Vegas. Costa Rica has become the world's preeminent offshore-betting mecca, with many casinos operating desks where you can place a wager on sporting events back home.

The term "casino" gets tossed around loosely in Costa Rica: a hotel can put a couple of video poker machines in its lobby and claim it operates a casino. The casino at the Hotel del Rey in Barrio El Carmen—arguably the city's most famous and definitely its most notorious gambling establishment—swarms with prostitutes. Avoid it.

Most of the city's larger hotels have legitimate casinos, including the Clarion Amón Plaza, the Aurola Holiday Inn (the view from the casino is breathtaking), and the Gran Hotel Costa Rica.

The 24-hour **Casino Colonial** (✉ Avda. 1, between Cs. 9 and 11, Barrio El Carmen ☎ 258–2807) has a complete casino, bar, restaurant, and cable TV, and a betting service for major U.S. sporting events. **Jungle Casino** (✉ Balmoral Hotel, Avda. Central, between Cs. 7 and 9, Barrio La Soledad ☎ 222–5022) is a casino, bar, and restaurant in one.

## Dance Clubs

San José's discos attract a very young crowd. Quite frankly, you'll feel ancient if you've passed 30. Live-music halls draw dancers of all ages, but most of these populate rougher neighborhoods on the city's south side and are best avoided.

**Ebony 56** (⊠ Centro Comercial El Pueblo, Avda. 0, Barrio Tournón ☎ 223–2195) does triple duty as disco, sports bar, and café and draws an under-25 crowd. **Friends** (⊠ Centro Comercial El Pueblo, Avda. 0, Barrio Tournón ☎ 233–5283) plays mostly pop and Latin music, draws a still young clientele, but slightly older than that of Ebony 56 next door. For an international scene, head to **Planet Mall** (⊠ Mall San Pedro, C. 42 and Avda. 2 ☎ 280–4693) on the top floor of the massive San Pedro Mall, which bills itself as the largest disco in Central America. Dress to impress; this is one of the city's most expensive dance bars.

For a dance-hall experience in a good neighborhood, we recommend the enormous **El Tobogán** (⊠ 200 m north and 100 m east of La República, Barrio Tournón ☎ 223–8920), an alternative to the postage stamp–size floors of most discos. Live Latin bands get everyone on their feet Friday and Saturday nights.

### Gay & Lesbian

San José has a few bars, restaurants, and dance places patronized primarily by a gay and lesbian clientele, although all are welcome. Another tier of businesses, exemplified by the venerable Café Mundo, draws a mixed gay-straight crowd. The gay-and-lesbian resource center **1@10 Café Internet** (⊠ C. 3 and Avda. 7, Barrio Amón ☎ 258-4561 ⊕ www.1en10.com) can provide you with information on gay and lesbian San José. Many more establishments dot the city than the tried-and-true places we mention below. A couple we visited preferred not to be listed in a guidebook. Others cater to tastes not quite so conventional. The popularity of still others waxes and wanes with changing fashions. The good folks at 1@10 can clue you in on what's hot and what's not.

**Al Despiste** (⊠ Across from Mudanzas Mundiales, Zapote ☎ 283–7164) is a gay bar that serves light bocas. A gay and lesbian crowd frequents **La Avispa** (⊠ C. 1, between Avdas. 8 and 10, Barrio La Soledad ☎ 223–5343), which has two dance floors with videos and karaoke, and a quieter upstairs bar with pool tables. The last Wednesday of each month is ladies' night.

**El Bochinche** (⊠ C. 11, between Avdas. 10 and 12, Barrio La Soledad ☎ 221–0500) is a gay bar that doubles as a Mexican restaurant. **Déjà Vu** (⊠ C. 2, between Avdas. 14 and 16A, Barrio El Pacífico ☎ 223–3758) is a mostly gay, techno-heavy disco with two dance floors and weekly drag shows. Take a taxi to and from here; the neighborhood's sketchy. Restaurant and bar **.G** (⊠ 50 m southeast of the higuerón [fig tree], San Pedro ☎ 280-3726) draws a primarily gay and lesbian clientele. Pronounce the name *pun-to hay.*

# SHOPPING

Although it might seem more "authentic" to buy your souvenirs at their out-country source, you can find everything in the city, a real bonus if you're pressed for time. Shops such as San José's venerable Galería Namu have assembled an amazing collection of folkloric and indigenous art from around Costa Rica. And there is indeed native San José–area art. Kaltak Artesanías in the suburb of Moravia deals in Pefi and Osenbach ceramics, trademark products of two well-known artisans in the capital.

If the capital has any real tourist shopping district, it's found loosely in the cluster of streets around Parque Morazán, just north of downtown, an area bounded roughly by Avenidas 1 and 7 and Calles 5 and 9. Stroll and search, because many other businesses congregate in the area as well. The northeastern suburb of Moravia contains a cluster of high-quality crafts and artisan shops in the three blocks heading north from the Colegio María Inmaculada. The street is two blocks behind the city's church.

> ## TALKING SHOP
>
> Shopping in Costa Rica will seem blissfully low-key, especially if you've earned your stripes in places with high-pressure sales pestering, such as Mexico and Jamaica. Vendors will ask *"¿En qué puedo servirle?"* ("How can I help you?") as you walk by their stands, but if you're just looking, a simple *"No gracias"* ("No, thank you") reply suffices to be left alone. Prices are fixed, but fair. There's no haggling here.

## Shopping Malls

Old-timers lament the malling over of San José, but several huge enclosed shopping centers anchor the metro area, complemented by dozens of smaller malls. Expect all the comforts of home—food courts and movie theaters included. **Mall San Pedro** (⊠ Rotonda de la Hispanidad, San Pedro ☎ 283–7540) sits in its namesake suburb, a short 10-minute taxi ride from downtown San José. **Multiplaza del Este** (⊠ Across from Registro Nacional, Curridabat ☎ 289–9300) lies east of San José, and is the counterpart to the west-side Multiplaza between Escazú and Santa Ana. The west-side **Plaza Rohrmoser** (⊠ 200 m east of U.S. Embassy, Pavas ☎ 258–9122) dispenses with food courts and movie theaters, and focuses instead on upscale shopping of the Liz Claiborne type. The mammoth **Terramall** (⊠ Autopista Florencio del Castillo, Tres Ríos ☎ 278–6970) is the far eastern suburbs' prime shopping destination.

## Specialty Stores

### Books & Maps

With several locations around the metro area, **Casa de las Revistas.** (⊠ C. 5, between Avdas. 3 and 5, Barrio El Carmen ☎ 256–5092 ⊠ Plaza del Sol, Curridabat ☎ 283–0822 ⊠ Plaza Mayor, Blvd. de Rohrmoser, Rohrmoser ☎ 296–7943) has San José's best selection of magazines in English. At **Lehmann** (⊠ Avda. Central, between Cs. 1 and 3, Barrio El Carmen ☎ 223–1212) you'll find some books in English on the first floor although the Spanish-language selection is more extensive. The store also stocks large-scale topographical maps.

**Librería Internacional** (✉ 300 m west of Taco Bell, Barrio Dent ☎ 253–9553) is San José's largest bookstore and the closest it has to a Borders or Barnes and Noble. It stocks English translations of Latin American literature and myriad coffee-table books on Costa Rica. **Mora Books** (✉ Avda. 1, between Cs. 3 and 5 ☎ 255–4136) is the place to grab a used paperback or two before heading out to the beach. If it's been in print, it's probably passed through the four walls here. And if you need tunes for your portable CD player on that long trip, you'll find second-hand discs here too. **Papyrus** (✉ C. 42 and Avda. 5, Sabana Norte, next to the Más x Menos ☎ 221–4664) has a wonderful selection of magazines in English. The affable owners of **7th Street Books** (✉ C. 7, between Avdas. Central and 1, Barrio La Soledad ☎ 256–8251) make this store *the* place to stop in and see what's going on in the expat community. It has the city's best selection of books in English and is also strong on Latin America and tropical ecology. You can pick up *The Tico Times* here.

## Crafts

The arts-and-crafts tradition in Costa Rica is not as strong as in, say, Guatemala or Peru, and at first glance you might be disenchanted with what you see in the run-of-the-mill souvenir shops around town. Keep your disappointment in check until you visit two of San José's outstanding purveyors of fine artisan work.

**Fodor's**Choice    Downtown San José's must-stop shop is **Galería Namu** (✉ Avda. 7, be-
★    tween Cs. 5 and 7, behind Aurola Holiday Inn, Barrio Amón ☎ 256–3412), which sells Costa Rican folkloric art and the best indigenous crafts in town. Its inventory brims with colorful creations by the Guaymí, Boruca, Bribri, Chorotega, Huetar, and Maleku peoples—all Costa Rican indigenous groups. You can also find exquisitely carved ivory-nut "Tagua" figurines made by Wounan Indians from Panama's Darién region. Take note of carved balsa masks, woven cotton blankets, and hand-painted ceramics. The store looks expensive when you first walk in—and indeed, the sky is the limit in prices—but if your budget is not so flush, say so: the good folks here can help you find something in the $10–$20 range that will make a more cherished souvenir of your trip than a *Pura Vida* T-shirt. And as an added bonus you'll get an information sheet describing your work's creator and art style. Namu has a reputation for fair prices for customers, and for fair pay to artists or artisans.

★    The staff and selection at **Kaltak Artesanías** (✉ 50 m north of Colegio María Inmaculada, Moravia ☎ 297–2736) make it a real standout from all the Moravia shops. Walk in with some unformulated "I'm not sure what I want" notions, and the folks here will help you find that perfect souvenir or gift from among the selection of ceramics (Pefi and Osenbach designs are well represented), wood-and-leather rocking chairs, oxcarts of all sizes, orchids, and carvings from native *cocobolo* and *guápinol* woods and ash wood.

## Food & Beverages

Costa Rica's foremost product is its foremost souvenir: Café Rey, Café Volio, and the ubiquitous Café Britt are superior brands of arabica **coffee,** and you'll find their foil-wrapped export-quality packages in supermarkets—which have the best prices—or souvenir shops. Their labels read *grano entero* (whole bean) or *molido* (ground); and *tostado claro* (light roast) or *tostado oscuro* (dark roast). The good ground stuff will also say *puro* (pure), and will not be mixed with sugar the way that Costa Ricans drink it. Britt is the only one that offers you the more sedate *descafeinado* (decaffeinated) option. And while you're at it, pick up a *chorreador,* too. Most souvenir stores sell the small stands with a cloth through which you can brew coffee the time-honored Tico way. (It's more tedious than Mr. Coffee, but is guaranteed to generate more conversation among your guests back home.)

Costa Rica's best **rum** is the aged Centenario—pick up a bottle for about $10. In addition to *añejo* (aged), it also comes *blanco* (white), and *conmemorativo* (commemorative), a premium aged, limited-production edition. There are several brands of **coffee liqueurs** (*licor de café*), including Café Rica and Golden Cream, but Britt makes the best one (although the Don Braulio–brand hand-painted bottles add visual pizzazz to your home bar). Buy these at any of San José's abundant supermarkets and liquor stores. FANAL, the government distillery, bottles Cacique-brand **guaro**, a 60-proof sugarcane liquor. "Firewater" might be a better description for it; try it only if you dare.

Any self-respecting Tico home or restaurant keeps a bottle of **Salsa Lizano,** one of the country's signature food products, on hand. Its tang brightens up meat, vegetable, and rice dishes, and a bottle fits nicely into your carry-on.

**Más x Menos** (⊠ Avda. Central, between Cs. 11 and 13 ☎ 233–7811 ⊠ C. 42 and Avda. 5 Sabana Norte ☎ 248–2096 ⊠ 50 m west of higuerón (fig tree), San Pedro ☎ 225–0636), Costa Rica's largest supermarket chain, beats souvenir stores' prices for coffee, food, liquor, and other beverages. (That *x* in the name is pronounced "*por,* " by the way.)

## Music

San José's music stores stock the Latin sounds of every artist from Chayanne to Shakira, but Costa Ricans take special pride in their home-town Latin-fusion group, the Grammy award–winning Editus.

Tunes waft outside from branches of **Music Box** (⊠ Avda. Central and C. 5, Barrio La Soledad ☎ 258–1359 ⊠ Avda. Central and C. 2., Barrio La Merced ☎ 256–4922), a small chain. The staff is always happy to offer recommendations. In addition to selling everything else imaginable, downtown department store **Universal** (⊠ Avda. Central, between Cs. Central and 1, Barrio El Carmen ☎ 222–2222) stocks a good selection of Latin CDs in its first-floor music department.

## Souvenirs

Hotel gift shop **Boutique Annemarie** (⊠ Hotel Don Carlos, C. 9 and Avda. 9, Barrio Amón ☎ 221–6063) has a huge selection of popular souvenirs and CDs of Costa Rican musicians. Café Britt operates souvenir shops **Casa Tica** and **El Cafetal** in the **Aeropuerto Internacional Juan Santamaría** (⊠ 16 km [10 mi] northwest of downtown San José, just outside Alajuela) for those last-minute purchases. Choose from Britt coffee ($5 per pound)—the only brand sold here—and a terrific selection of good-quality merchandise, such as hand-carved bowls and jewelry, aromatherapy candles, banana-paper stationery, and Costa Rica travel books. There's nary another store in the country carrying such a variety all in one place. The catch is that the shop charges U.S. prices for this luxury.

Some 100 souvenir vendors congregate in the block-long covered walkway known as the **Calle Nacional de Artesanía y Pintura.** (⊠ C. 13, between Avdas Central and 2, western side of Plaza de la Democracia), and offer some real bargains in hammocks, wood carvings, and clothing.

Dozens of souvenir vendors set up shop on the two floors of **La Casona** (⊠ C. 2, between Avdas. Central and 1, Barrio El Carmen ☎ 222–7999), in a rickety old downtown mansion. It's much like a flea market, and it's a fun place to browse. **La Ranita Dorada** (⊠ Avda. 1, between Cs. 9 and 11, Barrio El Carmen ☎ 256–6808) sells pretty standard souvenir fare—although it has quite a large selection of wood products—but the friendly staff, who happily take the time to give personalized service, make this place worth a stop.

**Mercado Central** (⊠ Bordered by Avdas. Central and 1 and Cs. 6 and 8, Barrio La Merced), an 1880 precursor to the modern shopping mall, doesn't bill itself for souvenir shopping—the maze of passageways is where the average Costa Rican comes to stock up on day-to-day necessities—but a few stalls of interest to tourists congregate near the entrances. If you can't find it at **Mundo de Recuerdos** (⊠ Across from Colegio María Inmaculada, Moravia ☎ 240–8990), it probably doesn't exist. Here's the largest of the Moravia shops with simply everything—at least of standard souvenir fare—you could ask for under one roof. The tour buses always find their way to **Plaza Esmeralda** (⊠ 800 m west of Jacks, Pavas ☎ 506/296–0312 or 506/232–7949 ⊕ www.plaza-esmeralda.com), and the place hums with all the activity of a port when a cruise ship is docked. There are lots of souvenirs to be found; we like the place because the quality is high and you can watch your souvenir being created in front of you. Jewelry is a mainstay here, and there's even a replica of an emerald mine.

# SAN JOSÉ ESSENTIALS

## Transportation

### BY AIR

ARRIVING & DEPARTING  Two airports serve San José. Aeropuerto Internacional Juan Santamaría is the destination for all international flights as well as those of domestic airline SANSA in a terminal a couple of blocks away. Domestic NatureAir flights depart from Aeropuerto Internacional Tobías Bolaños. Arrival and departure at the tiny Tobías Bolaños Airport is very informal. For in-depth information about arriving at Juan Santamaría airport, getting to and from the airport, and airlines *see* Air Travel *in* Smart Travel Tips A to Z.

🛪 Airports **Aeropuerto Internacional Juan Santamaría (SJO)** ⊠ 16 km [10 mi] northwest of downtown San José, just outside Alajuela ☎ 437–2400. **Aeropuerto Internacional Tobías Bolaños (SYQ)** ⊠ 3 km [2 mi] west of the city center, Pavas ☎ 232–2820.

## BY BUS

ARRIVING &
DEPARTING San José has no central bus terminal, and buses to many destinations depart from street corners. The four largest bus stations—the Gran Terminal del Caribe, the Terminal Atlántico Norte, the Terminal de Puntarenas, and the Terminal Coca-Cola—are all in dicey neighborhoods. Always take a taxi to and from the bus station, and at the Coca-Cola never take your eyes off your belongings. Call your individual bus line for information about schedules rather than the terminal itself. Consider the comfort of a shuttle-van service in an air-conditioned minivan for travel out of the capital. For bus and shuttle-van information and departure points from San José to other areas of the country, *see* Bus Travel *in* Smart Travel Tips A to Z.

🚌 Bus Terminals **Gran Terminal del Caribe** ⊠ C. Central and Avda. 13, Barrio Tournón. **Terminal Coca-Cola** ⊠ C. 16, between Avdas. 1 and 3, Barrio México. **Terminal Atlántico Norte** ⊠ C. 12 and Avda. 9, Barrio México. **Terminal de Puntarenas** ⊠ C. 16, between Avdas. 10 and 12, Barrio Cuba.

GETTING
AROUND City bus service is absurdly cheap (30¢–50¢) and easy to use. For Paseo Colón and La Sabana, take buses marked SABANA–CEMENTERIO from stops at Avenida 2 between Calles 5 and 7, or on Avenida 3 next to the *correos* (post office). For the suburbs of Los Yoses and San Pedro near the university, take one marked SAN PEDRO from Avenida Central, between Calles 9 and 11.

## BY CAR

ARRIVING &
DEPARTING San José is the hub of the national road system. Paved roads fan out from Paseo Colón west to Escazú and northwest to the airport and Heredia. For the Pacific coast, Guanacaste, and Nicaragua, take the Carretera Interamericana (Pan-American Highway) north (CA1), which continues beyond the airport. Calle 3 runs north into the highway to Guápiles, Limón, and the Atlantic coast through Braulio Carrillo National Park, with a turnoff to the Sarapiquí region. If you follow Avenida Central or 2 east through San Pedro, you'll enter the Pan-American Highway south (CA2), which has a turnoff for Cartago, Volcán Irazú, and Turrialba before it heads southeast over the mountains toward Panama. For car-rental information, *see* Car Rental *in* Smart Travel Tips A to Z.

GETTING
AROUND Almost every street in downtown San José is one-way. Try to avoid driving at peak hours (7–9 AM and 5–6:30 PM), as traffic gets horribly congested. Parking lots, scattered throughout the city, charge around $1 an hour. Outside the city center you can park on the street, where *guachimen* ("watchmen" or car guards) usually offer to watch your car for a 500-colón tip, more if you're going to be away from the car for a few hours. Even so, never leave shopping bags or valuables inside your parked car. For car-rental information, *see* Car Rental *in* Smart Travel Tips A to Z.

## BY TAXI

GETTING
AROUND Taxis are a good deal within the city. You can hail one on the street (all licensed taxis are red with a gold triangle on the front doors) or have your hotel or restaurant call one for you, as cabbies tend to speak only Spanish and addresses are complicated. (A good way to avoid get-

ting lost is to have someone write down the address to show to the driver.) A 3-km (2-mi) ride costs around $2, and tipping is not the custom. Taxis parked in front of expensive hotels charge about twice the normal rate. By law, all cabbies must use their meters—called *marías*—when operating within the metropolitan area; if one refuses, negotiate a price before setting off, or hail another. ■ TIP➔➔ The surest way to antagonize a driver is to slam the door; be gentle. Cab companies include Alfaro, San Jorge, Coopetaxi, and, if you need to go to the airport, the orange Taxis Unidos. Many unofficial taxis (*piratas*) ply the streets as well. They might be red cars with a margarine container on the dashboard painted to resemble a taxi sign. Some locals use them, but they have no meters, are illegal and often unsafe, and carry no insurance in the event of an accident.

🚖 Taxi Companies **Alfaro** ☎221-8466. **Coopetaxi** ☎235-9966. **San Jorge** ☎221-3434. **Taxis Unidos** ☎ 221-6865.

## Contacts & Resources

### BANKS & EXCHANGING SERVICES
Get all the cash you need before you head out of San José. Outside the capital there are fewer banks and ATMs, making it more difficult to change money (although the situation is improving). It is virtually impossible to change currency other than U.S. dollars or traveler's checks outside of San José. It's even difficult to change non-U.S. dollars *in* San José. Lines at the state banks—Banco Nacional, Banco de Costa Rica (BCR), Bancrédito (BCAC), and Banco Popular—move very slowly, but you can change dollars and cash traveler's checks. The private Scotiabank and BAC San José (formerly Banco San José) perform the same services with more palatable lines, but they have many fewer outlets. You can get local currency using your MasterCard or Visa at the Juan Santamaría Airport: there are machines in the check-in area, near Gate 4 of the boarding area, and near the baggage-claim carousels. The ATH (A Toda Hora) and Red Total networks accept Plus- and Cirrus-affiliated cards. A few—very few—Red Total machines give cash against American Express and Diners Club cards as well. Ask at your hotel for the location of the nearest bank or *cajero automático* (ATM), and specify whether you need a MasterCard- or Visa-friendly machine.

🏦 Banks **BAC San José** ✉ Avda. 2, between Cs. Central and 1, Barrio El Carmen ☎ 295-9797. **Banco de Costa Rica** ✉ Avda. Central between Cs. 4 and 6 ☎ 287-9008. **Banco Nacional** ✉ Avda. 1, between Cs. 2 and 4, Barrio La Merced ☎ 212-2000. **Bancrédito** ✉ Avda. 4, between Cs. Central and 2 ☎ 212-7000. **Scotiabank** ✉ Avda. 1, between Cs. Central and 2, Barrio La Merced ☎ 287-8700.

### EMERGENCIES
🏥 Hospitals **Clínica Bíblica** ✉ Avda. 14, between Cs. Central and 1, Barrio El Pacífico ☎ 522-1000. **Clínica Católica** ✉ Attached to San Antonio Church on C. Esquivel Bonilla, Guadalupe ☎ 246-3000.

💊 Late-Night Pharmacies **Fischel Pharmacy** ✉ Clínica Católica, attached to San Antonio Church on C. Esquivel Bonilla, Guadalupe ☎ 283-6616 ✉ Across from Banco Popular, San Pedro ☎ 295-7694.

**INTERNET**

There are Internet cafés on almost every block in downtown San José. Many of those just south of the Universidad de Costa Rica in San Pedro are open 24 hours. Competition keeps prices at $1 or less per hour.

🖪 Internet Cafés **1@10 Café Internet** ⊠. 3 and Avda. 7, Barrio Amón ☎ 258-4561. **Café Digital** ⊠ Avda. Central, between Cs. 5 and 7, Barrio La Soledad ☎ 223-8051 ⊠ C. 7, between Avdas. Central and 1, Barrio La Soledad ☎ 248-2033. **Cafe Internet** ⊠ Paseo Colón, between Cs. 36 and 38, Paseo Colón ☎ 256-6842. **Café Net California** ⊠ Avda. 1, between Cs. 19 and 21, Barrio La California ☎ 258-2324. **Cafenet** ⊠ C. 19 at Avda. 10, Barrio La Soledad ☎ 255-1910. **CepiaNet** ⊠ Avda. Central and C. 5, Barrio La Soledad ☎ 258-5050. **CyberCafé Las Arcadas** ⊠ Avda. 2, between Cs. 1 and 3, ground floor of Las Arcadas building, Barrio La Soledad ☎ 233-3310. **Estudio Net Café** ⊠ C. de la Armargura, San Pedro ☎ No phone. **Internet Café Costa Rica** ⊠ 50 m west of Banco Popular, San Pedro ☎ 283-5375 ⊠ Avda. Central, between Cs. 7 and 9, Barrio La Soledad ☎ 255-1154 ⊠ Avda. Central and C. 4, Barrio La Merced ☎ No phone ⊠ Paseo Colón, between Cs. 38 and 40, Paseo Colón ☎ No phone. **RACSA** ⊠ C. 1 at Avda. 5, Barrio La Merced ☎ 287-0087. **SuperNet** ⊠ C. de la Armargura, San Pedro ☎ 234-8200.

**MAIL & SHIPPING**

The Correos de Costa Rica (Post Office of Costa Rica) is notorious for losing letters, but if you must use it, head to the Central Postal Office in Barrio La Merced, open weekdays 7:30–6 and Saturday 7:30–noon. Routine mail, such as postcards to the folks back home, should make it, and takes about two weeks to reach the U.S. and Canada, three weeks to Europe. You can also mail letters from large hotels. For important packages, rely on DHL, FedEx, or UPS. (DHL is the shipping service favored by locals.)

🖪 Post Office **Correos de Costa Rica (main branch)** ⊠ C. 2, between Avdas. 1 and 3, Barrio La Merced.

🖪 Shipping Services **DHL** ⊠ C. 34, between Paseo Colón and Avda. 2, Paseo Colón ☎ 210-3838. **FedEx** ⊠ Paseo Colón, between Cs. 40 and 42, Paseo Colón ☎ 800/052-1090 in Costa Rica. **UPS** ⊠ East of Pizza Hut offices, Zona Industrial, Pavas ☎ 290-2828.

# The Central Valley

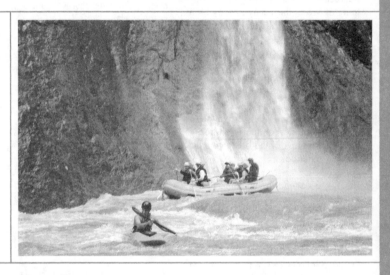

Pacuare River

**WORD OF MOUTH**

"In Cartago we visited . . . the most awesome church: the Basilica de Nuestra Senora de los Angeles—a must-see. Lankaster Gardens was a very pleasant stop. The orchids are obviously beautiful, but so are all of their gardens. (Bug spray is a good idea.) Then onto the Orosi Valley—oh my gosh! What a spectacular view! Coming down the mountain, you get glimpses of the valley, just beautiful."

—dfarmer

www.fodors.com/forums

# WELCOME TO THE CENTRAL VALLEY

View from Irazú Volcano

## TOP 5
## Reasons to Go

**1 Coffee:** Get up close and personal with harvesting and processing on coffee tours at two of the valley's many plantations: Café Britt and Doka Estate.

**2 The Orosi Valley:** Spectacular views and quiet, bucolic towns make this area a great day trip or overnight from San José.

**3 Rafting the Pacuare River:** Brave the rapids as you descend through tropical forest on one of the best rivers in Central America.

**4 The views:** Ascend the volcanic slopes that border the valley, meeting superb views almost anywhere you go.

**5 Avian adventures:** Flock to Tapantí National Park to see emerald toucanets, resplendent quetzals, and nearly every species of Costa Rican hummingbird. Rancho Naturalista is the bird-lovers' hotel of choice.

The areas North and West of San José are dominated by coffee farms and small valley towns whose beautiful hotels attract lots of tourists on their first and last nights in the country. Café Britt and Doka Estate are both here, as is the international airport, near Alajuela.

Coffee beans

Guayabo National Monument

# Getting Oriented

The Central Valley is something of a misnomer, and its Spanish name, the *meseta central* (central plateau) isn't entirely accurate either. The two contiguous mountain ranges that run the length of the country—the Cordillera Central range (which includes Poás, Barva, Irazú, and Turrialba volcanoes) to the north and the Cordillera de Talamanca to the south—don't quite line up in the middle, leaving a trough between them. The "valley" floor is 3,000 feet above sea level. In the valley, your view toward the coasts is obstructed by the two mountain ranges. But from a hillside hotel, your view of San José and the valley can be spectacular.

In the eastern Central Valley are Cartago and Irazú Volcano. Cartago is an older city than San José, with some significant historic attractions. Irazú is Costa Rica's tallest volcano. On a clear day you can see both the Atlantic and Pacific oceans from its peak.

Rafting trips on the Pacuare and Reventazón are based in Turrialba, a bustling little town. The nearby Guayabo Ruins, of a city deserted in AD 1400, is Costa Rica's only significant archaeological site.

An often overlooked beauty is the Orosi Valley. The drive into the valley is simply gorgeous, and a tranquil way to spend a day. Birding destination Tapantí National Park is at the southern edge of the valley.

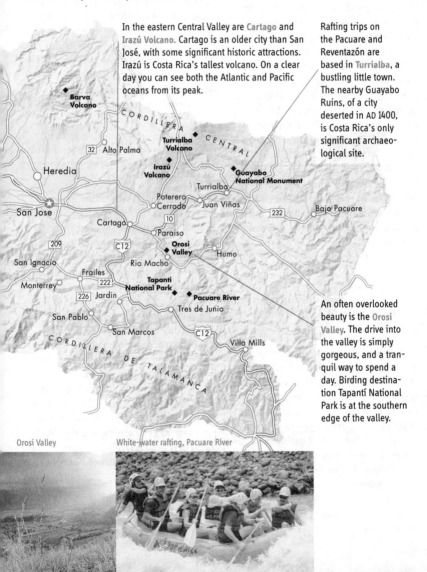

Orosi Valley

White-water rafting, Pacuare River

# CENTRAL VALLEY PLANNER

## When to Go

Known for its "eternal spring, " the Central Valley lacks the oppressive seasonal heat and rain of other parts of the country and is almost always suitable for a visit. Average highs are 24–27°C (75–80°F). Afternoon downpours are common from mid-May to December (with a slight drop-off around August), but the amount of rain is modest compared to the Caribbean coast and the southern Pacific. Don't rule out the rainy season—fewer travelers mean you won't need reservations, rain is usually during afternoon siesta hours, and the valley is swathed in green after a few months of moisture. Holy Week (the week before Easter) and the last two weeks of the year are prime vacation times for Ticos, so reserve cars and hotel rooms in advance.

## Choosing a Place to Stay

For getting away from it all and still being close to the country's primary transportation hub, the lodges around San José are ideal. Rustic *cabinas* (cottages), sprawling coffee plantations, nature lodges, and hilltop villas with expansive views are some of your options. The large chains are here as well, but the real gems are the so-called "boutique" hotels, many of which have unique designs that take advantage of exceptional countryside locations. Tropical gardens are the norm, rather than the exception, and air conditioning is usually not necessary.

## Getting There

The region has an extensive network of paved roads in relatively good shape. The Pan-American Highway runs east–west through the valley and the center of San José. Mountains ring the valley, so most trips to or from the lowlands require a drive up in elevation then back down. The bus network is good, but since sights tend to be spread out it's less time-consuming to travel by car. Consider taking taxis. They're plentiful, they know the roads (most of the time), and the prices are reasonable. Even several $10 taxi rides per day—and $10 gets you quite a ways—are cheaper than a rental car.

■ TIP➜➜ Navigating the winding roads around the Central Valley is difficult at best, and absurd at its worst. Call ahead for directions, and don't hesitate to ask a local for assistance along the way.

## How Much Time?

You could spend an entire week in the Central Valley without getting bored, but if you have only a week or two in Costa Rica, we recommend a maximum of two days before heading to rain forests and beaches in other parts of the country. Spending a day after you arrive, then another day or two before you fly out gives you a taste of the region, breaks up the travel time, and makes your last day interesting, rather than spent in transit back to San José. The drive between just about any two points in the Central Valley is two hours or less, so it's ideal for short trips. In a day you can explore the Orosi Valley and Cartago, raft the Pacuare River, or hop from the Butterfly Farm to a coffee plantation.

■ TIP➜➜ Bring a jacket—it can get chilly at night in any of the Central Valley towns, and downright cold at higher elevations.

## Recommended Tour Operators

These San José–based tour operators arrange transport from some hotels (generally those in San José and around the airport). Costa Rica Sun Tours, Costa Rica's Temptations, Grayline, and Swiss Travel have myriad tour options:

Crowned Woodnymph

■ **Costa Rica Sun Tours** (☎ 296-7757 ⊕ www.crsuntours.com).

■ **Costa Rica's Temptations** (☎ 239-9999 ⊕ www.crtinfo.com).

■ **Grayline Tours Costa Rica** (☎ 220-2126 ⊕ www.graylinecostarica.com).

■ **Horizontes** (☎ 222-2022 ⊕ www.horizontes.com) has countrywide natural-history and adventure trips

■ **Swiss Travel** (☎ 231-4055 ⊕ www.swisstravelcr.com).

### WHITE-WATER OUTFITTERS

Most outfitters are based in San José. Tico's River, Costa Rica Ríos, and Rainforest World are in Turrialba. Many have both rafting and kayaking.

■ **Costa Rica Expeditions** (☎ 257-0766 ⊕ www.costaricaexpeditions.com).

■ **Costa Rica Nature Adventures** (☎ 225-3939 or 224-0505, 800/235-6150 in North America ⊕ www.toenjoynature.com).

■ **Costa Rica Ríos** (☎ 556-9617 or 556-8482 ⊕ www.costaricarios.com).

■ **Exploradores Outdoors** (☎ 222-6262 ⊕ www.exploradoresoutdoors.com).

■ **Rainforest World** (☎ 556-0014 or 357-7250 ⊕ www.rforestw.com).

■ **Ríos Tropicales** (☎ 233-6455 ⊕ www.riostropicales.com).

■ **Tico's River** (☎ 556-1231 or 394-4479 ⊕ www.ticoriver.com).

Rafting, Pacuare River

## Price Categories

**WHAT IT COSTS in Dollars**

|  | $$$$ | $$$ | $$ | $ | ¢ |
|---|---|---|---|---|---|
| **Restaurants** | over $25 | $15–$25 | $10–$15 | $5–$10 | under $5 |
| **Hotels** | over $250 | $150–$250 | $75–$150 | $50–$75 | under $50 |

Restaurant prices are per-person for a main course at dinner. Hotel prices are for two people in a standard double room in high season, excluding service and tax (16.4%).

# WEST OF SAN JOSÉ

Updated by
Ryan Sarsfield

As you drive north or west out of San José, the city's suburbs and industrial zones quickly give way to arable land, most of which is occupied by coffee farms. Within Costa Rica's coffee heartland are plenty of tranquil agricultural towns and two provincial capitals, Alajuela and Heredia. Both cities owe their relative prosperity to the coffee beans cultivated on the fertile lower slopes of the Poás and Barva volcanoes. The upper slopes, too cold for coffee crops, are dedicated to dairy cattle, strawberries, ferns, and flowers, making for markedly different and thoroughly enchanting landscapes along the periphery of the national parks. Since the hills above these quaint valley towns have some excellent restaurants and lodgings, rural overnights are an excellent alternative to staying in San José.

## Escazú

❶ A traditional coffee-farming town at the foot of a small mountain range (the Cordillera de Escazú), Escazú is a bedroom community for San José. As you exit the highway and head gradually uphill, you might think you made a wrong turn and ended up in southern California—Hugo Boss outlets, strip malls, fast food, Persian rugs for sale—nothing to indicate that you're in Costa Rica. There's even a bagel shop! But farther up you return to small-town Central America. Narrow roads wind their way up the steep slopes of the *cordillera* (mountain range) past coffee fields and well-tended farmhouses with tidy gardens and the occasional oxcart parked in the yard—precisely the kind of scene that captured the attention of many a Costa Rican painter in the early 20th century. There are also plenty of fancy homes and condos between the humble farmhouses, especially in the San Antonio and San Rafael neighborhoods. Escazú's ancient church faces a small plaza, surrounded in part by weathered adobe homes. Several blocks downhill from the town center is the busy road to Santa Ana, lined with a growing selection of restaurants, bars, and shops.

### Exploring

High in the hills above Escazú stands the tiny community of **San Antonio de Escazú**, famous for its annual oxcart festival held the second Sunday of March. The view from here—of nearby San José and distant volcanoes—is impressive by both day and night. If you head higher than San Antonio de Escazú, brace yourself for virtually vertical roads that wind up into the mountains toward **Pico Blanco**, the highest point in the Escazú Cordillera, which is a half-day hike to ascend.

### Where to Stay & Eat

$$–$$$$  ✕ **Le Monastère.** This monastery turned formal restaurant high in the San Rafael hills has a great view of the Central Valley. The dining room is dressed up in antiques, with tables set for a five-course meal; waiters don friar robes, which makes the atmosphere too theatrical for some tastes, but the classic French dishes are outstanding. La Cava, the bar beneath the dining room, has live music Monday through Saturday and

is open into the wee hours. ⊠ *San Rafael de Escazú; take old road to Santa Ana, turn left at the Paco Shopping Center, and follow signs* ☎ *289–4404* ⊟ *AE, DC, MC, V* ⊘ *Closed Sun. No lunch.*

**$$–$$$$** ✕ **Restaurante Cerutti.** The diva of San José's Italian eateries, this little restaurant occupies a lovely century-old adobe house near a busy intersection called El Cruce (The Cross). Whitewashed walls are adorned with antique prints. The extensive menu, focusing on modern Italian cuisine, ranges from saffron penne with New Zealand mussels to aragona rabbit with escargots and polenta to the more traditional *cordero al horno* (rack of lamb roasted with vegetables). No one disputes that the quality of the food is high—with prices to match. ⊠ *Cruce de San Rafael de Escazú* ☎ *228–4511* ⊟ *AE, DC, MC, V* ⊘ *Closed Tues.*

> ## HOCUS POCUS
>
> During colonial days, Escazú was dubbed the City of Good Witches because many native healers lived in the area. Locals say that Escazú is still home to witches who will tell your fortune or concoct a love potion for a small fee, but you'd be hard-pressed to spot them in the town's busy commercial district. Try a soccer field instead; the city's team is christened *Las Brujas* (The Witches).

**★ $–$$$$** ✕ **El Invernadero.** The name translates as "The Greenhouse, " which could refer to the ferns hanging from the ceiling of the main dining room or the orchids that decorate the tables. At night the low lighting and candles make this an especially cozy spot. The menu is a mix of French and Italian, with a few Costa Rican touches, such as the heart of palm salad and salmon with a *pejibaye* (peach palm) sauce. Choose from the likes of risotto de *mariscos* (seafood), mushroom ravioli in a four-cheese sauce, and corvina *al invernadero* (sea bass in a creamy asparagus and shrimp sauce). ⊠ *800 m south and 75 m west of El Cruce, Escazú* ☎ *228–0216* ⊟ *AE, DC, MC, V* ⊘ *Closed Sun.*

**$–$$** ✕ **Barbecue Los Anonos.** Established in 1960, Los Anonos expanded from its original rustic collection of deep booths with wooden benches in the late 1990s, adding a more elegant room decorated with historic photos. It is a popular spot with Costa Rican families on weekend nights, and businesspeople on weekdays, for the economical three-course lunches. The best bet is the grilled meat, and there is plenty to choose from, including imported U.S. beef and less expensive Tico cuts. Despite the name, barbecue sauce is not used. Fresh fish, shrimp, and half a dozen salads are other choices. ⊠ *400 m west of Los Anonos Bridge* ☎ *228–0180* ⊟ *AE, DC, MC, V* ⊘ *Closed Mon.*

**$–$$** ✕ **El Descanso del Cardenal.** This recent addition to the Escazú scene has had mixed reviews, but is a less expensive Italian alternative to Cerutti. The menu is also more traditional, offering staples such as spaghetti, lasagna, and ravioli, as well as poultry and seafood dishes. The setting is lavish and intimate, with various rooms to choose from on two levels, and a terrace overlooking a stream. ⊠ *600 m south of Scotia Bank* ☎ *289–8208* ⊟ *AE, DC, MC, V* ⊘ *No lunch Mon.–Tues. Closed Sun.*

**$$$$** ✕ ▣ **White House Hotel.** Formerly the Tara Resort Hotel, this luxurious little inn and spa near the top of Pico Blanco reopened in December 2004 after a renovation with a White House theme, and it appears that the

LIMÓN

2

0       5 miles

0       5 km

C O R D I L L E R A   C E N T R A L

◆ **Volcán Turrialba**

**Volcán Irazú** 8

**Guayabo National Monument** ◆

Santa Cruz

218

CARTAGO

Pacayas

Juan Vinas

*Río Reventazón*

**Turrialba** 9

Cot

**Cartago** 7

**Jardín Lankester** ◆

Paraíso

◆ **Cachí Dam**

*Lago Cachí*

TO CATIE →

Tejar

2

Ujarrás

**Orosi Valley**

see map page 82

Orosi

Cachí

O R O S I VALLEY

*Tapantí National Park*

# The Central Valley

transition from the Old South to Pennsylvania Avenue has been success-
ful. Most rooms are named for a president, so fans of Clinton, Bush, or
say, Warren G. Harding, are in luck. The rooms are very spacious and
expensively furnished, with French doors that open onto the public veranda. You can even come and go in a limo or helicopter if you so de-
sire. The restaurant, The Capital Grille ($$$–$$$$) features American-style
surf and turf dishes like filet mignon, prime rib, and swordfish, and the
glass walls do the view justice.  ⊠ ½ km/¼ mi south of the cemetery of
San Antonio de Escazú ☎ 288–6362 ⬚ 288–6365 ⊕ www.
whitehousecostarica.com ⤴ 4 rooms, 10 suites, 2 bungalows ⟁ Restau-
rant, room service, fans, in-room safes, cable TV, pool, whirlpool tub,
fitness room, massage, sauna, spa, bar, laundry service, Internet, airport
pickup, helipad, no-smoking rooms;no a/c, no kids under 12 ⊟ AE, DC,
MC, V ▮⊙▮ BP.

$$   ▦ **Courtyard Marriott San José.** You generally know what to expect here:
rooms mirror those in Marriotts the world over. You won't necessarily
feel that you're in Costa Rica when you bed down here—especially since
the surrounding "landscape" consists of a mall, a highway, and a parking lot—but it can be ideal if you are traveling on business or just need
a quality, no-nonsense place to sleep. ⊠ Just off the highway (Autopista
Prospero Fernandez) heading west, next to the Itskatzu Mall ☎208–3000
⬚ 288–0808 ⊕ www.courtyard.com ⤴ 120 ⟁ Restaurant, a/c, in-
room safes, cable TV, pool, bar, laundry service, in-room high-speed and
data ports, Internet, business center, airport shuttle, no-smoking rooms
⊟ AE, DC, MC, V.

$–$$   ▦ **Posada El Quijote.** Perched on a hill in the Bello Horizonte neighbor-
hood, with a great view of the city, this bed-and-breakfast strikes the
right balance between a small inn and a private residence. Being here
feels like visiting a friend, albeit a friend with great taste. The best view
is from the sundeck, just off the spacious living room, which has a couch,
a fireplace, and lots of modern art. The apartments and the two "deluxe"
rooms have comparable views. Smaller "standard" rooms overlook the
surrounding gardens, and aren't nearly as nice. The staff is extremely
helpful. It's a bit hard to find, so you may want to take a taxi, or call
for directions. ⊠ Bello Horizonte de Escazú, first street west of Anonos
Bridge, 1 km/½ mi up hill ⬚ Dept. 239–SJO, Box 025216, Miami, FL
33102-5216 ☎ 289–8401 ⬚ 289–8729 ⊕ www.quijote.co.cr ⤴ 8
rooms, 2 apartments ⟁ Fans, cable TV, travel services, laundry service,
Internet, some pets allowed, airport pickup; no-smoking rooms, no a/c
⊟ AE, DC, MC, V ▮⊙▮ BP.

$   ▦ **Casa de las Tias.** The name means "The Aunts' House, " which is ap-
propriate for this yellow house with a front porch and picket fence at
the end of short road in San Rafael de Escazú. A few simple antiques
and old photos of the aunts themselves complete the effect. The rooms
and furnishings feel slightly aged, but make up for it in charm, and the
large backyard and gardens give the illusion of being much farther than
a mere 150 m from a major commercial street. ⊠ 100 m south and 150
m east of the Cruce Escazú ⬚ SJO 478, PO Box 025216 Miami FL
33102-5216 ☎ 289–5517 ⬚ 289–7353 ⊕ www.hotels.co.cr/casatias.

*html* ↪ *5 rooms* ♿ *Fans, laundry service, no-smoking rooms, airport pickup; no a/c, no kids under 12* ▭ *AE, MC, V* ⏐◯⏐ *BP.*

**$** ⊡ **Costa Verde Inn.** Rooms at this large and quiet B&B on the outskirts of Escazú make nice use of local hardwoods, and their white walls display traditional Peruvian art. South American art also adorns the main building, where a large sitting area has comfortable chairs and a fireplace. The inn is surrounded by gardens, and at night you can see the lights of San José twinkling to the east, though just three of the rooms take advantage of the view. Since the inn is at the end of a narrow driveway with an unassuming gate, you may not be sure you've found the right place—just ring the bell. ✉ *From southeast corner of second cemetery, 200 m west and 100 m south* ⌖*SJO 1610, Box 025216, Miami, FL 33102-5216* ☎ *228–4080* 🖷 *289–8591* ⊕ *www.costaverdeinn. com* ↪ *17 rooms* ♿ *Fans, refrigerators, cable TV, pool, whirlpool tub, airport pickup; no a/c, no room phones* ▭ *AE, MC, V* ⏐◯⏐ *BP.*

## Nightlife

Escazú is the Central Valley's hot spot for nightlife—many Josefinos head here for the restaurants, bars, and dance clubs that cater to a young, cell phone–toting crowd. The highest concentration of nightspots is in the **Trejos Montealegre shopping center** (✉ Next to the highway between San José and Ciudad Colón), which has several bars and dance clubs.

One of the more popular watering holes with the under-30 set is **Henry's Beach Bar** (✉ Plaza San Rafael, 2nd fl. ☎ 289–6250), which features Caribbean music and a pseudo-"islands" decor, with beach paintings and surfboards. Costa Ricans refer to this style bar as an "American Bar" which is fairly accurate. **Q'Tal** (✉ 100 m east of El Cruce, San Rafael ☎228–4091), part of Quiubo Restaurant, has recorded music, with occasional live Latin music per-

> **KEEPING COOL**
>
> The Central Valley's climate is often a great surprise to first-time visitors—it's not at all the steamy tropics you've imagined. It's usually cool enough at night to go without air-conditioning, so don't be surprised if many hotels don't have it.

formed by the house band Réquete. **Orale** (✉ 120 m east of El Cruce, San Rafael ☎ 228–6436 or 228–6437), in the Trejos Montealegre mall, has live Latin music Fridays and Saturdays.

## Shopping

If you get the shopping bug and absolutely must visit a mall while on vacation, Escazú is the place to do it. **Itskatzu,** which lies on the north side of the highway (Autopista Prospero Fernandez) heading west, and **Paco,** on the old road to Santa Ana, are a couple of possibilities.

★ You can watch local craftsmen ply their trade at **Biesanz Woodworks** (✉ Bello Horizonte, 800 m south of the Escuela orizonte; follow signs ☎289–4337), where expat artist Barry Biesanz creates unique items from Costa Rican hardwoods, which are carved on-site. It's difficult to find, so take a taxi or call for directions from your hotel.

## To & From Escazú

*5 km/3 mi (15 min) southwest of San José.*

To drive to Escazú from San José, turn left at the western end of Paseo Colón, which ends at the Parque La Sabana. Take the first right, and get off the highway at the first exit. Turn right at the traffic light for San Rafael addresses, and right again at the bottom of the hill for the old road to Santa Ana. Buses for Escazú leave downtown San José every 20 minutes daily; buses to Santa Ana leave every 10 minutes.

## Escazú Essentials

🏧 Bank/ATM **Banco Nacional** ⊠ Southwest side of Parque Central. **Banco de Costa Rica ATM** ⊠ North side of church.

🏧 Hospital **HospitalCIMA** ⊠ Next to PriceSmart, west of town ☎ 208-1000.

🏧 Pharmacy **Farmacia San Miguel** ⊠ North side of Parque Central.

🏧 Internet **Café Teem Internet** ⊠ 25 m from northwest corner of Parque Central.

🏧 Post Office **Correos** ⊠ 100 m north of church.

🏧 Taxis **Coopetaxi** ☎ 224-7979.

# Santa Ana

❷ This once-tranquil agricultural community on the opposite side of the *cordillera* (mountain range) from Escazú is in the midst of a boom, and shopping malls and housing developments are popping up along its periphery. But the town center, with its rugged stone church surrounded by homes and businesses, has changed little in the past decade. The church, which was built between 1870 and 1880, has a Spanish-tile roof, carved wooden doors, and two pre-Columbian stone spheres flanking its entrance. Its rustic interior—bare wooden pillars and beams and black iron lamps—seems appropriate for an area with a tradition of ranching. Because it is warmer and drier than the towns to the east, Santa Ana is one of the few Central Valley towns that doesn't have a good climate for coffee, and is instead surrounded by pastures and patches of forest. It isn't unusual to see men on horseback here, and on a quiet night you may hear coyotes howling at the edge of town.

## Where to Stay & Eat

$-$$ ✕ **Bacchus.** Take a Peruvian chef trained in France and a Italian owner and you get Bacchus, a welcome addition to the local dining scene. The cuisine is a mix of French and Italian dishes such as duck breast in a port sauce, baked mushroom-and-polenta ragout, and a variety of pizzas. Modern art decorates the simple but elegant interior, and outdoor seating is available. An extensive wine list and reasonable prices make it a great pick for dinner. ⊠ *200 m east and 100 m north of church* ☎ *282-5441* ▭ *AE, DC, MC, V.*

$-$$ ✕ **Tex Mex.** This place serves a fairly standard Mexican menu—tacos, burritos, quesadillas, and so on—plus a few grilled meat items, such as the Argentinian *churrasco* (a thick tenderloin cut), complete with *salsa chimichuri* (diced garlic and parsley in olive oil). There are about two dozen *bocas* (appetizers, or snacks), which are mostly smaller versions of entrée items. The enchiladas may not be as good as what you find in San Antonio, but the setting is pleasant, next to an old house with a

# Speaking Costa Rican

CLOSE UP

**SPANISH IN COSTA RICA TENDS TO BE** localized and has many of its own peculiarities. Costa Rica is a land where eloquent speech and creative verbal expression are highly valued. For example, here the response to a "thank you" is the gracious, uniquely Tico *"Con mucho gusto"* ("With much pleasure") instead of *"De nada"* ("It's nothing"), which is used in much of Latin America. In other cases,

informality is preferred: the conventional *Señor* and *Señora*, for example, are eschewed in favor of the more egalitarian *Don* and *Doña*, used preceding a first name. Even President Abel Pacheco is called "Don Abel." Exercise caution when selecting from the list below. While young Costa Rican men address everyone as *maje* (dude), you might get a withering look if you, a visitor, follow suit.

## Words and Common Phrases

| | | | |
|---|---|---|---|
| *adios* | good-bye; but also used as "hello" in rural areas | *Muy bien, por dicha* | very well, luckily |
| *agarrar de maje* | to deceive someone | *paño* | towel |
| *birra* | beer | *pelo de gato* | cat hair; or fine, misty rain that falls during December |
| *brete* | work | | |
| *cachos* | shoes; any coin; a dumb person | *peso* | colón |
| *chunche* | any thingamajig | *pinche* | a tight-fisted person |
| *clavar el pico* | to fall asleep | | |
| *Con mucho gusto* | used in response to "thank you" instead of "de nada" | *ponerse hasta la mecha* | get drunk |
| | | *porfa* | please |
| | | *pura vida* | fantastic, great |
| *estar de chicha* | to be angry | *rojo* | red; also a 1,000-colón note |
| *estar de goma* | have a hangover | | |
| *harina* | money | *Si Dios lo quiere* | God willing |
| *jupa* | head | *soda* | an inexpensive local restaurant |
| *macho, macha* | a person with blonde hair | | |
| *matar la culebra* | waste time | *torta* | a big mistake or error |
| *maje* | buddy, dude, mate | *tuanis* | cool |
| *mamá de Tarzán* | know-it-all | *tucán* | toucan; also a 5,000-colón note |
| *maría* | a woman's name; also a taxi meter | | |
| | | *upe* | anyone home? |
| *montón* | a lot | | |
| *Muy bien, gracias a Dios* | very well, thank goodness | | |

2

yard shaded by massive trees. Seating is on a covered brick patio or in an adjacent dining area enclosed by windows, for cool nights. A few simple, inexpensive rooms are available for rent. ☒ *Northeast of Catholic church* ☎ *282–6342* ▭ *AE, DC, MC, V* ☉ *Closed Mon.*

★ $$$ ✕▣ **Alta.** The view from this Iberian-style hotel perched on a hillside above Santa Ana is impressive, but then, so is the hotel. The sloping stairway entrance lined with tall columns and palms is reminiscent of a narrow street in southern Spain, an effect reinforced by the barrel-tile roof and ocher-stuccoed walls; the narrow hallways feel like an old castle. Guest rooms are hardly spacious, but are nicely done in earth tones, with colonial-style furniture and bathrooms with hand-painted tiles. The restaurant, La Luz ($$), has a hardwood floor, beamed ceiling, and plenty of windows for admiring the distant hills and the pool and gardens below. The eclectic and unusual menu includes veal with stuffed grape leaves, shrimp tempura, marinated lamb chops, and Moroccan chicken. ☒ *Old road between Santa Ana and Escazú* ☝ *Interlink 964, Box 02–5635, Miami, FL 33102* ☎ *282–4160, 888/388–2582 in U.S.* ☒ *282–4162* ⊕ *www.thealtahotel.com* ↘ *18 rooms, 5 suites* ⌂ *Restaurant, in-room safes, minibars, cable TV, pool, gym, whirlpool tub, sauna, laundry service, Internet, airport pickup* ▭ *AE, DC, MC, V* ◯ *EP.*

$ ▣ **Hotel Posada Canal Grande** This small hotel tucked in the hills to the west of Santa Ana is a great value. Each room is different, but most have unique wicker beds and Guatemalan bedspreads. The second-floor rooms open to the balcony over the pool and have the view, but the first floor isn't bad either. Two four-poster beds are placed in the shade by the pool, just to lounge on. On a clear day you can see the Gulf of Nicoya to the west. If the hills behind the hotel catch your eye, the staff can arrange horseback riding. ☒ *500 m north of the Piedades de Santa Ana Bus Terminal. Or, take the Piedades exit off of the highway to Ciudad Colón.* ☎ *282–4089 or 282–4101* ☒ *282–5733* ⊕ *www.hotelcanalgrande.com* ↘ *12 rooms* ⌂ *Restaurant, cable TV, pool, sauna, bar, laundry service, Internet, airport pickup; no a/c* ▭ *AE, DC, MC, V* ◯ *BP.*

## Shopping

Large, glazed pots with ornate decorations that range from traditional ★ patterns to modern motifs are the specialties at **Cerámica Las Palomas** (☒ Old road to Santa Ana, opposite Alta Hotel ☎ 282–7001). Flowerpots and lamps are also common works, and the staff will eagerly show you the production process, from raw clay to art.

## To & From Santa Ana

*12 km/7 mi southwest of San José.*

From San José, turn left at the western end of Paseo Colón, which ends at the Parque La Sabana. Take the first right, and get on the highway. Get off at the third exit. Buses leave San José for Santa Ana every 20 minutes from 5 AM to 11 PM. Buses for Escazú run every 10 minutes or so.

## Santa Ana Essentials

🏦 Bank/ATM **Banco de Costa Rica** ☒ Southwest corner of church.
🏥 Pharmacy **Farmacia Sucre** ☒ 25 m south of church.

**El** Internet Internet Café El Sol ⊠ Southwest corner of church.
**El** Post Office Correos ⊠ Northwest corner of church.

# NORTH OF SAN JOSÉ

2

As you set out from San José or the international airport to explore the towns to the north, you're first faced with pavement, hotels, and malls—not especially scenic. It's only when you reach the centers of these small towns that you feel you've arrived in Central America. Santo Domingo and San Antonio de Belén blend into the outskirts of San José. Farther north, Alajuela and Heredia are bustling provincial capitals with charismatic central parks. Throughout this area, tucked into the urban scenery and lining volcanic slopes, are fields of that great Costa Rican staple, coffee.

## San Antonio de Belén

❸ San Antonio de Belén has little to offer visitors but its rural charm and proximity to the international airport. The latter led developers to build several of the San José area's biggest hotels here. The town also lies on the route of entry for Alajuela's Butterfly Garden. It's also a convenient departure point for trips to the western Central Valley, Pacific coast, and northern region. If you stay at the Marriott, you likely won't even see the town, just the busy highway between San José and Alajuela.

### Where to Stay & Eat

$–$$ ✕⊡ **El Rodeo.** This quiet hotel has spacious rooms with polished hardwood floors, high ceilings, and narrow balconies overlooking small gardens and rooms in the adjacent building. It bills itself as a "country hotel, " though this is more in image than fact. An open-air lounge on the second floor has a pool table and wicker furniture. Breakfast is served on a porch overlooking the pool, which gets very little use, since most of the guests are business travelers. The large wooden restaurant ($–$$) in front of the hotel is quite popular with Ticos, who pack it on weekends. Decorated with saddles, steer skulls, and other ranching paraphernalia, the restaurant serves an array of grilled meats, from the Argentinean churrascos to T-bones, as well as several fish and shrimp dishes. ⊠ *Road to Santa Ana, 2 km/1 mi east of Parque Central* ☎*293–3909* 🖷*239–3464* 🛏 *20 rooms, 9 suites* ⚖ *Restaurant, in-room safes, minibars, cable TV, 2 tennis courts, pool, whirlpool tub, sauna, laundry service, Internet, meeting rooms, travel services* ▤ *AE, DC, MC, V* ⃝*BP.*

★ $$$–$$$$ ⊡ **Marriott Costa Rica Hotel.** Towering over a coffee plantation west of San José, the stately Marriott's thick columns, wide arches, and central courtyard are re-creations straight out of the 17th century, and hand-painted tiles and abundant antiques complete the historic appearance. Guest rooms are more contemporary, but they're elegant enough,

**WORD OF MOUTH**

"[We] stayed at the Marriott Costa Rica Hotel, which I recommend. The pictures on the Internet don't really convey the beauty of the hotel!"
–TVL

with hardwood furniture and sliding glass doors that open onto tiny balconies. The service is comprehensive; if, for instance, you would like ballboys to help you fine-tune your tennis game, then this may be your place. ☒ ¾ km/½ mi west of Firestone, off Autopista General Cañas, San Antonio de Belén ☎ 298–0000, 800/228–9290 in U.S. ☎ 298–0011 ⊕ www.marriott.com ⌂ 244 rooms, 7 suites ⌂ 4 restaurants, café, in-room safes, in-room data ports, driving range, putting green, 3 tennis courts, 2 pools, gym, health club, hair salon, sauna, lobby lounge, shop, babysitting, dry cleaning, laundry service, concierge, business services, meeting rooms, airport shuttle, car rental, travel services, free parking ▤ AE, DC, MC, V.

### To & From San Antonio de Belén
17 km/10 mi, or 20 mins, northwest of San José.

From San José, turn right at the west end of Paseo Colón onto the Pan-American Highway (Carretera General Cañas). The San Antonio de Belén exit is at an overpass several miles west of the Heredia exit, by the Cariari Real Mall. San Antonio is only 10 minutes from the airport.

### San Antonio de Belén Essentials
🏦 Bank/ATM **Banco de Costa Rica** ☒ 50 m west of rear of church.
🌐 Internet **Belén Web Café** ☒ West end of soccer field.
✉ Post Office **Correos** ☒ 2 blocks west and 25 m north of northwest corner of soccer field.

## Alajuela

❹ Because of its proximity to the international airport (5–10 minutes away) many travelers spend their first or last night in Alajuela, but the beauty of the surrounding countryside persuades some to stay longer. Alajuela is Costa Rica's second-largest city (population 50,000), and a mere 30-minute bus ride from the capital, but it has a decidedly provincial air. Architecturally it differs little from the bulk of Costa Rican towns: it's a grid of low-rise structures painted in primary colors.

### Exploring
Royal palms and massive mango trees fill the **Parque Central** (☒ C. Central, between Avdas. 1 and Central), which also has a lovely fountain imported from Glasgow and concrete benches where locals gather to chat. Surrounding the plaza is an odd mix of charming old buildings and sterile concrete boxes, including a somewhat incongruous McDonald's.

The large, neoclassic **Catedral** (☒ C. Central, between Avdas. 1 and Cen-

**CORRUPTION CRACKDOWN**

Long a proponent of do-as-I-say, not-as-I-do anti-corruption policies, Costa Rica got tough on bigwigs in 2004. Three former presidents were taken into custody for allegedly accepting bribes in a telecommunications deal. One—Miguel Ángel Rodríguez—was forced to step down two weeks after taking over the presidency of the Organization of American States (OAS). The sight of former leaders being led away in handcuffs has shaken many Costa Ricans' faith in their democracy, but others see it as a positive sign that no one is above the law.

tral ☎ 443–2928) has interesting capitals decorated with local agricultural motifs and a striking red metal dome. The interior is spacious but rather plain, except for the ornate cupola above the altar. It's open daily 8–6.

Alajuela was the birthplace of Juan Santamaría, the national hero who lost his life in a battle against the mercenary army of U.S. adventurer William Walker when the latter invaded Costa Rica in 1856. The **Parque Juan Santamaría** (⊠ C. 2 and Avda. 3.) has a statue of the young Santamaría. After a restoration in early 2005, Juan should keep his youthful good looks for years to come.

Juan Santamaría's heroic deeds are celebrated in the **Museo Juan Santamaría,** one block north of Parque Central. It's worth a look, but not a linger, which is too bad because Santamaría's story is an interesting one. The orchid collection is impressive. ⊠ *C. 2 and Avda. 3* ☎ *441–4775* 🎫 *Free* ⊙ *Tues.–Sun. 10–6.*

☾ Spread over the lush grounds of **Zoo Ave** (Bird Zoo) is a collection of large cages holding macaws, toucans, hawks, and parrots, not to mention crocodiles, turtles, monkeys, wild cats, and other interesting critters. The zoo, the best in Costa Rica, runs a breeding project for rare and endangered birds, all of which are destined for eventual release. It has a total of 120 bird species, including such rare ones as the quetzal, fiery-billed aracari, several types of eagles, and even ostriches. An impressive mural at the back of the facility shows Costa Rica's 850 bird species painted to scale. ⊠ *La Garita de Alajuela; head west from Alajuela center past cemetery, turn left after stone church in Barrio San José; or head west of Pan-American Hwy to Atenas exit, then turn right* ☎ *433–8989* ⊕ *www.zooave.com* 🎫 *$9* ⊙ *Daily 9–5.*

★ ☾ Observe and photograph butterfiles up close at the **The Butterfly Farm** (La Finca de Mariposas), in the suburb of La Guácima. The farm's several microclimates keep comfortable some 40 species of tropical butterflies; it also has an apiary exhibit. Come when it's sunny if you can—that's when butterflies are most active. This is the original butterfly farm, but there are other butterfly gardens near Volcán Poás at La Paz Waterfal Gardens and in Monteverde. ⊠ *From San José, turn south (left) at the intersection just past Real Cariari Mall, turn right at church of San Antonio de Belén, then left at the corner, then follow the butterfly signs* ☎ *438–0400* ⊕ *www.butterflyfarm.co.cr* 🎫 *$15, $25 with transportation from San José* ⊙ *Daily 8:30–5.*

Considering the amount of coffee you'll drive past in the Central Valley, you might want to dedicate 90 minutes of your vacation to learning about the crop's production. **Doka Estate,** a working coffee plantation with more than 70 years in the business, offers a comprehensive tour that takes you through the fields, shows you how the fruit is processed and the beans are dried, and lets you sample the local brew. The best time to take this tour is during the October to February picking season. ⊠ *10 km/6 mi north of Alajuela's Tribunales de Justicia, turn left at San Isidro and follow signs, San Luis de Sabanilla* ☎ *449–5152* 🖷 *449–6427*

# Alajuela

### KEY

● Restaurants
① Hotels

---

**TAMBOR**

**SANTA BARBARA**

TO SANTA BARBARA

TO SAN PEDRO

TUETAL NORTE

TO SAN ISIDRO, POÁS VOLCANO

TO TACARES, GRECIA, SARCHÍ, ARENAL

TO LA GARITA

TO INTERSECTION MANOLOS, ARENAS

Zoo Ave

**ALAJUELA**

Calle 3
Calle 8
Calle 12

see inset

**Aeropuerto Internacional Juan Santamaría**

TO SAN JOSÉ

TO SAN JOSÉ

Hospital San Rafael
Tribunales de Justicia

Soccer Stadium

Catedral

Calle 7
Calle 5
Calle 3
Calle 1
Calle Central
Calle 2
Calle 4
Calle 6
Calle 8

Calle 9
Calle El Meson
Calle Ismael Chavern
Calle 14

Avenida Antonio Arroyo
Avenida Jesús Ocah

Avenida 3
Avenida 1
Avenida Central
Avenida 2
Avenida 4
Avenida 6
Avenida 8
Avenida 9

Parque Juan Santamaría

Cemetery
TO ZOO AVE

Alajuela Station

TO BUTTERFLY FARM

---

0 — 1 mile
0 — 1 km

### Restaurants

Bar y Restaurante El Mirador ............ **2**
Delicias de Mi Tierra ..... **1**

### Hotels

Buena Vista Hotel ...... **9**
Hotel Alajuela .......... **5**
Hotel La Rosa de América ........... **2**
La Princesa Marina ...... **4**
Martino Resort and Spa .......... **1**
Orquídeas Inn ......... **3**
Pura Vida Hotel ........ **6**
Pura Vida Yoga Retreat & Spa ........ **8**
Xandari Resort Hotel & Spa ......... **7**

CLOSE UP

## A National Hero

**WHEN THE COSTA RICANS DROVE** invader Walker's troops from their country in 1857, they chased his troops to Rivas, Nicaragua. The filibusters took refuge in a wooden fort. Juan Santamaría, a poor, 17-year-old drummer boy with a militia from Alajuela, offered to burn it down to drive them out. Legend says that Santamaría ran toward the fort carrying a torch, and that although he was shot repeatedly, he managed to throw it and to burn the fort down. His bravery wasn't recognized at the time, probably because of his modest origins, but in 1891 a statue depicting a strong and handsome soldier carrying a torch was placed in Alajuela, thus immortalizing Santamaría. For this occasion, Ruben Darío, the great Nicaraguan writer, dedicated a poem to him. The entire account may be apocryphal; some historians doubt there ever *was* such a person. But don't tell that to the average Tico. April 11 is now a national holiday in Costa Rica, called Juan Santamaría Day, which celebrates the Costa Rican victory at the Battle of Rivas.

⊕ *www.dokaestate.com* ⌨ *$16, $30 with transportation (2 person minimum) from San José, Alajuela, Heredia, Escazú, or San Antonio* ⊙ *Tours Sun.–Sat. at 9, 10, 11, 1:30, 2:30, and 3:30, Sat. and Sun. last tour at 2:30.*

**en route**  If you head straight through Alajuela, with the Parque Central on your right, you'll be on the road to Poás Volcano; you should pass the Tribunales de Justicia (the county courthouse) on your right as you leave town. If you turn left upon reaching the Parque Central, and pass the town cemetery on your right, you'll be on the old road to Grecia. About 3 km (2 mi) northwest of town on that road, you'll come upon an old concrete church on the right, which marks your arrival in Barrio San José, a satellite community of Alajuela. A left turn after the church will take you to a lovely rural area called **La Garita** (the Guardhouse), from where the road continues west to Atenas and the Central Pacific beaches. La Garita is a popular weekend destination for Tico families, who head there for the abundant restaurants.

### Where to Stay & Eat

**$–$$** ✕ **Bar y Restaurante El Mirador.** Perched on a ridge several miles north of town, El Mirador has a sweeping view of the Central Valley that is impressive by day but more beautiful at dusk and night when the basin is filled with twinkling lights. Get a window table in the dining room, or one on the adjacent porch if it isn't too cool. The menu, which includes *lomito* (tenderloin) and corvina served with various sauces, and several shrimp or chicken dishes, plays second fiddle to the view. You could just stop in around sunset for drinks and appetizers. Free transportation from most Alajuela hotels is sometimes available. There are at least two other restaurants nearby with similar names and views—this one is on the main road, close to the Buena Vista Hotel. ⊠ *Road to Poás, 5 km/3 mi north of Tribunales de Justicia* ☎ *441–9347* ⊟ *AE, DC, MC, V* ⌆ *Reservations essential on weekends.*

¢–$ ✕ **Delicias de Mi Tierra.** The name translates as "Delicacies of my Land," and tasty and traditional Tico favorites are in fact served here: arroz con pollo, *pozol* (corn and pork soup), *casado campesino* (stewed beef with rice, beans, corn, potatoes, and plantains), and *chorreada con natilla* (a corn-bread pancake with sour cream). Long wooden tables and benches are surrounded by cane walls, decorative oxcart wheels, dried gourds, and tropical plants—the kind of decor trying so hard to be traditional that it's anything but. Ordering a few *entraditas* (appetizers) is a good way to sample dishes, as is the *tablita mi tierra,* a platter with grilled chicken, beef, pork, rice, beans, fried plantains, and salad, or the larger *fiesta de gallos,* a mixed platter of corn tortillas with various fillings. Closing time is 8 PM. ⊠ *1½ km/1 mi west of Barrio San José* ☎ *433–8536* ⊟ *AE, DC, MC, V.*

¢–$ ✕ **La Princesa Marina.** This large open-air eatery (part of a chain) at the intersection of the old Alajuela-Grecia road and the road to La Garita is popular with Ticos, who pack it on weekends to feast on inexpensive seafood. The selection is vast, with 10 types of fish, shrimp, or octopus ceviche, fish fillets served with various sauces, three sizes of shrimp prepared a dozen ways, whole fried fish, lobster tails, and several *mariscadas* (mixed seafood plates). Pastas, rice dishes, beef, and chicken are some other choices, but the seafood is your best bet here. The decor is utilitarian—bare tables, ceiling fans, and dividers of potted plants separating the sections, but you avoid that feeling of being in a contrived tourist venue. ⊠ *Barrio San José, across from church* ☎ *433–7117* ⊟ *AE, DC, MC, V.*

$–$$ ✕▥ **Orquideas Inn.** This friendly and spirited hotel has a colorful, Spanish-style main building, a bar dedicated to Marilyn Monroe, and tropical gardens with nature trails. Deluxe rooms, on a hill with a view of three volcanoes, are spacious, with bamboo furniture. Smaller rooms have terra-cotta tile floors and Guatemalan fabrics; those on the garden side are quieter, and worth the extra $10. A sumptuous breakfast buffet is served on the bar's patio. The restaurant's ($–$$) eclectic selection ranges from Costa Rican *casados* (plates of rice, beans, fried plantains, salad, and meat, chicken, or fish) to chateaubriand, and includes some unusual dishes, like talapia in a shrimp and corn sauce. The over-the-top presentation (ceviche served in a half-coconut adorned with plantains, for one) has to be seen to be believed, and it tastes as good as it looks. ⊠ *5 km/3 mi west of Alajuela cemetery* ▱ *29 rooms, 4 suites* ☎ *433–9346* 🖷 *433–9740* ⊕ *www.orquideasinn.com* ⌆ *Restaurant, fans, cable TV, pool, whirlpool tub, massage, bar, shops, laundry service, Internet, meeting room, airport pickup, travel services; no room phones* ⊟ *AE, DC, MC, V* ℡ *BP.*

$$$–$$$$ ▥ **Pura Vida Yoga Retreat & Spa.** Yoga workshops are an integral part of your stay here, and you should have at least some interest in the discipline to fully enjoy your stay. The spa has the full range of traditional offerings, as well as cutting-edge treatments like *watsu* (water shiatsu)

and hot-stone massage. The variety of rooms ranges from large suites to carpeted and furnished tents; all are quite nice, if not super-luxurious. Most of the bamboo furniture–filled rooms have large windows and look out over the valley or tropical gardens. The weekly rate includes two daily yoga classes, tours, transfers, three healthful meals per day, and one massage. You can drop in for 1 to 3 days, but the experience is structured around the 5- to 7-day "Mind, Body & Spirit" package. ✉ ½ km/¼ mi south of the Nuevo Penca Bar, Pavas de Carrizal, Apdo. 1112, 4050 🖉 R&R Resorts, Box 1496, Conyers, GA 30012 ☎392–8099, 888/767–7375 in U.S. 🖷483–0041 ⊕ www.puravidaspa.com 🛏 30 rooms, 12 tent bungalows, 3 suites, 1 villa ⚒ Dining room, spa, airport shuttle, travel services; no a/c, no room phones, no room TVs ▤ AE, MC, V ⭗ FAP.

**$$$–$$$$** 🖾 **Xandari Resort Hotel & Spa.** The
Fodor'sChoice tranquil and colorful Xandari is a
★ strikingly original inn and spa. Its bold design is the brainchild of a talented couple—he's an architect, she's an artist. Contemporary pueblo-esque villas along a ridge overlooking Alajuela and San José are spacious, with plenty of windows, colorful paintings, large terraces, and secluded lanais (sunbathing patios). It's the kind of place that makes you want to take pictures of your hotel room. Some villas stand alone and some share a building, but nearly all of them have spectacular views. So does the restaurant, which serves tasty, low-fat food. A 4-km trail through the hotel's forest reserve winds past five waterfalls. ✉ 5 km/3 mi north of Tribunales de Justicia, turn left after small bridge, follow signs, Apdo. 1485–4050 ☎ 443–2020, 800/686–7879 in U.S. 🖷 442–4847 ⊕ www.xandari.com 🛏 21 villas ⚒ Restaurant, fans, in-room safes, minibars, 2 pools, whirlpool tub, spa, bar, shop, laundry service, Internet, airport shuttle, travel services, no-smoking rooms; no a/c, no room TVs ▤ AE, DC, MC, V ⭗ CP.

**$$$** 🖾 **Martino Resort and Spa** This relatively small Italian-style resort hotel has a casino, spa, and spacious grounds, with the occasional classical sculpture to catch your eye. It's a small step below the international luxury chains in both quality and price, but still a good value. The rear of the main building is gorgeous, with a restaurant balcony that looks over the pool. The rooms have terraces, wood furnishings, and carved wooden doors, and

> **WORD OF MOUTH**
>
> "I thought Xandari was just okay. It [has] great architecture and the staff was very friendly but there were a lot of bugs (more than in the rain forest–a ton of ants and flies in the room). The pools are just lap pools and our room (no. 11) was very close to the restaurant, making it very loud. . . . We did have amazing couples massages in the private jalapa (soo pretty)."
> —RChandler1118
>
> "We spent our first night in CR at [Xandari] and I was very impressed. . . . They upgraded our room since it was my birthday and the room and view were fabulous. I've traveled quite a bit and this was one of the nicest rooms I have ever stayed in–very clean, comfortable bed, huge pivate patio area, beautiful grounds, and a great dinner. . . . Loved it!"
> —ltilson

the restaurant, which is well regarded locally, serves pastas and Italian-style meat and seafood dishes. ✉ *Across from Zoo Ave on the road to La Garita* ☎ *433–8382* 🖨 *433–9052* ⊕ *www.hotelmartino.com* ⇗ *34 junior suites, 3 standard, 4 deluxe suites, and 1 villa* ⌂ *Restaurant, room service, cable TV, pool, beauty salon, gym, spa, tennis court, travel services, nature trails, casino, laundry service, Wi-Fi, Internet, meeting rooms, airport shuttle, no-smoking rooms* ▤ *AE, DC, MC, V* ⦿ *BP.*

**$–$$** 🏨 **Buena Vista Hotel.** Perched high above Alajuela, this hotel does have the "good view" it is named for, but few of its rooms share in that vista, which is best appreciated from the back lawn. Three balcony rooms on the second floor in back have decent views of the Central Valley, but even better are the views of Poás Volcano from the three rooms above the lobby. Most rooms, however, overlook the lawns, or pool area. They are fairly standard—carpeted and sparsely decorated, with small baths and TVs—with none of the pizzazz of similarly priced options. The staff are superb, and the restaurant behind the lobby serves international dishes and grilled items. ✉ *7 km/4 mi north of Alajuela's Tribunales de Justicia on road to Poás* ☎ *442–8595, 800/506–2304 in U.S.* 🖨 *442–8701* ⊕ *www.hotelbuenavistacr.com* ⇗ *21 rooms, 4 junior suites* ⌂ *Restaurant, fans, cable TV, pool, bar, shop, Internet, airport shuttle, travel services, no-smoking rooms, handicapped accessible; no a/c, no room phones* ▤ *AE, DC, MC, V* ⦿ *CP.*

★ **$–$$** 🏨 **Pura Vida Hotel.** Thanks to its location on a ridge north of town, several of this hotel's rooms have views of Poás Volcano, and all of them offer tranquillity and abundant birdsong. The two rooms in the main house have the best views, but *casitas* (little houses) scattered around the large garden offer more privacy. Some of these bright and cheery bungalows have separate bedrooms, and most of them have small terraces with chairs. Continental breakfasts, light lunches, and delicious dinners are served on a covered terrace behind the house. The helpful owners and proximity to the airport (15 minutes) make this a good place to begin and end a trip. ✉ *Tuetal, 2 km/1 mi north of Tribunales de Justicia, veer left at Y* ☎🖨 *441–1157* ⊕ *www.puravidahotel.com* ⇗ *2 rooms, 4 bungalows* ⌂ *Restaurant, fans, Internet, laundry service, airport shuttle, travel services, no-smoking rooms; no a/c, no phones in some rooms, no room TVs* ▤ *AE, DC, MC, V* ⦿ *CP.*

**$** 🏨 **Hotel La Rosa de América** This small hotel tucked off the road to La Garita is a simple and relaxed place to unwind. There are six buildings, most divided into two units, arranged around the pool and gardens. The white-walled rooms are a little boring and lacking in personality, but it's a quiet place to sleep. Calling ahead for directions is a good idea, but once you're there, you'll have easy access to nearby restaurants and Zoo Ave. ✉ *1.5 km from La Princesa Marina, on the left; look for the small sign,* ☎🖨 *433–2741 or 433–2455* ⊕ *www.larosadeamerica.com* ⇗ *11 rooms* ⌂ *Fans, in-room safes, cable TV, pool, laundry service, Internet, no smoking rooms; no a/c, no room phones* ▤ *AE, DC, MC, V* ⦿ *BP.*

**¢** 🏨 **Hotel Alajuela.** This slightly worn three-story concrete hotel across from the Parque Central's southwest corner has basic rooms with tile floors, ceiling fans, and tiny bathrooms. But it's cheap, plenty of restaurants are within walking distance, the airport is a 10-minute taxi ride away, and just a few blocks away is the bus stop for La Garita, Poás, and most destinations in central and northwest Costa Rica. ⊠ *C. 2 and Avenida Central, southwest corner of Parque Central* ☎ *441–1241* 🖷 *441–7912* ☞ *30 rooms* ☾ *Fans, free parking a block away; no a/c, no phones in some rooms, no room TVs* ☰ *AE, MC, V* ᛌ *EP.*

### To & From Alajuela
*20 km/13 mi northwest of San José.*

To reach Alajuela, follow directions to San Antonio de Belén ( ⇨ *above*). Continue west on the highway past the San Antonio turnoff and turn right at the airport. Buses travel between San José, the airport, and Alajuela every 10 to 40 minutes daily. The bus stop is 100 m south of Hotel Alajuela (C. 2 and Avda. Central).

### Alajuela Essentials
🔢 Bank/ATM **Banco de Costa Rica** ⊠ Southwest corner of Parque Central. **Banco Nacional** ⊠ West side of Parque Central.

🔢 Hospital **Hospital San Rafael** ⊠ San Rafael, between Alajuela and San José ☎ 436–1001.

🔢 Pharmacy **Farmacia Chavarria** ⊠ On Parque Central. **Farmacia Catedral** ⊠ On Parque Central.

🔢 Internet **A-1 NetCafe** ⊠ In front of BAC San José bank, 100 m north of Parque Central.

🔢 Post Office **Correos** ⊠ 200 m north and 100 m east of Parque Central.

🔢 Taxis **Cotaxi** ☎ 443–3030.

---

## Santo Domingo

❺ Between Heredia and San José, the town of Santo Domingo de Heredia has plenty of traditional architecture and a level of tranquillity that belies its proximity to the capital, a mere 15-minute drive away. Established in the early 19th century, Santo Domingo is surrounded by coffee farms and several smaller, even qui-

> **COFFEE'S MELTING POT**
>
> Coffee is touted as a quintessential part of Costa Rica's history and culture; paradoxically, the majority of coffee-plantation workers in the country today are Nicaraguan.

eter communities. It has two Catholic churches, including one of the country's two basilicas. The Iglesia del Rosario, which faces the town's sparsely planted Parque Central, was built in the 1840s and is open for mass every morning from 8 to 10. The larger Basilica de Santo Domingo, which stands across from a soccer field on the north end of town, is open for evening mass from 4 to 6, and is a venue for classical music concerts during the July to August International Music Festival.

### Exploring
♺ Santo Domingo's main attraction is **INBioparque,** which does a good job of exhibiting the country's various ecosystems. It's a useful, if slightly expensive, primer before you head out to the hinterlands. Wander trails through climate-controlled wetlands and out to tropical dry forest. The

forests may not look much different, but your English-speaking guide will explain the subtleties. Along the way, stop at the butterfly farm, snake and insect exhibits, and bromeliad garden. The tour is packed with information—perhaps too much—but if you're visiting Costa Rica for its ecology, it's a worthwhile lesson. A restaurant serves typical Costa Rican fare, and the gift shop has souvenirs and books on natural history. ⊠ *Road between Santo Domingo and Heredia, 400 m north and 300 m west of Shell gas station; follow the signs—you can't miss it* 🕾 *507–8107* 🖃 *$15 adults, $8 kids* ☉ *Daily 8–4. Tours every hour.*

## Where to Stay & Eat

★ **$$** ✕🖫 **Hotel Bougainvillea.** You might forget that you're only 15 minutes from San José on the Bougainvillea's extensive grounds surrounded by coffee farms. The spacious and carpeted but otherwise unremarkable rooms are furnished with local hardwoods and have large balconies; get one with a view of the gardens behind the hotel. The gardens, which are shaded by large trees, hold an extensive bromeliad collection, and have ample open areas for kids, are so big that they have their own brochure. Pre-Columbian pottery and paintings by Costa Rican artists decorate the lobby and restaurant ($–$$), which serves a small but excellent selection of Continental cuisine. An hourly shuttle takes you to the Hotel Villa Tournón in San José. ⊠ *2 km/1 mi east of Santo Domingo de Heredia, Santo Tomas* 🖃 *Apdo. 69–2120, San José* 🕾 *244–1414* 🖷 *244–1313* ⊕ *www.bougainvillea.co.cr* 📥 *77 rooms, 4 suites* ♻ *Restaurant, fans, cable TV, tennis court, pool, sauna, bar, shop, laundry service, Wi-Fi, Internet, travel services, no-smoking rooms; no a/c* 🖃 *AE, DC, MC, V.*

### To & From Santo Domingo

*18 km/11 mi northeast of Escazú, 7 km/4 mi northwest of San José.*

From San José, turn right at the west end of Paseo Colón onto the Pan-American Highway (aka the Carretera General Cañas), then turn right off the highway just before it heads onto an overpass, just after the Hotel Irazú (on the right).

# Heredia

**6** With a population of around 30,000, Heredia is the capital of one of Costa Rica's most important coffee provinces, with some of the country's best-preserved colonial towns. Founded in 1706, the city bears witness to how difficult preservation can be in an earthquake-prone country: most of its colonial structures have been destroyed by the tremors and tropical climate. Still, the city and neighboring towns retain a certain historic feel, with old adobe buildings scattered amid the concrete structures. The nearby villages of Barva and Santo Domingo de Heredia have more colonial and adobe buildings, and the roads that wind through the hills above those towns pass through charming scenery and rural enclaves, making them excellent routes for exploration.

## Exploring

Heredia proper is centered around a tree-studded **Parque Central**, which is surrounded by a few historic buildings. The park has a cast-iron fountain imported from England in 1897 and a simple kiosk where the municipal band sometimes plays Sunday-morning concerts. ✉ *C. Central and Avda. Central.*

The impressive **Iglesia de la Inmaculada Concepción** is a whitewashed stone church built between 1797 and 1804 to replace an adobe temple dating from the early 1700s. Its thick stone walls, small windows, and squat buttresses have kept it intact through two centuries of quakes and tremors. It has a pale interior with marble floors and stained-glass windows, and is flanked by tidy gardens. ✉ *Eastern end of Parque Central* ☎ 237–0779 ☉ *Daily 6–6.*

To the north of the Parque Central stands a strange, decorative tower called the **Fortín** (Little Fort), which was built in the 1880s by the local oligarch Fadrique Gutiérrez. Once used as a prison, it now serves as a symbol of the province. The old brick building next to the Fortín is the Palacio Municipal (Town Hall). ✉ *C. Central and Avda. Central* ☎ *No phone* ✍ *Free* ☉ *Weekdays 8–4.*

Two blocks south of the Parque Central is Heredia's **Mercado Viejo** (Old Market), which has fewer souvenirs for sale than San José's Mercado Central but is less cramped and safer. On the next block to the southeast is the **Mercado Nuevo** (New Market), which holds dozens of *sodas* (simple restaurants). ✉ *C. Central and Avda. 6* ☉ *Mon.–Sat., 7–6.*

At the edge of a middle-class neighborhood between Heredia and Barva is the **Museo de Cultura Popular** (Museum of Popular Culture), which preserves an early-20th-century farmhouse built with an adobelike technique called *bahareque*. Run by the National University, the museum is furnished with antiques and surrounded by a small garden and coffee fields. An adjacent open-air restaurant serves inexpensive Costa Rican lunches on weekends. ✉ *Between Heredia and Barva; follow signs* ☎ 260–1619 ✍ *$1* ☉ *Daily 9–4.*

★ The producer of Costa Rica's most popular export-quality coffee, **Café Britt,** gives a lively tour that highlights Costa Rica's history of coffee cultivation through a theatrical presentation that is admittedly a bit hokey. From the get-go, your "tour guides" are professional actors, but good actors to be sure, and if you don't mind the song and dance, it's fun. Take a short walk through the coffee farm and processing plant, and learn how professional coffee tasters distinguish a fine cup of java. One major difference between this tour and that of Doka Estate in Alajuela is that Doka takes you through the processing mill. Britt, ever the innovators, are adding this aspect as well as bike tours through coffee fields. ✉ *From Heredia, take road to Barva; follow signs* ☎ 260–2748 ⊕ *www.cafebritt.com* ✍ *$19, $26 with transportation, $34 with transportation and lunch* ☉ *Tours Dec.–May daily at 9, 11, and 3, and June–Nov. daily at 11.*

## Where to Stay

**$$$–$$$$**
FodorśChoice
★

☒ **Finca Rosa Blanca Country Inn.** There's nothing common about this luxurious little B&B overlooking coffee farms; you need only step through the front door of the Gaudí-esque main building to marvel at its soaring ceiling, white-stucco arches, and polished wood. Each guest

# Coffee, the Golden Bean

WHEN COSTA RICA'S FIRST elected president, Juan Mora Fernandez, began encouraging his compatriots to cultivate coffee back in 1830, he could hardly have imagined how profound an impact the crop would have on his country. Over the last 100 years coffee has transformed Costa Rica from a colonial backwater into a relatively affluent and cosmopolitan republic.

It was the "golden bean" that financed the construction of most of the nation's landmarks. Lured by plantation jobs, tens of thousands of immigrant families from Europe and elsewhere in the Americas moved to Costa Rica in the 1800s and early 1900s, and were given land in exchange for cutting down the forest and planting coffee. They formed the backbone of a middle-class majority that has long distinguished Costa Rica from most of the rest of Latin America.

Thanks to its altitude and mineral-rich volcanic soil, the Central Valley is ideal for growing coffee, and the crop covers nearly every arable acre of this region. But coffee is not actually native to Costa Rica: plants first arrived in Costa Rica from the Caribbean, probably in the early 1820s.

The coffee-growing cycle begins in May, when rains make the dark-green bushes explode into a flurry of white blossoms. By November the fruit starts to ripen, turning from green to red, and the busy harvest begins as farmers race to get picked "cherries" to *beneficios* (processing plants), where the beans—two per fruit—are removed, washed, dried by machine, and packed in burlap sacks for export. Costa Rica's crop is consistently among the world's best, and most of the high-grade exports wind up in Europe and the United States.

Traditionally, coffee bushes are grown in the shade of trees. Recently, however, many farmers have switched to sun-resistant varieties, cutting down shade trees to pack in more coffee bushes, and destroying habitats for migratory birds in the process. Environmentalists and many farmers are promoting a return to the old system by labeling shade coffee ECO-OK. (And shade coffee *does* actually taste better.) Though coffee prices have declined sharply since 2000, the crop still remains king in the Central Valley.

Ticos are fueled by lots of coffee, and generally make it in a *chorreador*, a wooden stand with a cloth filter—it makes a strong cup of java. Sadly, many Ticos drink the low-grade stuff, often mixed with molasses, peanuts, or corn for bulk. Most of the good stuff is exported. Reliable brands are Café Rey's Tarrazú, Café Britt, Américo, Volio, and Montaña.

room is different, but all have original art, local hardwoods, and colorful fabrics. The spacious two-story suite is out of a fairy tale, with a spiral staircase leading up to a window-lined tower bedroom. On the grounds, which are planted with tropical flowers and shaded by massive fig trees, are two two-bedroom villas. The owners try very hard to make the hotel as eco-friendly as possible, utilizing composting, solar panels, and other methods. Four-course dinners are available. ⊠ *1 km/½ mi east and 800 m north of Santa Barbara de Heredia, Barrio Jesus* ⏚ *SJO 3475, Box 025369, Miami, FL 33102-5216* ☎ *269–9392* 🖷 *269–9555* ⊕ *www.fincarosablanca.com* ⤳ *7 rooms, 2 villas* ⚭ *Dining room, fans, in-room safes, pool, whirlpool tub, horseback riding, laundry service, Internet, airport shuttle, travel services; no a/c, no room TVs* ▤ *AE, MC, V* 🍴 *BP.*

**$$** 🖼 **Hotel Valladolid** This is hands down the best hotel in downtown Heredia. The tall (for Heredia) and narrow building with a rooftop terrace has just 11 modern rooms, designed for business travelers and visiting professors at the nearby National University. The tile floors and white walls aren't exactly inspired, but are just fine for a night's sleep. ⊠ *400 m north and 100 m west of the main entrance of La Universidad Nacional (C. 7 and Avda. 7).* ☎ *260–2905* 🖷 *260–2912* ⌨ *valladol@racsa.co.cr* ⤳ *11 rooms* ⚭ *In-room safes, microwave, refrigerator, cable TV, whirlpool tub, sauna, bar, laundry service, Internet, airport pickup, no-smoking rooms* ▤ *AE, DC, MC, V* 🍴 *BP.*

**¢** 🖼 **Hotel Ceos.** Occupying an old wooden home a block north of the Parque Central, the Hotel Ceos has basic accommodations for travelers on a tight budget. Historic photos decorate the ground floor, and the rooms are painted bright colors, but are small and time-worn. The nicest spot in the place is the large balcony on the second floor, furnished with a sofa and chairs—perfect for shooting the breeze with a beer. The restaurant serves inexpensive breakfasts and light meals. ⊠ *Avda. 1 and C. Central (100 m north and 25 west of the Central Park)* ☎ *262–2628* 🖷 *262–2639* ⊕ *www.hamerica.net* ⤳ *10 rooms* ⚭ *Restaurant, fans, cable TV, laundry service; no a/c, no room phones* ▤ *AE, MC, V* 🍴 *EP.*

## To & From Heredia
*4 km/3 mi north of Santo Domingo, 11 km/6 mi northwest of San José.*

Follow directions to San Antonio de Belén (⇨ *above*). Pass by the San Antonio turnoff, and turn right off the highway just before it heads onto an overpass, just after the Hotel Irazú (on the right). To get to the center of Heredia, follow that road for several miles, then turn left at the Universidad Nacional; continue straight on this road to reach the Britt Coffee Tour, Museo de Cultura Popular, Sacramento, Barva, and points beyond. Buses run between San José and Heredia every 10 to 15 minutes daily (between 5 AM and 11 PM). If you're without a car, taxi is the recommended method for getting to Café Britt or Barva.

## Heredia Essentials
🏧 Bank/ATM **Banco Popular** ⊠ 50 m east of northeast corner of Parque Central. **Banco Nacional** ⊠ Southwest corner of Parque Central.

💊 Pharmacy **Farmacia Chavarria** ⊠ Southwest corner of Parque Central.

🌐 Internet **Internet Kfexion** ⊠ 100 m north and 25 m east of Parque Central.

✉ Mail **Correos** ⊠ Northwest corner of Parque Central. **DHL** ⊠ 300 m east of San Antonio intersection ☎ 210–3939 or 209–6000 ⊕ www.dhl.com.

en route At the center of Barva de Heredia, a small community about 3 km (2 mi) north of Heredia proper, is the **Parque Central,** surrounded by old adobe houses with Spanish tile roofs on three sides and a white

★ stucco church to the east. Flanked by royal palms, the stout, handsome church dates from the late 18th century; behind it is a lovely little garden shrine to the Virgin Mary. On a clear day you can see verdant Volcán Barva (⇨ Chapter 3) towering to the north, and if you follow the road that runs in front of the church and veer left at the Y, you will wind your way up the slopes of that volcano to Vara Blanca, where you can either drive north to the La Paz Waterfall Gardens, or continue straight to Poás Volcano National Park (⇨ Chapter 3). If you veer right at the Y and drive up the steep, narrow road, you'll pass through San José de la Montaña and Paso Llano to reach Sacramento, where the road turns into a rough dirt track leading to the Barva sector of Braulio Carrillo National Park (⇨ Chapter 3). If you turn left when you reach Barva's central plaza, you'll head to San Pedro and Santa Barbara, where roads head south to Alajuela and north to Vara Blanca.

# CARTAGO AND IRAZÚ VOLCANO

Cartago, due east of San José, was the country's first capital, and thus has scattered historical structures and the impressive Basílica de Los Angeles. To the north of Cartago towers massive Irazú Volcano, which is covered with farmland and topped by an impressive crater.

## Cartago

❼ Although it's a small city, Cartago was the country's first capital and held that title for almost three centuries. It's much older than San José, but earthquakes have destroyed most of its colonial structures, leaving just a few interesting buildings among the concrete boxes. Cartago became Costa Rica's second most prominent city in 1823, when the seat of government was moved to the emerging economic center of San José. You'll see some attractive old buildings as you move through town, most of them erected after the 1910 quake. The majority of the architecture in tiny Cartago is bland, with one impressive exception: the gaudy Basílica de Nuestra Señora de Los Angeles.

Most visitors see Cartago on their way to or from the Orosi Valley or Turrialba, and there is little reason to stay the night. The Orosi Valley, a short drive away, has better choices.

### Exploring

Churches in some form or another have stood at the site of the present-day Parque Central since 1575, and have been knocked down by earthquakes and reconstructed many times. Undetered by complete destruction in 1841, the citizens of Cartago began work on a Romanesque cathedral some years later, but the devastating earthquake of 1910 halted work and put an end to the last attempt at building a structure on the site. **Las Ruinas** (⊠ C. 1 and Avda. 2), or "the ruins" of this unfinished house of worship, now stand in a pleasant park planted with tall pines and bright bougainvillea. The friendly caretaker, *Don* Orlando, can let you in if the gates are locked. Among the many legends attributed to the ruins is the gruesome story of the priest of one of the earlier churches at the site, who after falling in love with his sister-in-law, was murdered by his brother. His ghost, dressed as a priest but headless, still haunts the grounds.

The **Basílica de Nuestra Señora de los Angeles** (Our Lady of the Angels Basilica; ✉ C. 16, between Avdas. 2 and 4, 10 blocks east of central Sq. ☎ 551–0465) is a hodgepodge of architectural styles from Baroque to Byzantine, with a dash of Gothic. The interior is even more striking, with a colorful tile floor, intricately decorated wood columns, and lots of stained glass. The church is open daily 6 AM to 7 PM. The basilica is also the focus of an annual pilgrimage to celebrate the appearance of La Negrita, or the Black Virgin, Costa Rica's patron saint.

## Where to Eat
*Haute cuisine* just doesn't exist here. Instead, Cartago gives you a fine opportunity eat some *comida típica*. On just about any street downtown you'll find a *soda* (simple café), and the women in the kitchen will serve you the same style food they cook at home for their own families. There are literally dozens of places of comparable quality. One rule of thumb: the busier the better—the locals know where to eat well.

## To & From Cartago
*22 km/14 mi southeast of San José.*

From San José, drive east on Avenida 2 through San Pedro, then follow signs from the intersection to Cartago. Shortly before Cartago, a traffic light marks the beginning of the road up Irazú, with traffic to Cartago veering right. Buses between San José and Cartago leave every 5 minutes daily, from 5 AM to midnight.

## Cartago Essentials
🏦 Bank/ATM **Banco de Costa Rica** ✉ Av. 2 and C. 8. ATM ✉ Avda. 2 and C. 6.
🏦 Pharmacy **Farmacia Central** ✉ Just south of Las Ruinas.
🏦 Internet **Internet Alta Velocidad** ✉ 50 m south of southwest corner of Las Ruinas in small shopping center.
🏦 Post Office **Correos** ✉ 25 m west of Avda. 2 and C. 13.

# Volcán Irazú

**❽** Volcán Irazú is Costa Rica's highest volcano, at 11,260 feet, and its summit has long been protected as a national park. The mountain looms to the north of Cartago, and its eruptions have dumped considerable ash on the city over the centuries. The most recent eruptive period lasted from 1963 to 1965, beginning the day John F. Kennedy arrived in Costa Rica for a presidential visit. Boulders and mud rained down on the countryside, damming rivers and causing serious floods. Although farmers who cultivate Irazú's slopes live in fear of the next eruption, they're also grateful for the soil's richness, a result of the volcanic deposits.

The road to the summit climbs past vegetable fields, pastures, and native oak forests. You pass through the villages of Potrero Cerrado and San Juan de Chicoá before reaching the summit's bleak but beautiful

CLOSE UP

## La Negrita

ON THE NIGHT OF AUGUST 1 and well into the early morning hours of August 2, the road to Cartago from San José clogs with worshippers, some of whom have traveled from as far away as Nicaragua to celebrate the 1635 appearance of Costa Rica's patron saint, La Negrita (the Black Virgin). At a spring behind the church, people fill bottles with water believed to have curative properties. Miraculous healing powers are attributed to the saint, and devotees have placed thousands of tiny symbolic crutches, ears, eyes, and legs next to her diminutive statue. Tour buses and school groups, along with shops selling the saint's likeness, make the scene a bit of a circus. The statue has twice been stolen, most recently in 1950 by José León Sánchez, now one of Costa Rica's best-known novelists, who spent 20 years on the prison island of San Lucas for having purloined the Madonna.

crater. Irazú is currently dormant, but the gases and steam that billow from fumaroles on the northwestern slope are sometimes visible from the peak above the crater lookouts. ■ TIP→→ Set out as early in the morning as possible—before the summit is enveloped in clouds—and wear warm, waterproof clothing. When conditions are clear, you can see the chartreuse crater lake and, if you're lucky, views of nearby mountains and either the Pacific or Caribbean in the distance. There are no trails at the summit, but a paved road leads all the way to the top, where a small coffee shop sells hot beverages and there's a tiny visitor's kiosk (often closed). Before reaching the park's main entrance, about 1 km (½ mi) from the village of Potrero Cerrado, Volcán Irazú's **Area Recreativa de Prusia** (Prusia Recreation Area) has hiking trails through oak and pine forest. It also has picnic areas. ☎ 551–9398, or 200–5025 for the ranger station, 192 in Costa Rica ☒ $7 ☉ Daily 8–3:30.

### Where to Eat

¢–$ ✕ **Restaurant 1910.** Decorated with vintage photos of turn-of-the-20th-century buildings and landscapes, this restaurant documents the disastrous 1910 earthquake that rocked this area and all but destroyed the colonial capital of Cartago. The menu is predominantly Costa Rican, with such traditional specialties as *pozol* (corn and pork soup) and arroz con pollo (chicken and rice). One of the less common dishes is corvina fillet with béarnaise sauce. ☒ *Road to Parque Nacional Volcán Irazú; 300 m north of Cot–Pacayas turnoff* ☎ 536–6063 ☒ AE, MC, V.

### To & From Volcán Irazú

*31 km/19 mi northeast of Cartago, 50 km/31 mi east of San José.*

Follow directions to Cartago ( ➪ *above*), but shortly before the city a traffic light marks the beginning of the road up Irazú; traffic to Cartago veers right. From downtown Cartago, take the road to Irazú at the north-

*Continued on page 87*

# DRIVING THE OROSI VALLEY LOOP

**Gardens, Churches, and Landscapes.** This classic day trip—popular with locals but still off the beaten tourist path—is not something you find in most guide books. But if you've got a day to spend near San José, we highly recommend this route past coffee plantations, small towns, and verdant landscapes, with countless breathtaking views. The region is unique because it is one of the few areas in Costa Rica that still has remnants (ruins and churches) of 17th-century Spanish colonialism. But the highlight of the tour is spending at least a couple of hours in Tapantí National Park tracking the resplendent quetzal or marveling at the many orchid species.

■ TIP→→Traffic jams are rarely a problem, but expect company on weekends from fellow motorists—and mountain bikes. (Costa Rica's Olympic cycling team trains here.)

## The Drive

Start from Cartago, 22 km (14 mi) southeast of San José. At the basílica in the center of town turn left onto the busy road to Paraíso and Orosi. After 6 km (4 mi), a blue sign on the right marks the short road to the lush gardens of the **Jardín Botánico Lankester** (☎ 552-3247 ☞ $5 ☉ Daily 8:30–4:30), one of the world's foremost orchid collections, with more than 1,100 native and introduced species of orchids. Bromeliads, heliconias, and aroids also abound, along with 80 species of trees, including rare palms. The best time to come is January through April, when the most orchids are in bloom. The garden's gift shop is one of the few places in Costa Rica to buy orchids that you can take home legally. (They come in small bottles and don't flower for four years, so you'll need some serious patience.) Admission is $5; the garden is open daily 8:30–4:30.

Head east toward Paraíso and then into the town itself. Hang a right at the central park. Some 2 km (1 mi) beyond is the **Sanchiri Mirador,** one of the valley's best *miradores* (lookout points). But our favorite vantage point is at a point on the road just beyond Sanchiri where the earth appears to drop away, and the valley comes into view as you make the steep descent to the town of Orosi. Here's a case for letting someone else do the driving.

Many a visitor has wondered, upon first seeing dreary Paraíso, with its concrete-block buildings and crowded

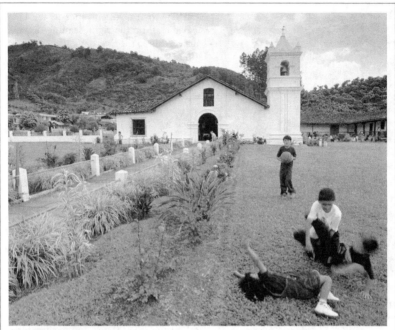

Orosi church

roads, how it ended up with so prodigious a name as "Paradise." But you need merely drive a couple of kilometers south from the central park and gaze down at the vast Orosi Valley to understand what inspired the town's founders. For travelers, Paraíso is on the map for only two reasons: it is the gateway to Orosi, and it has one of the country's best botanical gardens.

The town of Orosi, in the heart of the valley, has but one major attraction: the beautifully restored 1743 **Iglesia de San José de Orosi** (⊠ Across from soccer field, center of town ☎ No phone). It's the country's oldest church still in use, and one of the only structures still remaining from the colonial era. It has a low-slung whitewashed facade; the roof is made of cane overlaid with terra-cotta barrel tiles. Inside are an antique wooden altar and ancient paintings of the stations of the cross and the Virgin of Guadalupe, all brought to Costa Rica from Mexico. If you can find someone to open it for you, also take a look inside the religious-art museum next door. Admission to the museum is 50¢ and hours vary. The church is open daily 9–5.

It's not a must-do stop, but if you're craving relaxation, the **Balneario** (Thermal Baths; ⊠ South of Orosi on road to Orosi Lodge), fed by a hot spring, are open to the public for a nominal fee (less than $1) Wednesday through Monday, 7:30–4.

South from Orosi, the road becomes a rugged track following the Río Grande de Orosi past coffee plantations, elegant *fincas* (farmhouses), and seasonal barracks for coffee pickers before it's hemmed in by the steep slopes of thick jungle. At the bottom of the loop road, deviate (follow signs) to enter **Tapantí**

Resplendent quetzal

**National Park** (⊠ 14 km/8 mi south of Orosi ☎ 551–2970). Though it's worth the trip for just an hour or two of exploring, you could easily fill a day in the park. Stretching from the southern corner of the Orosi Valley up into the Talamanca Mountains, Parque Nacional Tapantí encompasses 47 square km (18 square mi) of largely pristine, remote cloud forest. It provides refuge for more than 350 bird species, including the emerald toucanet, violaceous trogon, most of the country's hummingbirds, and the resplendent quetzal. Quetzals are most readily visible in the dry season (mid-December to April), when they mate.

The rangers' office and visitor center are on the right just after the park entrance. You can leave your vehicle at a parking area 1½ km (1 mi) up the road. From here loop trails head off into the woods on both sides. One trail passes a picnic area and several swimming holes with (cold) emerald waters. The other trail is along a forested hillside. About 2½ km (1½ mi) up from the

parking area is an entrance to the La Pava Trail on the right, leading down a steep hill to the riverbank. If you continue 1½ km (1 mi) past the trailhead you arrive at a 500-foot trail leading to a lookout. Since the park clouds up in the afternoon, it's best to get an early start. Admission to the park is $7; it's open weekdays 8–4, weekends 7–5.

Amid coffee farms on the eastern end of the Orosi Valley, the village of Cachí survives on two industries: coffee and electricity. In the 1960s the national power company, ICE, dammed the Reventazón River near Cachí to create a reservoir for what was once the country's biggest hydroelectric project. The Represa de Cachí (Cachí Dam) is the closest thing the town has to a tourist attraction, and is worth stopping at for the view of the reservoir and narrow Reventazón Valley, but most people stop here to eat at the Casona del Cafetal, just north of town, and to shop for crafts at the Casa del Soñador.

Head back to the loop road and drive 15 km (9 mi) north, past the town of Cachí. Just before the Cachí Dam lies the immensely popular restaurant **La Casona del Cafetal** (⇨ Where to Eat *in* Cachí). It is touristy, but great fun, and well worth a stop for a late lunch. You'll have lots of company on a Sunday, the traditional maid's day off in Tico homes. Stop in at the unique artisan shop **Casa del Soñador** (House of the Dreamer; ⊠ 1 km/½ mi south of the Cachí Dam ☎ 577–1186 or 577–1983), established by local wood sculptor Macedonio Quesada. Though Macedonio died years ago, his son Miguel and a former apprentice are still here, carving interesting, often comical little statues out of coffee roots. You can learn about the carving process through a day-long apprenticeship, free of charge. The shop is open daily 11–6.

Continue past the dam into the small hamlet of Ujarrás, then follow the signs to the site of the ruins of Costa Rica's first church, **Iglesia de Ujarrás** (✉ In a small park, 1 km/½ mi from Restaurante Típico Ujarrás, Ujarrás). Built between 1681 and 1693 in honor of the Virgin of Ujarrás, the church, together with the surrounding village, was abandoned in 1833 after a series of earthquakes and floods wreaked havoc here, at the lowest point of the Orosi Valley. An unlikely Spanish victory in 1666 over a superior force of invading British pirates was attributed to a prayer stop here. The site is open daily 8–5. A final 6-km (3½-mi) drive to Paraíso from Ujarrás completes the loop.

### Logistics

Renting a car in San José is the best way to go. Public transportation is a partial option only; buses run clockwise from Paraíso to Cachí or counterclockwise to Orosi, but neither route completes the loop. Several San José tour operators offer this excursion as a guided day

Coffee Fields

trip from the capital. One such company is **Lava Tours** (☎ 278–2558, 888/862–2424 in the U.S. 🖷 413/410–2583 in U.S. ⊕ www.lava-tours.com), whose loop tour around Cachí Lake is $85.

2

DRIVING THE OROSI VALLEY LOOP

## WHERE TO STAY AND EAT

### PARAÍSO

**$–$$ ✕ 🖼 Sanchirí Mirador.** The greatest asset of this rustic place is its amazing view, from a hillside high above the valley. The large open-air restaurant ($–$$), partially enclosed by windows, has simple wooden chairs, flowery tablecloths, and a menu dominated by Costa Rican standards such as *arroz con pollo* (rice with chicken). Twelve modern rooms were built in early 2005 to go with 10 older wooden cabins. All of the new rooms have the view, but only 3 of the cabins do. The rooms themselves are nothing spectacular, but waking up to the view is well worth the modest price. ✉ *2 km/1 mi south of Parque Cen-* *tral* ☎574–5454 🖷 574–8586 ⊕ *www.* *sanchiri.com* ➷ *22 rooms* ♻ *Restaurant, cable TV, bar, playground, laundry services, Internet; no a/c in some rooms* 🖃 *AE, DC, MC, V* ⏏ *BP.*

### CACHÍ

**★ $–$$ ✕ La Casona del Cafetal.** The valley's best lunch stop is on a coffee plantation overlooking the Cachí Reservoir. It's firmly on the beaten path, which means frequent visits from tour groups. The spacious brick building has a high barrel-tile roof, with tables indoors and on a tiled portico on the lake side. Casados and other Costa Rican staples accompany inventive dishes such as *arroz* *tucurrique* (baked rice with cheese and heart of palm) and corvina *jacaranda* (stuffed with shrimp). After lunch, take a stroll down to the lake. The **gift shop** sells similar sculptures to those fashioned at Casa del Soñador. But unless you'll be at the restaurant anyway, go directly to the latter shop for crafts—it's far superior. ✉ *2 km/ 1 mi south of Cachí Dam* ☎ *577–1414* 🚪 *AE, DC, MC, V* ☾ *No dinner.*

¢–$ ✕ **Soda El Chilito Mexicano.** A great alternative to the touristy La Casona is this little café with some vaguely Mexican choices on the menu, but prepared Tico-style. This is where the locals eat, and it's good. ✉ *Next to the soccer field* ☎ *No phone.*

## OROSI

¢–$ ✕ **Bar y Restaurante Coto.** The only show in town, this place has good food and a location right on the plaza. Options range from sandwiches to filet mignon, seafood dishes, and tenderloin in a "secret" *Orosi* sauce. ✉ *North side of Plaza de Deportes (soccer field)* ☎ *533–3032* 🚪 *AE, DC, MC, V.*

$$–$$$$ 🏨 **Hotel Rio Perlas Spa & Resort.** Thermal springs fill one of the pools at this hotel squeezed into a small valley. The place has a condo community feeling, with a driveway running the length of the property and the rooms divided among many smaller buildings. Rooms are nice, but not especially luxurious or artistic; they have dark tile floors and wood furniture. There is a replica of the Orosi church on the property. ✉ *6 km/3½ mi south of Paraíso, turn right at bridge, then 2 ½ km/1½ mi; look for large sign* ☎ *533–3341 or 533–2543* 🖨 *533–3085* ⊕ *www. hotelrioperlas.com* ⇆ *32 rooms, 17 suites, 20 cabins* ⚐ *2 restaurants, room service, fans, in-room safes, cable TV, 3 pools, spa, bicycles, bar, laundry service, Internet, meeting rooms, airport pickup, no-smoking rooms; no a/c* 🚪 *AE, DC, MC, V* ⋈ *BP.*

$ 🏨 **Orosi Lodge.** Run by a German couple who have built a warm rapport with the community, the little lodge blends in with Orosi's pretty, old-town architecture: whitewashed walls are trimmed in blue, ceilings are high, and natural wood is used throughout. Some furnishings, such as the clay lamps in the rooms, are done by local artisans. Common areas are colorful, with paintings and sculpture by local artists. Beds have a single sheet and two comforters. Second-floor rooms have views of the Orosi Valley and Irazú Volcano. The hip coffee shop brews a great cup of joe, and Latin music usually plays from a 1960s' jukebox in the foyer. ✉ *50 m east of Balneario thermal baths* ☎ *533–3578* ⊕ *www.orosilodge.com* ⇆ *6 rooms* ⚐ *Dining room, fans, kitchenettes, refrigerators, minibars, mountain bikes, canoes, travel services, Internet; no a/c, no room phones, no room TVs* 🚪 *AE, DC, MC, V* ⋈ *EP.*

$ 🏨 **Kiri Mountain Lodge.** This small, family-run hotel has easy access to the park and its own 123-hectare private reserve with waterfalls and most of the same wildlife seen at Tapantí. The number of bird species in the lodge's gardens alone is impressive, especially hummingbirds. Rooms are small and simple, with tile floors and tiny bathrooms, but their porches have views of a jungle-laden hillside. The restaurant serves a small selection of Costa Rican food; fresh trout, raised in nearby ponds, is the best option. You can also catch your own trout and have them cook it for you. ✉ *Turnoff 1 km/½ mi before Tapantí park entrance* ☎ *533–2272* ⊕ *www.kirilodge.com* ⇆ *6 rooms* ⚐ *Restaurant, hiking, laundry service; no a/c, no room phones, no room TVs* 🚪 *MC, V* ⋈ *BP.*

east corner of the Basilica. Signs from Cartago lead you to the park. Buses head to Volcán Irazú from San José weekends at 8 AM and return at 12:30 PM.

# THE TURRIALBA REGION

2

The agricultural center of Turrialba and the nearby Guayabo ruins lie considerably lower than the Central Valley, so they enjoy a more tropical climate. There are two ways to reach this area from San José, both of which pass spectacular scenery. The more direct route, accessible by heading east through both Cartago and Paraíso, winds through coffee and sugar plantations before descending abruptly into Turrialba. For the second route, turn off the road between Cartago and the summit of Irazú near the town of Cot. That narrow route twists along the slopes of Irazú and Turrialba volca-

> **WORD OF MOUTH**
>
> "There really isn't much in Turrialba. Probably why I want to live there."
>
> –Suzie2

noes past some stunning scenery—stately pollarded trees lining the road, riotous patches of tropical flowers, and white-girder bridges across crashing streams. From Santa Cruz, a hiking trail leads up to the 10,900-foot summit of Volcán Turrialba. As you begin the descent to Turrialba town, the temperature rises and sugarcane alternates with fields of neat rows of coffee bushes.

## Turrialba

➒ The relatively well-to-do agricultural center of Turrialba (population 30,000) suffered when the main San José–Puerto Limón route was diverted through Guápiles in the late 1970s. The demise of the famous Jungle Train that connected these two cities was an additional blow. But today, because of the beautiful scenery and a handful of upscale nature lodges, ecotourism is increasingly the focus of the town's efforts. The damming of the Reventazón river has cut down on the number of tourists, but significant numbers of kayakers and rafters flock here to run the Pacuare. Turrialba has two major factories: Conair, which you'll see on the road to Siquirres, and a Rawlings factory, which makes all the baseballs used in the Major Leagues. Though pleasant enough and with a youthful vibe from the nearby university and the white-water folk, Turrialba doesn't have much to offer, but the surrounding countryside hides some spectacular scenery and patches of rain forest. Finally, there's Volcán Turrialba, which you can ascend on foot or horseback, and it's well worth the effort.

### Exploring

Athough you can't easily drive up to its summit as you can at Poás and Irazú, **Volcán Turrialba** is still worth visiting. The easiest way to arrange the excursion is to call the **Volcán Turrialba Lodge** (☎ 273–4335) and request a guide. You can ascend the 11 km (7 mi) on foot in 3 to 4 hours or more quickly on horseback, and at 3,329 m (1,820 ft) with luck you'll see clear down to the Caribbean coast. On the road that runs from Pacayas

## White-Water Thrills

**★ Fodor's Choice**

**YOU'RE STRUGGLING TO HANG** on and paddle, you can't hear a thing over the roar, and you were just slammed with a mighty wall of water. Sound like fun? Then you're in the right place. The Río Pacuare and the Río Reventazón draw rafters and kayakers from all over the world to Turrialba. Right next to Turrialba, the Reventazón has Class II, III, and IV rapids. The Pacuare, farther from Turrialba, has a spectacular 32-km (20-mi) run with a series of Class III and IV rapids. The scenery includes lush canyons where waterfalls plummet into the river and expanses of rain forest.

Nearly every outfitter has day trips, but some also have multiday trips that include jungle hikes. Nature Adventures and Ríos Tropicales ( ⇨ *Central Valley Planner* at the beginning of this chapter) even have their own lodges on the river. Age requirements for children vary by outfitter. The typical trip starts with an hour-long van ride to the put-in. After the first half of the run, guides flip one of the rafts over to form a crude lunch table. Then you continue up the river to Siquirres, and pile back in the van for the ride home.

It would be unwise to choose your company based merely on price: those with bargain rates are probably skimping somewhere. Good outfitters require you to wear life vests and helmets, have CPR-certified river guides with near-fluent English skills, and have kayakers accompany the rafts in case of emergencies. A 5:1 guest-to-guide ration is good, 10:1 is not. Local Turrialba companies have better prices and allow you to book a trip at the last minute. Hotels and travel agencies book trips with larger outfitters, who can pick you up from nearly anywhere in the Central Valley. Prices range from about $70 to $100.

Falling out of the raft happens all the time, and is no big deal. The worst-case scenario is getting caught underwater or under the raft, but surprisingly, most fatalities are heart-attack victims, so don't participate if you're high-risk. You should also be able to swim. Almost every long-standing company has had a death—it is simply the reality of the business. Don't hesitate to ask about safety records. The vast majority of trips, however, are pure exhilarating fun.

Plans are in the works to dam the Pacuare. This would be the last nail in the coffin for the rafting industry (the Reventazón was dammed in the 1960s) and would destroy one of nature's real gems. Locals will surely put up a fight, but run it now while you can.

to Turrialba through Santa Cruz there is a signed turnoff west of Santa Cruz that leads up the mountain. The drive up is 15 km (9 mi) and starts paved, but the road gets worse the higher you go. In most cases you'll need a 4WD to make the last section before the trailhead, which is in a very small community called La Central de Turrialba. The road veers left toward the Volcán Turrialba Lodge, while a very washed out road leads right toward the summit (that's where you need to head if you're going on your own). You can park on the left just after the school; usually someone is around to charge you a few dollars for the privilege. Get an early start and dress for the weather—it can get quite chilly up there even during the day. There is no charge to enter, but this may change. For general National Park information, dial 192 in Costa Rica. Some claim that a 4WD vehicle can still make it up the "road" to the summit in the dry season, but don't count on this.

off the
beaten
path

A good place for bird-watching, the **CENTRO AGRONÓMICO TROPICAL DE INVESTIGACIÓN Y ENSEÑANZA** (Center for Tropical Agricultural Research and Education), better known by its acronym, CATIE, is one of the leading tropical research centers in the world. You might catch sight of the yellow-winged northern jacana or the purple gallinule in the lagoon near the main building. The 8-square-km (3-square-mi) property includes landscaped grounds, seed-conservation chambers, greenhouses, orchards, experimental agricultural projects, a large swath of rain forest, labs and offices, and lodging for students and teachers. A muddy trail leads down into the forest behind the administration building, where you can see the lake that once was rapids on the Reventazón River. The CATIE staff are working to improve visitor access, with a tour of the impressive Botanical Garden planned for the future (at which time an entrance fee will be levied. ⊠ *Just outside Turrialba, on the road to Siquirres* ☎ *558–2000 or 556–6431* ⊕ *www.catie.ac.cr* ☞ *Free* ⊘ *Weekdays 7–3.*

On the slopes of Turrialba Volcano is **Guayabo National Monument,** Costa Rica's most significant archaeological site. It's interesting, but definitely no Chichén Itzá. In 1968 a local landowner was out walking her dogs when she discovered what she thought was a tomb. A friend, archaeologist Carlos Piedra, began excavating the site and unearthed the base wall of a chief's house in what eventually turned out to be the ruins of a large community (around 20,000 inhabitants) covering 49 acres. The city was abandoned in AD 1400, probably because of disease or starvation. A guided tour in Spanish takes you through the rain forest to a *mirador* (lookout) from which you can see the layout of the excavated circular buildings. Only the raised foundations survive, since the conical houses themselves were built of wood. The hillside jungle is captivating, and the trip is further enhanced by bird-watching possibilities: sacklike nests of oropéndolas hang from many of the trees. If you arrive from the east via the Santa Teresita (Lajas) route, you can make it in any car, but via the alternative Santa Cruz route you'll need a four-wheel-drive vehicle to get here. ⊠ *A few blocks east of Turrialba's central plaza, take road north 19 km/12 mi; follow signs* ☎ *559–1220, 192 in Costa Rica* ☞ *$4* ⊘ *Daily 8–3:30.*

## Outdoor Activities

Foot and horseback are the best ways to reach the summit of Turrialba Volcano. **Volcán Turrialba Lodge** (☎ 273–4335) arranges guided horseback and hiking trips.

## Where to Stay & Eat

¢–$   ✕ **La Garza Bar y Restaurante.** Similar to La Feria in scope but slightly more atmospheric and with a bar, La Garza also runs the gamut from hamburgers to chicken, but has a better seafood selection. (Sorry veg-etarians, "beetsteak" is a misprint.) ⊠ *Northwest corner of the park* ☎ *556–1073* ☰ *AE, DC, MC, V.*

¢–$ ✕ **Restaurante La Feria.** This family-style restaurant has the usual midscale Costa Rican fare, ranging from fast food to "filet mignon." Casados and gallo pinto compete with more familiar chicken and seafood dishes. Even spaghetti is on the menu. ⊠ *Just west of Hotel Wagelia, at the entrance to town* ☎ *556–0386* ☰ *AE, DC, MC, V* ☉ *Tues. lunch only.*

$$$$ 🏨 **Rancho Naturalista.** Customized guided bird-watching and horseback tours within a 150-acre private nature reserve are the reasons to stay here. The ranch is a birder's paradise and the narrow focus may be too much for nonbird-watchers not interested in riding horses. More than 400 species of birds and thousands of different kinds of moths and butterflies live on the reserve and nearby sites, and a resident ornithologist helps you see and learn as much as you want. The two-story lodge is upscale modern with rustic touches, as are the separate cabins. Good home cooking is served in the indoor and outdoor dining rooms, both of which have beautiful views of Volcán Irazú and Turrialba Valley. Guided tours, meals, and your birding guide are all included in the price. ⊠ *20 km southeast of Turrialba, 1½ km/1 mi along a semipaved road from Tuís* ✆ *SBO 840, Box 025292, Miami, FL 33102* ☎ *433–8278 for reservations, 554–8100 for directions* 🖶 *433–4925* ⊕ *www.costaricagateway. com/lodges* ➳ *16 rooms, 14 with bath* ♿ *Dining room, horseback riding, Internet, airport pickup; no a/c, no room phones, no room TVs, no smoking* ☰ *No credit cards* ⧉| *FAP.*

★ $$$ 🏨 **Casa Turire.** Backed by a sugar plantation and overlooking an artificial lake, this timeless hotel looks like a manor house that has survived mysteriously intact from the turn of the 20th century. In fact, it's the product of more recent imaginations. From the royal palms that line the driveway to the tall columns and tile floors, Casa Turire is an exercise in elegance and attention to detail. High-ceilinged guest rooms have hardwood floors and furniture, small balconies, and bright bathrooms with tubs. The central courtyard is a civilized spot in which to relax after a day's adventure, and the restaurant serves reasonably priced international cuisine. The master suite is exceptional, built on two floors with a huge wraparound balcony. ⊠ *8 km/5 mi south on Carretera a la Suiza from Turrialba, Apdo. 303–7150* ☎ *531–1111* 🖶 *531–1075* ⊕ *www. hotelcasaturire.com* ➳ *12 rooms, 4 suites* ♿ *Restaurant, room service, fans, in-room safes, cable TV, pool, whirlpool tub, massage, bike rental, boating, bar, shop, laundry service, Internet, meeting rooms, travel services; no a/c in some rooms* ☰ *AE, MC, V* ⧉| *BP.*

$ 🏨 **Turrialtico.** Dramatically positioned on a hill overlooking the valley east of Turrialba, this hotel has impressive views of the surrounding countryside. An open-sided restaurant occupies the ground floor, above which are handsome rooms with hardwood floors and (in some rooms) colorful Guatemalan fabrics. Ask for one on the west side—these have dazzling views of Turrialba and, if there are no clouds, Volcán Irazú. The restaurant serves a small selection of authentic Costa Rican dishes cooked on a woodstove. The only problem is that the rustic wooden construction makes the rooms anything but soundproof. ⊠ *8 km/5 mi*

*east of Turrialba on road to Siquirres, Apdo. 121–7150* ☎ *538–1111
or 538–1415* 🖷 *538–1575* ⊕ *www.turrialtico.com* 🏷 *19 rooms*
♨ *Restaurant, fans, shop, laundry service, horseback riding; no a/c, no
room phones, no room TVs* ☰ *AE, MC, V* ⑩ *BP.*

**$** 🏨 **Volcán Turrialba Lodge.** On the slope of the volcano, usually accessible only by 4WD (which the lodge will arrange for a fee), the lodge has simple but comfortable rooms, most with a woodstove. You'll eat well too: the proprietors serve healthful Costa Rican food cooked on a wood-burning stove. Even more compelling are the tours, one of which goes deep into the Turrialba crater, and another of which visits the fumaroles and thermal waters of Volcán Irazú. Mountain-biking and horseback-riding trips can be arranged, as well as a 10-hour trek from the Volcán Turrialba to Guápiles via Braulio Carrillo National Park. This place is not for everyone—it gets chilly up here over 9,000 feet, but it's a unique mountain escape and a great value. ■ TIP→→ Day-trippers are welcome. ⊠ *20 km/12 mi east of Cot, turn right at Pacayas on the road to Volcán Turrialba, 4 km/2½ mi on dirt Rd.* 🖃 *Apdo. 1632–2050, San José* ☎☎ *273–4335* 🖷 *273–0703* ⊕ *www.volcanturrialbalodge.com* 🏷 *28 rooms* ♨ *Dining room, bar, handicapped accessible rooms; no a/c, no room phones, no room TVs* ☰ *AE, DC, MC, V* ⑩ *FAP.*

### To & From Turrialba
*58 km/36 mi east of San José.*

The road through Cartago and Paraíso continues east to Turrialba, where you pick up another road a few blocks east of that town's central plaza. Marked by signs, this road leads north to Guayabo National Monument. Buses between San José and Turrialba leave hourly from 8 to 8. Buses to Cartago, San José, and Limón depart frequently from Avda. 4, between Calles 2 and Central.

### Turrialba Essentials
🏧 Bank/ATM **Banco Nacional** ⊠ C. 1 at Avda. Central. **Banco de Costa Rica** ⊠ C. 3 at Avda. Central.

🏥 Hospital **Hospital Dr. William Allen** ⊠ Avda. 2, 100 m west of C. 4.

💊 Pharmacy **Farmacia Colón** ⊠ Avda. Central, between Cs. 2 and 4.

💻 Internet **Café Net Turrialba** ⊠ Avda. Central, between Cs. 1 and 3.

✉ Post Office **Correos** ⊠ Avda. 8 at C. Central.

🚕 Taxi **Transgalo** ☎ 556–9393.

# CENTRAL VALLEY ESSENTIALS

## Transportation

**BY AIR**

There is no regional air travel within the Central Valley.

ARRIVING &
DEPARTING The Juan Santamaría International Airport (10 km/6 mi) is just outside Alajuela. You can get taxis from the airport to any point in the Central Valley for $8 to $50. Immediately outside the terminal, you'll see a booth where you can hire a taxi. Some hotels arrange pickup. For more information, *see* Air Travel *in* Smart Travel Tips A to Z.

## BY BUS

ARRIVING &
DEPARTING

Buses leave the international airport for Alajuela several times an hour; from Alajuela you can catch buses to Grecia, Sarchí, and San Ramón. Less frequent buses (one to three per hour) serve Heredia. For travel between the airport and Escazú, Cartago, or Turrialba, you have to change buses in San José, which usually necessitates a taxi ride between bus terminals. All buses heading toward San José from Alajuela can drop you off at the airport, but you need to ask the driver when you board, and then remind him again as you draw near to the stop, *"Aeropuerto, por favor"* ("Airport, please"). For more information, *see* Bus Travel *in* Smart Travel Tips A to Z.

GETTING
AROUND

Many visitors never consider taking a local bus to get around, but doing so puts you in close contact with locals—an experience you miss out on if you travel by taxi or tour bus. It's also cheap. If your Spanish and sense of direction are up to snuff and you have the time, give it a shot. Your hotel can help you get to the correct bus stop and get you a current schedule. Always opt for the taxi at night or when you're in a hurry.

## BY CAR

ARRIVING &
DEPARTING

Nearly all points in the western Central Valley can be reached by car. For San Antonio de Belén, Heredia, Alajuela, and points beyond from San José, turn right at the west end of Paseo Colón onto the Pan-American Highway (Carretera General Cañas). All the attractions in the eastern Central Valley are accessible from San José by driving east on Avenida 2 through San Pedro, then following signs from the intersection to Cartago. To get to the Orosi Valley, head straight through Cartago, turn right at the Basílica de Los Angeles, and follow the signs to Paraíso. The road through Cartago and Paraíso continues east to Turrialba.

GETTING
AROUND

The best way to get around the Central Valley is by car. Most of the car-rental agencies in San José (⇨ chapter 1) have offices at the airport in Alajuela. They will deliver vehicles and contracts to any of the hotels listed in this chapter, except those in Turrialba and the Orosi Valley.

## BY SHUTTLE VAN

A more comfortable (air-conditioned!) and quicker alternative to regular bus service are the hotel-to-hotel shuttle services offered by Interbus and Gray Line. Both have a long list of destinations around the country. For more information, *see* Shuttle Van Services under Bus Travel, *in* Smart Travel Tips A to Z.

## BY TAXI

All Central Valley towns have taxis, which usually wait for fares along the central parks. Taxis in Alajuela, Cartago, and Heredia can take you up to Poás, Irazú, and Barva volcanoes, but the trips are quite expensive (about $50). If you don't have a car, the only way to get to Tapantí National Park is to take a cab from Orosi (about $10).

# Contacts & Resources

Banks, Internet cafés, post offices, and emergency contacts follow each town listed in the chapter.

## BANKS & EXCHANGING SERVICES

There are ATMs in just about every Central Valley town, and most of them accept both Visa and MasterCard, but some accept only one of the two. Shopping centers and some gas stations have ATMs. Bank branches in all but the tiniest Central Valley towns exchange U.S. dollars, though it's quicker to get *colones* from an ATM. Most hotels, restaurants, tour operators, taxi drivers, and gift shops accept or change U.S. dollars, though at slightly less than the bank rate.

## INTERNET

Internet cafés are very common in Central Valley towns, and tend to charge the equivalent of $1 per hour. In most towns you can find one or more within easy walking distance of the central park. Many hotels offer Internet access, but some of them charge as much as $3–$6 per hour.

## MAIL & SHIPPING

Nearly every town in the Central Valley has a post office, which is usually facing or near the central plaza, but letters mailed from San José arrive faster. Shipping is best done in San José, though DHL has an office in Heredia.

# The Northern Plains

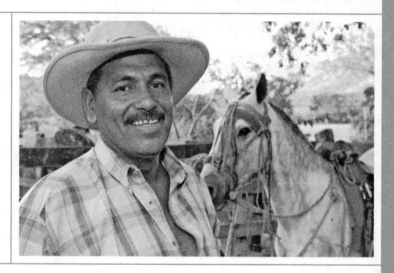

Guanacaste cowboy

**WORD OF MOUTH**

"I loved Tabacón and would go back to Arenal just for the hot springs. It's like a garden of Eden, very lush and green."

—vancouvergirl

"Just got back from Monteverde and I can easily say it was one of the highlights of our trip. The scenery is astounding and wildlife is amazing . . . The only negative [aspect] is the drive there, which is as unimaginably horrendous as it is beautiful."

—Skoob

# WELCOME TO THE NORTHERN PLAINS

Sky Trek, Monteverde

## TOP 5
## Reasons to Go

**1** **Walk in a cloud (forest):** Explore Monteverde's misty world on SkyWalk, a series of treetop walkways up to 138 feet off the ground.

**2** **Windsurfing:** Lake Arenal is one of the top windsurfing spots on earth; winds can reach 50-60 mph December through April.

**3** **Arenal Volcano:** You can hear the rumblings of the world's third most active volcano for miles around, and, on clear nights, watch crimson lava ooze down its flanks.

**4** **Watching wildlife:** Water birds, monkeys, turtles, crocodiles, jaguars, and sloths abound in the 25,000-acre Caño Negro National Wildlife Refuge.

**5** **Walk down to the waterfall:** The reward for a tough hike down to Catarata Fortuna is a magnificent series of waterfalls.

Home to the rainiest of rain forests, the Monteverde Cloud Forest Area is also the canopy-tour capital of Costa Rica. Hanging bridges, treetop tram tours, and zip-lines: it's got it all. As if that's not enough, there are horseback riding, rappelling, and nature hikes.

Sky Walk, Monteverde

Rincón de la Vieja National Park

# Getting Oriented

Geographically, the Zona Norte (Northern Zone), as it is known locally, separates neatly into two alluvial plains. The rich, lush terrain runs from the base of the Cordillera Central in the south to the Río San Juan, on the border with Nicaragua in the north. Most visitors begin their visit to Costa Rica in San José, and then head north to La Fortuna, using it as a base to explore the volcano, waterfall, and Caño Negro, and to participate in activities like sportfishing, windsurfing and kitesurfing at Lake Arenal, and rafting on the Sarapiquí River.

Egret, Caño Negro

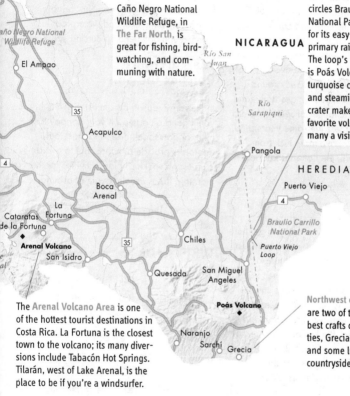

Caño Negro National Wildlife Refuge, in The Far North, is great for fishing, bird-watching, and communing with nature.

The Puerto Viejo Loop circles Braulio Carrillo National Park, rare for its easy-to-access primary rain forest. The loop's highlight is Poás Volcano; its turquoise crater lake and steaming main crater make it the favorite volcano of many a visitor.

The Arenal Volcano Area is one of the hottest tourist destinations in Costa Rica. La Fortuna is the closest town to the volcano; its many diversions include Tabacón Hot Springs. Tilarán, west of Lake Arenal, is the place to be if you're a windsurfer.

Northwest of San José are two of the country's best crafts communities, Grecia and Sarchí, and some luxurious countryside lodges.

Arenal Volcano

Hiking down to La Fortuna Waterfalls

# NORTHERN PLAINS PLANNER

## When to Go

Late November to April is considered high season. The rainy season is July–December, but the region is always hot and humid, with frequent rain. Expect highs of 32°C (90°F) and lows of 15°C (60°F). Nights are usually cool and comfortable. At almost 5,000 feet, Monteverde has a significantly different climate: It's cool and damp most of the time, with average highs around 20°C (70°F) and lows around 13°C (55°F). Visibility changes daily (and hourly), so your chances of seeing the craters are more or less the same year-round, though you may have more luck from February to April, the hottest and driest time of the year.

## Getting There

The cheapest and slowest way to get here is via public bus. The fastest and priciest is flying to La Fortuna (via NatureAir), driving yourself, or hiring a driver. A mid-range option is taking a private shuttle-bus service. Many San José–based tour companies arrange transportation and tours in the area. But La Fortuna, Arenal, and Monteverde are also full of tour companies that will arrange same-day or next-day transportation and tours for you.

## Rain Forests Are . . . Rainy

There's a reason they call it the rain forest! During the rainy season it's not unusual for it to rain for several days straight. But don't curse the wet weather—it's what keeps the forests green and gorgeous. Just bring a poncho or rain jacket and waterproof footwear so you don't end up cursing yourself.

## The Early Bird Catches the Sun

In the rainy season it's almost a given that you'll get a bit damp on your canopy tour, hike, or horseback ride, and most tour operators provide ponchos. But to avoid a thorough soaking, plan activities for the morning. Rains usually begin at around 2 PM, like clockwork, from July through December. The clearest time of day is before 8 AM.

## What to Do

| ACTIVITY | WHERE TO DO IT |
|---|---|
| Bungee Jumping | Colorado River (Grecia) |
| Canopy Tours | La Fortuna, Monteverde |
| Fishing | Lake Arenal |
| Hiking | Lake Arenal, Tilarán, La Fortuna |
| Horseback Riding | La Fortuna, Monteverde |
| Kitesurfing | Lake Arenal |
| Rafting | Sarapiquí River (La Fortuna) |
| Rappelling | La Fortuna |
| Wildlife-viewing | La Fortuna, Caño Negro, Monteverde |
| Windsurfing | Lake Arenal |

## How Much Time?

If your visit is limited to two or three days, make La Fortuna your base. Don't miss the volcano, the Tabacón Hot Springs, or Caño Negro Nature Preserve. Most tour operators who have volcano hikes end the day at the hot springs. "Half-day" tours to Caño Negro actually take most of a day, from around 7:30 AM to 4 PM. A week in the Northern Plains is more than enough time to experience a great deal of this area—especially if you're longing to get out and get moving. Give yourself four days in La Fortuna/Arenal for rafting trips on the Sarapiquí, horseback rides, and kitesurfing or windsurfing on Lake Arenal. Devote the rest of your week to Monteverde Cloud Forest.

## Choosing a Place to Stay

The La Fortuna/Arenal area has luxury resorts, mid-priced hotels, budget places, and campsites. While no longer as cheap as it was, hotel rates are low compared to American prices. If you plan to raft, hike, and go to the hot springs, a simple and comfortable cabina ($20–$40) in or around La Fortuna allows easy access to tours, restaurants, and buses—a good choice if you don't have a car. For privacy, quiet, luxury, and a volcano view, try the resorts west of Fortuna ($75–$185), closer to the volcano.

## Pack Right

It's hot and wet here much of the year, so don't think fashion, think comfort and utility. Must-haves include walking shoes (sneakers are fine unless you're planning on serious hiking), water sandals, and clothing made of quick-drying materials. Don't forget a good hat to shield your face from the sun and rain, and sunglasses. A light rain jacket or poncho, and mini umbrella are worth the space as well.

## Recommended Tour Operators

■ **Nature Adventures** (⊕ www.adventurecostarica.com) has five-day biking tours that combine Monteverde and Lake Arenal with the Central Valley.

■ **Costa Rica Expeditions** (⊕ www.costarica expeditions.com) customize almost limitless vacations.

■ **Costa Rica Study Tours** (☎ 645-7090 ⊕ www.crstudytours.com) can fix you up with all manner of excursions around Monteverde.

■ If you don't have much time, **Ecoscape Nature Tours** (☎ 297-0664 ⊕ www.escapetours.com) has an excellent daylong Sarapiquí loop tour. It also has nighttime jungle tours in the Selva Verde reserve.

■ A one-week tour with **Travel Wizard Costa Rica** (☎ 415/662-2683 in the U.S. or Canada ⊕ www.travelwizard.com) includes Arenal and Monteverde.

## Prices

| WHAT IT COSTS in Dollars | | | | | |
|---|---|---|---|---|---|
| | **$$$$** | **$$$** | **$$** | **$** | **¢** |
| **Restaurants** | over $25 | $15–$25 | $10–$15 | $5–$10 | under $5 |
| **Hotels** | over $250 | $150–$250 | $75–$150 | $50–$75 | under $50 |

Restaurant prices are per-person for a main course at dinner. Hotel prices are for two people in a standard double room in high season, excluding service and tax (16.4%).

■ TIP→→ The Web site www.monteverdeinfo.com has a wealth of information about the area.

# NORTHWEST OF SAN JOSÉ

Updated by
Joy Rothke

The rolling countryside northwest of San José and west of Alajuela holds a mix of coffee, sugarcane, and pasture, with tropical forest filling steep river valleys and ravines. The Pan-American Highway makes a steady descent to the Pacific coast through this region, which is also traversed by older roads that wind their way between simple agricultural towns and past small farms and pastoral scenery. West of San Ramón the valley becomes narrow and precipitous as the topography slopes down to the Pacific lowlands. An even narrower valley snakes northward from San Ramón to Ciudad Quesada and the northern lowlands beyond.

## Grecia

**1** Founded in 1838, the quiet farming community of Grecia is reputed to be Costa Rica's cleanest town, but the reason most people stop here is to admire its unusual church.

### Exploring

The brick-red, prefabricated iron **Iglesia** (Church) was one of two buildings in the country made from steel frames imported from Belgium in the 1890s (the other is the metal schoolhouse next to San José's Parque Morazán), when some prominent Costa Ricans decided that metal structures would better withstand the periodic earthquakes that had taken their toll on so much of the country's architecture. The frames were shipped from Antwerp to Limón, then transported by train to Alajuela—from which point the church was carried by oxcarts. ✉ *Avda. 1, between Cs. 1 and 3* ⊘ *Daily 8–4.*

On a small farm outside Grecia, the **Mundo de las Serpientes** (World of Serpents) is a good place to see some

> ### PURA VIDA, A WAY OF LIFE
>
> *Pura vida* means, literally, "pure life," and is used by Ticos—as Costa Ricans call themselves—to express agreement, greeting, leave-taking, and basically anything positive. If someone asks "¿Pura vida?" (basically, "How's it going?") the response could also be "¡Pura vida!" ("Excellent!") It might also be used to wish someone luck or to say "Have fun!" Once you set foot in this ecological wonderland, you realize that pura vida is also a philosophy of life, and undoubtedly one reason why nearly 2 million visitors come here each year.

of the snakes that you are unlikely—and probably don't want—to spot in the wild. Sequestered in the safety of cages here are some 50 varieties of serpents, as well as crocodiles, iguanas, poison dart frogs, and various other cold-blooded creatures. Admission includes a 90-minute tour. ✉ *2 km/1 mi east of Grecia, on road to Alajuela* ☎ *494–3700* ✇ *$11* ⊘ *Daily 8–4.*

### Outdoor Activities

BUNGEE JUMPING   A 265-foot-tall bridge that spans a forested gorge over the Río Colorado is the perfect place to get a rush of adrenaline in a tranquil, tropical setting. Even if you aren't up for the plunge, it's worth stopping to watch a few mad souls do it. **Tropical Bungee** (✉ Pan-American Hwy., 2 km/1 mi west of turnoff for Grecia, down a dirt road on the right ☎ 290–5629 🌐 www.bungee.co.cr) organizes trips to the bridge. The first jump is $60 and the second is $30. Reservations are essential. If it's your last hurrah in Costa Rica, a van can take you straight to the San José airport after your jump.

### Where to Stay

★ **$$–$$$** 🏨 **Vista del Valle Plantation Inn.** Honeymooners frequent this B&B on an orange and coffee plantation outside Grecia overlooking the canyon of the Río Grande. Cottages are decorated in minimalist style with simple wooden furniture and sliding doors that open onto small porches. Each has its own personality; the Nido, removed from the rest and with the nicest decor, is the most romantic. The hotel's forest reserve has an hour-long trail leading down to a waterfall. Breakfast is served by the pool or in the main house, where you can relax in a spacious living room. The food is quite good, and special dietary requests are accommodated with advance notice. It's a mere 20-minute drive from the airport. ✉ On highway, 1 km/½ mi west of Rafael Iglesia Bridge; follow signs 🏠 c/o M. Bresnan, SJO–1994, Box 025216 Miami, FL 33102-5216 ☎ 450–0800 🖨 451–1165 🌐 www.vistadelvalle.com ➷ 2 rooms, 10 cottages ᗧ Restaurant, fans, pool, whirlpool tub, horseback riding, tours; no a/c, no room phones, no room TVs ▤ AE, MC, V �101 BP.

> ### THE UBIQUITOUS *SODA*
>
> In Costa Rica the word *soda* has nothing to do with a carbonated beverage. (That's a *gaseosa* here.) Instead a soda is a small, often family-run restaurant frequented by locals that you'll find in every town and all over San José. Don't expect anything as fancy as a menu. A board usually lists specials of the day. The lunchtime *casado* (literally, "married")—a "marriage" of chicken, pork, or beef with rice, beans, cabbage salad, and natural fruit drink—sets you back about $2. Just pay the cashier when you're done.

### To & From Grecia

*26 km/16 mi (45 minutes) northwest of Alajuela, 46 km/29 mi (1 hr) northwest of San José.*

From San José continue west on the highway past the airport—the turnoff is on the right—or by head into Alajuela and turn left just before the Alajuela cemetery. Buses traveling between San José and Ciudad Quesada make stops in Grecia. From Alajuela, buses to Grecia/Ciudad Quesada pick up on the southern edge of town (C. 4 at Avda. 10).

### Grecia Essentials

🏦 Bank/ATM **Banco Nacional** ✉ Northwest corner of Central Plaza. **Banco de Costa Rica** ✉ South side of church.

## Sarchí

❷ Tranquil Sarchí is spread over a collection of hills surrounded by coffee plantations. Though many of its inhabitants are farmers, Sarchí is also one of Costa Rica's premier centers for crafts and carpentry. People drive here from all over central Costa Rica to shop for furniture, and caravans of tour buses regularly descend upon the souvenir shops outside town. Local artisans work native hardwoods into bowls, boxes, toys, platters, and even jewelry, but the area's most famous products are its brightly painted oxcarts—replicas of those traditionally used to transport coffee and other agricultural products. Trucks and tractors have largely replaced oxcarts on Costa Rican farms, but the little wagons retain their treasured place in Tico folklore and can be spotted everywhere from small-town parades to trinket shops.

## Exploring

The town's only real oxcart factory, **Taller Eloy Alfaro e Hijos** (Eloy Alfaro and Sons Workshop), was founded in 1923, and its carpentry methods have changed little since then. The two-story wooden building housing the wood shop is surrounded by trees and flowers—usually orchids—and all the machinery on the ground floor is powered by a waterwheel at the back of the shop. Carts are painted in the back, and although the factory's main product is a genuine oxcart—which sells for about $2,000—there are also some smaller mementos that can easily be shipped home. ⊠ *200 m north of soccer field* ☎ *No phone* 🖃 *By donation* ⊙ *Weekdays 8–4.*

### PAINTED OXCARTS

Coffee has come to symbolize the prosperity of the Central Valley and the nation; as such, this all-important cash crop has inspired a fair bit of folklore. Costa Rican artists have long venerated coffee workers, and the oxcart, once used to transport coffee to the coast, has become a national symbol. You can buy elaborately decorated carts in many different sizes at crafts shops throughout the Central Valley.

## Shopping

Sarchí is the best place in Costa Rica to buy miniature oxcarts, the larger of which are designed to serve as patio bars and can be broken down for easy transport or shipped to your home. Another popular item is a locally produced rocking chair with a leather seat and back.

★ There's one store just north of town, and several larger complexes to the south. The nicest is the **Chaverri Factory** (⊠ Main road, about 2 km/1 mi south of Sarchí ☎ 454–4944), and you can wander through the workshops in back to see the artisans in action. Chaverri is a good place to buy wooden crafts; nonwood products are cheaper in San José. Chaverri also runs a restaurant next door, **Las Carretas**, which serves international meals all day and has a good lunch buffet.

## To & From Sarchí

*8 km/5 mi west of Grecia, 53 km/33 mi (1½ hours) northwest of San José.*

To get to Sarchí from San José, take the highway well past the airport to the turnoff for Naranjo; then veer right just as you enter Naranjo. Direct buses to Sarchí depart from Alajuela (C. 8, between Avdas. 1 and 3) every 30 minutes 6 AM–9 PM; the ride takes 90 minutes.

## Sarchí Essentials

**Bank/ATM Banco Nacional** ⊠ Plaza Artesani.
**Post Office Correos** ⊠ 50 m west of central plaza.

# San Ramón

❸ Having produced a number of minor bards, San Ramón is known locally as the City of Poets. San Ramón hides its real attractions in the countryside to the north, on the road to La Fortuna, where comfortable nature lodges offer access to private nature preserves. There's not much to see in San Ramón other than its church.

## Exploring

Aside from the poets, the massive **Iglesia de San Ramón,** built in a mixture of the Romanesque and Gothic styles, is the city's claim to fame. In 1924 an earthquake destroyed the smaller adobe church that once stood here, and the city lost no time in creating a replacement—this great gray concrete structure took a quarter of a century to complete, from 1925 to 1954. To ensure that the second church would be earthquake-proof, workers poured the concrete around a steel frame that was designed and forged in Germany (by Krupp). Step past the formidable facade and you'll discover a bright, elegant interior. ⊠ *Across from Parque Central* ☎ *445–5592* ⊘ *Daily 6–11:30* AM *and 1:30–7* PM.

## Where to Stay & Eat

**$–$$** ✕ **La Colina.** This roadside diner, with its requisite plastic chairs, has an eclectic menu with some typical and some not-so-typical entrées. Start your meal with a delicious ceviche, moving on to the famous rice and chicken or, for the more adventurous, *lengua en salsa* (tongue in tomato sauce). Meals begin with complimentary chips and pickled vegetables. ⊠ *Highway to Puntarenas, 2 km/1 mi west of San Ramón* ☎ *445–4956* ⊟ *AE, DC, MC, V.*

**$$$$** 🏨 **Inn at Coyote Mountain.** Gourmet tropical-creole culinary vacations and a spacious teaching kitchen draw guests to this remote inn. The dark, rich gavilán ceilings against the whitewashed walls transport you to a rural Spanish villa. The blue washes of the Pacific and distant Nicoya Peninsula are extra eye-candy. Gregarious owners Daniel, Charles, and Vaughn are renowned for their organic gourmet revolution in New Orleans (chef Emeril was one of their early champions) and stand a good chance of realizing their goal: putting Costa Rica on the culinary map. The region itself paints a beautiful picture and provides options for an afternoon, but a 45-minute, jarring dirt road separates the inn from most activities and tourism establishments; if you don't do remote, you may be better served with a day trip for classes; either way, it's worth the effort. Groups of six or more can arrange for classes even when the inn is officially closed. ⊠ *Calle La Tabla de la Guaria de Piedades Sur; 15 km (9 mi) northwest of San Ramón* ☎ *383–0544, 902/742–0980 in the U.S.* ⊕ *www.cerrocoyote.com* ⇱ *5 rooms* ⚸ *Restaurant, fans; no a/c, no room phones, no room TVs* ⊟ *AE, MC, V* ⊘ *Closed Aug.–Jan.* ❡❍❡ *MAP.*

**$$** ✕🏨 **Valle Escondido.** "Hidden Valley" lies within an ornamental plant farm at the edge of a 250-acre forest preserve. You could spend days

**NICARAGUA**

## The Northern Plains

3

*San Juan*

*R. San Carlos*

*R. San Juan*

*R. Toro*

*R. Sarapiquí*

Boca Tapada

*R. Pital*

*R. Tres Amigos*

*R. Aguas Zarcas*

**Puerto Viejo de Sarapiquí**
**15**

**La Selva**
**16** **Biological Station**

*LA SELVA RESERVE*

*R. Sardinal*

Cariari

4

La Virgen

♦ **Magsasay Ranger Station**

Aguas Zarcas

*R. Sarapiquí*

Las Horquetas

140

San Miguel

**Rara Avis**
**17**

*JUAN CASTRO BLANCO N. P.*

126

Cinchona

*R. Sardinal*

Guápiles

**4**
**Ciudad Quesada (San Carlos)**

2

**Poás Volcano**
**13**

♦ **La Paz Waterfall Gardens**

*R. Puerto Viejo*

**Braulio**
**14** **Carrillo National Park**

32

Zarcero

*POÁS VOLCANO NATIONAL PARK*

Vara Blanca

**Carrillo** ♦ **Quebrada Gonzáles**
**Ranger Station** ♦ **Ranger Station**

141

**San Ramón**
**3**

**Sarchí**
**2**
**1**

Fraijanes

**Barva Volcano** ♦

**Zurquí Ranger Station** ♦

**Grecia**

**Barva Ranger Station**

Sacramento

♦ **Mundo de las Serpientes**

Atenas

Barva

Alajuela ✈

San Rafael

San José ★

Heredia

0        30 miles
0    45 km

exploring the 20 km (12 mi) of trails, which wind through primary forest past waterfalls and giant trees, or going on horseback rides and canopy tours. The rooms lack personality, but are spacious and have covered porches with wonderful views of a forested mountainside. Two restaurants ($–$$$), one by the road and one near the rooms, serve high-quality international fare, especially the Italian dishes such as fettuccine *a lo Marco* (with a shrimp cream sauce). You're welcome to hike in the preserve even if you just stop for lunch, which is a good option if you're traveling to or from Arenal. ⊠ *Road between San Ramón and La Fortuna, 32 km/19 mi north of San Ramón* ⬚ *Apdo. 452–1150, La Uruca* ☎ *231–0906 or 475–1082* 🖷 *232–9591* ⊕ *www.hotelvalleescondido. net* ⇄ *33 rooms* ⌂ *Restaurant, fans, pool, whirlpool tub, horseback riding, laundry service; no a/c, no room TVs* ▤ *AE, MC, V* ◉ *CP.*

★ **$$** ⊞ **Villablanca.** Built by former Costa Rican president Rodrigo Carazo, this charming hotel is on a working dairy and coffee farm. The farmhouse contains the reception desk, bar, and restaurant; down the hill are lovely casitas, which are tiny replicas of traditional adobe farmhouses complete with whitewashed walls, tile floors, cane ceilings, and fireplaces. Resident guides lead nature walks through the adjacent cloud-forest reserve, which is excellent bird-watching territory. Horses are available for exploring the rest of the farm, and you can arrange a canopy tour, as well. ⊠ *20 km/12 mi north of San Ramón on road to La Fortuna* ⬚ *Apdo. 3704, San José* ☎ *461–0300 or 461–0301* 🖷 *228–4004* ⊕ *www.villablancacr. com* ⇄ *34 casitas and suites* ⌂ *Restaurant, horseback riding, bar, gift shop; no a/c, no room TVs* ▤ *AE, MC, V* ◉ *BP.*

> ### AS TICO AS *GALLO PINTO*
>
> This how the saying goes, but how Tico is this rice-and-bean dish? Nicaraguans also claim it as their own, and the rivalry has led to three Guinness Book of World Records bids for the largest batch. Costa Rica captured the first title in 2003, only to have Nicaragua top them a mere 12 days later. After more than a year of grumbling, in 2005 Costa Rica snatched the title back with a 5,000 pounds of rice and beans.

## To & From San Ramón

*23 km/14 mi west of Sarchí, 59 km/37 mi (1½ hours) northwest of San José.*

San Ramón is on the Pan-American Highway west of Grecia. To reach the hotels to the north of town, head straight through San Ramón and follow the signs. Buses traveling to Ciudad Quesada from San José stop in San Ramón. From Alajuela, buses to San Ramón/Ciudad Quesada pick up on the southern edge of town (C. 4 at Avda. 10).

## San Ramón Essentials

🏦 Bank/ATM **Banco del Comercio** ⊠ West side of plaza. **BanCrecen** ⊠ C. 3 Norte.
🏦 Internet **Cybercafe San Ramón** ⊠ 100 m east of Banco Central ☎ 447–9007.

**en route**

The small town of **Zarcero**, 15 km (9 mi) north of San Ramón on the road to Ciudad Quesada, looks like it was designed by Dr. Seuss. Evangelisto Blanco, a local landscape artist, modeled cypress topiaries in fanciful animal shapes—motorcycle-riding monkeys, a lightbulb-eyed elephant—that enliven the park in front of the town church. The church interior is covered with elaborate pastel stencil work and detailed religious paintings by the late Misael Solís, a well-known local artist.

# THE ARENAL VOLCANO AREA

Whether you come here from San José or Liberia, prepare yourself for some spectacular scenery—and a bumpy ride. As you bounce along on your way to Arenal, you may discover that "paved" means different things in different places, and that potholes are numerous. Any discomfort you experience is more than made up by the swathes of misty rain forest and dramatic expanses of the Cordillera Central. Schedule at least 3 ½ hours for the trip.

## Ciudad Quesada (San Carlos)

❹ Highway signs point you to Ciudad Quesada, but it's simply "San Carlos" in local parlance. Like so many other places in Costa Rica, the landscape is splendid and what passes for architecture varies from ordinary to downright hideous. San Carlos is where Zona Norte residents come to shop, go to the movies, get medical care, and generally take care of the necessities. There's also an enormous bus station where you can make connections to almost anywhere in the country. If you're traveling from San José to points north, your bus will stop here (even if it's a so-called "express"). This lively mountain market town/provincial capital serves a fertile dairy region and is worth a stop for a soak in the soothing thermal waters.

### Exploring

**Termales del Bosque** lets you soak those tired muscles as you watch the birds, for under ten dollars. A variety of spa and massage treatments are also available for an additional fee. If you feel energized after your soak, take a horseback ride or a self-guided "eco-exploring" hike through the adjacent secondary-growth forest. Termales del Bosque is just west of Hotel El Tucano's grounds and is served by the same hot springs. ⊠ *Hwy. 140, 7 km/4½ mi east of Ciudad Quesada* 🕿 *460–1356* 🎫 *Day pass $8* ⊘ *Open daily 7* AM–9 PM.

### Where to Stay

★ $ 🖼 **Laguna del Lagarto Lodge.** One of Costa Rica's smaller eco-lodges is a hideaway in a 1,250-acre rain forest near the Nicaraguan border. Most of the rustic cabin rooms come with single beds. Some 380 bird species and counting have been logged here, including the endangered great green macaw. Buffet-style meals are served on a patio with river and forest views. Rates include one guided walk and use of canoes. Recommended extras include horseback riding and a boat trip up to the border on the San Carlos River. ⊠ *7 km/4 mi north of Boca Tapada* 🕿 *289–8163* 🖨 *289–5295* 🌐 *www.lagarto-lodge-costa-rica.com* ⮑ *20 rooms, 18 with bath* ⚉ *Restaurant, horseback riding, bar, laundry service; no a/c, no room phones, no room TVs* ▤ *MC, V.*

## To & From Ciudad Quesada

*45 km/28 mi (45 minutes) northwest of Zarcero.*

Quesada is on the Pan-American Highway north of Zarcero. Buses from San José leave Terminal Atlantico Norte on the hour, from 5 AM to 7 PM. The trip takes around 2½ hours. The Quesada bus terminal is a couple of kilometers outside of town; taxis wait at the terminal to take you downtown or to your hotel.

## Ciudad Quesada Essentials

📧 Bank/ATM **Banco Nacional** ✉ Across from cathedral. **Banex** ✉ 500 m north of Mercado Municipal.

📧 Hospital **Hospital de San Carlos** ✉ 2 km/1 mi north of park ☎ 460-1176.

📧 Internet **Internet Café** ✉ 150 m north of park ☎ 460-3653.

📧 Post Office **Correos** ✉ Across from Escuela Chávez.

➤ Arenal Volcano National Park    **See Page 110**

# La Fortuna

**❺** At the foot of massive Volcán Arenal, the small community of La Fortuna attracts visitors from around the world. Nobody comes to La Fortuna—an ever-expanding mass of hotels, tour operators, souvenir shops, and *sodas*—to see the town itself. Instead, thousands of tourists flock here each year to use it as a hub to visit the natural wonders that surround it. Volcanos, waterfalls, vast nature preserves, great rafting rivers, and an astonishing array of birds are to be found within an hour or less of your hotel. La Fortuna is also the best place to arrange trips to the Caño Negro National Wildlife Refuge (⇨ *below*).

After the 1968 eruption of Arenal Volcano, La Fortuna was transformed from a tiny, dusty farm town to one of Costa Rica's tourism powerhouses, where tourists converge to see the volcano in action. Volcano-viewing can be hit and miss though, especially during the rainy season (May–November). One minute Arenal looms menacingly over the village; the next minute clouds shroud its cone. Early morning is always the best time to catch a longer gaze.

**NAVIGATING LA FORTUNA** Taxis in and around Fortuna are relatively cheap, and public buses run throughout the day. Get a cab at the stand on the south side of Parque Central. The town itself is fairly compact, and it's easy to walk to restaurants, shops, and tour companies.

## Exploring

➤ Baldi Termae hot springs
Tabacón Hot Springs    **See Page 111**

The town's squat, pale, concrete **Church of San Juan Bosco,** unremarkable on its own, wins Costa Rica's most-photographed-house-of-worship award. The view of the church from across the central park, with the volcano in the background, a juxtaposition of serene and menacing, makes a great photo. This is also one of the few Catholic churches that doesn't follow the typical Costa Rican convention of facing west. Its entrance is on the east side of the building. ⊠ *West side of Parque Central* ☎ *No phone.*

**need a break?** The semi-open-air **Café Rainforest** (⊠ 30 m south of Parque Central ☎ 365–6370) is one of the best of the more American-style cafés and coffeehouses that have sprung up in La Fortuna. Ice cream is also served. **Lo Nuestro** (⊠ 50 m north of gas station ☎ 479–9489) brews coffee drinks, with pastries as accompaniment, and is a popular breakfast stop for tourists.

Arenal Hanging Bridges See Page 129

**Ecocentro Danaus** a small ecotourism project outside of town, exhibits 300 species of tropical plants, abundant animal life—including sloths and caimans—and butterfly and orchid gardens. It's also a great place to see Costa Rica's famed red poison dart frogs up close. It's an easy walk or inexpensive cab ride from town. 🏷 *$5* ⊙ *Daily 8–4. A guided evening tour ($12) should be reserved in advance* ⊠ *4 km/2½ mi east of La Fortuna* ☎ *393–8437 or 460–8005.*

> **CAUTION** ⚠
>
> The ubiquitous OFFICIAL TOURIST INFORMATION signs around La Fortuna and Monteverde aren't "official" at all, but are merely travel agencies and tour operators hoping to sell you tours.

**Fodor'sChoice** ★ Getting to the **Cataratas de la Fortuna** (La Fortuna Waterfall) requires a strenuous walk down ¼ mi of precipitous steps, but is worth the effort to see the amazing 177-foot falls. Depending on your pace, allow 25 to 50 minutes to reach the falls. Swimming in the pool under the waterfall is usually safe. You can work your way around into the cavelike area behind the waterfall for an unusual rear view, but you have to swim in turbulent waters and/or hike over slippery rocks. Wear sturdy shoes or water sandals with traction, and bring snacks and water or a picnic lunch to enjoy. You can get to the trailhead from La Fortuna by walking or taking an inexpensive taxi ride. ⊠ *Yellow entrance sign off the main road toward the volcano, 7 km/4 mi south of La Fortuna* 🏷 *$6* ⊙ *Daily 8–4*

**off the beaten path** In 1945 a farmer in the mountain hamlet of Venado fell in a hole, and thus were discovered the **Venado Caverns** (Cavernas de Venado). The limestone caves contain a series of eight chambers extending to about 2,700 m (8,858 ft, or 1½ mi), with an assortment of stalactites, stalagmites, underground streams, and other subterranean formations.

*Continued on page 112*

# ARENAL VOLCANO

★ Fodor's Choice

Costa Rica's most active volcano dominates the landscape here. Night is the best time to see it in action: on a clear evening you can see rocks spewing skyward and molten lava rolling down its sides.

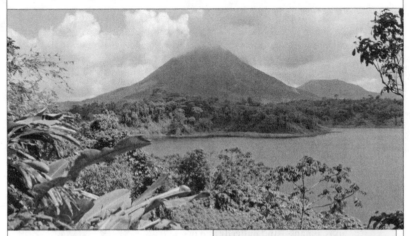

Volcán Arenal, at 1,624 meters (5,328 feet), dominates the landscape here.

Volcanologists estimate Arenal's age at around 4,000 years. It lay dormant for at least 400 years until 1968. It may be local folklore, but Ticos that homesteaded this area in the 1930s and '40s referred to Arenal as "the mountain" and apparently, despite its conical shape, did not realize it was a volcano. On July 29, 1968, an earthquake shook the area, and 12 hours later Arenal blew. The village of Arenal, to the west, bore the brunt of the shock waves, poisonous gases, and falling rocks. Some 100 people were killed in three days. Since then, Arenal has been in a constant state of activity—eruptions, accompanied by thunderous rumbling sounds, are sometimes as frequent as one per hour. An enormous eruption in 1998 put the fear back into the local community, though there were no casualties, and led to the closure of

## NOW YOU SEE IT, NOW YOU DON'T

The volcano is often hidden in cloud cover, so you may have to stay more than one day to get in a good viewing session. Your chances are best during the dry season (February–April), and dawn hours are the best for seeing the cone. The lava flow is most visible between midnight and pre-dawn, one reason to book a hotel on the lava side of the volcano. Tip: Wait until around 2 PM or so to see if the weather is clear, then book your afternoon volcano hike.

Route 42 and the evacuation of several nearby hotels. This earthshaking event reminded everyone what it really means to coexist with the world's third most active volcano.

The volcano is within 30,000-acre Arenal Volcano National Park, one of Costa Rica's largest parks and most popular destinations. Also in the park are Lake Arenal, the country's most important source of hydroelectric power, and Cerro Chato, an extinct volcano. Cerro Chato's collapsed crater, now an aquamarine lake, can be reached if you're up to a vigorous and steep four-hour hike. ⊠ *Turnoff to ranger station 3½ km/2 mi east of Lake Arenal, and 2 ½ km/1 ½ mi west of Tabacón* ☎ *695–5180* 🖃 *$7* 🕙 *Daily 8 AM–4 PM and at night with authorized guides and groups.*

## Volcano Hikes

Desafío and Jacamar get you close to the action, but still a safe distance away. Afternoon tours end with an optional stop at a hot springs (for an extra fee). Transportation is included.

**Desafío Adventures.** ⊠ *Behind the church, La Fortuna* ☎ *479–9464* ⊕ www.desafiocostarica.com 🖃 *$20* 🕙 Tours at 3:30 PM.

**Jacamar Naturalist Tours** ⊠ *Across from Parque Central, La Fortuna* ☎*479–9767 www.arenaltours.com* 🖃 *$30* 🕙 *Tours at 8 AM and 3 PM.*

⚠ Never hike beyond the warning signs, even if the volcano appears to be calm. Toxic hot gases are released by even small eruptions (which are frequent), and they move faster than you can.

---

# HOT SPRINGS

Tabacón Hot Springs & Resort

Where else can you lounge in a natural hot-springs waterfall with a volcano spitting fireballs overhead? Tabacón Resort's Tabacón Hot Springs is a busy day spa and hotel with gardens, waterfalls, hot mineral-water soaking streams, swimming pools, swim-up bars, and restaurants, all in a florid Latin interpretation of grand European baths. The best deal is the $45 zip-line canopy tour, which includes access to the waters. Make spa-treatment appointments at least one day in advance. A shuttle can bring you from central La Fortuna. ⊠ *Highway toward Nuevo Arenal, 13 km/8 mi northwest of La Fortuna* ☎ *460–2020 or 256–1500* ⊕ *www.tabacon.com* 🖃 *Day pass $29, package with lunch and dinner $45, 45-min massage $55* 🕙 *Daily noon–10.*

More economical and less crowded, Baldi Termae has 10 hot-springs-fed pools that vary in temperature and share views of Volcán Arenal. It has a swim-up bar, too. ⊠ *4 km/ 2½ mi west of La Fortuna* ☎ *479–9651* 🖃 *$12* 🕙 *Daily 10–10.*

## ROOMS WITH A VIEW

Some or all rooms at the following La Fortuna–area hotels have views of the volcano.

- Tabacón Hot Springs & Resort
- Arenal Lodge
- Arenal Observatory Lodge
- Arenal Country Inn
- Hotel Las Cabañitas Resort
- Montaña de Fuego
- Tilajari Hotel Resort
- Volcano Lodge
- Cabinas Los Guayabos
- Hotel San Bosco
- Lake Coter Eco-Lodge
- Lomas del Volcán
- Luigi's Lodge

Bobo Adventures ( ⇨ Outdoor Activities, *below*) runs trips. If your non-claustrophobic, willing to get wet and muddy, and don't mind bats, this could be just the ticket for you. ( ⊠ 45 min north of La Fortuna and 20 min southeast of San Rafael ☎ 479–9415 ⊠ $35 ⊙ Daily 7–8.)

## Outdoor Activities

★ **Desafío Adventures** ( ⊠ Behind the church ☎ 479–9464 ⊕ www.desafiocostarica.com) can take you rafting, horseback riding, hiking, and rappelling. **Bobo Adventures** ( ☎ 479–9390) specializes in excursions to the Venado Caverns and the Caño Negro Wildlife Refuge. **Jacamar Naturalist Tours** ( ⊠ Across from Parque Central ☎ 479–9767 ⊕ www.arenaltours.com) is one of the area's most established tour companies. Its wide variety of tours includes visits to Caño Negro Wildlife Refuge, birding excursions, and fishing trips.

ATV TOURS  **Fourtrax Adventure** ( ☎ 479–8444 ⊕ www.fourtraxadventure.com) leads guided three-hour ATV tours throughout the countryside around La Fortuna and the volcano. Tours are given daily at 7:30 and 11 AM and 2:30 PM. The price is $75 per couple; $15 for each additional person, and includes a guide, snacks, and transportation to and from hotels.

Canopy Tours See Page 126

FISHING  Where else can you fish in the shadow of a rumbling volcano? Lake Arenal is enormous and stocked with a wide variety of game fish, including tilapia, guapote (Central American rainbow bass), and machaca (Central American shad). Most tour operators and larger hotels can set you up with fishing guides for half- or full-day trips. Rates begin at around $150. **Jacamar Naturalist Tours** ( ⇨ *above*) has morning and afternoon sportfishing trips to Lake Arenal.

HIKING  A pleasant 6-km (4-mi) hike takes you from La Fortuna to the trailhead
★ for the 177-foot **Cataratas de la Fortuna** ( ⇨ *above*). After walking 1½ km (1 mi) from the trailhead and passing two bridges, turn right and continue straight ahead until you reach the river turnoff. You reach the waterfalls by walking down a steep series of steps that include a few vertiginous spots. Depending on your speed, it takes around 20 to 40 minutes. Wear sturdy sneakers, hiking shoes, or river sandals.

HORSEBACK  If you're interested in getting up to Monteverde from the Arenal–La For-
RIDING  tuna area without taking the grinding four-hour drive, there's an alter-
★ native: **Desafío Adventures** ( ⊠ Behind church ☎ 479–9464 ⊕ www.desafiocostarica.com) has a 4½-hour guided horseback trip ($65). The trip involves taxi or van service from La Fortuna to the southern shore of Lake Arenal, and from that trail's end to Monteverde, circumventing steep, muddy, poorly maintained trails at both ends. A boat ride across Laguna de Arenal is included. You leave La Fortuna at 7:30 AM and arrive in Monteverde around 2:30 PM. You can also take the trip in reverse, from Monteverde to La Fortuna ( ⇨ Monteverde, *below*). ⚠ Many

other agencies lead horseback tours between La Fortuna and Monteverde, but along treacherous trails, and some riders have returned with stories of terrified horses barely able to navigate the way. Stick with Desafío.

RAFTING  Several La Fortuna operators offer Class III and IV white-water trips on the Río Toro. The narrow river requires the use of special, streamlined boats that seat just four and go very fast. The easier Balsa, Peñas Blancas, Arenal, and San Carlos rivers have Class II and III rapids and are close enough to town that they can be worked into half-day excursions. **Canoa Aventura** (☎ 479–8200 ⊕ http://canoa-aventura.com) can design a rafting trip on the Río Peñas Blancas that fits your needs and skill level and also has daylong canoe tours of the Caño Blanco Wildlife Refuge. Tours are appropriate for beginners, and instruction is provided, but the folks here can tailor excursions if you're more experienced. **De-**
★ **safío Adventures.** (⊠Behind church ☎479–9464 ⊕www.desafiocostarica. com) has day trips on the Río Toro for beginning and experienced rafters ($45–$65).

RAPPELLING  Rappel down four waterfalls ranging in height from 60 to 150 feet with **Pure Trek Canyoning** (☎ 479–9940, 800/452–3195 in the U.S. ⊕ www. puretrek.com). Two guides lead small groups—10 is the maximum size—on the four-hour tour ($80) to a private farm near La Fortuna, with plenty of wildlife-watching opportunities along the way. The excursion includes transportation, all gear, breakfast, and a light lunch.

RIVER TOURS  **Jacamar Naturalist Tours** (⇨ *above*) operates a Safari Float tour ($40) on the Peñas Blancas River. This tranquil float in a rubber pontoon is a great choice for families with small children or visitors with limited stamina or mobility.

## Where to Eat

¢–$  ✕ **La Choza de Laurel.** The tantalizing rotisserie chicken and the cloves of garlic and bunches of onions dangling from the roof always draw in passersby to this open-air Costa Rican–style restaurant a short walk from the center of town. These folks open early; it's a great place to grab a hearty breakfast on your way to the volcano. ⊠ *100 m northwest of church* ☎ 479–9231 ▤ MC, V.

¢–$  ✕ **La Vaca Muca.** The food is good and the servings are generous at this small café just outside of La Fortuna. The exterior is draped with foliage, and the interior has turquoise paneling, glass tables, and bamboo and candles aplenty. Go for the steak, or if you're in the mood for something more basic, try the casado heaped with chicken, beef, or fish; rice; beans; fried egg; fried plantain; and cabbage salad. Stroll through the small orchid and butterfly garden next door after you're through. ⊠ *2 km/1 mi west of La Fortuna* ☎ 479–9186 ▤ AE, DC, MC, V.

¢–$  ✕ **Las Brasitas.** Chicken turns over wood on a rotisserie in a brick oven at this pleasant restaurant on the road heading out of town toward the volcano. Try the succulent chicken when it ends up in the tasty fajitas or any of the other ample-size Mexican dishes. You have your choice of three open-air dining areas arranged around a garden. Two are secluded and intimate; the third less so, being closer to the road. ⊠ *150 m west of church* ☎ 479–9819 ▤ MC, V.

¢–$  ✕ **Lava Rocks Café.** A step above the average *soda* in food and atmosphere (and a bit higher in price), this café has tasty *casados* (plates with rice, beans, fried plantains, and fish, chicken, or meat) and sandwiches, and we love their rich fruit *batidos* (milk shakes). ⊠ *50 m south of church* ☎ *479–8039* ▤ *MC, V.*

¢–$  ✕ **Rancho la Cascada.** You can't miss its tall, palm-thatch roof in the center of town. The festive upstairs contains a bar, whose large TV, neon signs, and flashing lights give it the appropriate ambience. Downstairs the spacious dining room—decorated with foreign flags—serves basic, midpriced Costa Rican fare. Its location right in the center of town makes it a favorite for tour groups. ⊠ *Across from northeast corner of Parque Central* ☎ *479–9145* ▤ *AE, DC, MC, V.*

¢  ✕ **Soda La Parada.** La Fortuna's only 24-hour eatery is a convenient place to grab a quick and cheap meal, and to stock up on snacks for long bus rides. ⊠ *Across from Parque Central and regional bus stop* ☎ *479–9547* ▤ *No credit cards.*

## Where to Stay

★ ¢  ▦ **Cabinas Oriuma.** Right in the center of town, Oriuma is a popular choice for budget travelers and tour groups. The modern rooms are sparkling clean. The second-floor balcony is a pleasant spot to relax and read, watch the happenings in the Parque Central across the street, or plan your next rain-forest adventure. ⊠ *15 m north of Parque Central* ☎ *479–9111* ⇨ *15 rooms* ⚿ *Fans; no a/c, no room phones, no room TVs* ▤ *No credit cards* ｜◎｜ *EP.*

$$  ▦ **Chachagua Rain Forest Hotel.** At this working ranch, intersected by a brook, you can see *caballeros* (cowboys) at work, take a horseback ride into the rain-forest, and look for toucans from the open-air restaurant, which serves local meat and dairy products. Each cabina has a pair of double beds and a deck with a picnic table. Large, reflective windows enclosing each cabina's shower serve a marvelous purpose: birds gather outside your window to watch their own reflections while you bathe and watch them. The lodge is 3 km/2 mi up a rough track—four-wheel drive is a must in rainy season—on the road headed south from La Fortuna to La Tigra. ⊠ *12 km/7 mi south of La Fortuna* ⌖ *Apdo. 476–4005, Ciudad Cariari* ☎ *239–6464* 🖷 *290–6506* ⊕ *www.chachaguarainforesthotel.com* ⇨ *27 cabinas* ⚿ *Restaurant, tennis court, pool, massage, bar, meeting rooms; no room TVs* ▤ *AE, MC, V* ｜◎｜ *EP.*

$  ▦ **La Pradera.** "The Prairie" is a simple roadside hotel with comfortable guest rooms that have high ceilings, spacious bathrooms, and verandas. Two rooms have whirlpool tubs. Beef eaters should try the thatch-roof restaurant next door. The steak with jalapeño sauce is a fine, spicy dish. ⊠ *About 2 km/1 mi west of La Fortuna* ☎ *479–9597* 🖷 *479–9167* ⇨ *20 rooms* ⚿ *Restaurant, a/c in some rooms, pool, hot tubs, bar; no a/c in some rooms* ▤ *AE, DC, MC, V* ｜◎｜ *BP.*

## Shopping

**Lunática** (⊠ 350 m east of town church ☎ 479–8255) sells vibrant, colorful works by artists both known and unknown from around the country, some of them local. Charming owner Francesa Maschi knows the area's arts, from the works of the nearby indigenous Maleku groups to those from a cooperative made up of women from local villages.

★ **Toad Hall** (⊠ Road between Nuevo Arenal and La Fortuna ☎ 692–8020), open daily from 7:30 to 5, sells everything from indigenous art to maps to recycled paper and used books. The owners can give you the low-down on every tour and tour operator in the area; they also run a deli-café with light snacks and views of the lake and volcano.

## Nightlife

People in La Fortuna tend to turn in early, though there are a few clubs and discos for the night owls. **Volcán Look Disco** (⊠ 5 km/3 mi west of La Fortuna ☎ 479–9616), which bills itself as the largest Costa Rican disco outside San José, erupts with dancing and music on weekends. Pizzeria **Vagabundo** (⊠ 3 km/2 mi west of La Fortuna ☎ 479–9565) turns into a lively bar in the evening with foosball and billiards in the back room.

## To & From La Fortuna

*50 km/30 mi (45 minutes) northwest of Ciudad Quesada, 17 km/11 mi east of Arenal Volcano, 190 km/118 mi (3 hours by car; 25 minutes by plane) north of San José.*

NatureAir has daily flights to La Fortuna. Shuttle-van service (⇨ The Northern Plains Essentials, *below*) is a cheaper way to get to La Fortuna, and the vans will pick you up from your hotel. Buses head to La Fortuna from San José three times daily, departing in the morning. Buses make multiple stops and can take much longer than driving yourself; for example, the trip from Ciudad Quesada can take 1½ hours by bus, but is only 45 minutes by car. **Desafío Adventures** (⊠ Behind church, La Fortuna ☎ 479–9464 ⊕ www.desafiocostarica.com) provides a fast, popular three-hour transfer between Monteverde and La Fortuna via taxi, boat, then another taxi, for $21 each way.

## La Fortuna Essentials

🏦 Bank/ATM **Banco Nacional** ⊠ Central Plaza. **Banco Popular** ⊠ 50 m east of Central Plaza. **Banco de Costa Rica** ⊠ 400 m east of Central Plaza.

🏦 Hospital **Seguro Social** ⊠ 300 m east of Parque Central ☎ 479–9643.

🏦 Pharmacy **Cathedral** ⊠ 50 m east of Central Plaza.

🏦 Internet **Destiny Internet** ⊠ 50 m north of Banco Nacional ☎ 479–9850 **Expediciones Fortuna** ⊠ Across the street from Central Plaza ☎ 479–9104.

🏦 Post Office **Correos** ⊠ Across from church.

# Lake Arenal

**❻** Shimmering Lake Arenal, all 125 square km (48 square mi) of it, lies between green hills and a rumbling volcano. It's Costa Rica's largest inland body of water. Many visitors are surprised to learn it's a man-made lake, created in 1973 when a giant dam was built. A natural depression was flooded, and a 20-mi-long by 9-mi-wide lake was born. The almost constant winds from the Caribbean make this area a windsurfing mecca. Outfitters in La Fortuna, Nuevo Arenal, and Tilarán run fishing, windsurfing, and kitesurfing trips on the lake. Desafío, an operator based in La Fortuna and Monteverde, has a half-day horseback trip between the two towns, with great views of the lake.

# Nuevo Arenal

**7** Much of the original town of Arenal, at one of the lowest points near Lake Arenal, was destroyed by the volcano's 1968 eruption, and the rest was destroyed in 1973, when Lake Arenal flooded the region. Nuevo Arenal, created about 30 km (19 mi) away from the site of the old town, doesn't have much to interest tourists, but is about halfway between La Fortuna and Tilarán, making it a good base.

## Exploring

More than 2,000 plant species from around the world are exhibited at the elegantly organized **Jardín Botánico Arenal** (Arenal Botanical Gardens). Countless orchids, bromeliads, heliconias, and roses; varieties of ferns; and a Japanese garden with a waterfall are among the many splendors laid out along well-marked trails. An accompanying brochure describes everything in delightful detail; well-placed benches and a fruit-and-juice stand provide resting places along the paths. The complex also includes a serpentarium and butterfly garden. ⊠ *5 km/3 mi east of Nuevo Arenal* ☎ *694–4305* ☜ *$8* ☉ *Nov.–Apr., daily 9–5; May–Oct., Mon.–Sat. 9–5.*

## Where to Stay

**$$** ⊡ **Villa Decary.** There's everything to recommend at this hillside lodg-

Fodor'sChoice ing overlooking Lake Arenal, but it all goes back to owners Jeff and Bill

★ and their attentive service. Rooms have large picture windows and private balconies—great places to take in the ample bird-watching opportunities—and bright yellow-and-blue spreads and drapes. Higher up the hill, spacious bungalows afford an even better view. Rates include a filling breakfast of eggs, pancakes, fruits, and juices. ⊠ *2 km/1½ mi east of Nuevo Arenal* ☎ *383–3012* 🖷 *694–4330* ⊕ *www.villadecary.com* ☜ *5 rooms, 3 bungalows* ♣ *Restaurant; no a/c, no room phones, no room TVs* ⊟ *AE, DC, MC, V* ¶⊙¶ *BP.*

**$** ⊡ **Chalet Nicholas.** John and Cathy Nicholas (and their resident Great

Fodor'sChoice Danes) have converted their hillside home into a charming bed-and-break-

★ fast with stunning views of the lake and volcano. The two rosewood rooms downstairs have tile floors. Up a spiral staircase lies the L-shape, all-wood double loft with three beds and a back porch that overlooks the large garden. All rooms have volcano views. Birds abound: 100 species have been cataloged on the grounds. Chat about your plans for the day with your fellow guests over one of Cathy's ample breakfasts. ⊠ *2 km/1½ mi west of Nuevo Arenal* ☎☎ *694–4041* ⊕ *www.chaletnicholas. com* ☜ *3 rooms* ♣ *Restaurant, gift shop; no a/c, no room phones, no room TVs, no smoking* ⊟ *No credit cards* ¶⊙¶ *BP.*

**$**   🏨 **Hotel Joya Sureña.** In the midst of a working coffee plantation, this Canadian-owned property with variously sized suites occupies a rather imposing three-story hacienda-style building surrounded by tropical gardens. It's fairly luxurious for up-country Costa Rica. Extensive trails in and around the place bring a rich diversity of plant, animal, and bird life to view. ⊠ *1½ km/1 mi down a rocky road that leads east from Nuevo Arenal* ☎ *694–4057* 📠 *694–4059* 🛏 *28 rooms* ♻ *Restaurant, fans, in-room safes, pool, health club, whirlpool tub, massage, sauna, boating, horseback riding, laundry service; no a/c, no room TVs* ⊟ *AE, MC, V* 🍽 *BP.*

### To & From Nuevo Arenal
*40 km/25 mi (1 hour) west of La Fortuna.*

Despite years of government promises to upgrade the major tourist route from Volcán Arenal to Nuevo Arenal, the highway around the north shore of Lake Arenal remains one of Costa Rica's most potholed (and that's saying something in a region notorious for terrible roads). Expect smooth sailing west of the Tabacón Resort as far as the Arenal Dam, after which sections of the road deteriorate badly until you arrive in Nuevo Arenal. Beware of deep, tire-wrecking washouts at all times. This stretch adds a bone-jarring hour to an otherwise lovely drive with spectacular lake and volcano views all the way. Public buses run several times daily from La Fortuna.

### Nuevo Arenal Essentials
🏧 Bank/ATM **Banco Nacional** ⊠ West side of church.
🌐 Internet **Tom's Pan** ⊠ 300 m south of gas station ☎ 694–4547.
📮 Post Office **Correos** ⊠ Next to Guardia Rural.

## Tilarán

**8**   Heading west around Laguna de Arenal, you pass a couple of small villages and several charming hotels ranging from the Cretan-inspired fantasy Hotel Tilawa to the rustic Rock River Lodge. The quiet whitewashed town of Tilarán, on the southwest side of the lake—a windmill farm in the hills high above the town attests to this being the windiest place in the country—is used as a base by bronzed windsurfers. For those days when you get "skunked" (the wind fails to blow), horseback riding and mountain biking can keep you busy. A lakeside stroll is a pleasant way to while away a few hours.

### Outdoor Activities

HORSEBACK RIDING   Uncounted miles of good horse trails cover a marvelous mix of terrain: verdant farmland, open meadows, rain forest, and plantations rich in bird life. The ride from La Fortuna to the Fortuna Waterfall is appropriate for both novice and experienced riders. **Chaves Horse Tours** (☎ 354–9159 or 479–9023) has guided horse tours to the waterfall.

MOUNTAIN BIKING   **Rock River Lodge** (⊠ 19 km/11 mi northeast of Tilarán ☎ 692–1180 ⊕ www.rockriverlodge.com) specializes in mountain bike trips in the Lake Arenal area.

**Rock River Lodge** ($\Rightarrow$ *above*) is one of several hotels that rent windsurfing equipment ($40/day). The best selection of wind- and kitesurfing equipment for rent or purchase can be found at lakefront **Tilawa Wind Surf** ($\boxtimes$ Hotel Tilawa, 8 km/5 mi north of Tilarán ☎ 695–5050). It's the only outfitter here open year-round. Full- and half-day lessons are also available for $150 and $100, respectively.

## Where to Stay

$ 🏨 **Hotel Tilawa.** This Costa Rican homage to the Palace of Knossos on Crete has neoclassical murals, columns, and plant-draped arches that somehow don't seem dramatically out of place. The large rooms have two queen-size beds with Guatemalan bedspreads and natural wood ceilings; the bathrooms are especially spacious. Sailing tours in a 39-foot catamaran, the windsurfing and kitesurfing school and shop, and the skateboarding park make this a practical place to base yourself if you want an active vacation. Packages include the use of windsurfing gear. The open-air patio restaurant dishes up steaks and seafood. $\boxtimes$ *8 km/5 mi north of Tilarán* ☎ *695–5050* 🖷 *695–5766* ⊕ *www.hotel-tilawa. com* 🖃 *Apdo. 92–5710, Tilarán* 🛏 *20 rooms* 👌 *Restaurant, pool, windsurfing, boating, mountain bikes, horseback riding, bar, laundry service; no a/c, no room TVs* 🖃 *MC, V.*

$ 🏨 **Rock River Lodge.** A handsome building on a grassy hill above the road leading from Tilarán to Nuevo Arenal houses wooden cabinas. They share a shaded front porch that has views of the volcano. Santa Fe–style cabinas are up the hill. The restaurant, bar, and lobby occupy a building closer to the road, with a porch and lounging sofas, an open kitchen, and a welcoming fireplace. The hotel rents windsurfing gear. The restaurant serves well-prepared food at reasonable prices. $\boxtimes$ *19 km/11 mi northeast of Tilarán* 🖃 *Apdo. 95–5710* ☎🖷 *692–1180* ⊕ *www.rockriverlodge. com* 🛏 *6 rooms, 8 cabinas* 👌 *Restaurant, windsurfing, mountain bikes, horseback riding, bar, laundry service; no a/c, no room phones, no room TVs* 🖃 *MC, V.*

¢ 🏨 **Hotel Naralit.** Spell Tilarán backward and you get the name of a great budget option in the center of town. It's basic but comfortable, run by friendly folks, and spotlessly clean. A large glass door fronts a porch in each pleasantly furnished room, letting in lots of light. The Naralit manages a small restaurant next door. $\boxtimes$ *Opposite south side of church* ☎ *695–5393* 🖷 *695–6767* 🛏 *25 rooms* 👌 *Fans, some refrigerators; no a/c, no room phones* 🖃 *MC, V.*

## To & From Tilarán

*22 km/14 mi (45 minutes) southwest of Nuevo Arenal, 62 km/38 mi (1½ hours) west of La Fortuna.*

The roads from La Fortuna to Nuevo Arenal are treacherous, narrow, and potholed, and Tico drivers are notorious for giving no quarter. Give yourself sufficient time—say, two hours—for the trip. Public buses travel to and from La Fortuna several times daily.

## Tilarán Essentials

🏧 Bank/ATM **Banco Nacional** $\boxtimes$ Central Plaza. **CooTilarán** $\boxtimes$ 150 m north of church.
🏥 Hospital **Red Cross** $\boxtimes$ 100 m east of church ☎ 692–5256.
📮 Post Office **Correos** $\boxtimes$ 115 m west of municipal stadium.

# MONTEVERDE CLOUD FOREST AREA

Monteverde is a rain forest, but you won't be in the tropics, rather in the cool, gray, misty world of the cloud forest. Almost 900 species of epiphytes, including 450 orchids, are found here; most tree trunks are covered with mosses, bromeliads, ferns, and other plants. Monteverde spans the Continental Divide, extending from about 1,500 meters (4,920 feet) on the Pacific slope and 1,350 meters (4,430 feet) on the Atlantic slope up to the highest peaks of the Tilaran Mountains at around 1,850 meters (6,070 feet).

## Monteverde Cloud Forest Biological Reserve

★ ❾ In close proximity to several fine hotels, the private Reserva Biológica Bosque Nuboso Monteverde is one of Costa Rica's best-kept reserves, with well-marked trails, lush vegetation, and a cool, damp climate. The collision of moist winds with the Continental Divide here creates a constant mist whose particles provide nutrients for plants growing at the upper layers of the forest. Giant trees are enshrouded in a cascade of orchids, bromeliads, mosses, and ferns, and in those patches where sunlight penetrates, brilliantly colored flowers flourish. The sheer size of everything, especially the leaves of the trees, is striking. No less astounding is the variety: 2,500 plant species, 400 species of birds, 500 types of butterflies, and more than 100 different mammals have so far been cataloged at Monteverde. A damp and exotic mixture of shades, smells, and sounds, the cloud forest is also famous for its population of quetzals, which can be spotted feeding on the *aguacatillo* (like an avocado) trees; best viewing times are early mornings from January until September, and especially during the mating season of April and May. Other forest-dwelling inhabitants include hummingbirds and multicolor frogs.

For those who don't have a lucky eye, a short-stay aquarium is in the field station; captive amphibians stay here just a week before being released back into the wild. Although the reserve limits visitors to 160 people at a time, Monteverde is one of the country's most popular destinations. Come early and allow a generous slice of time for leisurely hiking to see the forest's flora and fauna; longer hikes are made possible by some strategically placed overnight refuges along the way. At the reserve entrance you can buy self-guide pamphlets and rent rubber boots; a map is provided when you pay the entrance fee. A two-hour guided night tour starts each evening at 7:15, and the reserve provides transport from area hotels for an extra $2. ☎ 645–5122 ⊕ *www.cct.or.cr* ✉ *$12, $15 with guide, $13 night tour* ☉ *Daily 7–4.*

### To & From Monteverde Biological Reserve
*10 km/6 mi (30 minutes) south of Santa Elena, 35 km/22 mi (2 hours) southeast of Tilarán, 167 km/104 mi (5 hours) northwest of San José*

Buses from Santa Elena leave at 6 AM and 1 PM daily. Taxis from Santa Elena are $7. Buses from Tilarán leave once a day, at 1 PM. Buses from

## What Is a Cloud Forest?

CLOSE UP

CLOUD FORESTS ARE A TYPE OF rain forest, but are very different from the hot, humid lowland forests with which most people are familiar. First of all, they're cooler. Temperatures in Monteverde Cloud Forest, for example, are in the 65°F range year-round, and feel colder due to the near-constant cool rain. Cloud forests—also known as montane forest—occur at elevations of around 6,500 to 11,500 feet. At this altitude, clouds accumulate around mountains and volcanoes, providing regular precipitation as well as shade, which in turn slows evaporation. Moisture is deposited directly onto vegetation, keeping it lush and green. The trees here, on top of high ridges and near the summits of volcanoes, are transformed by strong, steady winds that sometimes topple them and regularly break off branches. The resulting collection of small, twisted trees and bushes is known as an elfin forest. The conditions in cloud forests create unique habitats that shelter an unusually high proportion of rare species, making conservation vital. Monteverde is Costa Rica's most touristed cloud forest, but not its only one. Other cloud forests are in nearby Santa Elena Reserve, the Los Angeles Cloud Forest Reserve near San Ramón (⇨ *above*), and around San Gerardo do Dota (⇨ chapter 6).

San José leave twice daily from the Terminal Atlántico Norte (C. 12 at Avda. 9), at 6:30 AM and 1:30 PM. The roads to the park are some of the worst in the country.

## Monteverde & Santa Elena

**10** **11** The area's first residents were a handful of Costa Rican families fleeing the rough-and-ready life of nearby gold-mining fields during the 1940s. They were joined in the early 1950s by Quakers, conscientious objectors from Alabama fleeing the Korean War. A number of things drew them to Costa Rica: just a few years earlier it had abolished its military, and the Monteverde area offered good grazing. But it was the cloud forest that lay above their dairy farms that soon attracted the attention of ecologists. Educators and artisans followed, giving Monteverde and its town center, the village of Santa Elena, a mystique all their own. Monteverde's Quakers, or more officially, the Society of Friends, no longer constitute the majority these days, but their imprint on the community remains strong.

"Monteverde" refers generally to the entire area, but officially it's the original Quaker settlement that congregates around its dairy-processing plant down the mountain from the reserve entrance. (Road signs designate it that way.)

The only way to really see the area's reserves, including the Monteverde Cloud Forest, is to hike them (⇨ Hiking *in* Outdoor Activities, *below*.)

# Monteverde & Santa Elena

TO MARÁN

TO LAS JUNTAS (1)

Sky Walk & Sky Trek

Camino Verde Info Center/Santa Elena Reserve Office

Selvatura Office

Sky Walk & Sky Trek Office

SANTA ELENA

Original Canopy Tour

Cerro Amigo Trail
T. V. Tower

3

CERRO PLANO

Original Canopy Tour Office

MONTEVERDE

Meg's Stables

La Lechería (Cheese Factory)

Hummingbird Gallery

CASEM

TO PANAMERICAN HIGHWAY

Bajo del Tigre Trailhead

TO LAGARTE, SAN JOSÉ

0        1 mile
0        1 km

TO SAN LUIS

TO SAN LUIS

### KEY

**1** Exploring Sights
(1) Hotels & Restaurants

It's becoming easier and easier to get around the Monteverde area without a car. Taxis are much more plentiful than they used to be, and it's easy to call one from your hotel. Many tour companies will pick you up from your hotel and bring you back at the end of the day, either free or for a small fee.

## Exploring

Several conservation areas that have sprung up near Monteverde make attractive day trips, particularly if the

**CAUTION**

Never take advice from the street "guides" who meet incoming buses in Fortuna, Arenal, Monteverde, and other destinations. They claim to want to help you find accommodations and tours, when in reality they're receiving kickbacks for sending tourists to less-than-desirable hotels or to unqualified "tour guides".

Monteverde Reserve is too busy. The **Santa Elena Reserve** just west of Monteverde is a project of the Santa Elena high school and has a series of trails that can be walked alone or with a guide. The **Camino Verde Information Center** (✉ Main street in town) operates a shuttle service to the reserve with fixed departures and returns. Reservations are required, and the cost is $2 each way. ✉ *6 km/4 mi north of Santa Elena* ☎ *645–5390* ⊕ *www.monteverdeinfo.com/reserve* ✆ *$9* ⊙ *Daily 7–4.*

If your time in Monteverde is limited, consider spending it at **Selvatura,** a kind of nature theme park—complete with canopy tour and bridge walks—just outside the Santa Elena Reserve. A 100-bird hummingbird garden and an enormous enclosed 50-species *mariposario* (butterfly garden) sit near the visitor center. Not to be missed is the world's largest private insect collection. Transportation from area hotels is included in the price. You can choose from numerous mix-and-match packages, depending on which activities interest you, or take it all in, with lunch included, for $78. ✉ *Across from church, Santa Elena* ☎ *645–5929* ⊕ *www.selvatura.com* ✆ *Prices vary, depending on package* ⊙ *Daily 8:30–4:30.*

Only in Monteverde would visitors groove to the nightlife at an exhibition of 20 species of frogs, toads, and other amphibians. Bilingual biologist-guides take you through a 45-minute tour of the terrariums in the **Ranario de Monteverde,** just outside Santa Elena. For the best show, come around dusk and stay well into the evening, when the critters become more active and much more vocal. There's a small frog-and-toad-theme gift shop. ✉ *½ km/¼ mi southeast of Supermercado La Esperanza, Santa Elena* ☎ *645–6320* ✆ *$8* ⊙ *Daily 9–8:30.*

At the **Serpentario Monteverde,** greet 40 species of live Costa Rican reptiles and amphibians with glass safely between you and them. Guided tours in English or Spanish are included in your admission price. ✉ *Just outside Santa Elena on road to Monteverde* ☎ *645–6002* ⊕ *www.snaketour.com* ✆ *$7* ⊙ *Daily 9–8.*

The 200-acre **Sendero Tranquilo Reserve** is bordered by the Monteverde Cloud Forest Biological Reserve and the Guacimal River. Narrow trails are designed to have as little impact on the forest as possible (only groups of two to six are allowed). A guide leads you through primary and secondary forest and a deforested area. Because of the emphasis on minimal environmental impact, animals here tend to be more timid than at some other reserves. ✉ *3 km/2 mi north of Monteverde Reserve entrance, Cerro Plano* ☎ *645–5010* 🖅 *$20* ☉ *Tours depart daily at 7:30* AM *and 1* PM; *reservations required.*

Bite your tongue before requesting Costa Rica's ubiquitous Café Britt up here. Export-quality Café Monteverde is the locally grown product.
★ The **Monteverde Coffee Tour** lets you see the process up close from start to finish, from shade growing on the area's Finca La Bella plantation; transport to the *beneficio*, the processing mill where the beans are washed and dried; and finally to the roaster. The tour starts and ends at the Café Monteverde coffee shop, which is the only place in the Monteverde region to buy authentic Café Monteverde coffee. (Almost all of it is exported.) Reservations are required. ✉ *At start of road to Jardín de Mariposas, Cerro Plano* ☎ *645–7090* ⊕ *www.crstudytours. com* 🖅 *$15* ☉ *Tours at 8* AM *and 1* PM.

**Finca Ecológica** is a private wildlife refuge with four trails on its 75-acre Ecological Farm, plus birds, sloths, agoutis, coatimundis, two waterfalls, and a coffee plantation. If you can't make it all the way up to the Monteverde Reserve for the evening hike, there's a top-notch guided, two-hour twilight walk that begins each evening at 5:30. Reservations are required. ✉ *Turnoff to Jardín Mariposas, off main road between Santa Elena and Monteverde* ☎ *645–5554* ⊕ *www.fincaecologicamonteverde. com* 🖅 *$7, twilight walk $14* ☉ *Daily 7–5.*

Forty species of tropical butterflies flit about in four enclosed botani-
☺ cal gardens at the **Jardín de Mariposas** (Butterfly Garden), all of which have terrific views of the Golfo de Nicoya. Morning visits are best, since the butterflies are most active early in the day. A guided tour helps you understand the stages of a butterfly's life. Don't miss the strangely compelling microparade on the leaf-cutter ant trail. A small theater presents an informational video in English, Spanish, French, Dutch, or German. ✉ *Near Pensión Monteverde Inn; take right-hand turnoff 4 km/2½ mi past Santa Elena on road to Monteverde, continue for 2 km/1 mi* ☎ *645–5512* 🖅 *$8* ☉ *Daily 9:30–4.*

The **Jardín de Orquídeas** (Orchid Garden) showcases more than 400 species of orchids, including two unnamed, one of which is the world's smallest. The Monteverde Orchid Investigation Project manages the gardens. ✉ *1½ km/1 mi southeast of Santa Elena on road to Monteverde Reserve* ☎ *645–5510* 🖅 *$5* ☉ *Daily 8–5.*

☺ The 54,000-acre **Bosque Eterno de los Niños** (Children's Eternal Rain Forest) dwarfs the Monteverde and Santa Elena reserves. Much of it is not open to the public, but for those seeking a rugged experience the Monteverde Conservation League offers stays at San Gerardo and Poco Sol, two remote field stations within the forest. The $34 packages include dormitory accommodation and meals. Hiking tours of the forest are available ( ⇨ Hiking, *below*). ✉ *100 m south of CASEM* ☎ *645–5305* 🖅 *Forest $5; transportation from area hotels $2* ☉ *Daily 8–4:30.*

**need a break?** Long before tourists flocked up here, dairy farming was the foundation of Monteverde's economy. Quakers still operate what is locally referred to as the Cheese Factory, or **La Lechería** (✉ ½ km/¼ mi south of CASEM, halfway between Santa Elena and Monteverde Reserve ☎ 645–2850, 645–7090 tours). It's a much grander milk-processing plant today than the original settlers ever envisioned. The factory store sells local cheeses and ice cream. Stop in for a cone. It's open Monday–Saturday 8–4 and Sunday 10–4; it's closed Sunday April–November. If you have more time, take a two-hour tour of the operation Monday–Saturday at 9 or 2. Tours are $8 and wind up with a cheese-sampling session. Reserve in advance.

## Outdoor Activities

Canopy Tours                                    See Page 126

HIKING    The Monteverde Conservation League's (MCL's) **Bajo del Tigre trail** in the Bosque Eterno de los Niños rain forest ( ⇨ Exploring, *above*) makes for a gentle, self-guided 1½-km (1-mi) hike through secondary forest. Along the trail are 27 points of interpretation, many with lessons geared toward kids. A separate guided twilight walk ($15) begins at 5:30 PM and lasts two hours, affording the chance to see the nocturnal side of the cloud forest; reservations are required. The trail is open daily 8 to 4:30; admission to the forest ($5) applies.

The 75-acre private wildlife refuge **Finca Ecológica** ( ⇨ Exploring, *above*) has four trails ranging from 1 to 3 km and a two-hour guided twilight walk ($14) each evening at 5:30. Reservations are required. The 1.4-km Youth Challenge Trail at **Santa Elena Reserve** ( ⇨ Exploring, *above*) takes about 45 minutes to an hour to negotiate; you can stop at an observation platform with views as far away as the Arenal Volcano—that is, if the clouds clear. If you're feeling hardy, try the 5-km (3 mi) Caño Negro Trail, clocking in at around 4 hours.

Hike 200 acres through four different stages of cloud forest at the **Sendero Tranquilo Reserve** ( ⇨ Exploring, *above*), including one area illustrating the results of cloud-forest devastation. Tours are arranged through Hotel El Sapo Dorado ( ⇨ Where to Stay & Eat, *below*) and require a two-person minimum and six-person limit.

Long-established **Desafío Adventures** (✉ Across from La Esperanza supermarket, Santa Elena ☎645–5874 ⊕www.monteverdetours.com) leads four-hour horseback tours to the San Luis Waterfall, an area not often taken in by Monteverde visitors, and also has shorter excursions on farms around Santa Elena. For the Monteverde–La Fortuna trip ($65), you travel by car and boat, with a three-hour horseback ride on a flat trail along Lake Arenal. Farms for resting the animals are at each end. It's infinitely more humane for the horses (and you) than the muddy, treacherous mountain trails used by dozens of other individuals who'll offer to take you to Arenal. Tour prices range from $25 to $48.

⚠ The ride from Monteverde to La Fortuna can be dangerous with outfitters that take inexperienced riders along steep trails. Desafío should be your only choice for getting from Monteverde to La Fortuna on horseback.

Escorted half-day horseback-riding tours ($40) with **Caballeriza El Rodeo** (⊠ West entrance of town of Santa Elena, at tollbooth ☎ 645–5764) are on a private farm. Excursions are for everyone from beginner to experienced rider. A two-hour sunset tour ($25) begins at 4 PM. Family-operated **El Palomino** (⊠ Just outside of Santa Elena ☎ 645–5479) gives escorted afternoon half-day horseback-riding tours ($25) on farm areas around Santa Elena. Transportation from your hotel is included.

On a horseback tour with **Gold Tours** (⊠ Monteverde Homestay, 150 m northeast of school, Cerro Plano ☎ 645–6914) you visit a 1920s gold mine. The excursion ($40) includes a demonstration of the panning methods used during those heady days, and on the trip back a visit to a *trapiche*, a traditional sugarcane mill. Everyone from small children to seasoned experts can participate on these guided horseback-riding trips ($15–$50) with **Meg's Stables** (⊠ Main road, across from CASEM ☎ 645–5419). Reservations are a good idea in high season, and essential if you want an English-speaking guide. A tour to the San Luis waterfalls is geared toward experienced riders.

■ TIP➔➔ Book horseback trips in the morning during rainy season (July–December). Rains usually begin at around 2 PM.

★ The Canyoneering Tour ($45) on the private El Mirador Reserve and Lodge with **Desafío Adventures** (☎ 645–5874 ⊕ www.monteverdetours.com), 30 minutes outside Santa Elena, begins with a half-hour hike to the first of four waterfalls that range in height from 50 to 100 feet. You lower yourself down the falls with the aid of a guide and very secure harnesses. The tour includes transportation and gear, and is appropriate for any level of experience. (The walk uphill at the end might tax you more than the rappelling did.) An optional lunch at the lodge is extra. Tours leave daily at 7:30 AM across from Supermercado La Esperanza and return early afternoon.

## Where to Stay & Eat

$–$$ ✕ **Cafe Flor de Vida.** This popular vegetarian restaurant has a menu that includes chili, a huge veggie burger, sandwiches, soups, salads, bagels, and plenty of desserts. ⊠ *In front of El Establo Resort, Cerro Plano* ☎ 645–6081 ▤ AE, MC, V ☺ *Breakfast served.*

$–$$ ✕ **De Lucía.** Cordial Chilean owner José Belmar is the walking, talking (in five languages) menu at this elegant restaurant, always on hand to chat with guests. All entrées are served with grilled vegetables and fried plantains, and include sea bass with garlic sauce and orange chicken. The handsome wooden restaurant with red mahogany tables is given a distinct South American flavor by an array of Andean tapestries and ceramics. An excellent dessert choice is *tres leches* (three milks), a richer-than-rich cake made with condensed, whole, and evaporated

*Continued on page 130*

# CANOPY TOURS

Why should monkeys have all the fun? Biologists have long known that much of the action in the rain forest happens off the ground, near the tops of trees. This is where the most eye-catching animals—birds and monkeys—make their homes.

## What Is a Canopy Tour?

There are two basic types of canopy tours: one that gives you a chance to see treetop animals up close; and one that lets you behave like them. The former are canopy tours in the literal sense, where you walk along suspension bridges, ride along in a tram, or are hoisted up to a platform to get a closer look at birds, monkeys, and sloths. They may also be called hanging-bridges tours, sky walks, or platform tours.

The latter, and much more popular, type of canopy tour has less to do with learning about nature. Instead, it is a fast-paced and fun experience where you are attached to a zip line with a safety harness and then "fly" from one tree platform to the next. When most people say "canopy tour" they are generally referring to a zip-line tour. These tours are great fun, but don't plan on seeing the resplendent quetzal as you zip from platform to platform. (Your shouts of exhilaration will probably scare them all away.)

Tree-to-tree zip lines date back to the 19th century, and were introduced as a means for rain-forest study in Costa Rica in the 1970s by U.S. biologist Donald Perry. Darren Hreniuk, a Dutch-turned-Tico entrepreneur, opened the country's first commercial canopy tour in Monteverde in the mid-1990s. It was an almost immediate success. Within a decade, there were close to 100 canopy tours operated by various companies and individuals. Canopy tours now generate some $120 million annually, and attract a reported 200,000 tourists each year.

■ **TIP** ➔➔ If the day is overcast, save your money. All you'll see are clouds, and you can do that for free back on the ground.

### Is It Safe?

Flying through the air, while undeniably cool, is also inherently dangerous. So before you strap into a harness, be certain that the safety standards are first rate. Like so much in Costa Rica, there is no government oversight of canopy tours, so you are dependent on the representations of the operators.

Since 1997 two zip-line tour deaths have been attributed to faulty equipment; one in 2000 on a San Lorenzo Canopy Tour in San Ramón, the other in 1997, at a canopy tour near La Fortuna (neither company is listed in this book). Both women plummeted to earth after their harnesses came apart. Considering that thousands of tourists enjoy the canopy tours each year, the safety record is quite good. Nevertheless, don't fall for sales pitches, and take your time to choose wisely. If anything seems "off" or makes you uncomfortable, walk away.

**Just as importantly:** Listen closely to the guides and follow their instructions. Don't attempt to take photos in flight and never argue with the guide when s/he is making a decision to preserve your safety. A good operator will refund your money or reschedule your tour if it's cancelled due to weather.

## ZIP-LINE TOURS IN MONTEVERDE & ARENAL

Reservations are required for all zip-line tours.

**The Arenal Rain Forest Reserve** ( ⇨ *Hanging Bridges and Trams*) is a suspension-bridge and gondola tour with a zip-line option.

**Aventura Canopy**, the newest zip-line operator in this region, takes you over 16 cables—some extending 2,000 feet—one rappel, and one Tarzan swing on a 2½-hour tour. ⊠ *Road to Santa Elena Reserve, across from bus terminal, Santa Elena* ☎ *645–6901* ⊕ *www. aventuracanopy.com* ⊠ *$45*.

★ **Fodor's Choice** **The Original Canopy Tour** near La Fortuna has well-trained guides who send you whizzing between trees that stand about 328 feet over the streams of Tabacón. If it's a small tour, they may be able to snap a picture of you. ⊠ *Tabacón Resort, 13 km/8 mi northwest of La Fortuna on highway toward Nuevo Arenal* ☎ *460–2020 or 256–1500* ⊕ *www. canopytour.com* ⊠ *$45 (includes Tabacón Hot Springs day pass)*.

★ **The Original Canopy Tour** near Santa Elena was the first zip-line tour in Costa Rica and is still one of the best, with 10 platforms in the canopy, and lasting 2½ hours. You arrive at most of the platforms using a cable-and-harness traversing system and climb 42 feet inside a strangler fig tree to reach one. ⊠ *Across from La Esperanza Supermarket, Santa Elena* ☎ *645–5243, 291–4465 in San José* ⊕ *www.canopytour.com* ⊠ *$45*.

**Selvatura** is the only zip-line tour built entirely inside the cloud forest. It has 18 lines and 20 platforms. ⊠ *Across from church, Santa Elena* ☎ *645–5929* ⊕ *www.selvatura.com* ⊠ *$35*.

**Sky Trek** has 11 cables that are longer than those of the Original Canopy Tour—the longest more than 2,500 feet. The zip lines here extend between towers above the canopy, rather than between trees, and you'll more likely notice the effects of the wind on this one. ⊠ *Across from Banco Nacional, Santa Elena* ☎ *645–5238* ⊕ *www.skytrek.com* ⊠ *$42*.

### CAN I DO IT?

You don't need any particular skills or athleticism to participate in a zip-line tour, but you do need some degree of fearlessness to allow yourself to be suspended hundreds of feet in the air. You'll also be asked to "brake" for yourself by squeezing the zip line before you get to the tree, so those with hand injuries or arthritis may have problems. Talk with the tour operator before you book. Tour operators usually have (and should have) weight and age restrictions; ask about these beforehand.

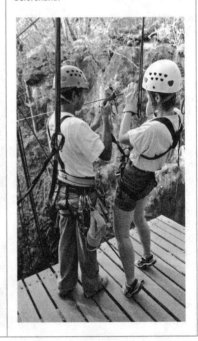

**ASK BEFORE YOU BOOK:**

■ How long has the company been in business, and are they insured?

■ Is the company a member of the Association of Adventure Tour Operators, and/or does it abide by the association's safety guidelines?

■ Are cables, harnesses, and other equipment manufacturer-certified?

■ Is there a second safety line that connects you to the zip line in case the main pulley gives way?

■ Are participants clipped to the zip line while on the platform? (They should be.)

■ What sort of training do the guides receive?

■ Does the tour operator give a thorough pre-tour safety briefing–in English–that addresses such issues as how much climbing and walking are involved?

■ What's the price? Costs vary from around $20 to $75. An extremely low price may indicate a second-rate operation.

## HANGING BRIDGES AND TRAMS

**The Natural Wonders Tram** is an hour-long ride through the rain-forest canopy in a two-person carriage on an elevated track. You control the speed of your carriage. Alternatively, a 1½-km (1-mi) walk gives you a ground-level perspective. The site opens for night visits with advance reservations. ⊠ *Off main road between Santa Elena and Monteverde, on turnoff to Jardín de Mariposas* ☎ *645–5960* ⊡ *$15* ⊘ *Daily 8 AM–6 PM.*

**Tree Top Walkways,** at Selvatura, takes you to heights of 500 feet on a 3-km (2-mi) walk along very stable bridges, ranging from 36 to 150 feet, through the same canopy terrain as the zip-line tour. ⊠ *Across from church, Santa Elena* ☎ *645–5929* ⊕ *www.selvatura.com* ⊡ *$20.*

**Sky Walk** allows you to walk along five hanging bridges, at heights of up to 138 feet, connected from tree to tree. Imposing towers, used as support, mar the landscape somewhat. Reservations are required for guided tours. ⊠ *Across from Banco Nacional, Santa Elena* ☎ *645–5296* ⊕ *www.skywalk.co.cr.eng* ⊡ *$15, $27 tours* ⊘ *Daily 7–4.*

**Arenal Hanging Bridges** is actually a series of trails and bridges that form a loop through the primary rain forest of a 250-acre private reserve, with great bird-watching and volcano-viewing. Fixed and hanging bridges allow you to see the forest at different levels. It's open rain or shine, and there are things to do in both climates. Shuttle service from La Fortuna can be arranged. ⊠ *Arenal Dam, 4 km/2½ mi west of Tabacón* ☎ *479–9686 or 253–5080* ⊕ *www.hangingbridges.com* ⊡ *$20; $30 bird tour, $35 evening tour* ⊘ *Daily 7–4:30; evening tour at 5:30.*

**The Arenal Rain Forest Reserve,** a canopy tour–bridge walk complex near La Fortuna, is operated by the Sky Trek–Sky Walk folks in Monteverde. Alpine-style gondolas transport you to the site, from which you can descend via a zip-line canopy tour or hike through the cloud forest along a series of suspended bridges. ⊠ *12 km/7 mi west of La Fortuna, El Castillo* ☎ *479–9944* ⊕ *www.arenalreserve.com* ⊡ *$60* ⊘ *Daily 7–4.*

**3**

**CANOPY TOURS**

milk. ✉ *Turnoff to Jardín de Mariposas, off main road between Santa Elena and Monteverde, Cerro Plano* ☎ 645–5337 ⊟ AE, MC, V.

$–$$ ✕ **Pizzería de Johnny.** Everyone makes it to this stylish but informal place with candles and white tablecloths. The Monteverde pizza, with the works, is the most popular dish, and pastas, sandwiches, and a decent wine selection round out the menu. ✉ *Road to Monteverde Reserve, 1½ km/1 mi southeast of Santa Elena* ☎ 645–5066 ⊟ MC, V.

$ ✕ **El Márquez.** Seafood is an unexpected treat up here in the mountains, and it's fresh: the owner gets shipments up from Puntarenas several times weekly. The place is nothing fancy; expect plastic tables and chairs, with lots of local flavor. Portions are big, but prices aren't. You could have trouble finishing the generous mixed seafood platter with shrimp, crab, and octopus in a white-wine sauce, or the jumbo shrimp with a sauce of mushrooms and heart of palm. ✉ *Catercorner from Banco Nacional, next to Suárez veterinary clinic, Santa Elena* ☎ 645–5918 ⊟ MC, V ☉ Closed Sun.

★ $ ✕ **Moon Shiva.** Costa Rican meets the Middle East at this casual place with large glass windows overlooking a forested garden. Falafel, pita, tahini, and baba ghanouj figure prominently on the menu, but fillings for the *gallos* (build-your-own tortilla-wrapped "burritos") include standard Tico black-bean paste as well as hummus. The house sauce of pineapple, curry, and coconut garnishes many a dish. Ice cream with fried bananas in rum and cinnamon is a sweet finale. ✉ *100 m east of CASEM, Monteverde* ☎ 645–6270 ⊟ AE, MC, V ☉ No lunch Sun.

$ ✕ **Morphos.** Casual Morphos serves meat dishes and quite a few vegetarian options. Inside this second-floor restaurant are stone walls, log-hewn chairs, artwork, and huge wooden light fixtures in the shape of the famed blue butterfly from which the restaurant takes its name. A large glass window lets you survey all that goes on in town. This tiny place fills up quickly—make reservations a week in advance. ✉ *Across from La Esperanza Supermarket, Santa Elena* ☎ 645–5607 ⚬ Reservations essential ⊟ MC, V.

¢–$ ✕ **Café Rainforest.** Here's a great, trendy place to warm up with a cup of coffee on a chilly evening, and there are plenty of those up here. If it's not too cold, check out the open-air second-floor balcony that overlooks the street. ✉ *Across from AyA, Santa Elena* ☎ 645–5841 ⊟ No credit cards.

¢–$ ✕ **Stella's Bakery.** This local institution is one of the few spots that open at 6 AM. It's a good place to get an early-morning fix before heading to the Santa Elena Reserve. Pastries, rolls, muffins, natural juices, and coffee are standard breakfast fare. Take them with you if you're running short of time. Lunch consists of light sandwiches, soups, and pastas. ✉ *Across from CASEM, Monteverde* ☎ 645–5560 ⊟ V ☉ Breakfast served. No dinner.

$$ ✕🏨 **Fonda Vela.** Owned by the Smith brothers, whose family was among the first American arrivals in the 1950s, these steep-roof chalets have large bedrooms with white-stucco walls, wood floors, and huge windows. Some have markedly better views of the wooded grounds. The most innovatively designed of Monteverde's hotels is also one of the closest to the reserve entrance. The restaurant ($$) prepares local and in-

Fodor's Choice
★

ternational recipes with flair, served indoors or on the veranda. ⊠ *1½ km/1 mi northwest of Monteverde Reserve entrance, Monteverde* ☎ *645–5125, 257–1413 in San José* 🖷 *645–5119, 257–1416 in San José* ⊕ *www.fondavela.com* 🕮 *Apdo. 70060–1000, San José* ⇲ *40 rooms* ⚒ *2 restaurants, minibars, refrigerators, horseback riding, bar, laundry service, Internet, meeting room; no a/c, no TV in some rooms* ▭ *AE, DC, MC, V* ⦿ *EP.*

**$$**  ✕🔲 **Hotel El Sapo Dorado.** After beginning its life as a nightclub, the "Golden Toad" became a popular restaurant and then graduated into a very pleasant hotel. Geovanny Arguedas's family arrived here to farm 10 years before the Quakers did, and he and his wife, Hannah Lowther, have built secluded hillside cabins with polished paneling, tables, fireplaces, and rocking chairs. The restaurant ($$) is well-known for its pastas, pizza, vegetarian dishes, and sailfish from Puntarenas. ⊠ *6 km/4 mi northwest of Monteverde Reserve entrance, Monteverde* ☎ *645–5010* 🖷 *645–5180* ⊕ *www.sapodorado.com* 🕮 *Apdo. 9–5655, Monteverde* ⇲ *30 rooms* ⚒ *Restaurant, massage, bar, laundry service; no a/c, no room phones, no room TVs* ▭ *V* ⦿ *EP.*

**$–$$**  ✕🔲 **Hotel Belmar.** Built into the hillside, Hotel Belmar resembles two tall Swiss chalets and commands extensive views of the Golfo de Nicoya and the hilly peninsula. The amiable Chilean owners have designed both elegant and rustic rooms, paneled with polished wood; half the rooms have balconies. In the restaurant ($$) you can count on adventurous and delicious *platos del día* (daily specials) of Costa Rican and international fare. ⊠ *4 km/2½ mi north of Monteverde* ☎ *256–8585* 🖷 *256–8585* ⊕ *www.hotelbelmar.com* 🕮 *Apdo. 17–5655, Monteverde* ⇲ *34 rooms* ⚒ *Restaurant, whirlpool tub, basketball, billiards, bar, laundry service, tours; no a/c, no phones in some rooms, no room TVs* ▭ *DC, V* ⦿ *EP.*

**$$**  🔲 **Monteverde Lodge.** The well-established Costa Rica Expeditions op-
**Fodor's**Choice  erates this longtime favorite close to Santa Elena. Rooms have vaulted
★  ceilings, bathtubs—an amenity rarely seen here—and great views. A table abuts the angled bay window overlooking the 15 acres of grounds, a perfect place to have a cup of coffee and bird-watch from indoors. The restaurant and bar congregate around an enormous but cozy lobby fireplace. Relax in the whirlpool tub in the enormous solarium, a perfect place to unwind after a day of tromping through the reserves. Or take in the evening slide presentation, showcasing cloud-forest life. ⊠ *200 m south of Ranario de Monteverde, Santa Elena* 🕮 *Apdo. 6941–1000, San José* ☎ *645–5057, 257–0766, or 222–0333* 🖷 *257–1665, 800/886–2609 from U.S.* ⊕ *www.costaricaexpeditions. com* ⇲ *27 rooms* ⚒ *Restaurant, whirlpool tub, bar, gift shop, Internet, meeting room, tours; no a/c, no room TVs* ▭ *AE, DC, MC, V* ⦿ *EP.*

**$–$$**  🔲 **El Establo Mountain Resort.** Mixing old and new, "The Stable" began life as just that, a stable near the road, remodeled and apportioned into comfortable rooms with basic furnishings. A newer pink building perches on the hill above with large suites with wood-and-stone walls. Some contain lofts; all come with amenities rarely seen up here, such as bathtubs, phones, and enormous windows with views of the Golfo de Nicoya. The newest building, higher on the hill, has rooms with hot tubs, private balconies, and even more commanding views. ✉ *3½ km/2 mi northwest of Monteverde* ☎ *645–5110* 🖷 *645–5041* ⊕ *www.hotelelestablo. com* ⇨ *63 rooms* ♻ *Restaurant, snack bar, cable TV, pool, whirlpool tub, massage, bar, tours; no a/c, no TV in some rooms* ▤ *AE, DC, MC, V* ▯◯▮ *BP.*

**WORD OF MOUTH**

"We stayed at El Establo. Beware that if you pay a lower rate you may get stuck in the old portion of the hotel by the road (not shown in pictures of the hotel)"

–Vet

**$–$$** ▦ **El Sol.** A charming family, natives of the Canary Islands, tends to guests at one of those quintessential get-away-from-it-all places just 10 minutes down the mountain from—and a noticeable few degrees warmer than—Santa Elena. Two fully furnished *ojoche*-wood cabins perch on the mountainside on the 25-acre farm. Every vantage point in the cabins—the living area, the bed, the desk, the shower, and even the toilet—has stupendous views. The property has 3 km (2 mi) of trails, a stone-walled pool, and a Finnish sauna, with massage services available. Cuisine is a mix of Spanish and German; meals can be taken in the main house or brought to your cabin. ✉ *4 km/2½ mi southwest of Santa Elena* ☎ *645–5838* 🖷 *645–5042* ⊕ *www.elsolnuestro.com* ⇨ *2 cabins* ♻ *Restaurant, pool, sauna; no a/c, no room phones, no room TVs* ▤ *No credit cards* ▯◯▮ *EP.*

*FodorsChoice* ★

**$–$$** ▦ **Swiss Hotel Miramontes.** Switzerland meets the cloud forest at this Swiss-owned and -operated small inn. Each room has a private porch. Guests have access to a private orchid garden with over 300 varieties. If you're tired of rice and beans, the restaurant serves a variety of Swiss, Austrian, and French dishes. ✉ *1 km south of Santa Elena* ☎ *645–5152* 🖷 *645–5297* ⊕ *www.swisshotelmiramontes.com* ⇨ *7 rooms, 2 chalets* ♻ *Restaurant, fans, tours; no a/c* ▤ *MC, V* ▯◯▮ *BP.*

**$** ▦ **Hotel Finca Valverde.** The Valverde family still farms the land around this hotel, as they have for over a half-century. They grow coffee for export and serve some of their vegetables in the restaurant's excellent dishes. This rustic (in need of some renovation) and quiet wooden enclave will give you the experience of Old Monteverde. All rooms have balconies with forest views. ✉ *300 m southeast of Monteverde* ☎ *645–5157* 🖷 *645–5216* ⊕ *www.monteverde.co.cr* ⇨ *22 rooms* ♻ *Restaurant, tours; no a/c* ▤ *No credit cards* ▯◯▮ *EP.*

**$** ▦ **Trapp Family Lodge.** The enormous rooms, with wood paneling and ceilings, have lovely furniture marvelously crafted from—you guessed it—wood. The architectural style is appropriate, as the lodge is surrounded by trees, just a 10-minute walk from the park entrance, making it the closest lodge to the reserve. (This means, though, that the trip into town is longer.) The friendly Chilean owners are always around to provide personalized service. ✉ *Main road from Monteverde Reserve, Monteverde* ☎ *645–5858* 🖷 *645–5990* ⊕ *www.trappfam.com* ✉ *Apdo. 70–5655, Monteverde* ⇨ *22 rooms* ♻ *Restaurant, bar, laundry service; no a/c, no room TVs, no smoking* ▤ *MC, V* ▯◯▮ *EP.*

★ **¢–$** ▦ **Arco Iris Lodge.** Just outside the center of town, this tranquil spot has cozy cabins set on 4 acres of birding trails. Cabin decor ranges from rustic to plush, but all lodgings come with porches. Start your day with a

# A Biological Superpower

**COSTA RICA'S FORESTS HOLD AN** array of flora and fauna so vast and diverse that scientists haven't even named thousands of the species found here. The country covers less than .03% of the Earth's surface, yet it contains nearly 5% of the planet's plant and animal species. Costa Rica has at least 9,000 plant species, including more than 1,200 types of orchids, some 2,000 kinds of butterflies, and 876 bird species.

Costa Rica's biological diversity is the result of its tropical location, its varied topography, and the many microclimates resulting from the combination of mountains, valleys, and lowlands. It can also be attributed to Costa Rica's geological youth. Five million years ago this patch of land didn't even exist—in its place was a huge canal separating North and South America, where the Pacific and Atlantic oceans flowed together. About three million years ago the movement of tectonic plates created the land bridge that is now Costa Rica and Panama, which became a pathway for flora and fauna that had never coexisted.

Costa Rica's enormous natural diversity is in many ways the result of the intercontinental exchange, but the country's flora and fauna actually add up to more than what has passed between the continents. Although it is a biological corridor, the isthmus also acts as a filter, a hospitable haven to many species that couldn't complete the journey from one hemisphere to the other. The rain forests of Costa Rica's Caribbean and southwestern lowlands, for example, are the most northerly home of such southern species as the crab-eating raccoon and the dreaded jungle pit viper known as the bushmaster. The tropical dry forests of the northern Pacific slope are the southern limit for such North American species as the white-throated magpie-jay and the Virginia opossum. And then there are the tourists—migrants, that is—such as the dozens of northern bird species that spend their winter holidays in Costa Rica, among them the Tennessee warbler, western tanager, and yellow-bellied sapsucker. Costa Rica's many physical barriers and microclimates have also fostered the development of indigenous plants and animals, such as the mangrove hummingbird and mountain salamander.

delicious breakfast buffet, including homemade bread and granola. The laid-back German management can provide good advice about how to spend your time in the area. ✉ *70 m south of Banco Nacional, Santa Elena* ☎ *645–5067* 🖷 *645–5022* ⊕ *www.arcoirislodge.com* ⤢ *12 cabins* ⚅ *Horseback riding, laundry service; no a/c, no room phones, no room TVs* ▤ *AE, MC, V* ⚏ *EP.*

¢–$ ⚏ **El Bosque.** Convenient to the Bajo del Tigre nature trail and Meg's Stables, El Bosque's quiet, simple rooms are grouped around a central camping area. A bridge crosses a stream and leads to the hotel. Brick-oven pizzas are served on the veranda. ✉ *2½ km/1½ mi southeast of Santa Elena on road to Monteverde Reserve, Monteverde* ☎ *645–5221* 🖷 *645–5129* ✍ *elbosque@racsa.co.cr* ⚏ *Apdo. 5655, Santa Elena*

## FODOR'S FIRST PERSON

**Joy Rothke**
*Writer*

Bugs were my primary concern on my first visit to Costa Rica. Insects and I don't get along, and two decades of living in San Francisco had put my entomophobia into remission. I was pleasantly suprised when, after six weeks in the Northern Plains, I had only a handful of mosquito and chigger bites to show for it. Was I lucky? Tasteless to Tico bugs? Whatever it was, I returned to the States unbitten and unbowed.

A year later, I relocated to La Fortuna. My luck had obviously run out. On my first day I saw the uniquely Central American horror, the flying cockroach. It's big, and drops in for visits on even the most spotless kitchens. Every meal meant sharing the table with a bug. Even one crumb or drop of iced tea attracted ants. And then there were mosquitoes—swooping, buzzing, biting. Each morning I woke covered with scores of itchy red bites.

About 300,000+ insect species live in this little country, with thousands yet to be categorized. Locals, in their typically passive Tico way, just live with it. We fought back.

First we bought and installed a mosquito net over the bed. It was only partially effective, since very fine netting was unavailable. Then we got high-tech. Window screens. Hardly anyone here has them, and they had to be built from scratch. A few weeks later, and fully screened, my quality of life returned to a tolerable level.

I recently moved back to the U.S., and while I miss Costa Rica, it's no small consolation that the only insects that bug me now are on the Discovery Channel.

🛏 *29 rooms* ⚒ *Restaurant, bar, laundry service; no a/c, no room TVs* 🖃 *AE, MC, V* 🍴 *EP.*

¢ 🏨 **Pensión Monteverde Inn.** One of the cheapest inns in the area is quite far from the Monteverde Reserve entrance, on a 28-acre private preserve. The bedrooms are basic, but they have stunning views of the Golfo de Nicoya as well as hardwood floors, firm beds, and powerful, hot showers. Home cooking is served by the chatty David and María Savage and family. ✉ *5 km/3 mi past Butterfly Garden on turnoff road, Cerro Plano* ☎ *645–5156* 🛏 *10 rooms* ⚒ *Restaurant; no a/c, no room phones, no room TVs* 🖃 *No credit cards* 🍴 *EP.*

¢ 🏨 **Quetzal Inn.** Three buildings ascend a hill at three levels, both in price and elevation, at this family-run inn near the center of Santa Elena. Opt for the rooms in cedar- and guanacaste-wood cabins with balconies, in the lower-level building: they're the nicest. The lowest-priced rooms with shared bath are on the upper floor of the main building. Highest on the hill are more spartan wood-and-plaster cabins, the medium-range rooms here. All are pleasantly furnished. This is a real budget find. ✉ *75 m south of Banco Nacional, Santa Elena* ☎ *645–6076* 🖷 *645–5358* 🛏 *15 rooms, 11 with bath* ⚒ *Restaurant; no a/c, no room phones, no room TVs* 🖃 *No credit cards* 🍴 *EP.*

## Shopping

Part gallery, part workshop, **Art House** (☒ 1½ km/1 mi southeast of Santa Elena on road to Monteverde Reserve ☎ 645–5275) has five rooms of colorful, locally made carvings, masks, wall hangings, and hammocks. **Atmosphera** (☒ Turnoff to Jardín de Mariposas, Cerro Plano ☎ 645–6555) specializes in locally made primitivist wood carvings. **Art of the Forest** (☒ Next to Supermercado La Esperanza ☎ 645–5881) sells art made from the large, native jícara bean—they look fragile, but really aren't—that artist Mitch Lantz turns into lamps and candleholders.

**Chorotega** (☒ Next to gas station, Cerro Plano ☎ 645–6919) sells ceramics made by the indigenous Chorotega from the artisan community of Guaitil in northwest Costa Rica as well as Nicaraguan woodworking. The **Cooperativa de Artesanía de Santa Elena y Monteverde** (CASEM; ☒ Next to El Bosque hotel, Monteverde ☎ 645–5190) artisans' cooperative sells locally made crafts, mostly by women. The prices are much higher than at most other places. **Coopesanta Elena** (☒ Next to CASEM ☎ 645–5901) is the area's distributor for packages of the area's gourmet Café Monteverde coffee and accoutrements.

The **Community Art Center** (☒ 50 m southwest of Cheese Factory ☎ 645–6121) exhibits and sells the works of local artists and artisans. Local artist and art instructor Marco Tulio Brenes exhibits and sells his wood reliefs and turning, painting, and ceramic works at **Galería Extasis** (☒ 100 m west of CASEM, Monteverde ☎ 645–5548). Artists from around the country exhibit here, too. The **Hummingbird Gallery** (☒ Just outside entrance to Monteverde Reserve ☎ 645–5030) sells books, gifts, T-shirts, great Costa Rican coffee, prints, and slides by nature specialists Michael and Patricia Fogden, as well as watercolors by nature artist Sarah Dowell.

## Nightlife

"Wild night" takes on a particular meaning here. You can still get up close with nature after the sun has gone down. Several of the reserves have guided evening walks—advance reservations and separate admission are required—and the Ranario and Serpentario keep evening hours. Noted area biologist Richard LaVal presents a slide show called **Sounds and Scenes of the Cloud Forest** at the Monteverde Lodge nightly at 6:15 ($5). Advance reservations are required.

## To & From Monteverde & Santa Elena

*Monteverde is 167 km/104 mi (5 hours) northwest of San José. Santa Elena is 6 km/4 mi (30 minutes) north of Monteverde and 35 km/22 mi (2 hours) southeast of Tilarán.*

Getting here means negotiating some of the country's legendarily rough roads, but don't let that deter you from a visit. Years of promises to pave the way up here have collided with politics and scarce funds, but many residents remain just as happy to keep Monteverde out of the reach

| CAUTION |  |
| --- | --- |

The San José-to-Monteverde bus route is notorious for theft; watch your bags, and never let your passport and money out of your sight–or off your person.

of tour buses and day-trippers. Your own vehicle gives you the greatest flexibility, but a burgeoning number of shuttle-van services connect Monteverde with San José and other tourist destinations throughout the country. And once you're here, if without wheels, the community's rugged taxis can get you from hotel to restaurant to reserve. **Desafío Adventures** (⊠ Across from Supermercado La Esperanza ☎ 645–5874 ⊕ www.desafiocostarica. com) provides a fast, popular three-hour transfer between Monteverde and La Fortuna. The taxi-boat-taxi service costs $21 one-way.

If your bones can take it, a very rough track leads from Tilarán via Cabeceras to Santa Elena, near the Monteverde Cloud Forest Biological Reserve, doing away with the need to cut across to the Pan-American Highway. You need a 4WD vehicle and you should inquire locally about the current condition of the road. The views of Nicoya Peninsula, Lake Arenal, and Volcán Arenal reward those willing to bump around a bit. Note, too, that you don't really save much time—on a good day it takes about 2½ hours as opposed to the 3 required via Cañas and Río Lagarto on the highway.

### Monteverde & Santa Elena Essentials

🏧 Bank/ATM **Banco Nacional** ⊠ 50 m north of bus station, Santa Elena.

🏥 Hospital **Red Cross** ⊠ North side of Santa Elena ☎ 645–5127. **Seguro Social** ⊠ Near supermarket, Santa Elena ☎ 645–1156.

💊 Pharmacy **Vitosi** ⊠ Next to police station, south end of the road, Santa Elena ☎ 645–5004.

🌐 Internet **Historias Internet Café** ⊠ Road to Jardín de Mariposas, 75 m down from Pizzería de Johnny, Cerro Plano ☎ 645–6914.

📮 Post Office **Correos** ⊠ Center of Santa Elena.

ℹ️ Tourist Information **CETAM** ⊠ 150 m downhill from La Esperanza Supermarket, across from hardware, Santa Elena ☎ 645–5771.

# THE FAR NORTH

Apart from the sportfishing and Caño Negro National Wildlife Refuge, there's little reason to venture this far north while on vacation. You can cross into Nicaragua via Los Chiles here, but it's a difficult way to access the rest of Nicaragua.

## Caño Negro National Wildlife Refuge

**⓬**

Fodor'sChoice
★

A lowland rain-forest reserve in the far northern reaches of Alajuela, Refugio Nacional de Vida Silvestre Caño Negro covers 98 square km (38 square mi). Caño Negro has suffered severe deforestation over the years, but most of the Río Frío is still lined with trees, and the park's vast lake is an excellent place to watch such waterfowl as jabiru, anhinga, and the roseate spoonbill, as well as a host of resident exotic animals. In the dry season you can ride horses, but the visit here chiefly entails a wildlife-spotting boat tour. Caño Negro can be reached from the Nuevo Arenal–La Fortuna area, or you can approach via Upala (a bus from here takes 45 minutes). Visiting with a tour company is the best way to see the park. Camping is permitted, or you can stay in a couple of surprisingly nice lodgings in Caño Negro village—ones you'd never expect to find in such a far-flung corner of the country. 🖅 $6 ⊙ Daily 7–4.

## Outdoor Activities

Several La Fortuna–area tour companies have trips to Caño Negro: **Aventuras Arenal** (☎ 479–9133) runs top-notch, informative daylong tours, among the best in the country, down the Río Frío to Caño Negro for $48. Bring your jungle juice: the mosquitoes are voracious. **Bobo Adventures** (☎ 479–9390) has

**WORD OF MOUTH**

"[Caño Negro Wildlife Refuge] is where we saw the most diversity in wildlife. We saw Jesus lizards, caimans, iguanas, a sloth taking a bath right at the river edge, white-faced monkeys right next to the boat, [and] howler and spider monkeys in the trees in the distance."
                                    –cachas

trips to the Caño Negro Wildlife Refuge. **Jacamar Naturalist Tours** (☎ 479–9767 ⊕ www.arenaltours.com) is a well-established tour operator with three-hour boat trips ($50) on the Río Frío in the Caño Negro Nature Preserve.

FISHING  If you're here to fish, stay at the Caño Negro Natural Lodge or Fishing Club Caño Negro ( ⇨ *below*), both of which have sportfishing packages.

HORSEBACK  Horseback riding is arranged via the Caño Negro Natural Lodge or Fishing Club Caño Negro ( ⇨ *below*).
RIDING

## Where to Stay

$$ 🏨 **Caño Negro Natural Lodge.** That such an upscale property exists in this remote place might amaze you, but this Italian-designed, family-operated resort on the east side of the reserve is never pretentious. Rooms have high ceilings, colorful drapes and bedspreads, and huge showers; some rooms have bunk beds. There are two- and three-day packages available for anglers and nonanglers alike. The lodge has a variety of meal options; most guests opt for taking all meals here, since there are few other restaurants in town. Miniature golf, croquet, and badminton are a few of the on-site diversions. ⊠ *Caño Negro village* ☎ *471–1428, 265–2560 in San José* 🖷 *265–4561* ⊕ *www.canonegrolodge.com* 🛏 *10 rooms* ⚴ *Restaurant, in-room safes, pool, whirlpool tub, laundry service, meeting room; no room phones, no room TVs* ▤ *AE, MC, V* ⧫ *CP.*

$ 🏨 **Fishing Club Caño Negro.** Despite the name, all are welcome here, though the lodge is best known for its fishing tours, equipment and boat rental, and nearby lake filled with tarpon and bass. Four white bungalows of high-quality wood each contain two bright, sparkling rooms with terra-cotta tile floors, and are arranged around the wooded property. The produce from the lodge's citrus orchard ends up on your breakfast plate. ⊠ *Caño Negro village* ☎ *656–0071* 🖷 *656–0260* ⊕ *www.canonegro. com* 🛏 *8 rooms* ⚴ *Restaurant, fans, fishing, bar; no a/c, no room phones, no room TVs* ▤ *AE, MC, V* ⧫ *CP.*

## To & From Caño Negro

*91 km/57 mi (1½ hours) northwest of La Fortuna.*

Owing to its importance to the tourist economy, the highway from La Fortuna to Los Chiles is one the best-maintained in the northern lowlands. You can catch public buses in San José at Terminal Atlántico Norte twice a day, a trip of about five hours. Public buses also operate between La Fortuna and Los Chiles. If they have room, most tour companies (Aventuras Arenal and Bobo Adventures included) will allow you to ride along with them on their shuttles, for a cost of around $10.

## Crossing into Nicaragua via Los Chiles

Costa Rica's northernmost border crossing is Los Chiles, your typical poor, dusty border town. From the crossing it's a short boat trip to San Carlos, Nicaragua. Few tourists cross here, because there are virtually no roads on the other side, meaning access to other areas of Nicaragua is by boat. Most tourists use the easier approach via Peñas Blancas, to the west ( ⇨ chapter 6).

If you do cross here, you have to take one of the funky boats ($7) that ply the hour-long Río Frío route from Los Chiles to San Carlos, Nicaragua, several times daily. In San Carlos (a depressed town that makes you appreciate the "charms" of Los Chiles), you pass through the ramshackle, riverfront immigration point. Twice-weekly public boat service travels up the river from San Carlos to Lake Nicaragua and stops at the Solentiname Islands, Ometepe, and Granada (11 hours). Alternatively, "river taxis," picked up at the San Carlos dock, travel up the San Juan several times a day, stopping at tiny villages, sportfishing resorts, and everything in between. Los Chiles is directly off the Pan-American Highway, 12 km (7 mi) north of the Caño Negro Wildlife Refuge.

# THE PUERTO VIEJO LOOP

The Sarapiquí River gave its name to this region at the foot of the Cordillera Central mountain range. To the west is the rain forest of Braulio Carrillo National Park, and to the east are Tortuguero National Park and Barra del Colorado National Wildlife Refuge. These splendid national parks share the region with thousands of acres of farmland, including palm, banana, and pineapple plantations, as well as cattle ranching. Cheap land and rich soil brought a wave of Ticos to this area a half-century ago. Until the construction of Highway 126 in 1957, which connects the area to San José, this was one of the most isolated parts of Costa Rica, with little or no tourism. Government homesteading projects brought many residents, who cleared massive swathes of the rain forest for cattle grazing and agriculture. Now, ironically, old-growth lowland rain forest, montane cloud forest, and wetlands exist only within the borders of the national parks.

## Poás Volcano

🚻 Towering to the north of Alajuela, the verdant mass of Volcán Poás is covered with a quilt of farms and topped by a dark green shawl of cloud forest. A paved road leads all the way from Alajuela to its 8,800-foot summit, winding past coffee fields, patches of forest, pastures, fern farms, and increasingly spectacular views of the Central Valley. Most of the volcano's southern slope is covered with coffee, but the higher altitudes, which are too cold for that crop, hold screened-in fern and flower farms, neat rows of strawberries, and the light green pastures of dairy farms. Only the volcano's upper slopes and summit are still covered with cloud forest, which stretches northward toward Cerro Congo and east toward Volcán Barva. The road divides at Poasito, not far from the summit, where the route to the left leads to the national park, and the one to the right heads toward the intersection of Vara Blanca. At Vara Blanca, you can turn left for the Waterfall Gardens and Northern Zone, or continue straight to wind your way down the slopes of Volcán Barva to Heredia.

## Exploring

Fodor'sChoice
★ The 57-square-km (22-square-mi) **Poás Volcano National Park** (Parque Nacional Volcán Poás) protects epiphyte-laden cloud and elfin (small-tree) forest near the summit as well as a blue-green crater lake and the volcano's massive active crater. The main crater, nearly 1½ km (1 mi) across and 1,000 feet deep, is one of the largest active craters in the world. The sight of this vast, multicolored pit with smoking fumaroles and a gurgling, gray-turquoise sulfurous lake is captivating. All sense of scale is absent here, as the crater is devoid of vegetation. No one is allowed to venture into the crater, or walk along its edge.

The peak is frequently shrouded in mist, and many who come here see little beyond the lip of the crater. Be patient and wait awhile, especially if some wind is blowing—the clouds can disappear quickly. ■ TIP→ **The earlier in the day you go, the better your chance of a clear view. Aim to get there before 10 AM.** If you're lucky, you'll see the famous geyser in action, spewing a column of gray mud high into the air. Poás last had a major eruption in 1953 and is thought to be approaching another active phase; at any sign of danger the park is closed to visitors. It can be very cold and wet up top, so dress accordingly. If you come ill equipped, you can duck under a *sombrilla de pobre* (poor man's umbrella) plant, the leaves of which grow to diameters of 4 to 5 feet.

The park has a paved road that leads from the visitor center to the edge of the active crater, from which two trails head into the forest. The second trail, on the right just before the crater, winds through a thick mesh of shrubs and dwarf trees to the eerie but beautiful **Laguna Botos** (Botos Lake), which occupies an extinct crater. It takes 30 minutes to walk there and back. **Sendero Escalonia,** named for a tree common to the area, runs through a taller stretch of forest between the picnic area and the parking lot; boards along the way bear sentimental ecopoetry (in Spanish). Mammals are rare on Poás, but you should see various birds on either of these trails, including several kinds of hummingbirds and large, black sooty robins. Quetzals live in the park, but they rarely venture near the trails and crater. Note that Volcán Poás is a popular spot and gets quite crowded, especially on Sunday. It's not the place to go to commune with nature in solitude, but it is definitely worth seeing. The large visitor center has a scale model of the park, a display on vulcanology, a modest gift shop, and a cafeteria that serves hot coffee—perfect for those chilly afternoons. ⊠ *From Alajuela, drive north through town, and follow signs.* ☎ *482–2424, 192 in Costa Rica* ☜ *$7* ⊙ *Daily 8:30–3:30.*

★ Five magnificent waterfalls are the main attractions at **La Paz Waterfall Gardens,** on the eastern edge of Volcán Poás National Park, but they are complemented by the beauty of the surrounding cloud forest, an abundance of hummingbirds and other avian species, and the country's biggest butterfly garden. A concrete trail leads down from the visitor center to the multilevel, screened butterfly observatory and continues to gardens where hummingbird feeders attract swarms of those multicolored creatures. The trail then enters the cloud forest, where it leads to a series of metal stairways that let you descend into a steep gorge to viewing platforms near each of the waterfalls. A free shuttle will transport you from the trail exit back to the main building, if you prefer to avoid the hike uphill. Several alternative paths lead from the main trail through the cloud forest and along the river's quieter upper stretch, providing options for hours of exploration—it takes about 1½ hours to hike down the waterfall trail. The visitor center has a gift shop and open-air cafeteria with a great view. The gardens are 20 km (12 mi) northeast of Alajuela. ✉ *6 km/3 mi north of Vara Blanca* ☎ *482–2720* ⊕ *www. waterfallgardens.com* 🖃 *$21, $31 with lunch* ☉ *Daily 8–3:45.*

## Outdoor Activities

HORSEBACK RIDING
Guided horseback tours with **Poás Volcano Lodge** (✉ 500 m west of gas station ☎ 482–2194) take place in the cloud forest of Finca Legua, a private reserve 5 km (3 mi) north of the lodge. Daily tours ($65), which include lunch, run from 9 AM to 2 PM. Make reservations.

## Where to Stay & Eat

$   ✕ **Chubascos.** Amid tall pines and colorful flowers on the upper slopes
Fodor'sChoice of Poás Volcano, this popular restaurant has a small menu of traditional
★ Tico dishes and delicious daily specials. Choose from the full selection of casados and platters of *gallos* (homemade tortillas with meat, cheese, or potato fillings). The *refrescos* (fresh fruit drinks) are top-drawer, especially the ones made from locally grown *fresas* (strawberries) and *moras* (blackberries) blended with milk. ✉ *1 km/½ mi north of Fraijanes* ☎ *482–2280* 🖃 *AE, MC, V.*

$   ✕ **Jaulares.** Named after the Jaul, a tree common in the nearby cloud forest, this spacious restaurant specializes in grilled meat, though there are also several fish dishes and *chicharrones* (deep-fried meaty pork rinds). All the cooking is done with wood, which adds to the rustic ambience of terra-cotta floors, bare wooden beams, and sylvan surroundings. The house specialty, *lomito Jaulares* (Jaulares tenderloin), is a strip of grilled meat served with *gallo pinto* (rice and beans) and a mild *salsa criollo* (creole sauce). Though primarily a lunch spot, Jaulares stays open until midnight on weekends for concerts—Latin music on Friday nights and rock on Saturday nights. Four basic cabinas in back are an inexpensive overnight option, though you'll need to reserve them early for concert nights. ✉ *2 km/1 mi north of Fraijanes* ☎ *482–2155* 🖃 *AE, DC, MC, V.*

★ $$$–$$$$ 🛏 **Peace Lodge.** These rooms overlooking the misty forest of La Paz Waterfall Gardens seem like something out of the *Lord of the Rings,* with their curved, clay-stucco walls, hardwood floors (note that all but top floors can be noisy due to creaky footsteps), stone fireplaces (gas), and four-poster beds made of varnished logs, complete with mosquito-net canopy. They are proper abodes for elfin kings, especially the spacious, grottolike bathrooms with two showers, a whirlpool tub, tropical gardens, and private waterfall. Most hotels settle for a room with a bath. Peace Lodge gives you a bath with a room. And as if that weren't enough, you can soak in your second whirlpool tub on a porch with a cloud-forest view. Being able to explore the waterfall gardens before they open is another perk. The cuisine here is a couple of notches below the accommodations. ⊠ *3 km/2 mi north of Vara Blanca* ☎ *482–2720* ⊟ *482–2722* ⊕ *www. waterfallgardens.com* ⇝ *17 rooms, 1 villa* ⟂ *Restaurant, fans, in-room hot tubs, minibars, cable TV, gift shop; no a/c, no room phones* ⊟ *AE, DC, MC, V* ⏿ *BP.*

> **WORD OF MOUTH**
>
> "[Peace Lodge has] very unique bathrooms, with waterfall sinks, [but] it was a little fake and reminded me of Disney World, with the huge, painted concrete, imitation trees."
>
> –floydf
>
> "[Peace Lodge] is the place! Rooms are just great[–s]ervice, people, just wonderful. . . . Only drawback: they make a big deal out of a four course dinner ($28 per person), and the menu looks great, but the food just doesn't deliver."
>
> –SJacobs509

**$–$$** ⊞ **Poás Volcano Lodge.** The rustic architecture of this former dairy farmhouse, with rough stone walls and pitched beam roof, fits perfectly into the rolling pastures and forests that surround it. The interior mixes Persian rugs with textiles from Latin America, and Guaitil Indian pottery with North American pieces. The oversize sunken fireplace may be the lodge's most alluring feature. All rooms are different, so if possible, look at a few before you decide: one has an exquisite stone bathtub. The less expensive rooms, while not as opulent, have a more dependable supply of hot water. A small dairy farm and garden supply the kitchen with ingredients for the hearty breakfasts. ⊠ *6 km/4 mi east of Chubascos restaurant, on road to Vara Blanca* ⌖ *Apdo. 5723–1000, San José* ☎ *482–2194* ⊟ *482–2513* ⊕ *www. poasvolcanolodge.com* ⇝ *11 rooms, 7 with bath* ⟂ *Restaurant, billiards, Ping-Pong, laundry service, Internet; no a/c, no room phones, no room TVs* ⊟ *AE, DC, MC, V* ⏿ *BP.*

**$** ⊞ **Siempreverde B&B.** A night at this isolated B&B in the heart of a coffee plantation might be as close as you'll ever come to being a coffee farmer. The attractive wooden house has four nicely decorated rooms upstairs, with hardwood floors and small windows; the room downstairs is a bit dark. There's also a living room, kitchen, lounge, and terrace in back where breakfast is served. Photos of the coffee harvest decorate the walls, and just beyond the yard and manicured gardens that surround the house, neat rows of coffee plants stretch off into the distance. ⊠ *12 km/5 mi northwest of Tribunales de Justicia de Alajuela, turn left at colegio (high school)* ☎⊟ *449–5134* ⇝ *4 rooms with bath* ⟂ *Restaurant; no a/c, no room phones, no room TVs* ⊟ *AE, DC, MC, V* ⏿ *BP.*

## To & From Poás Volcano

*37 km/23 mi (45 minutes) north of Alajuela, 57 km/35 mi (1 hour) north of San José.*

■ TIP→→ Avoid taking a public bus to the park, as it can take up to five hours. Taxis from San José are around $80 (and around $40 from Alajuela). From the Pan-American Highway north of Alajuela, follow the signs for Poás. The road is in relatively good condition.

## Braulio Carrillo National Park

⓮ In a country where deforestation is still rife, hiking through Parque Nacional Braulio Carrillo is a rare opportunity to witness dense, primary tropical cloud forest. The park owes its foundation to the public outcry provoked by the construction of the highway of the same name through this region in the late 1970s—the government bowed to pressure from environmentalists, and somewhat ironically, the park is the most accessible one from the capital thanks to the highway. Covering 443 square km (171 square mi), Braulio Carrillo's extremely diverse terrain ranges from 108 feet to about 9,500 feet above sea level and extends from the central volcanic range down the Caribbean slope to La Selva research station near Puerto Viejo de Sarapiquí. The park protects a series of ecosystems ranging from the cloud forests on the upper slopes to the tropical wet forest of the Magsasay sector; it is home to 6,000 tree species, 500 bird species, and 135 mammal species.

The **Zurquí ranger station** is to the right of the highway, ½ km (¼ mi) before the Zurquí Tunnel. Here a short trail loops through the cloud forest. Hikes are steep; wear hiking boots to protect yourself from mud, slippage, and snakes. The main trail through primary forest, 1½ km (1 mi) long, culminates in a *mirador* (lookout point), but alas, the highway mars the view. Monkeys, tapirs, jaguars, kinkajous, sloths, raccoons, margays, and porcupines all live in this forest, and resident birds include the quetzal and the eagle. Orchids, bromeliads, heliconias, fungi, and mushrooms live closer to the floor. Another trail leads into the forest to the right, beginning about 17 km (11 mi) after the tunnel, where it follows the Quebrada González, a stream with a cascade and swimming hole. There are no campsites in this part of the park. The **Carrillo ranger station,** 22 km (14 mi) northeast along the highway from Zurquí, marks the beginning of trails that are less steep. Farther north on this highway, near the park entrance/exit toward Guápiles is the **Quebrada Gonzalez** ranger station. To the east of Heredia, a road climbs **Barva Volcano** (⇨ *below*) from San Rafael. ☎ *283–8004 Sistemas de Areas de Conservación, 192 (national parks hotline)* ⊠ *$6* ⊙ *Daily 7–4.*

The 9,500-foot summit of **Barva Volcano** is the highest point in Braulio Carrillo National Park. Dormant for 300 years now, Barva is massive: its lower slopes are almost completely planted with coffee fields and hold more than a dozen small towns, nearly all of which are named after saints. On the upper slopes are pastures lined with exotic pines and the occasional native oak or cedar, giving way to the botanical diversity of the cloud forest near the top. The air is usually cool near the summit, which combines with the pines and pastures to evoke the European or North American countryside.

Barva's misty, luxuriant summit is the only part of Braulio Carrillo where camping is allowed, and it's a good place to see the rare resplendent quetzal early in the morning. Because it's somewhat hard to reach, Barva receives a mere fraction of the crowds that flock to the summits of Poás and Irazú. A two- to four-hour hike in from the Barva ranger station takes you to the main crater, which is about 540 feet in diameter. Its almost vertical sides are covered in *sombrillas de pobre* (poor man's umbrellas), a plant that thrives in the highlands, and oak trees laden with epiphytes (nonparasitic plants that grow on other plants). The crater is filled with an otherworldly, black lake. Farther down the track into the forest lies a smaller crater lake. ■ TIP➜➜ Bring rain gear, boots, and a warm shirt. Stay on the trail when hiking anywhere in Braulio; even experienced hikers who know the area have lost their way up here, and the rugged terrain makes wandering through the woods very dangerous. In addition, muggings of hikers have been reported in the park. Go with a ranger if possible.

For access to the volcano, start from Sacramento, north of Heredia. North of Barva de Heredia the road grows narrow and steep. At Sacramento the paved road turns to dirt, growing worse as it nears the Barva ranger station. We recommend a 4WD vehicle, especially during the rainy season. From the ranger station you can take a 4WD over the extremely rocky road to the park entrance (dry season only), or hike up on foot. The walk through the cloud forest to the crater's two lakes takes two to four hours, but your efforts should be rewarded by great views (as long as you start before 8 AM, to avoid the mist). ⊠ *Access via the park's Barva ranger station* ☎ *283–5906, 192 in Costa Rica* ⚏ *$7 (in addition to $6 Braulio Carrillo Park entrance)* ⊙ *Tues.–Sun. 7–4.*

**San Rafael de Heredia,** 2 km (1 mi) northeast of Heredia, is a quiet, mildly affluent coffee town with a large church notable for its stained-glass windows and bright interior. The road north from the church winds its way up Barva Volcano to the hotels Chalet Tirol and La Condesa, ending atop the Monte de la Cruz lookout point.

## Outdoor Activities

HIKING  The upper slopes of **Barva Volcano** have excellent hiking conditions: cool air, vistas, and plentiful birds. The crater lakes topping the volcano can be reached only on foot, and if you haven't got a 4WD vehicle you'll also have to trek from Sacramento up to the entrance of Braulio Carrillo National Park. The trails are frequently muddy; ask about their condition at the ranger station. The **Sendero Botello** trail, on the east side of the park (entrance near the Quebrada Gonzáles ranger station off the Guápiles Highway), is a better choice for casual hikers.

HORSEBACK  Horseback-riding tours along the upper slopes of Volcán Barva combine views of the Central Valley with close exposure to the cloud forest and resident bird life. **Canopy Adventure** (⊠ Passo Llano, 7 km/4 mi north of Barva de Heredia ☎ 266–0782) runs horseback tours suitable for all levels of riders in its private cloud-forest reserve above San José
RIDING

de la Montaña. Rides can be combined with a canopy tour and lunch ($75); reserve in advance.

## Where to Stay

**$$–$$$** ▣ **Hotel La Condesa.** The stone fireplace surrounded by armchairs and a small bar in the La Condesa lobby is one of the many facets of the hotel that suggest a lodge you'd expect to find in a more northern latitude. In the central courtyard, topped by a giant skylight, is one of the hotel's three restaurants. A tropical garden is similarly enclosed in the pool area. Guest rooms are carpeted and tastefully furnished, and each has a picture window. Suites have bedroom lofts, sitting areas, and the hotel's best views. The log-cabin villas with full kitchens are ideal for families. ⊠ *Next to Castillo Country Club, 10 km/6 mi north of San Rafael de Heredia* ☎ *267–6001* 🖷 *267–6016* ↙ *61 rooms, 31 suites, 4 villas* ♨ *3 restaurants, in-room safes, some kitchens, minibars, cable TV, indoor pool, whirlpool tub, horseback riding, 2 bars, laundry service, meeting room, car rental, tours; no a/c* ▭ *AE, DC, MC, V* ⏍*BP.*

**$** ▣ **Hotel Chalet Tirol.** The Austrian design here doesn't seem out of place amid the pines, pastures, and cool air of Volcán Barva's upper slopes. The replica of a cobbled Tirolean town square—complete with fountain and church—may be a bit much, but the cozy, bright two-story wooden chalets are charming, as is the restaurant, with its ivy, wooden ceiling, and elegant murals. High-quality French cuisine makes this a popular weekend destination for Costa Ricans. The suites have fireplaces and are more private than the chalets. ⊠ *Main road, 10 km/6 mi north of San Rafael de Heredia* 🏛 *Apdo. 7812–1000, San José* ☎ *267–6222* 🖷 *267–6373* ↙ *13 suites, 10 chalets* ♨ *Restaurant, cable TV, tennis court, bar, laundry service; no a/c* ▭ *AE, DC, MC, V* ⏍*CP.*

**$** ▣ **Las Ardillas.** Surrounded by old pines on a country road, these unpretentious log cabins are inviting retreats for those looking to lock themselves up in front of a fireplace and tune out the world. The small on-site spa is a good reason to venture from the comfortable, romantic rooms. The restaurant specializes in meats roasted over a wood fire and has a nice selection of Spanish wines. All rooms have modest wood furniture and queen-size beds. ⊠ *Main road, Guacalillo de San José de la Montaña* 🏛 *Apdo. 44–309, Barva* ☎ *260–2172* 🖷 *266–0251* ↙ *15 cabins* ♨ *Restaurant, kitchenettes, whirlpool tub, massage, sauna, spa, bar; no a/c, no room phones* ▭ *AE, MC, V* ⏍*BP.*

## To & From Braulio Carrillo National Park
*30 km/19 mi (45 minutes) north of San José.*

From San José, travel northeast on Calle 3, which become the Guápiles Highway (Hwy. 32), toward Limón. This highway winds through the park, entering at the main ranger station, Zurquí, and exiting at the Quebrada Gonzalez ranger station. The Barva station is on the west side of the park, north of Zurquí, and is the easiest to access. From Heredia, drive north to Sacramento on Hwy. 114. The station is 4 km (2½ mi) northeast of Sacramento on a trail that's accessible on foot or by 4WD (except during heavy rains).

Any bus going to Guapiles, Síquirres, and Puerto Viejo de Sarapiquí can drop you off at the Zurquí ranger station. Buses ($2) depart from San José Monday through Saturday from the TUASA bus station and Sundays from the central market and return from park at 2:30 PM. A cab from San José costs $40–$50. A number of tour companies offer one-day tours from San José.

## Puerto Viejo de Sarapiquí

**⑮** In the 19th century, Puerto Viejo de Sarapiquí was a thriving river port and the only link with the coastal lands straight east, now Barra del Colorado National Wildlife Refuge and Tortuguero National Park. Fortunes nose-dived with the construction of the coastal canal from the town of Moín, and today Puerto Viejo has a slightly run-down air. The activities of the Nicaraguan Contras made this a danger zone in the 1980s, but now that the political situation has improved, boats once again ply the old route up the Río Sarapiquí to the Río San Juan on the Nicaraguan frontier, from where you can travel downstream to Barra del Colorado or Tortuguero. A few tour companies have Sarapiquí River tours with up to Class III rapids in the section between Chilamate and La Virgen with plenty of wildlife to see. If you prefer to leave the driving to them, many of the lodges operate boat tours on the tamer sections of the river.

### Exploring

Bats are not blind, contrary to popular belief, and most have no interest in sucking your blood. Just a couple of things you learn on the **Bat Tour** at the nonprofit **Tirimbina Rainforest Center.** The center encompasses 750 acres of primary forest and 8 km (5 mi) of trails, some of them traversing hanging bridges at canopy level. Reservations are required for all tours. ⊠ *La Virgen de Sarapiquí, 17 km/11 mi southwest of Puerto Viejo* ☎ *761–1579* ⊕ *www.tirimbina.org* ⊠ *$10, $15 guided tour, $15 bat tour* ☉ *Daily 7–5, bat tour daily 7:30 PM, guided tours 8 AM and 2 PM.*

Costa Rica's indigenous peoples don't get the visibility of those in Guatemala or Mexico, probably because they number only 40,000 out
★ of a population of 4 million. The **Museo de Culturas Indígenas Doctora María Eugenia Bozzoli** (Dr. María Eugenia Bozzoli Museum of Indigenous Cultures), part of the Centro Neotrópico Sarapiquís, provides a well-rounded all-under-one-roof introduction to the subject. Nearly 400 artifacts of the Boruca, Bribri, Cabécar, Guaymí, and Maleku peoples are displayed, including masks, musical instruments, and shamanic healing sticks. Start by watching a 17-minute video introduction, *Man and Nature in Pre-Columbian Costa Rica*. A botanical garden next door cultivates medicinal plants still used by many traditional groups. In 1999 researchers discovered an archaeological site on the grounds that contains pre-Columbian tombs and petroglyphs dating from the 15th century. The site is still under study. ⊠ *La Virgen de Sarapiquí, 17 km/11 mi southwest of Puerto Viejo* ☎ *761–1418* ⊕ *www.sarapiquis.org* ⊠ *$12 (includes guide)* ☉ *Daily 9–5.*

## Certificate of Sustainable Tourism

CLOSE UP

**ONE TRIP TO COSTA RICA AND** you'll swear everything here is eco-lodges, eco-tourism, eco-this, eco-that. But "sustainability," the buzzword in Costa Rican tourism these days, also has to do with conserving cultural resources. The Certification for Sustainable Tourism (CST) program, administered jointly by the Costa Rican Tourism Institute, National Chamber of Tourism, Ministry of the Environment, and University of Costa Rica, recognizes businesses that adhere to those ideals. Those that submit to a rigorous assessment are evaluated on their employment of local people, respect for local culture, contribution to the economic and social well-being of the community, and preservation of natural resources. Businesses that rely heavily on foreign investment and whose earnings are mostly repatriated outside Costa Rica don't make the cut (but probably don't submit to an evaluation in the first place).

Instead of stars, 51 hotels have earned one to five leaves for their efforts. At this writing, Finca Rosa Blanca, north of Heredia, and Lapa Ríos, at Cabo Matapalo, are the only two lodgings to hold five leaves. The resort and hotels that are recognized are not all small "mom-and-pop" places: Manuel Antonio's Sí Como No and Arenal's Tabacón have been recognized as well. Nor are they only places in the middle of the rain forest: San José's large but unobtrusive Clarion Amón Plaza is among several city lodgings proudly displaying awards.

While other countries have their own rating systems for eco-friendly lodgings, many of these suffer from corrupt policies that allow ratings to be bought. The CST is one of the best and most thorough awards programs in the world. In fact, the World Tourism Organization has adopted it as its model, and countries from Mexico to Malawi now employ similar standards. You'll find a list of Costa Rican CST holders at the program's Web site, www.turismo-sostenible.co.cr.

A working dairy farm and horse ranch, the **Hacienda Pozo Azul** runs guided tours of the ecologically sound 360-cattle dairy operation. It also has many adventure tours (⇨ Outdoor Activites, *below*). ⊠ *La Virgen de Sarapiquí, 17 km/11 mi southwest of Puerto Viejo* ☎ *761–1360 or 438–2616* ⊕ *www.haciendapozoazul.com* ☞ *$10* ◷ *By reservation.*

Heliconias abound at the aptly named **Heliconia Island** in the Sarapiquí River. Some 70 species of the flowering plant, a relative of the banana, are among the collections that populate five acres of botanical gardens here. Expect to see ample bird and butterfly life too. ⊠ *La Chaves, 8 km/5 mi south of Puerto Viejo de Sarapiquí* ☎ *766–6247* ☞ *$7.50* ◷ *Daily 9–5.*

Curious about the life and times of Costa Rica's most famous yellow fruit? The **Standard Fruit Company**, known as Dole in North America, has two-hour Banana Tours to guide you through the process from plantation to processing to packing. Visits are best arranged through several San José travel agencies, who will transport you to any of the three sites. Options include a plantation in Sarapiquí or sites in Siquirres or south of Limón. ☏ 768–8683 or 383–4596 ⊠ $10 ⊙ *Tours daily at 10* AM.

## Outdoor Activities

**Hacienda Pozo Azul** (⊠ La Virgen de Sarapiquí, 17 km/11 mi southwest of Puerto Viejo ☏ 761–1360 or 438–2616 ⊕ www.haciendapozoazul. com) is a dairy farm and ranch with biking, horseback riding, rafting, canopy tours, float tours, and rappelling excursions that allow you to combine several activities in a day. **Hotel Gavilán Río Sarapiquí** (☏ 766–6743 ⊕ www.gavilanlodge.com) runs wildlife- and bird-watching tours from its site near Puerto Viejo de Sarapiquí up to the San Juan River. Passports are required for the trip, since the San Juan lies entirely within Nicaragua.

CANOPY TOUR  The canopy tour ($45) at **Hacienda Pozo Azul** (⇨ *above*) has 13 zip lines, one topping 300 feet.

HORSEBACK RIDING  Dairy farm **Hacienda Pozo Azul** (⇨ *above*) is also a horse ranch and has riding excursions for all experience levels through the region around La Virgen. A two-hour tour is $30; a half-day is $45.

MOUNTAIN BIKING  **Aventuras de Sarapiquí** (☏ 766–6768 ⊕ www.sarapiqui.com/biking. html) has half-day and multiday biking trips for casual and serious riders. **Costa Rica Biking Adventure** (☏ 225–6591 ⊕ www.bikingincostarica. com) runs one-day mountain-biking tours of the area. **Hacienda Pozo Azul** (⇨ *above*) has half-day, full-day, and two-day rough-and-tumble back-roads bike tours ($30–$50).

RAFTING  The Virgen del Socorro area is one of the most popular "put-in points" for white-water rafters, and offers both Class II and III rapids. Trips leaving from the Chilamate put-in are more tranquil, with mostly Class I rapids. The put-in point depends on the weather and season.

Several operators lead tours on the Sarapiquí River, including: **Aventuras Naturales** (☏ 225–3939 ⊕ www.adventure-costarica.com), **Costa Rica Expeditions** (☏ 222–0333 ⊠ 257–1665 ⊕ www.costaricaexpeditions. com), **Hacienda Pozo Azul** (⇨ Horseback Riding, *above*), and **Ríos Tropicales** (☏ 233–6455 ⊕ www.riostropicales.com). Prices range from $30 to $70.

RAPPELLING  **Hacienda Pozo Azul** (⇨ *above*) guides you on a 90-foot river canyon descent ($20).

## Where to Stay

$–$$ ▥ **Centro Neotrópico Sarapiquís.** Overlooking the Río Sarapiquí, the CNS is an environmental educational center, museum, gardens, and hotel all rolled into one. Three indigenous-inspired circular palenque buildings with palm-thatched roofs house the ample-size rooms. All come with a tile floor, pre-Columbian-style decor, and a private terrace. There's an extra cost to visit the center's numerous attractions. ⊠ *La Virgen de Sarapiquí, 17 km/11 mi southwest of Puerto Viejo* ☏ *761–1004* ⊠ *761–1415* ⊕ *www.sarapiquis.org* ⇲ *36 rooms* �ዽ *Restaurant, coffee shop, fans, bar, library, gift shop, laundry service, meeting room; no a/c, no room TVs, no smoking* ▤ *AE, DC, MC, V* ▯ *EP.*

★ **$$** ▦ **Selva Verde Lodge.** Built on stilts over the Río Sarapiquí, this expansive complex stands on the edge of a 2-square-km (1-square-mi) private reserve of tropical rain forest and caters primarily to natural-history tours. The buildings have wide verandas strung with hammocks, and the rooms come with polished wood paneling and mosquito blinds. Activities include guided walks, boat trips, canoeing, rafting, and mountain biking. Room prices include a bird-watching tour. Reserve a few weeks ahead, especially in high season; the place is very popular with tour groups. ⊠ *7 km/4 mi west of Puerto Viejo de Sarapiquí* ☐ *Apdo. 55, Chilamate* ☎ *766–6800, 800/451–7111 in North America* 🖷 *766–6011* ⊕ *www.selvaverde.com* ⇨ *40 rooms, 5 bungalows* ☐ *Restaurant, fans, boating, horseback riding, library, laundry service, meeting room; no a/c, no room phones, no room TVs* ▭ *AE, MC, V* ⊖ *FAP.*

$ ▦ **Hotel El Bambú.** Unlike the many isolated properties in this region, Bambú is in the heart of Puerto Viejo de Sarapiquí. The rooms are simple but comfortable. A dense cluster of tall bamboo stalks climbs like Jack's beanstalk out of the garden, lending shade for the bar and restaurant, the latter of which serves Costa Rican–influenced Chinese food at reasonable prices. ⊠ *Main street across from town square and soccer field* ☎ *766–6005* 🖷 *766–6132* ⊕ *www.elbambu.com* ☐ *Apdo. 1518–2100, Guadalupe* ⇨ *16 rooms* ☐ *Restaurant, pool, gym, bar, laundry service, tours, no-smoking rooms* ▭ *AE, MC, V* ⊖ *BP.*

$ ▦ **Hotel Gavilán Río Sarapiquí.** Beautiful gardens run down to the river, and colorful tanagers and three types of toucan feast in the citrus trees. The two-story lodge has comfortable rooms with white walls, terra-cotta floors, and decorative crafts. The food, Costa Rican *comida típica* (typical fare), has earned its good reputation. Prime activities are horseback jungle treks and boat trips up the Río Sarapiquí. ⊠ *700 m north of Comando Atlántico (naval command)* ⊕ *www.gavilanlodge.com* ☐ *Apdo. 445–2010, San José* ☎ *766–6743, 234–9507 in San José* 🖷 *253–6556* ⇨ *13 rooms* ☐ *Restaurant, fans, whirlpool tub, fishing, horseback riding; no a/c, no room phones, no room TVs* ▭ *AE, DC, MC, V* ⊖ *BP.*

$ ▦ **Posada Andrea Cristina.** Alexander Martinez and his wife Florabel own and operate this friendly and comfortable bed-and-breakfast. High-ceilinged rooms have private bathrooms and hot water. Two A-frame bungalows share a (cold-water-only) bathroom. All bungalows and rooms have private gardens with hammocks. ⊠ *½ km/¼ mi west of town, La Guai'ra* ☎ *766–6265* 🖷 *766–6265* ⊕ *www.andreacristina.com* ⇨ *4 rooms, 2 bungalows with shared bath* ☐ *Restaurant, tours; no a/c* ▭ *No credit cards* ⊖ *BP.*

## To & From Puerto Viejo de Sarapiquí
*6½ km/4 mi north of La Selva.*

The Carretera Braulio Carrillo (Braulio Carrillo Highway) runs from C. 3 in San José and passes the Zurquí and Quebrada Gonzáles sectors of Braulio Carrillo National Park. It branches at Santa Clara, north of the park, with the paved Highway 4 continuing north to Puerto Viejo de Sarapiquí. Alternatively, an older winding road connects San José with Puerto Viejo de Sarapiquí, passing through Heredia and Vara Blanca.

CLOSE UP

# Bird Country

3

**NEARLY 850 BIRD SPECIES** have been identified in Costa Rica, more than in the United States and Canada combined, and all in an area about half the size of Kentucky. Consequently, bird-watchers flock here by the thousands. The big attractions tend to be eye-catching species like the keel-billed toucan, but it is the diversity of shape, size, coloration, and behavior that makes bird-watching in Costa Rica so fascinating.

**Tropical superstars:** Parrots, parakeets, and macaws; toucans and toucanets; and the elusive but legendary resplendent quetzal are a thrill for those of us who don't see them every day.

**In supporting roles:** Lesser known but equally impressive species include motmots, with their distinctive racket tails; oropéndolas, which build remarkable hanging nests; and an amazing array of hawks, kites, and falcons.

**Color me red, blue, yellow . . . :** Two of the most striking species are the showy scarlet macaw and the quirky purple gallinule; tanagers, euphonias, manakins, cotingas, and trogons are some of the country's loveliest plumed creatures, but none of them match the iridescence of the hummingbirds ( ⇨ below).

**Singing in the rain:** The relatively inconspicuous and seemingly ubiquitous clay-colored robin is Costa Rica's national bird. It may look plain, but its song is melodious, and since the males sing almost constantly toward the end of the dry season—the beginning of their mating season—

local legend has it that they call the rains.

**The big and the small of it:** The scintillant hummingbird is a mere 2½ inches tall and weighs just over 2 grams, while the jabiru, a long-legged stork, can grow to more than 4 feet tall and can weigh up to 14 pounds.

**Hummingbirds:** Costa Rica hosts 51 members of the hummingbird family, compared with just one species for all of the United States east of the Rocky Mountains. Time spent near a hummingbird feeder will treat you to an unforgettable display of accelerated aerial antics and general pugnacity.

**"Snow birds":** If you're here between October and April, don't be surprised if some feathered friends from home made similar vacation plans. When northern birds fly south for the winter, they don't all head to Miami. Seasonal visitors like the Kentucky warbler make up about a quarter of the amazing avian panorama in Costa Rica.

Bird-watching can be done everywhere in the country—all you need is a pair of binoculars and a copy of *A Guide to the Birds of Costa Rica*, the excellent field guide by Gary Stiles and Alexander Skutch. And don't let the rainy season deter you: seasonal *lagunas* (lagoons) such as Caño Negro and the swamps of Palo Verde National Park, which disappear during the dry months, are excellent places to see birds. For more information, *see* the Wildlife Glossary *in* the Understanding Costa Rica chapter.

The former route is easier, with less traffic; the latter route is more scenic but heavily trafficked. The roads are mostly paved, with the usual rained-out dirt and rock sections; road quality depends on the time of year, the length of time since the last visit by a road crew, and/or the amount of rain dumped by the latest tropical storm. Heavy rains sometimes cause landslides that block the highway near the Zurquí Tunnel. Check conditions before you set out. ■ TIP→→ There are gas stations just outside Puerto Viejo de Sarapiquí. Fill the tank when you get the chance.

### Puerto Viejo de Sarapiquí Essentials

🏦 Bank/ATM **Banco Nacional** ⊠ 100 m east of soccer field. **Banco Popular** ⊠ West corner of soccer field.

🏦 Hospital **Red Cross** ⊠ West end of town ☎ 710-6901.

🏦 Internet **Internet Sarapiquí** ⊠ Next to Joyería Mary ☎ 766-6223.

🏦 Post Office **Correos** ⊠ 50 m north of soccer field.

## La Selva Biological Station

**⑯** At the confluence of the Puerto Viejo and Sarapiquí rivers, La Selva packs about 420 bird species, 460 tree species, and 500 butterfly species into just 15 square km (6 square mi). Spottings might include the spider monkey, poison dart frog, agouti, collared peccary, and dozens of other rare creatures. ■ TIP→→ If you want to see wildlife without having to rough it, skip Rara Avis and come here. Extensive, well-marked trails and swing bridges connect habitats as varied as tropical wet forest, swamps, creeks, rivers, secondary regenerating forest, and pasture. To see the place, take an informative 3½-hour morning or afternoon nature walk with one of La Selva's bilingual guides, who are some of the country's best. Walks start every day at 8 AM and 1:30 PM. You can add a noontime lunch to your walk for $9; schedule it in advance. For a completely different view of the forest, set off on a guided dawn walk at 5:30 AM, or the night tour at 7 PM. Or get a group of at least five together and enroll in the Saturday-morning Bird-watching 101 course ($40 per person). Advance reservations are required for the dawn and night walks as well as for the Saturday-morning course. ☎ 766-6565 or 240-6696 🖷 766-6535 or 240-6783 ⊕ www.ots.ac.cr ⌖ OTS, Apdo. 676-2050, San Pedro ⊠ Nature walk $26, morning and afternoon walks $40, night walks $30 ⊙ Walks daily at 8 AM and 1:30 PM.

### Where to Stay

**$$** ▦ **La Selva.** Other lodges provide more comfort for the money, but none can match La Selva's tropical nature experience. The dorm-style rooms have large bunk beds, tile floors, and lots of screened windows. The restaurant, something like a school cafeteria, serves decent food but has a very limited schedule (reserve ahead). It's a good idea to pay the full-board fee, which includes a guided nature walk and three meals a day with your room rate, since there's nowhere else to eat. Priority is given to researchers, so advance reservations are essential. ⊠ 6 km/3½ mi south of Puerto Viejo de Sarapiquí ☎ 766-6565, 240-6696 in San Pedro ⌖ OTS, Apdo. 676-2050, San Pedro 🖷 240-6783 ⇨ 60 bunk beds share 12 baths, 3 cabins ⌂ Restaurant, fans, laundry facilities; no a/c, no room phones, no room TVs ▤ AE, MC, V ⏀ FAP.

## To & From La Selva

*6 km/3½ mi south of Puerto Viejo de Sarapiquí, 79 km/49 mi (2–4 hours) northeast of San José.*

To get here, drive south from Puerto Viejo and look for signs on the west side of the road. For those without wheels, La Selva is a $4 taxi ride from Puerto Viejo de Sarapiquí.

# Rara Avis

3

⑰ Toucans, sloths, great green macaws, howler and spider monkeys, vested anteaters, and tapirs may be on hand to greet you when you arrive at Rara Avis, one of Costa Rica's most popular private reserves and open only to overnight guests. Ecologist Amos Bien founded Rara Avis with the intent of combining research, tourism, and the sustainable extraction of forest products. Bilingual guides take you along the muddy trails—boots are provided—and canopy observation platforms and help point out wildlife. Or go on your own to the orchid house and butterfly garden. Bring a camera: the reserve's lacy double waterfall is one of Costa Rica's most photogenic sights.

The town of **Las Horquetas** is the jumping-off point for the 13-square-km (8-square-mi) private reserve. The 16-km (10-mi) trip from Las Horquetas to the reserve can be accomplished in three hours on horseback, two to three hours by tractor (leaves daily at 8:30 AM), or one hour by four-wheel-drive vehicle, plus a rough 3-km (2-mi hike) up to the lodge proper. The trails are steep and rugged, but the flora and fauna en route are remarkable. ⚠ There have been some complaints that, although the reserve itself is lovely, the guides and services are considerably less impressive.

## Where to Stay

$$–$$$ 🏠 **Rara Avis.** There are three lodging options here. The Waterfall Lodge, near a 197-foot waterfall, has hardwood-paneled rooms with chairs, firm beds, balconies, and hammocks. Despite the prices, accommodation is rustic, with minimal amenities and no electricity. More basic, Las Casitas are three two-room cabins with shared bath. On the high end, ideal for a rustic honeymoon, is the River Edge Cabin, a 10-minute walk through the forest (it's dark at night, but you're given a flashlight), with private bath and balcony and solar panel–generated electricity. Rates include guides and transport from Las Horquetas. It's time-consuming to get here, so the recommended stay is two nights. ✉ *Las Horquetas* ☎ *764–3151* 🖷 *764–4187* ⊕ *www.rara-avis.com* ⇲ *16 rooms, 10 with bath* ⚓ *Restaurant; no a/c, no room phones, no room TVs* ▭ *AE, MC, V* ⏀ *AI.*

$$ 🏠 **Sueno Azul Resort.** This nature lodge and wellness retreat is the most luxurious property in the area, and a favorite for honeymooners and those attracted by the wide variety of yoga and other "wellness" disciplines. Spacious rooms have high ceilings, two double beds, large bathrooms, and a private porch overlooking either one of the rivers or a small lake. One large junior suite has its own outdoor whirlpool tub. Meals are served in an open-air dining room with a view. A wide range of tours and activi-

ties is offered, including rain-forest hikes, horseback riding, mountain biking, and fly-fishing, as well as trips to major attractions. The spa and yoga facility is impressive for this area. ✉ *Just west of Horquetas, off Hwy 4* ☎ *764–4244* 🖷 *764–3129* ⊕ *www.suenoazulresort.com* ⇋ *45 rooms* ♨ *Restaurant, fans, pool, whirlpool tub, spa, laundry service, gift shop, bar, meeting rooms; no a/c in some rooms* ▤ *MC, V* ⦿ *EP.*

### To & From Rara Avis
*17 km/11 mi (20 minutes) south of Las Horquetas, 100 km/62 mi (2 hours) north of San José.*

From Braulio Carrillo, turn left at signs for Puerto Viejo de Sarapiquí and continue on to Las Horquetas.

# THE NORTHERN PLAINS ESSENTIALS

## Transportation

**BY AIR**

ARRIVING & DEPARTING
NatureAir has flights from San José to La Fortuna. For more information, *see* Air Travel *in* Smart Travel Tips A to Z.

**BY BUS**

ARRIVING & DEPARTING
For more information about bus travel between the Northern Plains and San José, *see* Bus Travel *in* Smart Travel Tips A to Z.

GETTING AROUND
Buses in this region are typically large, clean, and fairly comfortable but often crowded Friday through Sunday. Don't expect air-conditioning. Even supposedly express buses marked *directo* (direct) often make numerous stops. Bus schedules are constantly changing. If your plans aren't flexible, go to the station the day before you depart to check the schedule.

**BY CAR**

ARRIVING & DEPARTING
Road access to the northwest is by way of the paved two-lane Pan-American Highway (Carretera Interamericana, or CA1), which starts from the west end of Paseo Colón in San José and runs northwest through Cañas and Liberia and to Peñas Blancas at the Nicaraguan border.

GETTING AROUND
Before you decide to drive here, think long and hard. On the plus side, a personal vehicle offers you freedom and mobility. On the minus, it's expensive, the roads are by and large terrible, and Ticos are reckless drivers. Four-wheel-drive vehicles are best on the frequently potholed roads. If you don't want to pay for 4WD, at least rent a car with high clearance. Many rental agencies insist you take a 4WD vehicle if you mention Monteverde as part of your itinerary. The roads here are some of the worst in the country.

Drivers here will attempt to pass you on even the narrowest roads and bridges. Resistance is futile, so take a deep breath and let them pass. If the triangular CEDA EL PASO sign faces you, yield to oncoming traffic before you proceed across the bridge. Prepare to be honked at, tailgated, and passed even on the narrowest roads.

🏛 Major Rental Agencies **Alamo** ✉ 100 m west of church, La Fortuna ☎ 479-9090.
🏛 Local Rental Agencies **Poás Rentacar** ✉ 50 m south of church, La Fortuna
☎ 479-8418.

### BY SHUTTLE VAN

ARRIVING &
DEPARTING

If you prefer a speedier, more private form of travel, consider taking a shuttle. Gray Line has daily service between San José, Fortuna and Arenal ($25), and Monteverde ($38). Comfortable air-conditioned vans leave various San José hotels around 8:30 in the morning and return midafternoon. During high season, purchase your tickets at least a day in advance. Service is also provided from Arenal and Monteverde to several Pacific-coast beaches. Interbus also connects San José with La Fortuna ($25) and Monteverde ($38) daily, with connections from there to a few of the North Pacific beaches. Apart from schedule, there's little difference between Gray Line and Interbus.

🏛 Shuttle Van Services **Gray Line Tourist Bus** ☎ 232-3681 or 220-2126 ⊕ www.graylinecostarica.com. **Interbus** ☎ 283-5573 ⊕ www.interbusonline.com.

## Contacts & Resources

Banks, Internet cafés, post offices, and emergency contacts follow each town listed in the chapter.

### BANKS & EXCHANGE SERVICES

Most hotels, tour companies, and retailers accept credit cards and debit cards. Visa and MasterCard predominate; a few retailers accept American Express. Changing U.S. dollars or traveler's checks is possible at Banco Nacional branches scattered throughout the region, but lines are long. Because of fraud, most retailers won't accept traveler's checks.

You'll find a small but growing number of *cajeros automáticos* (ATMs) out here: Banco Nacional offices in La Fortuna and Santa Elena, as well as Banex in Ciudad Quesada and CooTilarán in Tilarán, are affiliated with the ATH (A Todas Horas) network, and accept Cirrus- and Plus-linked cards.

There's no rush to change dollars for *colones*. American currency is accepted even in the smallest towns.

### INTERNET

Internet cafés are easy to find in most areas of the Northern Plains, with hourly rates averaging around $1.50–$2. Virtually all have only dial-up service. At upscale hotels or resorts, rates can run as high as $6–$7 per hour.

### MAIL & SHIPPING

The privatized Correos de Costa Rica (Post Office of Costa Rica) provides inexpensive but slow postal service from this region. Expect postcards to take at least two weeks to reach their destination in the U.S. The Costa Rican customs service is notoriously corrupt, and many outgoing packages containing valuables never make it past them. Shipping valuables via UPS or FedEx is a better bet, though San José is the closest place to do that.

# North Pacific

Conchal Beach

**WORD OF MOUTH**

"In the rainy season, go to Guanacaste, the driest region of Costa Rica. There are great beaches on the Nicoya Peninsula. At this time the nature is green, the beaches are not crowded, prices are lower, and it rains normally one hour a day in the late afternoon or in the night."

—costaklaus

# WELCOME TO THE NORTH PACIFIC

## TOP 5
## Reasons to Go

**1** **Beaches:** White sand, black sand, palm-fringed strands, beaches for swimming, partying, surfing, and sunbathing—you can't beat Guanacaste's beaches for sheer variety.

**2** **Rincón de la Vieja National Park:** Mud pools bubble and fumaroles steam on the forested slopes of this active volcano. Turn up the heat with a soak in a hot sulphur spring.

**3** **Surfing Witch's Rock and Ollie's Point:** The waves off the coast of Santa Rosa National Park are legendary.

**4** **Turtle tours:** From October through April at Playa Grande and Playa Ostional, witness the life-and-death drama of thousands of sea-turtle hatchlings scurrying to the sea past a daunting array of predators.

**5** **Scuba diving:** Forget the pretty tropical fish. Sharks, rays, sea turtles, and moray eels are the large-scale attractions for divers on the Guanacaste coast.

Dry, hot Far Northern Guanacaste is traditionally ranching country. But Rincón de la Vieja National Park, with wildlife and one of Costa Rica's five active volcanoes, is here; as is Bahía Salinas, second to Lake Arenal for wind- and kitesurfing.

Ostional Wildlife Refuge

# Getting Oriented

This vast, inland chunk of land in northwestern Costa Rica—which comprises Guanacaste Province—is bordered by the Pacific Ocean to the west and the looming Cordillera de Guanacaste volcanic mountain range to the east. To the south is the Nicoya Peninsula, with almost continuous beaches along more than 60 miles of Pacific coastline, as the crow flies. Roads are mostly unpaved, so absent your own boat, the best way to get around is in a four-wheel-drive vehicle. Take a plane, bus, or shuttle van to Liberia and pick up your rental car there.

Church of San Blas, Nicoya

Playa Hermosa

National parks Palo Verde and Barra Honda are the main attractions in The Tempisque River Basin. The former is a prime bird- and wildlife-watching park; the latter is filled with caves ripe for exploration.

The number and variety of beaches along The Nicoya Coast make it a top tourist destination. Each beach has its specialty, be it surfing, fishing, diving, or just plain relaxing. Top hotels and restaurants are in generous supply.

Tamarindo Beach

# NORTH PACIFIC PLANNER

## When to Go

Guanacaste is the driest region of the country, with only 65 inches of average annual rainfall, and the hottest, with average temperatures around 30–35°C (86–95°F). The best time to visit is the shoulder season (mid-November–January), when the landscape is green, the evening air is cool, and hotels and restaurants energetically gear up for the tourist influx. Rainy-season travel (May–December) means lower prices and fewer crowds, but some restaurants and hotels are closed, and nearly every afternoon brings downpours. Avoid the January–March high season; skies are clear, but the heat is intense (apart from evening breezes near the beach), the landscape is brown and parched, and beaches and trails are packed. Mid-December to February, when school is out in Costa Rica, is especially busy.

■ TIP➔➔ Always apply bug repellent if you're going to be on the beach around sunset, when no-see-ums feast on unprotected ankles

## Getting There

The Pan-American Highway heads northwest from San José to Liberia, then due north to the Nicaraguan border. But it's poorly maintained, potholed and hilly, and heavily trafficked by trucks and buses. The airport outside Liberia is the best way to access the region. Fly directly here from the U.S. or Canada or hop on a domestic flight from San José and save yourself four to five hours of difficult driving.

## Ground Transportation from Liberia

At Daniel Oduber Airport in Liberia, official red taxis and hotel vans wait to meet each flight. When making a hotel reservation for the first night, ask if the hotel provides a cab or shuttle. If not, ask how much you should expect to pay for ground transportation from the airport. Fares vary widely, depending on how far away the hotel is and how many people are traveling together. In Guanacaste, it's usually safe to take *pirata* (pirate, or unofficial) taxis, but always negotiate the price before getting into the cab.

## What to Do

| ACTIVITY | WHERE TO DO IT |
|---|---|
| Fishing | Playa Flamingo, Tamarindo, Puerto Carrillo, Playas del Coco |
| Diving | Playa Hermosa, Playa Panama (Papagayo Peninsula area), Playa Potrero, Playas del Coco |
| Surfing | Tamarindo, Playa Grande, Playa Avellanas, Playa Negra, Santa Rosa National Park |
| Volcanoes | Rincón de la Vieja National Park |
| Turtle-watching | Playa Grande, Playa Ostional |
| Wildlife-watching | Palo Verde National Park, Rincón de la Vieja National Park, Santa Rosa National Park |

## How Much Time?

Ten days is what we recommend to get a taste of the North Pacific. Ideally, schedule at least a week to get into the rhythm of beach life. Logistically, you also need time for slow travel over bumpy roads. (By boat is faster and easier; tour operators will collect you from almost any beach.) A beach with lots of restaurants and nightlife can keep you entertained for a week or more, whereas a more solitary beach might merit only a couple of days. Outdoorsy types should consider spending a few days around Rincón de la Vieja National Park, hiking, bird-watching, horseback riding, and doing canopy tours.

## Great Combinations

You can easily stop at Monteverde (⇨ chapter 3) en route to the coast from San José. From there, shuttle van connections to the beach are excellent. Macaw Air flies directly from Tamarindo or Liberia to Puerto Jiménez, where you can spend a few days in a jungle lodge off the grid in the Osa Peninsula, a contrast to developed Nicoya beaches.

## Recommended Tour Operators

■ **Swiss Travel Service** (☎ 282-4898 ⊕ www.swisstravelcr. com) specializes in Guanacaste. Despite the name, it's operated by Costa Ricans with lots of local experience. Custom-design a guided private or small-group tour.

■ The excellent **Horizontes** (☎ 222-2022 ⊕ www. horizontes.com) has independent, private tours with your own guide/driver and small group tours.

■ **Calypso Cruises** (☎ 256-2727 📠 256-6767 ⊕ www. calypsocruises.com) takes you to Pacific-coast beaches Punta Coral and Isla Tortuga.

## Choosing a Place to Stay

Balancing out super-expensive resorts like the Four Seasons are budget options like the $15/night grass shacks on the beach at Sámara. As in all of Costa Rica, the places we most recommend are the small owner-operated hotels and B&Bs that blend in with unspoiled nature and have one-on-one attention from the staff and owners. If your budget is tight, consider condo or apartment properties with kitchens (and no meals provided). That's how most Ticos travel. These places may not be fancy, but they put you where you want to be. Winter (January–March) tends to be the most stifling time of year, and a room with a/c is essential.

## Prices

WHAT IT COSTS in Dollars

|  | $$$$ | $$$ | $$ | $ | ¢ |
|---|---|---|---|---|---|
| **Restaurants** | over $25 | $15–$25 | $10–$15 | $5–$10 | under $5 |
| **Hotels** | over $250 | $150–$250 | $75–$150 | $50–$75 | under $50 |

Restaurant prices are for a main course excluding tax and tip. Hotel prices are for two people in a standard double room in high season, excluding service and tax (16.4%).

# FAR NORTHERN GUANACASTE

By Dorothy MacKinnon

The mountains, plains, and Pacific coastline north of Liberia up to the border of Nicaragua are encompassed in Far Northern Guanacaste. Liberia is the capital of Guanacaste province and is the closest town to Costa Rica's second-largest airport. You'll most likely pass through it on your way to the beaches west of the city or up north to the national parks of Guanacaste, Santa Rosa, or Rincón de la Vieja. Volcán Rincón de la Vieja, an active volcano that last erupted in 1991, is pocked with eerie sites such as boiling creeks, bubbling mud pools, and vapor-emitting streams—look, but don't touch!

Northwest of Rincón de la Vieja, on the coast, Santa Rosa National Park is a former cattle ranch where Costa Ricans defeated the invading mercenary army of American William Walker in 1856. Santa Rosa also protects some of the last remnants of the region's original dry tropical forest, as well as olive ridley sea turtles that come to lay their eggs on its beaches between August and November. Closer still to the Nicaraguan border are the remote beaches of Guanacaste National Park and the town of La Cruz, overlooking the lovely Golfo de Santa Elena and some windswept hotels on Bahía Salinas.

> ## THE FIRST GUANACASTECOS
>
> The Chorotega tribe first settled the Guanacaste area and grew corn and fished. Chief Nicoya was the Chorotegan leader who greeted the conquistadors in 1523 and bequeathed his name to the town and peninsula.

## Rincón de la Vieja National Park

★ ❶ Parque Nacional Rincón de la Vieja is Costa Rica's mini-Yellowstone, with volcanic hot springs and boiling, bubbling mud ponds. The park protects more than 177 square km (54 square mi) of the volcano's upper slopes, much of which are covered by dry forest. The wildlife here is diverse: 200 species of birds, including black-headed trogons and blue-crowned motmots; plus mammals such as brocket deer, monkeys, and armadillos. There may still be a jaguar or two left, but these large cats are elusive and rarely seen.

Rincón de la Vieja Volcano, often enveloped in a mixture of sulfurous gases and cloud, dominates the scenery to the right of the Pan-American Highway as you head north. The volcano has two peaks: **Santa María** (1,898 m/6,228 feet) and the barren **Rincón de la Vieja** (1,805 m/5,924 feet). Fumaroles on the latter, which has two craters—one of them still active—constantly let off steam, making it unlikely that it will erupt anytime soon. (The last violent eruptions were between 1966 and 1970, but there was a temporary increase in activity in 1995.) **Las Hornillas** (The Kitchen Stoves), on the southern slope of the Rincón de la Vieja peak, near the Las Pailas entrance to the park, are a 124-acre medley of hot-water pools, bubbling mud pots, and vent holes, most active during the rainy season. ⚠ Don't get too close to the mud pots—their edges are brittle, and several people have slipped in and been severely burned. To the east, **Los Azufrales** are hot sulfur springs in which you can bathe. Take off all jewelry before you soak (to avoid tarnish).

The Las Pailas park entrance is the most common place to enter the park because it has the most accessible trails and there are more hotels along the road leading up to it. △ If you want to explore the slopes of the volcano, go with a guide—the abundant hot springs and geysers have given unsuspecting visitors some very nasty burns. In addition, the upper slopes often receive fierce and potentially dangerous winds—before ascending, check at either ranger station for conditions. The park does not have guides; we recommend the guides at Hacienda Guachipelín ( ⇨ *below*). You must sign a personal injury waiver before being admitted into the park. ☎ 661–8139 *(after 1* PM *only)* ⌲ *$6* ⊙ *Daily 7–5, last entry at 3* PM.

## Outdoor Activities

**Buena Vista Lodge & Adventure Center** (⊠ Western slope of the volcano, 10 km/6 mi north of Cañas Dulces ☎ 661–8158 ⊕ www.buenavistacr. com) has horseback riding, waterfall hikes, a canopy tour, rappelling, tractor tours, and a 1,600-foot (long, not steep) waterslide through the forest. Tours are $15 to $30 per person; a combo ticket is $65. **Hacienda Guachipelín Adventure Center** (⊠ Road to Rincón de la Vieja park ☎ 442–2818 ⊕ www.guachipelin.com) has horseback riding, river tubing, and guided waterfall and volcano hikes. The popular canyon tour incudes rock climbing, rappelling, zip lines, suspension bridges, and a Tarzan swing. A one-day, all-you-can-do adventure pass is $70. Tours are designed for ages 8 to 80. Playa Hermosa–based Maynor Lara Bustos of **Tours Your Way** (☎ 697–0210) guides tours to Rincón de la Vieja National Park.

CANOPY TOURS The zip-line canopy tour ($20) with **Buena Vista Lodge & Adventure Center** ( ⇨ *above*) has cables that are up to 90 feet off the ground and up to 450 feet long. **Treetop Trails** (⊠ Rincón de la Vieja Volcano Mountain Lodge ☎ 200–0238) runs four-hour canopy tours ($50), which include a forest-floor hike and

> ### WORD OF MOUTH
>
> "I enjoy the fact that you can go to Rincón de la Vieja on a beautiful day and not see more than 10 cars in the parking lot."
> —rbrazill

canopy observation from 16 cable-linked treetop platforms. A more elaborate seven-hour tour ($70) also includes horseback riding to thermal springs and a box lunch.

HIKING Nearly all of the outfitters in the area have guided hikes through the park to volcano craters, hot springs, or waterfalls.

If you're doing a self-guided hikes stop for trail maps and hiking information at the park stations at both entrance gates. The 8-km (5-mi) **trail to the summit** heads up into the forest from the Las Pailas park entrance, then emerges onto a windy, exposed shale slope that's slippery and hard going, and has poor visibility due to clouds and mist. It's a trip for serious hikers, best done in dry season with preparation for cold weather at the top. A less strenuous option is the fascinating 3-km (2-mi) **loop**

## The North Pacific

Tilarán

Cañas

Isla Chira

Jicaral

Carmona

NICOYA PENINSULA **4**

Taiwan Friendship Bridge

Lomas Barbudal Biological Reserve

**25** **Palo Verde National Park**

R. Tempisque

Puerto Moreno

R. Corobicí

Filadelfia

Belén

**26** **Barra Honda National Park**

Guaitil

Santa Cruz

**27** **Nicoya**

Curime

Catalina Islands

**11** **Playa Pan de Azúcar**

**12** **Playa Penca** / **Playa Potrero**

**13** **Playa Flamingo**

Brasilito

Huacas

Villarreal

**14** **Playa Conchal**

**16** **Playa Grande**

Las Baulas Marine National Park

**15** **17** **Tamarindo & Playa Langosta**
see map page 201

**18** **Playa Avellanas**

**19** **Playa Negra**

**20** **Playa Junquillal**

**Vientisiete de Abril**

Paraiso

R. Rosario

**Ostional National Wildlife Refuge**

Ostional

Playa Ostional

Playa Nosara

Playa Peluda

Playa Guiones

R. Nosara

R. Montaña

**21** **Nosara**

Garza

**22** **Sámara**

Isla Chora

**23** **Playa Carrillo**

**24** **Punta Islita**

Playa Camaronal

20 miles
30 km

**through the park,** which takes about two hours to complete, starting at the Las Pailas entrance. Along the well-marked trail you'll see fumaroles exuding steam, a *volcáncito* (baby volcano), and Las Pailas, the boiling mud fields named after pots used for boiling down sugarcane. If you tread softly, you can spot many animals, including howler, white-faced capuchin, and spider monkeys and raccoonlike coatis, looking for hand-outs. ■ TIP➔➔ Remember the cardinal rule of wildlife encounters: Don't feed the animals. Another popular hike is a four-hour, 10-km (6-mi) **La Cangreja Waterfall loop.** The *catarata* (waterfall) has a cool swimming hole below; the surrounding rocks have pockets of hot springs.

HORSEBACK    **Buena Vista Mountain Lodge & Adventure Center** ( ⇨ *above*) has horseback
RIDING    trips to hot springs ($15) and to Borinquen Waterfall ($25). If not everyone in your party is a horse-lover, tractor transport ($20) is available to the hot springs as well. **Rincón de la Vieja Volcano Mountain Lodge** (☎ 200–0238) has guides for hiking or horseback riding near the park.

## Where to Stay

$$$$ 🏨 **Borinquen Mountain Resort Thermae & Spa.** The luxury villas on this 12,000-acre ranch are shaded by old-growth trees on the volcano's windy west slope. The spa has volcanic mud (*lodo*) baths, a wooden sauna heated by steam from a fumarole, and naturally heated mineral pools— all included in room rates. The sulfur smell takes a little getting used to. Actvities include hiking, horseback riding, ATV trips, a canopy tour, and a farm tour (with cow-milking). Getting to the restaurant and spa requires steep climbs, but the staff can transport you in a golf cart. The modern, two-room, hacienda-style villas have large private verandas; single villas are more private. The food is not on par with the rest of the hotel. ✉ *13 km/8 mi northwest of Liberia on the Pan-American Hwy., then 29 km/18 mi north on the dirt road toward Cañas Dulces* ☎ *690–1900* 🖶 *690–1903* ⊕ *www.borinquenresort.com* ⥹ *23 villas* ♨ *Restaurant, room service, a/c, refrigerator, cable TV, pool, whirlpool tubs, spa, horseback riding, tours, bar, laundry service, Internet station* ▤ *AE, DC, MC, V* ¶ *BP.*

$–$$ 🏨 **Posada El Encuentro B&B.** Cinematic views of valley, volcano, and the Gulf of Nicoya can be had from the main house and *casitas* (small houses) at this unexpectedly upscale B&B. The suites in the modern, hacienda-style house have queen-size four-poster beds, wicker sofas, and private baths. The casitas are similarly furnished, but a little more private. A big breakfast is served in a bright atrium room and there's a small dinner menu. After hiking in the nearby national park you can watch the sun set while lounging on the large pool terrace. ✉ *9 km/5 mi off the Pan-American Hwy., on road to Las Pailas park entrance* ☎ *848–0616, 389–1456* ⥹ *3 suites, 2 casitas* ♨ *Dining room, fans, pool, bar; no a/c, no room phones, no room TVs* ▤ *AE, MC, V* ¶ *BP.*

$–$$ 🏨 **Rincón de la Vieja Mountain Lodge.** This is the closest you can stay to the Las Pailas park entrance, and the best thing about staying at this place, which feels like a camp in the woods, is access to hiking and horse trails leading to a hot sulfuric pool and a blue lake and waterfall. It's also home to the exciting Treetop Trails canopy tour. Apart from a few newer, brighter bungalows, the rooms—which each sleep four, in a double bed and bunk beds—are dark and sparsely furnished. But they all have verandas, with views of the gardens and a man-made lake. The dining room is claustrophobic, with mediocre food served buffet-style, but the alfresco bar is lively in the evening, usually filled with small groups of international ecotourist types. ⊠ *2 km/1 mi south of the Las Pailas park entrance, near the end of the Curubandé Rd.* ☎ *200–0238* 📠 *666–2441* ⊕ *www.rincondelaviejalodge.net* ↗ *49 rooms, 30 cabins, 11 bungalows* ⚮ *Dining room, fans, pool, horseback riding, bar, Internet station; no a/c, no room phones, no room TVs* ▤ *AE, DC, MC, V* ⦾ *EP.*

★ $ 🏨 **Hacienda Guachipelín.** Day-trippers come here for hair-raising adventure tours ( ⇨ Outdoor Activities, *above*), but this 3,706-acre working ranch is also famous for its horses—all 120 of them—and its nature trails leading to waterfalls. Rugged ranch hands swaggering around give the place a real cowboy flavor. Rooms are large, with windows front and back to let in cool mountain air. The newest rooms, Nos. 40–49, are the most elegant and quiet, though a bit of a walk from the restaurant. Avoid Rooms 24–31, right beside the corral, unless you enjoy the aroma of horses. Above-average buffet meals are served in the open-air restaurant. Dairy products come fresh from the hacienda's own herd. Large groups often stay here, but you can always find a quiet trail or corner somewhere on the landscaped property. ⊠ *17 km/10 mi north of the Pan-American Hwy., on road to Las Pailas park entrance* ☎ *666–8075* 📠 *442–1910* ⊕ *www.guachipelin.com* ↗ *50 rooms* ⚮ *Restaurant, fans, pool, horseback riding, tours, bar, playground, laundry service, Internet station; no a/c, no room phones, no room TVs* ▤ *AE, DC, MC, V* ⦾ *BP.*

¢ 🏨 **Rancho Curubandé Lodge.** Convenient to Rincón de la Vieja and Santa Rosa, these equipped bungalows and modern rooms are part of a working farm owned by a Costa Rican family. Rooms in the wooden ranch home that used to host large family gatherings share two cold-water bathrooms and a kitchen. The villas and newer rooms have modern comforts, including hot water, plus a view of the volcano from a deck under a giant Guanacaste tree. ⊠ *Just off Pan-American Hwy. on road to Las Pailas* ☎ *665–0374 or 369–8563* ⊕ *silviamgutierrez£hotmail.com* ↗ *7 rooms, 2 villas* ⚮ *Dining room, a/c, fans, horseback riding; no a/c in some rooms, no room phones, no room TVs* ⦾ *EP.*

## To & From Rincón de la Vieja National Park
*25 km/15 mi (1 hour) northeast of Liberia.*

There are two park entrances: at Hacienda Santa María on the road leading northeast from Liberia; and at Las Pailas, past Curubandé off the Pan-American Highway. To get to the Las Pailas entrance from Liberia, take the first entrance road 5 km (3 mi) northwest of Liberia off the Pan-American Highway. The turnoff is easy to miss—follow signs for Hacienda Guachipelín or the town of Curubandé. It's a rough 17-km (11-mi) dirt road, and you have to pay a small toll. The Santa María entrance is 25 km (15 mi) northeast of Liberia along the Colonia Blanca route, which follows the course of the Río Liberia. The turnoff from the Pan-American Highway to the hotels on the western slope of the volcano is 12 km (7 mi) northwest of Liberia, via Cañas Dulces. A 4WD

## More Texan than Tropical

CLOSE UP

GUANACASTE, COSTA RICA'S "Wild West," looks different from the rest of Costa Rica. It was originally covered in vast, dry tropical forests, but beginning in early colonial times, and then picking up speed in the 1950s when cattle ranching became big business, the dry forest was cleared to create vast cattle ranges. (The harder-to-access forests covering the volcanic slopes survived.) The resulting flat, sun-baked landscape makes the inland parts of the province look a little like the American Southwest. Cowboy culture still takes center stage during seasonal fiestas and a few rodeos. But these days more and more *sabaneros* (cowboys) are turning in their horses for Toyota HiLux trucks.

vehicle is recommended, though not essential, for all of these slow and bone-rattling rides. Taxi or with a tour company is the only way to go if you're without wheels.

## Santa Rosa National Park

➋ Intrepid bird-watchers, naturalists, backpackers and campers who like to rough it are the sort that visits this national park. Renowned for its wildlife, which is easy to spot due to less luxuriant, low-density foliage, Santa Rosa is the largest swath of tropical dry forest in Central America. Treetop inhabitants include spider, white-faced capuchin, and howler monkeys. If you station yourself next to water holes during the dry season, you may also spot deer, coyotes, coatis, or ocelots by day and armadillos and tapirs by night. This is also the southernmost distribution of many North American species such as the Virginia opossum and the cantil, a pit-viper snake. Typical dry-forest vegetation includes oak, wild cherry, mahogany, calabash, bullhorn acacia, and gumbo-limbo.

Santa Rosa's wealth of flora and fauna is due in part to its remoteness, which also makes it very difficult to access. To get anywhere in the park, you must first hike the 7-km (4½-mi) paved road to park headquarters from the entrance gate. About halfway along this road is a wooden sign signaling that you are entering the old-growth area, with trees as old as 500 years. Within this dense, shady forest, temperatures drop by as much as 5° C.

⚠ Visit areas beyond La Casona and accessible trails near the park headquarters only if you are a hardy hiker and backpacker. In rainy season the park's rough trails cannot be accessed by even 4WD vehicles and require hours of trekking on foot. From the park's entrance it's 8 km (5 mi) to the park headquarters, another 13 km (8 mi) to **Playa Naranjo**—where famed Witch's Rock surf break is located (most surfers get there by boat)— and **Playa Nancite**—the world's only totally protected olive ridley turtle *arribada,* or mass nesting (accessible primarily to biologists and students; permit required)—is an additional 5 km (3 mi) beyond that. Only the first 20 km (12 mi) of trail is accessible by 4WD in the dry season. There are no services in the park—that includes restrooms.

✉ *Km 269, Pan-American Hwy., 35 km/22 mi north of Liberia*
☎ *666–5051* 🕔 *$6* 🕙 *Daily 8–4.*

## Outdoor Activities

HIKING  The short **La Casona nature-trail loop** from the park headquarters is worth taking to get a brief sampling of the woods. Look for the INDIO DESNUDO, or "Naked Indian," path, named after the local name for gumbo-limbo trees. ■ TIP➔➔ Carry your own water; water holes are none too safe.

The grueling **trails to the beaches** in Santa Rosa all start at the park headquarters, which is itself a 7-km (4-mi) hike along a hot, sunny road. The hike to Playa Naranjo is another 13 km (8 mi) and Playa Nancite is 5 km (3 mi) beyond that. You can get a map of the trails at the park entrance.

SURFING  **Witch's Rock,** one of the oldest rock formations in the country, creates
★  a near-perfect beach break off Playa Naranjo in Santa Rosa Park. If you are interested in surfing Witch's Rock, take a boat tour from Playas del Coco, Playa Hermosa, or Playa Tamarindo, to the south.

## Where to Stay

There are some campsites within Santa Rosa Park, but they are very basic, remote, and have limited availability. Call the park headquarters (☎ 666–5051) for information.

★ $ 🏨 **Los Inocentes Lodge.** So you want to be a cowboy? You can start by staying at this ranch in a private reserve bordering Guanacaste National Park. The ranch has more than 100 horses, cattle, a herd of farm-raised peacocks (which account for the shrill shrieks you hear), and two pet scarlet macaws. The exquisitely maintained 115-year-old hardwood hacienda still has the original rooms, which are big, with high ceilings, huge closets, carved headboards, and only transom windows for ventilation. They're a little like elegant stables for people. Hot showers are across the corridors. Bungalows, about 200 meters from the hacienda, have private, solar-heated

> **WALKER'S LAST STAND**
>
> Santa Rosa Park was the site of the 1856 triumph over American invader William Walker in the famous Battle of Santa Rosa—one of the few military historic sites in this army-less country. The rambling colonial-style **Hacienda La Casona** farmstead was the last stand of a ragged force of ill-equipped Costa Ricans who routed the superior mercenary army of the notorious Walker. Disgruntled poachers burned La Casona to the ground in 2001, but it has since been rebuilt.

baths. The restaurant, which serves good traditional meals, and the second-floor veranda have views of verdant Orosi Volcano. Experienced guides, friendly horses, and miles of trails get you into the forests. ✉ *15 km/9 mi west of La Cruz* ☎ *679–9190* 🖷 *679–9224 or 265–4385* ⊕ *www.losinocentesranch.com* 🕮 *Apdo. 228–3000, Heredia* 🛏 *11 rooms with shared bath, 12 bungalows* 🍴 *Dining room, fans, pool, whirlpool tub, horseback riding, bar; no a/c, no room phones, no room TVs* 🚮 *AE, MC, V* 🍽 *FAP.*

**To & From Santa Rosa National Park**
*35 km/22 mi (30 min) northwest of Liberia.*

The turnoff for Santa Rosa National Park from the CA1 (Pan-American Hwy) is well marked. From Liberia you can hop on a bus heading north to La Cruz and get off at the park entrance.

## Playa Bahía Junquillal

❸ This 2½-km (1½-mi), tree-fringed, Blue Flag beach is as close as you can get to a soft white-sand beach in this part of Guanacaste. The warm, calm water makes it one of the best swimming beaches on the Gulf of Santa Elena. Not to be confused with the Playa Junquillal on the western coast of the Nicoya Peninsula farther south, this beach is part of the Guanacaste National Wildlife Refuge to the north of Santa Rosa. Stay for the day or camp out in the shaded camping area close to the beach. You can snorkel if you've got your own gear. ⊠ *$4* ☎ *679–9692* ⊙ *7 AM–7 PM.*

**To & From Playa Bahía Junquillal**
*22 km/14 mi north of Santa Rosa National Park.*

From the Pan-American Highway, take the road signed for Cuajiniquil, 43 km (26 mi) northwest of Liberia and 8 km (5 mi) north of Santa Rosa Park. Follow the paved road 10 km (6 mi) to the beach turnoff, along a dirt road for another 4 km (2 ½ mi). From the Bahía Salinas area, take the scenic dirt road (4WD recommended); then follow the road near Puerto Soley (signed for Cuajiniquil) 7 km (4 mi) to the beach entrance. You can also take a public bus from Liberia to Cuanijiquil and walk 7 km (4 mi) to the beach.

## La Cruz

❹ North of Guanacaste National Park on the west side of the highway is the turnoff to La Cruz, a scruffy, bustling little town. For travelers, it's noteworthy only for the stunning views of Bahía Salinas from its bluff and its proximity to the windswept beaches on the south shore of Bahía Salinas, the hamlet of Jobo, and the gentler beaches of the Golfo de Santa Elena. The Nicaraguan border lies just north of La Cruz at Peñas Blancas. ⚠ All travelers are stopped at two preborder checkpoints south of La Cruz for passport and cursory vehicle inspection. Police vigilance is heightened in the region.

### Where to Stay

¢ 🏨 **Amalia's Inn.** This breezy, bright, white inn on the cliff overlooking Bahía Salinas has big rooms furnished with a hodge-podge of mismatched furniture. Large-scale, dark, modern paintings and prints haunt the otherwise cheerful place. The view of the bay, from the garden or swimming pool, is the main selling point. A *soda* (informal restaurant) serving a *tipico* breakfast is a block away. ⊠ *East of Central Park, on left of road heading into town* ☎ *679–9181* ⇱ *7 rooms* ⚐ *Pool, laundry service; no a/c, no room phones, no room TVs* ▭ *No credit cards* ⊙ *EP.*

## Guanacaste National Park

CLOSE UP

THE 325-SQUARE-KM (125-square-mi) Parque Nacional Guanacaste, bordering the east side of the Pan-American Highway 30 km (18 mi) north of Liberia, was created in 1989 to preserve rain forests around Cacao Volcano (5,437 feet) and Orosi Volcano (4,847 feet), which are seasonally inhabited by migrant wildlife from Santa Rosa. The park isn't quite ready for tourism yet. There are no facilities (not even a toilet) and no well-marked trails. In rainy season, roads are impassable; a 4WD vehicle is required year-round. The park is a mosaic of interdependent protected areas, parks, and refuges; the goal is to eventually create a single Guanacaste megapark to accommodate the migratory patterns of animals, from jaguars to tapirs. Much of the park's territory is cattle pasture, which, it is hoped, will regenerate into forest. Today the park has more than 300 different birds and more than 5,000 species of butterflies.

To really explore the park, you must stay in the heart of it, at one of three biological stations. They are mostly reserved for students and researchers, but you can request accommodations from the **park headquarters** (☎ 666–5051).

### To & From La Cruz
*65 km/40 mi (1 hour) northwest of Liberia.*

La Cruz is a straight shot north of Liberia on the Pan-American Highway. Buses leave Liberia for La Cruz or you can flag down a bus anywhere along the highway north of Liberia that says LA CRUZ on its windshield.

### La Cruz Essentials
🏦 Banks **Banco Nacional** ⊠ Entrance to town, just off Pan-American Hwy. **Banco Popular** ⊠ South of Central Park.

🏦 Hospital **Hospital Area de Salud La Cruz** ⊠ Main highway at entrance to town.

🏦 Pharmacies **Farmacia San Angel** ⊠ 2 blocks north of Central Park ☎ 679–8048.

🏦 Internet **Internet Café** ⊠ Beside the Banco Popular.

🏦 Post Office **Correo** ⊠ Behind police station on west side of Central Park.

## Crossing into Nicaragua at Peñas Blancas

Costa Rica and Nicaragua share a busy border crossing at Peñas Blancas, 12 km (7 mi) north of La Cruz along a paved highway. ⚠ Rental vehicles may not leave Costa Rica. Tica Bus and Transnica bus companies ( ⇨ Bus Travel *in* Smart Travel Tips A to Z) cross into Nicaragua. The fee to cross the border is $7 (paid on the Nicaraguan side), plus a $2 surcharge if you cross from noon to 2 PM or on weekends. You can negotiate the border crossing on foot; taxis on the Nicaraguan side will take you to Rivas, the first city of any size, about 30 km (18 mi) from the border. Returning to Costa Rica is basically the same process in reverse; you are charged a $1 municipal tax and $2 exit tax to leave Nicaragua by land. The crossing is open daily 6 AM–8 PM; get there with time to spare or you *will* be stranded. Banks on both sides of the border change their own currency and U.S. dollars. Colones are not accepted or exchanged in Nicaragua; likewise for córdobas in Costa Rica. Overland border crossing procedures can be confusing if you don't speak Spanish.

## Bahía Salinas

**⑤** The large windswept bay at the very top of Costa Rica's Pacific coast is the second windiest area in Costa Rica, after Lake Arenal, making it ideal for windsurfing and kitesurfing. The wind usually blows strong November through August (September and October are the height of the rainy season). Winds are generally not as powerful as those at Lake Arenal, but they're strong enough to make this a viable alternative. The south (bay) side has the strongest winds, and choppy, cold water. But on the sheltered Golfo Santa Elena to the west are two beaches that rank among the most beautiful in all of Costa Rica: Playas Rajada and Jobo.

### Exploring

**Playa Copal** (✉ About 2 km/1 mi east of the branch road that leads to Ecoplaya) is the main venue for kitesurfing. It also has villas and rooms for rent, along with hostel accommodations.

Gorgeous, horseshoe-shaped **Playa Rajada** (✉ 5 km/3 mi west of Ecoplaya Beach Resort or 3 km/2 mi north of the town of Jobo) is a wide sweep of almost-white, fine-grain sand. Shallow, warm waters make it perfect for swimming, and an interesting rock formation at the north end invites snorkelers. It's also a favorite beach for watching sunsets.

★ **Playa Jobo** (✉ 3 km/2 mi walk or drive, west from Ecoplaya Beach Resort) is a gem with fine sand, calm water, and rocky claws at each end of its horseshoe. It's fringed with acacia trees that have sharp thorns, so keep your distance. There's a shady parking area about 150 m off the beach where you have to leave your car.

Just offshore from the Ecoplaya Resort in Bahía Salinas is tiny **Isla Bolaños,** a rocky bird refuge and nesting site for thousands of frigate birds, brown pelicans, and cormorants. You can visit by boat, but your tour operator needs a government permit to land, and visitors can only disembark for a very short time, so as not to disturb the birds. **Ecoplaya Beach Resort** (☎ 676–1010 ⊕ www.ecoplaya.com) arranges tours for $35 per person.

### Outdoor Activities

**Ecoplaya Beach Resort** (☎ 676–1010 ⊕ www.ecoplaya.com) organizes local adventure tours like kayaking, fishing, horseback riding, and diving, as well as farther-afield adventure tours to Bolaños, Los Inocentes, and Hacienda Guachipelín, and overnight tours to Granada in Nicaragua.

KITESURFING & **Kite Surfing Centre and School** (☎ 826–5221 ⊕ www.suntoursandfun.com/
WINDSURFING kitesurfing.htm) on Copal Beach gives 10 hours of kitesurfing lessons for $225, including equipment use. The multilingual instructor has lots of experience. The school also offers basic hostel accommodation, with 8 curtained-off rooms and the use of a shared kitchen for $12.50 per person. **Eco-Wind** (☎ 676–1010 ⊕ www.ecoplaya.com) at Ecoplaya

Beach Resort will fix you up for all your windsurfing needs. Equipment rental runs around $60 a day.

## Where to Stay

**$$** 🏨 **Ecoplaya Beach Resort.** How windy is it? Even with glass buffers and windbreak trees and shrubs, the large swimming pool usually has waves. This sprawling collection of villas and poolside rooms with bathtubs and king-size beds is bordered by a nearly 1-km-long (½-mi-long) beach with coarse brown sand flecked with sharp broken shells. Bird- and wildlife-filled estuaries hem in the beach. Jobo and Rajada beaches are just a short drive or hike away. The hotel organizes activities and tours, but many entail a jolting ride back to La Cruz and beyond. The restaurant serves good food. ✉ *La Coyotera Beach, 15 km/10 mi west of La Cruz on a rough dirt Rd.* 🕾 *676–1010, 228–7146 in San José* 🖨 *Plaza Colonial, Escazú, No. 4, San José* 🖻 *289–4536 in San José* ⊕ *www. ecoplaya.com* ⟿ *16 villas, 20 rooms* ⌂ *Restaurant, in-room safes, some kitchens, pool, beach, windsurfing, horseback riding, tour operator, bar, kids' programs (high season only), playground, recreation room, laundry service* ▤ *AE, MC, V* ¶⃝ *BP.*

**¢–$** 🏨 **Pura Vida Residence.** An affordable, unusually upscale base for exploring the area, this Italian-built and -managed hilltop residence overlooks Playa Copal, the premier beach for windsurfing and kitesurfing. Studio rooms are in a modern residence. Fully equipped villas are perfect for sharing. High ceilings, lots of cool stone, tile, and huge windows to catch the winds off the bay help you keep your cool despite the lack of a/c. ✉ *Playa Copal, 13 km/8 mi west of La Cruz* 🕾 *389–6794* 🖨 *676–1055* ⊕ *www. progettopuravida.com* ⟿ *8 rooms, 7 villas* ⌂ *Restaurant (high season only), fans, some kitchens, some kitchenettes, pool, beach; no a/c, no room phones, no room TVs* ▤ *No credit cards* ¶⃝ *EP.*

## To & From Bahía Salinas

*15 km/9 mi (45 minutes) west of La Cruz.*

From a high point in La Cruz, the road to Salinas descends both in altitude and condition. It's only 15 km (9 mi) southwest to Hotel Ecoplaya, but they are the most jolting miles of broken road you can imagine. The road is actually signed for Puerto Soley and Jobo, an end-of-the-road hamlet, about 2 km (1 mi) past the turnoff for Ecoplaya. Playa Copal is about 13 km (8 mi) along the same road from La Cruz.

# Liberia

**❻** Liberia is the gateway to the national parks to the north and to the Nicoya Peninsula beaches to the south. The drive from San José takes between four and seven hours, so it makes sense to fly directly into Liberia if you're going to the North Pacific. It's easy to rent a car near the airport, which you should do as soon as you arrive: the attractions of the city don't compare to the wonders of the nearby parks and beaches. Liberia is essentially a good place to have a meal and make a bank stop.

Once a dusty cattle-market town, Guanacaste province's capital city is now galloping toward modernization. Though you can spot the occasional *sabanero* (cowboy) on horseback, you'll see them mainly only at fiesta time. The town is well on its way to becoming a giant shopping mall, complete with Burger King and multiplex cinema (the only movie theater in the province). The whitewashed adobe houses for which Liberia was nicknamed "The White City," are traces of its colonial past.

NAVIGATING
LIBERIA The *avenidas* (avenues) officially run east–west, while the *calles* (streets) run north–south. Liberia is not too big to walk easily, but there are always taxis lined up around the central park.

## Exploring

For a true-grit taste of the sabanero life that is fast disappearing from Liberia, mosey on over to **Rancho Santa Alicia** (⊠ Pan-American Hwy., 12 km/7 mi south of Liberia ☎ 671–2513) south of the city for a scenic trail ride by day or a romantic moonlight ride. The highlight is the Saturday-night **rodeo** when cowboys from all over Guanacaste come to compete in bull riding, bronco busting, and precision riding in a covered rodeo stadium. Barbecued beef, ribs, and some lighter choices are served ($6–$10). Additional entertainment includes *ranchero* music, mariachis, and a late-night disco.

## Where to Eat

**$**  ✕ **La Toscana.** Billing itself as "spaghetteria, pizzeria, and cafe, " this restaurant uses authentic Italian ingredients like real Parmigiano cheese and real Parma prosciutto in its pastas and 33 types of wood-oven pizzas. Risotto is the chef's specialty: a nutty, brown, three-mushroom version cooked perfectly *al dente* and flavored with truffle oil, rare in these parts. Décor is classy, in an elegantly restored mansion. ⊠ *400 m west of the main church, then 150 m north* ☎ 665–0653 ▭ *AE, DC, MC, V.*

**¢–$**  ✕ **Café Europa/The German Bakery.** The aroma of baking bread is irresistible as you pass this bakery just south of the Liberia airport, whose baked goods are delivered all over the peninsula. Stop in for strudels, bundt cakes, and flaky fruit pastries. Lunch choices include (non-German) pizza and bratwurst with sauerkraut. It's open from 6 AM to 6 PM. ⊠ *2 km/1 mi south of Liberia airport* ☎ 668–1081 ▭ *AE, D, MC, V.*

**¢–$**  ✕ **El Café Liberia.** The smell of roasting coffee is the best advertisement for this sophisticated café in the center of Liberia, where cheerful owner/chef Catherine Miller whips up cool, refreshing soups—the Mint Pea is a winner—and homemade desserts. Along with quiche, cakes, and hot sandwiches, Catherine dishes out local information and advice. Imported wines, single-malt Scotches, and sherries can accompany meals. The café runs an English-language used-book exchange. ⊠ *From Liberia's main street, 75 m south of Banco de Credito Agricola* ☎ 665–1660 ▭ *No credit cards* ◷ *Closed weekends.*

## Where to Stay

**$$**  ▣ **Best Western Hotel El Sitio.** Lacking warmth but with plenty of conveniences, this hotel has airy and spacious rooms with lots of storage space and some king-size beds. Elevated wooden walkways framed with greenery lead to rooms. Even-numbered rooms all have views of the pools shaded by an ancient Guanacaste tree in the hotel's garden court. The

# Liberia

**Restaurants**
Café Europa ............ **1**
El Café Liberia ......... **4**
La Toscana ............. **5**

**Hotels**
Best Western Hotel
El Sitio .................... **3**
Best Western
Las Espuelas ........... **2**
Hostal Ciudad Blanca ... **6**

**KEY**
**1** Restaurants
**①** Hotels

## FODOR'S FIRST PERSON

**Dorothy MacKinnon**
*Writer*

We were rolling along the nearly deserted highway near Liberia when an aluminum ladder came loose from an open-bed truck and flew straight for our windshield. My colleague swerved, catching the concrete abutment, flipping our rented KIA Sportage. We landed right side up, inches from a large tree.

Seconds later the highway was alive with people rushing to our aid. Two men, including the flying-ladder truck's driver, pried open our crumpled doors and pulled us out. Amazingly we had only minor cuts, but

the car was totaled and my driver was passing out from shock. An ambulance arrived in under five minutes. A passerby reported the accident to the traffic police and called my rental company. An elderly woman ran home to fetch salve for my injuries. A neighbor offered a glass of cold water and stayed with me for two hours.

Everyone, officials or not, was efficient. But more importantly, they were warm, treating two *extranjeras* (foreigners) like family. Within five hours of a potentially fatal accident our new KIA was loaded up we were on our way with a better appreciation for Tico culture.

restaurant is Italian. ⊠ *South of Burger King, on road heading west toward airport and beaches* ☎666–1211 🖷666–2059 ⊕*www.bestwestern. com* 🖅 *Apdo. 134–5000, Liberia* 🛏 *50 rooms* ᎠᏞ *Restaurant, a/c, in-room safes, cable TV, 2 pools, spa, bar, casino, laundry service, Internet, meeting room, car rental* ▤ *AE, MC, V* ¶◯¶ *BP.*

**$** 🏨 **Best Western Las Espuelas.** Smaller and with more personal attention than the Best Western El Sitio on the other side of town, this motel-style hotel has some character thanks to local paintings and indigenous stone statues. Rooms are a little institutional, but there's great water pressure in the showers (hard to find in Costa Rica) and the air-conditioning is quiet. The suites, by the pool, have private whirlpool tubs. Rooms facing the highway can be a little noisy; Nos. 17 and up are quieter. The restaurant serves excellent coffee and a good buffet breakfast, but it's dark and gloomy. ⊠ *2 km/1 mi south of Liberia* ☎ *666–0144* 🖷 *666–2441* 🖃 *espuelas@racsa.co.cr* 🛏 *44 rooms, 2 suites* ᎠᏞ *Restaurant, a/c, cable TV, pool, outdoor whirlpool tub, bar, meeting rooms* ▤ *AE, D, MC, V* ¶◯¶ *BP.*

**¢** 🏨 **Hostal Ciudad Blanca.** This two-story, minimansion built of stone feels more like a guest house than a hotel. It's in a quiet, older section of town where there are still remnants of colonial architecture. The rooms are small, and those downstairs, lined up along a stone patrio, are dark but well maintained. Upstairs rooms are brighter. There's a cheerful patio restaurant up front and Pizza Pronto just around the corner. ⊠ *200 m south of the old government house, then 150 m (1 ½ blocks east)* ☎ *666–3962* 🖷 *666–4382* 🛏 *12 rooms* ᎠᏞ *Restaurant, a/c, fans, cable TV* ▤ *No credit cards* ¶◯¶ *EP.*

*Continued on page 179*

# CHOOSING A BEACH

Tamarindo Beach, Guanacaste, Costa Rica

Each beach along Nicoya's coast, most lined with palms and tamarind trees, has its distinct merits. Sand varies from pulverized black volcanic rock (Playa Negra) to crushed white shells (Playa Conchal) to picture-perfect, soft white sand (Playa Carrillo), with every shade of brown in between. Atmospherically, beaches vary from tranquil, secluded, Robinson Crusoe–like strands (Playa Rajada) to civilized beaches with restaurants so close to the ocean the surf spray salts your food (Playa Brasilito) to family-friendly spots with calm, swimmable waters and shade (Playas Hermosa and Sámara) to beaches with buff and beautiful, tattooed surfers (Playas Tamarindo and Negra) to those made for contemplative walks or dramatic sunsets (Playas Langosta and Pelada).

**Playa Hermosa**

**Tamarindo**

### BEACHES KEY

- Diving
- Snorkeling
- Fishing
- Surfing
- Kayaking
- Sailing
- Swimming
- Blue Flag Ecological Award

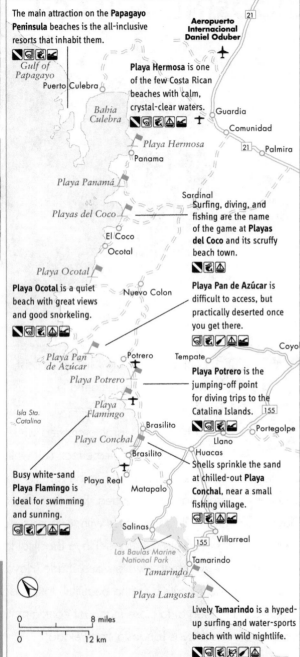

The main attraction on the **Papagayo Peninsula** beaches is the all-inclusive resorts that inhabit them.

**Playa Hermosa** is one of the few Costa Rican beaches with calm, crystal-clear waters.

Surfing, diving, and fishing are the name of the game at **Playas del Coco** and its scruffy beach town.

**Playa Ocotal** is a quiet beach with great views and good snorkeling.

**Playa Pan de Azúcar** is difficult to access, but practically deserted once you get there.

**Playa Potrero** is the jumping-off point for diving trips to the Catalina Islands.

Busy white-sand **Playa Flamingo** is ideal for swimming and sunning.

Shells sprinkle the sand at chilled-out **Playa Conchal**, near a small fishing village.

Lively **Tamarindo** is a hyped-up surfing and water-sports beach with wild nightlife.

Aeropuerto Internacional Daniel Oduber

Gulf of Papagayo
Puerto Culebra
Bahía Culebra
Playa Hermosa
Panama
Playa Panamá
Playas del Coco
El Coco
Ocotal
Playa Ocotal
Nuevo Colon
Playa Pan de Azúcar
Potrero
Playa Potrero
Playa Flamingo
Isla Sta. Catalina
Playa Conchal
Brasilito
Playa Real
Matapalo
Salinas
Las Baulas Marine National Park
Tamarindo
Playa Langosta

Guardia
Comunidad
Palmira
Sardinal
Coyol
Tempate
Portegolpe
Llano
Huacas
Villarreal

0    8 miles
0    12 km

Playa Langosta

Nosara

Playa Carrillo

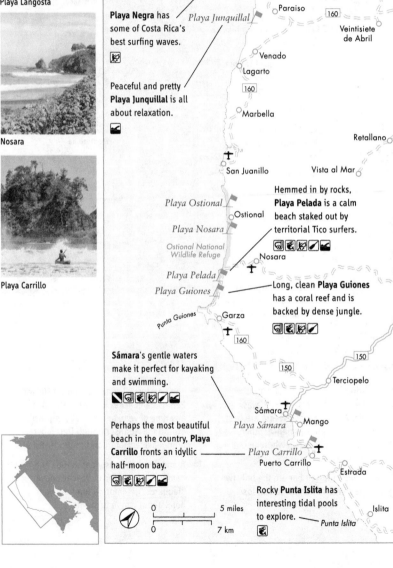

Black-sand **Playa Langosta** is great for walks up its estuary and watching dramatic sunsets.

**Playa Avellanas** is a no-frills backwater surf spot.

**Playa Negra** has some of Costa Rica's best surfing waves.

Peaceful and pretty **Playa Junquillal** is all about relaxation.

Hemmed in by rocks, **Playa Pelada** is a calm beach staked out by territorial Tico surfers.

Long, clean **Playa Guiones** has a coral reef and is backed by dense jungle.

**Sámara**'s gentle waters make it perfect for kayaking and swimming.

Perhaps the most beautiful beach in the country, **Playa Carrillo** fronts an idyllic half-moon bay.

Rocky **Punta Islita** has interesting tidal pools to explore.

Tamarindo
Tamarindo
Playa Langosta
Villarreal
155
Playa Avellanas
Playa Negra
152
Paraiso
160
Veintisiete de Abril
Playa Junquillal
Venado
Lagarto
160
Marbella
Retallano
San Juanillo
Vista al Mar
Playa Ostional
Ostional
Playa Nosara
Ostional National Wildlife Refuge
Nosara
Playa Pelada
Playa Guiones
Punta Guiones
Garza
160
150
150
Terciopelo
Sámara
Mango
Playa Sámara
Playa Carrillo
Puerto Carrillo
Estrada
Islita
Punta Islita
0    5 miles
0    7 km

4

CHOOSING A BEACH

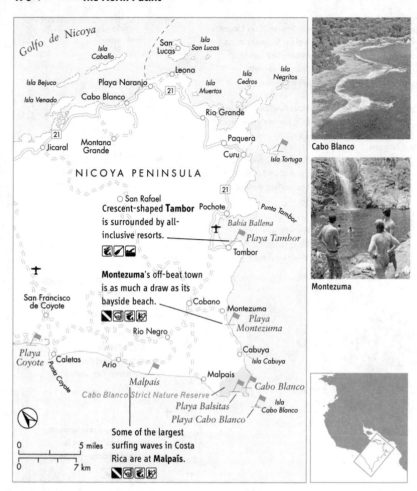

Cabo Blanco

Montezuma

Crescent-shaped **Tambor** is surrounded by all-inclusive resorts.

**Montezuma**'s off-beat town is as much a draw as its bayside beach.

Some of the largest surfing waves in Costa Rica are at **Malpaís**.

0 ___ 5 miles
0 ___ 7 km

## MAKING THE MOST OF YOUR BEACH VACATION

■ Tamarindo, Nosara, and Sámara are good for beginning surfers. Playas Grande, Avellanas, and Negra are best left to those with experience; other surfing waters are somewhere in between.

■ Tamarindo and Tambor are the only two beaches with air service to San José.

■ The beach road connecting most Nicoya Peninsula beaches is hard to stomach any time of year, and virtually impassible during the August through December rains. Take easier inland routes instead.

■ Riptides are seriously dangerous and hardly any Costa Rican beaches have lifeguards; get information from your hotel about where to swim.

## To & From Liberia

*234 km/145 mi (4 hours) northwest of San José.*

From San José, follow the Pan-American Highway west past the Puntarenas exit and north past Cañas to Liberia. The road is paved but is in various states of disrepair. It's a heavily traveled truck and bus route and there are miles and miles where it is impossible to pass, but many drivers try, making this a dangerous road. Frequent direct buses leave San José for Liberia each day, so it might be worth busing up to Liberia and renting a car from there.

### Liberia Essentials

⬛ Banks **BANEX** ⊠ C. 4 and Avda. 0.

⬛ ATMs **Bancredito** ⊠ Avda. 0, 2 blocks north of Hwy. **Burger King ATH** ⊠ Pan-American Hwy., at entrance to town.

⬛ Hospital **Liberia Hospital** ⊠ North end of town ☎ 666-4250.

⬛ Pharmacies **Farmacia Lux** ⊠ C. 4 and Avda. 0 ☎ 665-0182 ⊙ Weekdays 8-6, Sat. 8-noon.

⬛ Internet **Ciber Enl@ce** ⊠ C. 4 and Avda. 0 ⊙ Daily 8 AM-10 PM.

⬛ Post Office **Correo** ⊠ 300 m west of hwy, 200 m north of Avda. 0.

# THE NICOYA COAST

Strung along the coast of the Nicoya Peninsula are sparkling sand beaches lined with laid-back fishing communities and hotels and resorts in every price category. As recently as the 1970s, fishing and cattle ranching were the area's mainstays. Development is picking up speed, bringing with it sophisticated restaurants, hotels, and shops selling international surf gear and beachwear. But roads are only starting to catch up, so you'll find the interesting anomaly of a fabulous restaurant or hotel plunked at the end of a tortuous dirt road. At night you have your pick of open-air bars, beach barbecue parties, traditional marimba folk music, and sports bars with satellite TVs showing *Monday Night Football*. But after watching one of Nicoya's magnificent sunsets, most visitors head to bed early to catch early-morning waves, fishing boats, and wildlife walks. The key to enjoying Nicoya is to slow down—you'll soon be as mellow as the locals.

## Papagayo Peninsula

❼ If you are looking for resort or all-inclusive hotels in which to isolate yourself, Papagayo Peninsula, a crooked finger of land cradling the west side of Bahía Culebra (Snake Bay), is the place to do it. As of mid-2005, four large hotels and resorts were situated around the Papagayo Bay; upwards of 15 additional hotels have contracts to build in the near future. Though the hotels are modeled on Caribbean Island resorts, beaches are distinctly Costa Rican, with brown sand and cloudy, rough water not recommended for swimming. Isolation is the name of the game, which means that getting out of man-made "paradise" to explore wilderness or anything off-property often entails hours in a van on a pricey tour.

High season here coincides with dry season, so there's guaranteed sun January to April, but there's also intense heat and the landscape is brown and brittle. The sparkling water and spectacular sunsets are beautiful year-round. In the rainy season (August–December) the landscape is green and lush, and you can be outdoors comfortably.

## Outdoor Activities

CANOPY TOUR  Taking advantage of one of the few remaining patches of dry tropical forest on the Papagayo Peninsula, **Witch's Rock Canopy Tour** (☎ 666–7546) gives you your money's worth: 23 platforms, with a thrilling 450-meter cable zip between two of them; four hanging bridges; a waterfall; and hiking trails. The 1½-hour tour is $50 per person.

## Where to Stay

$$$$   ☷ **Four Seasons Resort Costa Rica.** By far the most luxurious hotel in Costa Rica, the Four Seasons is extremely secluded (it's nearly 30 minutes from the main road). From the time you arrive to the time you sip your last umbrella drink, you won't have to lift a finger. Service, provided by a cream-of-the-crop, bilingual Tico staff, is faultless. Huge rooms have king-size beds, marble baths, and screened-in living-room terraces. The breezy 18-hole Arnold Palmer signature golf course has breathtaking views—and prices ($180 per round). Players report

> **WORD OF MOUTH**
>
> "The Four Seasons was amazing: A beautiful resort with outstanding service. My wife's all-time favorite. We did not leave the resort–a few days of R&R was badly needed."
> —elizabean
>
> "To me, going to the Four Seasons kind of cancels out the whole point of going to Costa Rica in the first place. [You] might as well be anywhere." —tully

hard greens, with a lot of bounce. The state-of-the-art spa is impressive but a little sterile. Dishes created at the dinner-only Di Mare restaurant are worth their wildly expensive price tags. ⊠ *25 km/15 mi west of Guardia; follow signs to Papagayo Allegro Resort, and continue to the end of the Rd.* ☎ *696–0000* 🖷 *696–0010* ⊕ *www.fourseasons.com* ↪ *123 rooms, 36 suites, 21 villas* ⚴ *3 restaurants, room service, a/c, fans, in-room safes, refrigerators, cable TV, 18-hole golf course, 3 pools, gym, spa, beach, tours, 2 bars, babysitting, kids' programs, laundry facilities and service, concierge, in-room broadband, business center, meeting rooms, airport shuttle, car service* ⊟ *AE, DC, MC, V* �101 *EP.*

$$$$   ☷ **Premier Fiesta Resort & Spa Papagayo.** This is the coziest of the large hotels around the bay; it also has the best beach. Pretty bungalows are spread out on the hills overlooking the bay. Half have king-size beds. The pool and beach are the noisy hubs for most of the organized activities. But an adults-only resistance lap pool is near the spa and fitness center. Ask for a bungalow near the spa if you seek quiet. Avoid the high-rise block of rooms at the top of the hill. Book early in the morning for à la carte meals. ⊠ *Playa Arenilla, just north of Playa Panama* ☎ *664–4250* 🖷 *663–3112* ⊕ *www.fiestapremier.com* ↪ *100 rooms in 50 bungalows, 60 high-rise rooms* ⚴ *Two restaurants, a/c, fans, in-room*

safes, refrigerator, cable TV, 2 pools, gym, spa, beach, dive shop, tours, bicycles, kayaking, 3 bars, casino, nightclub, babysitting, kids' programs, laundry facilities, concierge, Internet 🖴 AE, DC, MC. V ⦿ AI.

**$$$–$$$$**  **Occidental Grand Papagayo.** This Mediterranean-style hotel has lodgings staggered on a hillside fronting the bay. A sweeping exterior double staircase leads down to the pool and

> ### ECO-OK?
>
> The Papagayo Peninsula has been the center of controversy for a decade, pitting development companies against local environmentalists concerned about shrinking habitat and low water levels in this already parched area.

snack bar. More stairs lead to the brown-sand beach. The pricier (and higher-up) Royal Club rooms and suites have terra-cotta floors, dark-wood furniture, king-size beds, and floor-to-ceiling windows with bay views. Standard rooms, in two-story buildings, have wall-to-wall carpeting and overlook the pool. Concrete staircases leading to the higher rooms are, at this writing, without railings. But vans can transport you nearly anywhere on-site. Make dinner reservations for your entire stay when you arrive. The hotel is not kid-oriented. ⊠ *Playa Buena* ☎ *506/ 672–0191* 🖷 *506/672–0058* ⊕ *www.occidentalhotels.com* ➷ *150 rooms, 12 Royal Club rooms, 7 suites ⌂ 3 restaurants, room service in some rooms, snack bar, a/c, in-room safes, minibars, whirlpool baths in master suites, cable TV, pool, whirlpool tub, massage, spa, beach, tennis court, tours, 3 bars, nightclub, laundry service, in-room broadband in some rooms, Internet, airport shuttle, car rental, no-smoking rooms* 🖴 *AE, MC, V* ⦿ *AI.*

### To & From Papagayo Peninsula

All hotels here have airport pickup. To get to the Four Seasons from the Liberia airport, drive 10 km (6 mi) south of Guardia, over the Río Tempisque Bridge, then take the turn on the right signed for Papagayo Allegro Resort. Follow this road about 20 km (12 mi) to its end at the entrance to the resort. For Fiesta Premier, the best route is via Comunidad, then 20 km (12 mi) north to Playa Panamá, all on paved roads. The Grand Papagayo is 30 km (19 mi) north of Guardia toward Nacascolo, then follow signs.

## Playa Hermosa

❽ Beautiful Playa Hermosa is one of the last laid-back beach towns on this part of the coast. It's the kind of place where the beach is still the town's main throroughfare and is filled with joggers, people walking their dogs, families out for a stroll, and fishermen setting off in the mornings and hauling in their catch in the evenings. Not to be confused with the mainland surfers' beach of the same name south of Jacó, this Playa Hermosa is experiencing some development pressures, with rows of sunny villas springing up and filling up with American and Canadian expatriates, and condominiums climbing up the surrounding hillsides. Luckily, though, the full length of the beach has long been occupied by small hotels, restaurants, and homes, so the newer hotel behemoths and other developments are forced to set up shop off the beach or on other beaches in the area. There is a positive side to all this growth: new restaurants and a wider choice of accommodations.

Hermosa's mile-long crescent of dark gray volcanic sand attracts heat, so the best time to be out on the beach is early morning or late afternoon, in time for the spectacular sunsets. The beach fronts a line of trees, so there's a welcome respite from the heat of the sun. The crystal-clear water—it's a Blue Flag beach—is usually calm, with no strong currents and with comfortable temperatures of 74–80° F. Sea views are as picturesque as they get, with bobbing fishing boats, jagged profiles of coastline, rocky outcroppings, and at night the twinkling lights of the Four Seasons Resort across the bay. At the beach's north end, low tide creates wide, rock-lined tidal pools.

## Outdoor Activities

**Aqua Sport** (⊠ Beach road; heading south, take second entrance to Playa Hermosa and follow signs ☎ 672–0050 ⊕ www.costarica-beach-hotel.com) organizes fishing, surfing, and snorkeling trips. **Charlie's Adventure** (⊠ Hotel Condovac, north end of beach ☎ 672–0275) organizes ATV tours, horseback riding, fishing trips, snorkeling, diving, and sunset sails, as well as boat tours of a mangrove estuary and Hermosa Bay. At the north end of the beach, below Hotel Condovac, an independent **kiosk** rents Boogie boards, plastic kayaks, Jet Skis, and other water toys. **Tours Your Way** (☎ 697–0210) has jungle canopy tours and horseback riding.

BOATING  **Cool Runnings** (☎ 824–1875, 672–0103 ⊕ www.sailcoolrunnings.com), a spacious 46-foot trimaran, sets sail at 3 PM for a three-hour sunset cruise ($55 per person) with open bar and *bocas* (snacks). The boat, which holds up to 25, can pick you up at nearby beaches as well. Daytime snorkeling cruises ($65) include lunch, gear, and open bar. **The *Giuseppina*** (☎ 305–1584), a 48-foot replica of a Grand Banks trawler, can be chartered by the hour (three-hour minimum) or overnight, from $200/hour to $245 per person overnight (four-person minimum). **Hotel el Velero** (⊠ 100 m north of Aqua Sport ☎ 672–0036 ⊕ www.costaricahotel.net) will take you out for a five-hour sunset cruise on their 38-foot sailing yacht ($45 per person). Tours include snorkeling, cave exploring, and sunbathing.

DIVING &  Average temperatures of 75 to 80 degrees, 20 to 60 feet of visibility, and
SNORKELING  frequent sightings of sea turtles, sharks, manta rays, moray eels, and very big fish make Hermosa a great place to dive. **Charlie's Adventure** ( ⇨ *above*) organizes snorkeling and diving trips. **Diving Safaris** (⊠ Second entrance road to Playa Hermosa, across from Villa Huetares Hotel ☎ 672–0012, 877/853–0538 in U.S. ⊕ www.costaricadiving.net) has a range of scuba activities, from beginner training to open-water PADI certification courses. Multitank dives are organized at more than 30 sites. Guides and trainers are very good, and their safety standards have the DAN (Divers Alert Network) seal of approval. This dive shop has also earned the coveted five-star, gold–palm status from PADI. Prices range from $65 for two-tank morning dives to $375 and up for PADI open-water and Dive Master certification courses.

There are no reefs for snorkeling here, but there are coral formations and rocky outcroppings to explore. You need a boat and a guide to find the best spots. **Aqua Sport** ( ⇨ *above*) sends snorkelers out with a knowledgeable local guide who's excellent at finding marine life. A three-hour tour with guide, boat, and equipment is $25 per person.

FISHING The fishing at Playa Hermosa is mostly close to the shores, and yields edible fish like dorado (mahi-mahi), amberjack, and yellowfin tuna. Local restaurants are happy to cook your catch for you. You can rent a boat with **Aqua Sport** ( ⇨ *above*). **Charlie's Adventure** ( ⇨ *above*) runs fishing trips.

## Where to Stay & Eat

★ ¢–$  ✕ **Ginger Restaurant Bar.** This all-appetizer restaurant, in a modernistic glass-and-steel treehouse cantilevered on the side of a hill, is a big hit. The Cordon Bleu–trained chef has created a half Asiatic, half Mediterranean menu with fun offerings like seasoned shoestring fries dipped in roasted garlic mayonnaise and a taco basket filled with seared pepper–crusted tuna and pickled ginger slaw. Portions look small, but layerings of condiments and garnishes make them satisfying. ⊠ *Main highway, just south of Hotel Condovac entrance* ☎ 672–0041 ☰ AE, DC, MC, V ⌨ *Reservations essential Jan.–Mar.* ☉ *Closed Mon. No lunch.*

★ $$  ⊡ **Hotel El Velero.** This hotel is always hopping, with local expats and visitors exchanging fishing, boating, and real-estate stories. The Canadian general manager is an ebullient host, full of local lore and advice. Spacious, attractive rooms at this two-story, white beachfront hotel have arched doorways, terra-cotta tiles, bamboo furniture, and large windows. The hotel runs daily snorkeling and sunset cruises on its own handsome 38-foot sailboat. In the restaurant, jumbo shrimp and always-fresh mahimahi are fixtures. Come on Wednesday or Saturday for beach barbecue nights, when there's live music. ⊠ *Second entrance to Playa Hermosa, then north 100 m along beach Rd.* ☎ 672–0036 ☐ 672–0016 ⊕ *www.costaricahotel.net* ⤴ *22 rooms* ⌂ *Restaurant, in-room safes, cable TV, pool, snorkeling, boating, jet skiing, bar, laundry service* ☰ AE, MC, V ⎺⎺ EP.

$–$$  ✕⊡ **Villa del Sueño Hotel.** While the handsome garden restaurant ($–$$$) is the main attraction at this elegant hotel, superior rooms are spacious and comfortable, with bamboo furniture in sitting areas, two double beds, new closets, and freshened-up fabrics and paint. The smaller standard rooms around the pool have no air-conditioning. But high ceilings, fans, and good ventilation keep them surprisingly cool. Apartments for longer stays are available in the villa development across the street. The restaurant has formal food and polished service, but a casual atmosphere. Filet mignon with a brandy-and-peppercorn sauce, perfectly cooked mahimahi in shrimp sauce, and garlicky butterfly shrimp are always on the menu. ⊠ *First entrance to Playa Hermosa, 350 m west of main Hwy.* ☎☐ 672–0026 ⊕ *www.villadelsueno.com* ⤴ *14 rooms, 12 apartments* ⌂ *Restaurant, fans, in-room safes, some refrigerators, some kitchens, pool, bar, shop, Internet; no a/c in some rooms, no room phones, no room TVs* ☰ AE, MC, V ⎺⎺ EP.

$  ⊡ **Hotel Playa Hermosa Bosque del Mar.** Shaded by massive, hundred-year-old trees, this low-lying hotel is pleasantly low-key. The most popular activity here is lounging in hammocks strung around the garden. Flashes of sunlit ocean, just a few barefoot steps away, periodically penetrate the cool greenery. The rooms, lined up in one-story brick blocks, were updated in 2004 with new mattresses, color-washed walls, ceramic bathrooms with hot water, and quiet, remote-controlled air conditioners in 12 rooms. Beachfront rooms are the smallest, but you can open the screened windows at night and catch the breeze and the sound of the ocean. The restaurant serves truly fresh fish and beef tenderloin raised on the owner's ranch. ⊠ *End of the first entrance to Playa Hermosa* ☎ *672–0046* 🖷 *672–0019* ⊕ *www.hotelplayahermosa.com* 🗷 *20 rooms* ⚓ *Restaurant, a/c, fans, beach, bar* ▭ *AE, DC, MC, V* ☉❙ *BP.*

$ 🖾 **Villas Huetares.** The best bargain in town, this long-established family hotel with two-bedroom garden bungalows has a pleasant, two-story annex with 16 spacious rooms. In a quiet corner of the large garden, behind the pool, the newer rooms have two double beds, small fridges, cable TV, and air conditioning. One of the ground-floor rooms is wheelchair accessible. Oddly, a few rooms only have cold water, or as the Ticos like to say, *agua corriente* (room-temperature water). If you're willing to cook for yourself, the bungalows are a bargain, especially for families or groups. Be prepared for the sound of kids playing in the pool and garden. The walk to the beach is about 10 minutes. ⊠ *Second entrance road to Playa Hermosa, 100 m (1 block) in from the main hwy.* ☎ *672–0052* 🖷 *672–0051* 🗷 *16 rooms, 15 bungalows* ⚓ *Snack bar, a/c, fans, some kitchens, some refrigerators, cable TV, 2 pools* ▭ *AE, DC, MC, V* ☉❙ *EP.*

## Nightlife

**Hotel El Velero** (⊠ Second entrance to Playa Hermosa, then 100 m north of Aqua Sport on beach Rd.) hosts beach barbecues with live music on Wednesday and Saturday nights in high season. The crowd is 30-ish and up. Weekend nights in high season there's live mellow jazz, as well as some classic rock at **Villa del Sueño** (⊠ First entrance to Playa Hermosa, 350 m west of main hwy). The band takes its cues from what the audience wants to hear.

## Shopping

You can shop for a beach picnic at the **Aqua Sport** (⊠ Second entrance to Playa Hermosa; follow signs heading south on beach Rd.) minimarket and liquor store and buy souvenirs in the gift shop. The **Villa del Sueño gift shop** (⊠ First entrance to Playa Hermosa, 350 m west of main Hwy.) has original oil paintings, exotic crafts from around the world, and locally made mother-of-pearl jewelry and unique ivory bracelets made of local Brahman cow bones. **Kaltak Art and Craft Market** (⊠ South of airport on road to Santa Cruz) has five rooms of high-quality crafts and gifts, including organic-cotton blouses and dresses and traditional leather-and-wood rocking chairs, which they will ship for you. **La Gran Nicoya** (⊠ Just north of small bridge over Río Tempisque, on road to Santa Cruz) has an excellent jewelry selection plus an international shipping service and tourist information and maps. Kaltak and La Gran Nicoya, both on the road between the Liberia airport and the turnoff for Playa Hermosa, have nearly any souvenir you could want.

### To & From Playa Hermosa
*27 km/17 mi (30 minutes) southwest of Liberia airport.*

From the Comunidad turnoff from Hwy 21, heading from Liberia, Playa Hermosa is about 15 km (9 mi) northwest. The paved road forks after the small town of Sardinal, with the right fork heading into Hermosa and the left leading to Playas del Coco. Local directions usually refer to the first and second entrance roads to the beach, the first entrance being the southern one. There is no through beachfront road, so you have to approach the beach from either of these two roads. Empresa Esquivel buses leave from Liberia for Playa Hermosa daily at 4:45, 7:30, and 11:30 AM and 1, 3:30, and 5:30 PM.

### Playa Hermosa Essentials
Playa Hermosa has few resources. Get what you need in Liberia or Playas del Coco, to the south.

🌐 Internet **Villa Acacia** ✉ Second entrance to Playa Hermosa; south on beach Rd. ☎ 672–1000.

## Playas del Coco

**❾** Messy, noisy, colorful, and interesting, Playas del Coco is first and foremost a fishing port, with a Port Captain's office, a fish market, and an ice factory for keeping fish fresh—not for cooling margaritas, although many are drunk here. The town (called "El Coco" by locals) is not particularly scenic. The dark-sand beach is mostly a workplace, and it hasn't yet met the Blue Flag standards of cleanliness. The unpaved main street becomes a sea of mud when it rains and a dustbowl when it doesn't. So why do visitors flock here? They come to eat at the many excellent seafood restaurants and to shop at the big supermarket and myriad souvenir shops. But primarily they come to dive, surf, and fish. If you like your resorts to have some local color, Coco's slightly down-at-the-heels appearance can be appealing. It's also one of the most accessible beaches from San José in Guanacaste, so it serves as a playground for Costa Rica's college kids. Christmas and Semana Santa in March are impossibly crowded. The quieter, north part of the beach has some lovely grown-up restaurants and hotels, although condominium developers have moved in and the sounds of construction will be ringing out for a few years to come.

### Outdoor Activities

BOATING  You can sail off into the sunset for $55, including open bar and appetizers, on **Drums of Bora Bora** (☎ 670–1033), a 50-foot teak yacht.

DIVING & SNORKELING  Half a dozen dive shops crowd into this small town. This coast doesn't have the coral reefs or the clear visibility of the Caribbean coast, but it does have a lot of plankton (hence the lower visibility) that feeds legions of fish, some of them really, really big. Manta rays and sharks (white-tipped, nurse, and bull varieties) are among the stars of the undersea show. It takes about 20 to 45 minutes to reach the local sites.

Most of the dive shops have instruction, but the owner of **Summer-Salt Dive Center** (✉ Main St. ☎ 824–7258 ⊕ www.summer-salt.com) is the only PADI course director based in Costa Rica. **Deep Blue Diving Adventures** (⊠ Main street, in Hotel Coco Verde parking lot ☎ 670–1004 ⊕ www.scuba-diving-in-costa-rica.com) has the cheapest dives. **Drums of Bora Bora** (⇨ Boating, *above*) runs daytime snorkeling trips ($65). **Rich Coast Diving** (⊠ Main street, across the street and one block north of Hotel Coco Verde ☎ 670–0176 ⊕ www.richcoastdiving.com) has enthusiastic guides and instructors and limits tours to five divers per dive master and 10 divers per boat.

FISHING   Fishing charter boats go out 15 to 40 miles seeking yellowfin tuna, mahimahi, grouper, and red snapper close-in, and sailfish, marlin, and roosterfish offshore (beyond 40 miles). Boats, moored here and in nearby Ocotal, can pick you up from a beach near your hotel. **TranquilaMar** (⊠ Behind Louisiana Bar & Grill, off main St.) has three 28-foot Cummins diesel-powered boats moored in nearby Ocotal and can pick you up at any local beach. Just bring sunscreen and your hat, says the owner. Trips are $350 for a half-day and $550 for a full day. **Blue Marlin Service** (⊠ Main St. ☎ 670–0707, 353–5011) goes out in either a 24-foot boat for close-in fishing ($285/half-day) or in a luxury, 52-footer for a full day offshore ($1,400).

SURFING   Legendary **Witch's Rock and Ollie's Point** surfing spots are a 1½-hour boat
★   ride away from Playas del Coco off the coast of Santa Rosa National Park. Overcrowding led the park authorities to limit the number of daily surfers to 25 in 2004, but that stricture has gone by the boards. Now you can surf as long as you pay the $7 park entrance fee.

You can sign up for a surfing trip with any beach-town tour operator, but local authorities only allow excursions to Witch's Rock and Ollie's Point to originate from the main dock at Playas del Coco, in boats owned by local boat owners, in order to curb overcrowding and undue environmental stress. **World Class Waves** (⊠ Main street, about 3 blocks from beach ☎ 670–1020 ⊕ www.costaricasurftrips.com) is the operator that officially represents the local association of boat operators. The trip is around $50 per person, plus the park entrance fee.

## Where to Stay & Eat

**$–$$**   ✕ **Louisiana Bar & Grill.** This second-story restaurant is cool and breezy, but the Cajun cuisine is hot, with the best authentic jambalaya in town and a spicy gumbo loaded with shrimp, crab, and sausage. Fish is fresh, thanks to the owner's fleet of fishing boats (⇨ TranquilaMar, above), and it's served any way you like it, with a choice of 10 intriguing sauces, including macadamia pesto or orange-chipotle sauce. ⊠ *Main road through town, across from Hotel Coco Verde* ☎ 670–0400 ▭ *AE, MC, V.*

**$–$$**   ✕ **Restaurante Papagayo Pura Vida.** The best way to enjoy the beach and the bay is to set yourself down at an outdoor table at this beachfront Tico restaurant. The food is straightforward, reliably fresh, and flavorful. Sip a fruit smoothie, sample a ceviche of fish and shrimp, or slurp up a seafood soup generously packed with shrimp, calamari, fish, and crab. The lobster is a little expensive, at $28; if you want one, wait until after 4 PM, when the lobster boats come in with the day's catch. ⊠ *Main street, right at the beach* ☎ 670–0272 ▭ *AE, DC, MC, V.*

★ $  ✕ **El Sol y La Luna.** Finding haute-Italian cuisine in a romantic alfresco restaurant in Playas del Coco is a pleasant surprise. Host Alessandro Tolo brought his design ideas and superb jazz CD collection from Rome, and his wife, Silvia Casu, brought her culinary skills from her native Sardinia. Diners are often repeat visitors, returning for homemade pasta and homegrown basil, along with other distinctively Italian tastes, including a wide selection of Italian wines, sparkling San Pellegrino mineral water, and aromatic Sambuca liqueur. For dessert, try the Arenal, a moist, chocolate cake floating in a lake of chocolate sauce. ⊠ *La Puerta del Sol hotel, 180 m to right, off main road to Playas del Coco* ☎ *670–0195* ⊟ *AE, MC, V.*

$  ✕ **Tequila Bar and Grill.** Home of the Howler, a spicy shot of tequila laced with jalapeño and habañero peppers, this popular gringo hangout with a concrete floor and old wooden tables is created in the image of a grubby Mexican restaurant. The meals are authentic and tasty, especially the fajitas, which come with chicken, beef, shrimp, or *pulpo* (octopus). Along with its excellent margaritas, the bar is famous for its cool jazz, blues, and Latin recordings. ⊠ *Main strip, 130 m east of (away from) beach* ☎ *670–0741* ⊟ *No credit cards* ☾ *Closed Wed.*

$$  ▦ **Hotel Coco Verde.** Right in the middle of main street, this freshly painted green-and-white Best Western with modern, motel-style rooms is well maintained and comfortable. What the hotel lacks in charm is made up for by a pleasant pool area and its location: you can walk (or stagger) to almost anywhere in town. The hotel has lots of man appeal, with a steak and ribs restaurant, a pizza parlor, and an on-site casino that has dealer tables and machines. Amusing fish-themed decor gives it more class than the typical Tico casino. And there's a spa to keep nonfishers and nonsurfers busy. ⊠ *Main St.* ☎ *670–0494* 🖷 *670–0555* ⊕ *www.cocoverde.com* ↝ *33* ⌂ *Two restaurants, a/c, fans, cable TV, pool, spa, dive shop, tours, bar, casino* ⊟ *AE, MC, V* ▯◎▯ *BP.*

$$  ✕▦ **La Puerta del Sol.** The most luxurious hotel in the area is a tranquil enclosure of stylish suites sitting in a formal garden with sculpted shrubs and a lovely pool. The modern, airy Mediterranean-style guest rooms have cool, pastel color schemes and filmy fabrics. King-size beds roost atop adobe platforms, and gleaming white, tiled bathrooms have high ceilings. Pasha, the resident Newfoundland dog, can usually be found lolling around the reception area, and there are various pet cats prowling in the garden. The restaurant, El Sol y La Luna (⇨ *above*), is excellent. ⊠ *180 m to right (north) off main road to town* ☎ *670–0195* 🖷 *670–0650* ⊕ *hotelsol@racsa.com.cr* ↝ *10 suites* ⌂ *Restaurant, a/c, in-room safes, refrigerators, cable TV, pool, gym* ⊟ *AE, MC, V* ▯◎▯ *BP.*

$$  ▦ **Rancho Armadillo.** The eye-popping avenue of pink bougainvillea lining the long drive to this B&B is just a hint of the riotous garden beyond that attracts hummingbirds, butterflies, birds, and small beasts. At the foot of a forested mountain, the hotel has views of greenery as far as the eye can see, and azure sea in the distance. There's nothing fussy here: this is a place to relax, with decks, terraces, and an elevated hammock house. The handsome rooms are large, with queen- and king-size beds with carved-wood headboards. Big bathrooms have rain-forest shower heads. You are welcome to cook in the commercially equipped

kitchen, but owner and former culinary arts teacher Rick Vogel will cook dinner for you on request. He also gives cooking lessons ($10 plus cost of the ingredients). ⊠ *First left turn, just before divided boulevard, at entrance to Playas del Coco* ☎ *670–0108* 🖷 *670–0441* ⊕ *www. ranchoarmadillo.com* ⬐ *5 rooms, 2 2-bedroom suites* ⟁ *Shared kitchen, a/c, fans, cable TV, pool; no room phones* ☰ *AE, MC, V* ⥷ *BP.*

**$–$$** 🔲 **Villa Flores.** Extremely popular, this comfortable B&B with floral motifs inside and out books up quickly all year round. Comments in the guest book uniformly praise the homey feeling and the personalized attention by the American owners. The high-ceilinged upstairs suites are spacious, while the downstairs rooms are fairly small but cozy, with smallish bathrooms. The gardens are awash in flowering shrubs and the pool is inviting, as are the hammocks slung between an avenue of tall palm trees. A hearty breakfast is served in a tiled terrace restaurant and, in high season, dinner, too. Restaurant Sol y Luna is just around the corner. ⊠ *180 m east of main Rd.* ☎ *670–0269* 🖷 *670–0787* ⟟ *Apdo. 2, Playas del Coco* ⊕ *www.hotel-villa-flores.com* ⬐ *7 rooms, 2 suites* ⟁ *Restaurant, a/c, fans, pool, gym, whirlpool tub, laundry service; no room phones, no TV in some rooms* ☰ *V* ⥷ *BP.*

## Nightlife

**Banana Surf** (⊠ Across from Coco Verde casino), a second-floor disco-restaurant, has very loud music and dancing on a tiny dance floor until 2 AM. The crowd can be pretty scruffy, including older guys looking for one-night stands—with professionals or amateurs. At **The Lizard Lounge** (⊠ Across from Banana Surf, next to Hotel Coco Verde) there's dancing every night on a big thatched-roof dance floor. The reggae and rap beats appeal to a very young surfing crowd. There's a happy hour and gambling every night at the **Hotel Coco Verde** (⊠ Main road through town). Occasionally, there are dances down by the dock at the **Coco Mar** (⊠ On beach, turn left from plaza), when a live band comes to town and the locals come from miles around. Dancing doesn't get under way until after 10 PM.

## Shopping

If you can't find it at **Galería & Souvenirs Susy** (⊠ Main street, next to Coco Verde Hotel), chances are they don't make it in Costa Rica. Along with a huge selection of interesting notebooks and albums made of botanical materials, they also sell locally made shell belts ($11). At **El Tucán** (⊠ Beside Papagayo Seafood, main street), among the souvenirs and racks of beach wear, you can find interesting coconut-shell buttons and a line of high-gloss, colorful pottery with toucan and macaw motifs.

## To & From Playas del Coco

*25 km/16 mi (30 minutes) southwest of Liberia airport*

It's an easy drive from the Liberia airport to Playas del Coco. This is the first major town, with lots of services, south of Liberia. The paved highway turns into a grand, divided boulevard as you enter town and then dissolves into the dirt-road main street that leads directly to the beach. If you don't have a car, the best way to get here from Playa Hermosa is in a taxi, for about $7.50 each way.

### Playas del Coco Essentials

🏧 Bank/ATM **Banco Nacional** ✉ Main street, at entrance to town.

🏥 Hospital **Public Health Clinic** ✉ Next to Hotel Coco Verde.

💊 Pharmacies **Farmacia Cocos** ✉ 100 m east of Banco Nacional ⊗ Mon.–Sat. 8:30–8, Sun. 10–6 ☞ resident doctor.

💻 Internet **Internet@Juice Bar** ✉ Main street, next to Lizard Lounge.

📮 Post Office **Correo** ✉ Beachfront, beside police station.

## Playa Ocotal

⑩ One of the most dramatic beaches in the country, this serene crescent is ringed by rocky cliffs. The sparkling, clean turquoise water contrasts with the black sand. It's only ⅓-mile long but the vistas are endless, with offshore islands and the jagged profile of the Santa Elena Peninsula 21 miles away. Right at the entrance to the Gulf of Papagayo, it's a good place for sportfishing enthusiasts to hole up between excursions. There's good diving at Las Corridas, just 1 km (½ mi) away, and excellent snorkeling in nearby coves and islands, as well as right off the beach around the rocks at the east end of the beach.

### Outdoor Activities

DIVING & SNORKELING  The **dive shop** at **El Ocotal Beach Resort** (✉ 3 km/2 mi south of Playas del Coco ⊕ www.ocotaldiving.com) is the only PADI Gold Palm Resort in Costa Rica, so it's pretty much a sure thing that they have excellent equipment, safety standards, and instruction. It rents snorkeling equipment for $10 per day. The rocky outcrop at the north end of the beach near Los Almendros is good for snorkeling.

FISHING  **El Ocotal Beach Resort** (✉ 3 km/2 mi south of Playas del Coco ⊕ www.ocotalfishing.com) has a sportfishing operation.

HIKING  Take an exhilarating and engrossing morning walk ($10) in the hills of Ocotal with retired vet and very active naturalist **Dr. Will Abrams** (☎ 670–0553). The energetic, knowledgeable Tennessee native entertains and educates with stories about the secret lives of trees, plants, and animals spotted along the way.

### Where to Stay & Eat

$–$$  ✕ **Picante.** It's hot and it's tropical. As the name warns (*picante* means "spicy") everything here makes your tastebuds tingle. The menu spices up (literally) local fish and tropical fruits in dishes like fresh-tuna *salade niçoise* and grilled mahimahi with spicy mango sauce. The large terrace restaurant is poolside, facing the gorgeous beach backed by an cookie-cutter condominium development at Bahía Pez Vela. The cheap dinette furniture is out of sync with the innovative food. ✉ *At the beach, Bahía Pez Vela, 1 1//2 km/1 mi south of Ocotal* ☎ 670–0901 ⊟ *AE, DC, MC, V.*

$$$  🏨 **Los Almendros.** If you don't mind cooking for yourself, consider settling into this residential hotel complex right on the beach. Its pleasant, two-bedroom, two-bath apartments are in a great location with mature gardens and good snorkeling right at their doorstep. Kitchens are modern and well equipped. The best apartment is No. 14, with a trail right

CLOSE UP

## The Ecological Blue Flag

RECOGNIZING THAT THREE-QUARTERS OF TRAVELERS to Costa Rica visit the beaches, the national water utility, Aqueductos y Alcantarillados, in conjunction with the Costa Rican Tourism Board (ICT), began evaluating and ranking beaches' water and environmental quality in 1996. Those that achieved a 90-percent score were awarded a blue flag to fly as a symbol of excellence. The program, modeled on one begun in Spain in 1986 and now used in the European Union, awards flags to communities, rather than to individual hotels. Participating areas must form a Blue Flag committee bringing together diverse sectors of the population that might otherwise fiercely compete for tourist dollars.

Officials inspect heavily visited beaches once a month. More isolated communities get an assessment every two months. Water quality—ocean and drinking water—trash cleanup, waste management, security, signage, and environmental education are evaluated. The competition is now open to inland communities and schools as well as beach communities. Only 10 beaches won a Blue Flag that first year; 19 succeeded the following year. In 2005, out of 124 that applied, 65 communities—

50 beaches and 15 inland towns—won flags. Evaluators do yank flags: long-time Blue Flag holder Tamarindo lost its status in 2005, due to problems with water quality and security. Blue flags fly in the following communities covered in this guide:

Northern Plains: La Fortuna, Las Horquetas (near Rara Avis).

North Pacific: Nosara (Playa Guiones, Playa Pelada), Ostional, Playa Carrillo, Playa Conchal, Playa Flamingo, Playa Grande, Playa Hermosa, Playa Junquillal, Playa Langosta, Playa Ocotal, Playa Pan de Azucar, Playa Panamá, Punta Islita.

Central Pacific: Isla Tortuga, Malpaís, Manuel Antonio (Playa Manuel Antonio, Playa Espadilla Sur, Puerto Escondido, Playa Gemelas), Punta Leona (Playa Blanca, Playa Limoncito).

South Pacific: Ballena National Marine Park (Playa La Colina, Playa Piñuela, Playa Ballena, Punta Uvita), Playa Zancudo, San Gerardo de Rivas, San Marcos de Tarrazú.

Caribbean: Cahuita (Puerto Vargas, Playa Blanca, Playa Negra), EARTH, Puerto Viejo de Talamanca (Playa Negra, Playa Chiquita, Playa Cocles, Punta Uva), Gandoca-Manzanillo National Wildlife Refuge.

---

down to a tidal-pool natural bathtub. There are also four-bedroom, cottage-style houses for rent, but these are a little scruffy and poorly furnished. ⊠ *East end of Playa Ocotal* ☎ *670–0582* 📠 *670–0526* ⊕ *www. losalmendros.com* ➥ *20 apartments* ♨ *A/c, fans, kitchens, cable TV, 2 pools, beach* ☰ *AE, DC, MC, V* ⊺⊙⫯ *EP.*

**$$–$$$**   🏨 **El Ocotal Beach Resort.** A little frayed at the edges, this luxury resort still has the best sea and coastline views and is one of the best dive resorts in the country. The lobby and restaurants, however, are in sad shape. The rooms with the best views are in the hilltop 400 series; they share a small pool and whirlpool. Down the hill to the beach, comfortable triangular bungalows each have two separate large suites that share a semiprivate pool. The food in the recent past has been lamentable, but at this writing a new chef is updating the menu with Mediterranean and Asian flavors. It remains to be seen whether the new owner can revive this fading beach queen. ⌖ *3 km/2 mi south of Playas del Coco, down newly paved Rd.* ☎ *670–0321* 🖷 *670–0083* ⊕ *www.ocotalresort.com* 🖃 *Apdo. 1, Playas del Coco* ⇴ *42 rooms, 5 suites, 12 bungalow suites* ♿ *Restaurant, a/c, fans, in-room safes, cable TV, tennis court, 3 pools, spa, dive shop, bicycles, kayaking, horseback riding, bar, laundry service, Internet* ☰ *AE, MC, V* ⏍�‖ *BP.*

★ **$$** 🏠 **Hotel Villa Casa Blanca.** For romance you can't beat this Victorian-style, all-suite B&B in a hillside building buried in a bower of tropical plantings. Suites have four-poster beds, plush furniture, and Victorian detailing. The Honeymoon Suites have deep soaking tubs built for two. The pool is small but pretty. There's no room service, but the obliging staff can arrange for local restaurants to deliver dinners *à deux*, to be enjoyed by candlelight at the pool or on the terrace. Waffles, pancakes, muffins, and savory dishes provide fuel in the morning, and breakfast entertainment is provided by two pet parrots who are vociferous as well as notorious mooches. Judging by the guest comments, people love them. ⌖ *Just inside gated entrance to El Ocotal Beach Resort* ☎🖷 *670–0448* ⊕ *www.hotelvillacasablanca.com* 🖃 *Apdo. 176–5019, Playas del Coco* ⇴ *12 suites* ♿ *Pool, a/c, fans, outdoor whirlpool tub; no room phones, no room TVs, no smoking* ☰ *AE, MC, V* ⏍�‖ *BP.*

### Nightlife

Enjoy a quiet margarita with an ocean view at **Father Rooster Sports Bar & Grill** (⌖ El Ocotal Beach Resort, 3 km/2 mi south of Playas del Coco) on the beach. The action heats up later in the evening with big-screen TV, music, pool, beach volleyball, and Tex-Mex bar food. During peak holiday weeks, huge crowds of partyers descend on the bar to dance by torchlight.

### To & From Playa Ocotal

*3 km/2 mi (10 minutes) of Playas del Coco.*

The drive from Playas del Coco is on a paved road to the gated entrance of Playa Ocotal. The road winds through a heavily populated Tico residential area, so be on the lookout, especially at night, for bicyclists without lights, children, dogs, cows, and horses on the road. There are no buses from Playas del Coco to Ocotal, but it's only $5 by taxi.

## Playa Pan de Azúcar

⓫ Playa Pan de Azúcar (Sugar Bread Beach) has a quality that can be hard to come by in this area: privacy. With only one built-up property, the entire stretch of brown-sugar sand feels practically deserted. The north end of the beach has some good snorkeling, and the swimming is good here—the ocean floor is soft and sandy. Playa Penca, a short walk south along the beach, has good swimming as well.

### Outdoor Activities

Most of the operators who work out of Flamingo (⇨ *below*) cover this whole area, which is very close as the boat speeds, although more spread out via road.

## Where to Stay

**$$–$$$** 🏨 **Hotel Sugar Beach.** Picture a thin, curving beach and a secluded hotel and shimmering pool shaded by trees. But with major construction adding suites and beach houses, the new owners may be undermining the very reasons to come here: peace and quiet. Many of the original rooms have idyllic ocean views, and each room's wooden door has a hand-carved

> **WORD OF MOUTH**
>
> "The sunsets at Sugar Beach are spectacular. The pelicans are in a feeding frenzy and dive repeatedly into the waves as the sun goes down—it is really a show!"
>
> –jamamac

image of a local bird or animal. Bright yellow-and-blue fabrics along with watermelon, aqua, and yellow walls make rooms festive and fresh. If you like serenity, opt for a room in the cool, maturely landscaped garden. The open-air rotunda restaurant serves good seafood dishes. Before you reserve, make sure all the construction is completed. ⊠ *8 km/5 mi north of Playa Flamingo* ☎ *654–4242* 🖷 *654–4239* ⊕ *www.sugar-beach.com* ✉ *Apdo. 90, Santa Cruz* 🛏 *18 rooms, 7 suites, 1 apartment, 2 houses* ♨ *Restaurant, in-room safes, some kitchens, minibars, cable TV, pool, snorkeling, boating, horseback riding, bar, laundry service, airport shuttle* 🖃 *AE, D, MC, V* ⑩ *EP.*

### To & From Playa Pan de Azúcar

*8 km/5 mi (20 minutes) north of Flamingo Beach.*

Getting to this beach is an adventure in itself. It's still a very bumpy road from Flamingo Beach. If you have four-wheel drive and an excellent sense of direction, you can attempt to drive (dry season only) the 16-km (11-mi) Monkey Trail, which cuts through the mountains from Coco to Flamingo. But even some Ticos get lost on this route, so keep asking directions along the way. There are buses to Playa Pan de Azúcar, but it's easier to get there by car or taxi.

## Playa Potrero

⑫ The small town of Potrero is a classic Tico community, with a church, school, and supermarket arranged around a soccer field. But Potrero Beach stretches for 4 km (2½ mi) all the way south from the village to the concrete skyline of Flamingo. Development is picking up speed, with large houses and condominium developments springing up on any hill that has a view. There's a large Italian contingent here, adding some style and flavor to area hotels. There are also some affordable, self-catering resorts, where you can set yourself up comfortably for a week or more. The brown-sand beach is safe for swimming, and the quietest stretch is midway between Flamingo and Potrero town. The best beach view and best breeze are from a bar stool at Cantina Las Brisas. About 10 km (6 mi) offshore lie the Catalina Islands, a barrier-island mecca for divers and snorkelers.

### Outdoor Activities

DIVING  Marked as Santa Catarina on maps, the **Catalina Islands,** as they are known locally, are a major destination for dive operations based all along the coast. These barrier islands are remarkable for their variety, and appeal to different levels of divers. On one side the islands have 20- to 30-foot drops, great for beginner divers. The other side has deeper drops of 60 to 80 feet, better suited to more experienced divers. The two premier diving sites around the Catalina Islands are **The Point** and **The Wall.** From January to May, when the water is colder, you are almost guaranteed mantaray sightings at these spots. Cow-nosed and devil rays are also spotted here in large schools. Dive operators from Playa Hermosa south to Tamarindo offer trips to these islands. Reserve through your hotel.

**Costa Rica Diving** (⊠ 1 km south of Flamingo on the main Hwy. 📠 654–4148) has been specializing in Catalina Islands dives for 16 years, with two-tank, two-location trips limited to five divers. The German owners also offer courses and are noted for their precision and high standards.

## Where to Stay & Eat

¢–$$ ✕ **Harden's Garden Bakery & Cafe.** You won't find a better peanut-butter cookie in the country. Harden's is also famous for its gooey cinnamon buns and pizza by the slice or pie. You can call in your order and pick up your pizza to eat on the beach or in your hotel. Good Mexican food—from breakfast burritos through lunchtime taco salads to grilled seafood dinners—is served at casual terrace tables shaded by an ancient fig tree lit with fairy lights at night. ⊠ *Across from Club Bahía Potrero* 📞 *654–4271* 🚫 *No credit cards.*

$ ✕ **Ristorante Marco Polo.** They came, they saw, they built a whole Tuscan-style village and imported a chef from Italy to cater to a demanding Italian clientele. Marco Polo, the main restaurant at the Villagio Flor de Pacífico mega-development of red-roofed villas east of Potrero, serves properly *al dente* pasta with homemade sauces and excellent wood-oven pizza. The poolside restaurant always looks nice, with elegant tablecloths and table settings. Lunch is served from noon to 3 PM, dinner from 6 to 9:30 PM, and the pizzeria is open from noon to 10:30 PM. ⊠ *1 km/½ mi east of Potrero* 📞 *654–4664* 🚫 *AE, DC, MC, V.*

¢–$ ✕ **Cantina Las Brisas.** The perfect beach bar, Las Brisas is a shack with a view, and what a view: the entire sweep of Playa Potrero. The Texan owner serves excellent Mexican-inspired food and seafood. The fish tacos are outstanding—breaded strips of fish smothered in lettuce, tomato, and refried beans and encased in both a crisp taco and a soft tortilla shell. Wednesday is ladies' night and karaoke, and the joint really jumps. The place is decorated with old surfboards, rusty U.S. license plates, and wall murals. ⊠ *Beside the supermarket* 📞 *654–4047* 🚫 *No credit cards.*

$$ ✕🛏 **Club Bahía Potrero.** It has the premier location on the beach, but this luxury hotel doesn't rest on its location laurels. The food and service are a match for the unbeatable surroundings. At the restaurant ($–$$), next to the gorgeous palm-fringed pool, smartly uniformed waiters serve jumbo shrimp, lobster, and fish fresh from the sea with Costa Rican accents, such as hearts of palm and *pejibaye* (a nutty palm fruit). The Continental breakfast includes heavenly rich coffee and homemade bread. The hotel's design is modern, with elegant Costa Rica–made wood furniture and patterned ceramic-tile floors. Rooms are

arranged round an impressive topical garden and are spacious, with two double beds, but a little bare. Three rooms have outdoor showers and soaking tubs in private patio gardens. ⊠ *South end of Potrero Beach, across from Harden's Garden* ☎ *654–4671* 🖷 *654–5182* ⊕ *www. potrerobay.com* ⤳ *25 rooms, 14 suites* ⚭ *Restaurant, a/c, some in-room whirlpool tubs, cable TV, pool, massage, beach, bar, laundry service, concierge, Internet* ⊟ *MC, V* ⫯⊘⫯ *EP.*

$ 🏨 **Bahía Esmeralda Hotel & Restaurant.** Although it's not on the beach, this Italian-run hotel has lots of style at an affordable price. It's a great place for families or groups. Ochre-colored villas are spread out around a pretty pool in a sunny garden. Large glass doors bring in lots of light and clay-tile roofs keep the villas cool. The equipped apartments ($$–$$$) are for four, six, or eight people. All rooms and apartments have handsome, modern fabrics and elegant Italian bathrooms tiled in cool green. An alfresco restaurant serves breakfast and light Italian dishes. The friendly, owner/manager is always on site. It's a five-minute walk through the village to the beach. ⊠ *1 block east of Potrero village* ☎ *354–6322* 🖷🖷 *654–4480* ⊕ *www.hotelbahiaesmeralda.com* ⤳ *4 rooms, 14 apartments* ⚭ *Restaurant, a/c, fans, some kitchens, cable TV, pool, laundry service; no room phones* ⊟ *MC, V* ⫯⊘⫯ *rooms BP, apartments EP.*

## To & From Playa Potrero

*4 km/2 ½ mi (15 minutes) north of Flamingo.*

Just before crossing the bridge at the entrance to Flamingo, take the right fork signed for Potrero. The road, which is alternately muddy or dusty, is rough and follows the shoreline. You don't need four-wheel drive as long as you take it nice and slow. If you've come via the four-wheel-drive-only Monkey Trail from Coco, you'll reenter civilization at Potrero. Local buses run from Flamingo to Potrero, but it's so close that you're better off taking a taxi.

# Playa Flamingo

⑬ Flamingo was one of the first of the northern Nicoya beaches to experience the wonders of overscale resort development, a fact immortalized in the huge concrete towers that straggle up the hill overlooking Flamingo Bay. The place is still a bevy of real estate activity, only now the realtors are selling condominiums and house lots all around the bay. The beach, hidden away to the south of the town, is one of the few truly white-sand beaches in Costa Rica. This beach is great for swimming, with a fine-sand bottom and no strong currents. There's a bit of surf, so keep your eye on little paddlers. Except for a few spindly trees, there is no shade along the beach's kilometer-long stretch. The beach is so well hidden you could pass by Flamingo proper and never know it was there. Just as you enter town, instead of going up the hill, turn left past Marie's Restaurant and follow the road past the entrance to the Flamingo Beach Resort to the end, where it becomes a dirt beach road.

Flamingo is perhaps most famous for its large sportfishing fleet, temporarily moored out in the bay until the government grants a new concession to update and operate the marina here. As you enter town there's a jokey road sign, warning: DESPACIO/ PESCADORES EN LA VIA ("Slow down/ Fishermen in the roadway"). Lured by boatloads of single-for-the-week fishermen, working girls abound here, adding a faint, salacious whiff to the hangouts around the defunct marina.

## Outdoor Activities

**Aquacenter Dive Shop** (⊠ Flamingo Marina Resort, hill above Flamingo Bay ☎ 654–4141 ⊕ www.aquacenterdiving.com) has diving trips, kayaking, snorkeling, cruises, kids' activities, and more.

BOATING With **Lazy Lizard Sailing Catamaran Adventures** (☎ 832–5773 or 844–9096 ⊕ www.sailingcostarica.com), sail off for an afternoon of snorkeling and sunbathing on a 38-foot Australian-built catamaran. The catamaran's two hulls make for smoother sailing, minimizing seasickness. A four-hour sail leaving at 2 PM is $75, including guided snorkeling, kayaking, beer, wine, rum, and lots of food. Sunsets appear as you sail into port. If you're up for a more energetic sea expedition, paddle with **Costa Rica Outriggers** (☎ 383–3013) to hard-to-reach beaches for snorkeling, swimming, beachcombing, and kayaking ($45, including fruit buffet). Canoes seat seven, plus two guides.

> ### HELP ON THE ROAD
>
> The more remote the area, the more likely that someone will stop to help you change a tire or tow you out of a river. Usually, good samaritans won't accept any payment and and are more trustworthy than those who offer to "help" in the States. Near Ostional there's a farmer named Valentin who regularly pulls cars out of the flooded river with his tractor. So he is known as Valentin *con chapulin* (with a tractor).

FISHING Although the marina is closed down while officials consider proposals (and incentives) for reopening it, there are plenty of sportfishing boats bobbing in Flamingo Bay. In December the wind picks up and many of the smaller, 31-foot-and-under boats head to calmer water farther south. But marlin (blue, black, and striped) love colder, choppier water, so January to April is prime catch-and-release marlin season. Sailfish abound, too, and there are tournaments galore. Closer in, the edible catch usually includes dorado, yellowfin tuna, wahoo, grouper, and red snapper. One of the established fishing operations that sticks around all year is **Billfish Safaris** (⊠ Lower level, Mariner Inn, at entrance to town ☎ 828–2173 or 654–4272). Its 42-foot boat with twin 350-horsepower diesel engines can go anywhere in any kind of sea. Trips on smaller boats are also available. Half-day close-in trips are $550 for up to five fishers; or $800 for a day. Offshore trips are $650 (for up to seven people) for a half-day; $900 for the whole day.

## Where to Stay & Eat

★ $–$$ ✕ **Marie's Restaurant.** A Flamingo institution, this veranda restaurant serves reliably fresh and delicious seafood in large portions at reasonable prices. Settle in at one of the sliced-tree-trunk tables painted with sea creatures for delightful ceviche and a delicious *plato de mariscos* (shrimp, lobster, and fish fillets served with garlic butter, potatoes, and salad). Save room for the dark and delicious banana-chocolate bread pudding.

At breakfast, try unusual papaya pancakes and French toast made with cream cheese and jam. ⊠ *Main road, near north end of beach* ☎ 654–4136 ▤ V.

$ ✕ **Licks'n'Wicks.** Homemade ice cream in 20 flavors, with 20 aromatic candles to match, is the concept of Toronto transplant Mary

> **THE GUANACASTE TREE**
>
> Massive and wide-spreading, with ear-like seed pods, the guanacaste—named for the province—is Costa Rica's national tree.

Ann Marlow, a good cook and a trained aromatherapist. Her candles, nestling in coconut shells, smell as delicious as her exotic ice creams taste. Try an avocado-vanilla smoothie for something different. The casual menu includes health-conscious quiches, salads, fish, and chicken burgers. Prices are a little high for the area, but the produce is organic and fresh. Mary Ann also bakes her own bread. It's open 6 AM to 9 PM daily. ⊠ *On hillside above Marie's Restaurant* ☎ 654–4226 ▤ No credit cards.

★ $$$$ ▥ **Colores del Pacífico.** High atop a commanding cliff, this small, exquisite, family-run hotel presiding over Potrero Bay looks like a page out of *Architectural Digest,* with a very modern, minimalist design that incorporates terra-cotta walls, Mexican-tile floors, sculptural cactus plantings, and indirect lighting. Each room has a dramatic bed "treatment" by the Belgian interior designer–owner. Fresh flowers and fruit greet you in your room, and each room has a private terrace and hammock. Breakfast and lunch, along with sunset cocktails and canapés, are served in a thatch-roof restaurant with an ocean view. Aqua exercise sessions in the infinity-edge pool and yoga sessions are offered every day. ⊠ *At intersection of roads leading out of Flamingo and to Playa Potrero* ☎ 654–4769 🖷 654–4976 ⊕ *www.coloresdelpacifico.com* ⇥ *6 rooms, 1 suite* ♿ *Restaurant, a/c, minibars, pool, fitness classes, bar; no TV in some rooms, no kids under 12* ▤ *AE, MC, V* ◉ *BP.*

$$-$$$ ▥ **Flamingo Marina Resort.** With more personality than other large resorts in the area, this upscale collection of hillside pink buildings with brightly colored tile roofs has lots to do, with four pools, tennis courts, a beach, a dive shop, and a tour desk. The fashionably decorated rooms, color washed in a mango hue, have terra-cotta lamps, hand-carved wooden furniture, and shell-shape sinks. The luxurious condos have modern kitchens and spacious sitting areas with leather couches. Nearly all rooms and condos have large verandas with excellent views of the sea below. One suite has a private whirlpool tub. ⊠ *Hill above Flamingo Bay* ☎ 654–4141, 290–1858 in San José 🖷 654–4035, 231–1858 in San José ⊕ *www.flamingomarina.com* ⒹApdo. 321–1002, San José ⇥ *22 rooms, 8 suites, 57 condos* ♿ *Restaurant, a/c, fans, in-room safes, some kitchens, minibars, cable TV, 4 pools, wading pool, outdoor whirlpool tub, beach, dive shop, kayaking, 2 bars, laundry service, meeting room* ▤ *AE, DC, MC, V* ◉ *BP.*

$$ ▥ **Flamingo Beach Resort.** After years of lying dormant, this modest concrete hotel, the only hotel actually fronting Flamingo Beach, has risen again, under new management that seems to have its act together, renovating rooms and landscaping. The family-friendly hotel isn't stylish, but it's a good value and has a secluded location. The centerpiece is a huge

swimming pool, with Olympic-length laps along one side. The kids' pool has a sunburn-preventive cover. There's a dive shop on site and lots of water equipment, plus game rooms and lots of kids' activities. The beach is just across the beach-access road. Rooms are huge, each with a private balcony. The restaurants are not exciting, so if you're looking for spectacular cuisine, don't take the all-inclusive option. There are lots of restaurants within walking distance, including Marie's, and some beach-front seafood places at the entrance to Flamingo. ⊠ *Hotel entrance just past Marie's Restaurant, on left side of Rd.* ☎ *654–4444, 283–8063 in San José* 🖷 *654–4060, 253–1593 in San José* ⊕ *www.resortflamingobeach. com* 🗪 *83 rooms, 8 2-bedroom suites* ⌂ *Restaurant, a/c, fans, high-speed Internet, in-room safes, refrigerators, cable TV, fitness room, 2 pools, beach, dive shop, 2 bars, casino, babysitting, kids' programs, laundry service, Internet, meeting rooms* ▤ *AE, DC, MC, V* ◉⦿ *BP.*

**$** 🏨 **Hotel Guanacaste Lodge.** On the outskirts of Flamingo this quiet Tico-run lodge sits on manicured grounds with tall trees. The 10 large rooms are in five houses with high beamed ceilings, and are comfortably furnished with wood furniture and walk-in closets. Bathrooms are tiled and spacious. Each room has a picture window looking out onto the pool and a cascading fountain. The attached Rancho Grande Restaurant/Bar serves Tico, Mexican, and Spanish dishes in a huge, open rancho with handmade wooden furniture. There's a big-screen TV for karaoke and occasional live music, so there could be some noisy times here. ⊠ *200 m south of the Potrero-Flamingo crossroads* ☎ *654–4494* 🖷 *654–4495* 📧 *portolsa@racsa.co.cr* 🗪 *10 rooms* ⌂ *Restaurant, fans, in-room safes, cable TV, pool, bar, laundry service* ▤ *MC, V* ◉⦿ *BP.*

## Nightlife

The **Mariner Inn Bar** (⊠ Bottom of the hill, entering Flamingo) is always boisterous and thick with testosterone, as fishermen trade fishtales. If you're interested in fishing of a different sort, or just like to watch, restaurant, disco, and casino **Amberes** (⊠ Halfway up hill in Flamingo) is the late-night meeting place.

## To & From Playa Flamingo

*80 km/50 mi (3 hours) southwest of Liberia.*

To get to Playa Flamingo from Liberia, drive 45 km (28 mi) south to Belén on a good, paved road and then 35 km (22 mi) west on a not-so-good potholed road to Flamingo. (Pre-potholes, the trip from Liberia took only 1½ hours.) If you're coming from the Playas del Coco and Ocotal area, you can take a 16-km (10-mi) shortcut, called the Monkey Trail, starting near Sardinal and emerging at Potrero. It's then 4 km (2½ mi) south to Flamingo. Only attempt this in dry season and in a four-by-four. You can also take a bus from Liberia (⇨ Bus Travel *in* Smart Travel Tips A to Z).

## Playa Flamingo Essentials

🏧 Bank/ATM **Banco de Costa Rica** ⊠ Main street, halfway up hill.

🏥 Hospital **Pacific Emergencies** ⊠ Crossroads at Huacas ☎ 653-8787 or 378-8265 🕗 Daily 8–8.

🕿 Pharmacy **Santa Fe Medical Center & Pharmacy** ⊠ Halfway up hill ☎ 654-9000 ⊙ Daily 8-8.
🕿 Internet **Shark Point at Costa Rica Diving** ⊠ 1 km south of town ☎ 654-4148 ⊙ Daily 8-8.

# Playa Conchal

**⑭** Lovely, secluded Playa Conchal is aptly named—it's sprinkled with shells atop a base of fine white sand. Although you can access the beach from the water and by walking south from Brasilito at low tide, you can't get to it from the road without passing through the rigid security of the sprawling Paradisus Playa Conchal resort. The road north of the resort is also sprinkled—but with a cluster of restaurants and shops.

## Exploring
A small, scruffy fishing village just 1 km (½ mi) north of Conchal, **Brasilito** has ramshackle houses huddled around its main square, which doubles as the soccer field. It's cluttered, noisy, and totally Tico, a lively contrast to the controlled sophistication of Playa Conchal. Fishing boats moor just off a wide beach, about 3 km (2 mi) long, with golden sand flecked with pebbles and a few rocks. The surf is a little stronger here than at Flamingo Beach, but the shallow, sandy bottom keeps it swimmable. The beach is lined with casual, Tico *marisquerias* (seafood snack bars) and a couple of notable restaurants.

## Outdoor Activities
GOLFING One of the best golf courses in the country, the Paradisus Playa Conchal mega-resort's **Garra de Léon Golf Course** (⊠ Paradisus Playa Conchal, entrance less than 1 km/½ mi south of Brasilito ☎ 654-4123) is a par-72 course designed by Robert Trent Jones Jr. Hotel guests and nonguests who reserve at least one day in advance can try out their swing on 18 holes for $140 or go nine holes for $75, cart included.

## Where to Stay & Eat
**$-$$** ✕ **El Camarón Dorado.** Much of the appeal of this bougainvillea-drenched bar-restaurant is its shaded location on Brasilito's beautiful beach. Some tables are right on the beach, with the surf lapping just yards away, perfect for sunset drinks. The white-plastic tables and chairs are not up to the standards of the food and service. A small-vessel fishing fleet anchored offshore assures you of the freshness of the bountiful portions of seafood on the menu. If you have a reservation, a van can pick you up from Flamingo or Tamarindo hotels. ⊠ *200 m north of Brasilito Plaza, Brasilito* ☎ *654-4028* 🖃 *AE, DC, MC, V.*

**$-$$** ✕ **Perro Plano Bar y Restaurante.** This large, breezy restaurant facing the beach is a global village of flavors: Russian borscht, Japanese tempura, Thai green curries, and fat Irish fries in homage to the Irish owners' heritage. In the hands of the Argentine chef, all dishes are authentic and delicious, as is the well-prepared local seafood. Unusual desserts include a strawberry soup with lemon sorbet. Service is a little slow, but the food is worth the wait. ⊠ *50 m north of the church, Brasilito* ☎ *654-9028* 🖃 *AE, MC, V.*

¢–$$ ✕ **Il Forno Restaurant.** For a break from seafood, try lunch or dinner at this romantic Italian garden restaurant. There are 15 versions of thin-crust pizzas, plus fine, homemade pastas and risotto, and veal marsala. Vegetarians have lots of choices (if you can get past the thought that veal is on the menu), including an eggplant lasagna and interesting salads. At dinner, fairy lights and candles glimmer all through the garden, and some private tables are set apart under thatched roofs. Spanish and Italian wines are available by the glass or bottle. ⊠ *Main road, 200 m south of the bridge in Brasilito* ☎ *654–4125* ☐ *No credit cards* ☉ *Closed Mon.*

$$$$ ▣ **Paradisus Playa Conchal Beach & Golf Resort.** So vast that guests ride around in trucks covered with striped awnings and staff get around on bicycles, this all-inclusive resort, the top of the line of the Spanish Meliá hotel chain, is luxurious, if lacking a bit in personality. The grounds encompass almost 4 square km (1½ square mi) that include a distant, picture-perfect beach. But in the labyrinthine guest village the ocean disappears, and the only views are of gardens and other villas exactly like yours. The split-level Spanish colonial–style villas have huge marble bathrooms and elegant sitting rooms. There are two kids' clubs for different ages, and grown-ups amuse themselves with nightly live shows, a casino, a gorgeous 18-hole golf course, and the largest pool in Central America. ⊠ *Entrance less than 1 km/½ mi south of Brasilito* ☎ *654–4123* 🖷 *654–4181* ⊕ *www.paradisusplayaconchal.com* ⤳ *292 villas* ⚐ *7 restaurants, a/c, fans, in-room safes, minibars, cable TV, 18-hole golf course, pro shop, 4 tennis courts, pool, gym, beach, jet skiing, bicycles, casino, nightclub, babysitting, children's programs, laundry service, Internet, meeting room* ☐ *AE, DC, MC, V* ⦿ *AI.*

¢ ▣ **Hotel Brasilito.** For adventurers only, this vintage all-wood hotel is definitely sans frills, including hot water. But its seafront location makes it the best—and only—choice if you want to stay right at Playa Brasilito. Be prepared for some noise: kids playing, dogs barking, and motors revving. The sparely furnished rooms occupy both floors of an old but well-maintained two-story wooden building behind the restaurant. Ask for one of the two larger rooms above the restaurant; they share a veranda with unobstructed sea views. You can't beat the price for seaside rooms. ⊠ *Next to the square and soccer field, Brasilito* ☎ *654–4237* 🖷 *654–4247* ⊕ *www.brasilito.com* ⤳ *15 rooms* ⚐ *Restaurant, fans, beach, laundry service, Internet; no a/c, no room phones, no room TVs* ☐ *MC, V* ⦿ *EP.*

## Nightlife

Live music, both acoustic guitar and rowdier dance bands, keeps the **The Happy Snapper** (⊠ Brasilito, at the beach) hopping on Friday and Saturday nights. Owner Mike Osborne mans the bar and spikes the drinks with his own brand of wry humor.

## To & From Playa Conchal

*8 km/5 mi (10 minutes) south of Flamingo.*

The drive south from Flamingo is on a paved highway. Both town and beach are just 1 km (½ mi) north of the entrance to Paradisus Playa Conchal. Buses run from Flamingo to Conchal three times daily, at 7:30 and 11:30 AM and 2:30 PM. A taxi from Flamingo is about $6.

## Playa Conchal Essentials

The closest bank and ATM are in Flamingo.

🏥 Hospital **Pacific Emergencies** ⊠ Crossroads at Huacas ☎ 653–8787 or 378-8265 🕒 Daily 8–8.

🏥 Pharmacies **Farmacia El Cruce** ⊠ Crossroads at Huacas ☎ 653–8787 🕒 Daily 8–8.

🏥 Internet **Supermarket Lopez** ⊠ 200 m south of school ☎ 654–4861 🕒 Daily 10–10.

---

**en route** | Gas stations are few and far between in these hinterlands. If you're heading down to Tamarindo from the Flamingo/Conchal area, fill up first. There's a station near Brasilito, but it's unreliable and often closed. Your best bet is the 24-hour Oasis Exxon, 3 km (2 mi) east of Huacas. A *ferreteria* (hardware store) on the northern outskirts of Tamarindo sells diesel and regular gas. It closes at noon on Sunday.

---

# Tamarindo

**⓯** Once a funky beach town full of spacey surfers and local fishermen, Tamarindo has become a hyped-up hive of commercial development with an ever-more-dazzling variety of restaurants, bars, and hotels. Strip malls and high-rise condominiums have obscured views of the still-magnificent beach, the streets are in a constant state of construction, and some low-life elements are making security an issue. But once you're on the beach, all the negatives disappear. Wide and flat, the sand is packed hard enough for easy walking and jogging. ⚠ Strong currents at both ends of the beach get a lot of swimmers into trouble, especially when they try to cross the estuaries during tidal changes. Surfing is the main attraction for the young crowd that parties hard at beachfront bars after a day riding the waves. Gray-haired veterans of the '60s surfing scene also come to surf and perhaps get in 18 rounds at one of the nearby golf courses—one of them, Hacienda Pinilla, is an 18-hole championship course with ocean views. An older, nonsurfing crowd is attracted by the upscale beachfront hotels away from the revved-up town center. With an airstrip just outside town, Tamarindo is also a convenient starting point for exploring the rest of the country.

## Outdoor Activities

BOATING  Rocky Isla El Capitán, just offshore, is a great **kayaking** destination, full of sand-dollar shells. Exploring the tidal estuaries north and south of town is best done in a kayak at high tide, when you can travel farther up the temporary rivers. Arrange kayaking trips through your hotel. Sail off into the sunset aboard a 50-foot traditional schooner with cruise company **Mandingo** (☎ 653–0623). Soft drinks, beer and wine, and bocas are included on the three-hour cruise. The boat leaves at 3 PM from the white tower on the beach ($50 per person).

FISHING  A number of fishing charters in Tamarindo cater to saltwater anglers. The best among them is probably **Tamarindo Sportfishing** (☎ 653–0090 📠 653–0161 ⊕ www.tamarindosportfishing.com), run by Randy Wilson, who has led the way in developing catch-and-release techniques that are easy on the fish. Wilson has roamed and fished the Guanacaste waters since the 1970s, and he knows where the big ones lurk. His boat,

# Tamarindo & Playa Langosta

**KEY**

▶ Restaurants

① Hotels

0 ────── 300 yards
0 ────── 300 meters

TO LIBERIA,
AIRPORT,
PLAYA AVELLANES

Playa Grande

SANSA ◆

Playa Tamarindo

Playa Langosta

**Restaurants** ▶

Dragonfly Bar & Grill ....**10**
Gecko's at
Iguana Surf ............**4**
Gil's Place ..............**5**
Hotel Pastiempo
Restaurant ............**11**
El Jardín del Edén .....**14**

La Laguna del
Cocodrilo Bistro .......**17**
Nogui's ................**6**
Pachanga ..............**8**
Zullymar's
Restaurant/Bar ........**7**

**Hotels** ①

Arco Iris ...............**9**
Best Western Tamarindo
Vista Villas ...........**19**
Cabinas La Laguna del
Cocodrilo ............**18**
Cabinas Marielos .......**16**
Casa Cook .............**2**

Hacienda Pinilla .......**20**
Hotel Capitán Suizo ....**1**
Hotel Pasatiempo .....**12**
El Jardín del Eden .....**15**
Luna Llena
Hotel & Restaurant ....**3**
Tamarindo El Diriá
Beach & Gol Resort ....**13**

the *Talking Fish,* is equipped with a marlin chair and a cabin with a shower. For up to six people, full days run $975, half days $575.

GOLFING  Mike Young, who has designed some of the best golf courses in the southern United States, designed the par-72 championship course at **Hacienda Pinilla** (⊠ 10 km [6 mi] south of Tamarindo via Villa Real ☎ 680–7062 ⊕ www.haciendapinilla.com). It has ocean views and breezes, and plenty of birds populate the surrounding trees.

SURFING  **Iguana Surf** (⊠ Road to Playa Langosta ☎☎ 653–0148 ⊕ www.iguanasurf.net) has information for surfers and visitors, as well as guided kayaking tours of the San Francisco Estuary. **Iguana Surf 2** (⊠ At beach near Frutas Tropicales) rents surfboards, Boogie boards, and snorkeling equipment and gives motorboat-driven snorkeling tours. **Maresias Surf Shop** (⊠ Next to Banco Nacional ☎ 653–0224) has equipment, lessons, and lots of local knowledge. Check out the **Robert August Surf Shop** (⊠ Tamarindo Vista Villas ☎ 653–0114) for boards to buy or rent, wax, surfing gear, swimsuits, and sunblock. **High Tide Surf Shop** (⊠ Tamarindo Aventuras ☎ 653–0108) has high-end surfing equipment and clothing and a large selection of beachwear; it also organizes kayaking, ATV tours, and surf lessons.

TURTLE TOURS  Numerous tour operators organize turtle tours in season for $35–$45 per person. **Papagayo Excursions** (⊠ Next to Banco Nacional, main St. ☎ 653–0254) is the oldest turtle-tour operator in Tamarindo. Tours ($45) include hotel pickup, boat transport to Playa Grande, park entrance fee, and an expert guide. Pickup is usually around 7:30 PM and the tour lasts until you see a turtle.

## Where to Stay & Eat

★ $$–$$$  ✕ **La Laguna del Cocodrilo Bistro.** It's not often you get to experience haute cuisine overlooking a crocodile-filled lagoon, but the unusual pairing works. Parisian chef Sebastien Couratier prepares—among other dishes—duck breast with a corn mousse and a vanilla-mango marmalade; and roasted almond-crusted Atlantic salmon. Wines by the glass are served out of a temperature-controlled dispenser, and the list is long and carefully conceived. The place is casual, but the food and service are anything but. Don't leave without trying the molten chocolate cake, served with vanilla ice cream and caramelized bananas. The bar opens at 4 PM. ⊠ *Hotel Laguna del Cocodrilo, north end of Tamarindo* ☎ 653–0255 ▤ *AE, MC, V* ☉ *Closed Sun. No lunch.*

$$  ✕ **Dragonfly Bar & Grill.** A huge tent with tree-trunk poles, simple but sculptural Ikea lamps, and a cool soundtrack are the components of this immensely popular, ultracool restaurant. The limited but enticing menu attracts standing-room-only crowds eager to tingle their tastebuds with ancho chile garlic shrimp, filet mignon with a cilantro-horseradish sauce, or—the standout—a smoky, chile-rubbed pork chop on a mountain of chipotle mashed potatoes, surrounded by roasted apples, chorizo, and fried onions. ⊠ *100 m east of Hotel Pasatiempo* ☎ 653–1506 ▤ *No credit cards* ⚹ *Reservations essential* ☉ *Closed Sun. No lunch.*

$$  ✕ **Gecko's at Iguana Surf.** Locals and visitors can't get enough of Chef John Szilasi's excellent cooking. The ambitious dinner-only menus re-

volve around fresh local ingredients such as tuna, plump calamari, and lobster. For people who like it hot, Gecko's Pasta is a mountain of garlicky linguine studded with jumbo shrimp, set on fire with jalapeño peppers and balanced by a bed of bitter arugula. The divine chocolate cake is worth the drive to Tamarindo; order early because it sells out quickly. Portion sizes seem to vary widely, not only from day to day but from diner to diner, and the food is a little pricey. The chef is sometimes absent and it shows in the food, so make sure he's going to be there the night you reserve a table. But there's always an excited buzz, and when the chef is hot there's no better place to dine in town. ⊠ *Beside Iguana Surf, on road to Playa Langosta* ☎ 653–0334 ▭ *No credit cards* ⊗ *Closed Tues. No lunch.*

**$–$$** ✕ **Nogui's.** Considered by a loyal legion of local fans as the most affordable seafood restaurant in town, Nogui's, practically on the beach, has been dishing out huge salads and fish tacos at lunch and a full seafood menu at dinner since 1974. The homemade pies are legendary. The newest addition to the menu is a meal-sized, garlicky steak sandwich, loaded with cheese, mushrooms, and onions on freshly baked bread. Instead of the ubiquitous rice and beans on the side, Nogui's has a purée of *tiquisque*, a local, potato-like vegetable. Nogui's location is practically on the beach. ⊠ *South side of Tamarindo Circle, on the beach* ☎ 653–0029 ▭ *AE, DC, MC, V* ⊗ *Closed Wed. and 2 wks in Oct.*

**★ $–$$** ✕ **Pachango.** In a casual but chic setting, Shlomi Koren, a Cordon Bleu–trained Israeli chef, transforms fresh local ingredients into elegant Mediterranean dishes you would pay a fortune for on the Riviera. Ours was red snapper fillet in a sauce of white wine, thyme, and sundried tomatoes, followed by a sublime chocolate soufflé. The small terrace restaurant shimmers in a golden light, with tangerine walls, a sunburst mural and an eerie, backlit Medusa-like mask. ⊠ *Across from Hotel Pasatiempo* ☎ 368–6983 ▭ *No credit cards* ⊗ *No lunch. Closed Sun. and two weeks in May.*

**¢–$** ✕ **Gil's Place.** You gotta love a guy who has the chutzpah to print this slogan on his menu: "No shoes, no shirt—we don't care; Come on in and grab a chair." Poetry it isn't, but the breakfast burritos are worthy of a laureate's praises. The hand-rolled, paper-thin tortillas are good enough to eat all on their own, but instead they wrap generous combinations of scrambled eggs, cheese, sautéed vegetables, and breakfast meats, served with a flavorful but mild salsa. (Hot sauce is kept under the counter.) Go. Eat. You won't be disappointed. ⊠ *Next to Iguana Surf shop on road to Playa Langosta* ☎ 836–3345 ▭ *No credit cards* ⊗ *Closed Sun.*

**★ $$$** ▦ **Casa Cook.** Life is a beach for the lucky few who get to stay here, on the prettiest, quietest part of Playa Tamarindo. You can play at owning your own beach house in one of the three furnished cabinas. Each comes with a kitchen, a spacious bathroom, queen-size beds, and queen sofa beds in the living room. Air-

## WORD OF MOUTH

"My two cents on Tamarindo: We would not have been happy staying in Tamarindo proper. I told my wife I think we were the only two Republicans within 50 miles."

—stepmoore

conditioning is $10 extra per night. There's a great family-size apartment overlooking the pool. Cabina Banyan is the most sought after—it comes with its own lap pool. The elegant restaurant at Capitán Suizo is right next door. Owners Ruth Ann and Chuck Cook and a friendly Tico staff are always around to offer help and advice. The true testimony to the popularity of this place is how many guests come back year after year. ⊠ *Road to Playa Langosta, north of the Hotel Capitán Suizo* ☎ *653–0125* ☐ *653–0753* ⊕ *www.tamarindo.com/cook* ✒ *3 cabinas, 1 apartment* ⚬ *A/c, fans, in-room safes, kitchens, cable TV, pool, beach; no smoking* ⊟ *AE, MC, V* ⏐◯⏐ *EP.*

$$$    ✕⊞ **El Jardín del Edén.** The only drawback to the "Garden of Eden" (this one, anyway) is that it's not right on the beach. Instead, the two-tier, Mediterranean-style pink building resides amid lush hillside gardens. Most rooms have been recently redecorated by new French owners with a penchant for crisp blue-and-white Moroccan and hot Polynesian decor. The lowest-priced double rooms are very tiny indeed, fine for one person but a little tight for two. Most rooms have ocean views, and two beautiful pools provide the missing water element. Unfortunately, new highrise condominiums are encroaching on the once-pristine view. The thatch-roof restaurant ($$) is excellent and one of the most romantic dinner places in town. It serves outstanding fresh seafood, pastas, and steaks. ⊠ *From Hotel El Milagro on main road, go up hill 180 m, then right for 180 m* ⌂ *Apdo. 1094–2050, San Pedro* ☎ *653–0137* ☐ *653–0111* ⊕ *www.jardindeleden.com* ✒ *19 rooms, 2 apartments* ⚬ *Restaurant, a/c fans, in-room safes, minibars, some kitchens, cable TV, 2 pools, whirlpool tub, 2 bars, laundry service, Internet* ⊟ *AE, MC, V* ⏐◯⏐ *BP.*

$$$    ⊞ **Hotel Capitán Suizo.** For folks who like luxury, small scale, and a beautiful beach setting, this is the best choice in town. On a relatively quiet stretch of Tamarindo's gorgeous beach, elegant balconied rooms and luxurious bungalows surround a large, shaded pool set in a mature garden. The stunning two-story rooms have high, angled ceilings and amusing flourishes of original art on the walls. The two-level bungalows have sybaritic bathrooms with sunken tubs, beautiful tile work, and outdoor garden showers. The four-bedroom apartment has a kitchen and whirlpool tub. A beautifully decorated restaurant serves contemporary cuisine and hosts lively beach barbecues. Service is friendly and polished. ⊠ *Right side of road toward Playa Langosta (veer left before circle)* ☎ *653–0075 or 653–0353* ☐ *653–0292* ⊕ *www.hotelcapitansuizo. com* ✒ *22 rooms, 8 bungalows, 1 apartment* ⚬ *Restaurant, in-room safes, refrigerators, pool, kayaking, fishing, bicycles, horseback riding, tours, shop, laundry service; no a/c in some rooms, no room TVs* ⊟ *AE, MC, V* ⏐◯⏐ *BP.*

FodorsChoice
★

$$$    ⊞ **Tamarindo El Diriá Beach & Golf Resort.** Tamarindo's first-ever luxury hotel, close to the beach, has spectacular sunsets from a terrace bar overhung by a gigantic strangler fig tree or from the large pool. Rooms in the contemporary three-story building have pre-Columbian design motifs, tile floors, modern furniture, and a spacious balcony, but feel spartan and bare. Avoid the rooms facing the noisy main road; "sunset-view rooms," facing the beach, deliver spectacular sunsets, as promised. No-

body raves about the food here, but you can eat well at a dozen restaurants within walking distance. Despite its name, the hotel has only a driving range (near the airport) but is close to two courses. At the end of rainy season (November), there is sometimes an unpleasant smell down by the beach, owing to flooded septic systems. ⊠ ¾ km/½ mi before Tamarindo center ☎ 653–0031, 291–2821 in San José 🖷 653–0208 ⊕ www.tamarindodiria.com 🖃 Apdo. 476–1007, San José 🛏 123 rooms ⚐ Restaurant, in-room safes, minibars, cable TV, driving range, tennis court, 2 pools, massage, bar, casino, laundry service, Internet, meeting rooms ▱ AE, MC, V ⍾ BP.

$$–$$$ 🏨 **Best Western Tamarindo Vista Villas.** If you're into surfing, this is where you want to be. Around the pool and bar the talk is all about waves. There's a surf school, a great surf shop, and surfing legends Robert August and Wing Nuts, of *Endless Summer* movie fame, are frequent guests. The large suites with kitchens could use freshening up and are slowly being redecorated. Avoid Rooms 101–107, which face the blank supporting wall of the pool. Poolside rooms can be noisy, with the pool filled with frolicking kids. The hotel has a helpful tour desk and an ATM machine in the reception area. ⊠ Main road entering Tamarindo ☎ 653–0114, 800/536–3241 in U.S. 🖷 653–0115 ⊕ www.tamarindovistavillas.com 🛏 17 rooms, 16 suites ⚐ Restaurant, a/c, fans, cable TV with movies, pool, bar ▱ AE, MC, V ⍾ CP.

$$–$$$ 🏨 **Hacienda Pinilla.** Golfers drive from miles around to play the beautiful par-72 championship course on the 4,500-acre grounds of this former ranch turned recreational community. Guests get good discounts on greens fees. At the colonial-style hotel, the Posada del Sol, even the standard rooms are luxurious, with soft indirect lighting, expensive fabrics, and spacious bathrooms. Villas are scattered around a garden and share a pretty pool and upscale outdoor restaurant-bar. The hotel is far from the beach and golf course, but there's a shuttle van to cart you around. You can get closer to the deserted beaches by staying in one of the two to four-bedroom Beach Houses. For golfers with a big family or lots of buddies, there's the castlelike Casa Golf Suites by the 18th hole, with its own pool, as well as three rustic, secluded beach houses. Horseback riding and tennis are the main nongolf activities. ⊠ 10 km/6 mi south of Tamarindo via Villa Real ☎ 680–7062 🖷 680–7063 ⊕ www.haciendapinilla.com 🛏 22 rooms, 8 suites, 6 houses ⚐ Restaurant, a/c, fans, minibars, cable TV, golf, pro shop, pool, beach, bicycles, horseback riding, bar, in-room data ports ▱ AE, MC, V ⍾ CP.

$$ ✕🏨 **Hotel Pasatiempo.** Come for Sunday football projected on a large screen, open mike on Tuesday nights, or great eggs Benedict any morning. One way or another, you are bound to pass some time at this friendly, laid-back place where there's always something happening. Energetic owners Ron and Janet Stewart throw legendary parties and raise money for community projects. Comfortable bungalow rooms

> **WORD OF MOUTH**
>
> "Ron, the owner at Hotel Pasatiempo, is a lot of fun, and is used to seeing surfers and helping them. He's even driven us to various 'off the path' surf breaks."
> —Oceangirl84

are scattered around the nicely landscaped grounds and a beautiful pool. Each unit, named after a Guanacaste beach, has a patio with a hammock or swinging chair and a unique hand-painted mural. Suites have one bedroom and daybeds in the living room. The restaurant ($–$$) serves a mix of above-average bar food and pizza, along with more sophisticated fare, like seared tuna with wasabi, or chicken in a Stroganoff sauce. ⊠ *Off dirt road to Playa Langosta, 180 m from beach behind Tamarindo Circle* ☎ 653–0096 🖶 653–0275 ⊕ *www. hotelpasatiempo.com* 🛏 *15 bungalows, 2 suites* ⚖ *Restaurant, a/c, fans, pool, bar, laundry service; no room TVs, no room phones* ▭ *AE, MC, V* ⦿ *EP.*

$$ 🏨 **Luna Llena Hotel & Residence.** This place looks a little like a Fellini film set of a fantasy tropical village. Bright-yellow conical thatched-roof huts on different levels circle a central pool. Interiors are colorful and whimsical, with unusual fabrics, furniture, and walls painted by co-owner Simona Daniela, who, along with husband Pino Trimarchi, adds Italian panache to the place. Downstairs the bungalows have a kitchen, a king-size bed, and a bathroom. Up a steep, curving ladder stair there's a loft right under the thatched roof, with its own air conditioner. Four double rooms in a two-story building are spacious and just as creatively decorated. One room sleeps four. The hotel is far from the beach in a quiet, woodsy area. ⊠ *From road to Playa Langosta, first left (uphill); one block past Iguana Surf* ☎ 653–0082 🖶 653–0120 ⊕ *www. hotellunallena.com* 🛏 *7 bungalows, 6 rooms* ⚖ *Dining room, a/c, fans, in-room safes, some kitchens, cable TV, pool* ▭ *AE, MC, V* ⦿ *CP.*

$ 🏨 **Cabinas Marielos.** In high season Tamarindo has few decent bargain rooms; among the best are these cabinas, decorated with painted floral motifs in the style of the artisans of Sarchí. Rooms (not literally cabinas) are in two wings, flanking a colorful flower garden well back from the road. Guests sometimes share their meals in the well-equipped common kitchen. The atmosphere is surprisingly serene. There is no hot water except in the three newest air-conditioned rooms. ⊠ *Across main dirt road from beach, north of town center (follow signs)* ☎🖶 653–0141 ✉ *cabinasmarielos@hotmail.com* 🛏 *20 rooms* ⚖ *Fans, some refrigerators; no a/c in some rooms, no room phones, no room TVs* ▭ *AE, MC, V* ⦿ *EP.*

¢–$ 🏨 **Arco Iris.** This arty hotel is on the hill above the road to Playa Langosta. The four funky cabinas are painted in primary colors and decorated with distinct themes by the creative Italian sisters who own the hotel. Aerobics, stretching, kickboxing, dance, art, and yoga sessions are available on-site, and a massage therapist is on hand in case it all gets too strenuous. There's a communal kitchen, and $1 of the room rate goes to a fund to keep the beach clean. ⊠ *Follow signs past Hotel Pasatiempo and go up hill to right* ☎ 653–0330 🛏 *4 cabinas* ⚖ *Fans, refrigerators, fitness classes, massage; no a/c, no room phones, no room TVs* ▭ *No credit cards* ⦿ *BP.*

¢–$ 🏨 **Cabinas La Laguna del Cocodrilo.** Yes, there really are crocodiles here, and the hotel owners feed them every evening at 5:30 PM. Rooms have African tribal motifs and ceramic bathrooms. There's no pool, but the ocean is a sandy path away and there's a sundeck for basking alongside the nearby crocs. Panaderia de Paris opens at 6 AM, selling baguettes, passable croissants, and excellent quiches. A French bistro is open for dinner (can you tell the owners are French?). Room rates drop from $65 to a bargain $30 without air-conditioning. The hotel has its own sport-fishing boat. ⊠ *North end of main road into Tamarindo* ☎ *653–0255* 🖷 *653–1029* ⊕ *http://art-spark.com/cocodrilo* ⇆ *10 rooms* ♿ *Restaurant, a/c in some rooms, fans, in-room safes, cable TV, beach; no a/c in some rooms* ¶⊙¶ *EP.*

## Nightlife

Tamarindo is one of the few places outside of San José, along with Jacó, in the Central Pacific, where the nightlife really jumps. In fact, it has the dubious distinction of being featured on Entertainment Television's explicit *Wild On* series, which spotlights the rowdiest party scenes around the world.

Despite Tamarindo's party-hearty reputation, it does have some low-key options. For a sedate evening, try barbecue on the beach at the **Capitán Suizo Hotel** (⊠ Right side of road toward Playa Langosta; veer left before circle), starting at 6:30 with a cocktail, then on to a lavish barbecue buffet and live folk music and dancing ($35, reserve in advance). During the week **Hotel Pasatiempo** (⊠ Off dirt road to Playa Langosta) has wildly popular Tuesday open-mike sessions, with a $5 cover or two-drink minimum charge. Friday nights at **The Monkey Bar** (⊠ Tamarindo Vista Villas, main road entering Tamarindo) is Ladies Night and usually a big party. The live Latin dance music (no cover) attracts locals who really know how to dance. **Restobar La Caracola** (⊠ Tamarindo Circle, beside Nogui's) often has live Latin music and dancing on weekends, and occasional tango, salsa, and merengue dance lessons. Acoustic and classical performances take place year-round.

## Shopping

Most stores in the strip malls lining the main road sell similar souvenirs and beachwear. It's hard to leave without at least one sarong in your suitcase. The first seriously upscale art gallery in town, **Galería Guacamole** (⊠ Across the street from Aster Commercial Center ☉ Closed Sun.), sells arresting ceramics and paintings by Costa Rican artists. Look for mixed-media basketwork pottery and ceramic masks that evoke a pre-Columbian Picasso. There's also high-design jewelry here.The most original clothing and jewelry are at **Azul Profundo** (⊠ Centro Comercial ☎ 653–0395), designed by a talented young Argentine woman. All her jewelry is made with real and semiprecious stones. **Souvenirs Guanacaste** (⊠ Centro Comercial Aster, 50 m south of Super Tamarindo at crossroads of main road into town and road up to Hotel Pasatiempo) stands out from the sarong-and-souvenir shops in this shopping center for its delicate wood carvings and handsome silver jewelry studded with polished stones, made by a local Italian artist. For a great selection of swimsuits, check out **Tienda Bambora** (⊠ On beach, south side of Tamarindo Circle; attached to Nogui's Restaurant).

# Understanding Costa Rica's Climate

ALTHOUGH YOU MAY associate the tropics with rain, precipitation in Costa Rica varies considerably, depending on where you are and when you're there. This is a result of the mountainous terrain and regional weather patterns. A phenomenon called rain shadow—when one side of a mountain range receives much more rain than the other—plays an important ecological role in Costa Rica. Four mountain ranges combine to create an intercontinental divide that separates the country into Atlantic and Pacific slopes; thanks to the trade winds, the Atlantic slope receives much more rain than the Pacific. The trade winds steadily pump moisture-laden clouds southwest over the isthmus, where they encounter warm air or mountains, which make them rise. As the clouds rise, they cool, lose their ability to hold moisture, and eventually dump most of their liquid luggage on the Caribbean side.

During the rainy season—mid-May to December—the role of the trade winds is diminished, as regular storms roll off the Pacific Ocean and soak the western side of the isthmus. Though it rains all over Costa Rica during these months, it often rains more on the Pacific side of the mountains than on the Atlantic. Come December, the trade winds take over again, and while the Caribbean prepares for its wettest time of the year hardly a drop falls on the western side until May.

Climate variation within the country results in a mosaic of forests. The combination of humidity and temperature helps determine what grows where; but whereas some species have very restricted ranges, others seem to thrive just about anywhere. Plants such as strangler figs and bromeliads grow all over Costa Rica, and animals such as the collared peccary and coati—a long-nosed cousin of the raccoon—can pretty much live wherever human beings let them. Other species have extremely limited ranges, such as the mangrove hummingbird, restricted to the mangrove forests of the Pacific coast, and the volcano junco, a gray sparrow that lives only around the highest peaks of the Cordillera de Talamanca.

## To & From Tamarindo

*82 km/51 mi (1 hour, 15 min) southwest of Liberia.*

Both NatureAir and SANSA fly to Tamarindo from San José. Macaw Air flies between Liberia and Tamarindo and to other Nicoya Peninsula towns. By car from Liberia, travel south on the highway to the turnoff for Belén, then head west and turn left at the Huacas crossroads to Tamarindo. The road from Belén is paved, in variable states of disrepair. There are no direct bus connections between Playa Grande or Playa Avellanas and Tamarindo. Taxi is the way to go from nearby towns if you don't have wheels.

### Tamarindo Essentials

🏧 Bank/ATM **Banco Nacional** ✉ Across from Hotel Diriá.

🏥 Hospital **Clínica** ✉ Next to Farmacia Tamarindo ☎ 653-1226. **Clínica Pública** ✉ Main road in Villareal, 4 km east of Tamarindo.

🏥 Pharmacies **Farmacia Tamarindo** ✉ Main road into town ☎ 653-0210 or 821-9605.
🏥 Internet **Internet Café** ✉ Road to Hotel Pasatiempo, next to ABC Realty.
🏥 Post Office **Super Tamarindo** ✉ Main road, across from Hotel Diría ☞ sells stamps and posts letters.

## Playa Grande

**16** A very bumpy 21 miles from Tamarindo by road, but only 5 minutes by boat across a tidal estuary, lies unspoiled Playa Grande. The beach has escaped overdevelopment, thanks in part to a surfer who came ashore more than 30 years ago and traded in his surfboard for a conservationist's agenda. Louis Wilson, owner of Las Tortugas Hotel, spearheaded the campaign to create a national park—now Las Baulas Marine National Park—to protect nesting *baulas* (leatherback turtles). Today, the brown-sand, Blue Flag beach, edged by creeping sea-grape, is a paradise for surfers and sunbathers by day and a haven for nesting turtles by night. The whole beach and miles of water offshore are, in fact, part of the national park.

Playa Grande isn't immune to development. More hotels and private houses are cropping up here, but well back from the beach, thanks to a legislated buffer zone and a decree that no lights can be visible from the beach, to avoid disrupting the turtles. The new hotels and restaurants make this a pleasant, tranquil alternative to Tamarindo. And if you crave the bright lights, Tamarindo is only a boat ride away.

### Exploring

**Las Baulas Marine National Park** (Parque Nacional Marino Las Baulas) protects the long Playa Grande and the **Tamarindo Wildlife Refuge,** a mangrove estuary with some excellent bird-watching that has been under some developmental pressure of late. Playa Grande hosts the world's largest visitation of nesting giant leatherback turtles. From October 1 to February 15, during the peak nesting season, the beach is strictly off limits from 6 PM to 5 AM. You can only visit as part of a guided tour, waiting your turn at the park entrance, beside Hotel Las Tortugas, until spotters find a nesting turtle. Then you silently sprint down the beach in darkness to witness the remarkable sight of a 500-pound creature digging a hole in the sand large enough to deposit up to 100 golfball-size eggs. Just as impressive is the sight of hundreds of hatchlings scrambling toward open water in the early morning about sixty days after. The best way to go is with a turtle-watching tour run by one of numerous Playa Grande or Tamarindo hotels and tour operators. Environmental activist Lewis Wilson, also the owner of the Hotel Las Tortugas, struggled for a decade to get Las Baulas established. An evening spent discussing ecotourism and ecopolitics with him is a real education. ✉ *North of Tamarindo, across an estuary* ☎ *653-0470* 🎟 *Free, Oct. 1–Feb. 15 $6 after 6 PM, guided tour (Spanish only) $7* ⊙ *24 hours, Oct. 1–Feb. 15 by reservation only after 6 PM.*

**El Mundo de la Tortuga** (Turtle World) is a museum with creative displays about the life cycle of the giant leatherback and the threats it faces. Audio tours (available in English) through the interactive exhibits last 20 minutes. The museum runs nighttime turtle tours ( ⇨ *below*). ✉ *Road to*

*Hotel Las Tortugas* ☎ *653–0471* ✉ *$5* ◷ *4* PM *until tours return. Closed May–Oct.*

Just south of Tamarindo, accessible by walking on the beach or by kayak at high tide, is the **San Francisco Wildlife Refuge,** with an estuary system that's rich in bird life. Unlike the Tamarindo Refuge, it's free of motorboats. The farthest reaches of the refuge are only accessible by boat. Iguana Surf ( ⇨ Tamarindo, above) is one of many tour operators that can take you there.

## Outdoor Activities

⚠ Unless you are a strong swimmer attached to a surfboard, don't swim here. There is some calmer water for snorkeling about a 20-minute walk north of Las Tortugas, at Playa Carbón.

**Hotel Las Tortugas** (✉ Las Baulas Marine National Park ☎ 653–0423 ⊕ www.cool.co.cr/usr/turtles) has a full menu of nature tours, including guided walks to pristine, remote areas; snorkeling at Playa Carbón; and canoeing and nature photography tours ($20–$30).

SURFING   Playa Grande is renowned for having the most consistent surf breaks in the country and impressive barrels. Only experienced surfers should attempt them. Some of the best breaks are right in front of Hotel Las Tortugas. The waves are best at high tide and it's customary to share waves. **Hotel Las Tortugas** ( ⇨ *above*) rents boards for $20 a day. **Hotel Bula Bula** (✉ Palm Beach Estates, 2 km east of Playa Grande ☎ 653–0975, 877/658–2880 in U.S. ⊕ www.hotelbulabula.com) rents both long and short boards for $25/day.

TURTLE TOURS   Lots of tour operators in Tamarindo organize turtle tours in season for about $35 to $45 per person. **El Mundo de la Tortuga** (✉ Road to Hotel Las Tortugas ☎ 653–0471) conducts excellent turtle tours almost every night from October 20 to February 15, depending on high tide, and returning not earlier than 11 PM (and sometimes as late as 3 AM). **Hotel Las Tortugas** ( ⇨ *above*) gives turtle tours for $25 per person. They include a visit to the Turtle Museum just steps from the hotel but do not include transport.

## Where to Stay & Eat

$$   ⊞ **Hotelito Sí Sí Sí.** Yes, yes, yes! Emphatically worth a visit, this little hotel is halfway between a boutique hotel and a B&B. The multicourse breakfast is sumptuous, and the large, luxurious rooms are designed for privacy, so you don't feel as though you're sharing someone's house. Modern and sleek, each room has a queen-size bed, handsome cedar bureau and desk, and a view of the split-level, blue mosaic pool. Bathrooms are also modern, with granite and glass block. Beyond the garden is a 75-meter buffer of mangrove and then the beach, realm of surfers by day and turtles by night. The upstairs master suite is the best room in the house, but requires reserving well in advance. ✉ *Palm Beach Estates, 2 km/1 mi south of Playa Grande* ☎ *653–0715* 🖨 *653–0982* ⊕ *www.hotelitosisisi.com* ⇝ *5 rooms* ♿ *A/c, fans, refrigerators, pool, whirlpool tub, beach, kayaking, bicycles; no a/c in 1 room; no room phones, no room TVs* ▤ *AE, MC, V* ⏀ *EP.*

**$$**  ×▥ **Hotel La Cantarana.** This hotel is essentially a restaurant with hotel rooms. Chef Manfred Margraf brings to the table 30 years of cooking experience in Switzerland, Germany, and the Caribbean. The menu changes depending on availability of local ingredients—think lots of seafood—and on the chef's inspired whims, but is always classically Continental, with elegant presentation. Clean lines, modern ceramic bathrooms, and twin beds make rooms, in a two-story terra-cotta building facing a beautifully landscaped pool, a comfortable if not exciting place to spend the night after an evening of feasting. The beach is a short walk away. ⊠*Palm Beach Estates, 2 km/1 mi east of Playa Grande, across from Hotelito Sí Sí Sí* ☎ *653–0486* 🖷 *653–0491* ⊕ *www.hotelcantarana.com* ⤸ *5 rooms* ⌂ *Restaurant, a/c, fans, in-room safes, cable TV, pool* ▭ *V* ℗| *BP.*

**$**  ×▥ **Hotel Bula Bula.** At the far east end of Palm Beach Estates, Bula Bula has its own dock and boat for ferrying customers the short distance to and from Tamarindo. Rooms march in two straight lines, forming a 45-degree angle to the curvy pool bordered by an impressive cactus garden (be careful where you walk in the dark!). Walls painted in brilliant jewel colors, king-size beds, and generous bathrooms make for lots of creature comforts, but some people may find the rooms too close together. Complimentary sarongs, bottled water, and fluffy pool towels are nice touches. The beach is about 300 m away. The menu at the alfresco Great Waltini Restaurant & Bar ($–$$) reads like that of a U.S.-style eatery: peel'n'eat shrimp, lobster tails, filet mignon, and New York strip steak. ⊠ *Palm Beach Estates, 3 km/2 mi east of Playa Grande* ☎ *653–0975, 877/658–2880 in U.S.* ⊕ *www.hotelbulabula.com* ⤸ *10 rooms* ⌂ *Restaurant, a/c, fans, pool, beach, bar, laundry service, boat service; no room phones, no room TVs* ▭ *AE, MC, V* ℗| *BP.*

**¢–$**  ▥ **Hotel Las Tortugas.** Just steps from the Las Baulas Marine Park entrance and El Mundo de las Tortugas, this hotel was designed with turtles in mind. Owner/conservationist Louis Wilson made sure, for instance, that room windows do not overlook the nesting beaches, since light disorients the turtles. Rooms are quiet, with good beds, stone floors, and stucco walls. Dirt-cheap rooms—as low as $15 per person—are available in the apartment annex, and student quarters that Louis reserves for ecotourists and turtle volunteers. Long-term-rental apartments have kitchenettes. The surf is famous here, but rip currents are dangerous and many guests retreat to the pool shaped like a leatherback turtle instead. Local guides lead turtle tours at night and the hotel organizes canoeing, snorkeling, and other guided nature tours. ⊠ *At entrance to Las Baulas Marine National Park, 33 km/20 mi north of Tamarindo* ☎ *653–0423* ☎🖷 *653–0458* ⊕ *www.cool.co.cr/usr/turtles* ☐ *Apdo. 164, Santa Cruz de Guanacaste* ⤸ *11 rooms, 7 apartments* ⌂ *Restaurant, a/c, fans, some refrigerators, some kitchenettes, pool, whirlpool tub, beach, canoeing, tour operator, bar, laundry service; no room phones, no room TVs* ▭ *MC, V* ℗| *EP.*

## To & From Playa Grande
*21 km/13 mi (40 min) north of Tamarindo.*

Ten km (6 mi) of the road from Tamarindo is paved, as far as Huacas, and then 11 km (7 mi) is a rough dirt road. Palm Beach Estates is about

3 km (2 mi) of bumpy but nicely shaded road east of the Playa Grande entrance of Las Baulas Marine National Park. Alternatively, you can take a small boat across the Tamarindo Estuary for about 50 ¢ per person and walk 40 minutes along the beach to Playa Grande; boats are at the guide kiosk at the north end of Tamarindo. Or you can take a ferry with Las Palmas Tours (☎ 653–1502) from the Tamarindo side and return with the Hotel Bula Bula ferry (☎ 658-2880) from the Playa Grande side. Ferries run 6 AM–11 PM during high season, for about $2 per person each way.

## Playa Langosta

⑰ Every foot of beachfront property has now been sold, and the cessation of contractors' hammers should soon restore peace and quiet to beautiful Playa Langosta. This formerly quiet, leatherback-turtle nesting beach is now an upscale, gentrified extension of Tamarindo, connected by a heavily traveled dirt road. The beach is separated from Tamarindo Beach by a rocky headland at high tide. Most of the development is tucked behind mangrove trees, so you can enjoy an unsullied dramatic beachscape, with surf crashing against rocky outcroppings. Most of the sand is coarse, black pulverized rock and shell, though there's a wider, whiter, softer stretch in front of the Barceló Resort. At low tide you can walk across the San Francisco estuary and walk a ways up the tidal river in search of wading birds: showy snowy egrets; hunting little blue herons; tail-bobbing spotted sandpipers; and if your eyes are sharp, tiny white-lored gnatcachers, endemic to these parts. The beach is quiet in the early morning, perfect for solitary walks. Big, well-shaped river-mouth waves near the north end of the beach make it popular with surfers. At sunset, light is refracted from surf spraying against rocks, and pelicans glide by, silhouetted against an orange sky.

### Outdoor Activities

Tour operators in Tamarindo, just a few miles north, offer activities in the Playa Langosta area.

### Where to Stay & Eat

★ $–$$ ✕ **Maria Bonita Restaurant.** This popular, intimate, Latin-Caribbean restaurant is owned by a couple with years of hotel and restaurant experience in Cuba and throughout the Caribbean. Cheerful Adela serves while Tom slaves away in the kitchen, turning out mouth-watering, perfectly spiced dishes. His orange chipotle sauce, served on juicy seafood cakes, tingles your tastebuds with pepperiness. There are just three tables in the pretty patio garden and four tables inside the restaurant—and they fill up fast. ⊠ *Beside the Playa Langosta supermarket* ☎ *653–0933* ▭ *MC, V* ⚑ *Reservations essential* ⊙ *Closed Sun. and Oct. No lunch.*

$$$–$$$$ 🏨 **Sueño del Mar.** A garden gate opens into a dreamy world of intimate
FodorsChoice gardens and patios with frescoes and antique tiles at this nearly flaw-
★ less B&B. Seashells are embedded in window frames and strung together in wind chimes. The adobe-style house, which descends a stepped passageway, has double rooms with queen-size beds, and Balinese showers open to the sky. Casitas have large kitchens, sitting rooms, and a loft bedroom. The downstairs rooms are a little dark and closed-in but

full of interesting *objets* in illuminated alcoves. If privacy is paramount, opt for the breezy honeymoon suite. A lavish breakfast is served on the patio looking onto a tiny garden pool. Or you can take your morning coffee on the beach, sitting on driftwood furniture—it's a bit like being on a desert island. ⊠ *130 m south of Capitán Suizo, turn right for 45 m, then right again for about 90 m to entrance gate, across from back of Cala Luna Hotel* 🖼🖼 *653–0284* ⊕ *www.tamarindo.com/sdmar* 🛏 *3 rooms, 1 suite, 2 casitas* ᴧ *Dining room, a/c, fans, some kitchens, pool, beach, bicycles, horseback riding, laundry service, Internet; no room phones, no room TVs* ▤ *MC, V* ⦿⧉ *BP.*

**$$$**  ✕🖼 **Cala Luna.** This gorgeous hotel can be alternately as lifeless as a tomb and raucously noisy, with parties around the pool. The secluded villas, with hidden driveways and private pools, impart a clandestine aura. The beach is a short walk away, across a road and through a stand of mangroves, where there's a posted security guard. Past a labyrinth of hibiscus hedges are the large, luxurious ocher-color rooms with king-size beds and softly lighted alcoves. Oversize bathrooms have curved bathtubs for two. The glorious pool in the garden is overlooked by the pretty Cala Moresca restaurant ($–$$$), whose cuisine leans toward Mediterranean, with Middle Eastern touches. Dinner prices can skyrocket if you order lobster or shrimp or overpriced extras such as bottled water. ⊠ *Across from Sueño del Mar* 🖼 *653–0214* 🖼 *653–0213* ⊕ *www.calaluna.com* 🛏 *20 rooms, 21 villas* ᴧ *Restaurant, a/c, fans, in-room safes, cable TV, pool, massage, tours, bicycles, bar* ▤ *AE, MC, V* ⦿⧉ *CP.*

★ **$$$**  🖼 **Villa Alegre.** A visit here is like coming to stay with friends who just happen to have a really terrific house on a fantastic beach. Owned by congenial and helpful Californians Barry and Suzye Lawson, this homey but sophisticated Spanish-style B&B is close to a stand of trees and a somewhat rocky but swimmable beach, which is visible from the pool. Rooms are furnished with souvenirs from the Lawsons' travels to Japan, Russia, Guatemala, and elsewhere. All but one room have a private terrace. Breakfast is lavish. The hotel often plans and hosts weddings; ceremonies take place at a huge boulder on the beach dubbed Marriage Rock. ⊠ *Playa Langosta, 300 m south of Hotel Capitán Suizo* 🖼 *653–0270* 🖼 *653–0287* ⊕ *www.villaalegrecostarica.com* 🛏 *4 rooms, 2 villas, 1 casita* ᴧ *A/c, fans, pool, beach, no-smoking rooms; no room phones, no room TVs* ▤ *AE, MC, V* ⦿⧉ *BP.*

## To & From Playa Langosta
*2 km/1 mi (5 minutes) south of Tamarindo.*

The dirt road from Tamarindo is alternately dusty or muddy, but reliably rough. Or you can walk along the beach, at low tide, all the way from Tamarindo Beach. Most car-free visitors get picked up from Tamarindo by their hotels. Or you can take a taxi.

# Playa Avellanas

**⓲**  Geographically and atmospherically separate from Tamarindo, this undeveloped beach's main claim to fame is surfing. As you bump along the very rough beach road, most of the cars you pass have surfboards tied on top. The beach is a beautiful 1-km (½-mi) stretch of pale-gold sand with rocky outcroppings, a river mouth, a mangrove swamp, and a very big pig named Lola, who likes to cool off in the surf.

## Outdoor Activities

SURFING  Apart from taking photos of Lola the pig with waves washing over her, the main action here is surfing. Locals claim there are eight surf spots when the swell is strong. There are no tour operators based in Playa Avellanas. Tamarindo-based surf shops bring surfers down here whenever the surf is up. You can rent boards and find kindred surfing spirits at **Cabinas Las Olas** (⊠ Road to Avellanas; follow signs ☎ 658–8315).

## Where to Stay & Eat

**$–$$**  ✕ **Lola's.** In deference to Lola, the owners' pet pig who freely roams the beach, the menu at this hip beach café is heavily vegetarian. Seating, or more precisely, lolling is all on the sand. The low driftwood tables, reclining wood chairs, and colorful throws and cushions slung around the beach recall a Roman-style beach banquet. Along with the fresh-fruit smoothies and vegetarian pizzas of past seasons, the menu includes organic chicken, mushroom crêpes, and "responsible fish" (fish caught in nets that don't mistakenly trap turtles). You can arrange in advance for private beach dinners by candlelight (pig not invited). ⊠ *At main entrance to Playa Avellanas* ☎ *658–8097* ▭ *No credit cards* ⊙ *Closed Mon. and mid-Sept.–mid-Nov.*

**$**  ▦ **Cabinas Las Olas.** Frequented mainly by surfers, the hotel's spacious glass-and-stone cabinas, divided into two units each, are scattered across a leafy, treed property behind Playa Avellanas and its renowned surfing waves. There's no air-conditioning, but high ceilings, tree shade, and ocean breezes keep cabins cool at night. Monkeys and other critters lurk in and around the extensive grounds. An elevated boardwalk leads from the cabinas to the beach through a protected mangrove estuary. The restaurant, under the shade of a giant guanacaste tree, serves reasonably priced breakfasts, lunches, and dinners. ⊠ *Road to Avellanas; follow signs for hotel* ☎ *658–8315* ▤ *658–8331* ⊕ *www.cabinaslasolas. co.cr* ✉ *Apdo. 1404–1250, Escazú* ⇩ *10 rooms* ⚅ *Restaurant, dive shop, boating, bicycles, bar, laundry service, Internet; no a/c, no room phones, no room TVs* ▭ *AE, MC, V* ⊙ *Closed Oct.* ᴉ⊙ᴉ *EP.*

**$**  ▦ **Cabinas El León.** Accommodations are basic, but surfers don't seem to mind, as long as they are near the beach. Comforts in these four simple, concrete-block rooms extend as far as fans and hot water. Rooms aren't pretty, but are cleaner than most of the shabby surfers' camps along the beaches here. The beach is a two-minute walk away. ⊠ *Beach road, just south of Cabinas Las Olas* ☎ *658–8318* ⊕ *www.cabinaselleon.com* ⇩ *4 rooms* ⚅ *Fans, beach.* ▭ *No credit cards* ᴉ⊙ᴉ *BP.*

## To & From Playa Avellanas

*17 km/11 mi (30 minutes) south of Tamarindo.*

You have to drive inland from Tamarindo to Villareal and then 13 km (8 mi) down a very bumpy road to reach Playa Avellanas. There are many rivers to cross in rainy season and huge potholes to avoid in dry season. If you're sans car, have your hotel pick you up in Tamarindo.

## Playa Negra

**⑲** Surfer culture is apparent here in the tiny wave of casual restaurants, a health-food bakery, a couple of Internet cafés, and bikini shops springing up along the road. A roadside tent bazaar sells sarongs and crafts during the high season. But there's also a big residential development here called Rancho Playa Negra, with

> ### A SURF CLASSIC
>
> Americans—American surfers at least—got their first look at Playa Negra in 1994's *The Endless Summer II*, a film by legendary surf documentarian Bruce Brown.

more upscale development on the drawing boards. The beach is rocky and, true to its name, has very dark, hard-packed sand. Spindly mangrove trees edge the beach and there are views north of the wavy coastline.

### Outdoor Activities

SURFING Surfing cognoscenti dig the waves here, which are almost all rights, with beautifully shaped barrels. The beach also has a spectacular rock-reef point break. Ask at Hotel Playa Negra where the best breaks are or just scan the ocean to see where everybody else is. **Hotel Playa Negra** (⊠ 4 km/2½ mi northwest of Paraíso on dirt road [watch for signs for Playa Negra], then follow signs carefully at forks in Rd. ☎ 658–8034 ⊕ www. playanegra.com) has surfing and Boogie-board lessons, and rents boards. Trips to Ollie's Point and Witch's Rock can be arranged.

### Where to Stay & Eat

**$** ✕ **Pablo's Picasso.** You can't miss the attention-getting road signs advertising this place: BURGERS AS BIG AS YOUR HEAD. Yes, the hamburgers are big at this Playa Negra institution. So are the giant wooden chairs that make you feel Lilliputian, and the impressive, wall-size surfing mural. ⊠ *Just past the turnoff for Hotel Playa Negra, left side of the Rd.* ☎ *658–8158* ▤ *No credit cards.*

★ **$** ▥ **Hotel Playa Negra.** This ocean-front place is gorgeous: a little village of brilliantly colored thatch-roof cabinas sprinkled across sunny lawns strewn with tropical plantings. The cabinas are perfectly round, as are the two swimming pools. Each hut has built-in sofas that can double as extra beds, and beautiful, curvaceous tile bathrooms. There's no air-conditioning, but the high, conical thatch roofs keep the cabinas cool. The ocean has tidal pools, swimming holes, and rock reefs providing some shelter. This is paradise found for surfers, with a good swell running. Surfing lessons and Boogie-board classes are available. The round rancho restaurant serves typical food with a few Continental touches left over from a now departed French chef. ⊠ *4 km/2½ mi northwest of Paraíso on dirt road (watch signs for Playa Negra), then follow signs carefully at forks in Rd.* ☎ *658–8034* ▤ *658–8035* ⊕ *www.playanegra. com* ⊅ *10 cabinas* ⚲ *Restaurant, fans, in-room safes, pool, beach, horseback riding, bar, laundry service; no a/c, no room phones, no room TVs* ▤ *AE, DC, MC, V* ⏍ *EP* ⊗ *Restaurant closed Sept. 15–Nov. 1.*

**¢–$** ▥ **Pablo's Picasso.** The signs for the hotel's restaurant (⇨ *above*), reading BURGERS AS BIG AS YOUR HEAD, are what direct you here. The cabinas aren't pretty but they have hot water, fans, and some kitchens. Only a few have air-conditioning. Most people head here for the restaurant, but the cabinas are a cut above the $10/night surfer camps. ⊠ *Just past the turnoff for Hotel Playa Negra, on the left side of the Rd.* ☎ 658–8158 ⤴ *7 cabins* ⚹ *Restaurant, some a/c, fans, some kitchens; no room phones, no room TVs.* ▭ *No credit cards* ⦿ EP.

### To & From Playa Negra

*3 km/2 mi (10 minutes) south of Playa Avellanas.*

From Playa Avellanas, continue south on the rough beach road to Playa Negra, or if you don't have 4WD or it's rainy season, approach along a more civilized route from Santa Cruz. Drive 27 km (16 ½ mi) west, via Vientisiete de Abril, to Paraíso, then follow signs for Playa Negra for 4 km (1½ mi). Taxi is the easiest way to get around if you don't have a car.

# Playa Junquillal

**㉒** Seekers of tranquillity need look no farther than Junquillal (pronounced hoon-key-*yall*). To the south of Playa Negra, this long swath of picturesque beach stretches about 3 km (2 mi), with only one old, wooden hotel/bar on the entire beach. A surprisingly cosmopolitan mélange of restaurants— Peruvian, German, Italian, Swiss—is adding an international flavor, and away from the beach Junquillal is definitely getting livelier. There's finally a small supermarket in the village with a public Internet connection. Although it qualifies as a Blue Flag beach, the surf here is a little strong, so watch children carefully. It's a perfect beach for taking long strolls.

### Outdoor Activities

HORSEBACK RIDING  At German-run **Paradise Riding** (658–8162, www.paradiseriding.com) the 14 horses are in tip-top shape, as is the impressive tack room, with top-quality saddles lined up in a neat row. There are two-hour trail rides ($29), sunset rides, or you can set off for a whole day of riding. The maximum number of riders they can handle is 10. You saddle up at the friendly owner's house, across from the entrance to Guacamaya Lodge.

> **THE YOUNGEST PROVINCE**
>
> Guanacaste was a political monkey-in-the-middle for centuries, bouncing between Spain, Nicaragua, and independence. In 1858 Guanacastecans finally voted to annex themselves to Costa Rica, an event celebrated every July 25 with a national holiday.

### Where to Stay & Eat

★ $$–$$$  ✕ **La Puesta del Sol.** Italian food aficionado Alessandro Zangari and his wife, Silvana, have created what he modestly calls "a little restaurant in my home." But regulars drive all the way from San José to sit at one of the four tables and enjoy the haute-Italian menu. Alessandro spares no expense or effort to secure the best ingredients, and each fall he travels to Italy to buy truffles in season. The softly lighted patio restaurant, tinted in tangerine and deep blue, evokes a Moroccan courtyard. All the pasta is made from scratch; the ravioli *boscaiolo* contains a woodsy trio of cremini, porcini, and Portobello mushrooms. ⊠ *Just north of Playa Junquillal* ☎ 658–8442 ⚹ *Reservations essential* ▭ *No credit cards* ⊘ *Closed Mon.; May, June, Sept., Oct. No lunch Nov. 10–Easter and July–Aug.*

**$$** 🏨 **Land Ho! at Hotel Villa Serena.** Cape Cod comes to Costa Rica in this tropical version of New England, with shell-motif quilts and wall stencils, and hooked rugs with palm trees. Rooms are spacious and comfortable; for the ultimate in romance, ask for No. 10, a round room with an ocean view. The landscaped garden has a large pool with a butterfly garden nearby. There's a full-service day spa on the property open only in high season. To reach the Spanish-tiled terrace restaurant overlooking the beach, you pass a collection of Costa Rican student art, some of it for sale. Coffee is delivered each morning to your room, but breakfast is à la carte. ✉ *Across the dirt road from Playa Junquillal* ☎658–8430 🖷 658–8091 ⊕ *www.land-ho.com* ⤳ *12 rooms* ⟑ *Restaurant, tennis court, pool, spa, snorkeling, boating, fishing, horseback riding, bar; no a/c in some rooms, no room phones, no room TVs* ☰ *AE, MC, V* ⊘ *Closed Oct.–early Nov.* ⦿| *EP.*

**★ $–$$** 🏨 **Guacamaya Lodge.** Secluded Guacamaya, on a breezy hill, has expansive views of surrounding rolling countryside and a river estuary below, making it ideal for bird-watching. The landscaping around the pool is exceptional, with chenille plants and tall, vibrant red gingers. The three-meal restaurant serves excellent, reasonably priced food, including such Swiss specialties as *rösti* potatoes, as well as calorie-conscious "fitness plates." The spacious cabinas have lovely curtains and bedspreads and modern bathrooms. Screened windows let in the cooling evening breezes. The modern house has a full kitchen; the suites are the newest addition to the property. The place fills up fast, so book early or come off-season. ✉ *275 m off Playa Junquillal* ☎ 658–8431 🖷 658–8164 ⊕ *www. guacamayalodge.com* ✑ *Apdo. 6, Santa Cruz* ⤳ *6 cabinas, 4 suites, 1 house* ⟑ *Restaurant, a/c, fans, some kitchens, pool, volleyball, bar, shop, playground, laundry service, Internet; no room phones, no room TVs* ☰ *AE, MC, V* ⦿| *EP.*

**$–$$** 🏨 **Hotel Iguanazul.** On a bluff overlooking black tidal pools, this hotel is a 10-minute walk from surfing waves to the north and a 30-minute walk from Playa Junquillal to the south. The joint is jumping for surfer-video nights, happy hours, and Monday-night football on a large screen. All the bones are there—great pool, alfresco restaurant, high-ceilinged bungalows, mature gardens—but the flesh is sagging. The stone stairs to the beach are steep and need repair; and rooms, with screened windows letting in ocean breezes and simply furnished with two double beds, are so poorly lit that it's hard to see yourself in the mirror. No. 6 has ocean views and the most privacy. Food is adequate but poorly presented, and service is friendly but slow. New condominiums set back from the beach should be ready by late 2005. ✉ *North end of Playa Junquillal* ☎ 658–8124 🖷 658–8123 ⊕ *www.hoteliguanazul.com* ✑ *Apdo. 130–5150, Santa Cruz* ⤳ *24 rooms* ⟑ *Restaurant, fans, in-room safes, pool, beach, bar, laundry service; no a/c in some rooms, no room phones, no room TVs* ☰ *AE, MC, V* ⦿| *CP.*

**$** 🏨 **Hotel Tatanka.** This Italian hotel has great style and great food, and it's a bargain. Ten big rooms are lined up under a tile-roofed veranda facing a kidney-shaped pool. They have firm mattresses, big windows, and Mayan-motif wall paintings, arty bamboo closets, and scarlet fixtures in the tiled bathrooms. Wood-oven pizzas and homemade pastas—

the *spaghetti a la carbonara* is *delicioso*—are served in a huge alfresco restaurant with elegant furniture. The beach is a three-minute walk away. ⊠ *Main Junquillal road, south of Guacamaya Lodge, 300 m from the beach* ☎ *658–8426* 🖶 *658–8312* ⊕ *www.crica.com/tatanka.com* 🛏 *10 rooms* ⚑ *Restaurant, some a/c, fans, pool; no room phones, no room TVs* ☰ *MC, V* ⊙ *Closed Sept.–Oct.* ⦿ *BP.*

### Shopping

The **Hotel Iguanazul gift shop** (⊠ North end of Playa Junquillal) has interesting glass jewelry made by a Peruvian artist who lives in Playa Negra. There is also truly different and fabulous shell jewelry, including cuff bracelets, made by a local company called Organic Jewelry.

### To & From Playa Junquillal

*4 km/2 ½ mi (30 min) south of Paraíso. 34 km/22 mi (1 hour) south of Santa Cruz.*

In rainy season the 4-km-long beach road from Playa Negra to Playa Junquillal is not passable, and even in dry season and with a 4WD vehicle it's challenging. Your safest bet is driving down from Santa Cruz on a road that's paved part of the way. Or take a bus. The Castillos company (☎ No phone) runs a bus to Junquillal from the central market in Santa Cruz once a day; the trip takes about an hour. If you don't have a car, Junquillal is a bit difficult to access.

### Playa Junquillal Essentials

The closest town for most services is Santa Cruz, 33 km/21 mi east.
🏥 Hospital **Clínica** ⊠ Vientesiete de Abril, 16 km/10 mi northeast of Playa Junquillal.
🌐 Internet **Supermercado Junquillal** ⊠ Near beach entrance.

# Nosara

㉑ One of the last beach communities for people who want to get away from it all, Nosara is a small, rather uninteresting Tico town set inland, but bordering the wild stretches of side-by-side Playas Pelada and Guiones, with surfing waves and miles of beach to comb. The Nosara Yoga Institute is increasingly a draw. Regulations here limit development to low-rise buildings 200 meters from the beach, where they are thankfully screened by trees. Americans and Europeans, with a large Swiss contingent, are building at a fairly rapid pace, but there appears to be an aesthetic sense here that is totally lacking in Tamarindo.

The access roads to Nosara are abysmal, and the labyrinth of woodsy roads around the beaches and hard-to-read signs make it easy to get lost. ■ TIP→→ It's a good idea to scout out your dinner spot earlier in the day. For local news and happenings, check out *The Voice of Nosara* (⊕ www. voiceofnosara.com).

### Exploring

With some of the best surf breaks around, **Playa Guiones** attracts a lot of surfboard-toting visitors. But the breezy beach, with tendrils of sea grape curling almost down to the high-tide mark, is also a haven for shell-seekers and sun lovers. The only building in sight is the bizarre, surreal Hotel

Nosara, chronically under construction. Otherwise, this glorious beach has 7 km (4 mi) of hard-packed sand, great for jogging and riding bikes. Since there's a 3-meter tide, it's safer to go swimming at either high or low tide, and avoid the strong currents when the tide is turning. Most hotels post tide charts. Guiones is at the south end of the Nosara agglomeration, with three public accesses. The easiest one to find is just past the Hotel Villa Taype.

North along the shore, Playa Guiones segues seamlessly into cres-

> **CAUTION**
>
> To approach Nosara along the coast from Junquillal to the north, you have to ford many rivers, including the Río Ostional, impossible during most of the wet season. This beach road is in really bad shape and is extraordinarily slow going even in dry season; 23 km (14 mi) can take two hours to drive. You are better off driving via Nicoya on the paved road.

cent-shaped **Playa Pelada,** where the water is a little calmer for swimming. There are tide pools to explore and a blowhole that sends water shooting up at high tide. Lots of trees provide shade. Local Ticos have staked out their claim to the surfing waves here and don't always take kindly to interlopers. This is also the locals' favorite vantage point for watching sunsets. Olga's Bar, a ramshackle Tico beach bar, is a great place for a cool beer; or sip a sunset cocktail at the funky La Luna Bar & Grill next door.

**Ostional National Wildlife Refuge** (Refugio Nacional de Fauna Silvestre Ostional) protects one of Costa Rica's major breeding grounds for olive ridley turtles. Locals have formed an association to run the reserve on a cooperative basis, and during the first 36 hours of the *arribadas* (mass nesting) they are allowed to harvest the eggs, on the premise that eggs laid during this time would likely be destroyed by subsequent waves of mother turtles, or stolen by poachers. Guided tours of the nesting and hatching areas are given October–April for $7 per person. Stop at the kiosk at the entrance road to the beach to ask for a tour. Before you go to the refuge, try to get a sense from the locals of when, if ever (some years they come in very small numbers), the turtles will arrive. ⊠ *7 km/4½ mi north of Nosara; during the rainy season a 4WD vehicle is needed to cross the river* ☎ *No phone* ⊠ *$7* ◷ *Oct.–Apr., by tour only.*

★ At the north end of Nosara the **Reserva Biológica Nosara** is a natural treasure. The 125-acre private reserve includes trails through a huge mangrove wetland and old-growth forest along the Nosara River. A concrete walkway passes over an eerily beautiful mangrove swamp, with fantastical roots and snap-crackling sound effects from respiring mollusks. More than 250 bird species have been spotted here, and there's an observation platform for observing wading birds. There are always crabs, lizards, snakes, and other creatures rustling in the grass or monkeys, iguanas, and boa constrictors hanging from the trees. Pick up a self-guided trail map from the Lagarta Lodge (near the trailhead); call ahead to the lodge if you want to hire a guide ($6 entrance fee). ⊠ *Trailhead 168 steps down from Lagarta Lodge, top of hill at the north end of Nosara* ☎ *682–0035.*

MASSAGE & YOGA **The Nosara Yoga Institute** (⊠ Southeast end of town, on main road to Sámara ☎ 682–0071, 866/439–4704 in U.S. ⊕ www.nosarayoga.com) focuses on teacher certification, but also offers daily yoga classes to the public, weeklong workshops, and retreats. Relaxing massages ($50/hour) are available by appointment at **The Body Workshop** (⊠ Shopping center on the Café de Paris road to Playa Guiones ☎ 848–8279 or 845–1498). At **Surf Till Ya Die Center for Health** (⊠ Across from Hotel Villa Taype ☎ 682–0096 ⊕ www.surftillyadie.com) you can workout in a well equipped gym ($10/day) or book a massage ($25/30-min neck and back; $40/60-min full-body).

## Outdoor Activities

**Iguana Expeditions** (⊠ Gilded Iguana, Playa Guione ☎ 682–0259 ⊕ www.iguanaexpeditions.com) organizes canopy tours, kayaking, horseback riding, fishing, and nature tours. The **Harbor Reef Lodge** (⊠ Follow signs from Café de Paris turnoff, Playa Guiones ☎ 682–0059 ⊕ www.harborreef.com) has an excellent tour desk that can arrange fishing, surfing, snorkeling, and nature tours.

BIRD-WATCHING On river trips with **Toni's Birdwatching** (⊠ Boat moored at bottom of hill leading to Lagarta Lodge, follow the yellow-fish signs to mouth of Nosara River ☎ 822–1806 or 682–0610) you glide up the Nosara and Montaña rivers in a flat-bottomed catamaran with an almost noiseless electric motor. Wading herons, egrets, roseate spoonbills, ospreys, and kingfishers are common sights. Guide Toni Kast, an enthusiastic German-born naturalist, also knows where river otters play and crocodiles hunker down in mud caves along the riverbank. Trips are $60 for two or three people; $25 per person for four or more.

HORSEBACK RIDING German equestrienne Beate Klossek and husband Hans-Werner take small groups of two to four people on 2½-hour horseback nature tours through the jungle and along the beach ($40) with **Boca Nosara Tours** (⊠ 150 m below Lagarta Lodge, at the mouth of the Nosara River ☎ 682–0610). Horses are well mannered and well treated. Up to eight people can go on day-long rides into the mountains, stopping at a comfortable hotel for lunch and a swim ($80).

SURFING If you ever wanted to learn to surf, Nosara is the place. Guiones is the perfect beginners' beach, with no strong undercurrents and no reef to worry about. Local surf instructors say that the waves here are so consistent that there's no week throughout the year when you won't be able to surf. In February there's a local tournament organized by Safari Surf School, with guest celebrity surfers. In March the Costa Rican National Surf Circuit comes here for surf trials. Especially recommended for beginners, **Safari Surf School** (⊠ Road to Playa Guiones; ask for directions at Nosara Surf Shop ☎ 682–0573 ⊕ www.safarisurfschool.com) is run by two surfing brothers from Hawaii, one of whom lives here year-round. It's closed in October. **Corky Carroll's Surf School** (⊠ Near Casa Romántica, on the Playa Guiones Rd. ☎ 682–0385 ⊕ www.surfschool.net) has its own hotel for surfing students. **Coconut Harry's Surf Shop** (⊠ Main road, across from Café de Paris ☎ 682–0574) has gear, boards, wax, and lessons. **Nosara Surf Shop** (⊠ Café de Paris road to Playa Guiones ☎ 682–0186), rents boards by the day or week and has lots of gear too.

## Where to Stay & Eat

**$**   ✕ **Café de Paris.** Despite the French-Swiss owners, this restaurant and bakery feels almost completely Tico-tropical. But the service is still efficiently Swiss. Fresh-baked French pastries and desserts are a major draw. Sweet and savory croissants are excellent, as is the divine chocolate tart. In addition to the tried-and-true wood-oven pizza, nachos, casados, huge salads, and hearty sandwiches, you can order low-fat vegetarian dishes catering to health-conscious guests, many of whom are studying at the Nosara Yoga Institute. ⊠ *Main road at Playa Guiones entrance* ☎ *682–0087* ▤ *AE, MC, V.*

**$**   ✕ **Chez Olivier.** A French couple, ecapees from overwrought Tamarindo, have set up their kitchen on a hill overlooking Playa Pelada. A gratinéed smoked salmon-and-avocado appetizer and steak tartare are a couple of the Gallic choices. Food is presented artistically on huge plates. A grouper filet sauced with a creamy, lemon *mousseline* was excellent. The breezy, tropical bistro is all very French, with homemade bread, complimentary *amuse-gueules* (tidbit appetizers), a blackboard menu, delicious profiteroles, and crème brûlée. ⊠ *Hotel Almost Paradise, top of hill over Playa Pelada* ☎ *682–0172* ▤ *AE, DC, MC, V* ☼ *No lunch.*

★ **$**   ✕ **Giardino Tropical Restaurant Pizzería.** Famous for its crispy-crusted, wood-oven pizzas loaded with toppings and homemade chili-pepper sauce, this thatch-roof, two-story restaurant casts a wider net to include excellent fresh seafood and fish—the carpaccio of sea bass is a sure bet. Service is always fast and friendly. ⊠ *Giardino Tropical Hotel, main street, past entrance to Playa Guiones* ☎ *682–0258* ▤ *AE, DC, MC, V.*

**$**   ✕ **La Mariposa Panadería Café–Bar.** For the best bread in town, visit this bakery/café started by Swiss bakers who sold their goods door to door. Now multigrain breads, baguettes, carrot cake, and brownies are sold from a garden café a stone's throw from Playa Pelada. Savory empanadas, quiches, sandwiches, daily hot specials, and a chicken salad plate that is an edible work of art are other menu items. Get takeout or

> **CAUTION**   ⚠
>
> Many restaurants do not include 13% tax and 10% service in their menu prices but tack it onto the bill at the end. It might be indicated somewhere on the menu that tax and tip are not included, but that's not always the case. If you're not sure, ask.

counter service, or sit at candlelit cedar tables under the sloping roof. ⊠ *Across from Los Condominios las Flores, Playa Pelada* ☎ *682–0545* ▤ *No credit cards.*

**$$**   ▦ **Condo Canadiense del Sol Villas.** Steps from Playa Guiones, these clean and comfortable white villas face the garden's riot of color surrounding a sparkling blue pool. They have great kitchens, all-wood furniture, and queen beds in the high-ceilinged bedrooms. Living areas have both a double and a single futon and large terraces have dining tables. The air-conditioning units are old and a little noisy, but there are quieter ceiling fans as well. ⊠ *Across from Casita Romántica, Playa*

*Guiones* ☎ 682–0350, 403/938–1112 *in Canada* ⊟ 403/938–3051 *in Canada* ⊕ *www.condocanadiense.com* ⊅ *4 villas* ♢ *A/c, fans, kitchens, pool* ⊟ *MC, V for online reservations; cash only in Costa Rica* †Ⓞ *EP.*

★ **$$** ⊡ **Luna Azul.** The most luxurious, tasteful hotel in the Nosara area, Luna Azul is full of clever designs and healthful attributes—supplied by the zoologist and homeopathist Swiss owners. Birds and wildlife are abundant thanks to the surrounding private nature reserve. There's a gorgeous inifinity pool. Three rooms are private and separate; four others share two buildings. They're all spacious, with individual tropical themes. Bathrooms are elegant, with hot-water showers open to nature. Acupuncture and homeopathic treatments and massages are given. The chic seafood restaurant is drawing customers from Nosara (even when the river is flooded) with seafood fondues and theme nights. The only drawback to this fabulous place is that it's hard to get to when the Ostional River overflows in rainy season. ⊠ *1 km north of Ostional, 5 km north of Nosara* ☎ *821–0075* ⊕ *www.hotellunaazul.com* ⊅ *7 rooms* ♢ *Restaurant, a/c, fans, refrigerators, in-room safes, pool, whirlpool tub, bar* ⊟ *AE, DC, MC, V* †Ⓞ *BP.*

**$–$$** ⊡ **Casita Romántica.** This small terra-cotta hotel used to be the annex to Casa Romántica next door. But it is now being run as a separate hotel. The five modern, comfortable suites, all with kitchenettes, share a pool, a garden, and a pathway to the beach. Each suite has a wonderful wall mural, loads of light, and stylish furnishings. One large suite has a kitchen and room for four. The management is Swiss. ⊠ *Beside Casa Romántica* ☎ *682–0019* ⊕ *www.hotelcasaromantica.com* ⊅ *5 suites* ♢ *Some a/c, fans, kitchenettes, pool, beach; no room phones, no room TVs, no a/c/ in some rooms* ⊟ *MC, V* †Ⓞ *EP.*

**$–$$** ✕⊡ **Giardino Tropical Hotel.** In the lush gardens downhill from the popular restaurant (⇨ *above*), are comfortable cabinas and a sparkling 17-meter swimming pool. The handsome suites have everything you need to make breakfast: electric kettle, coffeemaker, fridge, and sink. Two spacious apartments also have full kitchens. The four smaller cabinas have been renovated and have solar-heated hot water, ceiling fans, coffeemaker, and fridges. ⊠ *Main street, past entrance to Playa Guiones* ☎ *682–0258* ⊟ *682–0353* ⊕ *www.giardinotropicale.com* ⊅ *4 cabinas, 4 suites, 2 apartments* ♢ *Restaurant, fans, some kitchens, some kitchenettes, pool; no a/c, no TVs, no phones* ⊟ *AE, DC, MC, V* †Ⓞ *EP.*

**$–$$** ✕⊡ **Harbor Reef Lodge.** Lose yourself in five acres of jungly garden centered on a small pool presided over by a concrete crocodile. Your wake-up call is from a resident howler monkey. Rooms and suites cater to surfers of every age, with plenty of space for boards and families inside the large but sparely furnished rooms. Beach houses are great for stays of a week or more. The newest rental units, in a complex called Tortuga Suites ($$$–$$$$), are very spiffy. The surf breaks at Playa Guiones are a 300-meter walk away, and a surf school operates out of the hotel. The open-sided restaurant ($–$$) serves fresh fish, steak, and tasty low-cholesterol options—a rarity in Costa Rica. A large souvenir and beachwear shop and a small grocery are on the grounds. Owner Randy Bombard has a wealth of information about the area. ⊠ *Follow signs from Café de Paris* turnoff, *Playa Guiones* ☎ 682–0059 🖷 682–0060 ⊕ *www.harborreef. com* ⟿ *9 rooms, 10 suites, 12 houses* ⚘ *Restaurant, some kitchens, refrigerators, pool, fishing, bar, gift shop; no a/c in some rooms, no room phones, no room TVs* 🖃 *AE, DC, MC, V* ⦿ *EP.*

**$** ⌹ **Casa Romántica Hotel.** The name (Romantic House) says it all: the Spanish Colonial–style house has a balustrated veranda upstairs and a graceful arcade below. New Swiss owners have renovated the six downstairs rooms under the shady arcade. They are bright, with big bathrooms and views of the glorious garden and extra-large pool covered by a thatched cabana. The short path to the beach is lined with aloe, cactus, and costus (a type of flowering ginger) and populated with birds. There is a small patio restaurant where breakfast is served and a small, international menu at dinner. ⊠ *Turn down road at Il Giardino Tropicale, Playa Guiones* ☎ 682–0272 🖷 682–0272 ⊕ *www.casa–romantica.net* ⟿ *7 rooms* ⚘ *Restaurant, some kitchens, pool, massage, beach, Internet; no a/c in some rooms, no room phones, no room TVs* 🖃 *MC, V* ⦿ *BP.*

★ **$** ⌹ **Lagarta Lodge.** A birders' and nature-lovers' mecca, this magnificent property on a promontory has the best views of Ostional National Wildlife Refuge. The private Nosara Biological Reserve is directly below the lodge. A 10-minute steep walk down takes you through a monkey-filled forest to beautiful Playa Guiones and surfing waves. Swiss managers Regina and Amadeo Amacker have renovated and brightened up formerly dark rooms. The eagle's-nest lobby-restaurant, with great views, has family-style seating and a Swiss-inspired menu. The breakfast buffet is delicious, with fresh breads and homemade jams. ⊠ *Top of hill at the north end of Nosara* ☎ 682–0035 🖷 682–0135 ⊕ *www. lagarta.com* ⌺ *Apdo. 106–5233, Nosara* ⟿ *6 rooms* ⚘ *Restaurant, fans, pool, beach, laundry service, Internet; no a/c, no room phones, no room TVs* 🖃 *MC, V* ⦿ *EP.*

**$** ⌹ **The Gilded Iguana.** This lively hotel/bar/restaurant has been a Nosara fixture for more than 15 years. Televised sports, live music, and lots of friendly regulars keep this popular place casual. The on-site tour desk can arrange almost any outing you can think of. Six large, newer, air-conditioned rooms are lined up behind a beautiful pool, complete with a refreshing waterfall. For traditionalists, the original rooms have more character, in a shaded wooden building, with louvered, screened windows letting in fresh breezes. Spacious, woodsy No. 4 is the favorite. ⊠ *Playa Guiones, Nosara* ☎ 682–0259 ⊕ *www.gildediguana.com* ⟿ *9 rooms, 3 suites* ⚘ *Restaurant, a/c, fans, refrigerators, pool, kayaking, tours, bar, laundry service; no room phones, no room TVs, no a/c in some rooms* 🖃 *MC, V* ⦿ *EP.*

### Nightlife

There's always plenty of surfing talk at **Blew Dog's Surf Club** (⊠ Playa Guiones ☎ 682–0080). Friday nights **Café de Paris** (⊠ Entrance to Playa Guiones) shows DVD movies on a big outdoor screen. **The Gilded Iguana** (⊠ Playa Guiones), a popular sports bar, has live acoustic music on Tuesday nights that draws a big crowd. Sip a margarita or one of a myriad other cocktails and watch the sun set at tony **La Luna Bar & Grill** (⊠ Playa Pelada, 200 m north of Olga's). Sunset is the main evening event on the Nosara beaches, and people gather on Playa Pelada to down a local beer at **Olga's Bar** (✉ Playa Pelada), a ramshackle beach bar.

## Shopping

**Arte Guay** (✉ Commercial center, just past Café de Paris on road to Playa Guiones) has local crafts, including some "vegetable ivory" bracelets made from giant tagua nuts. Along with surfing wear and gear, **Coconut Harry's Surf Shop** (✉ Main road, across from Café de Paris) has an interesting selection of jewelry and bottled hot sauces made by Harry himself. (The Iguana Atomic Hot Sauce will rip your tongue out!) At the **Nosara Boutique** (✉ Commercial center, just past Café de Paris on road to Playa Guiones), the Nosara Yoga Institute sells yoga books, New Age CDs, and yoga wear. **Nosara Surf Shop** (✉ Café de Paris road to Playa Guiones) has a great selection of straw hats to keep the sun from frying your hair and face.

## To & From Nosara

*28 km/17 mi (1 hour) southwest of Nicoya.*

From Nicoya, drive south, almost to Sámara, but take the very first road signed for Nosara, 1 km south of the big gas station before Sámara. This higher road is rough too for about 8 km (5 mi) but there are bridges over all the river crossings. When you join up with the beach road near Garza, you still have a very bumpy 10 km (6 mi) to go. Whichever way you go, the roads into Nosara are in really bad shape, and a four-wheel-drive vehicle is definitely recommended. Even the high-speed highway buses for Nosara transfer passengers to crummy old buses to negotiate the last 20 km (12 mi). You can also fly directly to Nosara or take an air-conditioned shuttle van from San José.

## Nosara Essentials

🏧 Bank/ATM **Banco Popular** ✉ Beside Café de Paris, at entrance to Playa Guiones. ⊘ Bank open Mon. and Fri. only; ATM available some days.

🏥 Hospital **Clínica Pública** ✉ In front ot Super Nosara ☏ 682-0166.

💊 Pharmacies **Farmacia** ✉ Next to soccer field ☏ 682-0282 ⊘ Mon.–Sat. 8–noon and 2–4.

💻 Internet **Café de Paris** ✉ At entrance to Playa Guiones.

✉ Post Office **Correo** ✉ Next to soccer field.

---

# Sámara

**㉒** The drive to Sámara from Nicoya may be one of the most scenic in Costa Rica, past rolling hills and green vistas. Long a favorite with well-off Ticos, many of whom built summer houses on the beach, Sámara is flourishing and attracting a lot of Europeans. The town even has a sidewalk. A branch of the Heredia-based language school **Intercultura** (☏ 656–0127) attracts students of all ages. But despite a distinctively Italian flavor, Tico culture—school, soccer field, and church—still rules, along with a certain amount of characteristically Tico clutter.

Sámara's wide sweep of beach is framed by two forest-covered hills jutting out on either side. It's the perfect hang-out beach, with plenty of natural shade and snack bars to take refuge in from the sun. The waves break out on a reef that not only provides protection for this giant cove and keeps the water calm for swimming, but also provides a site for diving and snorkeling excursions. Isla Chora, at the south end of the light-sand beach, is also a popular destination for kayakers and snorkelers.

## Outdoor Activities

Sámara is known more for gentle water sports such as snorkeling and kayaking than for surfing or diving, although there are a couple of surfing and dive shops. There are also two high-flying adventures here: zipline tours and ultralight flying lessons. ATV tours, tearing along dirt roads, are also becoming popular.

**Tío Tigre Tours** (☎ 656–0098 ⊠ On the beach, across from police station) has a full line of guided outdoor tours, including snorkeling, kayaking, in-shore fishing, horseback riding, and dolphin- and whale-watching tours. **Carrillo Tours** (⊠ Main street, across from Las Brasas restaurant ☎ 656–0935) is a reputable general tour operator that can organize any kind of local activity.

CANOPY TOURS **Wing Nuts Canopy Tour** (⊠ In the hills above Sámara ☎ 656–0153) is a three-hour, 12-platform zip-line tour through dry tropical forest, with ocean views from some of the platforms ($50; $30 for 18 years and under).

DIVING & SNORKELING The reef just offshore is the best place to snorkel. Kayakers also paddle out to Isla Chora to snorkle around the island. The lone dive shop here, French-run **Pura Vida Dive** (⊠ Downtown Sámara, around corner from Villas Kalimba ☎ 843–2075) takes divers (five maximum) about five miles out for guided dives around rock formations off Playa Buena Vista and Playa Carrillo. Rays, turtles, and white-tipped sharks are the star sightings. They also rent scuba equipment and make snorkeling trips.

KAYAKING **Tío Tigre** (⇨ *above*) is the main kayaking outfitter in Sámara. **PoPo's Adventures** (⇨ Playa Carrillo, *below*) runs kayaking trips in the area.

SURFING The surf is relatively gentle around Sámara, so it's a good place for beginners. The challenging waves for more experienced surfers are farther south, past Puerto Carrillo at Playa Camaronal, which has both left and right breaks. **Jesse's Original Sámara Beach Surf School** (⊠ Northwest end of the beach ☎ 656–0055) specializes in teaching beginners and also rents boards. **C&C Surf Shop** (⊠ Across from Hotel Belvedere in town ☎ 656–0628) gives one free surf lesson with board rental.

ULTRALIGHT FLIGHTS **Flying Crocodile Lodge** (⊠ Playa Buena Vista, 4 km northwest of Sámara ☎ 656–8048 ⊕ www.flying-crocodile.com) gives ultralight flights and flying lessons ($60 for 20-min. tour; $110 for instruction plus cost of flights).

## Where to Stay & Eat

**$–$$** ✕ **Restaurante Las Brasas.** Seafood and meat grilled over hot *brasas* (coals) are the specialties at this Spanish restaurant, along with paella, gazpacho, and a variety of Spanish *tortillas* (hearty omelets). Avocado stuffed with shrimp salad makes an excellent shared starter or a light lunch. An upstairs balcony is perfect for sipping Spanish wines. Downstairs, enormous green elephant-ear leaves frame the rustic wooden-railed restaurant, decorated with oxen horns and yokes. Hungry groups can feast on an entire roast suckling pig with two-days' advance reservation. ⊠ *Main road to beach, beside soccer field* ☎ 656–0546 ▤ *V.*

$ ✕ **Restaurant El Dorado.** After one visit to Costa Rica, Andrea Dolcetti and his wife, Luigina Sivieri, sold their restaurant in Ferrara, Italy, and opened one here. We're glad they did. Their open-air *palenque* (wood-and-thatch building) specializes in seafood, pasta, and at dinner, wood oven–baked pizzas. Andrea brings home the fish and Luigina works magic in the kitchen. Pasta is made from scratch, and real Parmesan cheese and salami are imported from Italy. Luigina's lasagna is the lightest imaginable, and the spaghetti *al mare* is an inspired marriage of local shellfish and Italian cooking. For dessert there are fruit *crostatas* (tarts) and chocolate "salami." ⊠ *West off main road, just past church in Sámara* ☎ 656–0145 ▤ *AE, DC, MC, V* ☉ *Closed Thurs. No lunch May–early Dec.*

¢–$ ✕ **La Vela Latina.** Cool doesn't begin to describe this casually sophisticated nightspot right on the beach, the perfect place to sit back, enjoy a drink with a boca or two, a savory foccacia, a plate of nachos, or a light salad. Listen to the sounds of the surf, and have a conversation. Lights are soft and flattering and the seating is sleek and teak or swinging, in leather-and-wood rocking chairs. Tequila cocktails and rum daiquiris come in exotic fruit flavors, or you can drink sangria, wine, milk shakes, or smoothies. It opens at 4 PM to catch the sunsets, which are even more romantic accompanied by a chocolate fondue for two. ⊠ *Across from Villas Kalimba, on the beach* ☎ 656–0418 ▤ *No credit cards* ☉ *No lunch.*

★ ¢–$ ✕ **Pizza & Pasta a Go-Go.** Exceptionally fine Italian food, including 25 fabulous pizzas, 26 pasta choices, generous salads, and a lengthy Italian wine list are just a few reasons to drop in at this sidewalk trattoria with glass tabletops showcasing shells. Save room for a tiramisu that transcends the tropics and delivers your taste buds to Italy. ⊠ *Hotel Giada lobby, main strip, 150 m from beach* ☎ 656–0132 ▤ *AE, MC, V.*

¢ ✕ **Soda Ananas.** Fruit rules at this garden-gazebo café on the hill leading into town. Pure-fruit *naturales* (smoothies) are made with water or milk and tropical fruit salad, and fruity sundaes are made with homemade ice cream. The *ananas* (pineapple) sundae comes in a scooped-out pineapple. Breakfast is served Tico-style, with rice and beans, or health food–style, with granola and fruit. Baguette sandwiches, veggie burgers, and salads make a light lunch. Home-baked cakes and specialty coffees are available all day. ⊠ *Main road leading into Sámara* ☎ 656–0491 ▤ *No credit cards* ☉ *Closed Tues. May–early Dec. No dinner.*

$$$ ▦ **Villas Playa Sámara.** Families come back year after year for good reasons: there's lots to do; the villas are spacious; and the setting is fabulous. The long stretch of picture-perfect beach has clean, clear water that's shallow and safe enough for swimming. The pretty one-, two-, and three-bedroom, white-stucco villas are sprinkled throughout the property's gardens. Air-conditioning is of an older, noisier vintage (bedrooms only). Villa 11B, near the beach with a shaded terrace, has one of the most idyllic beach views. The restaurant food is not terrific; it's best to cook for yourself or dine in Sámara, which you can walk to in 20 minutes along the beach (it's perfectly safe at night). ⊠ *Off main road, 2 km/1¼*

*mi south of Playa Sámara* 📠📠 *656–0372; 256–8228 in San José* ✍*htlvilla@racsa.co.cr* 🛏 *58 villas* ⚱ *Restaurant, fans, kitchens, pool, beach, boating, fishing, bicycles, horseback riding, bar; no room phones, no room TVs* 🖃 *AE, MC, V* ⦿⦿ *EP.*

**$$** 🏠 **Villas Kalimba.** You may never want to leave this dream world hidden behind scrolled white and orange walls. The architecture is Spanish colonial but the style is all Italian, with filmy fabrics, custom ceramics, and artistic accents. Ochre-washed 2-bedroom villas circle a garden pool with a cool cascade. Kitchens are state of the art and dining is alfresco at a long wooden table on your own tiled terrazza. All the comforts of a luxury home—king-size bed, cable TV, a personal portable phone, dataports—are here, just 50 meters from the beach. Barbecues are held each week and coffee is brewing away all day at the pool rancho. ✉ *200 m east of the Sámara police station, along the beach Rd.* 📞 *656–0929* 🖨 *656–0930* ⊕ *www.villaskalimba.com* 🛏 *5 villas* ⚱ *A/c, fans, cable TV, kitchens, pool, beach, in-room dataports* 🖃 *MC, V* ⦿⦿ *EP.*

**$–$$** 🏠 **Las Brisas del Pacífico.** One of the few beachfront hotels in Sámara, Las Brisas has two rows of white, Spanish-style bungalows hugging the bottom of a steep, landscaped hill. The well-maintained bungalows face a gorgeous pool and thatch-roof restaurant. "Sky rooms, " in the two-story building at the top of the hill, have just been renovated. They have ocean-view balconies and a pool topside, as well as a separate parking lot, so you don't have to climb up and down the hill except for meals and beach walks. The hotel's tour desk can arrange diving trips and other outings. The only down side is the rather surly German owner. ✉ *South end of beach* 📞 *656–0250* 🖨 *656–0076* ⊕ *www.brisas.net* 🛏 *22 bungalows, 16 rooms* ⚱ *2 restaurants, in-room safes, cable TV, 2 pools, 2 outdoor whirlpool tubs, massage, beach, snorkeling, bar; no a/c in some rooms, no room phones, no TV in some rooms* 🖃 *AE, D, MC, V* ⦿⦿ *BP.*

**$** 🏠 **Casa del Mar.** Less than a block from the beach, you can't beat this pleasant, well-tended hotel for value. The bright, tidy rooms have darkwood furniture, white walls, and ceramic floors. Some have queen-size beds.The hotel has a giant cold-water whirlpool in a small garden and a big cage with pet parrots. Evening beach breezes help to cool down the rooms without air-conditioning. ✉ *Main strip, 45 m east of school* 📞 *656–0264* 🖨 *656–0129* ⊕ *www.casadelmarsamara.com* 🛏 *17 rooms, 11 with bath* ⚱ *Dining room, a/c in some rooms, fans, in-room safes, some refrigerators, bar; no a/c in some rooms, no room phones, no room TVs* 🖃 *AE, MC, V* ⦿⦿ *CP.*

**$** 🏠 **Hotel Belvedere.** After a day on the beach it's refreshing to retreat to this small hotel buried in a dense, cool garden. There's a shaded swimming pool with a trickling waterfall, and a cool whirlpool. Friendly German owners Manfred and Michaela run a tight ship, keeping the garden moisture out of the large, bright rooms housed in a two-story, white-stucco building. Breakfast comes with ocean views, and the total bill is a hard-to-beat bargain. The beach is a 10-minute walk through town. ✉ *Entering Sámara, go 100 m left at the first cross St.* 📞 *656–0213* 🖨 *656–0215* ⊕ *www.belvederesamara.net* 🛏 *20 rooms* ⚱ *Dining* room, a/c, fans, cable TV, in-room safes, some kitchenettes, refrigerators, pool, whirlpool tub; no room phones ▭ MC, V ¶⃝ BP.

★ **$** ⊡ **Hotel Giada.** The gem of Sámara's small hotels, Giada, which means "jade," is the polished creation of artistic Italian owners. Watermelon, terra-cotta, and yellow washes give the walls an antique Mediterranean look. In contrast, thatch roofs overhang private terraces, which overlook a tropical garden and curvaceous blue pool. The large rooms have elegant bamboo furniture, and whimsical sea creatures are hand-painted on the bathroom tiles. Pizza & Pasta a Go-Go (⇨ above) is an excellent Italian restaurant. The hotel's only drawback is that the upstairs roadside rooms can be noisy; ask for a room overlooking the pool or one of the newer rooms in the back garden. ⊠ *Main strip, 150 m from beach* ☎ *656–0132* 🖶 *656–0131* ⊕ *www.hotelgiada.net* ✉ *Apdo. 5235–67, Sámara* 🛌 *24 rooms* ৬ *Restaurant, a/c, fans, some refrigerators, cable TV, 2 pools, tours, car rental, laundry service; no room phones* ▭ *AE, MC, V* ¶⃝ *BP.*

## Nightlife

The liveliest, noisiest beach bar is at **Las Olas** (⊠ Northwest end of the beach). Three pool tables, bright lights and a pulsing Latin soundtrack attract locals and young backpackers staying in cold-water thatch huts next to the bar. **Sol y Mar** (⊠ Northwest end of the beach) has popular karaoke nights; just ask in town for the schedule. **Shake Joe's** (⊠ On beach, center of town) is the place for music, juices, drinks, and an in-
★ ternational menu. Ultracool **La Vela Latina** (⊠ Across from Villas Kalimba, on the beach) is the place for grown-up soft music and cocktails on the beach.

## Shopping

Souvenir stands set up along the main street and at the entrance to the beach. Most shops here have pretty much the same beachwear and souvenirs for sale. **Shopping Licia** (⊠ Main St.) has a wall hung with pretty glass fish and butterfly ornaments made by a San José artist. Arts and crafts gallery **Dragonfly Galería** (⊠ Across the street from Licia) sells local paintings and carvings, and shell, feather, and bead jewelry. It also paints temporary henna tattoos.

## To & From Sámara

*36 km/23 mi (1 hour) southwest of Nicoya. 26 km/16 mi (2 ½ hours) south of Nosara.*

The road from Nicoya is paved all the way for the scenic 36 km (23 mi) to Sámara. ⚠ Potholes are spreading, so keep your eyes on the road instead of the beautiful views. A rough beach road from Nosara is passable in dry season (it's more direct, but takes just as long); do not attempt this road when it rains. To get from Nosara to Sámara via the paved road, drive south, 5 km past Garza. At a T intersection, ignore the road toward Sámara (the beach road) and take the road to the left, toward Nicoya. This will take you uphill to merge with the main Nicoya-Sámara highway. No matter which way you go, the drive to Sámara is long and bumpy. Buses leave Nicoya at 8 AM and 3 and 4 PM daily for Sámara, from a stop 300 m east of the central park.

## Sámara Essentials

🏦 Bank/ATM **Mobile Banco Nacional** ⊠ Beach entrance, in front of police station ⊘ ATM available when satellite communication working.

🏥 Hospital **Medical Care Beach Services** ☎ 304-2121 ⊘ 24-hr emergency hotline.

💊 Pharmacies **Farmacia Sámara** ⊠ North end of soccer field ☎ 656-0123.

💻 Internet **Skynet** ⊠ Beside Galeria Dragon ☎ 656-0920 ⊘ Sun.-Fri. 9-9.

✉ Post Office **Correo** ⊠ Beside church, across from soccer field.

# Playa Carrillo

**㉓** With its long, reef-protected beach backed by an elegant line of sway-
**Fodor'sChoice** ing palms and sheltering cliffs, Playa Carrillo (interchangeably called
★ Puerto Carrillo) is a candidate for the most picturesque beach in Costa
Rica. Totally unmarred by even a single building, it's ideal for swimming, snorkeling, walking, and lounging—just remember not to sit
under a loaded coconut palm. There are some round concrete tables and
benches but they get snapped up quickly.

## Exploring

Most nature lovers are no fans of zoos, but **La Selva Zoo & Bromeliad
Garden,** a small zoo with mostly rescued small animals, is a great chance
to see them up close, in low, chest-high corrals under the shade of trees.
The zoo's focus is on hard-to-see nocturnal animals, so the best time to
visit is at sunset when the armadillo and big-eyed kinkajou are starting
to stir. There are also a skunk, spotted pacas, raccoons, and scarier species
like bats, boas, poison-dart frogs, caymans, and crocodiles (the latter
two very small babies). A bromeliad and orchid collection is artistically
arranged around the zoo. If you come early in the day, your ticket is
also good for a return evening visit. ⊠ *Road behind Hotel Esperanza*
☎ *305–1610* 🎫 *$5* ⊘ *Daily 10–9.*

## Outdoor Activities

ATV TOURS **Hotel El Sueño Tropical** (⊠ 2 km/1 mi south of Puerto Carrillo, along a
dirt Rd. ☎ 656-0151 ⊕ www.elsuenotropical.com) guides ATV tours
along beach trails south of Puerto Carrillo.

KAYAKING Energetic, friendly Tad Cantrell at **PoPo's Adventures** (⊠ Off main Carrillo road, just south of Hotel Esperanza ☎ 656-0086) knows his birds
and trees, and he'll point them out as you float down the Río Oro in
an easy-to-use inflatable kayak. He also has skirted, cockpit kayaks for
more experienced paddlers. The four-to-five-hour trip is designed for
anyone aged 2 to 102, he says, and includes a picnic lunch. Cantrell also
runs a sea kayaking school, organizes longer, more challenging kayaking trips, and has surfing and snorkeling trips as well.

FISHING From January to April, sportfishing boats moored off the beach take
anglers on fishing expeditions. Experienced local Captain Rob Gordon
lives right in Puerto Carrillo and runs fishing trips on *Kitty Kat*
(☎ 656-0170 or 359-9039 ⊕ www.sportfishcarrillo.com) a 28-foot aluminum boat with twin diesels. He'll find marlin and sailfish out in the
ocean as well as good-eating dorado, yellowfin tuna, and wahoo for you.

## Where to Stay

**$$** 🏨 **Puerto Carrillo Sunset Luxury B&B.** High on a hill, these rooms are a lit-
tle pricey, but can't be beat for spectacular views of distant Sámara Bay
and nearby Carrillo Beach. Rooms are spacious and sunny, with carv-
ings of fish adorning the wooden headboards. Huge blue-tiled bath-
rooms have solar-heated hot water. Breakfast is served poolside in an open
rancho facing the view. Surrounded by secondary forest, the garden has
flowers that lure hummingbirds and butterflies. The road to the hotel is
incredibly steep and often heavily rutted after rain, but you can usually
get up it in dry season without four-wheel drive. ⊠ *500 m up steep road
to left of public parking area in Playa Carrillo* ☎ *656–0011* 🖷 *656–0009*
⊕ *www.carrillosunset.com* ⇄ *6 rooms* ♦ *Fans, pool; no a/c in some rooms,
no room phones, no room TVs* ▤ *No credit cards* ✵◎� *BP.*

**$** 🏨 **El Sueño Tropical.** This resort has everything but the beach, but there
are two beaches just a shuttle-van ride away, one for surfing and one
for swimming and snorkeling. The pool has a teak deck for blissful loung-
ing and the property's expansive gardens are lush and cool. Lime-green
bungalows are in a valley, with steps to the pool and restaurant, which
specializes in Italian food. The rooms and two-bedroom apartments are
painted in hot, tropical colors and furnished with a mix of bamboo and
rustic wood pieces. Screened windows let in cool air at night. The hotel
has horseback riding, ATV tours, and a tour desk. ⊠ *2 km/1 mi south
of Puerto Carrillo, along a dirt Rd.* ☎ *656–0151* 🖷 *656–0152* ⊕ *www.
elsuenotropical.com* ⇄ *12 rooms, 4 apartments* ♦ *Restaurant, a/c,
fans, pool, horseback riding, tours, bar* ✵◎�Ⅰ *CP.*

**$** ✕🏨 **Hotel Esperanza.** The best thing about this modest but comfortable
B&B is the garden, an oasis with hammocks, lounge chairs, an old-fash-
ioned swing seat, and a pretty dining terrace. Marisa and Guy Orfali from
Montreal have created a homey place with tropical flair. Beds are comfy,
there's lots of hot water, and the rooms, which sleep two to seven, are al-
ways fresh and well maintained. At night, in high season, the breakfast
terrace becomes El Ginger Restaurant (¢-$), specializing in grilled jumbo
shrimp, fish and beef tenderloin, and a bananas flambé ending. The hotel
organizes a waterfall hiking tour and fishing excursions. ⊠ *90 m west of
Hotel Guanamar* ☎🖷 *656–0564* ⊕ *www.hotelesperanza.com* ⇄ *7 rooms*
♦ *Restaurant, fans; no a/c, no room phones, no room TVs* ▤ *MC, V* ✵◎ⅠBP.*

## To & From Playa Carrillo
*7 km/4 mi (15 minutes) southeast of Sámara.*

You can fly into Playa Carrillo on SANSA or NatureAir and land at the
airstrip, or head south on the smooth, paved road from Sámara. If
you're not staying at a hotel in Carrillo you'll have to park your car ei-
ther in a sun-baked concrete lot halfway along the beach or on the grassy
road median at the south end of the beach. You can also leave the driv-
ing to Interbus ( ⇨ The North Pacific Essentials, end of chapter) and get
here via air-conditioned van.

## Playa Carrillo Essentials
Sámara is the closest town for banks and other services.
🏧 Internet **Internet Café** ⊠ Carrillo Tours, Hotel Guanamar, 200 m south of Hotel Es-
peranza, main Rd.

## Punta Islita

**24** Punta Islita is named for a tiny tuft of land that becomes an island at high tide, but the name is synonymous in Costa Rica with Hotel Punta Islita, one of the country's most luxurious and gorgeous resorts. The curved beach is rather rocky but good for walking, especially at low tide when tidal pools form in the volcanic rock. Another interesting stroll is through the small village, which has become a work of art in progress, thanks to a community art project led by renowned Costa Rican artists recruited by Hotel Punta Islita, who use town buildings as their canvas. Everything—from outdoor activities to food—revolves around and is available through the resort.

> ### WORD OF MOUTH
>
> "I personally think that Costa Rica is a wonderful destination for honeymooners, but is best experienced in small hotels rather than all inclusive resorts, where you get very little of Costa Rica. There are a lot of luxurious places to consider that offer beautiful beaches and a lot of activities. Some of these include Hotel Punta Islita, Hotel Cala Luna, [and] Hotel Makanda by the Sea."
>
> –costaricafinca

### Where to Stay

**$$$$** **Hotel Punta Islita.** Overlooking **Fodor'sChoice** the Pacific from a forested ridge, ★ this exquisite, secluded hotel is luxury incarnate. Hidden around the hillside are villas, casitas, suites, and spacious rooms, each with a private porch and a hammock. Beds have rough-hewn wooden bedposts, and bathrooms are tiled, with deep tubs. Casitas have their own private plunge pools or outdoor whirlpools and private gardens, one of the main attractions for the many honeymooners. A massive thatched dome covers the restaurant and opens onto an infinity-edge pool with a sea view and a swim-up bar. If you overdo with activities here—which include golfing, zip-line canopy tours (shorter and lower to the ground than most canopy tours), and mountain biking—stop by the spa for unique massage treatments using local herbs. ⊠ *South of Playa Carrillo* 🕾 *661–3322, 231–6122 in San José* 🖷 *661–4043, 231–0715 in San José* ⊕ *www. hotelpuntaislita.com* ✆ *Apdo. 242-1225, San José* ⇆ *15 bungalows, 13 casitas, 6 suites, 5 villas* ⚘ *2 restaurants, minibars, cable TV (some with VCR or DVD), driving range, 2 tennis courts, 2 pools, gym, spa, beach, boating, fishing, hiking, horseback riding, tours, 2 bars, laundry service, Internet, airstrip, helipad* 🖃 *AE, DC, MC, V* ⧍ *CP.*

### To & From Punta Islita

*8 km/5 mi (15 minute) south of Playa Carrillo in dry season; 50 km/31 mi (1 ½ hours) south of Carrillo by alternate route in rainy season.*

In rainy season it's often impossible to cross the Río Oro south of Carrillo, so you have to make a much longer detour along dirt roads with spectacular mountain views but lots of potholes. Most guests fly into the hotel's private airstrip.

# THE TEMPISQUE RIVER BASIN

The parks in and around the Río Tempisque are prime places to hike, explore caves, and watch birds and other wildlife. The town of Nicoya is the commercial and political hub of the northern Nicoya Peninsula. By road, Nicoya provides the best access to Sámara, Nosara, and points south and north and is linked by a smooth, well-paved road to the artisan community of Guaitil and the northern Nicoya beach towns.

The Taiwan Friendship Bridge, built with donated funds from Taiwan and more commonly referred to as the Río Tempisque Bridge, has not only speeded up access to the Pacific Coast but has also speeded up the pace of life here. The bridge crosses the Río Tempisque just north of where passengers used to weather long waits for a ferry. To get to the bridge, head north from San José on the Pan-American Highway, turn left about 48 km (30 mi) north of the Puntarenas turnoff, and drive 27 km (17 mi) west.

## Palo Verde National Park

**❷⑤** One of the best wildlife- and bird-watching parks in Costa Rica, Palo Verde is bordered on the west by the Río Tempisque. Extending over 198 square km (76 square mi), the park protects a significant amount of deciduous dry forest. The forest is less dense than rain forest, which makes it easier to spot birds and animals. The terrain is fairly flat—the maximum elevation in the park is 268 meters (879 feet)—and the main attraction is bird-watching. Its swampland and the nearby river are temporary homes for thousands of migratory birds toward the end of the rainy season. From September through March you can see dozens of species of aquatic birds, including herons, wood storks, and jabirus and elegant, flamingo-like roseate spoonbills. ■ TIP→→ A raised platform near the ranger station, about 8 km (5 mi) past the park entrance, gives you a vantage point over a marsh filled with ducks and jacanas. But be prepared to climb a narrow metal ladder. Camping in rustic dormitory facilities ($7) and meals ($2.50 for lunch or dinner) can be arranged through the park headquarters. ☎ 200–0125 ☒ $6 ⊙ Daily 7–4; last admission at 1 PM.

Just 3 km north of the Palo Verde road at Bagaces, take the dirt road signed for **Llanos de Cortés** to get to this hidden waterfall less than 2 km (1 mi) off the highway. About half a kilometer along the dirt road you'll see on your right a large rock with CATARATAS scrawled on it. Follow this bumpy road about 1.3 km to its end and then clamber down a steep path to the pool at the bottom of a spectacular, wide, 50-foot waterfall. This is a great place for a picnic. ⚠ Don't leave anything of value in your car.

Sad but sobering, one of the few places left in the country where you are guaranteed to see large wildcats, including a jaguar, is **Las Pumas rescue shelter** (☒ 4 ½ km/3 mi north of Cañas on main hwy. ☎ 669-6044 ⊕ www.geocities.com/laspumas2000). The small enclosures also hold jaguarundis, pumas, margays, ocelots, and oncillas. Some small animals and birds are rehabilitated and released into the wild. But the larger cats

CLOSE UP

## Making a Difference

**YOUR NATIONAL-PARK** or -Reserve entrance fee helps support the preservation of Costa Rica's wildlife and protected places. You can also make your visit beneficial to the people living nearby by hiring local guides, horses, or boats; eating in local restaurants; and buying things (excluding wild-animal products) in local shops. You can go a few steps further by making donations to local conservation groups or to such international organizations as Conservation International, the Rainforest Alliance, and the Worldwide Fund for Nature, all of which support important conservation efforts in Costa Rica. It's also helpful to explore private preserves off the beaten path, and stay at lodges that contribute to environmental efforts and to nearby communities. By planning your visit with an eye toward grassroots conservation efforts, you join the global effort to save Costa Rica's tropical ecosystems and help ensure that the treasures you traveled so far to see remain intact for future generations.

are probably here for life; it's too dangerous (for them) to be released. The refuge relies on contributions.

### Outdoor Activities

The **Organization for Tropical Studies** (☎ 240–6696 ⊕ www.ots.ac.cr) runs half-day hiking, mountain-biking, and boat tours in Palo Verde Park, and has some nighttime tours. Packages combine a guided walk with three meals and lodging in small, bunk-bedded double rooms with private bath ($50 per person).

BIRD-WATCHING A boat excursion to Isla Pájaros along the Río Tempisque is a must for birders. At the end of rainy season this tiny 2.3-hectare island, across from Puerto Moreno, is an exciting place to see hundreds of nesting wood storks, cormorants, and anhingas. You can get close enough to see chicks being fed in nests. ■ TIP➔➔ The best time to go is very early in the morning, to avoid heat and to guarantee the most bird sightings. **Aventuras Arenal** (☎ 479–9133 ⊕ www.arenaladventures.com) guides have good eyes and usually know the English names for birds. The company specializes in ecological tours and runs bird-watching boat tours ($25 per person) to Isla Pájaros, leaving from docks along the Río Tempisque, including the dock at Palo Verde. It will pick up passengers from as far south as Tamarindo and Sámara. **CATA Tours** (☎ 674–0126, 296–2133 in San José ⊕ www.catatours.com) runs wildlife and bird-watching boating adventures down the Río Bebedero into Palo Verde. Arrange hotel pickup with your reservation.

RIVER RAFTING **Ríos Tropicales** (☎ 669–6262 ⊕ www.riostropicales.com) has relatively easy Class I and II rafting trips down the Río Corobicí. The one-, two-, or three-hour trips ($20–$45) start from the Restaurante Rincón Corobicí, on the main highway 5 km (3 mi) north of Cañas. It's a good way to get an introduction to rafting without being scared to death by fast rapids.

**WILDLIFE WATCHING** On a calm adventure trip with **Safaris Corobicí** (✉ Follow signs from highway to Km 193 ☎☎ 669–6191 ⊕ www.nicoya.com), guides do the rowing on large inflatable rafts while you look at the passing scene and wildlife. The three-hour float trips ($45, including snack) cover wildlife-rich territory not far from Palo Verde. Trips require two or more passengers. They have a kiosk at Restaurante Rincón Corobicí, on the main highway, 5 km (3 mi) north of Cañas. Another recommended operator is **CATA Tours** ( ⇨ Bird-Watching, *above*).

## Where to Stay Near Palo Verde

**$ ▥ La Ensenada Lodge.** This is the most comfortable base for bird-watching and nature appreciation near the Río Tempisque. Part of a national wildlife refuge, the property is also a 1000-acre cattle-fattening ranch and salt producer. The salt flats and nearby shallow waters attract wading birds, and crocodiles that snack on them. The good-sized pool has a gulf vista, and there's a motorboat for wildlife touring. The Isla Pájaros Biogical Reserve, the country's largest breeding grounds for black-crowned night herons, is a short boat ride away. The wood cabins are small but comfortable, with verandas and views and big screened windows for breezes. The rancho restaurant serves Italian/Costa Rican meals, buffet-style, including beef raised on the ranch. ✉ *13 km/8 mi along a dirt road from the Pan-American Hwy, 27 km south of Cañas* ☎ *289–6655* 🖷 *289–5281* ⊕ *www.laensenada.net* 🛏 *21 cabin rooms* ⚘ *Restaurant, fans, pool, horseback riding, bar, laundry service* ▤ *No credit cards* ⏺ *Al.*

## To & From Palo Verde

*52 km/32 mi (3 hours) south of Liberia.*

To get to Palo Verde from Liberia, drive south along the Pan-American Highway to Bagaces, then turn right at the small, easy-to-miss sign for Palo Verde, along a rough dirt road for 28 km (17 mi). Count on an hour to drive the distance from the main highway to the park entrance; it's a very bumpy road. The OTS station is about 7 km (5 mi) beyond the park entrance; the park headquarters is just another kilometer farther. The gatekeeper takes lunch from noon to 1 PM, so don't arrive during that time. Day visitors must be out of the park by 6 PM.

**en route** The approach to the town of Santa Cruz is like a giant pit stop, with one car-parts shop after another. One of the few reasons to visit is to eat at **Coope-Tortillas** (✉ Drive through business district, 200 m past church turn right and look for peaked-roof metal structure, Santa Cruz ☎ 680–0688) where you can watch hand-rolled corn tortillas being cooked the old-fashioned way over an open fire. Friendly women in blue uniforms, members of a local women's cooperative, heap your plate with your choice of traditional *Guanacasteco* foods and bring it to one of the picnic tables in a high-ceilinged, corrugated-metal building. Try the delicious *arroz de maiz,* a corn stew. The restaurant is open 4 AM to 6 PM. Tortillas sometimes run out before 4 PM.

## Barra Honda National Park

 Once thought to be a volcano, 1,184-foot **Barra Honda peak** actually contains an intricate network of caves, a result of erosion after the ridge emerged from the sea. Some caves in the almost 23-square-km (14-square-mi) park remain unexplored, and they're home to abundant animal life, including bats, birds, blindfish, salamanders, and snails.

Every day from 7 AM to 1 PM local guides take groups 58 feet down to the **Terciopelo Cave,** which shelters unusual formations shaped like fried eggs, popcorn, and shark's teeth. You must wear a harness with a rope attached for safety. The tour costs $12 for equipment rental, plus $16 for a guide for one to four people, in addition to park admission. Kids under 12 are not allowed to visit this cave, but they can visit the kid-size La Cuevita cavern that also has interesting stalagmites. Both cave visits include interpretive nature hikes.

If caving leaves you feeling claustrophobic, you can climb the 3-km (2-mi) Los Laureles trail (the same trail that leads to the Terciopelo cave) to Barra Honda's summit. From here you have fantastic views sweeping across the islet-filled Gulf of Nicoya. Wildlife includes howler monkeys, skunks, coatis, deer, parakeets, and iguanas. Hikers must be accompanied by local guides, members of the **Asociación de Guias Ecologistas** (☎ 659–1551). An off-site **park office** (✉ Across from colonial church, Nicoya ☎ 686–6760) provides information and maps of the park. It's open weekdays 7–4. The park has camping facilities; and a community tourism association provides guides and runs a simple, inexpensive restaurant and lodge ($4.50 per person) by the park entrance. Make reservations for weekend food or lodging in the park. ☎ 659–1551 ✉ $6 ☉ Daily 7–4.

### To & From Barra Honda
*100 km/62mi (2 hours) south of Liberia. 13 km/8 mi west of Río Tempisque Bridge.*

From the Río Tempisque Bridge, drive west along a paved highway. Then follow a dirt road (signed off the highway) for 10 km (6 mi) to the park entrance. There are buses from the town of Nicoya but they don't leave till 12:30 and 4 PM, which is a liitle late to start a hike. You can also take a taxi from Nicoya to the park entrance or go with one of many tour companies in beach towns on the Nicoya Peninsula.

## Nicoya

 Once a quaint, provincial town, known as Guanacaste's colonial capital, Nicoya is now a boomtown, thanks to increased traffic from the Río Tempisque Bridge. The town has spruced up old buildings and added modern new ones, and has Internet cafés and ATMs that take international cards.

Sadly, with all the commercial bustle Nicoya is rapidly losing what small-town charm it once had. But there are still a few historic remnants around the central park. The Chorotega chief Nicoya greeted the Spanish conquistadores upon their arrival here in 1523, a meeting that forever changed the peninsula that bears the chief's name. A noticeable Chinese population, descendants of 19th-century railroad workers, gives Nicoya a certain cosmopolitan air, manifested in part by numerous Chinese restaurants.

## Exploring

Nicoya's only colonial landmark, is the whitewashed, mission-style **Church of San Blas.** Originally built in 1644, the current church was reconstructed after an 1831 earthquake. The spare interior is made grand by seven pairs of soaring, carved-wood columns. Inside are folk-art wood carvings of the stations of the cross arrayed around the

> ### CHOROTEGA POTTERY
>
> In the country village of Guaitil ( ✉ 24 km/15 mi north of Nicoya) artists—most of them women—have revived a vanishing tradition by producing clay pottery handmade in the manner of the pre-Columbian Chorotega. The town square is a soccer field, and almost every house facing it has a pottery shop out front and a round, wood-fired kiln in back. Pottery designs range from imitation Mexican to inspired Cubist abstractions. Prices range from $12 to $300, depending on size; most are around $30. Pieces do crack easily, so pack them carefully.

stark white walls, a small collection of huge, 18th-century bronze mission bells, and some antique wooden statues of saints. Arched doorways frame views of park greenery and distant mountains. ✉ *North side of central park* ☎ *No phone* ✉ *By donation* ☉ *Erratic hours.*

## Outdoor Activities

Hiking in Barra Honda is the main outdoor adventure here. If that's too strenuous for you, **Tempisque Eco Adventures** (✉ 3 km west of Río Tempisque Bridge ☎ 687–1110 or 687–1212) can show you flora and fauna similar to Barra Honda's on their seven-cable canopy tour ($25). For a fun day you can combine the canopy tour with a Palo Verde boat tour for wildlife watching and lunch in their charming, open-air restaurant accompanied by traditional marimba music ($50).

## Where to Stay & Eat

¢–$ ✕ **Restaurante Nicoya.** There are many Chinese restaurants from which to choose in Nicoya. This one is the most elegant, with hanging lanterns, a colorful collection of international flags, and an enormous menu with 85 Asian dishes, such as stir-fried beef with vegetables, along with some familiar favorites, such as fried chicken. The fresh sea bass sautéed with fresh pineapple, chayote, and red peppers is excellent. ✉ *Main road, 70 m south of Coopmani Bldg.* ☎ 685–5113 ✉ *No credit cards.*

¢ ✕ **Soda Colonial.** One of the last vestiges of local color in town is this vintage all-day restaurant with white-adobe walls. Facing the shady central park, it's a great place to watch small-town life go by. Sit at a wooden bench in the wainscotted interior and sip a tamarindo refresco or order hearty portions of typical Tico food, heavy on the beans and rice. ✉ *Southeast corner of central park* ✉ *No credit cards* ☉ *Open 1 AM–11 PM daily.*

$ ▥ **Hotel de Lujo Río Tempisque.** There aren't many reasons to stay overnight in Nicoya, unless you're on a shopping spree. But if you're staying, the rooms here, with high wooden ceilings and big picture windows, are luxurious by any standards, and on the road to Santa Cruz they are a marvel. The owner is in the hardware business, and the hotel has high-quality materials inside and out, including palatial iron gates at the entrance. Huge white-tiled bathrooms have mirrored closets and showers big enough for two. The gardens and pool area are beautifully landscaped. There is no restaurant, but room fridges are stocked with juice and soft drinks. ⊠ *Highway north to Santa Cruz, just outside Nicoya* ☎ *686–6650* ➥ *30 rooms* ♿ *Restaurant, a/c, fans, refrigerators, cable TV, pool; no room phones* 🖃 *AE, MC, V* 🍴 *EP.*

## To & From Nicoya
*27 km/15 mi (40 minutes) west of the Río Tempisque Bridge.*

The town of Nicoya is west of the Río Tempisque Bridge on a newly paved road. If you're running out of gas, oil, or tire pressure, the Servicentro Nicoyano on the north side of Nicoya, on the main road, is open 24 hours.

### Nicoya Essentials
🏦 Banks **Banco Nacional** ⊠ Main St.

🏧 ATMs **Coopmani ATH** ⊠ Main street, beside Fuji Film store.

🏥 Hospital **Hospital de L'Anexion** ⊠ Main road into town from hwy. ☎ 685-5066.

💊 Pharmacies **Farmacia Clinica Medica Nicoyana** ⊠ Main street, near Restaurante Nicoya ☎ 685-5238 🕑 Weekdays 8-7:30, Sat. 8-6.

💻 Internet **CiberClub** ⊠ Across from Hotel Yenny, 1 block south of central park. 🕑 Mon.-Sat. 8:30 AM-9 PM.

📮 Post Office **Correo** ⊠ Southwest corner of park.

# NORTH PACIFIC ESSENTIALS

## Transportation

### BY AIR

ARRIVING & DEPARTING
International Aeropuerto Internacional Daniel Oduber (LIR) in Liberia is a good gateway to the coast. Tamarindo, Playa Nosara, Playa Carrillo, Punta Islita, and Tambor also have airstrips. Flying in from San José to these airports is the best way to get here if you are already in the country. If your primary destination lies in Guanacaste and/or Nicoya, make sure you or your travel agent investigate the possibility of flying directly into Liberia instead of San José, which saves some serious hours on the road. For more information, *see* Air Travel *in* Smart Travel Tips A to Z.

GETTING AROUND
Macaw Air, based in Tamarindo, flies five-passenger Cessna 206 planes between Liberia, Tamarindo, Nosara, and Tambor on the Nicoya Peninsula, and over to Quepos on the mainland and as far south as Puerto Jiménez in the South Pacific.

🛪 **Macaw Air** ☎ 653-1362 ⊕ www.macawair.com.

### BY BUS

ARRIVING & DEPARTING
For information about bus travel to and from the North Pacific, *see* Bus Travel *in* Smart Travel Tips A to Z.

GETTING
AROUND Bus service connects the larger cities to each other and to the more popular beaches, but forget about catching a bus from beach to beach; you'll
generally have to backtrack to the inland hubs of Nicoya and Liberia
unless you take a minibus, which may take just as long as a bus, although
they're usually more comfortable. Your hotel front desk should be able
to confirm which station specific buses and lines depart from. Buses don't
serve Rincón de la Vieja and Guanacaste National Parks.

## BY CAR

ARRIVING &
DEPARTING The northwest is accessed via the paved two-lane Pan-American Highway (CA1), which begins at the top of Paseo Colón in San José. Take
the bridge across the Río Tempisque to get to the Pacific beaches south
of Liberia. Paved roads run down the spine of the Nicoya Peninsula all
the way to Playa Naranjo, with many unpaved and potholed stretches.
Once you get off the main highway the pavement holds out only so far,
and then dirt, dust, mud, potholes, and other factors come into play.
The roads to Playa Sámara, Playas del Coco, and Ocotal are paved all
the way; every other destination requires some dirt-road maneuvering.
If you're headed down to the coast via unpaved roads, be sure to get
advance information on road conditions.

GETTING
AROUND If you want to drive around the Nicoya Peninsula, be prepared to spend
some serious time in the car. The road to Nicoya's southern tip is partly
paved and partly just gravel, and it winds up and down and around various bays. Some roads leading from Liberia to the coast are intermit-
tently paved. As you work your way toward the coast, pay close attention
to the assorted hotel signs at intersections—they may be the only indi-
cators of which roads to take to your lodging.

Stick with the main rental offices in San José—they have more cars
available and you're more likely to reach an English-speaking agent
on the phone; some have local satellite offices. Alamo has pickup and
car delivery in Liberia. Budget has branches in San José and also 6 km
(4 mi) west of Liberia's airport. Economy, Alamo, and Elegante rent
cars in Tamarindo; Economy has a good supply of automatic four-wheel-
drive vehicles.

■ TIP→→ Four-wheel-drive vehicles are recommended, but not essential, at
least not in the dry season, for most roads. If you don't rent a four-wheel-drive
vehicle, at least rent a car with high clearance—you'll be glad you did.

🚗 Major Rental Agencies **Alamo** ⊠ 2 km/1 mi north of Liberia airport, Liberia
🕾 668-1111, 800/462-5266 in U.S. 🖂 Hotel Diriá, main road, Tamarindo 🕾 653-0727.
**Budget** ⊠ 6 km/4 mi southwest of Liberia airport, Liberia 🕾 668-1024 or 668-1126
🖂 Hotel Zullymar, main road just past Hotel Diriá, Tamarindo 🕾 653-0756. **Economy**
⊠ 3½ km/2 mi south of Liberia airport, Liberia 🕾 666-2816 or 666-7560 🖂 Main road
entering Tamarindo, next to Restaurant Coconut, Tamarindo 🕾 653-0728.

🚗 Local Rental Agencies **Elegante** ⊠ 5 km/3 mi south of Liberia airport, Liberia
🕾 667-0511 🖂 Pueblo Dorado Hotel, main road as you enter town from north,
Tamarindo 🕾 653-0015. **Sol Rentacar** ⊠ In front of Hotel El Bramadero, across from
Burger King at intersection of Pan-American Hwy. and entrance to town, Liberia
🕾 666-2222 🖂 Second entrance to Playa Hermosa, beside Aqua Sport 🕾 356-9872.

### BY SHUTTLE VAN

ARRIVING &
DEPARTING You can ride in a comfortable, air-conditioned minibus with Gray Line Tourist Bus, connecting San José, Liberia, Playa Flamingo, Playa Hermosa, Tamarindo, and other destinations in Guanacaste. Fares range from $25 to $58, depending on destination. The Gray Line Tourist Bus from San José to Tamarindo and Liberia begins picking up passengers from hotels daily around 6 AM. The return bus leaves Tamarindo around 2 PM and passes through Liberia around 3:30 PM. Interbus has door-to-door minivan shuttle service from San José hotels to all the major beach destinations (Papagayo, Panama, Hermosa, Flamingo, Tamarindo, Hermosa, Cocos, and Ocotal in Nicoya) for $25 per person. Reserve at least one day in advance.

🚍 Shuttle Van Services **Gray Line Tourist Bus** ☎ 232-3681 or 220-2126 ⊕ www.graylinecostarica.com. **Interbus** ☎ 283-5573 ⊕ www.interbusonline.com.

## Contacts & Resources

Banks, Internet cafés, post offices, and emergency contacts are listed at the end of each town entry.

### BANKS & EXCHANGING SERVICES

ATMs that accept international bank cards are few and far between in Guanacaste. ATH (A Todas Horas) machines are the most reliable, although even they may be out of cash during peak holiday times. You can get a cash advance on a Visa card at a bank, but be prepared for a long wait and be sure you have your passport (not a copy) with you. Your best bets for ready cash are the Burger King ATH near Liberia and the Coopmani ATH in Nicoya. Branches of Banco Nacional and Banco de Costa Rica can be found in Filadelfia, Liberia, Nicoya, and Santa Cruz. Banco Nacional also has a branch in Playas del Coco. Banco de Costa Rica is in Playa Flamingo and at the Liberia airport.

### INTERNET

Apart from beach communities, public Internet access is not widespread in this part of the country. Expect to pay about $2 per hour of access time. Dial-up services are less zippy than connections in San José.

### MAIL & SHIPPING

Finding a post office in beach towns is almost impossible, since most beach areas are not incorporated towns. Liberia, La Cruz, Nicoya, Nosara, Playas del Coco, Sámara, and Santa Cruz all have post offices.

# Central Pacific

Scarlet Macaw

**WORD OF MOUTH**

"Manuel Antonio National park is my favorite. There is so much to do there . . . comb the mountain's many trails, zip through the trees like Tarzan, or go horseback riding."

—hopabout

"Montezuma is a place that I am glad I visited . . . I most definitely saw more hippies than I have seen since the '60s. But . . . we enjoyed ourselves."

—dfarmer

www.fodors.com/forums

# WELCOME TO THE CENTRAL PACIFIC

Surfing at Playa Jacó

## TOP 5
## Reasons to Go

1. **Nature and wildlife:** Explore seaside flora and fauna at Manuel Antonio National Park, Curú National Wildlife Refuge, and Cabo Blanco Nature Reserve.

2. **Fishing:** Deep-sea fishing at Quepos almost guarantees your snapshot alongside a swordfish, marlin, or yellowfin tuna.

3. **Waterfalls:** In Montezuma, hike to a waterfall with two swimming holes or ride horseback to a cascade falling into the sea. Near Tárcoles, get refreshed in a majestic 656-foot waterfall.

4. **Surfing:** This is Costa Rica's surf central. Jacó, Malpaís and Playa Hermosa swarm with surfers, from beginners to pros.

5. **Adventure sports:** Snorkel among colorful fish, get muddy on ATV mountain rides, and zip through treetops near Jacó, Manuel Antonio, or Montezuma.

On **the Southern Nicoya Tip,** across the gulf from the "mainland," towns are more tranquil and more spread out. Beaches and surfing dominate. Montezuma is a popular hub.

Kayaking, Quepos

# Getting Oriented

Most of the Central Pacific is mountainous, and beach towns are backed by forested peaks. Humid evergreen forests, coffee fields, and cattle pastures blanket the land. The coastal highway connects all towns from Tárcoles to the southern Pacific. The hub town of Jacó makes a good base for visiting surrounding beaches and wildlife areas. Farther south are Quepos and its neighbor, Manuel Antonio, followed by smaller towns barely touched by tourism. Across the Gulf of Nicoya, the more tranquil southern tip of the Nicoya Peninsula is also surrounded by impressive mountains, but with dry tropical forests that change radically from the rainy to the dry season. Distances are longer between towns here. Many folks like to use Montezuma as a regional hub.

Carara National Park

Boy jumping through waterfalls, Montezuma

Humid evergreen forests, coffee fields, and cattle pastures blanket the Inland portions of the Central Pacific. Lagoon-ridden Carara Biological Reserve is here.

Carara Biological Reserve

Tárcoles

34

Jacó    Pavona

PUNTARENAS

Parrita

Esterillos Este

Quepos    Manuel Antonio

34

*Pacific Ocean*

Manuel Antonio National Park    Rey

From Tárcoles, the highway along the Coast connects lively tourist hubs Jacó, Quepos, and Manuel Antonio, and on down to the South Pacific. This is the place to surf, do a multitude of active tours, laze on the beach, and explore Manuel Antonio National Park.

Manuel Antonio National Park

# CENTRAL PACIFIC PLANNER

## When to Go

Masses arrive during the dry season (late December–May), driving hotel prices up; in Manuel Antonio high-season prices kick in even earlier. Holy Week and the last week of December are the hardest times to find a room. Consider May to August, when the weather tends to sunny days and occasional light rain. Avoid the tip of Nicoya in September and October— heavy rains make road crossing difficult, and many businesses close.

## Crowd Control

Most tourist towns in Costa Rica spring into action after Christmas, but Manuel Antonio's high season activates at the start of December, with rising hotel prices, long park entrance lines, and overcrowded beaches. To avoid the crunch, go June–November. To beat the crowds at the park, get there early—around 7 AM.

## Great Combinations

South of Quepos along the coastal highway lie tranquil beaches, where time seems to stand still, a real contrast with the busy Manuel Antonio area. Dominical makes a great surf spot after Jacó, and Punta Uvita has calm waters and more wildlife than people. From the southern tip of Nicoya, head up the west coast to hop along the endless stretch of beaches. Or ferry back to the mainland to explore Monteverde's cloud forest.

## Getting There

If you're not pressed for time, rent a car or travel by bus, shuttle, or private driver instead of flying from San José to experience beautiful landscapes and typical rural towns. Distances from San José are not overwhelming, and the ferry ride across the Gulf of Nicoya has great views of the mountainous coast and its islands. Buses are timely and economical, but if you prefer an air-conditioned ride, shuttles leave from San José and can drop you off at your hotel's doorstep. Most travelers heading to the southern tip of the Nicoya Peninsula arrive by car from points north or take the ferry from Puntarenas to Paquera. You can also fly into Tambor's airstrip.

## What to Do

| ACTIVITY | WHERE TO DO IT |
| --- | --- |
| Fishing | Quepos, Playa Herradura, Tambor, Malpaís |
| Snorkeling | Isla Tortuga, Manuel Antonio, Cabo Blanco Nature Reserve |
| Surfing | Jacó, Playa Hermosa, Malpaís |
| Wildlife-viewing | Manuel Antonio National Park, Tárcoles River, Cabo Blanco Nature Reserve, Curú National Wildlife Refuge, Carara National Park |
| Yoga | Montezuma, Malpaís, Jacó, Manuel Antonio |
| Zip-line tours | Malpaís, Montezuma, Jacó, Playa Herradura, Playa Hermosa, Manuel Antonio, Quepos |

## Choosing a Place to Stay

The southern Nicoya Peninsula has a good mix of high-quality hotels, nature lodges, and *cabinas* (low-cost Tico-run hotels, often laid out like motels). The Central Pacific "mainland" has some of the country's priciest lodgings, but as a rule, prices drop 20 to 30 percent during the rainy season. Reserve as far in advance as possible during the busy dry season. Near Manuel Antonio National Park, Manuel Antonio is the more activity-rich, attractive, and expensive place to stay (though we've culled the best budget options). Quepos has a wider range of economy hotels and is not as popular, making it ideal for last-minute reservations.

## Recommended Tour Operators

■ **Costa Rica's Temptations** (CRT; ☎ 777-0607 ⊕ www.costarica4u.com) has a variety of Central Pacific tours, plus car rentals, private drivers, shuttle vans, and a 4WD off-the-beaten-path "adventure" transfer between San José and Manuel Antonio.

■ **Cruceros del Sur** (☎ 232-6672 ☐ 220-2103) runs a seven-day natural-history cruise through the Central and South Pacific and to some islands off Panama aboard the *Temptress*, a 63-passenger ship.

■ **King Tours** (☎ 637-7343, 643-2441 ⊕ www.kingtours.com) arranges trips to the top Central Pacific attractions, including Manuel Antonio National Park and Carara Biological Reserve.

■ **Ríos Tropicales** (☎ 233-6455 ⊕ www.riostropicales.com), a high-quality adventure tour company, runs a four-day, three-night sea-kayaking trip ($600) that leaves from Curú National Wildlife Refuge and meanders among the islands of the Gulf of Nicoya. Transport is provided from San José or from Paquera.

### Spring Break All Year

Nightlifers of all ages, including Ticos and tourists, flock to Jacó to party till sunrise, making it the country's liveliest beach town. Jacó draws everyone from partying college kids to groups of men seeking to savor the local beer and ladies, some too young to be legal. (That's a *warning*, not a tip.)

### How Much Time?

A week gives you enough time to visit several beaches on the central coast or get a good grasp of the tip of Nicoya. Don't try to hit every beach in the Central Pacific or you'll defeat the purpose of your vacation: to relax. The larger towns of Manuel Antonio, Jacó, and Montezuma take more time to explore.

## Prices

WHAT IT COSTS in Dollars

| | $$$$ | $$$ | $$ | $ | ¢ |
|---|---|---|---|---|---|
| **Restaurants** | over $25 | $15–$25 | $10–$15 | $5–$10 | under $5 |
| **Hotels** | over $250 | $150–$250 | $75–$150 | $50–$75 | under $50 |

Restaurant prices are per-person for a main course at dinner. Hotel prices are for two people in a standard double room in high season, excluding service and tax (16.4%).

# THE SOUTHERN NICOYA TIP

Revised by
Yolanda
Hernandez

Catch a breathtaking ferry ride that lasts about an hour from Puntarenas to the southern tip of the Nicoya Peninsula, and you'll be just a bumpy bus hop away from gorgeous beaches with waterfalls and tidal pools. Within the region are quiet, well-preserved parks where you can explore caves and pristine forests or travel by boat or sea kayak to remote islands and wildlife preserves for bird-watching, snorkeling, diving, and even camping. Not too remote, and thus at times overcrowded with tours, Isla Tortuga is ringed by some of Costa Rica's most beautiful beaches. If you like to mix nightlife with your outdoor adventures, the towns of Montezuma and Malpaís are often jammed with an international cast of surfers, ecotourists, and eccentrics of all sorts, from practitioners of alternative lifestyles to expatriate American massage therapists living out their dreams. For those who prefer the convenience of luxury resorts, Tambor's got several to choose from.

## Puntarenas

**❶** A stroll around Puntarenas's once glorious neighborhoods quickly reveals that the city's golden age has long since passed. Today, it's a docking point for international cruise ships and the launching pad for ferries heading to the southeast coast of the Nicoya Peninsula. Unless you're waiting to catch the ferry, there's really no other reason to stay in Puntarenas. But if you have some down time here, walk along the Paseo de los Turistas, a beachfront promenade lined with sidewalk lamps and concrete benches along which locals pass on bicycles. From this narrow spit of sand—*punta de arenas* (literally, "point of sand")—which protrudes into the Gulf of Nicoya, you get impressive sunsets and vistas toward the peninsula. On days when cruise ships arrive, the town really livens up and local artisans sell their wares at a market near the dock.

### Where to Eat

**$–$$** ✕ **Gugas.** Simple but elegant, Gugas receives high praises from locals for its fine dining al fresco. "Chicken of the Sea" (fish stuffed with shrimp and spices), pasta dishes, vegeterian options, seafood, and meat plates are all on the menu of this German-owned restaurant. ✉ *100 m north of the cruise-ship port or 100 m from the bus terminal* ☎ *661–4231* ⊟ *AE, DC, MC, V* ⊙ *Closed July.*

**¢–$$** ✕ **Restaurante La Yunta.** This steakhouse is one of Puntarenas's best restaurants. In a 1928 wooden building that originally served as a vacation house for San José's upper class, the old-fashioned restaurant is presided over by mounted ox heads (*la yunta* means a yoked pair of oxen), and has a veranda with a view of the ocean and of passersby strolling down the Paseo. Its specialty is *churrasco* (tenderloin), though its diverse menu includes seafood dishes like sea bass cooked 10 different ways. The liquor list is impressively long. ✉ *West end of Paseo de los Turistas, 100 m east of Hotel Tioga* ☎ *661–3216* ⊟ *AE, DC, MC, V.*

## A Darker Side of Tourism

CLOSE UP

**DESPITE COSTA RICA'S RELATIVE** affluence in Central America—in large part due to its thriving tourism industry—the fact remains that 10% of the country's population still lives in poverty. And while burgeoning tourism has benefitted portions of the population, it has manifested itself in less fortunate ways in more impoverished sectors of society by giving rise to a sex-for-sale trade that some experts say rivals that in Thailand.

The case is bleak for impoverished Costa Ricans, but is worst for women and young girls. Forty percent of girls do not attend school and 41% of births in Costa Rica are to unwed mothers. Prostitution is legal for those over 18 in Costa Rica, but pimping is not, and prostitution of minors certainly is not. There are no statistics on the number of minors involved in prostitution, but it's clear from the many Web sites promoting travel to Costa Rica as a sex-tourism paradise

with plenty of young girls available, that the problem is ongoing. In 1996 the National Institute for Children (PANI) targeted Limón, San José, and Puntarenas as the places where poor children are most susceptible to entering into prostitution; Jacó is another problem area.

In 2004 the U.S. Human Trafficking Report listed Costa Rica as one of the world's worst offendors in the trafficking of women and children into prostitution. To its credit, the administration of President Abel Pacheco has take steps to combat the the problem of the underage sex trade, a refreshing change from his predecessor Miguel Angel Rodríguez, who famously denied in an interview on the ABC News program 20/20 in 2001 that such a problem existed. Steps taken thus far have included crackdowns on brothels, closer surveillance, harsher penalties for offenders, and a Web site that lists photos of missing children.

### To & From Puntarenas
*110 km/68 mi (3 hours) west of San José.*

Buses to Puntarenas leave every hour from San José. From Puntarenas, jump on the ferry to Paquera to explore the southern tip of the Nicoya Peninsula. Located near Puntarenas's tip, the ferry dock is about a 20- to 25-minute walk from the bus station; taxis frequently drive by and can get you there in minutes. Ferries cross with passengers and cars (and livestock). If you don't have a car and you're heading on to a beach town, grab a bus or taxi from the Paquera ferry dock.

Passenger and car ferries run by **Naviera Tambor** (☎ 661–2084) and the **Asociación de Desarrollo Integral Paquera** (☎ 641–0118) connect Puntarenas with Paquera. The trip takes on average 1½ hours, and ferries leave nine times daily at 4, 6:30, 8, and 10:30 AM, noon, and 3:30, 4, 8, and 8:30 PM, with an equal number of return trips at 4:30, 6, 8:30, and 10 AM, and noon, 5:30, 6, and 9:30 PM. Expect long waits on all

The
Central Pacific

*Refugio Silvestre
de Peñas Blancas*

San Ramór

CA1

Esparza

**Puntarenas**
**1**

Caldera

27

Sa

Or

*R. Cuarros*

*R. Tárcol*

Playa
Naranjo

**Carara
Biological
Reserve** **10**

Paquera

**Curú National
Wildlife Refuge**

*San Rafael*

**2**

**Tárcoles** **11**
*Playa la Pita*

Agujas

*Nicoya
Peninsula*

**4**

**Isla
Tortuga**

*Punta Leona*

Herradura

**3** **Playa Tambor
Area**

**Playa Herradura** **12**

Cobano

**5** **Montezuma**

**Santa Teresa**
**8** Carmen
**7**
*Playa
Sta. Teresa*

Cabuya

**Malpaís**
**6**

**Cabo Blanco Absolute
Nature Preserve**

**Jacó**
**13**

see map
page 274

34

**14**

*Cabo Blanco*

*Pta.*

*Isla Cabo Blanco*

0                    20 miles

0                    30 km

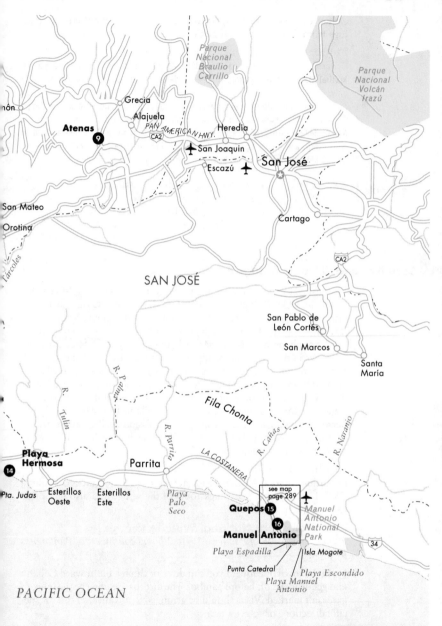

Parque
Nacional
Braulio
Carrillo

Parque
Nacional
Volcán
Irazú

ón

Grecia

**Atenas**
**9**

Alajuela
PAN AMERICAN HWY.
CA2

Heredia

✈ San Joaquin

San José ⊛

Escazú ✈

San Mateo

Orotina

Cartago

CA2

SAN JOSÉ

San Pablo de
León Cortés

San Marcos

Santa
María

Fila Chonta

R. Tárcoles

R. Tulín

R. Palo seco

R. Parrita

LA COSTANERA

R. Cañas

R. Naranjo

**Playa
Hermosa**
**14**

Parrita

Pta. Judas

Esterillos
Oeste

Esterillos
Este

Playa
Palo
Seco

see map
page 289
✈

**Quepos** **15**

**16**

**Manuel Antonio**

Manuel
Antonio
National
Park

34

Playa Espadilla

Isla Mogote

Punta Catedral

Playa Escondido

Playa Manuel
Antonio

*PACIFIC OCEAN*

| KEY |
|---|
| 🚢 · *Ferry lines* |

car ferries in high season and on weekends. Avoid Sunday afternoon crossings from Paquera at any time of the year.

**Puntarenas Essentials**

🏦 Bank/ATM **Banco de Costa Rica** (BCR) ✉ 100 m north of the municipal market. **Mutual Alajuela ATH** ✉ Across from Ferretería Tung Sing, near central market ☞ ATM only.

🏦 Internet **Millennium Cyber Café** ✉ Paseo de Los Turistas, just east of Hotel Tioga.

🏦 Tourist Information **La Camera de Turismo** ✉ Plaza de las Artesanias, in front of Muelle de Cruceros ☎ 661-2980 🕐 Open weekdays 8-noon and 2-5; weekends when cruise ships are in port. **La Oficina de Información Turistica** ✉ Near car ferry terminal ☎ 661-9011 🕐 Open daily 8-5.

---

**en route**

If you take the ferry from Puntarenas to the southern tip of the Nicoya Peninsula, you'll arrive at a ferry dock 5 km (3 mi) north of the small community of **Paquera.** The only reason to spend time here is to pick up supplies or fill up your tank on the way to the beach.

---

# Curú National Wildlife Refuge

🐚 ❷ Established by former farmer and logger turned conservationist Federico Schutt in 1933, Refugio Nacional de Vida Silvestre Curú was named after the indigenous word for the pochote trees that flourish here. Trails lead through the forest and high-salinity mangroves where you see hordes of phantom crabs on the beach, howler and white-faced capuchin monkeys in the trees, and plenty of hummingbirds, kingfishers, woodpeckers, trogons, and manakins (including the coveted long-tailed manakin). The refuge is working to reintroduce spider monkeys and scarlet macaws into the wild. Some very basic accommodations, originally designed for students and researchers, are available by the beach ($25 per person, including three meals and park admission); call ahead to arrange for lodging, guides, and early morning bird-watching walks. ☎ 710–8236 ✉ *refugiocuru@yahoo.com* 🎫 $6 🕐 Daily 7–4.

**Outdoor Activities**

**Luis Schutt Tours** (✉ Main road, across from Esso station, Paquera ☎ 641–0004) gives horseback tours of the refuge and also has a ride to a sparkling white beach.

**To & From Curú National Wildlife Refuge**

*7 km/4½ mi south of Paquera; 1½ to 2 hours southwest of Puntarenas by ferry.*

From the town of Paquera you can drive or catch a bus toward Cóbano and get dropped off before Tambor. The dirt road leading to the refuge's gate isn't marked. Visits should be arranged in advance, so call for specific directions or to get a taxi.

---

**en route**

Paquera is the closest city to Tambor, but if you're headed to Montezuma or Malpaís, you'll pass through **Cóbano,** 12 km (7½ mi) west of Tambor, a bustling crossroads with supermarkets, a bank, restaurants, shops, and a gas station.

## Playa Tambor Area

**❸** Known for luxe hotels and high-end housing developments, wide, tree-less Playa Tambor runs along the large half-moon Bahía Ballena, whose waters are much more placid than other beaches in Nicoya's southern tip. Its cleanliness, however, remains dubious after environmental infractions pinned on the mammoth Barceló resort, owner of most of the land in Tambor. On a brighter note, the tiny fishing village of Tambor hasn't developed as much as Montezuma or Malpaís, which means that its handful of sleeping and eating options are cheap, it's safer, and the locals are more open and less jaded by tourism. Aside from a couple of gift shops, a SANSA airline office, and a FedEx delivery point, there's virtually no sign of tourism in Tambor village. And since guests at the large hotels tend to stay on-site, you won't see many other foreigners walking around. The town's 1910 pink wooden church is worth more than a quick glance.

### Outdoor Activities

Unlike other beach towns, in Tambor you won't find tour operators on every corner or rentals of any kind, not even for a basic bike. The Barceló has a tour desk and all other hotel receptions have information on organized tours. Eduardo at Cabinas Cristina, across from the church, gives tourist information and the inside scoop on the area's hidden treasures.

HIKING One of the few things that you can do on your own in Tambor is hike. From the town's beach access, swing a right and walk along a shady trail, over rocks and sand around the Piedra Amarilla point to Tango Mar Resort—about 8 km (5 mi). The trees along the way resound with the throaty utterings of male howler monkeys.

SPORTFISHING Sailfish, marlin, dorado, tuna, and wahoo are in abundance from December to February, when deep-sea fishing is best. Peak coastal fishing season is November and December, but local fisherman and their small boats are your best guides to finding fish almost year-round. Prices range from $250 half-day trips to $400 for a full-day excursion. Tambor's best catch and release, deep-sea fishing boat is the 29-foot *Phoenix* owned by **End of the Line Sportfishing.** Robert, the owner, captains the boat for nine-hour full-day excursions ($900/group) or half-day trips that last around five hours ($400/group). The boat can carry six people. Lunch, drinks, and fishing gear are included. ✉ *Road from Paquera, just before Tambor's entrance* ☎ *683–0453* ✐ *endofthelinefishing@yahoo.com.*

### Where to Stay & Eat

¢–$$ ✕ **Bahía Ballena Yacht Club.** Get fishing tips and the day's catch in butter and garlic or grilled at this old dockside fisherman's haunt. Don't bother asking for a menu—this laid-back joint doesn't have one. Fridays is rotisserie chicken day, and Saturday serves up thick-crust pizza. Burgers and other basics can be cooked to order. A large central bar, TVs, a pool table, and dart board provide entertainment. ✉ *Road from Paquera, after the entrance to Tambor, left before hill; at the dock* ☎ *683–0213* ▭ *No credit cards.*

**¢–$** ✕ **Perla Tambor.** Between the row of private residences built along the right-hand side of Playa Tambor is this Swiss-owned restaurant that serves a dozen different pasta dishes, cheese fondue, and chicken *cordon bleu,* among other international plates. Surrounded by thick foliage, tables are arranged on an open-air terrace area beneath a white stucco building. The restaurant is a couple of minutes from town on foot along the beach. ⊠ *From Paquera, 50 m after Tambor* ☎ *683–0152* ▭ *MC, V* ☉ *Breakfast served.*

**$$$–$$$$** ⊞ **Tango Mar Resort.** This resort, featured on the TV series *Temptation Island,* lives up to most people's idea of a tropical paradise. Golf carts buzz around the huge 150-acre grounds. The "Tropical Suites," ideal for honeymooners, form a semicircle around a hilltop pool with partial ocean views. Between the reception area, two restaurants, and main pool, "Oceanfronts" are standard hotel rooms with balconies facing the sea. Behind them, the "Tiki Suites" are raised bungalows with ocean views, whirlpool tubs, and other luxurious touches. The plush villas, near the golf course or by the sea, resemble houses that you might see in Beverly Hills. On-site activities abound, such as trails through a nature reserve and to a beachfront waterfall, yoga, and snorkeling. ⊠ *3 km (2 mi) west of Tambor* ☎ *683–0001* 📠 *683–0003* ⊕ *www.tangomar.com* 📑 *4 villas, 18 rooms, 17 suites* ♣ *2 restaurants, a/c, some fans, some kitchens, refrigerators, cable TV, 9-hole golf course, 2 pools, massage, beach, horseback riding, 2 bars, laundry service, Internet, airport shuttle, car service* ▭ *AE, MC, V* ⦿| *BP.*

**★ $$$** ⊞ **Tambor Tropical.** In the town of Tambor, a stone's throw from the beach, this small hotel offers many of the fine touches of bigger hotels, but in a more intimate setting. The floors, ceilings, walls, and even toilet seats of its cabins are made from strips of more than 14 tropical Costa Rican woods. (The fact that many of these trees are rare should raise the eyebrows of any nature lover.) That said, the cabins are beautifully constructed and maintained, with every inch perfectly varnished. The large windows running across the front keep them full of light. Beds are on a platform so you can view the sunrise; second-floor cabins have the best views. The sea breeze and ceiling fans cool the rooms better than air-conditioning, and the TV-less living room area inspires reading and resting. ⊠ *Main street of Tambor toward beach, left* ☎ *683–0011* 📠 *683–0013* ⊕ *www.tambortropical.com* 📑 *10 suites* ♣ *Restaurant, room service, fans, kitchens, golf privileges, pool, whirlpool tub, massage, beach, horseback riding, bar, laundry services, airport shuttle; no a/c, no room phones, no room TVs, no children under 16* ▭ *AE, MC, V* ⦿| *BP.*

## To & From Tambor
*27 km/17 mi south of Paquera.*

You can fly directly to Tambor from San José on SANSA and NatureAir ( ⇨ Air Travel *in* Smart Travel Tips A to Z for schedules). Otherwise, when you arrive by ferry from Puntarenas, hop on the bus to Montezuma and ask to get dropped off at Tambor's entrance. Buses depart daily at 6:15, 7:30, and 10 AM and 12:30, 4:30, and 6:15. Drivers, head down the road toward Cóbano.

### Tambor Essentials
🔲 Internet **Compu-Office del Pacífico** ✉ In small strip mall on left after Costa Coral Hotel, coming from Paquera ☎ 683-0582.

## Isla Tortuga

☾ ❹ Soft white sand and casually leaning palms fringe this island of tropical dry forest off the southern coast of the Nicoya Peninsula. Sounds heavenly? It would be if there weren't so many people. Tours from Jacó, Herradura, San José, Puntarenas, and Montezuma take boatfuls of visitors to drink from coconuts and snorkel around a large rock. You'll see a good number of colorful fish, though in the company of many tourists. But it does make for an easy day trip out to sea. On the boat ride from Montezuma you might spot passing dolphins. A 40-minute hiking trail wanders past monkey ladders, strangler figs, bromeliads, orchids, and the fruit-bearing *guanabana* (soursop) and *marañón* (cashew) trees up to a lookout point with amazing vistas. Though state-owned, the island is leased and inhabited by a Costa Rican family who funded efforts to reintroduce such species as deer and wild pigs to the island some years ago.

### Outdoor Activities
KAYAKING   **Luis Schutt Tours** (✉ Main road, across from Esso station, Paquera ☎ 641-0004 ⊕ www.curuturismo.com), run by the son of the owner, arranges year-round kayak excursions to Isla Tortuga for $20; snorkeling equipment is extra. **Calypso Tours** (☎ 256-2727 🖷 256-6767 ⊕ www.calypsotours.com) takes you to Isla Tortuga from San Jośe, with bus and boat transportation included.

### To & From Isla Tortuga
*90 minutes by boat from Puntarenas.*

Every tour operator in Montezuma ( ⇨ below) offers trips to Isla Tortuga, one of the area's biggest activities, or take a kayak trip from the nearby Curú National Wildlife Refuge. Admission to the island is $7 (included in tour prices).

## Montezuma

❺ Beautifully positioned on a sandy bay, Montezuma is hemmed in by a precipitous wooded shoreline. Its small, funky town center is a pastel cluster of New Age health-food cafés, trendy beachwear shops, and jaunty tour kiosks mixed with older Tico *sodas* (casual eateries) and noisy open-air bars. Most hotels are clustered in or around the town's center, making it very pedestrian friendly. Montezuma has been on the international vagabond circuit for years, attracting backpackers and alternative-lifestyle types. It has an infamous drug reputation, but the community has been changing over the past years, with Internet cafés and more sophisticated hotels and restaurants. Thankfullly, its development remains manageable, compared to other beach towns that have been invaded by large franchise hotels and strip-mall developers. Despite its growth, Montezuma retains its very green atmosphere and holistic personality.

While it mostly fills up with tattooed travelers in their 20s and 30s, today more than ever you are likely to come across older, outdoorsy European tourists. The main attraction for everybody is the beautiful virgin beach that stretches across one national park and two nature preserves to the north. A good walk (about 2½ hours) or horseback ride leads to a beachfront waterfall; swimming at the waterfall is prohibited.

The **Karen Mogensen Fischer Museum** (✉ Internet Café, El Sano Banano Restaurant) details conservation contributions to the area's forests made by Nicolas and Karen Wessberg, who founded the Cabo Blanco Absolute Nature Preserve (⇨ *below*). It includes photos of the Wessbergs living in the virgin jungle.

## Outdoor Activities

Almost every second storefront is occupied by a tour operator in central Montezuma. They seem to work together more than against each other, and have standarized costs for the most popular activities, saving you the hassle of comparing prices. **Aventuras en Montezuma** (⇨ ATV Tours, *below*) can give you information about the area's activities, like boat and fishing trips. The oldest and most experienced tour group in Montezuma, **Cocozuma Traveller** (✉ Main road, next to El Sano Banano Internet Montezuma ☎ 642–0911 ⊕ www.cocozuma.com) offers just about every activity that's popular in the area, including horseback riding tours to the beachfront waterfall, full-day snorkeling trips to Isla Tortuga, fishing trips, canopy rides, and excursions to the nearby Curú reserve.

ATV TOURS   **Aventuras en Montezuma** (✉ Main Rd. ☎ 642–0050 ⊕ www.zumatours. com) is your only connection to ATV tours, which visit the other side of the peninsula.

HORSEBACK RIDING   A Montezuma favorite is the horse ride along the beach to the "Chorro" oceanfront waterfall, which used to be more impressive and swimmable prior to a landslide. Guides usually will take you afterward for a refreshing dip in a nearby river. Hop on an organized tour with any operator in town, including Cocozuma Traveller (⇨ *above*). Trips around sunset are highly recommended.

HIKING   Hiking is one of the best ways to explore Montezuma's natural treasures, including beaches, jungles, and waterfalls. There are plenty of options around town or in nearby parks and reserves. Just over a bridge, 10 minutes south of town, a slippery path patrolled by howler monkeys leads upstream to two waterfalls, the second one an impressive 108 feet, ★ with a fun **swimming hole.** If you value your life, don't jump or dive from the waterfalls. Guides from any tour operator in town can escort you, but save your money. This one you can do on your own. To reach the famous **El Chorro waterfall** on the beach, head left from the main beach access. The beautiful cascade lost some height and magnitude after a rough rainy season instigated a landslide that left it smaller and unswimmable, but still impressive. The roughly 2½-hour walk along the sand takes you across seven adjacent beaches. Bring water and good sunblock.

### Where to Stay & Eat

**$$** ✕ **Playa de los Artistas.** This open-air Italian restaurant with driftwood
Fodor'sChoice  tables scattered along the beach specializes in modern Mediterranean-
★  style seafood. Flickering lanterns combine with crashing surf to create
a romantic and relaxed dinner experience. Portions are plentiful and dra-
matically presented on huge platters. Eighty percent of the eclectic menu
changes daily, and an outdoor, coffee-wood oven gives a tropical aroma
to pizza, fish, and pork. Try the tuna carpaccio, a raw tuna appetizer
seasoned with oregano and garlic, and soak up the marinade with
freshly baked, savory focaccia. The smaller lunch menu lists primarily
homemade pasta dishes. ⊠ *275 m south of town, just past Los Man-
gos Hotel* ☎ *642–0920* ▤ *No credit cards* ⊘ *Closed Sun. and Oct.*

**$-$$** ✕ **El Sano Banano Restaurant.** Seafood, hormone-free chicken, and half
a dozen pasta dishes are included on the mostly vegetarian menu at Mon-
tezuma's first natural-food restaurant, named after the dried bananas
the owners originally sold. A terrace café provides excellent people-watching, as well as tall glasses of sinfully delicious Mocha Chiller, made with
frozen yogurt, and a wide variety of coffee drinks and desserts. A bat-
talion of ceiling fans keeps the air moving in the spacious, adobe-style
restaurant with green plastic chairs. It's open for breakfast from 7 AM;
a free movie is shown nightly at 7:30 PM in the dining room. ⊠ *Main
Rd.* ☎ *642–0638* ▤ *AE, MC, V.*

**¢** ✕ **Cafe Iguana.** On Montezuma's busiest corner, this colorful café with
modern ambient music serves up real Italian espresso, hot chocolate, fresh
fruit juices, and an impressive selection of baked goods, including huge
muffins, banana bread, and exotic coconut crumble. Overstuffed sandwiches, made on fresh, crusty home-baked bread or bagels, are big
enough for two. Ice cream is homemade. Wooden stools on a terrace are
perfect perches for watching the passing parade of colorful locals and
visitors. It opens at 6 AM. ⊠ *Town center, in front of Hotel Montezuma*
☎ *642–0422* ▤ *No credit cards* ⊘ *Breakfast served; closed in May.*

**$-$$** ✕▦ **Luz de Mono.** About 50 meters from the beach, downtown Mon-
tezuma's most elegant hotel has comfortable, tastefully decorated rooms
surrounded by large trees and rich vegetation. The front open-air dome
contains a low-key bar and restaurant and sometimes has live rock and
electronic music. Gravel trails lead to ample, all-white rooms with
wooden trim and furniture and original artwork. Fully equipped, secluded
concrete villas have the comforts of home and large wooden decks with
sea views. ⊠ *End of the main road, across from beach entrance*
☎ *642–0090* 🖷 *642–0010* ⊕ *www.luzdemono.com* ⇆ *12 rooms, 7 villas* ⚒ *Restaurant, fans, in-room safes, some kitchens, refrigerators, bar,
nightclub, laundry service, Internet, airport shuttle; no room phones*
▤ *AE, MC, V* ⎯ʘⱴ *BP.*

**$** ✕▦ **El Sano Banano Hotel Village.** Smack in the middle of Montezuma,
above the restaurant of the same name, guests of this hotel can walk to
Ylang-Ylang to swim in the pool and use its other facilities. Rooms have
huge showers. Aside from faint traces of music, the place is amazingly
quiet for its location near the town's nightlife. Cooking smells sometimes drift into the hallway from the kitchen below. Ask for a room with
a window to the garden or street, or you'll be staring at the wall of an

adjacent building. ✉ *Main Rd.* ☎ *642–0638* 🖨 *642–0631* 📧 *elbanano@reservation.com* 🛏 *14 rooms* ⚭ *Restaurant, a/c, cable TV, bar, laundry service, Internet café, no-smoking rooms; no room phones* 🖃 *AE, MC, V* ⦿ *BP.*

**$$–$$$**
Fodor'sChoice
★
🏨 **Ylang-Ylang Beach Resort.** Secluded and quiet, this tropical resort (formerly the El Sano Banano Beach Hotel) with a holistic slant is a 10-minute beach walk from town. Nestled between the sea and a lush forest, the geodesic-dome bungalows are snug but charming, with outdoor showers and terraces. Some have direct sea views and cozy loft sleeping areas for two. Facing the beach, a two-story building has three comfortable suites with balconies and three double rooms below. Adding to the romance is a garden-fringed pool with a waterfall. An array of yoga classes and spa services are offered, and a restaurant with tables under the stars serves some of the tastiest fusion dishes in Montezuma. The reception desk is at the El Sano Banano Restaurant in town. ✉ *700 m north of school in Montezuma, on the beach* ☎ *642–0636* 🖨 *642–0068* ⊕ *www.ylangylangresort.com* 🛏 *3 rooms, 3 suites, 8 bungalows* ⚭ *Restaurant, fans, in-room safes, refrigerators, pool, massage, beach, bar, shop, laundry service; no a/c, no room phones, no room TVs* 🖃 *AE, MC, V* ⦿ *BP.*

**$**
🏨 **Horizontes de Montezuma.** Montezuma's only Spanish-language center is perched on a hill a mile from town, and rents its rooms to students and travelers. The impressive white Caribbean-style house has wooden verandas, French doors, and a black-and-white tile floor. Its elegant stairway leads to three corner rooms with ample balconies and four smaller airy ones. Some rooms have views of the sea, others of the surrounding jungle. Tastefully decorated, the white rooms are simple, but sufficient. A large terrace evokes a Parisian café (though no food or drinks are served), and has a reading area with comfortable wicker chairs. The small pool in front is surrounded by a green lawn and gardens. Enjoy beautiful sunsets, cool nighttime temperatures, and a jungle trail through the 6-acre property. ✉ *1.8 km north of Playa Montezuma* ☎ *642–0534* 🖨 *642–0625* ⊕ *www.horizontes-montezuma.com* 🛏 *7 rooms* ⚭ *Fans, pool, massage, laundry service; no a/c, no room phones, no room TVs* 🖃 *No credit cards* ⦿ *EP.*

**$**
🏨 **Hotel Amor de Mar.** Take the time to walk the ¼ mi south of town to find this ruggedly handsome, two-story wooden hotel across from the waterfall's entrance. A grassy lawn stretches to the rocky seashore, where you can cool off in a natural tidal pool or in a palm-shaded hammock. It has a peaceful and intimate atmosphere, coupled with great homemade breakfasts. The wood-paneled rooms are rustic but comfortable; second-floor rooms have more windows. Two of the rooms share a bathroom and are a few bucks cheaper. A two-story, equipped oceanfront house has four bedrooms. ✉ *300 m south of town, just past bridge, left-hand side* ☎ *642–0262* ⊕ *www.amordemar.com* 🛏 *11 rooms, 9 with bath; 1 house* ⚭ *Restaurant, fans, some refrigerators, laundry service; no a/c, no room phones, no room TVs* 🖃 *MC, V* ⦿ *EP.*

**$**
🏨 **Hotel El Jardín.** On a hill in a tranquil section of town, this hotel has panoramic ocean views. True to its name, the rooms are scattered around a garden lush with ginger flowers and populated by stone sculptures of indigenous peoples. Teak paneling and furniture, stained-glass pictorial panels, and terraces with hammocks give this hotel style as well as com-

fort, though not all rooms have hot water. Request a top-floor room with sea views. There's no formal breakfast, but fresh fruit and coffee are laid out in the reception area each morning. ⊠ *Main road, top of northern hill* ☎ 642–0548 🖷 642–0074 ⊕ *www.hoteleljardin.com* 🖘 *14 rooms, one house* ⚲ *Some a/c, some fans, refrigerators, pool, whirlpool tub; no phones in some rooms, no room TVs* ▤ *AE, DC, MC, V* ⦿| *EP.*

$ 🏠 **Hotel El Tajalín.** A short walk from the beach and in a quiet part of town, this hotel has spacious rooms but a somewhat sterile atmosphere. Rooms are spread out across the concrete building's three floors, and only one has a private balcony. Skip the dull first-floor rooms; those on the second level are much roomier, and have refrigerators and wood floors. On the top floor an open-air lounge has hammocks, tables, and books. During the high season (December–May) a complimentary breakfast is offered at a nearby Italian café. ⊠*Behind the soccer field* ☎642–0061 🖷642–0527 ⊕ *www.tajalin.com* 🖘 *12 rooms* ⚲ *A/c, some fans, some refrigerators; no room phones, no room TVs* ▤ *MC, V* ⦿| *BP* ⊘ *Closed Sept. and Oct.*

★ $ 🏠 **Nature Lodge Finca los Caballos.** A long dirt road leads to this cozy equestrian paradise high on a hill, with 10 horses grazing around its vast 14 acres, just a short ride from Montezuma center. Five different horse tours are offered to nearby waterfalls, mountains, or the Curú Reserve. Bird-watching is also a popular activity here. The open-air restaurant, reading chairs, and pool have bird's-eye views of the ocean and valley below. Designed with a southwestern U.S. motif, the small, simple rooms have pastel walls decorated with stencils of lizards and frogs; all have hammocks in front, but only four have forest views. The others have views of the property. The restaurant serves dinner to nonguests by reservation. ⊠ *3 km (2 mi) north of Montezuma on main Rd.* ☎ 642–0124 🖷 642–0664 ⊕ *www.naturelodge.net* 🖘 *8 rooms* ⚲ *Restaurant, fans, pool, massage, horseback riding, bar, laundry service, airport shuttle, no-smoking rooms; no a/c, no room phones, no room TVs* ▤ *MC, V* ⦿| *EP* ⊘ *Closed Sept. and Oct.*

¢–$ 🏠 **Los Mangos Hotel.** Within sight and sound of the sea, these affordable octagonal wood cabins with wraparound decks are spread out across a wide shady mango grove. Even more affordable are the rooms in the rose-colored two-story building with verandas and rocking chairs facing the sea. Some rooms share (cold-water) baths, and all cabins have one double and one single bed. The secluded, scenic pool has ocean views. Yoga classes are given in an open-air pavilion. ⊠ *Just before entrance to waterfall trail, ¼ mi south of town* ☎ 642–0076 🖷 642–0259 ⊕ *www.hotellosmangos.com* 🖘 *10 rooms, 6 with bath; 9 cabins* ⚲ *Fans, some refrigerators, pool, whirlpool tub, massage; no a/c, no room phones, no room TVs* ⦿| *EP* ▤ *MC, V.*

¢ 🏠 **Hotel Lucy.** Montezuma's first hotel is still run by the same hospitable family and retains some of the lowest prices in town. The two-story renovated structure stands directly facing the sea, and though not every room enjoys the view, a communal veranda facing the ocean is open to all. Most of the spartan rooms share a cold-water shower. Private (cold-water) baths cost extra. Rooms on the second-floor heat up during the day. There's no formal reception, so you may have to walk to the side of the building, where family members are usually sitting under the shade. Lucy, the owner's daughter, runs a seaside restaurant next door that serves good and inexpensive breakfasts, lunches, and dinners. ⊠ *200 m south of town, in front of Hotel Los Mangos* ☎ *642–0273* ⬎ *19 rooms, 7 with bath* ⛁ *Fans, laundry service; no a/c, no room phones, no room TVs* ⊟ *No credit cards* ⍥ *EP.*

¢ ▦ **Mochila Inn.** As its name suggests, "Backpack Inn" draws globetrotters hunting a bargain. This rustic and friendly hotel is tucked within a forest of immense trees on the fringe of town. Though it's several blocks from the main beach entrance, its tranquillity ushers in the sound of crashing waves. Four cozy wooden cabins keep cool under the shady trees and have outdoor showers; "La Vista" cabin has a view of the sea. One room near the communal kitchen is also available for rent. ⊠ *From the center of Montezuma, 75 m toward Cabuya* ☎ *642–0030* ⬎ *4 cabins, 1 room* ⊕ *www.mochilainn.com* ⛁ *Fans, some kitchenettes, refrigerators, laundry facilities; no a/c, no room phones, no room TVs* ⍥ *EP.*

## Nightlife

Though options are extremely limited, Montezuma's nightlife scene is growing. Locals and foreigners mix at pool tables or late-night clubs, refreshing after larger beach towns where the clientele tends to be more segregated. Streetside artisans selling their creations oftentimes animate the area with drumming and dancing that draws passerbys to stop and shake their hips too.

The only bar in Montezuma, **Chico's Bar** (⊠ Center of town, next to Hotel Moctezuma) blasts music from its dark, uninviting entrance, but farther back is a brighter, spacious deck with pool tables and dancing. Directly behind Chico's Bar is **Chico's Playa**, an open-air bar with has softer music, tables in the sand, and a more laid-back atmosphere. The bar at the entrance of open-air seafood eatery **Restaurante Montezuma** (⊠ Center of town, next to Hotel Moctezuma ☎ 643–0657) is a favorite with locals and serves the cheapest beers in Montezuma. At night, tables in the sand are lit by candles and moonlight. Once Chico's closes next door, the crowd comes in for the late-night party shift, which is sometimes animated by house music or other DJ-generated styles.

## Shopping

Beachwear, banana paper, wooden crafts, and indigenous pottery are some of what you find in colorful shops in the town's center. During the dry season, traveling artisans from around the world unfold their streetside tables just before the sun begins to set; candles light up the handmade leather-and-seed jewelry, dreamcatchers, and knit tops. For some intellectual stimulation at the beach, head to **Librería Topsy** (☎ 642–0576 ⊠ Across from the school), where you can buy, exchange, or rent a book—one whole room is devoted to a lending library. Some foreign newspapers are available.

## To & From Montezuma

7 km/4½ mi southeast of Cóbano, 45 km/28 mi (15 minutes) south of Paquera, 18 km/11 mi (1½–2 hours) south of Tambor.

There are two routes into town, both bumpy and unpaved. Buses to Montezuma stop in Cóbano. They depart from Paquera daily at 6:15, 7:30, and

10 AM and 12:30, 4:30, and 6:15. Buses drop you off in the center of town. To continue to Malpaís, you have to switch buses in Cóbano. For Tambor, take a Paquera bus and ask the driver to stop at the town's entrance. Air-conditioned bus transfers can be arranged with any tour operator.

### Montezuma Essentials

🏧 ATM **Yacamares** ⊠ In front of Super Mamatea.

🖥 Internet **Surf the Banana Internet Café** ⊠ Main road, next to El Sano Banano Restaurant.

📮 Post Office **Librería Topsy** ⊠ Across from school ☞ Posts letters.

---

## Cabo Blanco Absolute Nature Preserve

**6** Conquistadores named this area Cabo Blanco on account of its white earth and cliffs, but it was a more benevolent pair of foreigners—Nicolas Wessberg and his wife, Karen, arriving here from Sweden in 1950—who made it a preserve (Reserva Natural Absoluta Cabo Blanco, in Spanish). Appalled by the first clear-cut in the Cabo Blanco area in 1960, the couple launched a pioneering and international appeal to save the forest. In time their efforts led not only to the creation of the 12-square-km (4½-square-mi) reserve but also to the founding of Costa Rica's national park service, the National Conservation Areas System (SINAC). Wessberg was murdered on the Osa Peninsula in 1975 while researching the area's potential as a national park. A reserve just outside Montezuma was named in his honor. A reserve has also been created to honor his wife, who dedicated her life to conservation after her husband's death.

Informative natural-history captions dot the trails in the moist evergreen forest of Cabo Blanco. Look for the sapodilla trees, which produce a white latex used to make gum; you can often see V-shape scars where the trees have been cut to allow the latex to run into containers placed at the base. Wessberg cataloged a full array of animals here: porcupine, hog-nosed skunk, spotted skunk, gray fox, anteater, cougar, and jaguar. Resident birds include brown pelicans, white-throated magpies, toucans, cattle egrets, green herons, parrots, and turquoise-browed motmots. A fairly strenuous 4-km (2½-mi) hike, which takes about two hours in each direction, follows a trail from the reserve entrance to **Playa Cabo Blanco.** The beach is magnificent, with hundreds of pelicans flying in formation and paddling in the calm waters offshore—you can wade right in and join them. Off the tip of the cape is the 7,511-square-foot **Isla Cabo Blanco,** with pelicans, frigate birds, brown boobies, and an abandoned lighthouse. As a strict reserve, Cabo Blanco has bathrooms and a visitor center but no other tourist facilities. Rangers and volunteers act as guides. ☎ 642–0093 ⊕ *www.asepaleco.org* ✉ *$8* ☼ *Wed.–Sun. 8–4.*

### To & From Cabo Blanco Preserve

*10 km/6 mi southwest of Montezuma, about 11 km/7 mi south of Malpaís.*

Roads to the reserve are usually passable only in the dry season, unless you have a 4WD. From Montezuma or Malpaís, take the road to Cabuya. Taxis can take you to or from Montezuma, but buses toward the park also leave from Montezuma daily at 8 AM and 10 AM.

## Malpaís & Santa Teresa

 This remote fishing village was once frequented only by die-hard surfers in search of some of the country's largest waves and by naturalists en route to the nearby Cabo Blanco Nature Preserve. The town and its miles of beach are accessible only down a steep gravel road. But now hotels, restaurants, and shopping centers are springing up at an alarming rate—especially toward the Santa Teresa side—despite the bad roads. Coming from Montezuma, the road ends at a T intersection, with the beach (the west coast of the peninsula) ahead of you. To the left is Malpaís, a tranquil fishing village with a handful of hotels and restaurants along its gravel road, but primarily residential homes. (Rumor has it that a large chain hotel is on its way though.) Playa Malpaís is rockier than Playas Santa Teresa and Carmen, but has tidal pools and is ripe for beach-combing. To the right at the intersection is the Santa Teresa area, which is more commercial, with more hotels, restaurants, markets, and a strip mall. Santa Teresa is parallel to Playa Carmen, the area's best place for surfing and swimming. Malpaís and Santa Teresa are so close that locals disagree on where one begins and the other ends. You could travel up the road parallel to the ocean that connects them and not realize you've moved from one town to the other.

The crowds in both beach towns are are fairly young, with tanned-and-buff surfers walking or bicycling their boards to wherever the surf is up, especially in Santa Teresa. But increasingly, older, more upscale visitors are drawn to the tranquillity of luxury retreats that cater to mind and body. The Malpaís-Santa Teresa road is long and challenging for walkers. But a car isn't obligatory; you can get around on bikes and ATVs, which can be rented at multiple places of comparable quality in each town.

> ### WORD OF MOUTH
>
> "The best part of Santa Teresa is the beach. I guarantee you will never see a beach like this ever! You have to see it to believe me. This town is so great and you really get a feel for the culture and life here. There are hardly [any] tourists here except for surfers, which is wonderful. So if you go, do not expect to be pampered."
> –audraf

### Outdoor Activities

Your hotel's reception is probably the best resource for area activities. Otherwise, the Internet café next to Frank's Place offers tourist information. If you speak some Spanish, you can ask locals in Malpaís's fishing village to take you out to sea or horseback riding along the beach or into nearby mountains.

CANOPY TOUR **Canopy del Pacífico** (⊠ In front of fisherman's village, Malpaís ☎ 640–0360, 640–0071 ⊕ www.malpais.net/canopy.htm) is the only canopy tour in the area. You can walk, glide, or rappel through 64 acres of forest.

SURFING **Playa Carmen** is the area's most consistent surf spot for all levels. In rocky Malpaís, across from **Mar Azul**, more advanced surfers like to catch stronger waves that result from swells. The handful of surf shops in Santa Teresa can connect you with experienced surfing teachers and board rentals and repairs.

## Where to Stay & Eat

**$$–$$$** ✕ **Nectar.** Resort Florblanca's alfresco restaurant is laid out by the pool with some tables enjoying calming sea views. Aside from a vegetarian and pasta menu, expect to find grilled filet mignon and fresh seafood that changes according to the day's catch. Green salads are organic, and the restaurant's international chef stresses a French-Asian influence in his dishes. From December to May, buffet-style BBQ dinners are offered each Sunday with live music. ⊠ *Resort Florblanca, 2 km/1 mi north of soccer field, Santa Teresa* ☎ *640–0232* ▭ *AE, DC, MC, V* ☉ *Breakfast served.*

★ **$$** ✕ **Soma.** This small restaurant within the Milarepa hotel serves up delicious and creative Latin-inspired plates. Specials change each night, and can include garlic papaya soup, seared tuna with plaintains, or pork chops with mashed sweet potatoes. A vegetarian special is also always offered in this tranquil restaurant, whose name comes from the Huxley classic *Brave New World*. Tables are arranged under an open-air poolside deck. ⊠ *Milarepa hotel, toward the end of town, beside Resort Florblanca, Santa Teresa* ☎ *640–0023* ▭ *No credit cards* ☉ *Closed mid-Sept. to mid-Oct. Breakfast served.*

**¢–$** ✕ **Piedra Mar.** With all the new restaurants popping up along the beach road, the favorite standby is still this old shack down on the beach. Tables and plastic chairs are set up under a corrugated tin roof, and the only decor is the rocky seascape, 10 feet away. Your shrimp or lobster (for less than $10) comes flavored with garlic and—on windy days—the sea spray crashing against the rocks. Sunset is popular with locals in the know, so come early. Or come for breakfast at 7 and watch the early morning sun lighting up the ocean. ⊠ *275 m south of Blue Jay Lodge, Malpaís* ☎ *640–0069* ▭ *No credit cards* ☉ *Breakfast served.*

**$$$$** ✕⌂ **Resort Florblanca.** Named for the white flowers of the frangipani
Fodor'sChoice    trees that shade the beachfront property, this collection of simply lux-
★    urious villas ministers to body and soul with a heavy Eastern-influenced decor. Secluded at the northern end of Santa Teresa, the handsome and spacious villas have outdoor Balinese-inspired bathrooms and sunken tubs. Most villas have one air-conditioned bedroom with a king-size bed; two-bedroom villas have a second room with twin beds. Three villas have sea views. A dojo for yoga classes faces the ocean, and a massage therapist is on staff to work out your kinks. The only TV is in a comfortable lounge. Two pools flow into each other in front of Nectar (⇨ *above*), the hotel's restaurant. ⊠ *2 km (1 mi) north of soccer field, Santa Teresa* ☎ *640–0232* 🖷 *640–0226* ⊕ *www.florblanca.com* ⇥ *10 villas* ⌂ *Restaurant, room service, a/c, fans, in-room safes, refrigerators, 2 pools, fitness room, massage, spa, beach, snorkeling, mountain bikes, hiking, horseback riding, bar, shop, Internet; no room TVs, no children under 8* ▭ *AE, DC, MC, V* ⦿| *BP.*

★ **$$** ✕⌂ **Milarepa.** Named after a famous Buddhist saint from Tibet who gained enlightenment in just one lifetime, Milarepa is a perfect place for peaceful renewal, whether romantic or spiritual. The four bamboo bun-

5

galows are spaced apart to ensure privacy and are furnished in ascetic but exquisite taste, with carved Indonesian wooden beds draped with mosquito netting, and bamboo armoires. Bathrooms are open to the sky, with alcoves for Buddhist deities. Each bungalow has a veranda looking out onto the carefully raked white beach, shaded by a grove of palms. Beachfront bungalows cost a bit more than those with ocean views but set farther back. A large

> **WORD OF MOUTH**
>
> "My husband has been surfing for over 30 years and has made 14 trips to CR to surf. He had GREAT surf [in Malpaís.] In fact, it was so big on our last morning he couldn't even get out. Just paddled and paddled and got nowhere. I thought it was funny, but he was not amused!"
>
> –Ally

pool lies next to Soma (⇨ *above*), the hotel's restaurant. ⊠ *2 km (1 mi) north of school, beside Resort Florblanca, Santa Teresa* ☎ *640–0023* 🖷 *640–0168* ⊕ *www.milarepahotel.com* ⤳ *4 cottages* ♨ *Restaurant, fans, in-room safes, pool, massage, yoga, beach, surfboards, bar laundry service; no a/c, no room phones, no room TVs* 🖃 *MC, V* ¶◎¶ *BP.*

**$$** 🏠 **Blue Jay Lodge.** This enchanting nature lodge evokes the old Disney flick *Swiss Family Robinson*. Tucked in a forested mountainside, the wood cabins feel like treehouses. Raised walkways lead to the rustic aeries built on stilts, with only screens for walls on three side. Hot-water showers and balconies with hammocks add to the simple comforts. Ceiling fans keep the air moving, but warm blankets are on hand for cool, breezy nights. Breakfast is in the wooden-terrace restaurant at ground level. The beach is 200 meters away, or you can climb the mountain trail to look for birds and howler monkeys. Apart from campsites, it's rare to find a place where you're so entrenched in the forest. ⊠ *From the crossroads, 800 m south toward Malpaís* ☎ *640–0089 or 640–0342* 🖷 *640–0141* ⊕ *www.bluejaylodgecostarica.com* ⤳ *7 cabins* ♨ *Restaurant, fans, pool, massage, bicycles, horseback riding, snorkeling, laundry service; no a/c, no room phones, no room TVs* 🖃 *AE, D, MC, V* ¶◎¶ *BP.*

Fodor'sChoice
★

**$** 🏠 **Ritmo Tropical.** Tranquil, comfortable, and nicely priced, the red-tile roof cabins here are simple, yet tasteful, with wooden ceilings, a rack for surfboards, and front terraces with chairs. Some cabins, arranged in a semicircle around a gravel garden, have views of the sea and the jungle behind. A pizzeria, in front of the property, also serves breakfast. ⊠ *Shortly after the crossroads on road toward Malpaís* ☎ *640–0174* ✉ *ritmotropical@racsa.co.cr* ⤳ *8 rooms* ♨ *Restaurant, fans, in-room safes, bar; no room phones, no a/c, no room TVs* 🖃 *No credit cards* ☉ *Closed Sept. and Oct. Breakfast served* ¶◎¶ *EP.*

☾ ¢ 🏠 **Frank's Place.** This is the first hotel you'll see when you arrive in the area, and it was the second hotel built in Malpaís. Owned by a former fisherman, it has grown significantly and is oftentimes full due to its location and low prices. Some rooms share a bathroom, others have their own (cold-water) shower, and the most expensive ones have air-conditioning, cable TVs, and hot water, and include breakfast. Rooms lie around the pool and gardens. The friendly staff is helpful in giving tourist information and rents ATVs. Skip the restaurant; local food can be found at better prices elsewhere. An Internet café is just next door. ⊠ *At the crossroads, on main road into Malpaís* ☎☎ *640–0096* ✆ *frank5@racsa. co.cr* ↘ *20 rooms, 6 with shared bath* ⚭ *Restaurant, room service, some a/c, some fans, some kitchens, some cable TV, pool, massage, bicycles, ATVs, bar; no room phones* ▤ *AE, D, MC, V* ❢❢ *EP.*

¢ ▦ **Los Tres Pinedas.** Behind Soda la Sirenita, a low-cost local eatery in front of Playa Carmen, this small, family-run motel has some of the cheapest rooms in the area. Two rows of rooms face each other, separated by a large green lawn with mountains in the background. The sky-blue rooms have either two twin beds or one double. Those with their own bathroom also have a refrigerator; bathrooms do not have hot water. A front porch has chairs for reading and relaxing. ⊠ *50 m north of Frank's Place, Malpaís* ☎☎ *640–0172* ↘ *8 rooms with shared bath* ⚭ *Restaurant, fans, some refrigerators; no room phones, no room TVs, no a/c* ▤ *No credit cards* ❢❢ *EP.*

### To & From Malpaís & Santa Teresa
*12 km/7½ mi southwest of Cóbano, 52 km/33 mi south of Paquera.*

From Paquera, take the road to Cóbano and then on to Malpaís passing by San Isidro. The dirt road to Malpaís can become quite muddy in the rainy season. There are no direct buses from Paquera to Malpaís; you have to change buses in Cóbano. Paquera–Cóbano buses depart at 6:15, 7:30, and 10 AM and 12:30, 4:30, and 6:15 daily. Cóbano–Malpaís buses depart at 10:30 AM and 2:30 PM. To head to Montezuma or back to Paquera, catch corresponding buses from Cóbano. **Extreme Boat** ( ☎ *640–0600* ⊕ *www.extboat.com.*) shuttles surfers between Malpaís and Jacó, Monday through Thursday.

# INLAND

Beaches may be this region's biggest draw, but the countryside holds some splendid scenery, from the steep coffee farms around Atenas to the tropical forests of the lowlands. In the wilderness of Carara Biological Reserve and surroundings, you might encounter white-faced capuchin monkeys in the trees or crocodiles lounging on a riverbank. Because it's an ecological transition zone, the region is extremely diverse biologically, making it a boon for bird-watchers and other wildlife enthusiasts.

## Atenas

❾ Known for its excellent cool-evening climate, Atenas is a pleasant, friendly town surrounded by a hilly countryside of coffee and cane fields, cattle ranches, and patches of forest. The small city has some charming mountaintop bed-and-breakfasts with breathtaking views that make for a relaxing stay on your way to or from the Central Pacific beaches. Plus, the fact that it's not on the tourist circuit means that here, unlike other highly popular destinations, you'll walk alongside more Costa Ricans than foreigners and get a more authentic idea of the country. Gazing at the tree-covered peaks and exploring the forest by horseback or mountain motorcycle are the main activities in this traditional town. Atenas's center has a concrete church, some well-kept wooden and adobe houses, and a central park dominated by royal palms.

## Outdoor Activities

Local hotels can recommend guides for horseback trips. **Villas de la Colina** (⊠ 4 km/2 mi west and 2 km/1 mi north of Coopeatenas ☎ 446–5015 🖷 446–8545) rents motorcycles and leads motorcycle tours through the nearby mountains.

**SIDESTEP SAN JOSÉ**

Some visitors to Costa Rica prefer using Atenas as their first- and last-night base camp instead of San José, since Atenas is smaller, friendlier, more tranquil, and safer. The international airport is geographically closer to Atenas, but the hilly roads make the ride slightly longer than on San José's express highway.

## Where to Stay & Eat

¢–$  ✕ **Mirador del Cafetal.** An obligatory stop even if it's just for a cup of coffee, this open-air restaurant next to the road between Atenas and Jacó is a great spot to enjoy the view of steep hillsides covered with coffee trees. The best view is from the long countertops with stools that line the edge of the building, but the wooden tables and chairs might be more comfortable. A mix of Costa Rican and Mexican cuisine is served, including side orders like miniature tamales, black-bean purée, and *patacones* (fried, squashed plantain slices). If you're hungry for more, try chicken in a tomato-and-onion sauce or *sopa azteca* (a tomato-based soup). The restaurant's own brand of coffee is sold by the pound. ⊠ *Road to Jacó, 6 km (3 mi) west of Atenas* ☎ 446–7361.

¢  ✕ **C@fé K–puchinos.** A good place to get a bite and check your e-mail (via a high-speed connection), this corner café in a papaya-colored 1900s house stands across from the town's palm-shaded central park. The Spanish owners serve a good selection of breakfast items, coffee drinks, pizzas, pastas, sandwiches, and salads, as well as meals such as sautéed shrimp and salmon in a wine sauce. Spanish culture influences menu items such as sangria and the *tortilla española* (Spanish omelet, with potatoes and onions). This is the only place we found in town with tourist information. ⊠ *Across from northwestern corner of central park* ☎ 446–8771 🖷 *No credit cards* ☉ *Closes at 8 PM Apr.–Dec (and at 10 PM Jan.–Nov.).*

$$  🖭 **El Cafetal Inn.** This extremely charming bed-and-breakfast feels and

FodorsChoice  looks more like a friend's house than a hotel. The living-room area has
★  wedding pictures of the friendly Salvadorean-Colombian owners, who go out of their way to make you feel at ease and help with your travel plans. On a hilltop coffee farm, the two-story concrete lodge has comfortable accommodations with fabulous vistas. The second-floor corner rooms are larger and have curved windows for panoramic views. Breakfast, which includes home-grown and -roasted coffee, is served on the back garden patio. ⊠ *8 km (5 mi) north of Atenas; heading west from San José on highway to Puntarenas, turn left (south) just before bridge 5 km (3 mi) west of Grecia, then follow signs, Santa Eulalia de Atenas* ☎ 446–5785 🖷 446–7028 ⊕ *www.cafetal.com* ☞ *12 rooms* ⟁ *Restaurant, fans, pool, bar, laundry service, no-smoking rooms; no a/c, no room phones, no room TVs* 🖷 *AE, MC, V* ⦿ *BP.*

$  🖭 **Ana's Place.** This former residence turned bed-and-breakfast is close to Atenas's center, so you can easily get to it by foot. Rooms within the house have parquet floors and big windows, but not all have private bathrooms. The basic cabinas next to the tree- and flower-filled garden area in the back have more privacy and their own bathrooms. The larger apartments toward the back of the garden have kitchenettes and are convenient for long-term rentals. The communal kitchen-and-dining area is under a thatched roof. ⊠ *200 m east of AyA (Acuaductos y Acantarrillados, the national water company), behind church* ☎ *446–5019* ⊜ *446–6975* ➟ *4 rooms (2 with bath), 4 cabinas, 2 apartments* ☆ *Fans, pool, laundry service; no a/c, no room phones, no room TVs* ⊟ *No credit cards* ‖⊙‖ *BP.*

$ ⊡ **Villas de la Colina.** A Costa Rican family owns and operates this hilltop retreat in the countryside north of town with rustic wooden cabinas and sweeping views of the surrounding countryside. A green lawn with an archway of flowers covers the footpaths to most rooms. Hummingbirds add to the natural beauty. The upper rooms cost a bit more but are brighter and have private balconies with hammocks. You can also rent motorcycles here for exploring the area's forested mountains. ⊠ *4 km (2 mi) west and 2 km (1 mi) north of Coopeatenas* ☎ *446–5015* ⊜ *446–8545* ➟ *6 cabinas* ☆ *Fans, kitchenettes, pool, horseback riding, laundry service; no a/c, no room phones, no room TVs* ⊟ *No credit cards* ‖⊙‖ *BP.*

### To & From Atenas
*42 km/26 mi (1 hour) west of San José.*

Buses to Atenas leave frequently from the Coca Cola station in San José and arrive near the center of town. You can also catch a bus to Jacó and request to be dropped off at the entrance to Atenas. If you're driving from San José, hop on the Pan-American Highway west towards Alajuela past the airport, and turn right on overpass after the giant RECOPE storage tanks (on left). Turn left from the exit, stay on the main road and follow the signs.

### Atenas Essentials
🖪 Bank/ATM **Banco de Costa Rica (BCR)** ⊠ 200 m west of Catholic church. **Banco Nacional** ⊠ Northern corner of central park.
🖪 Hospital **Clínica Pública** ⊠ 150 m south of the fire station ☎ 446–5522.
🖪 Pharmacy **Farmacia Don Juan** ⊠ West side corner of Catholic church ☎ 446–5055.
🖪 Internet **C@fé K-puchinos** ⊠ Northwest corner of Parque Central ☎ 289–0082.
🖪 Post Office **Correos** ⊠ 50 m southeast of northeast corner of market.
🖪 Tourist Information **C@fé K-puchinos** ⊠ Northwest corner of Parque Central ☎ 289–0082.

## Carara Biological Reserve

➓ On the east side of the road between Puntarenas and Playa Jacó, Parque Nacional Carara protects one of the last remnants of an ecological transition zone between Costa Rica's drier northwest and the more humid southwest. It consequently holds a tremendous collection of plants and animals. Much of the 47-square-km (18-square-mi) park is covered with primary forest on steep slopes, where the massive trees are laden with vines and epiphytes. The sparse undergrowth makes wildlife easier to see here than in many other parks, but nothing is guaranteed.

If you're lucky, you may glimpse armadillos, basilisk lizards, blue-crowned motmots, chestnut-mandibled toucans, trogons, coatis, and any of several monkey species.

The first trail on the left shortly after the bridge that spans the Río Tárcoles (a good place to spot crocodiles) leads to a horseshoe-shape *laguna meandrica* (oxbow lake). The small lagoon covered with water hyacinths is home to turtles, crocodiles, and waterfowl such as the northern jacana, roseate spoonbill, and boat-billed heron. It is a two- to four-hour hike from the trailhead to the lagoon. ⚠ Cars parked at the trailhead have been broken into, so ask at the main ranger station (several miles south of the trailhead) if there is a ranger on duty at the *sendero laguna meandrica* lagoon. If there isn't, you may be able to leave your belongings at the main ranger station, where you can also buy drinks and souvenirs and use the restroom.

Two trails lead into the forest from the parking lot. One short stretch is wheelchair accessible. A longer trail connects with the Quebrada Bonita loop, which takes two to three hours to hike. The latter can be quite muddy during the rainy months, when you may want rubber boots. Carara's proximity to San José and Jacó means that tour buses arrive regularly in high season, scaring some animals deeper into the forest. Come very early or late in the day to avoid crowds. Bird-watchers can call the day before to arrange admission before the park opens. Camping is not permitted.

Local travel agencies and tour operators arrange transport to and guides through the park (⇨ Park Tours, *below*). The park itself has guides, but you have to arrange in advance. ☎ 383–9953 ⌨ $8 ⊙ *Daily 7–4.*

### Park Tours

**Costa Rica Expeditions** (☎ 222–0333 🖳 257–1665) and **Horizontes** (☎ 222–2022 🖳 255–4513), the country's two premier nature-tour operators, have expert guides and can arrange tours that visit Carara, Manuel Antonio, or both. Tour operators in Jacó and Herradura (⇨ *below*) have trips to Carara. The Jungle Crocodile Safari (⇨ Tárcoles, *below*) has a day tour from San José that combines Carara Reserve with the Tárcoles riverboat tour.

### To & From Carara Biological Reserve

*43 km/25 mi southwest of Atenas, 85 km/51 mi (2½ hours) southwest of San José.*

From Atenas, pass through Orotina and follow the signs to Tárcoles and Jacó. The reserve is on left after you cross Río Tárcoles. From San José, hop on a bus to Jacó, Quepos, or Manuel Antonio and ask to be dropped off near the entrance of the park.

# THE COAST

Along a short stretch of Costa Rica's Pacific Coast from Tárcoles to Manuel Antonio are patches of undeveloped jungle, the popular Manuel Antonio National Park, and some of the country's most accessible

## Diving the Deep at Coco Island

CLOSE UP

RATED ONE OF THE TOP DIVING DESTINATIONS in the world, Isla del Coco is uninhabited and remote, and its waters are teeming with marine life. It is no place for beginners, but serious divers enjoy 100-foot visibility and the underwater equivalent of a big-game park: scalloped hammerheads, white-tipped reef sharks, Galápagos sharks, bottlenose dolphins, billfish, and manta rays mix with huge schools of brilliantly colored fish.

Encompassing about 22½ square km, or 14 square mi, Isla del Coco is the largest uninhabited island on earth. Its isolation has led to the evolution of dozens of endemic plant and animal species. The rocky topography is draped in rain forest and cloud forest and includes more than 200 waterfalls. Because of Isla del Coco's distance from shore (484 km/300 mi) and its craggy topography, few visitors to Costa Rica—and even fewer Costa Ricans—have set foot on the island.

Costa Rica annexed Coco in 1869, and it became a national park in 1978. Today only extremely high-priced specialty-cruise ships, park rangers and volunteers, and scientists visit the place Jacques Cousteau called "the most beautiful island in the world." The dry season (November–May) brings calmer seas and is the best time to see silky sharks. During the rainy season, large schools of hammerheads can be seen, but the ocean is rougher.

Most dive cruises to Isla del Coco are about 10 days, and include three days of travel time on the open ocean. The *Okeanos Aggressor* (☎ 257-8686, 800/348-2628 in U.S. ⊕ www. okeanoscocosisland.com) and the *Undersea Hunter* (☎ 228-6613, 800/ 203-2120 in U.S. ⊕ www. underseahunter.com) run trips year-round at a cost of roughly $3,500.

5

beaches. The proximity of these strands to San José leads Costa Ricans and foreigners alike to pop down for quick beach vacations. Surfers have good reason to head for the consistent waves of Playas Jacó and Hermosa, and anglers and golfers should consider Playa Herradura for its links and ocean access. You might find most of these beaches overrated and overdeveloped. Manuel Antonio could be accused of the latter, but nobody can deny its spectacular natural beauty.

## Tárcoles

⑪ Crocodile boat tours on the Río Tárcoles are this small town's claim to fame and the only reason to stop here. In fact, you don't actually have to drive to Tárcoles to do the tour, since operators can pick you up in San José or Jacó. The muddy river has gained the reputation as the country's dirtiest thanks to San José's inadequate sewage system, but it amazingly remains an impressive refuge for wildlife. An inordinate diversity of birds results from a combination of transitional forest and the river, which houses crocodiles, herons, storks, spoonbills, and other waterbirds.

Spot them on a boat tour along the river or hiking in the private reserves nearby, one of which has a spectacular waterfall.

You can hike, ride by horseback, or drive to the beautiful 656-foot **Manantial de Agua Viva Waterfall** deep in a lush forest. Its 10 natural pools are great for a refreshing dip after your ride or hike. The waterfall is within the private Complejo Ecológico la Catarata (Waterfall Ecological Reserve), which has guides who lead tours to the waterfall. The horseback ride is four hours. A tough 2½-km (1½-mi) trail makes a loop through the woods, passing the waterfall and pools; it takes between 40 minutes and two hours to hike, depending on how much bird-watching you do. Good physical condition and hiking shoes are necessary. Parrots, monkeys, scarlet macaws, and most of the other animals found in the nearby Carara Biological Reserve live in the forest here. ⊠ *From the coastal highway south to Jacó, turn left onto dirt road at Hotel Villa Lapas sign. The reserve is about 9 km/5½ mi past Villa Lapas.* ☎ 661–8263 ☜ *$10, $40 guided horseback ride (includes entrance fee)* ⊙ *Daily 8–4.*

## Outdoor Activities

BOAT TOURS On the two-hour **riverboat tours** through mangrove forest you might see massive crocodiles, Jesus lizards, iguanas, and some of roughly 50 colorful bird species, including the turquiose browed motmot and boat-billed heron. Tours reach the river's mouth, providing nice sea views, especially at sunset. ■ TIP➜➜ Around noon is the best time to spot crocs sunbathing; bird enthusiasts prefer afternoon rides to catch scarlet macaws. During the rainy season (May–November), the river may grow too rough for boats.

Two brothers run **Crocodile Man Tour** (⊠ Main road into Tárcoles ☎ 637–0426 or 637–0771 ☜ crocodilemantour@hotmail.com), started by a pioneer in the area's crocodile encounters, for $25 per person. Small scars on their hands prove they continue the tour's original (and optional) attraction: feeding fish to the crocs. The boats are small enough to slide up alongside the mangroves for a closer look. Transportation is provided from nearby beaches, but not from San Jośe. **Jungle Crocodile Safari** (⊠ Main road into Tárcoles ☎ 637–0338 or 637–0656 ⊕ www.costaricanaturetour.com) runs a fairly sophisticated microphone-guided tour ($25) on a larger pontoon boat, which depends on tide levels to navigate. A full-color brochure with 56 different birds helps identify waterfowl. Transportation is provided from San Jośe and nearby beaches. A full-day tour includes a visit to the Carara Biological Reserve.

CANOPY TOUR **Hotel Villa Lapas** (⊠ Off Costanera, 3 km/2½ mi after bridge over Tárcoles River, turn left on dirt road, up 600 m ☎☎ 637–0232 ☎ 637–0227 ⊕ www.villalapas.com) manages a suspension-bridge nature walk and a zip-line tour. **Sky Way** consists of five suspension bridges spread out over a 2½-km (1½-mi) old-growth-forest nature trail. You can do the trail with a guide ($20) or without a guide ($15). A shuttle picks you up at the Hotel Villa Lapas. **Villa Lapas Canopy** has zip lines through primary forest. The tour is $35 per person.

HIKING Trails in this area—in Manantial de Agua; the Complejo Ecológico; and at Hotel Villa Lapas's Sky Way—can keep you afoot for a couple of days, crossing suspension bridges in old growth forests or trekking up to one of the country's highest waterfalls, which you can also reach on horseback.

## Where to Stay & Eat

¢–$  ✕ **Soda las Veraneras** This small and simple tiled-floor eatery serves standard homemade *soda* food, like filling *casados* (plates of rice, beans, salad, and fish, chicken, or meat). ⊠ *Near entrance to Tárcoles* ☎ 637–0418 ▭ *No credit cards.*

¢–$  ✕ **Soda los Mangos.** Next to Soda las Veraneras, this place is similar, with casados and fresh fried fish or fish fillets in garlic sauce. Most tables are outdoors except for one beneath the television indoors. ⊠ *Near entrance to Tárcoles* ☎ 637–0672 ▭ *No credit cards.*

♨ ★ $$  ▦ **Hotel Villa Lapas.** Within a tranquil rainforest preserve, far from other hotels (and the beach), Villa Lapas is a great escape for nature lovers, but also has on-site entertainment to keep you busy, such as a large-screen television, a pool table, and foosball. Cross a suspension bridge to a small replica of a Costa Rican colonial village with a restaurant, cantina, church, and gift shops. Follow the river flowing through the protected forest for a pleasant hike. For the adventurous, there is a canopy tour on the property. The austere rooms are nothing special, but have terra-cotta floors, hardwood ceilings, and large baths. An all-inclusive meal plan is available. ⊠ *Off Costanera, 3 km (2½ mi) after bridge over Tárcoles River, turn left on dirt road, up 600 m* ☎☎ 637–0232 ☎ 637–0227 ⊕ *www. villalapas.com* ⇆ *58 rooms* ⚐ *2 restaurants, a/c, fans, in-room safes, pool, 3 bars, recreation room, 3 shops, laundry service, meeting room; no room TVs* ▭ *AE, DC, MC, V* ⎀ *EP.*

## To & From Tárcoles

*90 km/54 mi (1½ hours) southwest of San José.*

Any bus traveling to Jacó can drop you off at the entrance to Tárcoles just let the driver know in advance. By car, follow the signs on the Costanera to Orotina and continue toward Jacó. The entrance to the town of Tárcoles is on the west side of the road; across the highway is a dirt road that leads to the Hotel Villa Lapas and the waterfall reserve.

**en route** Even if you choose to bypass Tárcoles and its crocodile tours, you can still get a peek of the huge reptiles as they lounge on the riverbanks: on the Costanera, pull over just after crossing the Río Tárcoles bridge and walk back onto it. Bring binoculars if you have them. As always, lock your car—vehicles have been broken into here.

## Between Tárcoles and Playa Herradura

Past Tárcoles, the first sizeable beachtown of the Central Pacific coast is Playa Herradura. In between, you'll pass two of the area's most exclusive hotels, hidden from roadside view at the end of long winding roads. About a kilometer (½ mi) south after the entrance to Tárcoles, the Costanera passes a small beach called **Playa La Pita,** which provides your first glimpse of the Pacific if you're coming down from the Central Valley. The beach is rocky, and its proximity to the Tárcoles River makes the water murky and unfit for swimming, but it's a nice spot to stop and admire the ocean. La Pita lies within a calm-water cove, where fishermen anchor their boats off its southern end. Watch pelicans diving into the water, and in the distance, you might see the mountains of the southern tip of the Nicoya Peninsula. Farther down, you'll come across the entrances of elegant lodgings Villas Caletas and Hotel Punta Leona, which have access to other small beaches along the coast.

## Where to Stay & Eat

**$$-$$$**  ✕ **El Mirador Restaurant.** White tablecloths, glass walls, and yellow-and-blue checkered curtains contribute to the sophisticated but not overly stuffy atmosphere of this restaurant at the Villa Caletas hotel. A reasonable prix-fixe includes your choice of appetizer, main dish, and dessert. Add a little more for nightly specials or choose à la carte. Mango snook, cognac chicken supreme, and beef tenderloin béarnaise are a few of the delectable entrées. A covered terrace is popular for sunset viewing over a cocktail. ⊠ *Villa Caletas hotel, off coastal highway, 3 km (1½ mi) south of Punta Leona, on the right* ☎ *637–0606* ▤ *AE, DC, MC, V* ⊘ *No lunch.*

**¢-$$**  ✕ **Steve n' Lisa's.** A convenient location, an ocean view, and good food make this roadside restaurant overlooking Playa La Pita a popular pit stop for those traveling between San José and the Central Pacific beaches. Sit on the covered porch or at one of the concrete tables on the adjacent patio, and enjoy the view of the Gulf of Nicoya through the palm fronds. The menu includes breakfast options and a wide selection of lunch and dinner entrées that ranges from tacos and hot dogs to a pricy surf and turf. There's a salad bar, and an eclectic mix of appetizers includes a chicken quesadilla, two types of *ceviche*, onion rings, and deep-fried cauliflower. ⊠ *On the Costanera, 1 km (½ mi) south of Tárcoles turnoff, on the right* ☎ *637–0594* ▤ *AE, DC, MC, V* ⊘ *Breakfast served.*

★ **$$**  ✕▤ **Hotel Punta Leona.** This 740-acre private reserve and resort community is an odd and overwhelming mix of nature, residential development, and vacation spot. Punta Leona's attractions include three beaches, a tropical forest, a butterfly farm, and guided bird-watching hikes. Punta Leona (Lion's Point) made headlines as the main site of the Ridley Scott film *1492: Conquest of Paradise* and more recently for controversially blocking the public's access to its beaches, which is illegal in Costa Rica. The little "city" contains everything from multiple restaurants and pools to a grocery store and church, plus plenty of amusements, including a zip-line tour, tennis court, and mini–golf course. Frequent shuttles travel between the rooms, restaurants, and beaches. Hotel guests, homeown-

### THE CART WITHOUT OXEN

If you're out late one night and hear a slow scraping of wheels against the road, it just might be the *carreta sin bueyes* (cart without oxen) of ghostly legend. Its owner reputedly stole building materials from a church, and was condemned to perpetually traverse the country's highways and byways in the cart he used to transport his stolen goods. (The oxen were blameless for their role and escaped the curse.) Hurry back to your hotel.

ers, and time-share members contribute to crowded beaches on weekends, especially in the dry season. Nonguests who choose to dine or use any facility at Punta Leona must pay a $20 surcharge. ⊠ *Off the Costanera, on road to Jacó* ☎ *231–3131 or 625–8825* 📠 *282–9701* ⊕ *www.hotelpuntaleona.com* ➥ *108 rooms, 13 suites, 92 apartments* ⚹ *3 restaurants, 2 snack bars, in-room safes, refrigerators, cable TV, 3 pools, beach, snorkeling, hiking, 3 bars, shops, laundry service, Internet* 🖃 *AE, DC, MC, V* ⭐ *EP.*

**$$$** ✕⬚ **Villa Caletas.** On a promontory south of Punta Leona, this collec-
**Fodor'sChoice** tion of elegant rooms sequestered in the jungle has amazing views of
**★** the surrounding foliage and sea below, making it one of the area's most remarkable hotels. Freestanding suites and villas are gorgeous, but rooms in the main building are far inferior; if you can't afford a suite, at least get a deluxe room. Victorian, French colonial, and Hellenistic motifs are combined throughout, with Ionic columns, varied artwork, cookie-cutter trims, and cane chairs. The infinity-edge pool seems to flow into the spectacular sea behind it. The closest beach, Playa Caletas, is small, rocky, and unfit for swimming. An amphitheater hosts concerts once a month and a music festival in July. Staff is friendly and attentive. ⊠ *Off coastal highway, 3 km (1½ mi) south of Punta Leona, on the right* ☎ *637–0606* 📠 *637–0404* ⊕ *www.villacaletas.com* ➥ *10 rooms, 12 suites, 16 villas* ⚹ *2 restaurants, a/c, fans, in-room safes, mini-bars, cable TV, pool, fitness room, spa, beach, bar, shop, laundry service, concierge, no-smoking rooms* 🖃 *AE, DC, MC, V* ⭐ *CP.*

# Playa Herradura

⓬ If sportsfishing and golf are your priorities, this is a good option. If you're looking for nature, seclusion, a beautiful beach, or a bargain, keep driving. Rocky Playa Herradura, a poor representative of Costa Rica's breathtaking beaches, gets its name from the Spanish word for "horseshoe," referring to the shape of the deep bay it which it lies. Its tranquil waters make it considerably safer for swimming than most central and southern Pacific beaches, and that, coupled with its proximity to San José, has turned it into a popular weekend getaway for Josefinos, who compete for shade beneath the sparse palms and Indian almond trees. The bay, defined by mountainous points, is a pleasant enough sight toward the left, but the right side is dominated by the Los Sueños Resort's yacht-filled marina and condo buildings, which blotch the natural backdrop. The handful of restaurants and scant souvenir shops are lined along a tiny commercial strip in front of the sea. Aside from the mammoth Marriott hotel and a couple of low-budget motels, there's little else by way of accommodations.

## Outdoor Activities

A few activities are available directly in Playa Herradura, but that doesn't mean you have to settle for less. Most of the area's diverse outfitters can pick you up at your hotel for activities near Jacó and Playa Hermosa. Your hotel's reception desk is often a good source of information.

**King Tours** (⊠ Main road into Playa Herradura, in front of Los Sueños resort ☎ 637–7343, 643–2441 ⊕ www.kingtours.com) arranges trips to renowned attractions like Manuel Antonio National Park and Carara Biological Reserve, as well as crocodile boat tours, deep-sea and coastal fishing trips, horseback riding, and canopy tours. It also books tours elsewhere in country, to destinations such as Poás and Arenal volcanoes, Monteverde Cloud Forest, and Isla Tortuga. **Marlin del Rey** (⊠ On the main road into Playa Herradura, shortly after the entrance to Los Sueños resort, on the left ☎ 637–7249 or 386–6786) specializes in fishing tours, snorkel trips to Isla Tortuga, and sunset catamaran rides.

## Where to Stay & Eat

**$$–$$$$** ✕ **Nuevo Latino.** The most formal restaurant at the Los Sueños Resort (though dress is still Costa Rica casual), softly lit Nuevo Latino has large arched windows facing cascading water on one wall and large still-lifes of fruits on the other. As the name implies, the menu uses basic Latin American ingredients, like yuca, sweet potato, corn, and beans, in creative ways, fusing them with flavors from other parts of the world. The menu includes pork chops with mint pesto and sea bass with curry and coconut. ⊠ *Marriott Los Sueños Resort* ☎ *630–9000* ▭ *AE, DC, MC, V* ⊘ *No lunch.*

**$–$$$** ✕ **Restaurante El Pelícano.** It may not look like much at first glance, but this open-air restaurant across the street from the beach serves some dishes you'd be hard-pressed to find in other casual beach-town places. The decor is limited to green-tile floors, thin wooden columns, lime tablecloths, and soft candlelight. Starters include fish croquettes in a lemon sauce, green pepper stuffed with shrimp and mushrooms, or clams *au gratin.* Grilled tuna in a mango sauce, sea bass in a heart-of-palm sauce, lobster, and tenderloin are a few of the main dishes. ⊠ *Turn left at end of main road into Playa Herradura* ☎ *637–8910* ▭ *AE, DC, MC, V.*

**$$$$** ✕▣ **Marriott Los Sueños Ocean and Golf Resort.** This mammoth multimillion-dollar resort contains condos and a hotel. The palatial terra-cotta, colonial-style buildings, reminiscent of a theme park, combine modern amenities with traditional Central American decorative motifs, like Nicaraguan barrel-tile roofing and hand-painted Costa Rican tiles. Its rooms, though attractive and some of the country's most expensive, are nothing special compared with those at other hotels in this price range. They have marble baths, wooden furniture, and tiny balconies. Be sure to get a room with an ocean view, or you'll be contemplating condominiums. An enormous pool with islands and swim-up bars, a Ted Robinson golf course, a modern marina, and various diversions are designed to keep you on-site and entertained. ⊠ *On road to Jacó from San José, follow signs on right at entrance of road to Playa Herradura; hotel's entrance on right, shortly before end of road, clearly marked* ☎ *630–9000, 800/228–9290 in U.S.* 🖷 *630–9090* ⊕ *www.marriotthotels. com* ⇋ *191 rooms, 10 suites* ♢ *4 restaurants, 2 bars, in-room safes, minibars, cable TV, 18-hole golf course, 2 tennis courts, pool, gym, massage, beach, casino, shops, children's programs (ages 5–15), laundry service, business services, meeting rooms, no-smoking rooms, Internet, airport shuttle* ▭ *AE, DC, MC, V* ⊙❙ *EP.*

## To & From Playa Herradura
*12 km/7 mi (20 minutes) south of Punta Leona.*

By bus, hop on one heading to Jacó. By car, head straight down the Central Pacific highway. The town's entrance is on right-hand side. A long paved road leads to the beach: follow the signs to the Marriott.

# Jacó

**❸** Its proximity to San José has made Jacó the most developed beach town in Costa Rica. Nature lovers and solitude-seekers should skip this place, which is known for its nightlife, surf scene, and blatant prostitution. More than 50 hotels and cabinas back its long, gray-sand beach, and the mix of restaurants, shops, and bars lining Avenida Pastor Diaz (the town's main drag), gives it a cluttered appearance devoid of any greenery. Any real Costa Rican-ness evaporated years ago; U.S. chain hotels and restaurants have invaded, and you can pretty much find anything you need, from law offices and dental clinics to DVD rental shops and appliance stores. In terms of tours and outdoor activities, it's also got a bit of everything and makes a hub for exploring neighboring beaches and attractions.

Long, palm-lined **Playa Jacó,** just east of town, is a pleasant enough spot in the morning, but can burn the soles of your feet on a sunny afternoon. Though the gray sand and beachside construction make it less attractive than most other Costa Rican beaches, it's a good place to enjoy a sunset. Playa Jacó is popular with surfers for the consistency of its waves, making it less than ideal for swimmers.

## Outdoor Activities

You don't have to physically step into any tour office, since everyone from a reception desk attendant to a boutique salesperson can book you a local adventure. Almost every tour can pick you up at your hotel's doorstep. ■ TIP→→ Keep in mind that part of your price tag includes the salesperson's commission, so if you hear higher or lower prices from two different people, it's likely a reflection of a shift in the commission. You can try negotiating a better deal directly from the outfitter.

**Costa Tropical Expeditions** (☎ 393–6622) is a small Jacó tour operator that specializes in trips to Carara Biological Reserve, but can arrange all kinds of personalized excursions. **Fantasy Tours** (✉ Best Western Jacó Beach Resort ☎ 643–3032) is the biggest operator in Jacó and deals primarily with large groups, arranging day trips from Jacó to Arenal and Poás volcanoes, Manuel Antonio National Park, Sarchí, Tortuga Island, and rafting on the Savegre River, plus local tours like zip-line adventures and kayak and snorkeling trips, among many others. **Pacific Travel and Tours** (✉ Centro comercial La Casona (La Casona shopping center) ☎ 643–2520, 643-2449 ⊕ www.pacifictravelcr.com) organizes tours for numerous activities in and around Jacó.

ATV TOURS  Since ATV tours are fairly new here, the vehicles are in good condition. But they're not exactly the most ecofriendly way to see the area's rain forest and wildlife. Some operators will ask you to put up a credit card

# Jacó

Boulevard

Calle Jardín

Avenida Pastor Díaz

Calle Ancha

Calle Anita

Calle Bri Bri

Calle Las
Palmeras

Calle LasOlas

Calle Bohío

Calle Cocal

Calle La Central

Calle Hicaco

Calle Las Brisas

Calle Barahona

Calle Morales

Calle Cocodrillo

Calle Mora

Calle Pastor

Calle Madrigal

Costanera Sur

Costanera Sur

PACIFIC
OCEAN

**KEY**

🔴 1  *Restaurants & Shopping*

⚪ 1  *Hotels & Nightlife*

voucher of roughly $500. **ATV Tours** (☎ 778–8172, 812–1789 ✎ quad-tours@yahoo.ca) runs two- or three-hour tours ($65–$85) through rain forests, rivers, and waterfalls that lie about 15 minutes south of Jacó. **Paraíso Adventures** (☎ 643–2724 ⊕ www.paraisocostarica.com) has shorter tours with longer breaks than most companies, which means you spend less time riding the quad. Trips are $65 for two hours, $85 for three hours, and $95 for four hours. **Ricaventura** (✉ In the center of Playa Jacó, behind Subway ☎818–6973 or 643–3395 ✎ricaventura2@yahoo.com) is considered by locals to be the best ATV tour with the longest routes. Ricaventura offers three options: a two-hour sunset tour ($65), a four-hour Carara Park and nearby river tour ($90), and a six-hour Pacayal Waterfall trip ($150).

CANOPY TOURS   In the hills across the highway from Jacó Beach, **Canopy Adventure Jacó** (☎ 643–3271 ⊕ www.adventurecanopy.com) takes you sliding through the forest along cables strung between 13 treetop platforms ($55), some of which have views of the coast. **Waterfalls Canopy Tour** (☎ 643–3322 ⊕ www.waterfallscanopy.com), in a private reserve 4 km/2½ mi from Jacó, is a zip-line tour ($55) through trees, with a view of rain forest and waterfalls. You can combine the tour with a visit to a butterfly and frog garden.

HANG GLIDING   A truly unique experience for the adventurous, hang gliding gives you
AND ULTRALIGHT   the chance to see not just Jacó, but a huge expanse of Pacific coastline
FLIGHTS   from above. With **Hang Glide Costa Rica** (☎ 778–8710 ⊕ www.hangglidecostarica.com) you can take a tandem hang-gliding flight or fly in a three-seat, open cockpit ultralight plane. You are picked up in Jacó and taken to the airstrip 6 km/3½ km south of Playa Hermosa. Prices start at around $70 per person.

HORSEBACK   **Horse Tours at Hacienda Agujas** (☎ 643–2218, 838–7940) are serene
RIDING   enough for all ages and skill levels. Late-afternoon tours are on a cattle ranch about 25 minutes north of Jacó, include a trail ride through the rain forest and down a beach, and end with a colorful sunset bang. For much less you can take a tour with one of the locals who are usually walking their horses along the beach, but don't expect insurance coverage in the price.

KAYAKING AND   **Kayak Jacó Costa Rica Outriggers** (☎ 643–1233 ⊕ www.kayakjaco.com)
CANOEING   takes you to less restless waters than those at Jacó Beach with sea-kayaking tours for novices and seasoned adventurers and Hawaiian-style outrigger canoe trips. Both include snorkel excursions (conditions permitting) at secluded beaches. For a bit more activity, you can take a white-water kayaking or rafting trip.

SURFING   Jacó has several beach breaks, all of which are best around high tide, specifically three hours before and three hours after (local maps and promotional magazines carry tide charts). Surfboard-toting tourists abound in Jacó, but you don't need to be an expert to enjoy the waves—the swell is often small enough for beginners. Surf shops, which have popped up on almost every corner, rent boards and give surf lessons, although pretty much any local can teach you how to stand on a board. (Jacó has no surf schools.) Prices range from $25 to $45 an hour and usually include a board and transportation. If you plan to spend more than a week surfing, it might be cheaper to buy a used board and sell it before you leave ( ⇨ Shopping, *below*). If you don't have much experience, don't go out when the waves are really big—Jacó sometimes gets very powerful swells, which result in dangerous rip currents. During the rainy season, waves are more consistent than in the dry months, which can bring flatter waves.

> ### CAUTION ⚠
>
> Riptides (or rip currents), common in Jacó and Manuel Antonio's Playa Espadilla, are dangerous and have led to deaths in the area. If you get caught in one, don't panic and don't try to swim against it. Let the current take you out just past the breakers, where its power dissipates, then swim parallel to shore. Once the current is behind you, swim back to the beach. The best policy is not to go in deeper than your waist when the waves loom large.

The beach's extreme southern end is the calmest, with smaller waves and flatter sand. Most beginner lessons take place here. Strong currents create the best waves in front and to the left of the Bohío Restaurant. Advanced surfers should head to nearby Playa Hermosa.

SWIMMING   The big waves and dangerous rip currents that make surfing so popular here make swimming dangerous. Lifeguards are on duty only sporadically, so plan on being on your own. If the ocean is really rough, stay on the beach—dozens of swimmers have drowned over the years. When the waves are small, this can be a good place for strong swimmers to body surf. In general, if you're swimming and a wave is about to break on top of you, dive deep underneath it.

When the ocean is calm, you can swim just about anywhere along Jacó Beach. But always avoid the northern and southern extremes, and the areas around any of several small rivers that flow into the ocean, where the beach and ocean bottom are littered with rocks. The most frequently voiced advice is to not go deeper than your waist and to make sure you're always touching the ground.

## Where to Stay & Eat

★ $-$$$    ✕ **Marisquería El Hicaco.** Not many restaurants in Jacó have an ocean view. This one does, along with tables on the beach (in dry season) and some of the freshest seafood in town. In fact, this elegant restaurant serves little else. Not only do you get to pick from half a dozen different ways of how you'd like your fish, squid, prawns, or lobster to be cooked, but you also select your side dish. On Wednesdays an all-you-can-eat dinner buffet includes all of the above cooked to order, plus side dishes, beer, wine, an large dessert selection, and live music. ⊠ *100 m south and 90 m west of Más x Menos supermarket* ☎ *643-3226* ▭ *AE, DC, MC, V.*

$-$$    ✕ **BBQ Tangerí.** Carnivorous cravings can be satisfied at this restaurant whose grilled meat selection ranges from pork ribs to *churrasco,* a thick, sauceless tenderloin cut. A number of seafood dishes are served, though marlin is the only fish that's grilled; everything else is sautéed. The menu also includes a vegetarian and lacto-vegetarian option. It's a pleasant enough spot on a tranquil section of the main street, with high ceilings and gardens around the dining areas. ⊠ *Avda. Pastor Diaz, next to Hotel Tanger´* ☎ *643–3669* ⊟ *AE, DC, MC, V* ⊙ *Breakfast served on weekends.*

★ **$–$$** ✕ **El Chaán.** This open-air, high-ceiling eatery distinguishes itself from the bulk of Jacó's restaurants for its unique Peruvian dishes. It has nice ocean views from its location across the street from the beach. The menu is long on seafood, from the signature ceviche and aromatic seafood stew to *picante de camarones* (shrimp in a spicy cream sauce), but it also includes some good meat and pasta plates. Warning: the hot sauce is volcanic. Also, not every dish is Peruvian; look for those with a star. ⊠ *Hotel Balcón del Mar* ☎ *643–2223* ⊟ *AE, DC, MC, V* ⊙ *Breakfast served.*

★ **$–$$** ✕ **Hotel Poseidon Restaurant.** One of Jacó's best restaurants, this spot has patio seating, friendly service, an intimate atmosphere, good music, and an open grill at the entrance. Its small selection of inventive dishes always includes seafood, meat, chicken, and vegetarian options whose preparation changes every few days. Cooking flavors you might come across are Caribbean jerk-style, oyster peppercorn sauce, toasted pecans, and balsamic demi-glace. ⊠ *C. Bohío, 25 m west of main Rd.* ☎ *643–1642* ⊟ *AE, D, DC, MC, V.*

⊙ **¢–$** ✕ **Rioasis.** With an eclectic menu of Tex-Mex dishes, pastas, and salads, this large, colorful place on the main drag is popular with families and surfers, who head here for cheap eats. Pizza is the best bet: 34 varieties are baked in an outdoor wood-burning oven. You can eat on the front patio or under a high roof hung with ceiling fans. There's a long bar in back, a pool table, and a foosball for after-dinner entertainment. ⊠ *Avda. Pastor Diaz, north of Banco Nacional* ☎ *643–3354* ⊟ *MC, V* ⊙ *Closed Tues. May–Nov.*

**$$$–$$$$** ✕▥ **Club del Mar.** Secluded on the beach's southern extreme, far from
**Fodor's**Choice Jacó's din and masses, Club del Mar is the area's priciest option. In the
★ main building, above the restaurant, bar, and reception, standard green-and-cream-hued rooms have private teak balconies with screen doors that keep the sea breeze circulating. For the price, you can find better options elsewhere. Instead, go for the comfortable condos, clustered in a dozen two-story buildings amid massive trees and verdant lawns. The one- and two-bedroom apartments have modern kitchens, pleasant decor, abundant windows, and washing machines. Some apartments stand in front of the sea (Nos. 13–16); those farthest back lie close to the highway. Restaurant Las Sandalias ($–$$) serves some of the area's finest dinners, from chateaubriand to grilled lobster. It also serves breakfast. The split-level, open-air space has a bar on top and tables below, all facing the pool and ocean. The penthouse has two bedrooms, one with a king-size bed and the other with two twins. ⊠ *Costanera, 275 m south of gas station* ⓓ *Apdo. 107–4023* ☎ *643–3194* ⊕ *www. clubdelmarcostarica.com* ⬎ *9 rooms, 22 condos, 1 penthouse* ⚐ *Restaurant, a/c, fans, in-room safes, kitchens, cable TV, pool, massage, bar, shop, beach, laundry service, laundry facilities, kayaking, in-room data ports, Internet* ⊟ *AE, MC, V, DC* ⍭ *BP.*

## Catch the Wave

COSTA RICA GETS HIGH MARKS among surfers for its warm, clean ocean water, beautiful tropical scenery, consistent waves, and not-too-crowded conditions. (The place hasn't yet turned into California or Hawaii.)

Tamarindo anchors a popular surfing region on the North Pacific coast. Its protected bay offers smaller waves that translate into great conditions for beginners. The exception is December and January, when the bay is exposed to southern swells that create bigger waves. North of town to Playa Grande and south to Playas Avellanas and Negra always get exposed to those swells and are experts-only destinations year-round.

Farther down the coast, Sámara is little mentioned in surfing circles, but is a good beginner's beach for its small waves.

Some of the country's finest surfing is at Malpaís, at the tip of the Nicoya Peninsula. The town is gradually becoming more popular, despite its remoteness.

The Central Pacific town of Jacó gets mixed reviews. As the closest surfing destination to San José, it draws the crowds. Surfers say its waves close out early (good for beginners) but tend toward quick shore breaks (conditions best negotiated by experts).

Playa Hermosa, just south, has 8- to 10- foot waves. The beach is

enormously popular, but the waves are long enough that crowding is rarely a problem.

The South Pacific's Dominical is a nice alternative to Jacó. It's a bit farther from San José and therefore less crowded, and its wide beach break and cool beach-town atmosphere make it worth the trip.

Staring at each other from across the entrance to the Golfo Dulce are the point breaks and resulting big waves at Matapalo and Pavones. The latter in particular is famed in surfing circles for being one of the world's longest left-breaking waves.

While the Pacific has consistent year-round conditions, the Caribbean coast has a narrower January–April window of top-notch surfing. In theory, the north coast has the waves, but it's tough enough to get yourself here, let alone a board, and shark-infested waters make it a no-go. Heading south, the reef breaks at Limón draw a few surfers. (It's just not a popular tourist destination.) Cahuita's Playa Negra is fairly consistent for a beach break.

Just beyond Puerto Viejo de Talamanca is the consistent beach break at Playa Cocles. The famed—and revered—Salsa Brava, an experts-only reef break, is visible from the town of Puerto Viejo.

**$$$–$$$$** FodorsChoice ★ ✕⊡ **Docelunas.** Most of Jacó's hotels and visitors huddle around the beach and bars, but "Twelve Moons" has a radically different holistic atmosphere across the highway. With a mountainous green backdrop, this choice hotel spreads out across 5 acres. Paintings (for sale) decorate the spacious teak furniture–filled rooms, and large bathrooms have showers, bathtubs, and double sinks. Yoga classes are given daily in a hilltop, hardwood-floor room with windows for walls. The full-service spa uses the hotel's own homemade beauty products and the open-air restaurant ($$–$$$) serves up creative seafood, meat, vegetarian, and vegan dishes that change weekly. A lovely sun mosaic decorates the large pool with a waterfall flowing into it. Each Sunday local residents arrive for movie night. ⊠ *On coastal highway, coming from San José, pass the first entrances to Jacó; take dirt road on left with signs for Docelunas to the end (if you reach the gas station on the right, next to the last entrance to Jaco, you passed it)* ☎ *643–2277* ⊕ *www.docelunas.com* ➘ *20 rooms* ⌂ *Restaurant, room service, bar, a/c, fans, in-room safes, refrigerators, cable TV, pool, spa, shop, laundry service, in-room data ports, business center, meeting room, no-smoking rooms* ▤ *MC, V* ⫪ *BP.*

$$  **Amapola.** Several blocks from the beach, near the more tranquil southern end, Amapola is a smaller, slightly tackier version of a resort hotel. It draws mostly families and retirees who appreciate that everything you need is on site. A restaurant with room service, bars, and a casino are among the facilities. Activities include billiards, foosball, and volleyball. Rooms have terraces or balconies that open up to the large pool area and palm-filled lawn. Accommodation options range from standard double rooms to villas with kitchens and a capacity for up to six people. The all-inclusive package costs only a bit more, but the food is mediocre, and better, off-site restaurants are within walking distance. ⊠ *200 m east of the municipality* ☎ *643–2255* 🖷 *643–3668* ⊕ *www.hotelamapola.com* ➘ *44 room, 6 suites, 3 villas* ⌂ *Restaurant, room service, some kitchens, 3 bars, casino, children's programs, a/c, in-room safes, refrigerators, cable TV, pool, laundry service, bicycles, Internet, no-smoking rooms* ▤ *AE, MC, DC, V* ⫪ *BP.*

☾ $$  **Aparthotel Girasol.** A great option for families or groups looking for comfort and quiet, Girasol is a small beachfront hotel with a neighborly feel. The cozy apartments face the small pool and grill area and include a living and dining room, a complete kitchen, lots of windows, and a terrace with chairs. A winding pathway crosses the well-maintained front lawn, with an impressive tree in the middle, and leads to a small gate that opens directly onto the beach, where you should take at least one evening to enjoy a spectacular sunset. ⊠ *End of C. Los Almendros; 300 m south and 75 m west of Más X Menos supermarket* 🖷🖷 *643–1591* ⊕ *www.girasol.com* ➘ *16 apartments* ⌂ *A/c, fans, kitchens, cable TV, pool, laundry service; no phones in some rooms* ▤ *MC, V* ⫪ *EP.*

$$  **Best Western Jacó.** We recommend this place as a reliable backup when other hotels are booked. Like most hotels within the Best Western franchise, this one has sterile, generic rooms and almost every type of service and facility under the sun. Two large buildings face each other, with the noisy pool and lawn area in between. None of the rooms has a direct ocean view, though corner rooms 314, 414, and 415 look out to quiet gardens. Rooms in one building have private balconies. Daily activities (posted in the open-air reception) and an all-inclusive package can easily trap you here for days. The beach area has a lifeguard, plenty of chairs, and a bar nearby. ⊠ *On the main road, toward northern end, in front of Banco de Costa Rica* ☎ *643–1000, 800-528-1234 in U.S.*

or Canada 🖷 643–3246 ✉ bwjboperaciones@grupomarta.coms ⚓ 122 rooms ⚐ Restaurant, room service, children's programs, a/c, in-room safes, cable TV, pool, health club, beach, tours, laundry service, 1 tennis court, shop, grills, meeting rooms, Internet, no-smoking rooms ▭ AE, MC, DC, V ⍾ BP.

**\$\$**

**FodorsChoice ★**

🏨 **Hotel Canciones del Mar.** The poetically named "Songs of the Sea" is a tranquil, intimate, and charming hotel with rooms that are among the closest to the ocean of those in any area hotel. Except for one bamboo-lined room, spacious suites are the only option. Tastefully and individually decorated, the one- and two-bedroom suites are in a two-story cream-colored building, with well-equipped kitchens. Each has a porch overlooking lush gardens and a blue-tile pool, except for the honeymoon suite, which faces the beach. Breakfast and drinks can be enjoyed under a thatch roof next to the beach or in the shade of palms on the beach itself. A communal treehouse-like space behind the pool makes a pleasant reading or relaxing spot. ⊠ End of C. Bri Bri 🖀 643–3273 🖷 643–3296 ⊕ www.cancionesdelmar.com ⚓ 1 room, 10 suites ⚐ A/c, fans, in-room safes, kitchens, refrigerators, cable TV, pool, laundry service, Internet, no-smoking rooms; no room phones, ▭ AE, MC, V ⍾ BP.

**\$\$**

🏨 **Hotel Poseidon.** Wood carvings of the Greek god of the sea grace the facade of this small and somewhat cramped hotel. In the center of town, the hotel is conveniently close to shops, bars, and restaurants. Its own tasty and popular restaurant stands in front, while the reception and rooms stretch out toward the back, closed in between tall walls that give it an urban feel—with some green tropical touches. The small pool is strung with tiny jalapeño-pepper lights. Rooms are not spacious, but comfortable and simply decorated. A small air-conditioned bar with a few outdoor tables and large-screen TV hides above the restaurant. ⊠ C. Bohío, 30 m west of Avda. Pastor Diaz 🖀 643–1642, 888/643–1242 in U.S. and Canada ⊕ www.hotel-poseidon.com ⚓ 14 rooms ⚐ Restaurant, bar, room service, a/c, fans, minibars, cable TV in some rooms, pool, laundry service, Internet ▭ AE, D, MC, DC, V ⍾ BP.

**\$**

🏨 **Aparthotel Flamboyant.** Though nothing special, this small tranquil hotel is a good deal, especially if you take advantage of the cooking facilities. Half the rooms have small kitchenettes, the others have air-conditioning instead. Larger apartments can fit five to six people. Terraces with chairs overlook a garden and pool area, where there's a grill for your use. Second-floor rooms have balconies with sea views. It's all just a few steps from the beach, and a block east of Jacó's busy main strip. ⊠ 100 m east of Centro Comercial Il Galeone 🖀 643–3146 🖷 643–1068 ✉ flamboya@racsa.co.cr ⚓ 16 rooms, 3 apartments ⚐ Fans, in-room safes, some kitchenettes, pool, no a/c in some rooms, no TV in some rooms ▭ AE, DC MC, V ⍾ EP ⊗ Closed mid-Sept.–mid-Oct.

**☾ \$**

🏨 **Mar de Luz.** It may be a few blocks from the beach, and it doesn't look like much from the street, but Mar de Luz is a surprisingly pleasant, quiet place full of flowering plants and shady, bird-attracting trees. The Dutch owner is dedicated to cleanliness and providing extra amenities, such as poolside grills, a kids' gameroom, microwaves and refrigerators in each room, plentiful common areas—like the large open-air reading lounge with comfortable couches—and inexpensive tours. Rooms vary in feel and decor: the bright, pastel-hue rooms have two queen-size beds and kitchenettes; top-floor rooms have a small living room with checkered sofas and a double bed; the cozy split-level rooms with kitchenettes and stone walls are reminiscent of European bed-and-breakfasts. Few places can match Mar de Luz's helpful and accommodating staff. Breakfast is served at an additional cost. ⊠ *45 m east of Avda. Pastor Díaz, behind Onyx bar* ☎ *643–3259* ⊕ *www.mardeluz. com* ⮑ *27 rooms, 2 suites,* ⌂ *A/c, in-room safes, some kitchenettes, refrigerators, microwaves, cable TV, 2 pools, massage, laundry service, Internet; no room phones* ⊟ *AE, MC, V* ⊙ *EP.*

★ **$** ⊞ **Tropical Garden Hotel.** As its name suggests, this hotel's special charm comes from the impressive lush gardens that fill almost every inch of its property, making it one of the most verdant places in Jacó. Meters from the beach and from the main strip, rooms lack decor but have convenient kitchenettes and comfortable front porches for iguana- and bird-spotting. Though one of Jacó's earliest hotels (formerly known as Villas Miramar), it has modern perks like wireless Internet. Poolside breakfast is served for an extra $5 and the deluxe suite's two rooms sleep up to six people. ⊠ *In front of Il Galeone mall, toward the beach* ☎ *643–3003* 🖷 *643–3617* ⊕ *www.tropicalgardenhotel.com* ⮑ *11 rooms, 1 suite* ⌂ *A/c, fans, in-room safes, kitchenettes, cable TV, pool, massage, in-room data ports, Wi-Fi* ⊟ *No credit cards* ⊙ *EP.*

¢ ⊞ **Hotel El Jardín.** Near the tranquil northern end of the beach, about a 15-minute walk from Jacó's flock of tourists, El Jardín is just half a block from the sand and surf. Simple rooms with wooden ceilings, small baths, and tiny TVs surround a large pool and concrete picnic tables shaded by coconut palms. An open-air restaurant in front, with draping red and yellow fabrics, specializes in French dishes. Rooms with air-conditioning cost a bit more. Guests rave about the young owners' hospitality. ⊠ *C. Jardín, 50 m west of Cabinas Antonio* ☎ *643–3050* ⊕ *www.hoteleljardin.com* ⮑ *10 rooms* ⌂ *Restaurant, fans, restaurant, bar, cable TV, pool, laundry service, bicycles; no a/c in some rooms, no room phones* ⊟ *AE, DC, MC, V* ⊙ *CP.*

## Nightlife & the Arts

While other beach towns may have a bar or two, Jacó has an avenue full of them, with enough variety for many different tastes. After-dinner spots range from restaurants perfect for a quiet drink to loud bars with pool tables to dance clubs or casinos.

BARS  For a laid-back cocktail, people-watching, and a tropical feel, head to **Restaurante El Colonial** (⊠ Avda.

---

### ¿HABLA INGLES?

Although some Central Pacific areas like Jacó and Manuel Antonio are very touristy, don't assume everyone speaks English. For example, oftentimes taxi and bus drivers won't understand your directions in English. To make traveling smoother, write down the Spanish name of the place your headed to or ask your hotel's reception desk attendee to write out directions in Spanish, which you can pass on with a smile to your driver.

Pastor Diaz, across from Il Galeone mall ☎ 643–3326), on the main drag, which has a large circular bar in the center and lots of wicker chairs and tables in the front. Sometimes it has live music. A mix of bar and disco, **Nacho Daddy's** (✉ Avda. Pastor Diaz, first floor of Il Galeone mall ☎ 643–2270) draws crowds of all ages and nationalities. Its carpeted floors and air-conditioning make it Jacó's cushiest nightspot. Music might be reggae, pop, techno, or Latin. It closes at 2 AM—earlier than most bars. **Onyx** (✉ Avda. Pastor Diaz, across from Hotel Tangerí, above Subway ☎ 643–3911), a large, top-floor, wall-less bar, has wide-screen TVs, several pool tables, dart boards, and a large bar that draws a primarily foreign, under-25 crowd.

DANCE CLUBS **La Central** (✉ On the beach, end of the street across from Más x Menos ☎ 643–3076) is a club that plays a mix of popular dance music in different genres, has air-conditioning, and attracts a wide variety of late-night partygoers. No one arrives before 11 PM, and it stays open until 5 AM. **Club Olé** (✉ Avda. Pastor Diaz, north of the Beatle Bar ☎ 643–3226) has a dance floor, pool tables, a dart board, and other diversions. It plays more Latin music than other clubs and tends to draw thirtysomethings.

## Shopping

Souvenir shops with mostly the same mass-produced merchandise are crowded one after the other along the main street in the center of town. Most of the goods, like wooden crafts, seed jewelry, are run-of-the mill souvenir fare, but a few shops have more unusual items. Not all items are made in Costa Rica: Indonesian masks and Guatemalan textiles abound, so ask if the piece's source is important to you.

The two neighboring shops at **Cocobolo** (✉ Avda. Pastor Diaz, next to Banana Café ☎ 643–3486) are jam-packed with merchandise hanging from the ceiling, walls, and shelves. It's much of what you find in other stores, but with more international and tasteful items and richer variety. **El Cofre** (✉ Avda. Pastor Diaz, across from Banco Nacional ☎ 643–1912) claims to sell only handmade goods and specializes in mostly wooden furniture, including heavy Guatemalan pieces and Indonesian teak, but sells masks, drums, Morroccan lamps, and even carved doors. Curious relgious statues of saints and angels from Central America are big sellers. **Guacamole** (✉ Il Galeone mall ☎ 643–3297 ✉ Across the street from Restaurante Pancho Villa, Avda. Pastor Diaz ☎ 643–1120) sells beautiful and comfortable batik clothing produced locally, along with Brazilian bathing suits, Costa Rican leather sandals and purses, and different styles of jewelry.

SURFBOARDS AND GEAR **Chosita del Surf** (✉ Avda. Pastor Diaz, next to La Hacienda ☎ 643–1308) sells new and used boards and has the best selection in surfwear, sunglasses, and accesories—at the highest prices. **El Pana Bikinis and Surf** (✉ Avda. Pastor Diaz, next to Cocobolo souvenir shop ☎ 812–2803) has less variety than the other three shops in town, but more affordable prices. It rents and sells new and used surfboards and boogie boards, and fixes small dings. **Jass** (✉ Centro comercial Ureña ☎ 643–3549) has a good variety of surf gear at decent prices. It sells new and used boards. ■ TIP→→ Most shops that sell boards also buy used boards.

### To & From Jacó

*2 km/1 mi south of Playa Herradura, 114 km/70 mi (2 ½ hours) southwest of San José.*

Buses leave from San José's Coca Cola station five times daily. From here it's easy to catch a bus to the surrounding beaches or back to the capital, and many private shuttles offer transfers to other parts of the country. If you're driving, head down the Costanera, past Playa Herradura; get off before Playa Hermosa. **Extreme Boat** (☎ 640–0600 ⊕ www.extboat.com) shuttles surfers between Jacó and Malpaís, Monday through Thursday.

### Jacó Essentials

🔳 Bank/ATM **BAC San José** ⊠ Il Galeone mall. **Banco Nacional** ⊠ Avda. Pastor Diaz.

🔳 Hospital **Ambulance** ☎ 643–1690 **Clínica Pública** ⊠ In front of the Plaza de Deportes ☎ 643–1767)

🔳 Pharmacy **Farmacia Jacó** ⊠ Diagonal from Mas X Menos supermarket ☎ 643–3205.

🔳 Internet **Centro de Computación** ⊠ Avda. Pastor Diaz, center of town ☎ 643–2713.

🔳 Post Office **Correos** ⊠ Avda. Pastor Diaz.

🔳 Taxis **Taxi services** ☎ 643–2020, 643–2121, or 643–3030

🔳 Tourist Information **Pacific Travel and Tours** ⊠ Centro comercial La Casona [La Casona shopping center] ☎ 643–2520 or 643–2449 ⊕ www.pacifictravelcr.com

## Playa Hermosa

⓮ Just over the rocky ridge that forms the southern edge of Jacó is Playa Hermosa, a swath of gray sand and driftwood stretching southeast as far as the eye can see. Despite its name, there's nothing really pretty about it. The wide beach lacks palm trees or other shade-providing greenery; its sand is scorchingly hot in the afternoon and frequent rip currents make it unsafe to swim when the waves are big. But board-toters find beauty in its jaw-dropping surf breaks. The beach's northern end is popular for its angle, which often has waves when Jacó and other spots are flat. For nonsurfers, outdoor options include horseback and canopy tours in the nearby forested hills or ultralight and hang-gliding flights along the coast. But all of these can be done from other beaches. As for the town itself, there's really not much. Most of the restaurants, bars, and hotels have cropped up one after the other on a thin stretch separating the highway and the beach. From August to December, olive ridley turtles nest on the beach, on nights when there's not much moonlight.

> **WORD OF MOUTH**
>
> "We left Quepos around 9:30 AM for our long ride to Arenal. Stopped at Playa Hermosa to see the surfing beach. While walking back to our car, saw a huge cloud of dust from the dirt road. When the dust cleared, what emerged was a Tican cowboy herding about two dozen cattle! What a great sight. Kodak picture moment! We would have missed opportunities like these without our rental car."
> –Kwoo

## Outdoor Activities

You can arrange activites throughout the Central Pacific from Playa Hermosa. Most tour operators and outfitters include transportation in their prices. For more options than we list here, *see* Outdoor Activities section *in* Jaco, *above,* or consult your hotel's reception.

CANOPY TOUR   **Chiclets Tree Tour** (⊠ West of Costanera, ½ km/¼ mi north of Hermosa ☎ 643–1880) has four guided tours daily that take you through the rainforest canopy. Cables strung between platforms perched high in a dozen trees have views of tropical foliage, wildlife, and the nearby coast.

HORSEBACK RIDING   Tours with **Discovery Horseback** (☎ 643–7550) lead you through the nearby mountains and along the beach.

SURFING   Most people who bed down at Playa Hermosa are here for the same reason—the waves that break just a shell's toss away. One of the country's most consistent surf spots, Hermosa often has waves when other beaches are flat. There are half a dozen beach breaks scattered along the beach, but the surf is always best around low and high tide. Because it is a beach break, though, the waves here often close out, especially when the surf is big. If you don't have much experience, don't go out when the waves are really big—Hermosa sometimes gets very powerful swells, which result in dangerous rip currents. In fact, if you're a beginner, don't go out at all. Surf instructors in Hermosa take their students to Jacó, an easier place to stand on a board for the first time.

Reggae-themed **Restaurante Jammin'** (⊠ In front of Cabinas Las Arenas ☎ 643–1853) also has surf trips and lessons (2-hr lesson is $45; package is $100/day) and buys, rents, and sells boards as they're available. Andrea, a professional, Quiksilver surfer with **Viva Costa Rica Surf Adventures** (⊠ Next to the Backyard ☎ 643–2983 ⊕ www.wavescr.com), takes surf students to calmer Playa Jacó for two-hour lessons ($45; $100 for day-long package). She also has surf camp packages for women, which include room and board, yoga sessions, and surf lessons.

## Where to Stay & Eat

¢–$  ✕ **Jungle Surf Cafe.** This colorful, open-air eatery next to the Costanera serves some of Hermosa's best food. Seating is on a patio shaded by tropical trees, with a view of the road and soccer field. Breakfasts are hearty, and the eclectic lunch selection ranges from shish kebabs to fish sandwiches. The dinner menu changes nightly, but usually includes fresh tuna and mahimahi, and pork chops or chicken (preparation varies). ⊠ *Costanera, north of soccer field* ☎ *643–1495* ▭ *No credit cards* ⛴ *BYOB* ☉ *Closed Wed.*

¢  ✕ **The Backyard.** The only bar in Playa Hermosa, the Backyard has a North American atmosphere and several seating areas, each with its own bar. Inside, TVs on the wraparound bar show sports matches and surf videos. A wooden deck with plastic tables closer to the beach gets great sea breezes. The usual bar food, like pizza, burgers, and sandwiches, accompanies local seafood starters, including ceviche and peel-and-eat shrimp. It's a popular nightspot, especially on Wednesday and Friday's Ladies Night. ⊠ *Next to the hotel by the same name* ☎ *643–3936* ▭ *No credit cards.*

**$$–$$$**  🏨 **Hotel Fuego del Sol.** Off the main road, separated from most of Hermosa's hotels, are Fuego del Sol's two-story white-stucco buildings. Just behind the beach, rooms overlook palms and other foliage, and a large blue-tile pool. The two second-floor rooms closest to the beach have slight ocean views. They all have tile floors, wall paintings, and small balconies. Larger rooms that can fit four to seven people have fully equipped kitchens. The open-air restaurant is right next to the beach, where hammocks and concrete tables are shaded by Indian almond trees. ✉ *100 m north of soccer field's northwest corner* ☎ *643–3737* 🖷 *643–3736* ⊕ *www.fuegodelsolhotel.com* ➲ *18 rooms, 3 apartments* ⚲ *Restaurant, cable TV, pool, bar, laundry service, Internet, meeting room, travel services* ⊟ *AE, DC, MC, V* ⊚*| BP.*

**$$–$$$**  🏨 **The Backyard.** Surfers—not the budget backpacking kind—are the main clientele at this small two-story, cream-colored hotel on the beach. Rooms have high ceilings, clay-tile floors, and sliding-glass doors that open onto semiprivate balconies and terraces, most of which have good views of Playa Hermosa. Second-floor rooms have better views, as do the two spacious corner suites with separate bedrooms and large balconies—they're a good deal for small groups. ✉ *Costanera, southern end of town, 4 km south of Jacó* 🖷🖷 *643–1311* ⊕ *www.backyardhotel. com* ➲ *6 rooms, 2 suites* ⚲ *Bar, a/c, fans, in-room safes, minibars, cable TV, pool, massage, bar, laundry service, Internet; no room phones* ⊟ *AE, DC, MC, V.*

**$$**  🏨 **Hotel Terraza del Pacífico.** Playa Hermosa's largest hotel is self-sufficient and secluded, about 500 meters from the other hotels and businesses. Loud lime-colored, two-story buildings with white verandas surround the large pool with a swim-up bar and a green lawn and beach chairs. Near the beach are a sand volleyball court, a raised tiki-hut bar, and an open-air restaurant with tables that are probably the closest to the ocean in Hermosa. Rooms have clay-tile floors, balconies, simple wooden furniture, and original oil paintings from a resident artist who sometimes displays his work by the restaurant. The more spacious superior rooms on the second floor are better kept than the regular standards, with surfboard racks. Suites, which are mostly occupied by time shares, have kitchens and DVD players, a rare luxury. ✉ *Costanera, at the start of Playa Hermosa, first hotel on right* ☎ *643–3222, 440–6862 for reservations* 🖷 *643–3424* ⊕ *www.terrazadelpacifico.com* ➲ *40 rooms, 2 suites* ⚲ *Restaurant, room service, 3 bars, a/c, in-room safes, minibars in some rooms, cable TV, pool, laundry service, some rooms with kitchen, beach, car service, airport shuttle* ⊟ *AE, MC, V.*

**$**  🏨 **Casa Pura Vida.** Hidden from public view behind tall walls and a large fortress-style wooden door, Casa Pura Vida seems as secretive as Oz. Inside, the extremely intimate and tiny hotel is elegant and secluded enough to please a recluse millionaire—at a working man's rates. The two-story, Spanish-style building has just three apartments, each with two bedrooms and a kitchenette. The second-floor apartment has an ocean view and private balcony; the two downstairs open onto a gravel patio with a small green-tile pool and a kiosk with tables and rocking chairs. The beach is just across a bare lawn with a playground. Perks such as filtered water, a fully equipped communal kitchen by the pool, and attentive owners who live on-site make this a homey place to stay. ✉ *Costanera, 100 m south of soccer field* 🖩🖩 *643–2039* ⊕ *www.casapuravida.com* ↻ 3 *apartments* ⚇ *A/c, fans, in- room safes, kitchenettes, cable TV, pool, massage, playground, laundry service* ▤ *AE, MC, V* ⦿ *EP.*

⟳ ¢–$ ▦ **Vista Hermosa.** Older and more rustic than other Hermosa hotels, this place facing the beach has rooms that sleep two to eight people. It's behind a shady palm-tree grove on the beach, hard to find in bare Playa Hermosa. Two small budget cabins in a separate building from the rooms share a bathroom. Only some rooms have hot water. The rooms and restaurant surround two pools shaded by large tropical trees. Common areas have hammocks and diversions like foosball and Ping-Pong. ✉ *Costanera, 150 m south of soccer field* 🖩🖩 *643–3422* ↻ *12 rooms, 2 cabins with shared bath* ⚇ *Restaurant, fans, a/c in some rooms, some kitchenettes, cable TV, 2 pools, laundry service; no room phones, no a/c in some rooms* ▤ *No credit cards* ⦿ *BP.*

### To & From Playa Hermosa
*5 km/3 mi south of Jacó, 113 km/70 mi southwest of San José.*

From Jacó take a taxi or local bus toward Quepos. Some hotels can pick you up from Jacó. On coastal highway, drive 5 km (3 mi) past Jacó. You'll see the cluster of businesses on the right.

### Playa Hermosa Essentials
🈁 Internet **Goola Café and Internet** ✉ Costanera, north of soccer field ☎ 643-3696.
🈁 Tourist Information **Restaurante Jammin'** ✉ In front of Cabinas Las Arenas ☎ 643-1853.

---

# Quepos

🅕 This tourist-rich party town draws visitors with its world-famous sportfishing, laid-back pace, and 24-hour bars. The somewhat seedy gateway to Manuel Antonio is also the area's hub for banks, supermarkets, and other services. Quepos's name stems from the indigenous tribe that inhabited the area until the violence, slavery, and disease that accompanied the Spanish conquest wiped them out. For centuries the town of Quepos barely existed, until the 1930s, when the United Fruit Company built a banana port and populated the area with workers from other parts of Central America. The town thrived for nearly two decades, until Panama disease decimated the banana plantations in the late 1940s. The fruit company then switched to less lucrative African oil palms, and the area declined. Only since the 1980s have tourism revenues lifted the town out of its slump, a renaissance owed to the beauty of the nearby beaches, to Manuel Antonio National Park, whose forests begin just south of town, and to the massive Talamanca Mountain Range, some 10 km (6 mi) to the east, which holds one of the largest expanses of wilderness in Central America. Forests immediately to the north and east of Quepos were destroyed half a century ago, and that landscape is now dominated by oil-palm plantations.

Spread over Fila Chota, a lower ridge of the Talamanca Range 22 km (13 mi) northeast of Quepos, **Rainmaker** is a private nature reserve which protects more than 1,500 acres of lush and precipitous forest. The lower part of the reserve can be visited on guided tours from Manuel Antonio, or as a stop on your way to or from Quepos. Tours ($45; entrance fee included) begin at 8:30 and 12:30, and can include lunch. There are two tours available: a walk up the valley of the Río Seco, which includes a dip in a pool at the foot of a waterfall; or a hike into the hills above the waterfall and over a series of suspension bridges strung between giant tropical trees. The better value is a half-day package ($75; entrance fee included) that includes transport from Manuel Antonio or Quepos, a guided tour, a river swim, and breakfast and lunch. The reserve is home to most of the species found in Costa Rica, and you may spot birds here that you won't find in Manuel Antonio. It isn't as good a place to see animals as the national park, but Rainmaker's forest is different from the park's—lusher and more precipitous—and the view from its bridges is impressive. It's best to visit Rainmaker in the morning, since—true to its name—it often rains in the afternoon. ⊠ *15 km (9 mi) north and 7 km (4 mi) east of Quepos* ☎ *777–3565* ⌑ *$35* ☉ *Mon.–Sat., 8–4.*

## Outdoor Activities

Your hotel's reception desk, a tour operator, or travel agency can can arrange most activities, but some outfitters give discounts if you book directly through them. **Costa Rica's Temptations** (CRT; ⊠ Downtown, next to Adobe car rental ☎ 777–0607 ⊕ www.costarica4u.com) has various area tours. For more options in the area, *see* Outdoor Activities *in* Manuel Antonio, *below.*

KAYAKING & RAFTING **Iguana Tours** (⊠ Downtown Quepos, across from the soccer field ☎ 777–1170 or 770–0161 ⊕ www.iguanatours.com) specializes in exploring the area's natural beauty through river-rafting excursions on the Naranjo and Savegre rivers and kayak adventures by sea or in a mangrove estuary.

CANOPY TOUR The dry season is the best time to glide through the area's rain forests. If you're here during the rains, do a tour first thing in the morning. There are many zip-line tours in the area, but **Canopy Safari** (⊠ Downtown, next to the Poder Judicial ☎ 777–0100 or 777–3079 ⊕ www. canopysafari.com) has a earned a reputation for long and fast-paced rides. Its privately owned forest is about a 45-minute car ride from Quepos, and the tour ($65) includes a meal and swim in a river pool.

HIKING Manuel Antonio National Park is the most popular place to hike, but Rainmaker (⇨ *above*) is more tranquil and lush.

SPORTSFISHING Quepos is one of the best points of departure for deep-sea fishing in southwestern Costa Rica. **Bluefin Tours** (⊠ Downtown, across from the soccer field ☎ 777–2222 or 777–1676 ⊕ www.bluefinsportfishing.com) has catch-and-release sportsfishing, conventional, and fly fishing on half- and full-day charters ($380–$800) aboard 25-, 28-, or 31-foot boats. **Costa Mar Dream Catcher** (⊠ Entrance to Quepos, next to Café Milagro ☎ 777–0725 ⊕ www.costamarsportfishing.com) has half- and full-day charters ($450–$1000) on the largest variety of boats in Quepos; 11 boats range from 25 to 42 feet. Half-, three-quarter-, and full-day catch-and-release fly and conventional trips ($625–$900) with **Luna**

**Tours Sportfishing** (⊠ Downtown, next to Casino Kamuk ☎ 777–0725 ⊕ www.lunatours.net) are available on 27-, 32-, or 33-foot boats.

MOUNTAIN BIKING
The area's green mountains are great for biking, but in the dry season it's hot—very hot. The rainy season is cooler, but be prepared to get muddy. **Cycling Estrella** (⊠ Downtown, in front of Hotel El Pueblo ☎ 777–1286 ⊕ www.puertoquepos.com) has bike tours for intermediate and expert riders. An overnight trip ($625–$900) includes equipment, meals, lodging in mountain cabins, and, in the dry season, nighttime rides. Single-day tours ($95) and 2-hour tours ($45) are also available.

## Where to Stay & Eat

★ $–$$  ✕ **El Gran Escape.** A favorite with sportfishermen ("You hook 'em, we cook 'em"), the Great Escape is the best place for seafood in this area. The menu is dominated by marine entrées, from shrimp scampi to the highly recommended fresh tuna with mushrooms, but you can also get hearty burgers and a handful of Mexican dishes. You won't find any cooked billfish, like marlin, or swordfish, due to its conservation policy, but the back wall is covered with pictures of them (and their proud reelers). Weathered fishing caps hang from the bar's ceiling. ⊠ *150 m north of Hotel Kamuk* ☎ 777–0395 ⊟ *AE, DC, MC, V* ☉ *Closed Tues.*

$–$$  ✕ **La Lanterna.** Owned by a Milanese member of Quepos's small but visible Italian community, La Lanterna has a healthy selection of pastas, seafood, and meat dishes, as well as 18 types of crunchy, thin-crust pizza, baked in a wood oven out front. In addition to many Italian standards, the menu includes such treats as *penne mare monti* (with shrimp and Gorgonzola) and *filetto pomodoro e olive* (sea bass with tomato sauce and olives). Tables covered with white cloths are distributed along the sidewalk of this corner restaurant, and beneath the ceiling fans inside. A wide variety of international wines is available. ⊠ *Southwest corner of Quepos waterfront, diagonal to Banco Nacional* ☎ 777–0650 ⊟ *AE, DC, MC, V.*

$–$$  ▦ **Best Western Hotel Kamuk.** On Quepos's oceanfront street, this local hotel turned Best Western offers the town's priciest accommodations with all the perks of a chain hotel. Only two rooms have sea views, though blotched by electric lines. The rest have private or semiprivate balconies that face the pool and its waterfall or a side street. They all have ho-hum landscape paintings and basic conveniences like irons and blow-dryers. ⊠ *Downtown, 100 m after last bridge into Quepos* ☎ 777–0811 ♨ 777–0258 ⊕ *www.kamuk.co.cr* ⬿ *35 rooms* ♿ *2 restaurants, a/c, fans, in-room safes, cable TV, pool, bar, casino, laundry service, no smoking rooms* ⊟ *AE, MC, DC, V* ❙⊘❙ *BP.*

¢–$  ▦ **Cabinas Ramase.** Within walking distance of the heart of Quepos, this budget hotel has rooms with fans or air-conditioners. A large Indian almond tree in the center and a talkative caged parrot provide a bit of greenery. Aside from the bars around some of the television sets, the no-frills tile-floor rooms are pleasant enough. ⊠ *Eastern corner of the Palí supermarket* ☎☎ 777–0590 ⬿ *6 rooms* ♿ *Some a/c, some fans, refrigerators, cable TV; no room phones* ⊟ *No credit cards* ❙⊘❙ *EP.*

¢–$  ▦ **Hotel Malinche.** The older rooms in the main building of this centrally located hotel are cooled by ceiling fans and have private baths without

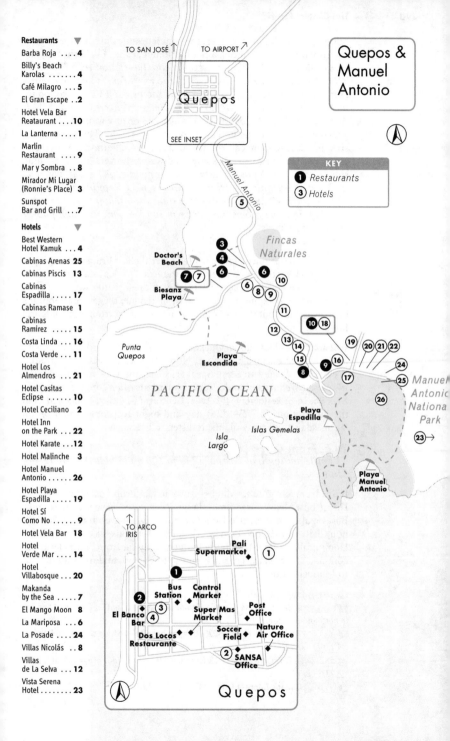

**Quepos & Manuel Antonio**

TO SAN JOSÉ ↑    TO AIRPORT ↗

Quepos

SEE INSET

**Restaurants ▼**

Barba Roja . . . . **4**

Billy's Beach
Karolas . . . . . . . **4**

Café Milagro . . . **5**

El Gran Escape . . **2**

Hotel Vela Bar
Reataurant . . . . **10**

La Lanterna . . . . **1**

Marlin
Restaurant . . . **9**

Mar y Sombra . . **8**

Mirador Mi Lugar
(Ronnie's Place) **3**

Sunspot
Bar and Grill . . . **7**

**Hotels ▼**

Best Western
Hotel Kamuk . . . **4**

Cabinas Arenas **25**

Cabinas Piscis **13**

Cabinas
Espadilla . . . . . **17**

Cabinas Ramase **1**

Cabinas
Ramirez . . . . . **15**

Costa Linda . . . **16**

Costa Verde . . **11**

Hotel Los
Almendros . . . **21**

Hotel Casitas
Eclipse . . . . . . **10**

Hotel Ceciliano **2**

Hotel Inn
on the Park . . . **22**

Hotel Karate . . .**12**

Hotel Malinche **3**

Hotel Manuel
Antonio . . . . . . **26**

Hotel Playa
Espadilla . . . . . **19**

Hotel Sí
Como No . . . . . **9**

Hotel Vela Bar **18**

Hotel
Verde Mar . . . . **14**

Hotel
Villabosque . . . **20**

Makanda
by the Sea . . . . . **7**

El Mango Moon **8**

La Mariposa . . . **6**

La Posade . . . . **24**

Villas Nicolás . . **8**

Villas
de La Selva . . . **12**

Vista Serena
Hotel . . . . . . . . **23**

**KEY**

**1** *Restaurants*

**3** *Hotels*

Manuel Antonio

*Fincas
Naturales*

Doctor's
Beach

Biesanz
Playa

Punta
Quepos

Playa
Escondida

PACIFIC OCEAN

Manuel
Antonio
National
Park

Playa
Espadilla

Isla
Largo

Islas Gemelas

Playa
Manuel
Antonio

↑
TO ARCO
IRIS

Palí
Supermarket

Bus
Station

Control
Market

El Banco
Bar

Super Mas
Market

Post
Office

Dos Locos
Restaurante

Soccer
Field

Nature
Air Office

SANSA
Office

Quepos

hot water. For double the price, the concrete annex holds larger, newer rooms with carpeted floors, air-conditioning, cable TV, hot water, and small balconies. ⊠ *½ block west of Quepos bus station* 🏠🏠 *777–0093* ✏ *hotelmalinche@racsa.co.cr* 🛏 *24 rooms* ⚐ *Fans, some have refrigerators, laundry service; no a/c in some rooms, no TV in some rooms, no hot water in some rooms, no room phones* ⊟ *No credit cards* ⵏ○ⵏ *EP.*

¢ 🖼 **Hotel Ceciliano.** If you arrive in town late or just want to sleep and go, consider this budget hotel with bare, basic rooms. The more expensive, but still economical, rooms include private bath, hot water, and cable TV. Half-price rooms share cold-water showers. It's a tranquil, simple hotel, with a green courtyard in the middle. ⊠ *Downtown, road to Manuel Antonio, in front of the Escuela Republica de Korea* 🏠 *777–0192* 🛏 *24 rooms* ⚐ *A/c in some rooms, fans in some rooms, cable TV in some rooms, hot water in some rooms; no room phones* ⊟ *No credit cards* ⵏ○ⵏ *EP.*

## Nightlife

Large, air-conditioned **El Arco Iris** (⊠ Over the last bridge into Quepos 🏠777–0449) is the only dance club in the area. Quepos locals and Manuel Antonio tourists of all ages pack in after midnight, after warming up in other bars. A DJ spins a mix of salsa, merengue, reggae, and pop. It's open every day, but there's not much activity apart from weekends and holidays.

**El Banco Bar** (⊠ Downtown Quepos 🏠 777–0478) is a laid-back bar with a pool table frequented by younger North American tourists. Happy hour is every day from 4 to 6 PM. Speakers blare pop/rock from the States. It's closed Wednesday. Older American expats often congregate at Tex-Mex **Dos Locos Restaurante** (⊠ Avda. Central at C. Central, diagonal from the bus station 🏠 777–1526) day and night to people-watch or, on Wednesday and Friday nights, to listen to live music.

## To & From Quepos

*23 km/14 mi south of Parrita, 174 km/108 mi (3 hours) southwest of San José.*

Buses from San José to Manuel Antonio can drop you off in Quepos. Direct buses leave three times daily; other buses leave six times daily. Buses make the short trip from Quepos to Manuel Antonio every half hour daily from 7 to 7, then hourly until 10 PM. Buses leave Quepos for Dominical (2½-hour trip) fairly frequently. By car from Playa Hermosa, continue south on the coastal highway to Quepos and from there head to Manuel Antonio.

## Quepos Essentials

🏧 Bank/ATM **BAC San José** ⊠ Avda. Central. **Banco Nacional** ⊠ 50 m west and 100 m north of bus station.

🏥 Hospital **Ambulance** 🏠 380–4125. **Quepos hospital** ⊠ 4 km on road to Dominical 🏠 777–0922.

💊 Pharmacy **Farmacia Fischel** ⊠ Near bus station, in front of municipal market 🏠 777–0816.

🌐 Internet **Quepos Internet Café** ⊠ C. 2 🏠 777–2183.

🚩 Post Office **Correos** ✉ C. Central.
🚩 Taxis **Taxi services.** ☎ 777-0425, 777-0734, or 777-1068
🚩 Travel Agency **Lynch Travel** ✉ Downtown, diagonal from Dos Locos restaurant, behind bus station ☎ 777-1170 ⊕ www.lynchtravel.com

## Manuel Antonio

**⓰** You need merely reach the top of the forested ridge on which many of Manuel Antonio's hotels are perched to understand why it is one of Costa Rica's most popular destinations. That sweeping view of beaches, jungle, and shimmering Pacific dotted with rocky islets confirms its reputation. And unlike the tropical forests in other parts of the country, Manuel Antonio's humid tropical forest remains green year-round. The town itself is spread out across a hilly and curving 5-km (3-mi) road that originates in Quepos and dead-ends at

> ### IN THE THICK OF IT
>
> There's more rain forest on private land than in Manuel Antonio National Park, which means it's not unusual to see many of the animals the park is famous for from the balcony of your hotel room or from your breakfast table. It also means that local landowners play an important role in conserving the area's flora and fauna.

the entrance to Manuel Antonio National Park. Along this main road, near the top of the hill or on its southern slope, are the area's most luxurious hotels and fine-dining restaurants, with amazing views of the rain forest, beaches, and offshore islands. The only problem with staying in one of those hotels is that you'll need to drive or take public transportation to and from the main beach and national park, about 10 to 15 minutes away. More hotel and restaurant options are available at the bottom of the hill, within the touristy center, which is lined with Internet cafées, tour operators, and souvenir shops. Nearly the entire ridge is covered with thick foliage.

Manuel Antonio is a very gay-friendly town. Many hotels and bars cater exclusively to foreign gay travelers and Costa Ricans who come on holiday from San José. The area doesn't cater to budget travelers, so backpackers may want to steer clear. While there are inexpensive accommodations, cheap eats are harder to find. Former *sodas* (low-cost Costa Rican eateries) have been turned into full-scale restaurants, and the overpriced central market lacks fresh fruits and vegetables. Hardly any locals live in touristy Manuel Antonio, and those that do work in hotels and restaurants and bus in from Quepos.

As the road approaches the national park, it skirts the lovely, forest-lined beach of **Playa Espadilla,** which stretches for more than a mile north from the rocky crag that marks the park's border to the base of the ridge. One of the most popular beaches in Costa Rica, Playa Espadilla fills up with sunbathers, surfers, volleyball players, strand strollers, and sand-castle architects on dry-season weekends and holidays, but for most of the year it is surprisingly quiet. Even on the busiest days it is long enough so that you can escape the crowd, which tends to gather around the restaurants

## FODOR'S FIRST PERSON

**Yolanda Hernandez**
*Writer*

As I hopped down the coast gathering information for this book, my birthday popped up on my last day in Manuel Antonio. After weeks of go, go, go, my body was itching to unwind. From the corner of my eye, I glimpsed my book's page holder—a pamphlet for one of the area's countless spas. Two minutes and a phone call later, I had an appointment for an "Energy Medicine" session. After

Reiki, acupressure, and chakra-openings, I left feeling like I was walking on clouds. I headed to quiet Biesanz Beach to float in its calm cove, surrounded by trees and mountains. I couldn't have imagined anything better, until I spotted a tree full of white-faced capuchin monkeys. A few hours later I was back in San José, delighted that I still enjoy being a visitor in this country that's been my home for three years.

and lounge chairs near its southern end. Though it is often safe for swimming, beware of rough seas, which create deadly rip currents.

**Fincas Naturales,** a former plantation, has been reforested to allow native trees to spring back and introduced not-so-native trees like teak. A footpath winds through part of the 30-acre tropical forest, and naturalist guides do a good job of ecological instruction and identifying birds. The reserve is home to three kinds of monkeys, as well as iguanas, motmots, toucans, tanagers, and large rodents called agoutis. Guided walks are given throughout the day: the first starts at 6:30 AM for bird-watching, and the last is a nighttime jungle trek that begins at 5:30 PM. Unfortunately, you can't explore the reserve at your own pace; only the Butterfly Botanical Garden can be seen without a guide. ⊠ *Entrance across street from Sí Como No Hotel* ☎ *777–0850* ⊕ *www. butterflygardens.co.cr* ⊠ *$15–$35, depending on the tour* ⊙ *Daily 6 AM–8 PM.*

### Outdoor Activities
Manuel Antonio's list of outdoor activities is almost endless. But all this excitement doesn't come cheap, and most tours range between $40 to $60 per person. Arrange tours through your hotel's reception desk or any of the tour operators in town, or contact outfitters directly. During the rainy season some outdoor options might lose their appeal; but clouds usually let loose in the afternoon, so take advantage of the sunny mornings. (⇨ For more activities, *see* Outdoor Activities *in* Quepos, *above.*)

TOUR OPERATORS  A small company run by friendly young locals with a good grasp of the area's activities, **Espadilla Tours** (☎ 777–5334 ✉ arellysmonge@yahoo. com) can arrange basically any kind of activity in the Quepos/Manuel Antonio area, from surf lessons to sunset sails. The Internet café next to the Marlin Restaurant has information.

CANOPY TOUR  **Tití Canopy Tours** (☎ 777–1020 or 777–3130 ⊕ www.titicanopytours. ★  com) has a slower-paced zip-line tour ($55) than the one at Canopy Sa-

*Continued on page 298*

# MANUEL ANTONIO NATIONAL PARK

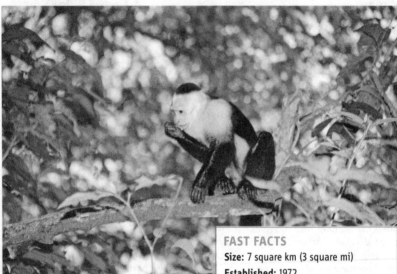

5

MANUEL ANTONIO NATIONAL PARK

★ **Fodor's Choice** | **GOOD THINGS COME IN SMALL PACKAGES.** Case in point, Costa Rica's smallest park packs in an impressive collection of natural attractions: lots of wildlife, rain forest, white-sand beaches, coral reefs, and rocky coves with abundant marine life. Trails are short, well maintained, and easy to walk. The forest is dominated by massive ficus and gumbo-limbo trees, and is home to two- and three-toed sloths, green and black iguanas, agoutis, four species of monkeys, and nearly 200 species of birds.

**FAST FACTS**

**Size:** 7 square km (3 square mi)

**Established:** 1972

**Dry season:** December–April

**Wettest months:** September–October

**What to do:** Nature hikes, bird-watching, wildlife-watching, kayaking, snorkeling, swimming

**Geography:** 5 km (3 mi) of coastline; 700 hectares (1,730 acres) of primary, secondary, and mangrove forest; 12 islands

**Number of species catalogued:** 184 birds, 109 mammals, 60 fish, 4 turtles

- One of two places in Costa Rica to see squirrel monkeys.
- One of two places in Costa Rica to see all four of Costa Rica's monkey species.
- One of the best places in Costa Rica to see three-toed sloths.
- Despite being Costa Rica's smallest national park, this is its second most-visited, after Poás Volcano.

Espadilla Beach

Make no mistake about it: Manuel Antonio is no undiscovered wilderness. It's one of Costa Rica's most-visited attractions, so if you're looking for an undisturbed natural oasis, this is not it. But what Manuel Antonio *does* have is great diversity of wildlife, all easily spotted from the well-marked trails. And because animals are so used to humans, this is one of the best places to see them up close.

## ATTRACTIONS

From the ranger station a trail leads through the rain forest behind **Playa Espadilla Sur,** the park's longest beach. It's also the least crowded because the water can be rough. ⚠ Riptides are brutal at Playa Espadilla when the surf is up; more than a few unsuspecting tourists have been swept away. Snorkeling, however, is good in the tidal pools. The coral reefs and submerged volcanic rocks of white-sand **Playa Manuel Antonio** also make for good snorkeling. The 1/2-mile-long beach, tucked into a deep cove, is safe for swimming. At low tide you can see the remains of a Quepos Indian turtle trap on the right—the Quepos stuck poles in the semicircular rock formation, which trapped turtles as the tide receded. Olive ridley and green turtles come ashore on this beach May through November. Espadilla and Manuel Antonio beaches lie on opposite sides of a tombolo, or a sandy strip that connects the mainland to **Punta Catedral** (Cathedral Point), which used to be an island. The steep path that leads up Punta Catedral's rocky hill draped with thick jungle, passes a lookout point from which you can gaze over the Pacific at the park's islands. ⚠ Theft is a problem on the beaches; don't leave your belongings unattended while you swim and don't leave anything of value in your car.

Farther east, **Playa Escondido** (Hidden Beach) is rocky and secluded, but it's also more difficult to access. Before you head out to Escondido, find out when the tides come in so you're not stranded. **Playa Playita,** south of Escondido, is Costa Rica's only nude beach, though unofficially so. It also tends to be a favorite of gay sun-seekers. It's quiet and secluded. Kayaking trips might take you down to **Punta Serrucho** near the southern border of the park, whose jagged peaks explain its name. (*Serrucho* means "saw.")

**Trails** from the entrance to Punta Catedral and Playa Manuel Antonio are in good shape. Trails farther east to Escondido and Playita are progressively rougher going.

Squirrel Monkey

## MONKEY BUSINESS

Monkeys are undoubtedly the superstars of Manuel Antonio wildlife. It's nearly impossible to tour the park without seeing at least one species. ⚠ Never feed or touch the monkeys: they have been known to bite overly friendly visitors and they can get sick, or even die from eating improper foods. Some monkeys are kleptomaniacs, so keep your backpack tightly zipped.

The **squirrel monkey** (*mono tití* in Spanish), the world's smallest monkey, is critically endangered, with only 1,200 to 1,500 remaining. Manuel Antonio is one of only two places in Costa Rica (the Osa Peninsula being the other) and three places in the world inhabited by squirrel monkeys.

Monkeys can't thrive only within the small park's border. To allow them to access areas outside the park, forested corridors have been built connecting the habitats. Suspended bridges allow monkeys to travel above roads around the park. Still, growing infrastructure around the park threatens the monkey population.

## A SHAKY START

Before 1972 the land that now constitutes the park had a succession of foreign private owners intent on making a profit from tourism. These owners alienated the local community by cutting off their access to the park and, in the case of the final owner, razing tracts of forest and allegedly dumping pesticides to throw a wrench in the government's plan to create a protected area. The government seized the land shortly thereafter.

## ACTIVITIES

### KAYAKING

**Iguana Tours** (☎ 777–1262 ⊕ www.iguanatours.com) runs sea-kayaking trips ($65) to the park's islands—which require some experience when the seas are high—and a mellower paddle through the mangrove estuary of Isla Damas, where you see monkeys, crocodiles and birds.

### SNORKELING

**Playa Manuel Antonio**, the third beach inside the national park, is a good snorkeling spot thanks to calm, clear waters and the varied marine life on and around submerged rocks. Snorkeling is best during the dry season, when tidal pools are clear.

### SWIMMING

Manuel Antonio's safest swimming area is sheltered **Playa Manuel Antonio**, whose white sand makes it attractive for lounging while keeping an eye on pint-sized swimmers.

## TOP WILDLIFE

Top on our list of animals to see here are:

- howler monkeys
- white-faced capuchin monkeys
- squirrel monkeys
- two- and three-toed sloths
- agoutis
- coatis
- magnificent frigate birds
- olive ridley turtles (May–November)
- green turtles (July–September)

For information on these and other species, *see* the Wildlife & Plant Glossary *in* Understanding Costa Rica, at the back of the book.

Sloth

## TIPS

- Hire a guide—you'll walk away with a basic understanding of the flora and fauna and see things you probably would have missed otherwise. Hire one at the entrance of the park or through any tour operator in town.

- Beware of *manzanillo* trees (indicated by warning signs)—their leaves, bark, and applelike fruit secrete a gooey substance that irritates the skin.

- Get here as early as possible—between 7 and 8 AM is ideal. Rangers permit only 600 to 800 people inside at a time, and during peak season visitors line up to enter. Early morning is also the best time to see animals. Avoid weekends and major holidays, particularly around Christmas and the week before Easter, when the park is packed.

- Camping is not allowed in the park, and there are no lodges or food.

- Park beaches do not have lifeguards, but that doesn't mean that swimming is always safe. Riptides are dangerous everywhere except at Manuel Antonio Beach.

- If you want to snorkel, come during the December–April dry season; at other times of the year, heavy rains cloud the water.

## A FRAGILE BEAUTY

Deforestation, development, cattle ranching, pollution, and tourism place environmental stress on the park. Tourism brings in enough revenue for the federal government to sustain the park, but the majority of the money goes to fund social programs. The major problems facing Manuel Antonio today are:

- Hotel and resort development that encroaches on natural wildlife corridors and traps animals within the park, diminishing their gene pool and threatening biodiversity

- Endangered squirrel-monkey population

- Solid-waste pollution

- Overwhelming growth that outruns development of infrastructure to handle it

- Lax regulations, corruption of park management, and poor relationship between the park and the municipality

## PARK INFO

**Hours of Operation:** Tuesday–Sunday 7–4. Closed Monday.

**Contacts:** 777–0654

**Admission:** $7

**Getting There:** From San José, 3½ hours by car, 4 hours by bus, or a 30-minute flight to Quepos, then 15 minutes by car. Entrance at the end of the main road from Quepos. Parking is less than $2.
■ TIP→→ The park entrance is across a shallow estuary that is so deep when the tide changes in the early morning and late afternoon that you have to pay a boatman (less than $1) to ferry you across it.

HOW MUCH TIME? A few hours is sufficient to tour the short trails and see some wild animals, but we recommend an entire day that includes lounging on the beaches, and/or hiking the challenging trails toward Puerto Escondido.

5

MANUEL ANTONIO NATIONAL PARK

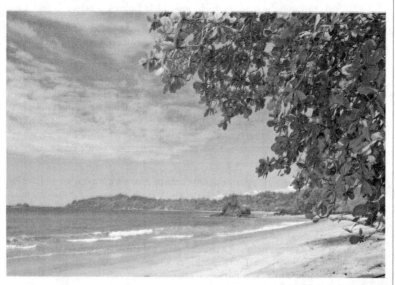

Manuel Antonio National Park

fari ( ⇨ Quepos, *above*), which gives you a better chance to spot animals and take in the scenery. It's also closer to Manuel Antonio. Guides go above and beyond to make you feel comfortable and safe.

HIKING    Highly visited Manuel Antonio National Park is the obvious place to go, but in private reserves like Fincas Naturales ( ⇨ *above*) and Rainmaker ( ⇨ Quepos, *above*) you can do more solitary hikes, gaining a richer appreciation of the local forests' greenery and wildlife. ■ TIP→→ Bring binoculars!

HORSEBACK RIDING    **Brisas del Nara** (☎ 779–1235 ⊕ www.horsebacktour.com) takes riders of all ages and levels through the protected Cerro Nara mountain zone, 10 miles from Manuel Antonio, and ends at a 350-foot waterfall within its property. Full-day tours include three hours on horseback, while the half-day tour lasts two hours on easier terrain. All tours include a meal. **Finca Valmy Tours** (☎ 779–1118 ⊕ www.valmytours. com) is known for its attentive service and expert guides. Its half-day horseback tours take you through the forested mountains above Villa Nueva, east of Manuel Antonio. Lunch and swimming in a pool below a waterfall are included.

Beach riding is the specialty of **Rancho Savegre** (☎ 777–0266 ✎ diegoso-lis@racsa.co.cr). Run by two cowboy hat–wearing brothers, trips set out from a cattle ranch about 15 minutes south of Manuel Antonio and include a stop at a waterfall for swimming or trail walking. Of the two half-day tours, only the morning tour includes a meal.

KAYAKING    **Iguana Tours** (☎ 777–1262 ⊕ www.iguanatours.com) runs sea-kayaking trips ($65) to the islands of Manuel Antonio National Park—which require some experience when the seas are high—and a mellower paddle through the mangrove estuary of Isla Damas, where you might see monkeys, crocodiles, and various birds.

SNORKELING    Multiple tour operators in town can put you on an organized snorkel excursion. Or for a more personalized and inexpensive experience, hire one of the locals waiting to take visitors on a short boat ride to the best snorkel spots. They're usually hanging out along Playas Espadilla and Biesanz. **Playa Biesanz,** near the Hotel Parador and ½ km (¼ mi) south of Makanda by the Sea, is in a protected cove full of rocks that provide habitat for marine life and calm swimming. **Playa Manuel Antonio,** the third beach inside the national park, is a good snorkeling spot thanks to calm, clear waters and the varied marine life on and around submerged rocks.

SWIMMING    When the surf is up, riptides are a dangerous problem on long Playa Espadilla ( ⇨ *above*), Manuel Antonio's main beach, which runs parallel to the road to the park's entrance. For a less turbulent swim and smaller crowds, head to **Playa Biesanz** (✉ Near Hotel Parador), which lies within a sheltered cove and also makes for great snorkeling. Manuel Antonio's safest swimming area is sheltered **Playa Manuel Antonio,** which lies within the national park. Its white sand makes it attractive for lounging around, and it's also good place for snorkeling. ⚠ Never leave your valuables unattended while you're swimming.

ULTRALIGHT
FLIGHTS AND
PARASAILING

Show up at **Gold Coast Parasail** (⊠ Espadilla Beach, in front of Mono Loco Restaurant ☎ 307–2606 [$60]) about 10 minutes before departure times—at 9 and 11 AM and 1 and 3 PM—to soar 800 feet into the air. **Sky Riders** (☎ 777–4101 ✐ skyriders@amnet.co.cr) has open-cockpit, slow-flying ultralights that glide between sea level and 1,000 feet. One tour is a one-passenger, 24-minute ride over Manuel Antonio and several surrounding beaches ($72). The other is a two-person 35-minute flight over Damas Island's canals and mangroves ($105).

WHITE-WATER
RAFTING

The three white-water rivers in this area have limited seasons. The rains from August to October raise the rivers to their perfect peak. **Río Savegre,** which flows past patches of rain forest, has two navigable stretches: the lower section (Class II–III), which is a mellow trip perfect for neophytes, and the more rambunctious upper section (Class III–IV). It is usually navigable from June to March. **Río Naranjo** (Class III–IV) has a short but exciting run that requires some experience and can be done only from June to December. **Río Parrita** (Class II–III) is a relatively mellow white-water route, and in the dry season it can be navigated only in two-person, inflatable duckies.

Manuel Antonio's original rafting outfitter, **Amigos del Río** (☎ 777–0082 ⊕ www.adventuremanuelantonio.com), leads trips down the Savegre and Naranjo on two-day, full-day, and half-day tours. Naranjo River tours can be combined with kayaking in the nearby estuary. **Rios Tropicales** (☎ 777–4092 ⊕ www.aventurash2o.com), the biggest rafting outfitter in the country, runs kayaking excursions and rafting trips on the Savegre and Naranjo.

## Where to Stay & Eat

$$ ✕ **Barba Roja.** Near the top of the hill, with a sweeping view of the sea and jungle, pirate-themed "Red Beard" is one of this town's oldest and most popular restaurants. Hardwoods furnish the open-air brick-floored dining room. The view, which is most impressive at sunset and equally good from any seat in the house, compensates for the sparse decoration. Tasty sandwiches are on the lunch menu; the most popular dinner plate is the seared ginger-soy tuna, or try a daily seafood special. The bar fills up for a happy hour lighted by crepuscular colors. There's often live jazz on Sundays. ⊠ *Main road to the park, in front of Hotel Divisamar, on the right* ☎ 777–0331 ▤ MC, V ☺ *Breakfast served* ☺ *No breakfast or lunch Mon.*

★ $$ ✕ **Billy's Beach Karolas.** Off the main road and tucked in the forest just below Barba Roja, plastic chairs and tables with candles are arranged under several covered and uncovered patio areas. The food is tasty, but some argue that it's overpriced. The tranquil setting makes up for the lack of ocean view. The most popular dishes are fresh tuna, shrimp, or the Plato Gordo, a mix of local seafood for two. Tenderloin, ribs, and Caribbean chicken are also top-notch, as are the desserts—leave room for a slice of macadamia pie. ⊠ *Down steep driveway south of Barba Roja* ☎ 777–1557 ▤ AE, MC, V.

★ $–$$ ✕ **Hotel Vela Bar Restaurant.** This small open-air, roadside restaurant retains an intimate atmosphere behind a minijungle of tropical foliage. Beneath a conical thatched roof it serves a variety of dishes in generous proportions, including shrimp in ginger, pork chops in pineapple sauce, vegetarian options, and nightly specials. Service can be slow when the place fills up. ⊠ *Up road from Marlin Restaurant, on left* ☎ 777–0413 ▭ *AE, DC, MC, V* ☺ *Breakfast served.*

**$–$$** ✕ **Sunspot Bar and Grill.** The open-air, poolside restaurant of the exclusive Makanda by the Sea hotel has tables beneath purple cloth tents, which overlook the sea and surrounding trees. Its kitchen is cleverly hidden beneath and serves up such succulent treats as jumbo shrimp in a ginger sauce and grilled beef tenderloin with different sauces. The menu also includes poultry and pasta dishes, along with nightly specials that sometimes list tender New Zealand lamb. ⊠ *Makanda by the Sea hotel, 1 km (½ mi) west of La Mariposa* ☎ 777–0442 ▭ *V* ⚞ *Reservations essential.*

**¢–$$** ✕ **Marlin Restaurant.** The outdoor tables of this two-story concrete restaurant are pretty much always full due to its location on Manuel Antonio's busiest corner, across the street from the beach. It's a convenient place to grab breakfast after an early-morning hike through the park—be it banana pancakes or a *típico*, with eggs and *gallo pinto* (black beans and rice). The lunch and dinner menu ranges from the ubiquitous *arroz con pollo* (rice with chicken) to pastas, tenderloin with homefries, and jumbo shrimp in garlic and lemon butter. The best place to sit is at the picnic tables with umbrellas in the front garden, nicely lighted at night. ⊠ *On corner across from bus stop* ☎ 777–1134 ▭ *AE, DC, MC, V* ☺ *Breakfast served.*

**¢–$$** ✕ **Mar y Sombra.** You haven't been to Manuel Antonio unless you've contemplated the sea from one of the circular concrete tables in the sand at Mar y Sombra, one of the area's first enterprises popular with nationals and internationals alike. The food may not win any awards, but it's hard to top the view of Playa Espadilla and the island-studded sea and the decor, a roof of Indian almond trees and thick lianas draped with moss, ferns, and orchids. Try a typical *gallo pinto* at breakfast or *casado* for lunch, but the best bet is the fresh dorado and other seafood. Even if you don't eat, have a drink here, preferably at sunset. ⊠ *Next to Cabinas Ramirez, on Playa Espadilla* ☎ 777–0003 ▭ *AE, MC, V* ☺ *Breakfast served.*

**¢** ✕ **Café Milagro.** The only place in town that serves its own fresh-roasted coffee, Café Milagro is a colorful, cozy place for breakfast food any time of the day, or to satisfy a chocolate-chip cookie craving. The North American menu includes bagels, breakfast burritos, baked goods like brownies and muffins, an inventive selection of sandwiches, and a fruit plate with granola. Tables on the front porch overlook the road, but there's also seating in the back garden. **El Patio,** an affiliated gourmet Latin bistro next door, is worth the drive for dinner (Monday–Saturday only). ⊠ *Main road to the park, across from Karolas, on the left* ☎ 777–0794 ▭ *AE, DC, MC, V* ☺ *Breakfast served.*

**¢** ✕ **Mirador Mi Lugar (Ronnie's Place).** A spectacular sunset view and friendly, attentive service are this simple, open-air restaurant's best qualities. The location is secluded: down a long dirt road that crosses a green valley on a narrow ridge in front of the sea. (Only attempt this route on foot during the day.) The small menu includes delicious sea-bass *ceviche,* pastas, sandwiches, grilled fish or shrimp on a skewer, and filet mignon wrapped with bacon and mushroom sauce. Sit at one of its concrete picnic tables close to the sea and sip on its popular sangria. ⊠ *Down dirt road 1 km (½ mi) west of main road from Amigos del Río* ☎ *777–5120* ⊟ *AE, DC, MC, V* ☾ *Breakfast served.*

☾ ★
$$$–$$$$
    **Hotel Sí Como No.** As is evident from the partial solar power, energy-efficient air-conditioning, and plantation wood, Sí Como No makes an effort to be eco-friendly and is a level-four member of Certificate of Sustainable Tourism. (Level five is the highest.) "Family-friendly" is another adjective that could be used to describe this place. Rooms of varying sizes (and prices) are in two-story concrete buildings. Request a room away from the road, and spring for a deluxe room for a sea view. Two pools—one for adults only—have cascades, swim-up bars, and adjacent restaurants. A free shuttle heads frequently to the beach, about 2 mi away, and movies are shown nightly. Concrete painted to resemble bamboo and palm trees evokes Disneyland, but the forest and ocean views are 100 percent Costa Rica. ⊠ *Road to park, just after of Villas Nicolás, right-hand side* ☎ *777–0777* 📠 *777–1093* ⊕ *www.sicomono.com* ⇲ *60 rooms, 4 honeymoon suites* ☾ *2 restaurants, a/c, fans, in-room safes, some kitchenettes, minibars, 2 pools, 2 whirlpool tubs, spa, 2 bars, shop, laundry service, Internet; no room TVs* ⊟ *AE, MC, V* ⍾⊙⍾ *BP.*

$$$$
Fodor'sChoice
★
    **Makanda by the Sea.** Hypnotic views of the jungle-framed Pacific Ocean and spacious villas for two make this secluded rain-forest retreat perfect for honeymooners. White-and-cream villas, which are among the country's best (and most expensive), have a comfortable seating area and king-size bed facing the glass doors that lead to large balconies with ocean views. The modern kitchens won't be necessary for breakfast, which is delivered to your room. Windows behind the bed maximize natural light, and the small Japanese-style garden out back adds to the subtle, well-designed touches. The smaller studios lack many villa amenities and have less private views. The Sunspot Bar and Grill ( ⇨ *above*) is one of the best restaurants in town. ⊠ *1 km (½ mi) west of La Mariposa* ☎ *777–0442, 888/625–2632 in U.S. and Canada* 📠 *777–1032* ⊕ *www. makanda.com* ⇲ *6 villas, 5 studios* ☾ *Restaurant, bar, room service, a/c, fans, in-room safes, kitchens, pool, massage, beach, laundry service, Internet; no a/c in one villa, no kids under 16* ⊟ *AE, MC, V* ⍾⊙⍾ *BP.*

$$$–$$$$
Fodor'sChoice
★
    **La Mariposa.** The best view in town—a sweeping panorama of verdant hills, the aquamarine Pacific, and offshore islands—is Mariposa's claim to fame. Accommodations range from standard rooms overlooking the rain forest to bright suites with ocean-view balconies to a comfortable master suite to a penthouse. All are spacious, with hand-carved furniture and large baths, and are located in a series of buildings between the jungle and gardens ablaze with colorful flowers. The white four-story main building with external spiraling stairways on both sides holds the lobby, restaurant, pools, and suites, which have semiprivate balconies. Transportation is provided to the beach, about 2½ mi away. ⊠ *Road to park, 100 m past Café Milagro, on the right* ⊕ *www. hotelmariposa.com* ☎ *777–0355, 800/368–2121 in U.S.* 📠 *777–0050*

🛏 *60 rooms* 🍴 *Restaurant, room service, a/c, in-room safes, some kitchenettes, 3 pools, 2 bars, shop, laundry service, concierge, Internet, in-room broadband; no room TVs* ▤ *AE, DC, MC, V* 🍽 *EP.*

★ $$$ 🏨 **El Mango Moon.** This bed-and-breakfast's intimate atmosphere and hospitable owners make you feel like you're with a friend rather than at a hotel. The comfy, open living-room area extends to a balcony lined with a wooden counter and stools with views to the mango-shaped pool below and a tranquil cove dotted with boats. The cream-color rooms vary in size and amenities; some have private or semiprivate balconies. Rooms on the top floor can connect for families and functions. Monkey-attracting mango trees surround the building, and a 15-minute trail leads to a secluded beach. Plush bathrobes and fine chocolates are among the hotel's personal touches. ✉ *Between La Mariposa and Hotel El Parador, on the right if coming from La Mariposa* 🕿 *777–5323* 🖷 *777–5128* 🌐 *www.mangomoon.net* 🛏 *8 rooms* 🍴 *A/c, fans, some kitchens, some refrigerators, cable TV, pool, massage, Internet, no-smoking rooms; no room phones, no kids under 12* ▤ *V* 🍽 *BP.*

★ $$–$$$ 🏨 **Costa Verde.** You're likely to see monkeys, iguanas, and all kinds of birds on the forest trails surrounding this extensive hotel's buildings, which are scattered on both sides of the main road, about 800 meters from the beach. Adult-only studios are spacious, with large balconies and screened walls that let the breeze through. Those in the other buildings are smaller, but can be closed and air-conditioned. Splurge for a Studio-Plus, which means it has an ocean view. Three fully-equipped bungalows are also available for groups of six or less. The cheaper, standard rooms are a mixed lot—only those in Building D, in the jungle overlooking the sea, are recommended. Transportation vestiges, like a plane from 1954, stand curiously next to two of the hotel's restaurants, and its reception and Internet café are inside antique train wagons. ✉ *Road to park, at Km 6* 🕿 *777–0584, 777–0187* 🖷 *777–0560* 🌐 *www.costaverde.com* 🛏 *3 rooms, 36 studios, 3 bungalows* 🍴 *3 restaurants, a/c in some rooms, fans, kitchenettes, cable TV, 3 pools, 4 bars, laundry service, Internet; no a/c in some rooms, no room phones* ▤ *AE, MC, V* 🍽 *EP.*

★ $$–$$$ 🏨 **Hotel Casitas Eclipse.** Perched on a hilltop about half a mile from the beach, this hotel with its Mediterranean-style architecture gives you the impression you're in the Greek Isles, until you spot the exuberant tropical forest below. The spacious two-story, white casitas with clay-tile roofs can be rented out entirely to include two separate bedroom areas and a kitchen, or by floors. Though the dull interior decor falls far behind the exterior, the casitas are comfortable, luminous, and ideal for groups. The balconies of the bottom casitas are closest to the jungle. The charmless standard rooms in the hotel section are worth skipping. ✉ *Road to park, at Km 5, in front of El Avíon restaurant* 🕿 *770–0408* 🖷 *777–1738* 🌐 *www.casitaseclipse.com* 🛏 *10 casitas, 13 rooms* 🍴 *Restaurant, a/c, fans, in-room safes, kitchenettes, refrigerators, cable TV, 3 pools, fitness room, massage, 2 bars, laundry service, no-smoking rooms* ▤ *AE, MC, V* 🍽 *BP.*

$$–$$$ 🏨 **Villas Nicolás.** Built on a hillside about two miles from the beach, villas—each with one bedroom—scale down into the jungle and have im-

# Getting Married in Costa Rica

COUPLES LONG AGO DISCOVERED that Costa Rica's rain forests, volcanoes, beaches, and sunsets make the country a prime honeymoon destination. A growing number are deciding to start that honeymoon early and tie the knot here as well.

First the marriage legalities:

• Any two people of the opposite sex at least 18 years old may marry in Costa Rica.

• Your passport must have at least six months' remaining validity.

• Your witnesses, who may not be your relatives, must meet the same requirements.

• You need to demonstrate that any former marriage is no longer in effect by providing a copy of a divorce decree or death certificate of a prior spouse; a Costa Rican consulate in the country where those documents were issued must translate them into Spanish and notarize them.

• A woman must wait at least 10 months after the end of a previous marriage or provide a medical statement attesting to not being pregnant (presumably with her ex-husband's child); a man has no waiting period.

Judges, attorneys, and Catholic priests have legal authority to certify a marriage in Costa Rica. While the law provides for complete freedom of religion, it grants the Catholic Church special "state church" status, meaning that if you have an official other than a Catholic priest preside over your service, a lawyer or judge will have to make it legal, either at the ceremony or at his or her office later. The priest (in a Catholic ceremony), a lawyer, or a judge will register the marriage with the Civil Registry and your own embassy. The license takes three months to issue and is sent to your home address. Virtually all Western countries recognize the legality of a Costa Rican marriage.

While the country offers no shortage of impressive backdrops for a ceremony, the Central Pacific coast sees the most tourist weddings, hands down. (May and June are the most popular months.) Manuel Antonio's Makanda by the Sea, La Mariposa, and Sí Como No and Punta Leona's Villa Caletas are among the many lodgings here with events staffs well versed in planning ceremonies and tending to the legalities. You need only say, "I do." Private wedding planner Tropical Occasions (☎ 249-0773 ⊕ www. tropicaloccasions.com) comes highly recommended and has over 450 weddings under its belt. It also has arranged a few same-sex commitment ceremonies, although Costa Rican law does not recognize these as legally binding.

5

pressive views of the ocean. Narrow walkways wind through the small and tranquil property, with its large pool, gardens, and nine two-story villas. Those on the upper levels have Pacific views, lower-level villas have jungle views, and those in the lower left corner overlook the hotel next door. Though each unit is decorated differently, most have balconies, some of which are large enough to hold a table, chairs, and hammock. In the high season, the small poolside restaurant serves breakfast and dinner. ⊠ *Road to park, across from Hotel Byblos, on the right* ☎ 777–0481 🖷 777–0451 ⊕ *www.villasnicolas.com* ⌁ *19 villas* ⚘ *Restaurant, fans, in-room safes, some kitchenettes, refrigerators, pool, laundry service, travel services; no smoking rooms, no a/c in some rooms, no room TVs* ⊟ *AE, DC, MC, V* ⑩ *CP.*

☾ ★ $$ 🏨 **Hotel Inn on the Park.** This family-friendly inn has a quiet central location, personalized service, and spacious rooms. From the outside it looks like an apartment building, and has three floors with two rooms each. Half are larger master suites, which have a separate bedroom and sizable kitchen. Upper rooms in the papaya-colored building share balconies. A small pool area with a wooden deck has a grill, and the gregarious English owner, who lives next door, is very attentive. The hotel has boogie-board and surfboard rentals. ⊠ *Up the road to the right of the Marlin Restaurant, turn right at Hotel Villabosque, on the left* ☎ 777–5115 *or* 777–5232 🖷 777–3468 ⊕ *www.innontheparkhotel. com* ⌁ *6 rooms* ⚘ *A/c, fans, in-room safes, some kitchens, cable TV, pool, laundry service, no-smoking rooms* ⑩ *BP.*

☾ $$ 🏨 **Hotel Playa Espadilla.** Close to the beach and park, this friendly hotel spreads back across rectangular-shaped grounds, bordered on two sides by the tall trees of its private reserve, with a trail. The simple but spacious mint-green rooms with big windows are housed in two-story concrete buildings surrounded by green lawns; for a bit more, some rooms have good-sized kitchens with modern appliances. A small blue-tile pool and patio area have a pleasant adjacent bar area with a billiard table. Directly behind is a large, open-air restaurant with elegant table settings, followed by a tennis court. ⊠ *End of dirt road, to the right of Marlin Restaurant* ☎☎ 777–2135 ⊕ *www.espadilla.com* ⌁ *16 rooms* ⚘ *Restaurant, snack bar, room service, a/c, some fans, in-room safes, some kitchenettes, cable TV, tennis court, pool, bar, laundry service, in-room data ports* ⊟ *AE, DC, MC, V* ⑩ *BP.*

$$ 🏨 **Hotel Verde Mar.** This whimsical little hotel and its helpful staff are in the rain forest, with direct access to the beach and minutes away from the park. The rooms are in a long two-story concrete building, and have colorfully artistic interiors, kitchenettes, and large windows with views of the ubiquitous tropical foliage. Suites are a bit bigger than standard rooms, which are closest to the beach, and have two queen beds and a walk-in closet. There's a small pool in back, from which a wooden catwalk leads through the woods to the nearby beach. The hotel has boogie-board rental. ⊠ *½ km (¼ mi) north of park* ☎ 777–1805 🖷 777–1311 ✉ *verdemar@racsa.co.cr* ⌁ *22 rooms* ⚘ *A/c, fans, kitchenettes, pool, no-smoking rooms; no room phones, no room TVs* ⊟ *AE, MC, V* ⑩ *EP.*

★ $$ 🏨 **Hotel Villabosque.** In "downtown" Manuel Antonio, this cramped, overbuilt hotel has pleasant rooms with wooden furniture, soft-colored walls, and one small painting each. Most are in a two-story motel-style building facing the gravel parking lot out front; others open onto a communal TV area and have less natural light. Rooms above the restaurant are smaller, but have private balconies with a table and chairs (Room 11 has the best forest view). A peaceful river runs behind the hotel amid tall trees and intertwined lianas (corner Room 18 is the closest), but unfortunately it's mostly hidden behind the construction. The shadeless pool is raised above the reception area. ✉ *From the Marlin Restaurant, 200 m east, end of the Rd.* ☎ 777–0463 🖷 777–0401 ✐ *hotelvilla-bosque@racsa.co.cr* 🗩 *17 rooms* ⚴ *Restaurant, a/c, in-room safes, cable TV, pool, massage, bar, laundry service; no room phones* ▤ *AE, DC, MC, V* ⦿ *CP.*

**$$**
**Fodor'sChoice**
★

🖾 **La Posada.** Nestled on the edge of the national park, this small group of bungalows is a rare gem within Manuel Antonio, and only a short walk from the beach. Each bungalow has its own theme—Fisherman, Birds of Paradise, and Jungle are a few—and is decorated accordingly. The palm-thatched covered terraces face the small pool and lush greenery of the rain forest next door. As the charming North American owner who lives on-site says, it's as close as you'll get to sleeping in the park. ✉ *Next to the park's exit* ☎🖷 777–5347 ⊕ *www.laposadajungle.com* 🗩 *5 bungalows, 1 apartment* ⚴ *A/c, fans, microwaves, refrigerators, pool, whirlpool tub, laundry service, no smoking rooms; no room phones* ▤ *MC, V* ⦿ *BP.*

**★ $–$$$**

🖾 **Villas de la Selva.** Hidden from the main road behind a mural of monkeys, almost as if to keep this place a secret, lies this unique, tiny hillside hotel with comfortable accommodations and great views of the Pacific. Straight down the long stairway, and perched on a cliff facing the ocean, stand three charming and airy rooms, each with its own colorful decor, kitchenette, and ample terrace. There's also a casita that fits several people. Up the side of the hill, two much smaller rooms have reduced balconies with more distant, but great views and local artesanal decor, but small bathrooms. A 300-meter trail leads to the beach. ✉ *Road to park, on right (coming from Quepos) after Costa Verde and La Arboleda hotels* ☎ 777–1137 🖷 777–0434 🗩 *7 rooms, 1 casita* ⚴ *Some a/c, some fans, some in-room safes, some kitchenettes, pool, laundry service; no room phones* ▤ *No credit cards* ⦿ *EP.*

**$**

🖾 **Cabinas Espadilla.** Across the street from Hotel Playa Espadilla, which is owned by the same family, these quiet concrete cabinas close to the beach are more affordable but have fewer amenities. Rooms open onto porches overlooking a wide lawn shaded by hammock-strung palm trees near a pool. The rooms with kitchenettes are ventilated by fans and less expensive than those with air-conditioning. Guests have access to the hotel's private reserve and trail. ✉ *Up dirt road to the right of Marlin Restaurant* ☎🖷 777–2113 ⊕ *www.espadilla.com* 🗩 *16 cabinas* ⚴ *Some fans, some a/c, in-room safes, some kitchenettes, pool, laundry service; no room phones, no room TVs* ▤ *AE, MC, V* ⦿ *EP.*

**★ ¢–$$**

✕🖾 **Hotel Vela Bar.** Abutting the jungle a mere 100 meters up a dirt road from Playa Espadilla, this low-key eclectic hotel has rooms of varying size and amenities at competitive rates. Though small, each room has its own rustic charm, with simple wooden furniture, terra-cotta tile or wooden floors, and minimal decor. For two, white-walled Room 7 is particularly charming, with large windows and a bathtub. Balconies and terraces with rocking chairs and hammocks overlook the tall, lush gardens. The casita, with a private patio, air-conditioning, and TV, sleeps four. The restaurant (⇨ *above*) is excellent. ✉ *Up road from Marlin*

**5**

*Restaurant, on left* ☎ 777–0413 🖷 777–1071 ⊕ *www.velabar.com*
🛏 *10 rooms, 1 casita* ♻ *Restaurant, a/c in some rooms, fans, some in-room safes, some kitchenettes, some refrigerators, cable TV in some rooms, bar, laundry service, Internet; no a/c in some rooms, no room phones* 🖃 *AE, DC, MC, V.*

★ ¢–$ 🏨 **Cabinas Arenas.** On a quiet street next to the park's exit, this tiny hotel rents three basic but comfortable rooms only a few minutes from the beach. Two have a double bed and one single; the third contains two doubles. Directly next to it stands an Italian eatery and souvenir shop with park-themed items. ✉ *Next to the park's exit* ☎ 777–5113 🛏 *3 rooms* ♻ *A/c, fans, microwaves, refrigerators; no room phones* 🖃 *No credit cards* ¶○¶ *EP.*

¢–$ 🏨 **Cabinas Piscis.** Shaded by tall trees a short walk through the woods from the beach, this older, tranquil hotel is one of the area's best deals. Most rooms are in a concrete building with a wide porch; they are simple but spacious, with small bathrooms and lots of windows. The tiny, lower-price rooms that share a separate, cold-water bathhouse are geared toward backpackers. Also available is a separate cabin with a refrigerator and an open-room, fully equipped *casita* for four. A small restaurant serves breakfast and light lunches. Bathrooms do not have hot water. ✉ *Road to park, right after Hotel Karahe, on right* 🖷🖷 777–0046 or 777–5320 ✉ *vivipisc@racsa.co.cr* 🛏 *15 rooms (9 with bath), 1 casita, 1 cabin* ♻ *Restaurant, fans, laundry service; no a/c, no room phones, no room TVs* 🖃 *MC, V* ¶○¶ *EP* ⊗ *Closed Oct.*

★ ¢–$ 🏨 **Hotel Los Almendros.** On a large palm-filled lot, these budget rooms are within walking distance of Manuel Antonio's main attractions, are well kept, and are a good deal for the price. But light sleepers keep away; the on-site Argentinian grill has live music every night until about 11 PM. Choose from air-conditioned or economical fan-ventilated rooms. Bathrooms are small, and front porches with plastic chairs face the large tiled pool. The restaurant serves all three meals. ✉ *From the Marlin Restaurant, 300 m west* 🖷🖷 777–0225 🛏 *21 rooms* ♻ *Some a/c, some fans, pool, bar, Internet; no room phones, no room TVs* 🖃 *No credit cards* ¶○¶ *EP.*

★ ¢–$ 🏨 **Hotel Manuel Antonio.** One of Manuel Antonio's original hotels, this economical place has the closest beds you'll find to the park's entrance and is across the street from the beach. Choose from rustic rooms above an open-air restaurant, which are a good option for budget travelers, or larger, newer rooms in a two-story yellow concrete building next

---

**HIGH-WIRE ACTS**

Though the construction of hotels and other buildings has altered the natural landscape, the surrounding forest has largely been left intact, and the wildlife seems to have grown used to the development. The greatest danger most animals face is the traffic that flows between Quepos and Manuel Antonio, which is why local conservationists have strung ropes over the road between large trees, so that monkeys can cross the street without risking their simian necks. Conservation group **ASCOMOTI** (⊕ www.ascomoti.org) is working with local landowners to preserve forest corridors for the monkeys between remaining islands of wilderness.

door, with cable TVs and air-conditioning. The new rooms have simple pastel drapes and bedspreads and large balconies; be sure to get one with an ocean view, preferably on the second floor. ✉ *End of the road to the park, across from beach* ☎ *777–1237 or 777–1351* 🖷 *777–5172* ✉ *hotelmanuelantonio@racsa.co.cr* ➯ *29 rooms* ᗌ *Restaurant, room service, some a/c, some fans, in-room safes, some cable TV, massage, bar, laundry service, Internet, no-smoking floors* ▭ *AE, MC, V* ⎟⎙⎟ *EP.*

★ ¢ ▦ **Cabinas Ramirez.** Manuel Antonio's first cabinas, owned by the same family as owns Mar y Sombra, Ramirez retains its cheap and simple accommodations that sleep up to 12 people, only 50 m from the beach. Some have kitchenettes, but a communal kitchen is also available. Not all private baths have hot water. Rooms and their front terraces face the parking lot or garden areas. Campers can pitch their tents in a palm-shaded area. ✉ *Road to the park, to the right of the entrance to "downtown" Manuel Antonio* ☎ *777–5044* ➯ *22 rooms* ᗌ *Fans, some kitchenettes, laundry service; no a/c, no room phones, no room TVs* ▭ *No credit cards* ⎟⎙⎟ *EP.*

¢ ▦ **Vista Serena Hostel.** The spectacular ocean view makes up for this youth hostel's distance from the beach and park, a 10-minute bus ride away. Cabinas have private terraces; their décor is less than spectacular. Bunk beds are in a light-filled dorm-style room with lockers, and share one patience-cultivating bathroom. The front terrace looks out to a green valley with a working farm and its grazing goats below. Lie in one of the many hammocks and watch the sun dip into the sea. The tranquil atmosphere is less busy than Costa Linda. Bilingual mother and son owners offer attentive service difficult to find elsewhere. A communal kitchen, TV-room, complimentary tea and coffee, and a hot water shower are some perks. Boogie boards and surfboards are available to rent. ✉ *Road to park, after La Colina hotel, on the right* ☎ *777–5162* ⊕ *www.vistaserena.com* ➯ *20 single beds and 1 double bed in a dorm-style room with shared bath, 2 cabinas* ᗌ *Fans, laundry service; no a/c, no room phones, no room TVs* ▭ *No credit cards* ⎟⎙⎟ *EP.*

## Nightlife

BARS **Barba Roja** (✉ Road to park, in front of Hotel Divisamar ☎ 777–0331)
★ has a popular sunset happy hour. It's primarily a restaurant, but the bar sometimes stays busy until 10 or 11. Try its famous nachos. The **Billfish Bar** (✉ Byblos Hotel, across from Barba Roja ☎ 777–0411) fills up on game nights for its large-screen TVs and pool tables. The casino next door is the only one in Manuel Antonio. **Bambu Jam** (✉ Road to park, ½ mi from Quepos ☎ 777–3369), an open-air French-and-tropical-fusion restaurant, has live music on Fridays in a variety of styles. **La Cantina** (✉ Across from the Costa Verde Hotel ☎ 777–0384) has live reggae and Latin music nightly from 7 to 11 PM, and serves dinner. The **Tutu** (✉ Above Gato Negro, Casitas Eclipse ☎ No phone) is Manuel Antonio's late-night gay bar. **Vikingos** (✉ Next to Marlin Restaurant, second floor ☎ 777–3323) is one of the few bars in the heart of Manuel Antonio. Its loud dance music attracts younger crowds, especially on Mondays, Wednesdays, and Fridays for Ladies Night.

DANCE CLUB **Cockatoo** (✉ 200 m north of Barba Roja, above La Hacienda Restaurant ☎ No phone) plays dancable music in a Spanish-style building. It has a gay bar on the second floor. **Mar y Sombra** (⊠ Next to Cabinas Ramirez ☎ 777–0003), the most popular restaurant on the beach, becomes an open-air dance party Thursday through Saturday after 10:30. Saturday is the busiest night, when the locals come in from Quepos.

## Shopping

There's no shortage of shopping in this town. Near the entrance to the park vendors in kiosks sell T-shirts and Indonesian fabrics. More authentic handicrafts, like seed jewelry, are sold at night by artisans positioned along the sidewalk in central Manuel Antonio. Plenty of souvenir shops across the main road sell typical Costa Rican crafts, similar to those you'd find anywhere else in the country. Quepos (⇨ *above*) has a handful of tasteful gift shops worth exploring.

**La Buena Nota** (⊠ Road to park, on right after Hotel Karahe ☎ 777–1002) has an extensive selection of beachwear, souvenirs, sunscreen, hats, postcards, international newspapers, Costa Rican CDs, and magazines. The second floor has English-language used books and a café. The friendly owner, one of the first North Americans to settle in Manuel Antonio, relates historical anecdotes about the area. **Regalame** (⊠ Next to Sí Como No Hotel ☎ 777–0777) is primarily an art gallery, with paintings, drawings, pottery, and jewelry by dozens of artists, but it also sells wood handicrafts and other souvenirs.

## To & From Manuel Antonio

*3 km/2 mi south of Quepos, 179 km/111 mi (3 ½ hours) southwest of San José.*

Buses from San José leave for Manuel Antonio (via Quepos) nine times daily; three buses are direct. When leaving Manuel Antonio, head to the bus terminal in Quepos, which has service to San José. Buses make the short trip from Quepos to Manuel Antonio every half hour daily from 7 to 7, then hourly until 10 PM. Buses leave Quepos for Dominical (2½-hours trip) fairly frequently. By car, once you cross the Quepos Bridge the road swings inland several kilometers, through forested hills until you reach downtown Manuel Antonio. To get to Dominical, return to the coastal highway and head straight south.

## Manuel Antonio Essentials

Along the road to the park's entrance there are multiple Internet cafés.

🏦 Bank/ATM **Banca Proamerica** ⊠ Next to Economy Rent A Car.

💊 Pharmacy **Farmacia Manuel Antonio** ⊠ Across from Marlin Restaurant ☎ 777–5370.

🌐 Internet **Cantina Internet** ⊠ Across from Costa Verde ☎ 777–0548.

🚕 Taxis **Taxi services.** ☎ 777–0425, 777–0734, or 777–1068

---

# CENTRAL PACIFIC ESSENTIALS

---

## Transportation

**BY AIR**

ARRIVING & DEPARTING    The 30-minute flight between San José and Quepos can save you the 3 ½-hour drive or bus trip, which involves a steep mountain road. Flights from San José get you to Tambor in a fraction of the time it takes to drive to Puntarenas and ferry over. For more information about bus travel between the Central Pacific and San José, *see* Air Travel *in* Smart Travel Tips A to Z.)

## BY BUS

ARRIVING & DEPARTING  Buses are very inexpensive and easy to use. From San José to Puntarenas you'll pay about $2. Buses to Manuel Antonio vary; the faster and slightly fancier direct ones cost about $4; a "collective" that makes several stops costs about $3. All buses heading toward San José that pass through Alajuela can drop you off at the airport, but you need to ask the driver when you board, and then remind him again as you draw near the stop. For more information about bus travel between the Central Pacific and San José, *see* Bus Travel *in* Smart Travel Tips A to Z.)

GETTING AROUND  The ratty buses might look and feel a bit nerve-wracking, especially as they slowly vroom up the hills (sometimes reversing to gain more momentum), but don't sweat it. You'll make it. Not every town has direct buses, so you may have to hop on a connecting bus to get to some destinations. Ask any local or your hotel's reception where the oftentimes unmarked bus stop is located and for departure times. Before handing a bill over to the bus driver, ask how much the fare costs to ensure you get the proper change.

## BY CAR

ARRIVING & DEPARTING  The quickest way to get to this region from San José is to take the Pan-American Highway (CA1) west to the exit for Atenas, where you turn left (south). Once you leave the highway the road is one lane in each direction for the rest of the route, and between Atenas and Orotina it is steep and full of curves. If you don't have experience in mountain driving, you're better off taking a bus, shuttle van, or flight to the coast. The coastal highway, or Costanera, heads southeast from Orotina to Tárcoles, Jacó, Hermosa, and Quepos. It is well marked and, except for a few stretches near bridges, well paved. An asphalt road winds its way over the hill between Quepos and Manuel Antonio National Park.

From San José the best way to get to the southern tip of Nicoya is to drive to Puntarenas, and from there board your car on the ferry bound for Paquera. Take the road to Cóbano, which passes Tambor. From Cóbano the road south to Cabuya branches out to Montezuma and Malpaís.

GETTING AROUND  It's best to stick with the main rental offices in San José, because they have more cars available and you're more likely to reach an English-speaking agent on the phone; some have local satellite offices. Montezuma Expeditions coordinates the delivery of rental cars from major agencies in Liberia.

🏠 **Major Rental Agencies Alamo** ✉ Downtown, 50 m south of Korean school, Quepos ☎ 777-3344, 800/462-5266 in U.S. ⊕ www.alamo.com. **Budget** ✉ Avda. Pastor Diaz, Jacó ☎ 643-2665 ⊕ www.budget.com. **Economy** ✉ Avda. Pastor Diaz, Jacó ☎ 643-1098 ✉ Next to Banca Proamerica, Manuel Antonio ☎ 777-5353 ⊕ www.economycarrental.com. **National** ✉ Avda. Pastor Diaz, Jacó ☎ 643-1752 ⊕ www.nationalcar.com.

🔲 Local Rental Resources **Elegante/Payless** ✉ Avda. Pastor Díaz, Jacó ☎ 643-3224 Jacó, 777-0115 Quepos ✉ 75 m east of Catholic church, Quepos ☎ 777-0115. **Montezuma Expeditions** ✉ Main road, near El Sano Banano restaurant, Montezuma ☎ 440-8078 🌐 www.montezumaexpeditions.com.

## BY SHUTTLE VAN

ARRIVING & DEPARTING  A more comfortable, air-conditioned, and quicker alternative to regular bus service to Montezuma, Tambor, Paquera, Puntarenas, Punta Leona, Playa Herradura, Jacó, Manuel Antonio, and some destinations in between is the hotel-to-hotel shuttle service offered by Interbus. Another luxury bus service, Gray Line Tourist Bus, has service to Jacó and Manuel Antonio. Prices on Interbus range from $17 to $38, depending on distance from San José. Gray Line is $21 to Jacó and $25 to Manuel Antonio. You can request that vans to Jacó drop you off at Carara Biological Reserve. Vans to Manuel Antonio can drop you off in front of Playa Hermosa's hotels.

🔲 Shuttle Van Services **Gray Line Tourist Bus** ☎ 232-3681 or 220-2126 🌐 www.graylinecostarica.com. **Interbus** ☎ 283-5573 🌐 www.interbusonline.com.

## Contacts & Resources

Banks, Internet cafés, and post offices, and emergency contacts are listed at the end of each town entry.

### BANKS & EXCHANGING SERVICES

There are various ATMs in Jacó, Puntarenas, Atenas, and Quepos that accept either Visa or MasterCard, or both. Ask the receptionist at your hotel where the nearest one is. In the unlikely event that you come upon an ATM that's out of order, you should be able to find another one nearby. Malpaís and Montezuma also have ATMs. Banks in Jacó, Puntarenas, Herradura, Cóbano, Atenas, Manuel Antonio, and Quepos exchange U.S. dollars, though it's quicker to get Costa Rican currency from an ATM, when available. Most hotels, restaurants, tour operators, taxi drivers, gift shops, and supermarkets will accept or change U.S. dollars, though at slightly less than the bank rate. Canadian, Australian, and New Zealand dollars and English pounds must be exchanged in banks.

### INTERNET

There are plenty of Internet cafés in Jacó, Montezuma, Puntarenas, and the Quepos/Manuel Antonio area, and at least one each in Atenas, Tambor, Malpaís, and Playa Hermosa. They charge the equivalent of $1–$3 per hour.

### MAIL & SHIPPING

Atenas, Jacó, Cóbano, and Quepos all have post offices, but letters mailed from them tend to take a good bit longer than if they were posted from San José. Manuel Antonio and Jacó both have DHL offices; Tambor has a FedEx dropoff. If you're not near these towns, ship your goods from San José.

# South Pacific

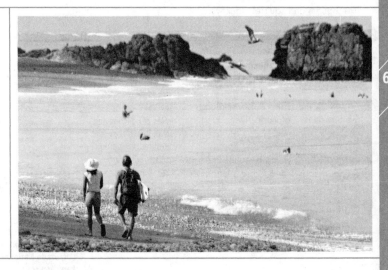

Matapalo Beach

**WORD OF MOUTH**

"Everything that everyone talks about being great and wonderful about Costa Rica is in the Osa! . . . It is hot and humid but you can't beat the beaches or the rain forest."

—coryandcarissa

"There are some great things to be said about the [Golfo Dulce] area. Hardly any tourism, which means long stretches of beach with no tourists. Great fishing, horseback riding, swimming, and surfing."

—Ally

# WELCOME TO THE SOUTH PACIFIC

Howler monkeys, Corcovado National Park

## TOP 5
## Reasons to Go

**1** **Enormous Corcovado National Park** is the last refuge of endangered species like jaguars and squirrel monkeys.

**2** **Mountain hikes** range from easy daytime treks from luxurious lodges to Costa Rica's toughest: 12,500-foot Cerro Chirripó.

**3** **Kayaking** the Golfo Dulce or along the Sierpe or Colorado rivers' jungly channels.

**4** **Bird-watching** yields beauties like scarlet macaws and the resplendent quetzal.

**5** **Wild places to stay** include top ecolodges, platform tents on the beach, and mountain retreats.

Cerro de la Muerte

Cerro Chirripó/Chirripó National Park

San Isidro

SAN JOSÉ

C2

Juntas

Dominical

VALLE DE EL GEN

Ballena National Park

244

34

Palmar Norte

**The Coast** consists of miles of beaches and small beach communities, including unassuming surfer town Dominical, which is just starting to be developed for tourism.

The wild **Osa Peninsula** consists almost enirely of Corcovado National Park, 445 square miles of primary and secondary rain forest straight out of a Tarzan film.

Rincón

San Pedrillo

Corcovado National Park

Pacific Ocean

Sirena

Iguana-crossing road sign, Dominical

Cerro de la Muerte Mountain

**CUIDADO !
BE CAREFUL !**

Iguana

**Yo también uso el camino
I use the road too**
ASANA · MINA

# Getting Oriented

The most remote part of Costa Rica, the South Pacific encompasses the southern half of Puntarenas Province and La Amistad National Park. The region descends from mountainous forests just a couple of hours south of San José to the humid Golfo Dulce and the richly forested Osa Peninsula, 8 to 10 hours from the capital by car.

Matapalito Beach

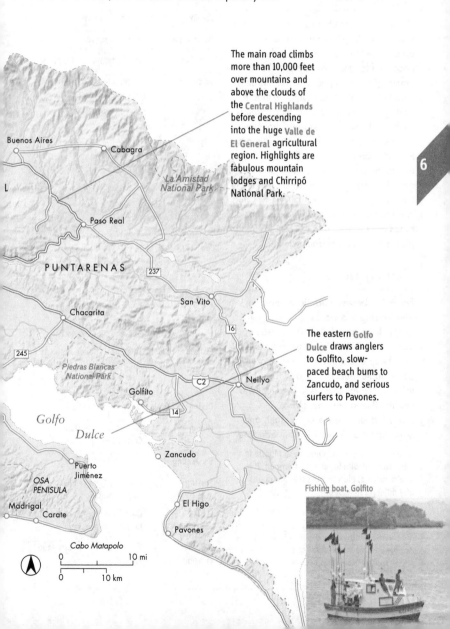

The main road climbs more than 10,000 feet over mountains and above the clouds of the **Central Highlands** before descending into the huge **Valle de El General** agricultural region. Highlights are fabulous mountain lodges and Chirripó National Park.

The eastern **Golfo Dulce** draws anglers to Golfito, slow-paced beach bums to Zancudo, and serious surfers to Pavones.

Buenos Aires

Cabagra

*La Amistad National Park*

Paso Real

PUNTARENAS

237

San Vito

Chacarita

16

245

*Piedras Blancas National Park*

C2

Neilyo

Golfito

14

*Golfo*

*Dulce*

Zancudo

Puerto Jiménez

*OSA PENINSULA*

Madrigal

Carate

El Higo

Pavones

*Cabo Matapolo*

0        10 mi
0        10 km

Fishing boat, Golfito

6

# SOUTH PACIFIC PLANNER

## When to Go

The May to December rainy season is the worst in the Osa Peninsula, where rains usually last through January, and roads flood and lodges might close in the rainiest months (Oct.–Nov.). Elsewhere, mornings tend to be brilliant and sunny, with rain starting in mid-afternoon. Climate swings wildly in the south, from frigid mountain air to steamy coastal humidity. In the mountains it's normally around 24°C (75°F) during the day and 10°C (50°F) at night, though nighttime temperatures on the upper slopes of Cerro de la Muerte can be close to freezing. Temperatures in coastal areas are usually 24–32°C (76–90°F), but it's the humidity that does you in.

## Getting There

For points between San José and San Vito, driving is a viable option, as long as you have lots of time. Direct buses to San Isidro, Golfito, and Puerto Jiménez are cheap and reliable and most are quite comfortable. But the best and fastest way to get to the far south is to fly directly to Golfito, Puerto Jiménez, Drake, or Carate. Many lodges arrange flights, taxi, and boat transfers all the way from San José.

DRIVING ALERT: The Cerro de la Muerte is often covered with fog in the afternoon. If you're driving, plan to cross the mountains at a different time of day.

■ TIP→→ Don't try to cover too much ground. You can't easily hop from one destination in the south to the other. It is impossible to estimate how long it takes to drive the roads or make transportation connections in this part of the country.

## What's Your Beach Style?

| Family | Playa Platanares |
| --- | --- |
| Relaxation | Playa Zancudo |
| Safe Swim | Playa Platanares, Playa Uvita |
| Water Sports | Ballena Marine Park, Playa Dominical, Playa Pavones |

## What to Do

| ACTIVITY | WHERE TO DO IT |
| --- | --- |
| Bird-watching | San Gerardo de Dota, San Gerardo de Rivas, Ballena Marine Park, San Vito, Corcovado Park |
| Fishing | Dominical, Ballena Marine Park, Golfito, Playa Zancudo, Puerto Jiménez, Cabo Matapalo |
| Diving | Ballena Marine Park |
| Hiking | San Gerardo de Dota, Chirripó Park |
| Snorkeling | Ballena Marine Park |
| Surfing | Dominical, Playa Pavones, Cabo Matapalo |
| Whale-watching | Ballena Marine Park, Puerto Jiménez, Drake Bay |
| Wildlife-viewing | La Amistad Park, Corcovado Park |

## Choosing a Place to Stay

Expect reasonable comfort in unbelievably wild settings. Small hotels and lodges are run by hands-on owners, many of them foreigners who fell in love with the place on a visit and stayed. Generally speaking, the farther south and more remote the lodge, the more expensive it is. Bad roads (causing supply problems) and lack of electricity and communications make hotel-keeping costly, especially in the Osa Peninsula and Golfo Dulce. But most of these places include meals, transport, and guides in the price.

## How Much Time?

You need at least a week to truly experience any part of the Osa Peninsula. Even if you fly, transfers to lodges are slow, so plan two days for travel. Choose one home base and take day trips. In three weeks you can experience the entire Southern Zone: mountains, beaches, and the Osa Peninsula. If you only have a few days you could make a quick mountain sortie from San José to tour the Route of the Saints and go hiking in the Cerro de la Muerte.

## Recommended Tour Operators

■ **Horizontes Nature Tours** (☎ 222-2022 ⊕ www.horizontes. com) is an expert generalist.

■ **Costa Rica Expeditions** (☎ 257-0766 ⊕ www. costaricaexpeditions. com) organizes trips with overnights at the Corcovado Lodge Tent Camp.

## Prices

| WHAT IT COSTS in Dollars | | | | | |
|---|---|---|---|---|---|
| | **$$$$** | **$$$** | **$$** | **$** | **¢** |
| **Restaurants** | over $25 | $15–$25 | $10–$15 | $5–$10 | under $5 |
| **Hotels** | over $250 | $150–$250 | $75–$150 | $50–$75 | under $50 |

Restaurant prices are per-person for a main course at dinner. Hotel prices are for two people in a standard double room in high season, excluding service and tax (16.4%).

## Living off the Grid

Many hotels in the South Pacific generate their own electricity, so don't count on air-conditioning, using a hair dryer, or paying with a credit card (unless it's arranged in advance). Pharmacies are few, and often low on supplies. Pack with Mother Nature in mind. Bring:

■ Flashlight with extra batteries

■ Insect repellent (lots of it)

■ Sunscreen (ditto)

■ All toiletries or medicine that you might conceivably need

■ Sturdy, breathable hiking shoes and lots of socks (your feet *will get wet*)

■ Waterproof walking sandals

■ Binoculars

■ Sun hat

■ Water bottle

6

# THE CENTRAL HIGHLANDS

By Dorothy
MacKinnon

Less than an hour south of San José the Pan-American Highway climbs up into the scenic Central Highlands of Cerro de la Muerte, famous for mountain vistas, high-altitude coffee farms, cloud-forest eco-lodges, and challenging mountain hikes.

## Zona de Los Santos

Empalme, at Km 51 of the Pan-American Highway, marks the turnoff for Santa María de Dota, the first of the blessed coffee-growing towns, all named after saints, that dot this mountainous area known as the Zona de Los Santos (Zone of the Saints). The scenic road that winds through the high-altitude valley from Empalme to San Pablo de León

★ is appropriately called **La Ruta de Los Santos** (Route of the Saints). It's well paved to facilitate shipping the coffee produced in the region, which is central to Costa Rica's economy. On the 45-minute (24-km [15-mi]) drive from Santa María de Dota to San Pablo de León Cortés you see misty valleys ringed by precipitous mountain slopes terraced with lush, green coffee plants. The route also captures the essence of a traditional Tico way of life built around coffee growing. Stately churches anchor bustling towns full of prosperous, neat houses with pretty gardens and 1970s Toyota Landcruisers in a rainbow of colors parked in front.

NAVIGATING THE
ROUTE OF THE
SAINTS

*Santa María de Dota is 65 km/40 mi (1½ hours) south of San José. The Route of the Saints is 24 km/15 mi long.*

From San José, drive southeast on the paved Pan-American Highway, heading toward Cartago, then follow the signs south for San Isidro de El General. The two-lane road climbs steeply and there are almost no safe places to pass heavy trucks and slow vehicles. Make an early start, because the road is often enveloped in mist and rain in the afternoon. At Km 51 turn right at Empalme to reach Santa María de Dota, 14 km (8 ½ mi) along a wide, curving, paved road.

### Where to Stay & Eat

¢ ✕ **Café de Los Santos.** This pretty café, run as a community project to showcase the region's coffee, serves more than 30 different kinds. The most typical of the region, billed on the menu as "a celestial drink of the land of the saints," is high-altitude *arabica* Tarrazú, for which this area is famous. The café also has homemade sweet and savory pastries. It's open weekdays 9–7 and weekends 2–6. There's also a more conveniently located outpost on the highway at Empalme (open daily 8–6). ✉ *50 m east of church, 6 km west of Santa María de Dota, San Marcos de Tarrazú; look for the sign with a chubby monk with a halo, pouring a cup of coffee* ☎ *No phone* 🖿 *No credit cards* ⊘ *Closed Sun.* ✉ *Pan-American Hwy., at entrance to Ruta de Los Santos, Empalme* ☎ *571–1118* 🖿 *No credit cards.*

$ 🏠 **El Toucanet Lodge.** For serenity and mountain greenery, you can't beat this family-run lodge with a 270-degree panorama of pastoral scenery from its dining room. Each of the six large rooms in three wooden cabins above the main lodge has its own private veranda and skylit tiled bathroom. No. 5 is the newest and most private room. One private three-bedroom cabin has a kitchen and fireplace. Owners Gary and Edna Roberts are excellent

> **THE FINAL FRONTIER**
>
> The Southern Zone was the very last part of Costa Rica to be settled. The first road, from San José to San Isidro, was built in the 1950s.

cooks, well-known for hearty breakfasts, baked trout dinners, and creative vegetarian dishes. Gary leads guests on a free quetzal hunt every day at 7 AM. He also arranges horseback rides, mountain hikes, and tours of neighboring coffee *fincas* (farms). With at least six hours' notice, Gary can fire up the natural-stone hot tub for an end-of-day soak under the stars. ⊠ *6 km/3½ mi east of Santa María de Dota (along steep, winding paved road), Copey; or from Km 58 of the Pan-American Hwy, turn right at sign for Copey and follow dirt road 7 km/4 mi* 🖷 *541–3045* ☎ *541–3131* ⊕ *www.eltoucanet.com* 🛏 *6 rooms, 1 cabin* ⚐ *Dining room, hot tub, horseback riding; no a/c, no room phones, no TV* ▤ *MC, V* ❂ *Sept.* ❍| *BP.*

6

## Shopping
The best—and cheapest—place to buy local coffee is where the farmers themselves bring their raw coffee beans to be roasted and packed into jute bags, the **Coopedota Santa Maria** (⊠ Main road, just after the bridge, as you enter Santa María de Dota ☎ 541–2828). You can buy export-quality coffee here for less than $5 per kilo (2.2 pounds) *en grano* (whole bean) or *molido* (ground), and choose between light or dark roast. It's open Monday through Saturday 6–11:30 AM and weekdays 12:30–5 PM. You can also arrange for a tour of the coffee co-op by calling ahead.

# San Gerardo de Dota

➊ Cloud forests, cool mountain air, pastoral scenery, and excellent birdwatching make San Gerardo de Dota one of Costa Rica's premier nature destinations. The village is in the narrow Savegre River valley, 9 km (5½ mi) down a twisting, partially asphalted track that descends abruptly to the west from the Pan-American Highway. The peaceful surroundings look more like the Rocky Mountains than typical Central America, but hike down the waterfall trail and the vegetation quickly turns tropical again. Beyond hiking, activities include horseback riding and trout fishing, but you might well be content just to wander around the pastures and forests, marveling at the valley's avian inhabitants.

## Outdoor Activities
BIRD-WATCHING  This area is a must for bird-watchers, who flock here with small package tours (⇨ Tours & Packages *in* Smart Travel Tips A to Z). Individual birders can choose from a roster of expert local guides; check with
★  your hotel for recommendations. **Savegre Hotel de Montaña** (☎ 740–1028 ⊕ www.savegre.co.cr) has the best bird guides in the area ($55/half day) and organizes hiking tours in the surrounding mountains.

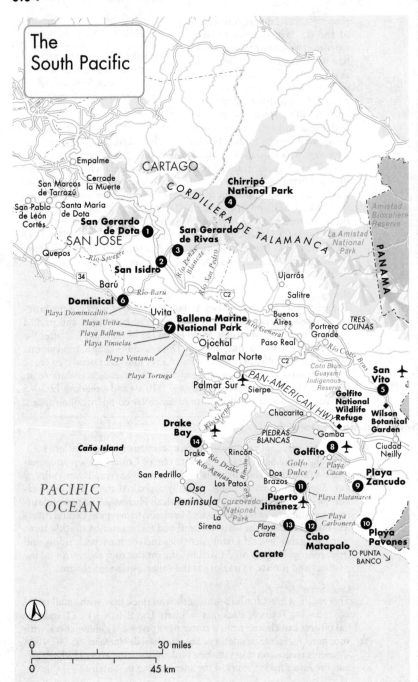

The
South Pacific

The windswept heights of **Cerro de la Muerte,** at Km 89 off the Pan-American Highway, offer your best chance to spot volcano juncos and fiery-throated hummingbirds. The **Savegre River valley** is reliable for sighting quetzals and other highland birds such as the elusive zeledonia (or wrenthrush) and silvery-fronted tapaculo.

Although you can see many birds from your cabin porch, most bird-watching requires hiking, some of it along steep paths made extra challenging by the high altitude (from 7,000 to 10,000 feet above sea level). Come fit and armed with binoculars and layers of warm clothing. The early mornings are brisk up here, but you'll warm up quickly with the sun and the exertion of walking.

> ## THE RESPLENDENT QUETZAL
>
> The damp, epiphyte-laden oak-tree forest around San Gerardo de Dota is renowned for its numbers of resplendent quetzals, considered by many to be the most beautiful bird in the Western world. Male quetzals are more spectacular than females, with metallic green feathers, crimson stomachs, helmetlike crests, and long tails—especially dramatic in flight. Quetzals commonly feed on *aguacatillos* (avocadolike fruits) in the valley's trees. Ask guides or hotel staff about common quetzal hangouts; early morning during the March–May nesting season is the best time to spot them.

**HIKING** Some of the best hiking in the country is in this valley. Expert birder Marino Chacón of Hotel de Savegre (⇨ *above*) leads a daylong natural-history hike that starts with a drive up to the *páramo* (high-altitude, shrubby ecosystem) near **Cerro de la Muerte.** The trail begins near the cluster of communication towers, near Km 89, and descends through the forest into the valley. Miles of prime bird-watching/hiking trails wind through the forest reserve belonging to the Chacóns. ⚠ Night temperatures near Cerro de la Muerte can approach freezing—it's called the Mountain of Death for the very simple reason that long-ago travelers attempting to cross it on foot often froze to death during the night. Pack accordingly.

★ The most challenging trail in the area is the one that begins at the Hotel Savegre and follows the **Río Savegre** down to a spectacular waterfall. To get to the trailhead, follow the main road past Savegre Hotel to a fork, where you veer left, cross a bridge, and head over the hill to a pasture that narrows to a footpath. Although it is only 2 km (1¼ mi) each way, the hike is steep and vigorous, especially near the bottom, and takes about three hours.

### Where to Stay & Eat

$ 🏠 **Albergue Mirador de Quetzales.** The main attraction at this 8,530-foot-high perch is the resplendent quetzal, which swoops its famous tail feathers around the 106-acre cloud-forest reserve, also known as Finca Eddie Serrano (Eddie Serrano's Farm). The price of a room in a rustic A-frame cabin overlooking a misty valley includes a hearty breakfast, dinner, and a guided tour. Electric space heaters and hot-water bottles at the foot of your bed take the chill off at night, when the temperature can drop close to freezing. The reserve's 4-km (2½-mi) El Robledal trail wends past gnarly 1,500-year-old cypress trees and 14-million-year-old marine fossils. Day visitors can pay $6 to walk the trail. You can also take a horseback ride past a sobering, old plane wreck to a waterfall. ✉ *Km 70 off Pan-American Hwy.* 📠 *381–8456* ⊕ *www. exploringcostarica.com/mirador/quetzales.html* ⬎ *11 cabins* ☆ *Restaurant, hiking, horseback riding; no a/c, no room phones, no room TVs* ▣ *No credit cards* ◉⃝ *MAP.*

¢–$  ✕▥ **Las Cataratas.** One of the best deals—and meals—in the valley is at this restaurant and cabins run by a lovely Tico family, who all join in (kids, too) to help serve meals. The property has three simple, wooden cabins with wood-burning fireplaces. The red-velvet decor borders on bordello, but the cabins are cheap and comfortable enough. There are also some short, steep forest trails to explore. At the restaurant you can dine on fresh trout—pulled directly out of the adjoining pond when you place your order—with salad, vegetables, dessert, and juice for under $5. If you haven't got the time or the courage to face the steep road all the way down to San Gerardo, this is a good compromise, only 3 km (2 mi) in from the highway. ✉ *3 km/2 mi down steep road to San Gerardo de Dota* 📞 *308–9213, beeper 257–8585* ⊕ *www.cataratas.guiapz. com* ⬎ *3 cabins* ☆ *Restaurant, fishing, hiking; no a/c, no room phones, no room TVs* ▣ *No credit cards.*

★ $–$$  ▥ **Savegre Hotel de Montaña.** Famous for quetzals and miles of bird-watching trails, this formerly rustic hotel has been upgraded to a new level of luxury, with handsome furniture, tiled baths, space heaters, and hair dryers—unthinkable luxuries back in the 1950s when Don Efrain Chacón first bushwhacked his way through the mountains to homestead here. Nine cabin-suites even have fireplaces and deep bathtubs. If you want to feel alone, the most secluded cabin is No. 105, across a bridge over a small stream. Still run by Efrain's affable sons, the main lodge has a big fireplace, a cozy bar, and a veranda with hummingbird feeders. Meals are served on a sunny terrace. Home-grown trout is the restaurant's specialty. You can avoid the twisting drive here by taking a bus to Km 80 on the Pan-American Highway and arranging to get a lift to the hotel ($10). On the hotel grounds, the **Quetzal Education Research Center** (QERC; 📞740–1010) hosts students and researchers; many take their meals at the hotel and are a great source for natural lore. ✉ *Turn right at sign to San Gerardo de Dota on Pan-American Hwy, about 80 km/50 mi southeast of San José, and travel 9 km/5½ mi down very steep, gravel road with some paving* 📞740–1028 📠740–1027 ✉Apdo. 482, Cartago

> **WORD OF MOUTH**
>
> "As we were approaching [Savegre Hotel de Montaña] my husband caught a glimpse of a quetzal on the post on the side of the road. We were beside ourselves! We had seen one from a great distance in Monteverde a few years earlier. This one (a female) was within 10 feet of us. We got great pictures. Another female (immature male?) flew in. And then the MALE. He was farther away but within very clear sight and we got great pictures of him as well! So we said, Well, okay, we can go home now, ha ha."
>
> –glover

⊕ *www.savegre.co.cr* ⇦ *22 cabinas, 9 cabin-suites* ♿ *Restaurant, fishing, bird-watching, hiking, horseback riding, bar, Internet; no a/c, no room TVs* ▭ *AE, MC, V* ⊙ *FAP.*

$ ▦ **Trogon Lodge.** It overlooks the same cloud forest and boulder-strewn river as Savegre Hotel de Montaña, but Trogon Lodge is more of a relaxing hideaway than a hiking-heavy destination. The green wood cabins, nestled in a valley, are surrounded by a riot of roses, calla lilies, and geraniums. Each cabin has two separate rooms with big windows, queen-size beds, white-tile baths with hot showers, and gas heaters and extra blankets for chilly mountain nights. The only drawback is that the verandas are shared. The honeymoon cabin is perched at the top of the property in solitary splendor, with a king-size bed and a whirlpool tub with a panoramic view. Meals are served in a restaurant with tree-trunk tables, adjoined by a bar with a river view. Quetzal-watching, horseback riding, waterfall hikes, and an 11-platform canopy tour are some of the diversions. Be prepared to be awakened by four roaming, pet peacocks that sometimes emit shrill screams at 2 AM. ⊠ *Turn right at the sign to San Gerardo de Dota on the Pan-American Hwy, about 80 km/50 mi southeast of San José, and follow signs; lodge is 7½ km/4½ mi down a dirt Rd.* ☎ *740–1051, 293–8181 in San José* ⊟ *229–8082 in San José* ⊕ *www.grupomawamba.com* ⊡ *Apdo. 10980–1000, San José* ⇦ *24 rooms, 1 suite* ♿ *Restaurant, bicycles, hiking, horseback riding, bar; no a/c, no room phones, no room TVs* ▭ *AE, MC, V* ⊙ *EP.*

## To & From San Gerardo de Dota

*89 km/55 mi (3 hours) southeast of San José. 52 km/32 mi (1 hour) south of Santa María de Dota.*

At Km 80 on the Pan-American Highway, turn down the dirt road signed SAN GERARDO DE DOTA. It's a harrowing, twisting road for most of the 9 km (5½ mi), with signs warning drivers to gear down and go slow. Some newly paved sections help to make the worst curves easier to take. Tourist vans often stop along the road when the guides spot birds; grab your binoculars and join them!

# VALLE DE EL GENERAL REGION

The Valle de El General (The General's Valley) is bounded to the north and west by the central highlands of the massive Cordillera de Talamanca and to the south by La Amistad International Park, above San Vito. The valley is named for the Río de El General, one of the many rivers that rise in the Talamancas and run down through the valley, making it ideal for farming. This area includes vast expanses of highland wilderness, on the upper slopes of the Cordillera de Talamanca and the high-altitude *páramo* (shrubby ecosystem) of Chirripó National Park, as well as prosperous agricultural communities amid vast, sun-baked fields of pineapple and sugarcane.

## San Isidro

❷ Although San Isidro has no major attractions, the bustling market town is a good place to have lunch, get cash at one of the many ATMs (the vast majority accept only Visa/Plus cards) or fill your tank: the main high-way into town is lined with service stations, some operating 24 hours.

## Exploring

The **National Parks Service** (✉ Across from Cámara de Cañeros ☎ 771–3155) has information and maps of Chirripó and is the central reservation agent for lodging in the park's hostel. Before you head up to the park entrance in San Gerardo de Rivas, you need to stop in here and pay up front for your park lodging.

In a lush valley 7 km (4½ mi) northeast of San Isidro, the community-managed **Las Quebradas Biological Center** is a *centro biológico* (nature reserve) that protects 1,853 acres of dense forest in which elegant tree ferns grow in the shadows of massive trees and where colorful tanagers and euphonias flit about the foliage. A 3-km (2-mi) trail winds through the forest and along the Río Quebradas, which supplies water to San Isidro and surrounding communities. Overnights in lodges (⇨ Where to Stay & Eat, *below*) are available. ✉ *At bottom of mountain as you approach San Isidro, take sharp left off Pan-American Hwy. at sign for Las Quebradas, go 7 km/4½ mi northeast; center is 2 km/1 mi north of town, along unpaved Rd.* ☎ *771–4131* ✉ *Apdo. 8000–30, Peréz Zeledón, San Isidro* 🖃 *$5* ☉ *Tues.–Sun. 8–3.*

**Los Cusingos Neotropical Bird Sanctuary** is the home of the late Dr. Alexander Skutch, Central America's preeminent ornithologist/naturalist and the author of *A Guide to the Birds of Costa Rica,* the birders' bible. His 190-acre estate, an island of forest amid new farms and housing developments, is now run by the Tropical Science Center, which, at this writing, is improving the trails and restoring the simple house where Dr. Skutch lived—without electricity—from 1941 until his death in 2004, just a week shy of his 100th birthday. Bird species you might see include fiery-billed aracaris, colorful, small members of the toucan family, and mixed tanager flocks. The plan is to make the sanctuary more accessible to visitors. ✉ *20 km/12 mi southeast of San Isidro, near Santa Elena; phone for precise directions, Quizarrá* ☎ *253–3267* ⊕ *www.cct.or.cr* 🖃 *$8* ☉ *By appointment only, daily 7 AM–sunset.*

## Outdoor Activities

**Selva Mar** (✉ Half a block south of the cathedral ☎ 771–4582 ⊕ www.exploringcostarica.com) is the most experienced Southern Zone tour operator. Before there were telephone lines, Selva Mar was the main booking agents for most of the remote southern hotels.

HIKING  The major tourist draw is climbing Mount Chirripó (the highest peak is

---

### HITTING THE TRAILS

The hiking in the south is simply splendid, so don't leave home without your boots. The most challenging hike in the country is Chirripó Mountain, an 8- to 10-hour haul up to the national-park hostel, a base camp for exploring surrounding peaks. Dramatic but less challenging hikes include the well-maintained, wide trails in the cool high-altitude forests of the Savegre Valley; the narrow Coastal Path south of Drake; and forest trails to waterfalls and swimming holes in the Golfo Dulce, Osa Peninsula, and around Dominical.

3,812 meters or about 13,500 feet high) in Chirripó National Park. **Costa Rica Trekking Adventures** (☎ 771–4582 ⊕ www.chirripo.com), run by Selva Mar, can arrange everything you need to climb the mountain, including transportation, guide, porters to carry your gear, meals, snacks, and beverages. But you still have to make the tough climb yourself, about eight hours uphill to the park lodge, and five hours to come down. The three-night, four-day packages are around $400 per person. The company also arranges multiday hikes across the Talamanca Mountains.

BIRD-WATCHING   **Birding Escapes** (☎ 771–4582 ⊕ www.birdwatchingcostarica.com), run by Selva Mar, has multiday bird-watching packages and arranges customized tours. At the **Los Cusingos Neotropical Bird Sanctuary** ( ⇨ Exploring, *above*), the home of the late Dr. Alexander Skutch, author of *A Guide to the Birds of Costa Rica,* you might spot scarlet-rumped tanagers, blue-crowned motmots, green honeycreepers, and turquoise cotingas.

## Where to Stay & Eat

¢–$   ✕ **El Trapiche de Nayo.** This rustic open-air restaurant with a panoramic valley view serves the kind of food Ticos eat at *turnos* (village fund-raising festivals), including hard-to-find *sopa de mondongo* (tripe soup). Easier to stomach are the *gallos* (do-it-yourself filled tortillas), which you can stuff with heart of palm, other root vegetables, and wood-fire-cooked chicken. On Saturdays, raw sugarcane is pressed in an antique mill and boiled in huge iron cauldrons to make smooth *sobado*, a molasses-flavored fudge. The restrooms—with seatless toilets—leave much to be desired. ⊠ *Pan-American Hwy., 6 km/4 mi north of San Isidro* ☎ *771–7267* ⊟ *AE, MC, V.*

$   ▦ **Hotel del Sur Country Club & Casino.** An extensive and rambling complex with well-tended gardens, this hotel doubles as a local country club. Weekday stays are tranquil, but the casino makes for lively weekends. Rooms are spacious but sparsely furnished, and have large windows looking out onto a courtyard garden. Basic cabinas in back have kitchenettes, bunks, and separate bedrooms but no air-conditioning. The hotel has a kids' pool and a playground. ⊠ *Pan-American Hwy., 6 km/4 mi south of town* ☎ *771–3033* 🖷 *771–0527* ✑ *Apdo. 4–8000, Peréz Zeledón, San Isidro* ↪ *48 rooms, 10 cabinas* ⚹ *Restaurant, fans, some in-room safes, some kitchenettes, some minibars, cable TV, tennis court, pool, bar, casino; no a/c in some rooms, no TV in some rooms* ⊟ *AE, MC, V* ⦿ *BP.*

$   ▦ **Las Quebradas Biological Center.** This rustic wooden lodge with dormitory-style rooms and cold-water showers is just inside the gates of the *centro biológico* (nature reserve). Meals are prepared by women from the nearby village and served family-style. This is an ideal place to stay if you want to get an early start on the trails. ⊠ *At bottom of mountain as you approach San Isidro, take sharp left off Pan-American Hwy. at sign for Las Quebradas, go 7 km/4½ mi northeast; center is 2 km/1 mi north of town, along unpaved Rd.* ☎ *771–4131* ✑ *Apdo. 8000–30, Peréz Zeledón, San Isidro* ↪ *30 beds with shared bath, in dorm-style rooms and 3 double rooms* ⚹ *No a/c, no TV, no room phones* ⦿ *MAP.*

¢–$   ▦ **Hotel Los Crestones.** Flowers in window boxes give this pleasant, two-story motel-style building near the local stadium a homey feel. Affordable rooms are large and comfortable, and two have bathtubs. At a small, informal grouping of tables in the reception area coffee and pastries and light breakfasts are served. ⊠ *Southwest side of stadium, on road to Dominical* ☎ *770–1200* 🖷 *771–6012* ⊕ *www.hotelloscrestones.com* ↪ *20 rooms* ⚹ *A/c in some rooms, fans, cable TV, pool; no a/c in some rooms, no room phones* ⊟ *AE, MC, V* ⦿ *EP.*

¢ ▦ **Hotel Zima.** One of the newest accommodations in town, modern Hotel Zima is close to the bus station. The pleasant rooms are in a nicely landscaped row, reminiscent of a 1950s motel. Some rooms have queen-size beds and air-conditioning; others have double or single beds. Have breakfast at the small terrace restaurant or cross the highway and forage among the inexpensive sodas in town. ⊠ *Half a block east of main highway into San Isidro, across from MUSOC bus terminal* ☎☎ *770–1114* ↪ *19 rooms* ⚹ *Dining room, fans, cable TV, laundry service, Internet; no room phones; no a/c in some rooms* ⊟ *No credit cards* ⦿ *EP.*

## To & From San Isidro
*54 km/34 mi (1 ½ hours) south of San Gerardo de Dota.*

The Pan-American Highway takes you straight into San Isidro. It's 129 km (80 mi) south of San José and about 50 km (31 mi) south of the San Gerardo de Dota highway exit. Truck traffic can be heavy. Buses to Dominical leave San Isidro from a stop 100 meters south and 200 meters east of the cathedral, near the main highway. Buses to San Gerardo de Rivas, the starting point of the trail into Chirripó National Park, depart from San Isidro at 5 AM from the central park and at 2 PM from a stop at the central market.

### San Isidro Essentials
🏦 Bank/ATM **Banco de Costa Rica** ⊠ 1 block south of southwest corner of park. **ATH Coopealianza** ⊠ South side of central park, beside Hotel Chirripó (ATM only.)
🏦 Hospital **Hospital Escalante Pradilla** ⊠ North end of town ☎ 661-3122.
🏦 Pharmacy **Farmacia Santa Marta** ⊠ Across from the cultural center.
🏦 Internet **Brunc@Net** ⊠ Above Gallo Mas Gallo store, north side of park.
🏦 Post Office **Correo** ⊠ 200 m south of City Hall, south side of park.
🏦 Visitor Information **Ciprotur** ⊠ Behind the MUSOC bus station, where the San José buses arrive ☎ 771-2003. **Selva Mar** ⊠ 45 m south of central park ☎ 771-4582 ⊕ www.exploringcostarica.com.

# San Gerardo de Rivas

❸ Chirripó National Park is the main reason to venture to San Gerardo de Rivas, but if you aren't up for this physically challenging adventure there are less difficult hikes, and the town is still a great place to spend a day or two. Spread over steep terrain at the end of the narrow valley of the boulder-strewn Río Chirripó, San Gerardo de Rivas has a cool climate, good bird-watching, spectacular views reminiscent of Nepal, and an outdoor menu that includes waterfall hikes.

## Exploring
☽ The **Aguas Termales** (Hot Springs), on a farm above the road to Herradura, are a favorite tourist stop. To get here, you must cross a river on a rick-

CLOSE UP

# A Mosaic of Forests

THOUGH THE RAIN FOREST IS the most famous region in Costa Rica, there are other types of forests here equally rich in life and well worth exploring. The tropical dry forests of the northwestern lowlands are similar to rain forests during the rainy season, but once the weather turns dry, most trees lose their leaves, and some burst simultaneously into full flower, notably the yellow-blossom buttercup tree and the pink tabebuia. Cacti, coyotes, and diamondback rattlesnakes can be found, in addition to typical rain-forest flora and fauna.

The cloud forests on the upper reaches of many Costa Rican mountains and volcanoes are so deeply lush that it can be hard to find the bark on a tree for all the growth on its trunk and branches. Vines, orchids, ferns, aroids, and bromeliads are everywhere. More light reaching the ground means plenty of undergrowth, too. Cloud forests are home to a multitude of animals, ranging from delicate glass frogs, whose undersides are so transparent that you can see many of their internal organs, to the legendary resplendent quetzal. The foliage and mist can make it hard to see wildlife.

Along both coasts are extensive mangrove forests, extremely productive ecosystems that play an important role as estuaries. Mangroves attract animals that feed on marine life, especially fish-eating birds such as cormorants, herons, pelicans, and ospreys. The forests that line Costa Rica's northeastern coast are dominated by the water-resistant *jolillo* palm or *palma real*. Mangroves are home to many of the same animals found in the rain forest—monkeys, parrots, iguanas—as well as river dwellers such as turtles and crocodiles.

6

ety footbridge, then it's a steep climb on foot to a combination of natural rock and concrete pools in a forested area. It can be crowded with locals on weekends. In dry season only, the **Selva Mar travel agency** (☎ 771–4582) in San Isidro can arrange for a donkey or horse, as can local hotels. ⊠ *Above road to Herradura, about 1½ km/1 mi past the ranger station, north of town* ⊠ *$2* ☉ *Daily 7–6.*

**Cloud Bridge Reserve,** a private nature reserve, has an easy trail to a waterfall, plus almost 20 km (12 mi) of river and ridge trails bordering Chirripó National Park. It's a pleasant alternative for hikers who aren't up to the challenge of Chirripó. ⊠ *2 km/1 mi northeast of San Gerardo de Rivas* ⊠ *By donation* ☉ *Daily, sunrise to sunset.*

## Outdoor Activities

**Selva Mar** (⇨ San Isidro, *above*) runs tours around San Gerardo de Rivas.

HIKING   If Chirripó isn't on your hiking list, you can still get some good walks in the area around San Gerardo de Rivas. Guide **Eric Kang** (⊕ www.climbcostarica.com) at the Cloud Bridge Reserve, arranges longer hiking trips and naturalist tours.

## Where to Stay

**$** ☒ **Río Chirripó Retreat.** A popular place for yoga retreats, this lodge with its clear mountain air, rushing river, and huge conical-roofed adobe temple hung with a monastery bell and Tibetan prayer flags makes you feel as though you have arrived in the Himalayas. The bougainvillea-bedecked B&B is also great place for acclimatizing before climbing Chirripó, for bird-watching, and for clambering along the river rocks, strewn with Druidic-looking stone seats and altars. Two-story wood cabins are cantilevered over a steep ravine, with twig-railing porches. The comfortable rooms have large bathrooms and walls stenciled with runic symbols. ☒ *Down a steep drive, just past cemetery* ☎ *771–7065, 707/937–3775 in U.S.* ⊕ *www.riochirripo.com* ↘ *8 rooms, 1 cabin* ⌂ *Dining room, pool, hiking; no a/c, no room phones, no room TVs* ⊟ *No credit cards* ⫟ *BP.*

**$** ☒ **Talari Mountain Lodge.** A great place for bird-watchers, this lodge run by a Tico-Dutch family is a 10-minute drive northeast from San Isidro on the road to San Gerardo de Rivas, at a cool, comfortable altitude of 800 meters (2,600 feet). It's on a small farm near the gurgling Río General. Rooms are very simple, with big windows, tile floors, and porches. The surrounding fruit trees and forest patches attract more than 200 middle-elevation birds, according to the lodge's bird list. A resident naturalist guide leads tours in high season and organizes trips to climb Chirripó. Meals are good; the dining room is closed Saturday. ☒ *Take a left off Pan-American Hwy., 1 km/½ mi south of central San Isidro, then 6 km/3½ mi on road signed for Rivas* ☎☎ *771–0341* ⊕ *www.talari. co.cr* ⊡ *Apdo. 517–8000, Peréz Zeledón, San Isidro* ↘ *9 rooms* ⌂ *Dining room, pool, hiking; no a/c, no room phones, no room TVs* ⊟ *AE, MC, V* ⫟ *BP.*

**¢** ☒ **Albergue de Montaña El Pelícano.** On a ridge south of town, this wooden lodge is named for a chunk of wood that resembles a pelican— and that's not its only oddity. The property also has a museum to house the dozens of idiosyncratic wooden sculptures carved out of tree roots by owner Rafael Elizondo. Above the restaurant, which has a gorgeous view of the valley below San Gerardo, are economical small rooms with shared bath. There are also two private wooden cabins with kitchenettes, near the pool. The owners can arrange everything for a climb up Chirripó, including a free lift to the park entrance. The climb to the hotel itself is quite steep and requires 4WD. ☒ *260 m south of national parks office* ☎ *390–4194* ☎ *770–3526* ⊡ *Apdo. 942–8000, San Gerardo de Rivas* ⊕ *www.hotelelpelicano.net* ↘ *10 rooms with shared bath, 1 cabin* ⌂ *Restaurant, tennis court, pool, horseback riding; no a/c, no room phones, no room TVs* ⊟ *AE, MC, V* ⫟ *EP.*

## To & From San Gerardo de Rivas
*20 km/12 ½ mi (1 hour) northeast of San Isidro.*

More than half the distance from San Isidro is on a very rocky, very hilly, dirt road; 4WD is strongly recommended. There is a bus from San Isidro and it is a slow, dusty ride up the mountain.

## Chirripó National Park

❹ The ascent to Mount Chirripó, the highest mountain in Costa Rica, is the most popular and challenging hike in the country. Unfortunately, it is also the most exclusive. A recent environmental-impact study led officials to limit the number of hikers in the park on any one day to 35. Thirty reservations are prebooked, usually months ahead, leaving only five spaces for hikers who show up at the park. The park service office in San Isidro allows phone reservations only twice a year, on May 1 and November 1. To access the challenging trail you must first hike 5 km (3 mi) uphill to the park's entrance from San Gerardo de Rivas. From there it's a tough climb to the base camp—6 to 10 hours from the official park entrance, depending on your physical condition—so most hikers head out of San Gerardo at the first light of day. There is a modern but unheated (and chilly) **hostel** near the top ($10/night). This will be your base for a night or two if you want to continue your hike up to the peaks. The hostel has small rooms with four bunks each, cold-water bathrooms, and a cooking area. In 2004, bathrooms were newly tiled and the septic system was improved. You can rent camp stoves, blankets, and sleeping bags here, but you should bring a better-quality sleeping bag, and you must bring food and water. ■ TIP➜➜ Pack plenty of warm clothes. Trails from the hostel lead to the top of Chirripó—the highest point in Costa Rica—and the nearby peak of Terbi, as well as to glacier lakes and the *páramo*—a highland ecosystem common to the Andes, with shrubs and herbaceous plants.

You are required to report to the **San Gerardo de Rivas National Parks Service** (✉ Main St. ☎ 200–5348) the day before you start your climb. The office is open 6:30–4. Don't try to sneak in: a park ranger will stop you at a checkpoint on the trail and ask to see your reservation voucher. To get maps of Chirripó and to reserve or pay for lodging in the park, you must visit the **San Isidro National Parks Service office** ( ⇨ *above*).

🎫 *$10 ⊙ Jan.–Aug. and Nov.–Dec., daily dawn–dusk.*

### Outdoor Activities
Hikes and other activities in the park are arranged by **Selva Mar** ( ⇨ San Isidro, *above*).

### To & From Chirripó National Park
*5 km/3 mi northeast of San Gerardo de Rivas*

The park entrance is a 5-km (3-mi) hike uphill from San Gerardo de Rivas.

## San Vito

❺ Except for the tropical greenery, the rolling hills around the bustling hilltop town of San Vito could be mistaken for a Tuscan landscape. The town actually owes its 1952 founding to a government scheme whereby 200 Italian families were awarded grants to convert the rain forest into coffee, fruit, and cattle farms. The Italian flavor lingers in outdoor cafés serving ice cream and pastries and an abundance of shoe stores. A statue dedicated to the *pioneros* stands proudly in the middle of town. San Vito is also the center of the Coto Brus coffee region, and many of the coffee pickers are from the Guaymí tribe and live in a large reserve nearby and just over the border in Panamá. They're easy to recognize by the women's colorful cotton dresses.

## Exploring

Fodor'sChoice ★ The compelling tourist draw here is a visit to the world-renowned **Wilson Botanical Garden,** a must-see for gardeners and bird-watchers and enchanting even for those who are neither. The paths through the extensive grounds are lined with exotic plants and shaded by avenues of palm trees and 50-foot-high bamboo stalks. In 1961, U.S. landscapers Robert and Catherine Wilson bought 30 acres of coffee plantation and started planting tropical species, including palms, orchids, aroids, ferns, bromeliads, heliconias, and marantas, all linked by a series of paths. Today the property extends over 635 acres, and the gardens hold around 2,000 native and 3,000 exotic species. The palm collection—more than 700 species— is one of the largest in the world. Fantastically shaped and colored bromeliads, which usually live in the tops of trees, have been brought down to ground in impressive mass plantings, providing one of the many photo opportunities. The property was transferred to the Organization for Tropical Studies (OTS) in 1973, and in 1983 it became part of Amistad Biosphere Reserve. Under the name **Las Cruces Biological Station,** Wilson functions as a research and educational center, so there is a constant supply of expert botanists and biologists to take visitors on natural history tours in the garden and the adjoining forest trails. If you spend a night at the garden lodge you have the garden all to yourself in the late afternoon and early morning, when wildlife is most active. ⊠ *6 km/4 mi south of San Vito on road to Ciudad Neily* ☎ *Apdo. 73–8257, San Vito* ☎ *773–4004* 🖷 *773–4109* ⊕ *www.esintro.co.cr* ☎ *$6* ☉ *Daily 8–4.*

## Outdoor Activities

BIRD-WATCHING In addition to its plants, **Wilson Botanical Garden** ( ⇨ Exploring, *above*) is renowned for its birds. More than 320 species have been recorded here, along with more than 800 butterflies. Naturalist guides lead visitors on birding and natural history tours through the garden ($15 per person). The Río Java trail, open only to overnight guests of Wilson, is a great place to see birds.

WILDLIFE- WATCHING If you are an overnight guest at **Wilson Botanical Garden** ( ⇨ Exploring, *above*), you can walk the Río Java trail, through a forest thick with wildlife.

## Where to Stay & Eat

★ $ ✕ **Pizzeria Liliana.** Treat yourself to real Italian pizza at the classiest restaurant in town. The large, friendly, family-run restaurant has an elegant indoor dining room and an attractive garden terrace out back. Pizzas have crispy olive-oil crusts and are generously sized. Or dig into the macaroni *sanviteña*-style, with white sauce, ham, and mushrooms. The classics are here as well, and they're all homemade—lasagna, canneloni, and ravioli. The authentically Italian vinaigrette salad dressing is a welcome change from more acidic Tico dressings. ⊠ *150 m west of central Sq.* ☎ *773–3080* 🖃 *V.*

**CLOSE UP**

# La Amistad National Park

BY FAR THE LARGEST PARK IN COSTA RICA, at more than 1,980 square km (765 square mi), La Amistad it's a mere portion of the vast La Amistad Biosphere Reserve that stretches into western Panama. Altitudes range from 1,000 meters (3,280 feet) to 3,500 meters (11,480 feet). There are miles of rugged, densely forested trails and plenty of wildlife (two-thirds of the country's vertebrate species live here), but because access is extremely difficult, it's not worth visiting the park unless you plan to spend several days, making this a trip only for experienced hikers. Tour operators don't do trips (yet), but you can—and

should, unless you're comfortable being lost in the wilderness—hire a park guide. The three-day guided trips have overnights at a ranger station with potable water and restrooms. The alternative is rustic camp sites (bring your own tent) for $5 per person. Reserve space about a week in advance. To get to the park (4WD essential), drive 31 km (20 mi) west from San Vito along the road to Paso Real. Turn right at the park sign at Guacimo, near two small roadside restaurants. Then drive about 20 km (13 mi) uphill on a rough road. ☎ 730-0846 or 200-5355 ✉ $5 per day ⊘ Daily 8-4.

**6**

¢ ✕**Panaderia y Reposteria Flor.** In a town famous for coffee, ice cream, and pastry shops, this emporium stands out. You can't miss the hot-pink sign on the main street. Stop in and grab a pair of tongs and a tray and help yourself to sweet and savory buns, breads, and an array of doughnuts, cakes, cookies, and puddings. The *pièces de résistance* are the elegant pastry swans filled with pastry cream. Enjoy your treats at the sidewalk tables or bag them and eat them en route to your next destination. ⊠ *Main street, halfway down the hill.*

$$ 🏨**Wilson Botanical Garden.** A highlight of any Costa Rican visit for gardeners and bird lovers, this magical botanical garden has comfortable
Fodor'sChoice
★ rooms in two modern buildings built of glass, steel, and wood that blend into a forested hillside. Private balconies cantilevered over a ravine make bird-watching a snap even from your room. Each room is named after the exotic plant growing at the doorway. Room rates include three excellent home-style meals, a guided tour, and 24-hour access to the garden. Staying overnight is the only way to see the garden at dusk and dawn, and it's also the only way to walk the Sendero Río Java, a trail that follows a stream through a forest teeming with birds and monkeys. The staff here are cheerful and professional, and the youthful enthusiasm of visiting research students is contagious. ⊠ *6 km/4 mi south of San Vito on road to Ciudad Neily* ⌂ *OTS, Apdo. 676–2050, San Pedro* ☎ *524–0628* 🖷 *524–0629* ⊕ *www.esintro.com* ⟿ *12 rooms* ⚙ *Dining room, fans, hiking, tours, Internet; no a/c, no room TVs* ⊟ *AE, MC, V* ⏀ *FAP.*

¢ 🏨**Hotel El Ceibo.** The best deal in town, El Ceibo is a well maintained two-story hotel tucked in a quiet cul-de-sac behind the main street. The architecture is reminiscent of Italy, with graceful arcades and decorative balustrades. Rooms are compact but tidy, bright, and comfortable; Rooms 1–10 and 21–32 have small balconies that open onto a wooded ravine alive with birds. The restaurant, illuminated by a skylight, serves homestyle Italian and Tico food at reasonable prices. ⊠ *140 m east of San Vito's central park, behind Municipalidad* ☎ *773–3025* 🖷 *773–5025* ⚑ *40 rooms* ⚒ *Restaurant, fans, cable TV, bar; no a/c, no room phones* ▤ *V* ⫛⃝ *EP.*

## Shopping

In an old farmhouse on the east side of the road between San Vito and the botanical garden, **Finca Cántaros** (⊠ Road to Ciudad Neily, 3 km/2 mi south of San Vito ☎ 773–3760) sells crafts by indigenous artisans from near and far, including Guaitil ceramic figures and *molas* (colorful appliqué work) made by Kuna women from the San Blas Islands in Panama. You can also find a great selection of colorful, high-glaze ceramics from San José artists. Profits help support the adjacent children's library.

## To & From San Vito

*110 km/68 mi southeast of San Isidro, 61 km/38 mi northeast of Golfito.*

If you are driving south from San Isidro, your best route is along the wide, smooth Pan-American Highway via Buenos Aires to Paso Real, about 70 km (43 mi). Then take the scenic high road to San Vito, 40 km (25 mi) farther along. This road has its share of potholes but it is the most direct route and the prettiest. Another route, which many buses take, is via Ciudad Neilly, about 35 km (22 mi) northeast of Golfito, and then 24 km (15 mi) of winding steep road up to San Vito, at almost 1,000 meters (3,280 feet) above sea level. There are direct buses from San José three times a day; and buses from San Isidro six times a day. You can also fly to Coto 47 and take a taxi to San Vito.

## San Vito Essentials

Most of the banks in town have cash machines that accept foreign cards.
🏦 Bank/ATM **Banco Nacional** ⊠ Across from central park. **ATH Coopealianza** ⊠ Center of town, north of hospital ☞ ATM only
🏥 Hospital **Hospital San Vito** ⊠ South end of town on road to Wilson Botanical Garden ☎ 773–3103.
💊 Pharmacy **Farmacia Coto Brus** ⊠ Center of town across from La Flor pastry shop.
💻 Internet **Neurotec** ⊠ 1 block west of main street at north end of town.
✉ Post Office **Correo** ⊠ Far north end of town, beside police station.

| en route |

The 33-km (21-mi) road from **San Vito to Ciudad Neily** is twisting and spectacular, with views over the Coto Colorado plain to the Golfo Dulce and Osa Peninsula beyond. Much of this steep terrain is covered with tropical forest, making it an ideal route for bird-watching and picture-taking. The road from **San Vito to Paso Real** is equally scenic, traveling along a high ridge with sweeping valley views on either side. As you descend, the wide valley of the El General River opens up before you, planted with miles of spiky pineapples and tall sugarcane. Sadly, the formerly perfectly paved road is now pitted with potholes. But if you pick your way carefully, the scenery is still worth the drive.

# THE COAST

On the other side of a mountain ridge, just a scenic 50-minute drive southwest of San Isidro, you reach the southern Pacific coast with its miles of beaches for sunning, surfing, kayaking, and snorkeling. Ballena National Marine Park alone encompasses almost 10 km (6 mi) of protected beaches. Scattered along the coast are small communities with increasing numbers of international residents and interesting restaurants and lodging options.

## Dominical

**6** Sleepy fishing village turned scruffy surfer town, Dominical is changing again, as luxury villas pop up all over the hillsides above the beaches, bringing new wealth that is fueling the local economy. For now, it's still a major surfing destination, with a lively surfer-fueled restaurant and nightlife scene. Bars and restaurants come and go with the waves of itinerant young people, so don't hesitate to try something new. Dominical's real magic, though, lies beyond the town, in the surrounding terrestrial and marine wonders: the rain forest grows right up to the beach in some places, and the ocean offers world-class surfing.

### Exploring

★ ⓒ The **Hacienda Barú** nature reserve is a leader in both ecotourism and conservation, with a turtle protection project and nature education program in the local school. The bird-watching is spectacular, with excellent guides. You can stay at the cabins or just come for the day to walk the forest and mangrove trails, zip through the canopy on cables, or climb a tree or stake out birds on an observation platform. ⊠ *2 km/1 mi north of bridge into Dominical* ☎ *787–0003* ⊕ *www.haciendabaru.com* ▣ *$6, tours $20–$60/person* ☼ *Daily dawn–dusk.*

Five years in the making, **Parque Reptilandia** is an impressive reptile residence, with more than 150 species of snakes, lizards, frogs, turtles, and other reptilian creatures in terrariums and large enclosures. There's also a maternity ward showcasing newborn snakes. The snakes live under a retractable roof that lets in sun and rain. They become much more active when it rains, so this is a great rainy-day-at-the-beach alternative activity. Night tours ($10) can also be arranged to watch nocturnal animals at work. ⊠ *13 km/8 mi east of Dominical on road to San Isidro* ☎ *787–8007* ▣ *$10* ☼ *Daily 9 AM–4:30 PM.*

**Cataratas de Nauyaca** (Nauyaca Waterfalls), a massive double cascade tumbling down 45 meters (150 feet) and 20 meters (65 feet), is one of the most spectacular sights in Costa Rica. The waterfalls—also known as Barú Falls—are on private property, so the only way to reach them is to take a hiking or horseback tour (⇨ Outdoor Activities, *below*).

**Playa Dominical** is long and flat, rarely crowded, and good for beachcombing among all the flotsam and jetsam that the surf washes up onto the brown sand. Swimmers should beware of fatally dangerous rip currents. In high season, flags mark off a relatively safe area for swimming, under the watchful gaze of a professional lifeguard.

**Playa Dominicalito,** just 1 km (½ mi) south of Playa Dominical, is usually calmer and more suited to boogie boarding.

> ### PACK YOUR BOARD
>
> The surfing is great in Dominical, thanks to the runoff from the Barú River mouth, which constantly changes the ocean bottom and creates well-shaped waves big enough to keep intermediate and advanced surfers challenged. The best surfing is near the river mouth, and the best time is two hours before or after high tide, to avoid the notorious riptides.

A considerably smaller waterfall than Cataratas de Nauyaca, **Pozo Azul** is in the jungle about 5 km (3 mi) south of town. Off the main highway, head up the road toward Bella Vista lodge and take the first road to the right, past the new school and through a stream; follow the road straight uphill for about 300 meters to where the road widens. You can park here and climb down the steep trail to the river on the right, where there is a lovely swimming hole and waterfall. Be sure not to leave anything of value in your parked car; there have been reports of theft here.

### Outdoor Activities

**Southern Expeditions** (✉ At entrance to town on right ☎ 787–0100 ✉ Villas Río Mar hotel, 1 km/½ mi west of Dominical ☎ 787–0052 ⊕ www.southernexpeditionscr.com) is the major tour operator in the area, and can arrange kayaking, white-water rafting, scuba diving, fishing, and nature tours in and around Ballena Marine National Park, Caños Island, and all the way down to Corcovado National Park.

Much of the lush forest that covers the steep hillsides above the beaches is protected within private nature reserves. By leading hikes and horseback tours, several of these reserves, such as Hacienda Barú and La Merced (⇨ Ballena Marine National Park), are trying to finance preservation of the rain forest.

**Green Iguana Surf Camp** (☎ 787–0157 ⊕ www.greeniguanasurfcamp. com) gives two-hour individual lessons ($50) and has week-long packages that include lodging, board rental, lessons, and transport to whichever nearby beach has the best waves each day (from $240).

FISHING  Angling options range from expensive sportfishing charters to a trip in a small boat to catch red snapper and snook for supper. The five most common fish species here are yellowfin tuna, wahoo, dorado, marlin, and sailfish. **Mark Hendry** (☎ 787–8224 ⊕ www.dominical.biz/mako1) runs trips 28 nautical miles out to the Furuno Bank, which he claims is the most reliable area for finding the big ones, including sailfish and marlin. Trips ($550/day) are in a 21-foot Mako boat and include food, drinks, and gear. Hendry has been fishing here since 1992. **Steve Sandusky**

(☎ 787–0230) has a high-powered boat that can go long distances fast to find sailfish and marlin ($650/day, including food, drinks, gear).

**HORSEBACK RIDING** **Don Lulo's tour** (☎ 771–3187) to Nauyaca Falls departs daily at 8 AM from the road to San Isidro, 10 km (6 mi) northeast of Dominical. The tour is $45 and includes breakfast and lunch at Don Lulo's family homestead near the falls. You can swim in the cool pool beneath the falls, so bring a bathing suit. The ride is easy; horses proceed at a walk.

Friendly, well-trained horses at **Bella Vista Lodge & Horse Ranch** (⌂ 5 km/3 mi south of Dominical ☎ 787–8069 or 388–0155) take riders on a mountain tour, with a gallop on the beach, morning or afternoon, depending on tides. The $45 tour includes breakfast before morning tours or sunset beers and bocas after the afternoon ride. The three- to four-hour tours start at the lodge, then head left up the steep Escaleras road, 2 km (1 mi) past Pozo Azul.

## Where to Stay & Eat

Lodgings in the lowlands of Dominical and the area a little to the north are hot and muggy and not as nice (excluding Río Mar) as the more luxurious, private, and breezy places up in the hills above Dominical-ito, to the south.

**DOMINICAL AND THE LOWLANDS** **$–$$** ✕ **Coconut Spice.** If you like rice with spice, you came to the right place. This sophisticated restaurant has authentic Southeast Asian flavor in both the food and furnishings. Try the hot-and-sour Tom Yan Goong soup, tart with lemongrass and limes and heated up with chilies. The jumbo shrimp vary in price and can get quite expensive, but they're worth it: buttery and sweet, and cooked in spicy coconut sauce. There are also satays, curries, and other Indian dishes. The best tables at this second-floor restaurant are out on the veranda, where it's cooler. ⌂ *Second floor, Plaza Pacífica, on the highway just above Dominical* ☎ 829–8397 ▣ *MC, V* ⊘ *Closed Mon.*

**¢–$$** ✕ **Restaurante El Rincón.** Savory meat and fish dishes are served with a sea view at this octagonal alfresco restaurant. At this writing, new owners are upgrading the decor and menu but promise not to change the warm tuna dinner salad that is unlike any other: chunks of succulent tuna sautéed in spicy oil and arranged over shredded lettuce, tomatoes, carrots, and mozzarella cheese. Beef, chicken, or tuna empanadas make a light lunch, or you can go for broke with a T-bone steak grilled gaucho-style. Sunsets are stunning. ⌂ *Pueblo Comercial center at entrance to town* ☎ 787–0048 ▣ *AE, MC, V* ⊘ *Closed Mon.*

**¢–$** ✕ **Restaurant Su Raza.** Among the handful of sodas in town serving typical Costa Rican food, this one is notable for its whole fish and hearty portions of seafood served on a wooden veranda that's a great bird-watching spot. Bring your binoculars, especially if you come just before sunset or for breakfast. Stick to the *desayuno típico* for breakfast, with traditional rice and beans and eggs. The omelettes are great but they come with limp frozen french fries, the bane of Tico restaurants today. ⌂ *Across from San Clemente Grill, main St.* ☎ 787–0105 ▣ *No credit cards.*

**¢–$** ✕ **San Clemente Bar & Grill.** Signs you're in the local surfer hangout: dozens of broken surfboards affixed to the ceiling, photos of the sport's early years adorning the walls, and a big sound system and dance floor. Fresh seafood, sandwiches, and Tex-Mex standards like burritos and nachos make up the menu. The bargain "starving surfer's breakfast"—two eggs with gallo pinto or pancakes, plus coffee—is very popular. Owner Mike McGinnis is famous for making great hot sauces and for being a super source of information about the area. ⊠ *Main St.* 🖀🖀 *787–0055* 🖃 *AE, MC, V.*

¢–$ ✕ **Tortilla Flats.** A popular surfer hangout along the lines of the San Clemente Grill, this place has the advantage of being right across from the beach. Fresh-baked baguette sandwiches are stuffed with interesting combinations; the California grilled chicken, avocado, tomato, and mozzarella is the most popular. Light eaters can buy half a sandwich. Fresh fish specials and typical Mexican fare round out the casual menu. The margaritas are excellent and ladies drink free *guaro* (sugar-can liquor)-and-anise shots on Tuesday nights. ⊠ *On the beach, Dominical* 🖀 *787–0033* 🖃 *No credit cards.*

¢ ✕ **Hammerhead's.** Diner-style comfort food with some pizzazz best describes the menu at this alfresco bar/restaurant that has become a mainstay of the expat American community. The crowd is always noisy and friendly. Along with the spicy chicken wings, Philly cheesesteaks, and hamburgers—which come "naked" or "wild," with sautéed onions, mushrooms, and cheese—are huge salads and delicious red snapper sandwiches. Decadent desserts include a dense chocolate brownie topped with *dulce de leche* (caramel) ice cream. ⊠ *Plaza Pacífica, downstairs from Coconut Spice* 🖀 *787–0125* 🖃 *No credit cards* 🕑 *Closed Mon. and Tues.*

$$ 🏨 **Plaza Suites Luxury Rentals.** Seemingly straight from the pages of a home-decorating magazine are these tastefully furnished apartments, equipped with a multitude of appliances and comforts. The kitchens are picture-perfect, the stone-lined showers are enormous, and each unit has its own design theme, reflected in fabrics and accessories. The 1,000-square-foot units share a small pool and barbecue area and a glorious garden that backs onto a river and forested hill with a trail to a waterfall. Dominical Beach is a 10-minute walk. The only drawback here is the road noise from the nearby highway, which can be drowned out by the remote-controlled a/c. ⊠ *Main highway above Dominical, 100 m south of Plaza Pacífica* 🖀 *787–0012* 🖶 *787–0049* 🖅 *www.caracolicostarica.com* ⚴ *A/c, pool, cable TV, kitchens* 🖃 *AE, MC, V* 🅾 *EP.*

$$ 🏨 **Roca Verde.** The sunny, stylish rooms of this beachfront hotel have stucco walls painted with swirling wallflowers, luxurious bathrooms, and cane-balustraded verandas looking onto a garden. There's no TV reception in the rooms, but if you're lucky you'll be here on a night when the local little theater group is performing in the hotel's huge, open-air lobby. The lobby is also an art gallery for local artists. The hotel arranges surfing lessons and fishing trips. Late-night dances on Saturdays, sometimes with live music, draw *bailarinas* (dancers) from surrounding towns. ⊠ *1 km/½ mi south of Dominical* 🖀 *787–0036* 🖶 *787–0013* 🖅 *10 rooms* ⚴ *Restaurant, pool, beach, laundry service; no a/c, no room phones, no room TVs* 🖃 *AE, MC, V* 🅾 *EP.*

$–$$ 🏨 **Hotel Diuwak.** An oasis of tranquillity in slightly chaotic Dominical central, Diuwak—which means "people of the sun" in indigenous

Bribri—has clean, but not luxurious, rooms in white-stucco buildings, with high ceilings, tiled floors, and rainbow-striped linens. The lush, sun-dappled garden is visible from carved wooden benches on the verandas in each room. A palm-lined avenue leads to a palatial pool with a theatrical waterfall. Along with upgrades around the property, prices have risen—perhaps beyond what the rooms are worth. Arranged in straight lines, the rooms put you at the mercy of noisy neighbors. ⊠ *South end of main road, near turnoff to beach* ☎ *787–0087* 🖷 *787–0089* ⊕ *www. diuwak.com* ⃔ *18 rooms* ⌂ *Restaurant, a/c in some rooms, fans, some kitchens, some refrigerators, pool, beach, bar, Internet; no a/c in some rooms, no TV in some rooms; no room phones* ⊟ *AE, MC, V* ⏏ *EP.*

**$** 🏨 **Hacienda Barú National Wildlife Refuge and Ecolodge.** Base yourself in these spacious but simple cabinas to explore the surrounding forests, mangroves, and Blue Flag beach. Four of the six cabins were freshened up in 2004, so be sure to ask for one of them when you reserve. Cabins, with tiled floors and sitting rooms with bamboo furniture, sleep three or four people. Linger for an hour or two atop a lofty bird observation platform in the hotel's rain-forest canopy, zip along the canopy tour, climb a 114-foot-high tree with ropes, or stay overnight at a shelter in the heart of the forest. Excellent local guides interpret the miles of trails, or you can follow the self-guided trail with the help of a handbook. There's a great gift shop here with lots of local crafts. ⊠ *3 km/2 mi north of bridge into Dominical* ⌂ *Apdo. 215–8000, Pérez Zeledón* ☎ *787–0003* 🖷 *787–0057* ⊕ *www.haciendabaru.com* ⃔ *6 cabinas* ⌂ *Restaurant, fans, kitchens, hiking; no a/c, no room phones, no room TVs* ⊟ *AE, MC, V* ⏏ *CP.*

**$** 🏨 **Río Lindo Resort.** This modest, two-story, concrete hotel has an old-fashioned resort-like feel, with a round pool ringed by gardens, and an idyllic view of the wide Barú River as it meets the ocean. Hunkered under the highway bridge that crosses the same river, there's some road noise but the pool fountain helps to mask it. Simple rooms are five up, five down, with the top rooms open to breezes (and road noise) and the bottom ones air-conditioned. Breakfast is served on a veranda with a river view. At night there's occasional live music at the funky Rum Bar, decorated with fantastical wall murals; there's always great bar food, including spicy chicken wings and stand-out *stromboli* (pizza rolls), as well as the best pizza in town. A guard watches the parking lot all night. ⊠ *Entrance to Dominical, beside the river* ☎ *787–0028* 🖷 *787–0078* ⊕ *www. riolindo.com* ⃔ *10 rooms* ⌂ *Restaurant, pool, fans, 2 bars; no room phones, no room TVs, no a/c in some rooms* ⊟ *AE, MC, V* ⏏ *CP.*

**★ $** 🏨 **Villas Río Mar.** The fanciest hotel in town is upriver from the beach on exquisitely landscaped grounds adrift in clouds of terrrestrial orchids and aflame with bright bougainvillea and hibiscus. Rooms are in adobe-style cabinas with thatched roofs and cane ceilings, and have clean white bathrooms. The newer junior suites have cable TV, king-size beds, and a/c—which is necessary, since they are on a hill, baking in the sun. Every room has a private porch screened with mosquito netting and furnished with bamboo chairs and hammocks. Plants and elegant table settings fill the thatch-roof restaurant. The breakfast buffet ($6) is a good

**6**

deal. The luxurious, large pool has a swim-up bar and handsome teak pool furniture. The spa can arrange yoga sessions. ⊠ *1 km/½ mi west of Dominical; turn right off highway into town and then right again under bridge and follow bumpy river Rd.* ☎ *787–0052* 🖷 *787–0054* ⊕ *www. villasriomar.com* 🖃 *Apdo. 1645–2050, San José* ⟿ *40 rooms, 4 junior suites* ♦ *Restaurant, refrigerators, tennis court, pool, whirlpool tub, massage, spa, beach, bicycles, bar, convention center; no a/c in some rooms, no TV in some rooms* ⊟ *AE, MC, V* ⧆ *EP.*

¢ 🖿**Posada del Sol.** Here you'll find clean, no-frills accommodations in a tranquil atmosphere. Rooms are on the ground floor of a concrete building opening onto a narrow porch with hammocks. In back is a little garden with a table and an area for washing clothes (by hand). Mattresses are firm, and the hotel has its own freshwater well, so the water is safe to drink. The Costa Rican owners are friendly and helpful and recommend the simple but good cooking at the Soda y Restaurante Nanyoa across the street. ⊠ *Main road, just south of San Clemente Bar & Grill* 🕾🕾 *787–0085 or 787–0082* ⟿ *5 rooms* ♦ *Fans; no a/c, no room TVs, no room phones* ⊟ *No credit cards* ⧆ *EP.*

THE HIGHLANDS
SOUTH OF
DOMINICAL
$$$ 🖿**Casí el Cielo.** The name, which means "almost heaven," is accurate at this unequaled, luxury B&B with a twist: a full staff at your service all day. The views from the villa's lofty perch alone are worth the price tag: the Pacific coast stretching south to the Osa Peninsula and north to Manuel Antonio. The four rooms, all with queen beds topped by pillow-soft mattresses, have themes of shells, birds, jungle, or fish. Exquisite details echo the room motif, down to the towel racks in the bathrooms. A coffee tray appears at 6:30 AM on your private terrace with a view. Enticing you to leave your room are the pretty pool; a resident naturalist ready to lead tours; and the friendly Tico staff, who prepare creative breakfasts and elegant lunches and dinners on a breezy terrace. ⊠ *Top of Bella Vista road at Km 147 of the Costanera, then 4 km/2 mi up* ☎ *813–5614* ⊕ *www.casielcielo.com* ⟿ *4 rooms* ♦ *Dining room, pool, car service; no room phones, no room TVs* ⊟ *No credit cards* ⧆ *MAP.*

★ $–$$$ 🖿**The Necochea Inn.** Though the forest setting feels primeval, the decor at this handsome B&B mountain retreat is a sophisticated mix of plush, contemporary furniture, at home in the huge rooms. Downstairs living and dining rooms face a wall of sliding glass doors looking onto a stone-decked pool with jungle and a slice of ocean for a view. Two streams run through the forested property, supplying a natural sound track. A curved stone stairway leads up to two luxurious, large rooms that share a spacious bath; and two suites, each with private porch, decadent bathrooms with deep tubs or whirlpool tubs for two, antique armoires, and gleaming hardwood floors. Hosts Yvonne and Carlos, transplants from Los Angeles, are full of energy and make every guest feel at home. ⊠ *2 km/1 mi up Bella Vista road just south of Km 147, past the Pozo Azul, Dominicalito* ☎ *787–8072 or 395–2984* ⊕ *www.thenecocheainn. com* ⟿ *2 rooms with shared bath, 2 suites* ♦ *Dining room, some in-room whirlpool tubs, pool; no a/c, no room phones, no room TVs* ⊟ *MC, V* ⧆ *BP.*

**$-$$** ⊞ **Coconut Grove.** Right on the beach, this well maintained colony of cabins and beach houses is ideal for couples or families who want to fend for themselves. The two bamboo-furnished beach houses sleep two to four and have full kitchens; the smaller cabins have kitchenettes and room for three. At night you can

> **WORD OF MOUTH**
>
> "Pacific Edge has a fabulous setting on a ridge with what must be a 270-degree clear view of the coast. We saw whales from there."
> —glover

also open the screened windows and fall asleep to the sound of the sea. There's a pretty pool and a barbecue grill. The American owners have dogs, including a very large but lazy Great Dane. ⊠ *Turn off the main highway at Km 147, 3 km/2 mi south of Dominical* ☏ 787-0130 ⊕ *www.coconutgrovecr.com* ⇲ *3 cabins, 2 beach houses* ♿ *A/c, pool, beach, kitchens, some kitchenettes* ⊟ *No credit cards* ¶◎¶ *EP.*

★ **$-$$** ⊞ **Pacific Edge.** Unbeatable views and stylishly rustic cabins at affordable prices set this place apart. The forest grows right up to the edge of the property, high on a mountain ridge south of town. Private, spacious wood cabinas—one sleeps six; others sleep two to four—have newly tiled bathrooms, hammocks strung on wide porches, and comfortable orthopedic mattresses covered with colorful Guatemalan bedspreads. Host Susie Anderson serves great breakfasts in the lodge's bamboo-roofed, pagoda-style dining room. Dinner—spicy Thai shrimp, perhaps—is cooked on request. Two lookout towers at each end of the tiny pool catch the spectacular sunsets and passing whale pods. The road up to this lofty perch requires a 4WD vehicle, but a hotel shuttle can pick you up in town with advance notice. Be prepared for a barky welcome; Susie and her husband George love big (but gentle) dogs. The reception desk closes at 6 PM. ⊠ *Turn inland 4 km/2½ mi south of Dominical on a rough road, follow road 2 km/1 mi* ⊕ *Apdo. 531–8000, Dominical* ☏ 787-8010 ⊕ *www.pacificedge.info* ⇲ *4 cabinas* ♿ *Dining room, refrigerators, pool, bar; no a/c, no room phones, no room TVs* ⊟ *AE, MC, V.*

**$** ⊞ **Cabinas Punta Dominical.** Picture a dream location: a high headland jutting out to sea with vistas up and down the Pacific coast. Add four simple wooden cabins on stilts (renovated in 2004), all facing the ocean, each with three walls of screened, floor-to-ceiling louvered windows to welcome in the constant breezes, a veranda with a hammock, and inside, bamboo furniture, good reading lights, and airy bathrooms. Throw in a breeze-swept restaurant, with spectacular views, despite none-too-exciting seaside cuisine. If you're just passing through Dominical, this is a good place for a tall glass of fruit juice or a cool beer with a view. Some guests have complained about reservations not being honored here, largely owing to changes in ownership, so be sure you call ahead to confirm your arrangements. ⊠ *4 km/2 ½ mi south of Dominical* ☏ 787–0016 ☏ 787–0241 ⊕ *www.laparcela.com* ⇲ *4 cabins* ♿ *Restaurant, bar, fans, hiking, laundry service; no a/c, no room phones, no room TVs* ⊟ *AE, MC, V* ¶◎¶ *CP.*

6

### Nightlife

During the high season, Dominical hops at night, and when the surfers have fled to find bigger waves there are enough locals around to keep some fun events afloat. Wednesday night there's live music at **Jazzy's Riverhouse** (⊠ Behind the Pueblo El Rio complex), when a mix of professional and local musicians jam after a fixed-menu vegetarian dinner. At Friday night's **Movies in the Jungle** (⊠ High up on Marina Drive in a private home with no sign; call for directions ☎ 787–8065), a pot luck dinner is at 5 and the movies start at 6. Movie buff Harley "Toby" Toberman presents self-proclaimed weird shorts from his huge collection plus a full-length feature on a huge screen, with state-of-the-art equipment. Admission is by $4 donation to the projection bulb fund. Saturday nights the dance action is at the **Roca Verde** (⊠ 1 km/½ mi south of Dominical), with a mixed crowd that doesn't usually get warmed up until 11 PM. Friday night there's noisy, rowdy dancing at **Thruster's** (⊠ Near the beach at south end of town), which attracts a fairly young, boisterous crowd.

### Shopping

★ Shop in rare air-conditioned comfort at **Banana Bay Gallery & Gifts** (⊠ Plaza Pacífica shopping center, highway just above Dominical ☎ 787–0106). It's open 9–5 daily, and it's stocked with an always intriguing and amusing mix of arts and crafts and unusual items, along with indigenous crafts such as Boruca masks and lots of insect-themed toys for kids of all ages.

### To & From Dominical

*34 km/21 mi (40 minutes) southwest of San Isidro, 40 km/25 mi (1½ hours) south of Quepos.*

The paved road west over the mountains and down to Dominical is scenic at its best and fog-enshrouded at its worst. There are lots of curves, and potholes pop up unexpectedly, so take your time and enjoy the scenery along the route from San Isidro. From Quepos, the road south is the only section of the Costanera still not paved, and it's a bumpy, dusty ride past palm-oil plantations. Buses from San Isidro and Quepos leave twice a day.

### Dominical Essentials

🏦 Bank/ATM **Banco de Costa Rica** ⊠ Plaza Pacífica.

🏥 Hospital **Clínica González Arellano** ⊠ Next to pharmacy ☎ 787–0129.

💊 Pharmacy **Farmacia Dominical** ⊠ Pueblo del Río Center, at entrance to town.

💻 Internet **Dominical Internet** ⊠ Above San Clemente Bar & Grill, main St. **Super Diuwak** ⊠ Next to Hotel Diuwak.

📮 Post Office **San Clemente Bar & Grill** ⊠ Main St.

ℹ️ Visitor Information **Southern Expeditions** ⊠ Entrance to town ☎ 787-0100.

# Ballena Marine National Park

❼ There's great snorkeling and whale-watching at Parque Nacional Marino Ballena (Whale Marine National Park), which protects several beaches stretching for about 10 km (6 mi), a mangrove estuary, an important coral reef, and a vast swath of ocean with rocky isles and islets. Along with the tropical fish you'll see while snorkeling, there are also hump-back whales. They can be seen with their young from December to April and again in late July through late October. Dolphins are also common sights. Above the water there are frigate birds and brown boobies, a trop-ical seabird, nesting on the park's rocky islands. With your less than $1 park admission you receive a brochure and a plastic garbage bag to re-mind you to take your trash with you. ☎ 743–8236 ⌨ $6 ($1 if you enter at Playa Uvita) ⊙ Daily 6–6.

At the park's northern end, palm-fringed, Blue Flag **Playa Uvita** stretches out into Punta Uvita, a long swath of sand, or *tombolo,* connecting a former island to the coast. At low tide the brown sand bar resembles a whale's tail fanning out on either side of the point, hence the name of the bay: Bahía Ballena, or Whale Bay. This is the best place to enter the park, since it only costs $1 and there are nearby restrooms and lots of restaurants nearby. The other entrance at Playa Ballena, staffed by park rangers, costs $6.

**Playa Ballena,** 6 km (4 mi) to the south of Playa Uvita in the park, is a lovely strand backed by lush vegetation. The price to enter the park here is $6.

Tiny **Playa Piñuela,** 3 km (2 mi) south of Playa Ballena and outside the park boundaries, is in a deep cove that serves as the local port.

**Playa Ventanas,** just 1½ km (1 mi) south of Ballena Marine Park, is a beautiful beach that's popular for sea-kayaking, with some interesting tidal caves. The mountains that rise up behind these beaches hold rain forests, waterfalls, and wildlife.

At **La Merced National Wildlife Refuge,** owned by Selva Mar, you can ride the range on horseback, explore the forest on a nature hike, or go bird-watching with an excellent guide. Tours include transportation from your hotel and a guide; the full-day tour includes lunch. ⊠ *Road between Dominical and Playa Uvita* ☎ *771–4582* ⊕ *www.wildlifecostarica. com* ⌨ *$25 half-day tour; $65 full-day tour* ⊙ *By tour only.*

## Outdoor Activities

Outfitters in Dominical (⇨ *above*) run tours to the park and surround-ing beaches. **La Merced National Wildlife Refuge** (⇨ *above*) has birding, forest hikes, and horseback riding.

DIVING & **Mystic Dive Center** (☎ 788–8636 ⊕ www.mysticdivecenter.com) spe-
SNORKELING cializes in dive and snorkel trips to Caño Island, about 50 km (31 mi), or an hour and 15 minutes, from Playa Uvita.

The best spot for snorkeling in the park is at the north end of Playa Bal-lena, near the whale's tail. **Ballena Tour** (☎ 831–1617) has a combina-tion tour ($65) that includes snorkeling in the park, swimming in the ocean to hear the whales sing, or swimming with sociable bottlenosed dolphins when they're around, plus exploring the caves at Ventana Beach. The tours are led by Georgie, a British environmental biologist, and Chumi, a local who has fished and guided all his life here. Their boat's four-stroke engine is extra quiet and environment-friendly. **Delfin**

**Tours** (☎ 743–8169), with an office very close to the beach, rents snorkeling gear and organizes snorkeling and fishing trips.

FISHING **Ballena Tour** ( ⇨ Diving & Snorkeling, *above*) organizes fishing trips for mahimahi, tuna, and mackerel, as well as catch-and-release sailfish and marlin. A half day costs $250; a whole day $400, including drinks, snacks, and all equipment.

KAYAKING **Flying Dutchman River Tours** (✉ Hotel Posada Playa Tortuga ☎ 384–5489) operates 2 ½–3-hour kayak tours ($30), in which you paddle along the Térraba River through mangroves to the mouth of the river.

ULTRALIGHT For a bird's-eye view of Bahía Ballena and the park, take off in an
FLIGHTS ultralight flying machine with aeronautical engineer Georg Kiechle and **Skyline Nature Ultralight Flying Tours** (✉ Road into Uvita ☎ 743–8037 ⊕ www.flyultralight.com). Tours cost $65–$150 for 20 minutes to an hour.

WHALE & When you head out to snorkel, chances are you'll be on the lookout for
DOLPHIN TOURS whales and dolphins too. **Ballena Tour** (☎ 831–1617) has a popular combo tour ( ⇨ Diving & Snorkeling, *above*).

## Where to Stay & Eat

$–$$  ✕ **Citrús Floating Restaurant.** Breezy and pretty, this restaurant is on a beautifully restored riverboat floating in a blue lagoon with a green mountain backdrop. Run by a Belgian/French chef, Citrús is as refreshing as its name, with *haute cuisine*—for example, duck breast with cranberry sauce and baked goat cheese and smoked salmon—served Jungle Queen–style. You can dine dockside or charter the boat for an elegant lunch or sunset dinner cruise through the mangroves. It's open for lunch and dinner. ✉ *At Km 178 on the Costanera, at the dock, just south of Ojochal* ☎ 304–1717 ⊟ *No credit cards* ☉ *Closed Mon. Jan.–Apr.; Closed Mon.–Wed. May–Dec.*

$–$$  ✕ **Exotica Restaurant.** Nestled in the tiny French-Canadian enclave of Ojochal, this restaurant serves tropical fare with a French accent. For starters, there's a tangy refreshing avocado, pineapple, lime, and cilantro appetizer or an intriguing Tahitian fish carpaccio (with bananas!). Or try a hearty serving of fish in a spicy banana-curry sauce. Presentation is artistic, with flourishes of flowers and sprigs of exotic greenery. Desserts are all homemade and luscious. A clump of beach almond trees provides a canopy for the patio restaurant, which has only nine tables. ✉ *Main road into Ojochal, 15 km/9 mi south of Uvita* ⊟ *No credit cards* ☉ *Closed Sun.*

$  ✕ **Pizzeria El Jardín Tortuga.** Ordering a pizza doesn't get any simpler than this: vegetarian or meat. The German pizza baker can make only six individual pizzas at a time in his wood-fired clay oven, but it's worth the wait for thin-crust pies heaped with toppings. The only other menu items are lasagna and salad. ✉ *Ojochal, past supermarket, left on bridge and first right* ☎ *No phone* ⊟ *No credit cards* ☉ *Closed Tues.*

¢ The first pizza place in Ojochal, **Gringo Mike's** ( ✉ Hotel Posada La Tortuga ☎ No phone) is in a trendy new space with murals of cigar-smoking angels. The pizza is the same and just as good, and pasta, chicken, and seafood have been added to the menu.

**$–$$** ⛉ **Hotel Posada Playa Tortuga.** High above Playa Tortuga, this Spanish-colonial style hotel is just a few kilometers north of Ballena National Marine Park, and right at the entrance to the French-Canadian enclave of Ojochal. The ocean view and pool are fabulous. The original rooms, stacked five on top of five, face the sea. Screened windows front and back make for good cross breezes when it cools down at night. Enormous new rooms in a Mediterranean-style building have king-size beds and huge bathrooms; one has a whirlpool tub on a private terrace. The buffet breakfast is ample and varied, and the pizza and pasta are famous in the area. Unfortunately, the hotel seems to be constantly under construction—at this writing, the new annex and pizzeria have been in progress for more than a year. The chatty American owner, known as Gringo Mike, knows a lot about the area. But watch out, he also sells real estate! ✉ *Off the Costanera, 35 km/22 mi south of Dominical, at entrance to Ojochal* ☎ *384–5489* ⊕ *www.hotel-posada.com* ⤶ *16 rooms* ⚒ *Restaurant, a/c, fans, pool, beach, kayaking, tours, bar; no room phones, no room TVs* ☰ *MC, V* ⍾ *BP.*

**$** ⛉ **Diquis del Sur Resort.** An ideal—and affordable—tropical retreat for the winter-weary, this formerly rundown hotel in the hills above Ojochal has been given new life by a French-Canadian couple who abandoned the Great White North almost the moment they saw this property. The views look to mountains and ocean and a garden full of mature fruit trees and flowering shrubs. Four freshly painted white bungalows with two rooms each are spread around the pretty grounds. Some have kitchen and a/c some have only a fan. But the shade trees keep the cabins cool. The full breakfast has a French accent—crêpes, French toast, omelets—and is served in a thatched-roof dining room overlooking an inviting pool with a waterfall. Owners Renée and Pierre Beaupré are just as delighted as their guests to be in this "earthly paradise." ✉ *1 km/½ mi up dirt road signed Calle Papagayo, off Ojochal main Rd.* ☎ *No phone* ⊕ *www.diquiscostarica. com* ⤶ *8 rooms* ⚒ *Dining room, pool, fans, some kitchens, bar: no a/c in some rooms, no room TVs, no room phones* ☰ *No credit cards* ⍾ *BP.*

**$** ⛉ **Rancho La Merced.** Be a cowboy for a day, herding and riding the range, at this 1,235-acre hillside cattle ranch. Or hike mountain trails in search of wildlife and birds. The rambling, 60-year-old farmhouse where you bed down is made of woodthat was shipped in from Puntarenas and then carried uphill on men's backs, before there were roads or cars in this area. The avocado-green hacienda has four simple but comfortable rooms that can accommodate up to 10 people; they share a modern bathroom with two showers and toilets. A homey eat-in kitchen is equipped with a microwave, coffeemaker, stove, and fridge. A separate cabin sleeps three. Resident guides can take you on foot or horseback into the forest. ✉ *15 km/9 mi north of Uvita, then 700 m up steep mountain*

*road, Uvita* ☎ *771–4582* 🖷 *771–8841* ⊕ *www.wildlifecostarica.com*
↩ *4 rooms, 1 cabin* ⚒ *Fans, hiking, horseback riding; no a/c, no room
phones, no room TVs* ▭ *AE, MC, V* ⊚ *FAP.*

$ ⊡ **Villas Gaia.** Conveniently just off the highway, these spacious villas
are spread around the jungle on a ridge here behind Playa Tortuga, overlooking forest ravines. The colorfully painted villas have handsome
hardwood furnishings and balconies; the poolside villas catch the best
breezes. A luxurious house has air-conditioning and satellite TV. The
restaurant is decorated with chandeliers made of mangrove roots and
has banana stenciling on the walls. The eclectic menu ranges from Mexican to Thai. A forest trail leads from the villas to the beach, where you
can swim safely. Horseback, mangrove, and sea-kayaking tours can be
arranged through the hotel. ⊠ *15 km/9 mi south of Uvita on coastal
highway, Playa Tortuga* ☎☎ *244–0316 in San Jose:ac:* ☎ *363–3928 in
Uvita* ⊕ *www.villasgaia.com* ↩ *12 cabinas, 1 house* ⚒ *Restaurant, fans,
pool, bar, laundry service; no a/c, no room phones, no room TVs* ▭ *AE,
MC, V* ⊚ *EP.*

## Shopping

Next door to Mystic Dive Center is **Green Leaf Arts & Artesania** (⊠ Centro Comercial Ventanas, near Km 174, north of Ojochal ☎ 788–8636),
with a great selection of quality local art and indigenous crafts. You can
also find huge bowls and vases made of recycled ojoche wood, which
used to cover all of Ojochal. **Licorera Feliz** (⊠ Centro Comercial Ventanas, near Km 174, north of Ojochal ☎ 788–8636) stocks Canadian
gourmet cheeses and health foods, perfect for beach picnics.

## To & From Bahía Ballena

*20 km/12 mi (30 minutes) southeast of Dominical.*

The park area encompasses the communities of Uvita, Bahía Ballena,
and Ojochal, all easily accessed off the Costanera. The park officially
begins 20 km (12 mi) south of Dominical along a wide, newly paved
highway. As soon as you get off the highway, however, the roads are
bumpy and dusty. While Uvita and Bahía have phones, Ojochal is in a
communications "black hole" and has next to no phone service. The
communications hub is an Internet café in the center of the village, which
has radio contact with some hotels and restaurants. Alternatively, take
a taxi or bus from Dominical. Buses leave Dominical at 5:30 AM and 3
PM daily.

# THE GOLFO DULCE

One of only three tropical fjords in the world, the Golfo Dulce has 600-
foot-deep waters in the center of the gulf that attract humpback whales.
At Chacarita, 33 km (20 mi) South of Palmar Sur, the southern coast
assumes a multiple personality. Heading west, you reach the Osa Peninsula and, eventually, the Pacific Ocean and the wildest region of Costa
Rica. Continuing due south is the Golfo Dulce, a tropical fjord whose

name means Sweet Gulf, connoting tranquil waters. This gulf creates two shorelines: an eastern shore that is accessible only by boat above Golfito and a western shore, which is the eastern side of the Osa Peninsula. South of Golfito the coast fronts the Pacific Ocean once again (rather than the tranquil gulf), with beaches that beckon surfers and nature lovers.

## Golfito

**8** Overlooking a small gulf (hence its name) and hemmed in by a steep bank of forest, Golfito has a great location and little else—that is, unless you're an angler. Sport- and fly-fishing have taken off in this area, and many lodges here run world-class fishing trips. The gulf water is warm, salty, and crystal clear in the early mornings, great for snorkeling. The sun sets behind the rolling silhouette of the Osa Peninsula and some nights you can spot phosphorescent fish jumping. Golfito was a thriving banana port for several decades—United Fruit arrived in 1938—with elegant housing for its plantation managers. After United Fruit pulled out in 1985, Golfito slipped into a state of poverty and neglect. The town itself consists of a pleasant older section and a long, ugly strip of newer buildings, dilapidated former workers' quarters, and abundant seedy bars. Visiting U.S. Navy ships dock here, and small cruise ships moor in the harbor. The Costa Rica Coast Guard headquarters is also here.

NAVIGATING
GOLFITO
Taxis and boats take you wherever you need to go in and around Golfito. You can hire taxi boats at the city dock in Golfito (about $35). The only way to reach the remote Golfo Dulce lodges above Golfito is by boat. Early morning is the best time, when the water in the gulf is at its calmest. Most lodges include the boat transport in their rates.

### Exploring

The northwestern end of town is the so-called **American Zone,** full of wooden houses on stilts, where the expatriate managers of United Fruit lived amid flowering trees imported from all over the world. These houses were purchased by Costa Ricans when the company departed, and a few are now very basic B&Bs.

Golfito doesn't have a beach of its own, but **Playa Cacao** is a mere five-minute boat ride across the bay from town. Hire a boat at the city dock or from a mooring opposite the larger cruise-ship dock, north of Golfito's center. Playa Cacao has one restaurant and one run-down lodge, but it makes a cooler, quieter option when the heat in Golfito gets unbearable.

The hills behind Golfito are covered with the lush forest of the **Golfito National Wildlife Refuge (Refugio Nacional de Vida Silvestre Golfito)** known as Naranjal by the locals. At the entrance, just 500 meters along a dirt road that runs parallel to the airport, you find the botanical legacy of the United Fruit Company's experimental farm, with flora from all over the world. The forest paths have been rehabilitated by the local tourism chamber and University of Costa Rica students, with signs

6

CLOSE UP

# Going Fishing?

COSTA RICA TEEMS WITH A constant supply of *pescado* (fish), some of which might seem unique to North Americans. Below are some local catches and where you'll find them.

*Gaspar* (alligator gar), found in Barra del Colorado River and Lake Arenal, look like a holdover from prehistoric times and have a long narrow snout full of sharp teeth; they make great sport on light tackle. Gar meat is firm and sweet (some say shrimplike), but the eggs are toxic to humans.

*Guapote* (rainbow bass) make their home in Lake Arenal. It's a hard-hitting catch: 5- to 6-pounders are common. Taxonomically, guapote are not related to bass, but are caught similarly, by casting or flipping plugs or spinner bait. Streams near the Cerro de la Muerte, off the Pan-American Highway leading south from San José, are stocked with guapote. The fish tend to be small, but the scenery makes a day here worthwhile.

Marlin and sailfish migrate northward through the year, beginning about November when they are plentiful in the Golfito region. From December into April they spread north to Quepos, which has some of the country's best deep-sea fishing, and are present in large numbers along the Nicoya Peninsula at Carrillo and Sámara from February to April, and near Tamarindo and Flamingo from May to September. Pacific sailfish average over 45 kilos (100 pounds), and are usually fought on a 15-pound line or less. Costa Rican laws require that all sails, except record catches, be released.

Tarpon and snook fishing is big on the Caribbean coast, centered at the mouth of the Barra del Colorado River. The acrobatic tarpon, which averages about 85 pounds here, is able to swim freely between saltwater and freshwater and is considered by many to be the most exciting catch on earth. Tarpon sometimes strike like a rocket, hurtling 5 m (16 ft) into the air, flipping, and twisting left and right. Anglers say the success rate of experts is to land about one out of every 10 tarpon hooked. In the Colorado, schools of up to 100 tarpon following and feeding on schools of *titi* (small, sardinelike fish) travel for more than 160 km (100 mi) to Lake Nicaragua. Snook also make this long swim. The long-standing International Game Fishing Association all-tackle record was taken in this area.

---

leading you to waterfalls. ✉ *500 m past the airport* ☎ *No phone* 💵 *Free* ☉ *24 hours.*

**Piedras Blancas National Park,** adjacent to the Golfito National Wildlife Refuge, has some great birding. The park is covered in verdant forest and is home to many species of endemic plants and animals. It's an important wildlife corridor because it connects to Corcovado National Park, and it's one of the few places in Costa Rica where jaguars still live. Follow the main road northwest through the old American Zone, past the airstrip and a housing project: the place where a dirt road heads into the rain forest is ground zero for bird-watchers. ✉ *Adjacent to Golfito National Wildlife Refuge* ☎ *No phone* 💵 *Free* ☉ *Daily dawn–dusk.*

★ A Garden of Eden with mass plantings of ornamental palms, bromeliads, heliconias, cycads, orchids, and flowering gingers, **Casa Orquideas** is accessible only by boat. It has been tended with care for more than 25 years by American owners Ron and Trudy MacAllister. The two-hour tour includes touching, tasting, and smelling, plus spotting toucans and hummingbirds. Tours require a minimum of four people. The water taxi from Golfito to the garden (about $50 for up to four people, including the return trip) is a tour in itself. ⊠ *North of Golfito on the Golfo Dulce* ☎ *775–1614* 💲 *$5* 🕐 *Tours Sat.–Thurs. at 8:30 AM.*

## Outdoor Activities

FISHING The open ocean holds plenty of sailfish, marlin, and roosterfish during the dry months, as well as mahimahi, tuna, and wahoo during the rainy season; there's excellent bottom fishing any time of year. Captains are in constant radio contact with one another and tend to share fish finds.

**Banana Bay Marina** (☎ 775–0838 ⊕ www.bananabaymarina.com) has the biggest charter fleet in town, with a dozen boats and world-record-holding captains. **C-Tales** (⊠ Las Gaviotas Hotel ☎ 775–0062 ⊕ www.c-tales.com) operates fishing boats with English-speaking captains. **Golfito Sailfish Rancho** (☎ 380–4262, 800/450–9908 in U.S.) has a big fishing charter operation with 11 boats. **King & Bartlett Marina** (☎ 775–1624 ⊕ www.costaricasailfish.com) arranges sportfishing char-
★ ters. **Roy Ventura** (⇨ Playa Zancudo, *below*) has some of the area's best charter trips. **Tierra Mar** (⊠ Waterfront next to Banana Bay Marina ☎☎ 775–1614 ⊕ www.marinaservices-yachtdelivery.com) arranges day trips with independent captains in the area.

## Where to Stay & Eat

The atmosphere of the in-town Golfito hotels (Hotel Samoa del Sur and Hotel Las Gaviotas) differs dramatically from the lodges in the delightfully remote east coast of the Golfo Dulce above Golfito. The latter is a world of jungle and blue water, birds and fish, and desert-island beaches, with lodges accessible only by boat, from either Golfito or Puerto Jiménez.

GOLFITO ✗ **Banana Bay.** For consistently good American-style food, you can't beat
$–$$ this breezy marina restaurant with a view of very expensive yachts and fishing boats. Locals complain that the prices are high, but portions are hefty, and include generous salads, excellent chicken fajitas wrapped in homemade tortillas, interesting pastas, and a delicious grilled dorado fish sandwich with a mountain of fries—a deal at $7. Jumbo shrimp, for which Golfito's commercial fleet is famous, are expensive at $14 but worth it. ⊠ *Golfito main street, south of town dock* ☎ *775–0838* ▭ *AE, MC, V* 🕐 *Breakfast served.*

$ ✗ **Restaurante Mar y Luna.** Strings of buoys, nets, and fishing rods give a nautical air to this casual terrace restaurant that juts out into Golfito Harbor. Even after the hottest day, there are cool evening breezes here and the restaurant's twinkling fairy lights frame a pleasant harbor view. The seafood-heavy menu includes shrimp and grilled whole fish. Chicken fillets smothered in a mushroom sauce and vegetarian dishes are non-fish choices. Unfortunately, the quality varies, depending on who's in the kitchen. ⊠ *South end of Golfito main street, just north of Hotel Las Gaviotas* ☎ *775–0192* ▤ *AE, MC, V* ☺ *Closed Mon.*

**$** ╳▦ **Hotel Samoa del Sur.** Nautical kitsch at its best, this dockside hotel has a ship-shaped bar/restaurant ($–$$), complete with a sail and a mermaid figurehead. This is definitely fishermen territory, with a pool table, loud music, and big TVs. Unexpectedly, the breakfast omelets may be the best in Costa Rica. The seaside theme carries through to spacious rooms, from shell-patterned bedspreads to shell-shaped hand soap. Rooms have two double beds, remote-controlled quiet a/c, and tiled bathrooms with hot water (a rarity). Mattresses are a little soft, and you are at the mercy of adjoining neighbors and the bass from the bar, but things usually quiet down by 11 PM. At this writing, the eccentric French owner/architect just finished a swimming pool in the shape of two butterfly wings. After midnight you are warned not to leave your room to avoid a nasty encounter with the guard dogs. ⊠ *Main street, 1 block north of town dock* ☎ *775–0233* 🖶 *775-0573* ⊕ *SamoaSur£racsa.co. cr* ☞ *14 rooms* ⌂ *Restaurant, a/c, fans, cable TV, pool, bicycles, bar, laundry service; no room phones* ▤ *AE, MC, V* ⍑ *EP.*

**$** ▦ **Hotel Las Gaviotas.** Just south of town on the water's edge, this hotel has wonderful views over the inner gulf. Rooms have terra-cotta floors, teak furniture, and a veranda with chairs overlooking the well-tended tropical gardens and the shimmering gulf beyond. A pleasant open-air restaurant with fresh-tasting food looks onto the large pool, whose terrace is barely divided from the sea. The bar-restaurant has an extensive wine and cocktail list and the weekend barbecue buffets ($12) are the best deal in town. The hotel books sportfishing trips. ⊠ *3 km/2 mi south of Golfito town center* ☝ *Apdo. 12–8201, Golfito* ☎ *775–0062* 🖶 *775-0544* ☞ *18 rooms, 3 cabinas* ⌂ *Restaurant, fans, cable TV, inroom safes, pool, bar, gift shop* ▤ *AE, MC, V* ⍑ *EP*

THE GOLFO DULCE **$$$$** ▦ **Golfito Sailfish Rancho.** Embraced by gulf and jungle, this comfy white-stucco lodge attracts serious fishermen and celebrity sports figures who come to fish, fish, fish! All-inclusive, first-rate fishing packages range from $1,900 for three days to $3,900 for seven days and include San José transfers and hotel; flight, taxi, and boat transportation to the lodge; plus all meals, snacks, beer and wine, and fishing gear. Two wings of comfortable rooms with tiled verandas look onto a narrow strip of beach. The convivial restaurant serves buffet meals. Spacious rooms have racks for storing fishing rods. The Rancho's fleet includes 10 up-to-date fishing boats, where you spend the majority of your days. ⊠ *15-min boat ride north of Golfito* ☎ *775–2157, 877/726–2468 in U.S.* ☝ *427 58th St., West Palm Beach, FL 33407* 🖶 *561/848–8998 in U.S.* ⊕ *www.golfitosailfish.com* ☞ *10 rooms* ⌂ *Restaurant, fans, beach, fishing, bar; no a/c, no room phones, no room TVs, no kids under 12* ▤ *AE, MC, V* ⍑ *AI.*

★ **$$$$** ▦ **Playa Nicuesa Rainforest Lodge.** Hands down, this is the best lodge on the gulf, with friendly but professional service and an emphasis on adventure. Out the front door of the lodge are beach, bay, and mangroves, with kayaks, snorkeling, fishing, sailing, and swimming; out the back door is a forested mountain with hiking trails, a waterfall, and plenty of wildlife and a resident naturalist to interpret the trails. The two-story main lodge is a palatial treehouse, crafted from 15 kinds of wood. Luxurious, hexagon-shape wooden cabins with open-air showers are scattered around a lush garden that ensures privacy. A stucco guesthouse with four large, comfortable rooms is shaded by mango trees. Solar power ensures a steady supply of electricity and there's always lots of hot water. Imaginative meals are served in the second-story dining room–cum–lounge with an unbeatable tropical-garden view. ✉ *Golfo Dulce, north of Golfito; accessible only by boat from Golfito or Puerto Jiménez* ☎ *735–5237 voicemail* ⊕ *www.nicuesalodge.com* ⇄ *5 cabins, 4 rooms* ⚘ *Restaurant, beach, snorkeling, boating, fishing, hiking, bar; no a/c, no room phones, no room TVs, no kids under 6* ▤ *MC, V* ⊘ *Closed Oct.–Nov. 15* ⦿ *AI.*

> ## TO FLUSH OR NOT TO FLUSH
>
> Costa Rican toilets *do* flush, but in most of Costa Rica septic systems weren't designed to dissolve toilet tissue. If you don't want to be the *gringo* who clogs up the works, watch for signs asking you not to put anything in the toilet—that includes toilet paper. A wastebasket (*basurero*) is almost always provided to hold used tissue. Even upscale resorts with modern septic systems have the basket, since the habit has been ingrained in locals.

**$$$$** 🏨 **Rainbow Adventures Lodge.** An energetic new manager is slowly sprucing up this gem of a lodge after a slow downward slide. The three-story, pagoda-style hardwood lodge is a treasure of Art Nouveau antiques, whose sinewy shapes blend in beautifully with the jungle. Rooms are open to the air, with mosquito nets over the beds and suspended panels of antique stained glass in place of windows. Sitting in solitary splendor on its own beach with one of the most beautiful views of the gulf, the lodge has kayaks and jungle trails and can arrange fishing trips. The new manager is updating the menu but you can count on lots of fresh fish and fruit. An extensive natural-history library was bequeathed by a former resident. ✉ *Playa Cativo, 35 min north of Golfito by motorboat* ☎ *831–5677* ✉ *petrabrinkhoff@hotmail.com* ⇄ *4 rooms* ⚘ *Dining room, pool, beach; no a/c, no room phones, no room TVs* ▤ *No credit cards* ⦿ *FAP.*

**$$$** 🏨 **Buenavista La Dulce.** Rebuilt and renamed after a disastrous fire, the former Buenavista Lodge is now the newest and most casual lodge on the gulf. Rooms are in two handsome teak and purpleheart-wood wings, connected by covered stairs to the open-air dining room and lounge. The rooms have private baths, wood shutters, and mosquito nets—and a lot of hard edges to bump into, so be careful in the dark. There's a steep jungle trail up to a *mirador* (lookout), a small beach, and a tiny plunge pool, plus fishing, kayaking, and snorkeling. There's not much privacy here, but it's a great place for sociable people or a group of friends to hang out. ✉ *First beach north of Rainbow Adventure, accessible only by boat from Golfito or Puerto Jiménez* ☎ *842–2287* 🖷 *503/977–2021 in U.S.* ⊕ *www.buenadulce.com* ⇄ *8 rooms* ⚘ *Dining room, pool, beach, bar; no rooms phones, no a/c, no room TVs* ▤ *No credit cards* ⦿ *FAP.*

$$$ ▦ **Esquinas Rainforest Lodge.** This well-managed ecolodge is run by an Austrian nonprofit group who have tried to instill a sense of Teutonic order. But the tidy gravel paths winding past wooden cabins in manicured gardens is being encroached upon by wild forest, with the garden looking wilder every year. Rooms have tile floors, good reading lamps, and airy bathrooms with plenty of hot water. A spring-fed pool is delightful, and the candlelit dining room serves excellent food. Fragrant white ginger and ylang-ylang encircle a pond with resident caimans. Wild and thrilling trails head to the waterfalls and primary forest of Piedras Blancas Park. Local guides lead river walks and bird-watching tours. More than 80 percent of the guests here are from Germany and Austria. If you have 4WD you can get here by following the dirt road through the heart of Piedras Blancas National Park. In the dry season when it's passable, this back route can cut miles off a trip from the north, and it passes through some gorgeous wilderness. ⊠ *Near La Gamba, 5 km/3 mi west of Villa Briceño turnoff* ☎ *775–0901 lodge, 775–0140 Golfito office* ⊕ *www.esquinaslodge.com* ⇆ *14 rooms* ⌂ *Dining room, fans, pool, hiking, horseback riding, bar; no a/c, no room phones, no room TVs* ☰ *AE, MC, V* ⋈ *FAP.*

## Shopping

**Tierra Mar** (⊠ Waterfront next to Banana Bay Marina) has an excellent selection of painted Boruca wood masks. It also has one-of-a-kind local crafts, such as woven straw hats, cotton purses, and painted gourds. In ★ a class all its own, the **Mercado Artesania** (⊠ Hotel Samoa Sur, main street, 1 block north of town dock) is the biggest emporium in the Southern Zone, filled with every imaginable—and unimaginable—souvenir. Large paintings by local artists, huge painted fans from Thailand, hammocks, beach clothes, and life-size snake carvings are just a few of the offerings here. Even if you don't buy a thing, it's fun to look. Ask the hotel manager to unlock the door and visit the Shell Museum, the hotel owner's personal, life-long collection of shells.

## Nightlife

The bar at **Banana Bay Marina** (⊠ Main street, south of town dock) is usually full of English-speaking fishermen in the evening. Thursday to Sunday nights, **Bar Los Comales** (⊠ Near the large dry dock at the north end of town) has late-night dancing and karaoke till 2 AM in a rougher section of town, near the large dry-dock. Be a little careful here; go with a group and leave in a taxi.

**King & Bartlett** (⊠ Just south of Banana Bay) is a little quieter than Banana Bay in the evenings although sometimes it jumps. **Samoa del Sur bar** (⊠ Hotel Samoa del Sur, main street, 1 block north of town dock) has a mix of Ticos and foreigners, mostly of the male persuasion, and loud music until 11 PM.

## To & From Golfito

*339 km/212 mi (8 hours by car; 1 hour by plane) southeast of San José.*

From San José the trip is a long and often grueling drive along paved roads but over often-foggy mountains. Your best bet, especially if you are visiting one of the lodges on the gulf, is to fly to Golfito. Direct buses from San José leave twice daily.

## Golfito Essentials

**Bank/ATM** **ATH Coopealianza** ✉ Across from hospital, north end of town. **Banco Nacional** ✉ South of hospital.

**Hospital** **Regional Hospital** ✉ American Zone, near Deposito ☎ 775-1001.

**Pharmacy** **Farmacia Golfito** ✉ Main street, across from city park ☎ 775-2442.

**Internet** **Golfito Internet** ✉ Main street, between city dock and gas station, next to Servicentro Pacifico Sur.

**Post Office** **Correo** ✉ Across from soccer field; climb flight of stairs off the main road, just south of central park.

**Taxis** **Taxi service** ☎ 775-2020.

**Visitor Information** **Land Sea Services** ✉ Next to Banana Bay Marina on left as you enter town ☎ 775-1614.

# Playa Zancudo

⑨ For laid-back beaching involving hammocks strung between palms and nothing more demanding than watching the sun set, you can't beat breezy Playa Zancudo, with its miles of wide, flat beach and views of the Osa Peninsula. It isn't particularly beautiful: the 10 km (6 mi) of dark brown sand is strewn with flotsam and jetsam. But there's a constant breeze and a thick cushion of palm and almond trees between the beach and the parallel dirt road through town. The standout feature is the magnificent view across the gulf to the tip of the Osa Peninsula. The beach runs almost due north/south, so you have center-stage seats for sunsets, too. Away from the beach breezes, be prepared for biting *zancudos* (no-see-ums).

There's a flurry of new construction here, with Canadians and Americans building substantial beachfront homes. Most hotels and restaurants are within sight of the beach. Life here is laid-back and very casual, centering on walking the beach, fishing, kayaking, swimming, and hanging out at the local bars and restaurants. Zancudo has a good surf break, but it's nothing compared with Playa Pavones a little to the south. Swimming is good two hours before or after high tide, and if you get tired of playing in the surf and sand you can arrange a boat trip to the nearby mangrove estuary to see birds and crocodiles. Zancudo is also home to one of the area's best sportfishing operations, headquartered at Roy's Zancudo Lodge.

NAVIGATING PLAYA ZANCUDO
Getting around Playa Zancudo doesn't take much, as it's so small. Rent an electric golf cart ($75, two-day minimum) at a shop across from the Supermercado Buen Precio. Rent a bike at Cabinas Sol y Mar or Tres Amigos Supermercado, both on the main road in Zancudo, for about $10 per day.

## Outdoor Activities

FISHING
If you've got your own gear, you can do some good shore fishing from the beach or the mouth of the mangrove estuary, or hire a local boat to take you out into the gulf. The main edible catches are yellowfin tuna,

snapper, and snook; catch-and-release sportfish include marlin, rooster-fish, and swordfish.

**Roy Ventura** (✉ Roy's Zancudo Lodge, main road, 1 km/½ mi west of Cabinas Sol y Mar ☎ 776–0008) runs the biggest charter operation in the area, with 11 boats ranging in length from 25 feet to 28 feet. Packages include room, food, and drink, and you can arrange to be picked up in Golfito, Puerto Jiménez, or San José. Captain John Olson at **Sportfishing Unlimited** (☎ 776-0036) fishes from 28-foot, center-console boats with both fly and conventional tackle. The rate is $500 per day for two fishers, which includes lunch, drinks, and gear. Experienced **Captain Ronny** (☎ 776–0048) uses a VHF Radio fish finder on his 26-foot boat with 240 HP diesel engines. The daily rate is $575.

HORSEBACK RIDING  Early-morning rides over hills, through jungle, and along the beach ($50) set off at 7 AM from a farm 4 miles inland and finish at **Oasis on the Beach** (☎ 776–0087) for a full breakfast. A shorter ride, from 4 to 6 PM ($30), takes you to a hilltop for a sunset view over the gulf.

KAYAKING  The kayaking is great at the beach and along the nearby Río Colorado, lined with mangroves. **Cabinas Los Cocos** (✉ Beach Rd. ☎ 776–0012) has a popular tour ($40) that takes you for a 1½–hour motorboat ride up the river, then a two-hour kayak tour along a jungly mangrove channel, before motoring back to Zancudo. The company also rents user-friendly, sit-on-top kayaks with back rests for $5 per hour.

## Where to Stay & Eat

$–$$  ✕ **Oasis on the Beach.** Huge windows facing a picture-perfect beach view in this contemporary space allow you to enjoy fish, shrimp, and excellent *fajitas* in humidity- and bug-free comfort. Saturday and Sunday are pizza nights, when the wood-fired brick oven outside is heated up. Save room for banana crêpes or the Piña Diablo, pineapple cooked with black pepper, brown sugar, and butter and flambéed with rum. This is a great place for a breezy breakfast, too; for something different, try the ZBC Eggs, thick slices of tomato topped with cheese and a sunny-side-up egg, baked in a sizzling-hot fajita pan. ✉ *Main beach road at entrance to Zancudo* ☎ 776–0087 ▭ *V* ☺ *Breakfast served.*

★ $–$$  ✕ **Restaurant Sol y Mar.** On a breezy porch with a palm-fringed beach view, this restaurant has the most cosmopolitan food in Zancudo, with an eclectic menu of Mexican *quesadillas,* savory chicken *cordon bleu,* and fresh fish with elegant French sauces. There's a touch of Thai here too; one of the most popular dishes is mahimahi in a coconut-ginger sauce. Desserts are decadent and delicious. ✉ *Hotel Sol y Mar, main Rd.* ☎ 776–0014 ▭ *No credit cards.*

¢–$  ✕ **Macondo** There's absolutely nothing fancy about this tiny restaurant, but it serves the best homemade pasta in the Southern Zone. Chef Daniel Borello comes from the Piemonte region in northern Italy and his pasta is light, almost tissue-paper thin, and perfectly sauced. There's no written menu, just a recitation of pasta shapes available with your choice of sauce. There are also meat or spinach-and-cheese ravioli and, sometimes, lasagna, as well as jumbo shrimp and tenderloin. But stick to the pasta—it's a sure bet. The only disappointment is that none of the wine choices is worthy of the food. End your meal with an authentic espresso or cappuccino. ⊠ *Across from the Ferreteria, on beach road, center of town* ☎ 776-0157 ⊟ *No credit cards* ⊘ *Closed Sept.–Nov.*

$ ✕⬚ **Cabinas Sol y Mar.** As its name implies, Cabinas Sol y Mar has sun and sea, plus a beach fringed by coconut palms. Peach-colored cabinas with tiled porches and high ceilings look onto the gulf and have views of the Osa Peninsula. Each roomy cabina has a sunny bathroom with a pebble-paneled shower and sleeps four. The alfresco restaurant ( ⇨ *above*) consistently serves the best food in town. The popular U-shape bar is an easy place to meet new friends, including the friendly Canadian-American owners. A shop sells colorful sarongs and clothing from Thailand. ⊠ *Main road, south of Cabinas Los Cocos, Playa Zancudo* ☎ 776–0014 ⊕ *www.zancudo.com* ⇶ *5 cabinas, 1 house* ⚇ *Restaurant, fans, beach, bar, gift shop; no a/c, no room phones, no room TVs* ⊟ *No credit cards* ⏐◯⏐ *EP.*

$ ✕⬚ **Oasis on the Beach.** This is the ideal, laid-back beachfront hotel. The three wooden cabins are reminiscent of old Nantucket cottages, and sure enough, the owners are from New England. The cabins have two bedrooms each, bright ceramic bathrooms and porches to sit on to catch the constant breeze and admire the view of coconut palms, hammocks, blue sea and sky, and white surf. Mini-fridges are stocked with juice and milk. The newest additions are the two air-conditioned rooms in a two-story villa. The cool, contemporary restaurant/bar ( ⇨ *above*) is the most sophisticated place in Zancudo. ⊠ *Main beach road, as you enter town* ☎ 776–0087 ⊕ *www.oasisonthebeach.com* ⇶ *3 cabins, 2 rooms* ⚇ *Restaurant, refrigerators, beach, horseback riding, bar; no a/c in some rooms, no room phones, no room TVs* ⊟ *V* ⏐◯⏐ *EP.*

$$$$ ⬚ **Roy's Zancudo Lodge.** Most people who stay here are anglers on all-inclusive sportfishing packages, taking advantage of Roy's 11 fishing boats. But the comfortable, modern hotel is a good choice even if you've never caught anything but a cold. It's right on the beach—the ample, verdant grounds surround an inviting pool, and an open-air restaurant serves buffet meals. The nonfishing rate includes all meals and "national-brand" drinks (locally made brands of alcohol). The sea foam–green two-story hotel has huge rooms with hardwood floors, two firm double beds, and ocean views. Four suites are in cozy private cabinas, and three cheaper rooms don't have refrigerators. ⊠ *Main road, 1 km 1½ mi west of Cabinas Sol y Mar, Playa Zancudo* ⌖ *Apdo. 41, Zancudo* ☎ 776–0008 ⎙ 776–0011 ⊕ *www.royszancudolodge.com* ⇶ *15 rooms, 4 cabinas* ⚇ *Restaurant, fans, some refrigerators, cable TV, pool, whirlpool tub, beach, fishing, bar* ⊟ *AE, MC, V* ⏐◯⏐ *FAP.*

$ ⬚ **Cabinas Los Cocos.** This little beachfront colony of four self-catering cabins is designed for people who want to kick back and enjoy the beach. Artist Susan England and her husband Andrew Robertson are Zancudo fixtures and can organize any activity, including river safaris and kayaking tours. Two idyllic tropical cabins have thatched roofs and hammocks. The other two cabins are renovated 40-year-old banana-company houses moved here from Palmar Norte. These charming white-and-green wooden cottages give you the rare chance to live a little bit of Costa Rican history. ⊠ *Beach Rd.* ☎☎ 776–0012 ⊕ *www.loscocos.com* ⇶ *4 cab-*

*ins ♿ Kitchens, beach; no a/c, no room phones, no room TVs* ⊟ *No credit cards* ⦿I *EP.*

## Nightlife

Hanging out at the bar at **Sol y Mar** (✉ Main road, south of Cabinas Los Cocos) and Oasis on the Beach constitutes nightlife here, although there is sometimes karaoke or a disco in town. **Oasis on the Beach** (✉ At the south end of the main road into town) is a popular hangout every night, but shows DVD movies projected onto a screen on Tuesday nights.

## To & From Playa Zancudo

*51 km/32 mi (2 ½ hours) south of Golfito.*

The road from Golfito is paved for the first 11 km (7 mi), but after the turnoff at El Rodeo the trip entails almost two hours of bone shaking and a short ride on—but sometimes long wait for—a cable river ferry. You are much better off without a car here. You can hire a boat at the municipal dock in Golfito for the 25-minute ride ($25 for two) or take a *collectivo* boat that leaves Zancudo daily at 7 AM and docks at Hotel Samoa del Sur in Golfito; the return boat leaves Samoa del Sur at noon ($5 each way). **Cabinas Los Cocos** (✉ Beach Rd. ☎☎ 776–0012) has water-taxi service to Golfito ($12.50 per person; minimum 2 people) and service to Puerto Jiménez ($15 per person; minimum 3 people).

## Playa Zancudo Essentials

�e Internet **Internet Café** ✉ Cabinas Coloso del Mar, main beach road across from Bar Tranquilo.

# Playa Pavones

➓ One of the most scenic beaches to drive past is remote Playa Pavones, on the southern edge of the mouth of Golfo Dulce. Through a fringe of palms you catch glimpses of brilliant blue, white surf crashing against black rocks, and the soft silhouette of the Osa Peninsula across the gulf. The area attracts serious surfer purists, but also has pristine black-sand beaches and virgin rain forest. The beach is very rocky, so it's important to ask around for the best swimming areas. One of the best places to swim is in the Río Claro, under the bridge or at the river mouth (dry season only). The town of Pavones itself is an unprepossessing collection of *pensiones* and sodas clustered around a soccer field.

## Outdoor Activities

SURFING Pavones is famous for one of the longest waves in the world, thanks to the mouth of the Río Claro, which creates ideal sand banks and well-shaped waves. The ocean bottom is cobblestoned where the surfing waves break. The most consistent waves are from April to September, and that's when the surfing crowd heads down here from the Central Pacific Coast beaches.

Most surfers here are serious about their sport and bring their own boards, but you can rent surfboards—$25 long, $20 short—and boogie boards at **Sea Kings Surf Shop** (✉ In town, by the soccer field ☎ 393–6982 or 829–2409). Surf lessons are $20 for 2 hours. **Cabinas La Ponderosa**

( ⇨ Where to Stay & Eat, *below*) rents surfboards and boogie boards, as well as bicycles.

## Where to Stay & Eat

**¢–$** ✕ **Cafe de la Suerte.** Lucky for food-lovers, the "Good Luck Café" serves truly astonishing vegetarian food that even a carnivore could love, along with intriguing exotic juice combinations and thick fruit smoothies. The homemade yogurt is a revelation: light, almost fluffy, and full of flavor. The Israeli owners serve it over a cornucopia of exotic fruits, sprinkled with their own granola, and mix it into refreshing fruit-flavored *lassis* (yogurt-based drinks from India). Healthy sandwiches are heavy on excellent hummus, and hot vegetarian daily specials might include curried hearts of palm. Don't leave without buying a fudgy brownie or a brown-sugar oatmeal square for the road. ⊠ *Next to soccer field* ☎ *No phone* ▭ *No credit cards.*

**$$$** ⊡ **Tiskita Jungle Lodge.** One of the premier attractions in the Southern Zone for nature lovers, Tiskita was begun in 1977 by Peter Aspinall, a passionate farmer and conservationist, and his wife Lisbeth. The property includes a vast fruit orchard, with more than 100 varieties of trees that attract monkeys, coatis, birds, and other wildlife. Surrounding the orchard are 800 acres of primary and secondary forest, a habitat for the more than 275 species of birds and a 90-strong troop of squirrel monkeys. Peter leads tours of the orchard, and expert naturalist guide Luis Vargas leads bird-watching and nature tours. Comfortable, screened wooden cabins on stilts are surrounded by lush vegetation and have rustic furniture and modern, open-air bathrooms. Trails invite you to explore the jungle on your own and a cascading waterfall with freshwater pools. Very simple, rather meager buffet meals are served in an open-air dining room; but throughout the day you can help yourself to freshly squeezed tropical juices in the fridge, and the cookie jar is always full. Cabins are spread out, with lots of steps to climb. No. 6 has the most privacy, and a beautiful ocean view. The beach, with swimmable waters, is a steep 15-minute downhill walk. Most guests arrive by air taxi at the hotel's private airstrip. ⊠ *6 km/4 mi south of Playa Pavones* ⌂ *Apdo. 13411–1000, San José* ☎ *296–8125* 🖷 *296–8133* ⊕ *www. tiskita-lodge.co.cr* ⇆ *16 rooms in 3 single cabins, 3 doubles and 1 triple* ⌂ *Dining room, fans, pool, beach, bicycles, hiking, horseback riding, bar, airstrip; no a/c, no room phones, no room TVs* ▭ *AE, MC, V* ⊘ *Closed Sept. 15–Oct. 15* ⊙| *AI.*

**$–$$** ⊡ **Cabinas La Ponderosa.** The world-famous Playa Pavones surfing break is just a 10-minute walk from this surfer-owned hotel. It's a cut above the usual surfer place, and a bar-

> **CAUTION** ⚠
>
> In the unlikely event that you are bitten by a snake, stay calm, move slowly, and try to remember what the snake looked like, to tell the clinic staff. Only allow antivenin to be administered by a trained person, in case of side effects. Five hours is the window before any tissue loss. To avoid snakebites, stay on trails and wear long pants; in some areas high rubber boots are recommended. *Never* reach out to touch a snake or poke it with a stick, à la Jeff Corwin.

**6**

gain, with three meals included in the rate. High-ceilinged rooms sleep up to six and have hardwood furniture and walls. Screened porches overlook a lush garden, and nature trails wind through 14 acres. The house has two bedrooms and a screened balcony but no kitchen. The restaurant/common area has satellite TV and there are volleyball and basketball courts. You can rent surfboards, boogie boards, or bicycles here. Everything is within walking distance, so you don't need a car. ⊠ *On beach* ☎ *824–4145 for voice mail, 954/771–9166 in U.S.* ⊕ *www. cabinaslaponderosa.com* ⇨ *5 rooms, 1 house* ⚴ *Dining room, a/c in some rooms, fans, some refrigerators, beach, bicycles; no a/c in some rooms, no room phones, no room TVs* ⊟ *No credit cards* ⦿⊩ *FAP.*

$ ⊞ **Casa Siempre Domingo.** High on a breezy hill, this B&B has the best view in town of the Golfo Dulce meeting the Pacific Ocean. Two of the four enormous rooms have 20-foot ceilings and two double beds set high to catch the view out the large windows. The other two rooms have pretty garden views. Even the big outdoor stone shower has narrow slits to capture the view. Substantial breakfasts are served at a large communal table in a screened-in great room with wicker furniture, and there's a communal fridge to store food and drinks. Trails lead up into the forest. The only drawback here is the very steep driveway up to this lofty perch. You'll need 4WD and nerves of steel or else you can build up a set of steely muscles climbing up. ⊠ *2 km/1mi south of town; follow signs after Río Claro Bridge* ☎ *820–4709* ⊕ *www.casa-domingo. com* ⇨ *4 rooms* ⚴ *A/c, fans, hiking, surfing; no room phones, no room TVs* ⊟ *No credit cards* ⦿⊩ *BP.*

$ ⊞ **Riviera.** Brand new at this writing, each of these spacious, one-bedroom villas next to the Río Claro has a large modern kitchen, two double beds, and a futon. Huge tiled patios look out onto a garden and there's a trail to the river, great for a cool swim. You're close enough to the beach to hear the surf. ⊠ *300 m southwest of Supermercado Siete Mares* ☎ *823–5874* ⇨ *3 villas* ⚴ *A/c, kitchen, beach; no phone, no TV* ⊟ *No credit cards* ⦿⊩ *EP.*

## Shopping

At **Arte Nativo** (⊠ Beside soccer field ☎ 821–6563) the best buys are charming watercolors painted by owner/artist Candyce Speck and beautifully matted with decorated banana paper ($15–$50). They're a much more evocative souvenir of the beach than the usual T-shirt. There's also a selection of high-quality indigenous crafts and funky jewelry and mobiles made from natural materials.

## Nightlife

From late April to September, **La Manta** (⊠ 1 km/½ mi north of town, on beach Rd.) is the main event, an open-air surfer bar where surfer videos shot by the owner are played every day, DVD movies are shown on a big screen, and Mediterranean-style food, including great falafels, is served.

## To & From Playa Pavones

*53 km/33 mi (2 ½ hours) south of Golfito.*

There's no avoiding the bumpy road from Golfito to Conte, where the road forks north to Zancudo and south to Pavones. But the dirt road to

Pavones is usually well graded. A public bus leaves from Golfito very early in the morning. A taxi from the airstrip in Golfito costs more than $60.

# THE OSA PENINSULA

Costa Rica's most breathtaking scenery and most abundant wildlife thrive on the Osa Peninsula, one-third of which is covered by Corcovado National Park. You can hike into the park on any of three routes or fly in on a charter plane. Corco-

> **WORD OF MOUTH**
>
> "Save the Osa for last, unless you like eating your dessert first."
> —greenfieldhunter

vado also works for day trips from nearby luxury nature lodges, most of which lie within private preserves that are home for much of the same wildlife you might see in the park. And complementing the peninsula's lush forests and pristine beaches is the surrounding sea, with great sportfishing.

There are two sides to the Osa: the gentle Golfo Dulce side, much of it accessible by car, albeit along rocky roads; and the much wilder and dramatic Pacific side, which is only accessible by boat or charter plane, or by hiking a sublimely beautiful coastal trail.

## Puerto Jiménez

**⑪** Once you see Puerto Jiménez, it may surprise you to learn that this dusty, one-iguana town is the largest on the Osa Peninsula. Main-street traffic consists mostly of bicycles and ancient pickup trucks. But the place has a certain frontier charm, and new restaurants, hotels, Internet cafés, and "green" newcomers are lending an interesting, funky edge. Heading south, it's also the last civilized outpost on the peninsula before you're off the grid. South of Jiménez there is no public electricity or phone service. So make your phone calls, send e-mails, get cash, and stock up on supplies here. Be prepared for the humidity and mosquitoes—Jiménez has plenty of both. You won't find much relief in the Golfo Dulce at the town dock; the water is quite warm and not clean. If you need a refreshing dip, head south of the airport to Playa Platanares, where there is a long stretch of beach with swimmable (but still warm) waters.

The reason to come to Puerto Jiménez is to spend a night before or after visiting Corcovado National Park, since the town has the best access to the park's two main trailheads and an airport with flights from San José, and is the base for the *collectivo* (public transport via pickup truck) to Carate.

The **National Parks Service Headquarters** (✉ Next to airport ☎ 735–5036 🖷 735–5276) has information about hiking trails in Corcovado National Park. The office is open weekdays 8 AM to 4 PM.

NAVIGATING PUERTO JIMÉNEZ Once you get to the main street in town, you can get around by foot. If you don't have a car and are staying at one of the Playa Platanares hotels or at Bosque del Río Tigre or Villa Corcovado—all outside of town—

## FODOR'S FIRST PERSON

**Dorothy MacKinnon**
*Writer*

In search of wild nightlife, I set out with entomologist Tracie Stice one moonless night on the Osa Peninsula. Equipped with headlamps and night-vision optics, we carefully moved along the jungle trail. After studying, then steering clear of a venomous fer-de-lance snake, we came across a whip scorpion and a dozen huge, industrous spiders. At a rickety suspension bridge, Stice felt a vibration. She signaled for silence while she scanned the bridge with her infrared flashlight for an animal large enough to make the bridge move. In a flash we recognized the creature. Eyes wide with terror, we silently beat a hasty retreat, narrowly escaping an encounter with the most dreaded animal in the forest: the skunk.

you are at the mercy of taxis to get anywhere. Water taxis, hired at the city dock, can take you to waterfront lodges, nearby beaches, or Golfito.

### Outdoor Activities

**Escondido Trex** (✉ Restaurante Carolina, center of town, 200 m south of soccer field ☎ 735–5210 🖷 735–5196 ⊕ www.escondidotrex.com) arranges kayaking, charter-fishing, and small-boat outings for watching wildlife, in addition to a number of land-based outings. Isabel Esquivel, at **Osa Tropical** (✉ Across from Banco Nacional on main St. ☎ 735–5062 🖷 735–5043 ⊕ www.osatropical.com), runs the best generalist tour operation on the peninsula. Whatever travel question you ask the locals, they will usually say: "Ask Isabel." Along with arranging flights, ground transport, hotel bookings, and tours, Osa Tropical is the radio communications center for all the Osa lodges and tour operators.

BIRD-WATCHING The birding around the Osa Peninsula is world renowned, with more than 400 species. Endemic species include Baird's trogon, yellow-billed cotinga, whistling wren, black-cheeked ant tanager, and the glorious turquoise cotinga. There has even been a very rare harpy eagle spotted in the last year. One of the best spots on the peninsula to find a yellow-billed cotinga or a white-crested coquette is the bridge over the river at **Rincón** (✉ 40 km/25 mi north of Puerto Jiménez), if you get there before 7 AM.

★ The best English-speaking birding guides are Liz Jones and Abraham Gallo, who run **Bosque del Río Tigre Lodge** (✉ Dos Brazos del Tigre, 12 km/7½ mi northwest of Puerto Jiménez ☎ 735–5725 ⊕ www.osaadventures.com) They lead birding trips all around the peninsula, including in Corcovado National Park.

FISHING Along with Golfito across the water, Puerto Jiménez is a major fishing destination, with plenty of billfish and tuna, snapper and snook, almost all year, with the exception of June and July, when things slow down.

**Escondido Trex** (⇨ *above*) has charter-fishing trips and unique fishing-by-kayak trips. **Osa Sportfishing** (✉ Next to Restaurant Carolina ☎ 735–5675 ⊕ www.fishosa.com) runs offshore fishing trips on a 30-foot Stamas boat,

$750 for up to six fishers; inshore fishing trips are $500 for up to three. Sunset party cruises ($55) are aboard the *The Delfin Blanco,* a 50-foot custom tour boat, with the chance to see dolphins and bioluminescent microbes during a scenic 3½-hour cruise around the gulf.

**Parrot Bay Village** (☎ 735–5180 🖷 735–5568 ⊕ www.parrotbayvillage. com) is one of the biggest operations around. Its state-of-the-art boats have quiet four-stroke engines and custom rods and lures. Guides recommend arriving 10 days before or after the new moon to ensure lots of fish. Most fishers come on a fishing package tour, but a full-day offshore fishing in a boat for two costs $850. The largest charter company in the area is **Roy Ventura** ( ⇨ Playa Zancudo, *above*).

HIKING   If you have 4WD, it's just a 30-minute ride west to the village of Dos Brazos and the **Tigre Sector** of the park. Few hikers come here because it's difficult to access, which means it's more pristine and you'll likely have it to yourself. You can take a taxi to Dos Brazos and hike from here or use rustic but comfortable Bosque del Río Tigre Lodge as a base.

★ **Osa Aventura** (☎☎ 735–5670 ⊕ www.osaaventura.com) specializes in multiday Corcovado hiking adventures, led by Mike Boston, an ebullient tropical biologist who sounds like Sean Connery and looks like Crocodile Dundee.

HORSEBACK RIDING   The most popular horse trails in the area are at remote **Río Nuevo Lodge** (✉ Office next to La Carolina Restaurant, main St. ☎ 735–5411), about 12 bumpy km (7½ mi) west of town. Rides along the river and up onto scenic forested ridges last from three to seven hours and include transportation there and back and a home-cooked hot meal for $50–$65 per person.

KAYAKING   Puerto Jiménez is a good base for sea-kayaking trips on the calm Golfo Dulce and for exploring the nearby mangrove rivers and estuaries. Alberto Robleto, an enterprising local, has amassed an impressive fleet of kayaks with excellent safety equipment at **Aventuras Tropicales** (✉ South of airport on road to Playa Platanares ☎ 735–5195 🖷 735–5692 ⊕ www.aventurastropicales.com). Tours include snorkeling, dolphin-watching and bird-watching. The most popular is the three-hour mangrove tour ($25). A three- to nine-day kayaking tour teaches survival skills in the tropical forest. **Escondido Trex** ( ⇨ *above*) has sea-kayaking trips and rents sit-on-top kayaks by the hour for $5.

## Where to Stay & Eat

Playa Platanares is only about 7 km (4 mi) outside of Puerto Jiménez, but lodgings there have a very different feeling from those in town, as they are on a lovely and quiet beach. Bosque del Río Tigre, Villa Corcovado, and Río Nuevo Lodge are also outside of town, but in a forested area.

★ **$$** ✕ **El Restaurante Jade Luna.** Haute cuisine is not what you'd expect in Puerto Jiménez, but New York chef Barbara Burckhardt has set a whole new standard at her elegantly arcaded terrace restaurant. Already famous for her ice creams and sorbets, Barbara has scoured the country to find goat cheese, the best smoked trout, and the freshest herbs, and solicited local fishermen to deliver fresh seafood, to create outstanding

# Where Have All the Forests Gone?

**THE WORLD GIVES HIGH MARKS** to Costa Rica for its environmental awareness, but accolades don't always match reality. In the last half century more than two-thirds of Costa Rica's original forests have been destroyed. Forests have traditionally been considered unproductive land, and their destruction was for a long time synonymous with development. In the 1970s and 1980s, international and domestic development policies fueled the destruction of large tracts of wilderness. Fortunately, in the 1970s alarmed Costa Rican conservationists began creating what is now the best national park system in Central America. The government has since made progress in curbing deforestation outside the national parks too.

As you travel through Costa Rica, you see that its predominant landscapes are not cloud and rain forests but the coffee and banana plantations and cattle ranches that have replaced them. Deforestation not only spells disaster for endangered animals like the jaguar and the harpy eagle, but can have grave consequences for human beings. Forests absorb rain and release water slowly, playing an important role in regulating the flow of rivers—which is why severely deforested regions often suffer twin plagues of floods during the rainy season and drought during the dry months. Tree covers also prevent topsoil erosion, thus keeping the land fertile and productive; in many parts of the country erosion has left once-productive farmland almost worthless. Finally, hidden within Costa Rica's boundless living species are countless unknown or understudied substances that might eventually be extracted to cure diseases. The destruction of this country's forests is a loss for the entire world.

---

dinners as well. The menu changes daily, but you can count on pan-blackened Cajun fish with a pineapple salsa, roasted vegetable-and-goat-cheese tart, or a grilled loin pork chop with star anise, black peppercorns, and coffee-bean rub. The chef spares no expense in her ingredients, her raw materials, and her attention to presentation and service. For dessert, the pecan–praline ice-cream pie with caramel and chocolate is a hit. ⊠ *East of airport, across from old cemetery, on road to Playa Platanares* ☎ *735–5739* ⊟ *No credit cards* ☉ *No lunch. Closed Sun.*

¢–$ ✕ **Il Giardino.** Good northern Italian cooking, in the form of wood-oven pizzas, homeade pastas, and excellent salads, has arrived in Puerto Jiménez. The owner is also a master carpenter, so the curvy blond-wood bar and wood detailing in the casual restaurant with garden tables are handsome indeed. Sushi and dim sum make guest appearances on the menu. ⊠ *25 m west of ICE telephone office, downtown Puerto Jiménez* ☎ *735–5129* ⊟ *No credit cards* ☉ *No lunch May–Dec.*

¢–$ ✕ **Juanita's Mexican Bar & Grill.** Swing open the saloon doors of this cantina and you might think you're in another south-of-the-border frontier town. The popular bamboo bar dispenses signature margaritas to go along with the Tex-Mex menu of quesadillas, burritos, and taco salads. The food is only so-so, but the brightly colored tablecloths and art enliven the eating experience, as do the antics of patrons on special-event nights with crab races and hula-hoop contests. It's open for breakfast, too. ⊠ *Beside CaféNet El Sol, center of town* ☎ *735–5056* 🖃 *No credit cards.*

¢–$  ✕ **Restaurante Carolina.** This simple alfresco restaurant in the heart of Puerto Jiménez serves decent *comida típica* (typical food) and reliably fresh seafood. It's also the central meeting place for every tourist and foreigner in town, ergo a good place to pick up information. Don't count on using a credit card, as phone lines are dodgy. ⊠ *Main street, center of town* ☎ *735–5185* 🖃 *V.*

★ $$$$  🏨 **Iguana Lodge.** If a long stretch of deserted beach is your idea of heaven, this luxury lodge with breezy, screened-in cabins among mature trees is for you. The gentle Golfo Dulce waters are perfect for swimming, sea-kayaking, and boogie boarding. Cabins are furnished elegantly in bamboo, with thoughtful touches, including Egyptian cotton sheets and a raft of candles for romantic evenings. The pebble-lined showers have plenty of solar-heated hot water and excellent water pressure. Buffet-style dinners, with exotic foods reflecting the owners' worldwide travels, are served in a thatched-roof dining room with a huge table that can accommodate up to 32. The lavish breakfasts are worth getting up for. There's also a communal kitchen, a yoga platform, and a Japanese soaking tub. Birds are plentiful in the Playa Preciosa Platanares Mixed Refuge, which borders the lodge. ⊠ *Playa Platanares, 5 km/3 mi south of Puerto Jiménez airport* ☎ *848–0752* 🖷 *735–5436* ⊕ *www. iguanalodge.com* 🗢 *4 rooms (in 2 bungalows), 2 (2-bedroom) family cabins, 1 (3-story, 3-room) house* ⚐ *Restaurant, fans, beach, tours, snorkeling, kayaking, boogie boards, bar; no a/c* 🖃 *MC, V* ⌾ *AI.*

$$$$  🏨 **Parrot Bay Village.** A storybook collection of octagonal cottages in a tropical garden, this hotel has caimans lurking in the nearby mangrove lagoon. The main event here is fishing, both onshore and offshore, and the hotel has fishing packages that also include some nature activities off the water. The comfortable cabinas have king-size beds, wicker furniture, tile floors, hot-water showers, and intricately carved mahogany doors. They sleep up to eight; three cabinas have two stories. Some face the bar and restaurant, others face the gulf. The attractive alfresco restaurant ($) has a view of the beach, gulf, fishing boats, and the distant hills of Piedras Blancas. The short dinner menu changes daily (fish is excellent) and full breakfasts are served. ⊠ *500 m southeast of airport, on Puerto Jiménez beachfront; 20-min walk from town* ☎ *735–5180* 🖷 *735–5568* ⊕ *www.parrotbayvillage.com* 🗢 *8 cabinas* ⚐ *Restaurant, in-room safes, beach, snorkeling, boating, bar, laundry service, airport shuttle; no room phones, no room TVs, no smoking* 🖃 *AE, D, MC, V* ⌾ *BP.*

$$$$  🏨 **Villa Corcovado.** Extravagant ecotourism is the theme here. Argentine owners have built the sumptuous villas, each a symphony of rare hardwoods, with handmade four-poster beds, high-quality cotton sheets, outdoor garden showers as well as nice indoor bathrooms, and private verandas with Golfo Dulce views. The pool is the largest in the South Pacific, meant for serious swimmers (the owner's daughter swims com-

**6**

petitively for Argentina). Bright-blue wicker beach chairs add a touch of whimsy to the elegant grounds. Service is top-notch in the gulf-view alfresco restaurant, and the food has Italian and Argentine accents. Kayaking, dolphin- and whale-watching, fishing, and organic-farm tours are given by local guides and drivers. You can also hike steep forest trails within the property. The road down to the waterfront resort is so steep that you need 4WD and nerves of steel to drive it. Most guests arrive by boat from Puerto Jiménez. This place is not recommended (by the owners' admission) for kids under 6. ⊠ *30 km/19 mi north of Puerto Jiménez, at the top of the Golfo Dulce* ☎ *840–3636* 📠 *770–8061* ⊕ *www. villacorcovado.com* 🛏 *8 villas* ⚖ *Dining room, fans, refrigerators, pool, massage, beach, kayaking, tour operator, bar, laundry service, airport shuttle; no a/c, no room phones, no room TVs* ▤ *MC. V* ♨ *FAP.*

**$$–$$$** ▦ **Bosque del Río Tigre Lodge.** You can't get any closer to nature than this off-the-grid lodge wedged between forest and the banks of the Río Tigre. Rooms have chest-high walls, and then are open to nature to the roof with no screens, just mosquito nets, and the electricity is solar-generated and limited. Hot-water showers are in the garden. Comfortable beds have fresh linens, and the gourmet food rivals the best luxury-lodge kitchens. Early-morning birders and hikers set out fortified by fresh-baked banana bread and excellent coffee and return to a gargantuan breakfast. Guests gather around a communal table at dinner. Owners Liz Jones and Abraham Gallo are the best bird guides in the area, and more than 340 species have been spotted on the property. Abraham, who has lived here all his life, can show you hidden mountain trails into Corcovado National Park, less than a mile away. Miners still pan for gold in the nearby river, which has a great swimming hole. ⊠ *Dos Brazos del Tigre, 12 km/7 mi west of Puerto Jiménez* ☎ *735–5725, 888/875–9543 in U.S.* 📠 *735–5045* ⊕ *www.osaadventures.com* 🛏 *4 rooms, 1 cabin, all with shared bath* ⚖ *Dining room, hiking, bird-watching, airport shuttle; no a/c, no phones, no room TVs* ▤ *No credit cards* ⊘ *Closed Oct. and Nov.* ♨ *FAP.*

**$$** ▦ **Río Nuevo Lodge.** You have to cross five rivers to get to this Tico-run tent camp on the western edge of Corcovado National Park. But it's worth the trip, and the bumpy truck ride from Puerto Jiménez is included in the affordable rate, along with three meals. This is camping even ardent anticampers can enjoy. The mold-free, green plastic tents sit atop wooden platforms with private porches. Inside, mattresses and bed linens are fresh and clean; each tent sleeps two. The views from the tents are of misty mountains, Río Nuevo, and a gorgeous tropical garden. Family-style meals usually consist of hearty Costa Rican stews and lots of vegetables, cooked on a wood-fire stove. The shared bathhouse is clean and lit by one lightbulb at night (bring a flashlight). The main event is horseback riding and many day visitors come out just for a three-hour ride and a hot lunch ($50). It's also a starting point for hiking into Corcovado National Park. ⊠ *12 km/7 mi west of Puerto Jiménez; office in Puerto Jiménez, next to Carolina Restaurant* ☎ *735–5411* 📠 *735–5407* ⊕ *www.rionuevolodge.com* 🛏 *8 tents with shared bath* ⚖ *Dining room, shared cold-water bath, horseback riding, hiking; no a/c, no room phones, no room TVs* ▤ *MC, V* ♨ *FAP.*

CLOSE UP

## Wildlife-Watching Tips

**IF YOU'RE ACCUSTOMED TO** nature programs on TV, with visions of wildebeest and zebra swarming across African savannah, your first visit to a tropical forest can be a bewildering experience. If these forests are so diverse, where are all the animals? Web sites, brochures, and books are plastered with lovely descriptions and close-up images of wildlife that give travelers high hopes. Reality is much different, but no less profound. Below are some tips to make your experience more enjoyable.

• Don't expect to see rarely sighted animals. It might happen; it might not. Cats, especially jaguars, harpy eagles, and tapirs are a few rare sightings.

• Monkeys can be the easiest animals to spot, but while they are as reliable as the tides in some locations, in others they are rare indeed.

• Remember that nearly all animals spend most of their time avoiding detection.

• Be quiet! Nothing is more unsettling to a wary animal than 20 *Homo sapiens* conversing as they hike. It's best to treat the forest like a house of worship—quiet reverence is in order.

• Listen closely. Many visitors are surprised when a flock of parrots overhead is pointed out to them, despite the incredible volume of noise they produce. That low-pitched growl you hear is a howler monkey call, which is obvious if nearby, but easily missed over the din of conversation. Try stopping for a moment and closing your eyes.

• Slowly observe different levels of the forest. An enormous caterpillar or an exquisitely camouflaged moth may be only a few inches from your face, and the silhouettes in the tree 100 meters away may be howler monkeys. Scan trunks and branches where a sleeping sloth or anteater might curl up. A quick glance farther down the trail may reveal an agouti or peccary crossing your path.

• In any open area such as a clearing or river, use your binoculars and scan in the distance; scarlet macaws and toucans may be cruising above the treetops.

• Cultivate some level of interest in the less charismatic denizens of the forest—the plants, insects, and spiders. On a good day in the forest you may see a resplendent quetzal or spider monkey, but should they fail to appear, focus on an intricate spiderweb, a column of marching army ants, mammal footprints in the mud, or colorful seeds and flowers fallen from high in the canopy.

**$–$$** 🏨 **Pearl of the Osa Beach Resort.** Just down the beach from Iguana Lodge, and a few rungs down the price ladder, is this funkier option. The owners are the same, and you can arrange to have meals at Iguana. But this hotel, right on Playa Platanares, has simpler, second-story rooms atop a popular restaurant/bar. Bamboo furniture, high-pressure hot showers, and comfortable beds echo the good taste that you also find at Iguana Lodge. There's no a/c, but ceiling fans and good cross breezes cool down the rooms. It's a great place for singles to mingle, especially on Friday nights when there's live music and a special pasta menu. Because the rooms are in a line, with open windows, privacy is minimal. ⊠ *Playa Platanares, 100 m north of Iguana Lodge* ☎ *848–0752* ⊕ *www.pearloftheosa.com* ➘ *8 rooms* ⌂ *Restaurant, ceiling fans, beach, kayaking, tours, bar; no a/c, no room phones, no room TVS* ⊟ *MC, V* ⍾ *BP.*

$  ⊞ **La Choza de Manglar.** Just steps from the airport, this hotel has comfort with pizzazz. Spectacular hand-painted murals in the huge restaurant area create an indoor rain forest, and the bathrooms are immersed in a sea of painted underwater life. An amazing amount of real wildlife makes appearances in the surrounding mangrove forest. Rooms are on the small side, with tile floors and colorful, hand-carved wooden furniture made in Nicaragua. The garden cabins are larger, with ceiling fans instead of air-conditioning, and hammocks on the porches. ⊠ *100 m west of airport* ☎☎ *735–5002* ✉ *info@manglares.com* ➘ *6 rooms, 4 cabins* ⌂ *Restaurant, fans, bar; no a/c in some rooms, no room phones, no room TVs* ⊟ *No credit cards* ⍾ *BP.*

¢  ⊞ **Cabinas Marcelina.** Two elderly Italian sisters run the best bargain hotel in town. The lavish Continental breakfast, served in the garden ($3.50), is optional. Fresh, bright, spotlessly clean rooms look out onto the pleasant garden and have homey, old-fashioned touches like lace shower curtains. All have private bath and hot water and half the rooms are air-conditioned. If you're traveling solo or need a break from your traveling companion, two single rooms are $17 each. ⊠ *Main street, north side of the Catholic church* ☎☎ *735–5007* ⊕ *cabmarce£hotmail.com* ➘ *8 rooms* ⌂ *Fans, garden; no a/c in some rooms, no room phones, no room TVs* ⊟ *No credit cards* ⍾ *EP.*

## Nightlife

The sidewalks are usually rolled up by 9 PM in Puerto Jiménez, but there are a few evening options. **La Taberna** (⊠ 1½ blocks east of main street, at Oro de Verde hotel turnoff) is a mellow lounge with intimate seating arrangements, a jungle garden, and large-screen TVs that show music videos. It's a great place to hang out with the locals. **Pearl of the Osa** ( ⇨ Where to Stay & Eat, *above*) attracts a big crowd Friday nights with live salsa music and a special pasta menu. The crowd is a mix of ages, and of tourists and locals. The music is loud and a lot of fun. Some Saturday nights there's live music—usually salsa or rock—at **La Choza de Manglar** (⊠ Beside airport). At **Juanita's** (⊠ Next to CaféNet El Sol in the middle of town), free movies are shown on Tuesdays; Wednesday night is Ladies' Night, with half-price drinks for *señoritas*; and Thursday nights you can bet on your favorite crustacean at the crab races. A weekend **discotheque** (⊠ North end of town) is mostly frequented by teens.

## Shopping

Jewelry maker **Karen Herrera** (⊠ Beside airport) has collected the finest arts and crafts in the area and displayed them in an impressive shop.

★  **Tagua Arts & Crafts** (⊠ Beside airport) has some rare items, including colorful cotton dresses and original, woven Panamá hats made by the Guaymí people. Other interesting items are bird carvings made by a family in Rincón, stained-glass mosaic boxes, mirrors and trivets made by a San José artist, local paintings, and serious art ceramics. There's also a selection of natural-history field guides and books.

## To & From Puerto Jiménez

*130 km/86 mi (3 hours by car; 90 min by boat) west of Golfito, 364 km/226 mi (8 hours by car; 1 hour by plane) from San José.*

Most visitors fly to Puerto Jiménez from San José, since the bus ride or drive is grueling and long. The drive from Golfito is not recommended either—the road from Chacarita to Rincón is notoriously potholed and the road from Rincón to Jiménez is dusty dirt all the way. A better option is the 90-minute water-taxi ride from Golfito. You can hire taxi boats at the city dock. Prices are $45 to Golfito from Puerto Jiménez and $35 from Puerto Jiménez to Golfito. Water taxis can also take you to beach-front lodges. A rickety-looking launch ($2.50 each way) leaves from Golfito's *muellecito* (small municipal dock) at 11:30 AM every day. It returns the next morning from the concrete pier at Puerto Jiménez.

A *collectivo,* an open-air communal truck ($6), leaves Puerto Jiménez twice daily for Cabo Matapalo and Carate. It's the cheapest way to travel but the trip is along a very bumpy road—not recommended in rainy season (May–December). The collectivo leaves from Autotransportes Blanco, 200 m west of the Super 96, at 6 AM and 1:30 PM.

## Puerto Jiménez Essentials

🄵 Bank/ATM **Banco Nacional** ✉ 500 m south of Super 96, directly across from the church.

🄵 Hospital **Public Clinic and First Aid Station** ✉ 25 m west of post office ☎ 735-5063.

🄵 Pharmacy **Botiquín** ✉ Main street, one block south of Carolina Restaurant and across the St. ☞ Very limited selection.

🄵 Internet **CaféNet El Sol** ✉ Center of town, next to Juanita's.

🄵 Post Office **Correo** ✉ West side of soccer field.

🄵 Visitor Information **Osa Tropical** ☎ Across from Banco Nacional on main street ☎ 735-5062 🖷 735-5043 ⊕ www.osatropical.com.

# Cabo Matapalo

**⓬** The southern tip of the Osa Peninsula, where virgin rain forest meets the sea at a rocky point, retains the kind of natural beauty that people travel halfway across the world to experience. From its ridges you can look out on the blue Golfo Dulce and Pacific Ocean, sometimes spotting whales in the distance. The forest is tall and dense, with the highest and most diverse tree species in the country, usually draped with thick lianas. The name "Cabo Matapalo" means "cape strangler fig," a reference to the fig trees that germinate in the branches of other trees and extend their roots downward, eventually smothering the supporting tree by blocking the life-giving light with their roots and branches. Strangler figs are common in this area, as they are nearly everywhere else in the country, but Matapalo's greatest attractions are its rarer species, such as the *gallinazo* tree, which bursts into yellow blossom as the rainy season comes to a close. The brilliant scarlet macaw is another draw here.

A forested ridge extends east from Corcovado down to Matapalo, providing a continuous forest corridor protected within a series of private preserves, which results in Cabo Matapalo's having most of the same wildlife as Corcovado National Park. Most of the point itself lies within the private reserves of the area's three main hotels listed below, and that forest is crisscrossed by footpaths, some of which head to tranquil beaches or to waterfalls that pour into pools. Most of the lodges in this area do not have phones, only radio contact.

## Outdoor Activities

Outfitters in Puerto Jiménez run tours in this area. Each of the lodges listed here has resident naturalist guides to take guests on nature hikes. For extreme forest sports, **Everyday Adventures** (☎ 735–5138 or 353–8619 ⊕ www.everydaycostarica.com) takes you on not-so-everyday adventures: rappelling down waterfalls, climbing up a 140-foot strangler fig, ocean kayaking (with an optional 30-foot dive), and rain-forest hiking.

SURFING   On the eastern side of Cabo Matapalo, waves break over a platform that creates a perfect right, drawing surfers from far and wide, especially beginners. Mike Hennessey of **Captain Mike's Surf School** (☎ 382–7796) gives surfing lessons ($50) on long boards in the relatively safe waves at Playa Pan Dulce, in front of Lapa Ríos, where he lives. Mike guarantees you'll stand up on the board the first wave you try.

FISHING   **Cabo Matapalo Sportfishing** (☎☎ 735–5773 ⊕ www.cabo-matapalo. com), has excellent, experienced fishing captains and top-of-the-line, well-equipped boats ($925 full day; $700 half-day). Captain Mike Hennessey is always in demand as one of the most entertaining and fun guys to go fishing with in the Gulf.

## Where to Stay

★ $$$$   ▦ **Bosque del Cabo.** On a cliff at the tip of Cabo Matapalo, this lodge has unparalleled views of blue gulf waters meeting blue ocean. The property, with hundreds of acres of animal-rich primary forest, also has the most beautiful landscaping on the peninsula. Deluxe cabins have king-size beds, and all the luxurious thatch-roof cabins have private, outdoor (hot-water!) garden showers. For the ultimate in romantic seclusion, ask for the Mariposa cabin, which has the most private porch. A suspension bridge through the forest links the main lodge with three more rustic cabins. Appetizing meals are served in a rancho restaurant overlooking a garden alive by day with hummingbirds. Lantern-lighted dinners are accompanied by a chorus of frogs. Solar power and a small hydro-powered generator provide enough light to read by, and ocean breezes make air-conditioning superfluous. Resident guides are on hand to lead you along dense forest trails—on foot or along a canopy zip line—and down to the beach with its natural warm tidal whirlpools and river waterfalls. ✉ 22 km/14 mi south of Puerto Jiménez on road to Carate ☎☎ 735–5206 ⊕ www.bosquedelcabo.com ✈ 6 deluxe cabins, 4 standard cabins, 3 garden cabins, 2 houses ♿ Restaurant, some kitchens, pool, beach, kayaking, fishing, horseback riding, bar, Internet; no a/c, no room phones, no room TVs ▤ MC, V ⅠΟⅠ FAP.

★ $$$$   ▦ **El Remanso.** Find tranquillity and understated elegance at this retreat in a forest brimming with birds and wildlife, 400 feet above a beach studded with tide pools. Luxurious cabinas have louvered, screened windows, large verandas, and showers behind curving Gaudí-like walls. A two-story, hot-pink stucco-and-cane building has two rooms that sleep four to six each. Three additional rooms are in a new building that is under construction at this writing. Excellent meals use local produce and are served on a shaded deck restaurant. The property reflects the owners' conservationist ideals; they met as Greenpeace volunteers. Waterfall rappelling, zip-line access to a canopy platform, and biologist-guided nature walks are the highlights, apart from soaking in the serenity. This is the most relaxed lodge in the area. ⊠ *A few meters south of the entrance to Bosque del Cabo on road to Carate* 🕿 *735–5569* ⊕ *www. elremanso.com* 🖚 *5 rooms, 5 cabinas* ⚭ *Dining room, beach, hiking, bar; no a/c, no room phones, no room TVs* ▤ *MC, V* ‖◎‖ *FAP.*

$$$$
Fodor'sChoice
★

🍴 **Lapa Ríos.** This is the most luxurious eco-resort in Costa Rica, winning awards worldwide for its mix of conservation and comfort. It's one of only two hotels in the country to have (deservedly) garnered five leaves, the tourism ministry's top ecotourism designation. After you catch your breath on seeing the view from the high, breezy jungle ridge rife with wildlife, your next sharp intake may be when you see the bill. But in this case the price is not inflated. Spacious, airy cabins, built of gleaming hardwood with high, thatched roofs, have four-poster queen beds, up-to-date luxury bathrooms, and showers with one screened wall open to nature. Private teak-decked garden terraces allow you to view passing monkeys and toucans from a lounge chair. Inspired meals, served in a dramatic rancho, include lots of seafood, exotic local fruits and vegetables, and mouthwatering desserts, and you can eat whenever—and as much as—you want. Resident naturalist guides lead tours through pristine wilderness and to nearby beaches on foot or on horseback. Along with the high cost of transporting and providing all these luxuries in a remote location, it's the exceptional service that justifies the high price tag, which includes transfers from Puerto Jiménez, unlimited food, and nonalcoholic drinks. Lapa Ríos also has more of a luxury hotel feel than the other equally beautiful but more casual lodges nearby. ■ TIP→ *If you don't like to climb stairs, request a cabin close to the main lodge.* ⊠ *20 km/12 mi south of Puerto Jiménez* ⓓ *Apdo. 100, Puerto Jiménez, or Box 025216, SJO 706, Miami, FL 33102-5216* 🕿*735–5130* 🖷*735–5179* ⊕*www.laparios.com* 🖚*16 cabinas* ⚭ *Restaurant, pool, spa, beach, fishing, hiking, horseback riding, bar, laundry service; no a/c, no room phones, no room TVs* ▤ *AE, MC, V* ‖◎‖ *FAP.*

### To & From Matapalo
*21 km/14 mi (1 hour) south of Puerto Jiménez.*

If you drive south from Puerto Jiménez, be prepared for a bumpy ride and a lot of river crossings. In rainy season cars are sometimes washed out along rivers to the ocean. Most hotels arrange transportation in 4WD taxis or their own trucks. The cheapest—and the roughest—way to travel is by *collectivo,* an open-air communal truck ($6) that leaves Puerto Jiménez twice a day. Buses do not serve Cabo Matapalo.

## Carate

❸ Carate is literally the end of the road. There are no phones and only a few select lodgings. The black volcanic-sand beach stretches for over 3 km (2 mi), with surf that's perfect for boogie boarding and body surfing but not for serious board surfing. The main entertainment at the beach is watching the noisy but magnificent scarlet macaws feasting on almonds in the beach almond trees that edge the shore. Carate has no phones; the store and lodges have radio contact only.

### Outdoor Activities

Activities here revolve around Corcovado National Park and its surrounds. Hikes, canopy tours, and other adventures must be organized through your hotel.

### Where to Stay

**$$$** 🏨 **Lookout Inn.** The only hotel on Carate's beach, this casual, barefoot inn—shoes come off at the bottom step—is on a hillside (steep stairs are plentiful here). Three luxurious rooms in the lodge have huge ceramic bathrooms. Two large, screened-in wooden cabins are private, and two newer, tentlike cabinas are on 10-foot platforms. Dozens of scarlet macaws frequent the garden. The place is full of quirky artistic touches, like the ceramic iguanas and frogs that pop out of vases and walls. But the quirkiest element is owner Terry Conroy, an energetic host who makes sure everyone joins in on activities. His serene Tica wife Katya balances her husband and makes a mean margarita. Inventive meals with lots of fresh fish and Asian flavors are served on two breezy terraces with spectacular views of the coastline. There's also a spring-fed plunge pool, a bird-watching trail through primary forest, and a corral with five horses for beach and trail rides. ✉ *300 m east of Carate landing strip* 🖀 *735–5431 in Puerto Jiménez (satellite phone at inn for emergencies only)* ⊕ *www.lookout-inn.com* ⇥ *3 rooms, 2 cabins, 2 platform cabins with shared bath* ⚲ *Dining room, fans, pool, beach, fishing, hiking, horseback riding, 2 bars, laundry service, some pets allowed; no a/c, no room phones, no room TVs* ▤ *MC, V* �⚭ *AI.*

**$$–$$$** 🏨 **Luna Lodge.** Luna's charm lies in its almost ethereal remoteness and tranquillity. On a mountain overlooking the Pacific and the rain forest, it's a true retreat, with a huge hardwood pavilion for practicing yoga or contemplating magnificent sunsets. Round cabinas, spaced apart for privacy, have thatched roofs, garden showers, and decks for bird-watching or relaxing in wood-and-leather rocking chairs. Or you can semi-rough it in a well-ventilated, comfortable tent. Guided hikes to nearby waterfalls and swimming holes are precipitous and thrilling. Healthful meals have an imaginative vegetarian flair, tempered with servings of fish and chicken spiced with herbs from a hilltop organic garden. Host Lana Wedmore is a model of amiable helpfulness. Prices include a waterfall tour. ✉ *2 km/1 mi up a steep, partially paved road from Carate* 🖀 *380–5036, 358–5848, 888/409–8448 in U.S.* ⊕ *www.lunalodge. com* ✉ *Box 025216–5216, Miami, FL 33102* ⇥ *8 cabinas, 7 tents* ⚲ *Restaurant, massage, boating, horseback riding, bar; no a/c, no room phones, no room TVs* ▤ *MC, V* ⚭ *FAP.*

★ **$$** 🏨 **Corcovado Lodge Tent Camp.** Fall asleep to the surf pounding the beach in tents on wooden platforms at this rustic lodge. Ecotourist pioneer Costa Rica Expeditions owns the lodge and its 400 acres of forest reserve adjoining Corcovado National Park. Side by side facing the

*Continued on page 372*

# CORCOVADO NATIONAL PARK

**FOR THOSE WHO CRAVE UNTAMED WILDER-NESS,** Corcovado is the experience of a lifetime. Covering one-third of the Osa Peninsula, the park is blanketed primarily by virgin rain forest and has one of Central America's last remaining tracts of lowland rain forest. The remoteness of Corcovado and the difficult access to its interior results in its being one of the most pristine parks in the country—barely disturbed by human presence—where massive *espavel* and *nazareno* trees tower over the trails, thick lianas hang from the branches, and toucans, spider monkeys, scarlet macaws, and poison dart frogs abound.

---

**FAST FACTS**

**Size:** 445 square km (172 square mi)

**Established:** 1975

**Dry season:** February-April

**Wettest months:** October–November

**What to do:** Nature hikes, bird-watching, wildlife-watching, river walks, sea kayaking, camping, deep-sea fishing

**Geography:** 37 km (23 mi) of beach; 44,500 hectares (109,961 acres) of tropical wet forest

**Number of species catalogued:** 10,000 insects, 700 trees, 367 birds, 140 mammals, 123 butterflies, 117 amphibians and reptiles

- 15 of Costa Rica's 30 endangered animal species live here
- Corcovado has the largest population of scarlet macaws in Costa Rica
- Nearly 200 inches of rain falls here every year
- The hike between any two ranger stations takes at least a day
- The harpy eagle, thought to have been extinct, was sighted here in 2003

Your chances of spotting endangered species, such as boa constrictors, squirrel monkeys, and five wild cats, are better here than anywhere else in the country. The rarest and most sought-after are the jaguar and Baird's tapir. In and around the park are some of Costa Rica's most luxurious jungle lodges and retreats, all of which are contributing to the effort to save Corcovado's wildlife.

For day trips into the park, the most convenient place to base yourself is either in Drake Bay or at the Corcovado Lodge Tent Camp near Carate. There are three entrances: **La Leona** (to the south), **San Pedrillo** (to the north), and **Los Patos** (to the east). The park has no roads, however, and the roads that approach it are dirt tracks that require 4WD most of the year.

## ROUGHING IT

If you have a backpack, strong legs, and a reservation for a tent site or a ranger-station bunk, you can spend days deep in the wilds. Bunks at the Sirena ranger station (which is in a deplorable state of disrepair at the moment) are very limited. Bring your own sheets, a pillow, and a good mosquito net. Basic meals can be arranged at Sirena if you reserve in advance with the National Parks Service office in Puerto Jiménez.

During the dry season the park takes reservations for bunks and camping on the first day of each month for the following month. You may be asked to deposit money into the Environment Ministry's account in the Banco Nacional to reserve space. Reconfirm your reservation a few days before you enter the park. Camping is allowed at the Sirena,

## ENDANGERED ANIMALS

Corcovado has significant populations of species that are in danger of extinction, including:

- Baird's tapir
- boa constrictor
- crocodile
- harpy eagle
- howler monkey
- jaguar
- jaguarundi
- little spotted cat (*caucel*)
- margay
- ocelot
- puma
- scarlet macaw
- sea otter
- spider monkey
- squirrel monkey

## BIRD CHECKLIST

Check the following off your "life list":

- Baird's trogon
- black-bellied wren
- black-hooded antshrike
- black-cheeked ant-tanager
- black-headed brush finch
- brown pelican
- fiery-billed aracari
- golden-naped woodpecker
- harpy eagle
- laughing gull
- mangrove hummingbird
- orange-collared manakin
- riverside wren
- scarlet macaw
- spotted-crowned euphonia
- turquoise cotinga
- whistling wren
- white-crested coquette
- yellow-billed cotin

crocodile

scarlet macaw

squirrel monkey

jaguar

purple gallinule

roseate spoonbill

hummingbird

brown pelican

laughing gull

howler monkey

three-toed sloth

Baird's tapir

6

CORCOVADO NATIONAL PARK

## SAVING THE CATS

The park has been under heavy pressure from poachers who have been killing the peccaries and pacas (small mammals) that the jaguars, ocelots, margays, and other cats feed on. Local and international groups are raising money to fund new park rangers to stop illegal hunting. In 2004 one non-profit conservation fund in the U.S. earmarked $8 million to protect and preserve the park. Much of the money will go to hiring more park rangers.

ocelot

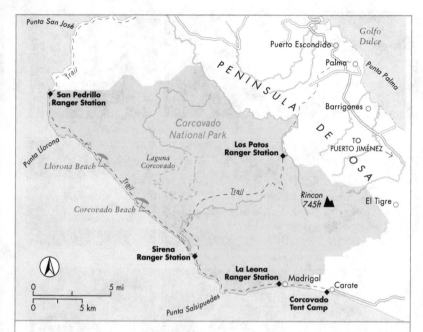

La Leona, Los Patos, and San Pedrillo stations, but only 35 people are allowed to camp at any given station, so reservations with the National Parks Service in Puerto Jiménez are essential in high season.

⚠ Swimming on the beach near Sirena is not advised due to rip currents and bull sharks. Also steer clear of the brackish Río Sirena, home to crocs, bull sharks, and snakes. The only advisable swimming area is the Río Claro.

## HOW MUCH TIME?

Most first-time visitors to Corcovado come on a day-long boat tour or hike. But to get to the most pristine, primary growth areas, you need to walk, and that means a minimum of three days: one day to walk in; one day to walk out out; and one day inside.

## HIRING A GUIDE

If your reason for coming to the Osa is Corcovado, choose a lodge that has resident naturalist guides. On the Drake Bay and gulf sides of the park, all the lodges arrange guided trips into Corcovado, most with their own guides, but some with freelance guides. Corcovado Lodge Tent Camp, on the southern edge of the park, has its own guides. Outdoors outfitters in Puerto Jiménez and Drake Bay also run guided trips in the park.

## HIKING

There are four main hiking routes to Corcovado. Two begin near Puerto Jiménez: one at the **Los Patos** entrance and the other an unmarked trail along the **Río Nuevo**; you will need a guide for this latter route. Osa Aventura (⇨ Outdoor Activities *in* Puerto Jiménez, *above*) specializes in guiding along the Río Nuevo trail. There are also two beach trails to the park: one begins in Drake Bay and follows the coast down to the **San Pedrillo** entrance to the park; the other is an easy 40-minute beach walk from Carate to the **La Leona** entrance. Hiking is always tough in the tropical heat, but the forest route (Los Patos) is cooler than the two beach hikes (La

Leona and San Pedrillo), and the latter are accessible only at low tide.

The hike between any two stations takes all day or more, and the longest hike is **San Pedrillo to Sirena**; it's 21 km (13 mi) along the beach, then 7 km (4 mi) on the forest trail. ■ TIPS →→This trail is passable only in the dry season, as the rivers get too high to cross in the rainy months and the river mouths fill up with snakes, bull sharks, and crocodiles! But for hardy hikers who attempt it, the reward is walking through majestic forest as you approach Sirena.

The hike from **La Leona to Sirena** is about 16 km (10 mi) and requires crossing one big river mouth and a stretch of beach that can only be crossed at low tide. It takes planning ahead, and some guides do it at night, by the light of the moon and stars, to avoid the blistering heat along the beach.

The 17.4-km (10.8-mi) trail from **Los Patos to Sirena** is lovely and forested. But to get to the Los Patos station you first walk 8 km (5 mi) along the verdant Río Rincón valley. The **Sirena ranger station** has great trails around it that can easily fill a couple of days.

## ESSENTIALS

**Hours of Operation:** Ranger stations are officially open from 8 AM to 4 PM daily, but you can walk in almost any time as long as you pay in advance.

**Contacts:** 735–5036 (National Parks Service in Puerto Jiménez)

**Admission:** $8 per day; $24 for 3 days; $32 for 4 days

**Getting There:** The easiest way to visit remote Corcovado is on a day trip via boat from a Drake Bay lodge or on foot from the Corcovado Lodge Tent Camp. The 20-minute boat trip from Drake Bay gets you to the San Pedrillo entrance in the dry season (January–April). The

## HIKING TIPS

- Stay on the trails, for your safety and for the well-being of animals and plants
- Animals here are less used to humans than those in more touristed parks; be quiet and keep your eyes and ears open
- Apply mosquito repellent and wear comfortable shoes
- Take plenty of water with you, even on short hikes. Don't ever drink water from streams. Every ranger station has potable water.
- Bring a flashlight. Darkness falls quickly in the forest.
- Plan your hikes around high tides, which can block park entrances
- Bring a sun hat and sunblock

Corcovado Lodge Tent Camp is a 10-minute walk from the La Leona entrance.

For getting to Corcovado from elsewhere, the most expensive option—but also the easiest way to get right to the heart of the park—is flying in on a small charter plane ($220) to the tiny La Sirena airstrip in the park. Contact **Alfa Romeo Aero Taxi** (✉ Puerto Jiménez airport ☎ 735–5178).

Less expensive is hiring a taxi in Puerto Jiménez ($45) to the Los Patos trailhead, or at least to the first crossing of the Río Rincón (from which you hike a few miles upriver to the trailhead).

The cheapest, and least convenient, option is to take a morning bus for less than $1 from Puerto Jiménez at 8 AM to La Palma and then hike or take a taxi to the Los Patos entrance.

ocean, tents have two single beds, no electricity, and share eight showers and toilets. Unsightly plastic lounge chairs are messily scattered
around, but the excellent naturalist guides still make this a prime destination for nature lovers. Family-style meals are served in an open-air
thatched restaurant with communal tables overlooking the ocean. Skip
the "canopy tour" that hoists you up into a 90-foot tree: you don't see
much wildlife, so it's not worth the $69 price tag. Bring a flashlight (there's
no electricity after 9 PM), insect repellent, and sandals for river hikes.
The package with all meals is a great deal, especially since there's
nowhere to buy food nearby. Your package can also include a charter
flight to Carate. The walk from Carate is 2 km (1 mi; 30–45 minutes)
along the beach. A horse and cart can pick up your luggage from the
store with advance notice. ⊠ *On beach 2 km/1 mi north of Carate; 30–45
min by foot* ☎ *257–0766 or 222–0333* 🖷 *257–1665, 800/886–2609
from U.S.* ⊕ *www.costaricaexpeditions.com* ⇨ *20 tents with shared bath*
⚐ *Dining room, beach, horseback riding, bar, laundry service; no a/c,
no room phones, no room TVs* ▭ *AE, MC, V.*

### To & From Carate
*60 km/37 mi (2 hours) west of Puerto Jiménez.*

The road from Matapalo to Carate covers 40 suspension-testing km (25
mi) and it is never easy; you're better off taking the *collectivo* from Puerto
Jiménez (⇨ To & From Puerto Jiménez, *above*). Or give yourself a
break and fly via charter plane to Carate's small airstrip, arranged
through your lodge. From here it's just a 3-km (2-mi), or roughly 40-
minute walk, along the beach to the La Leona ranger station entrance
to Corcovado National Park. In rainy season (May–December) it is sometimes impossible to cross the raging Río Carate that separates the landing strip from the beach path to the park, and you may end up stranded
on either side. Parking at the store in Carate is $5 per day.

## Drake Bay

 This is castaway country, a real tropical adventure, with plenty of hiking and some rough but thrilling boat rides. The rugged coast that
stretches south from the mouth of the Río Sierpe to Corcovado probably doesn't look much different than it did in Sir Francis Drake's day
(1540–96), when the British explorer
anchored here. Small, picture-perfect
beaches with surf crashing against
dark, volcanic rocks are backed by
steaming, thick jungle. Nature lodges
scattered along the coast are
hemmed in by the rain forest, which
is home to troops of monkeys, sloths,
scarlet macaws, and hundreds of
other bird species.

The cheapest accommodations in
the area can be found in the town
of **Drake**, which is spread out along

> **WORD OF MOUTH**
>
> "[S]wimming in the ocean near
> Drake Bay on the Osa was heav-
> enly! Warm water, tropical birds
> flying overhead, even able to do a
> bit of snorkling (fun, but not
> great). No crocs, but my husband
> did 'get' to share his swimmimng
> space with a poisonous water
> snake!"
>
> –Molly2

the bay. A trio of nature lodges—Drake Bay Wilderness Resort, Aguila de Osa Inn, and La Paloma Lodge—are also clumped near the Río Agujitas on the bay's southern end. They all offer comprehensive packages, including trips to Corcovado and Caño Island. Lodges farther south, such as Punta Marenco Lodge and Casa Corcovado, run excursions from even wilder settings. During the dry season you can reach the town of Drake via a graded dirt road from Rincón.

## Outdoor Activities

**Jinetes de Osa** (✉ Drake village, west side of bay ☎ 236–5637 ⊕ www. costaricadiving.com) has diving and snorkeling ($65) and dolphin-watching tours ($95), as well as a canopy tour ($55) with some interesting bridge, ladder, and rope transitions between platforms.

## Where to Stay

**$$$$** 🏨 **Aguila de Osa Inn.** The spacious rooms here have gorgeous hardwood interiors, huge bamboo beds, and luxurious tile bathrooms. Stained glass with tropical themes and hand-carved doors add artistic flair. Be prepared for a steep climb up a concrete path to your room with a view of Drake Bay. Morning coffee arrives outside your room before 6 AM, and the food is sophisticated and plentiful. The inn has two boats for sportfishing, its specialty. Scuba diving, snorkeling, and other excursions are easily arranged. ✉ *South end of Drake, at mouth of Río Agujitas* ☎ *296–2190 in San José* 🖷 *232–7722* ⊕ *www.aguiladeosa.com* 🕮 *Apdo. 10486–1000, San José* 🛏 *11 rooms* 🍴 *Restaurant, fans, massage, snorkeling, boating, fishing, horseback riding, bar, laundry service; no a/c, no room phones, no room TVs* ▤ *AE, MC, V* 🍽 *FAP.*

**★ $$$$** 🏨 **Casa Corcovado.** This hilltop jungle lodge has it all: a prime location on the edge of Corcovado National Park, resident naturalist guides, luxury accommodations, and first-class service and food. A trail leads right into the park from here, so you can explore its forests hours before anyone else arrives. Spanish colonial–style cabinas are spread around a garden for maximum privacy. The guest rooms have elegant Chinese-style furniture, four-poster beds, and huge tile bathrooms with separate vanity, shower, and toilet areas. There's a sunset bar near the top of the very steep hill that climbs up from the beach where you make a thrilling, very wet landing: a tractor-towed cart transports guests and luggage. The restaurant serves four-course gourmet dinners. The minimum stay is two nights, but the best deal is a three-night package that includes transportation from San José by plane, taxi, and boat, all meals, and a trip to Caño Island and Corcovado National Park. ✉ *Northern border of Corcovado* 🕮 *Apdo. 1482–1250, Escazú* ☎ *256–3181, 888/896–6097 in U.S.* 🖷 *256–7409* ⊕ *www.casacorcovado.com* 🛏 *14 rooms* 🍴 *Dining room, fans, 2 pools, beach, snorkeling, boating, hiking, horseback riding, 2 bars; no a/c, no room phones, no room TVs* ▤ *AE, MC, V* 🕓 *Closed Sept.–mid-Nov.* 🍽 *AI.*

**$$$–$$$$** 🏨 **Drake Bay Wilderness Resort.** Spread over a grassy point between the Río Agujitas and the ocean, with the best views of Drake Bay, this resort has lots of open ground for kids to play on and tidal pools to explore. The wooden cabins are camp-style with three to a building. But

CLOSE UP

## Snorkelers' Paradise

MOST OF UNINHABITED
2½-square-km (1-square-mi) Caño Island Biological Reserve is covered in evergreen forest that includes fig, locust, and rubber trees. Coastal Indians used it as a burial ground, and the numerous bits and pieces unearthed here have prompted archaeologists to speculate about pre-Columbian long-distance maritime trade. Occasionally, mysterious stones that have been carved into perfect spheres of varying sizes are still found on the island. The uninhabited island's main attraction now is the ocean around it, superb for scuba diving and snorkeling. The snorkeling

is best around the rocky points flanking the island's main beach; if you're a certified diver you'll probably want to explore Bajo del Diablo and Paraíso, where you're guaranteed to encounter thousands of good-size fish.

The only way to get to the island—19 km (12 mi) due west of the Osa Peninsula—is by boat arranged by your lodge or a tour company. Lodges and the Jinetes de Osa tour company in Drake Bay run day trips here, as do tour companies in Dominical and Uvita.

with hot water, tiled bathrooms, wall murals, and carved animal bed-posts supporting firm queen-size beds, this is very comfortable camping. Keep an eye out for the small troop of resident squirrel monkeys. Kayaks are at your disposal for paddles along the river. Most guests come here to see the rain forest, but you can also opt for scuba diving, sport-fishing, and dolphin- and whale-watching tours. The minimum stay is three nights. ⊠ *On peninsula at mouth of Río Agujitas, on southern end of bay* 🏨🏨 *770–8012* 📠 *384–4107* ⊕ *www.drakebay.com* 🖃 *Apdo. 30710–1000, San José* 📞 *561/371–3437 in U.S.* ⇄ *20 rooms* ⚐ *Restaurant, fans, saltwater pool, boating, fishing, horseback riding, bar, laundry facilities; no a/c, no room phones, no room TVs* ⊟ *AE, MC, V* ⎟⎜*FAP.*

★ **$$$–$$$$** 🏨 **La Paloma Lodge.** Sweeping views and jungle seclusion make these deluxe cabinas the area's most romantic. Planted in a jungle garden on a high hill just south of Drake Bay, the elegant wooden villas have bedroom lofts and large porches with pretty green wicker furniture, huge wooden armoires, and hammocks. The tiled pool overlooks forest and ocean. The hotel runs a diving school and offers river kayaking, along with trips to Corcovado and Caño Island. The flower-filled restaurant serves delicious, fresh tropical fare. La Paloma is closest to Playa Cocolito, a gem of a beach just down the hill along the coastal path that eventually leads to Corcovado. There's a three-night minimum stay; packages are the best bet and include transportation from San José, all meals, and some tours. ⊠ *Drake Bay, 300 m past Drake Bay Wilderness Resort* 🖃 *Apdo. 97–4005, Heredia* 📞 *293–7502* 📠 *239–0954* ⊕ *www.lapalomalodge. com* ⇄ *4 rooms, 7 cabinas* ⚐ *Restaurant, pool, beach, snorkeling, fishing, horseback riding; no a/c, no room phones, no room TVs* ⊟ *AE, MC, V* ☯ *Closed Oct.* ⎟⎜*FAP.*

**$$–$$$** ⬚ **Jinetes de Osa** The most comfortable and reasonably priced place to stay right in the village of Drake, this bay-side hotel and open-air restaurant has simple rooms, some larger and more expensive than others, all with tile floors and hot-water showers. The on-site tour and diving operations are well run and the lodge is often filled with groups of divers. A nice touch is the coffee delivered outside your room early in the morning. ⬚ *Drake village, west side of bay* ☎ *826–9757* 🖷 *241–2906 in San José* ⊕ *www.costaricadiving.com* ⤶ *9 rooms* ♣ *Restaurant, fans, beach; no a/c, no room phones, no room TVs* ▭ *MC, V* ⑩ *FAP.*

**$$** ⬚ **Punta Marenco Lodge.** This small, rustic lodge has the best location on the Pacific side of the Osa, with idyllic, thatched-roof cabins along a ridge overlooking the sea. Private porches with two hammocks each are perfect for siestas, sunsets, and stargazing. Toucans and scarlet macaws are reliable visitors every morning. Trails lead down to the beach and coastal trail and deep into the Río Claro National Wildlife Refuge, and a resident guide is on hand to interpret the trails. Oceangoing tours include diving, dolphin-watching, Caño Island, and Corcovado. The cozy rancho restaurant has a family feel, with communal tables and typical Tico food. There is electricity for only a few hours in the evening and no hot water. You can hike here from Drake or take a boat from Drake or Sierpe (not included). ⬚ *Beachfront, directly east of Caño Island and north of Casa Corcovado* ☎☎ *234–1308 in San José, no phone at lodge* 🖃 *Apdo. 6028-1000, San José* ⊕ *www.corcovadozone.com* ⤶ *10 cabinas, 4 rooms* ♣ *Dining room, beach, hiking, tours; no a/c, no room phones, no room TVs* ▭ *MC, V* ⑩ *FAP.*

**$** ⬚ **Eco-Manglares Sierpe Lodge.** For a taste of simple Tico-style river life, cross a narrow suspension bridge across the Río Sierpe to reach this ecolodge. Five well-ventilated, thatched-roof cabins with screened windows line a flower-bordered stone path leading to the river. Bed frames made of mangrove wood, rustic furniture made of *caña blanca* (cane), and homemade curtains appliquéd with birds and flowers add a homey touch. Bathrooms are airy, and despite the rustic setting there's plenty of hot water. The restaurant serves hearty portions of expertly cooked fish and is also renowned for its pizza. Kayaks and boat trips to explore the mangroves are the major activities, along with bird-watching. Rates include the use of kayaks. ⬚ *14 km/8½ mi southwest of Palmar Sur turnoff on Pan-American Hwy., Sierpe* ☎ *786–7414* 🖷 *786–7441* ⊕ *www. costaricasur.co.cr* ⤶ *5 cabins* ♣ *Restaurant, fans, boating, kayaking, Internet; no a/c, no room TVs* ▭ *MC* ☉ *Restaurant closed Sept. and Oct. if there are no reservations* ⑩ *BP.*

## Nightlife

★ ☾ When you're on the Osa Peninsula, the wildest nightlife is outdoors. Join entomologist Tracie Stice, also known as the Bug Lady, on the **Night Tour** (☎ *382–1619* ⊕ www.thenighttour.com) of insects, bats, reptiles, and anything else moving around at night. Tracie is a wealth of bug lore, with riveting stories from around the world. Special night-vision optics and infrared flashlights help you see in the dark. Tours are $35 per person; Tracie will meet you at your hotel.

### To & From Drake Bay
*18 km/11 mi north of Corcovado, 40 km/25 mi southwest of Palmar Sur, 310 km/193 mi (7 hours by car; 50 min by plane) south of San José*

The fastest way to get to Drake Bay is to fly directly to the airstrip. You can also fly to Palmar Sur and take a taxi to Sierpe and then a boat to Drake Bay. Many lodges arrange boat transportation from Drake Bay or Sierpe. From Rincón you can drive to Drake on a 20-km (12-mi) graded dirt road. The drive from San José to Drake is scenic, but exhausting.

Exceptionally fit backpackers can hike to the northern entrance of Corcovado along a 18-km (11-mi) coastal path that follows the shoreline, cutting through shady forest when the coast gets too rocky. But it is impossible to walk during rainy season (September–December), when rivers flood and tides are too high.

### Drake Bay Essentials
Drake just got electricity in 2004, so there are still very few services.

🚩 Internet **Internet Cafe** ✉ Corcovado Expeditions office, Drake ☎ 818-9962 open 10 to 8 daily; 1,000 colones per hour.

🚩 Visitor Information **Corcovado Expeditions** ☎ 818-9962, beside the high school in Drake village.

# THE SOUTH PACIFIC ESSENTIALS

## Transportation

### BY AIR
SANSA and NatureAir have direct flights to Golfito, Drake Bay, and Puerto Jiménez. For more information about air travel to the South Pacific from San José, *see* Air Travel *in* Smart Travel Tips A to Z.)

Alfa Romeo Aero Taxi, at the Puerto Jiménez "airport" (really more of an airstrip), flies small charter planes to Carate and Corcovado National Park's airstrip at La Sirena.

🚩 **Alfa Romeo Aero Taxi** ☎ 735-5178.

### BY BUS
ARRIVING & DEPARTING   Bus fares from San José to destinations in the South Pacific range from about $2 to $7, depending on distance and number of stops. For more information about bus travel between the South Pacific and San José, *see* Bus Travel *in* Smart Travel Tips A to Z.)

GETTING AROUND   The best way to get around the region's roads is by bus—let someone else do the driving. Bus fares are cheap and you'll meet the locals. But the going is generally slow, buses often leave very early in the morning, and schedules change frequently, so check the day before you want to travel.

### BY CAR
ARRIVING & DEPARTING   Owing to the dismal state of the roads and hazardous driving conditions—flooded rivers and potholes—we don't recommend driving to the

South Pacific, especially in rainy season. If you decide to drive, make sure your vehicle has 4WD and a spare tire. Give yourself lots of time to get to where you are going.

GETTING
AROUND
Driving is fairly straightforward, if slow, around Cerro de la Muerte, San Isidro, Dominical, and Uvita. But as soon as you get off the main paved highways the roads are rough and slow-going and require 4WD. On the Osa Peninsula and around the Golfo Dulce, the last thing you want is a car. Boat taxis and land taxis will save you time, if not money, and save your energy for activities that are more fun than navigating really rough roads.

There aren't many car-rental agencies in the Southern Zone; the closest agency outposts are in Quepos. Selva Mar can arrange for a rental car to be picked up in San Isidro, and you can drop off the car anywhere down south and avoid the drive back. Alamo, in Dominical, also allows drop-off at various points south. But with both agencies, drop-off fees, which range from $50 to $125, are incurred.

🗂 Major Rental Agencies **Alamo** ✉ Hotel Villas Río Mar, Dominical ☎ 787-0052. 🗂 **Selva Mar** ☎ 771-4582 ⊕ www.exploringcostarica.com.

**6**

### BY SHUTTLE VAN

ARRIVING &
DEPARTING
Interbus has van service from Quepos to Sierpe ($30); a minimum of four passengers is required.

🗂 Shuttle Van Services **Interbus** ☎ 283-5573 ⊕ www.interbusonline.com.

## Contacts & Resources

Banks, Internet cafés, post offices, and emergency contacts are listed at the end of each town entry.

### BANKS & EXCHANGING SERVICES

In the major centers—San Isidro, Golfito, and San Vito—banks and ATMS are plentiful. But in Puerto Jiménez there is only one bank with one ATM, which may or may not be working. Many other places have no banking facilities at all. Don't count on being able to use a credit card, since phone lines—where they exist—are often out of order. Arrange in advance to pay lodges.

### INTERNET

Internet cafés are popping up in all the major towns, but major portions of the south are still without phone service or even electricity. Internet service costs anywhere from $1 to $5 per hour, depending on the location and the type of connection.

### MAIL & SHIPPING

Post offices are few and far between. You are better off saving up your postcards and mailing them from San José.

# Caribbean

La Selva Biological Station

## WORD OF MOUTH

"Don't miss out on Tortuguero! We loved it. Take the boat in—it is definitely part of the experience. The wildlife viewing is incredible there. We saw everything, and plenty of it."

—tanya0070

"I'm a big fan of the Caribbean side of CR. It's less crowded, less touristy, and generally cheaper than the usual destinations. The beaches all down the coast are beautiful and practically deserted."

—rbrazill

www.fodors.com/forums

# WELCOME TO THE CARIBBEAN

Braulio Carrillo Park

## TOP 5
## Reasons to Go

**1** **Turtles:** People from around the world flock to the northern Caribbean for the annual nesting of four species.

**2** **Food and flavors:** Leave gallo pinto behind in favor of mouthwatering *rondon* (meat or fish stew), or *caribeño* (Caribbean) rice and beans, stewed in coconut milk.

**3** **Dolphin-watching:** Bottlenose, tucuxi, and Atlantic-spotted dolphins ply the southern Caribbean coast.

**4** **Music:** Mix reggae and calypso with your salsa. Rhythms waft in from the far-off Caribbean Islands; and home-grown musicians are making names for themselves, too.

**5** **Sportfishing:** World-class tarpon and snook attract serious anglers to the shores off Barra del Colorado and Tortuguero national parks.

**The Northern Lowlands** have little to offer tourists in their own right, but are close to Braulio Carrillo Park and rafting-trip put-in points.

Pichara Lodge

# Getting Oriented

This flat, expansive region just a few meters above sea level stretches from the eastern slope of the Cordillera Central, east through banana-growing country, and down to pristine beaches. North to the Nicaragua border, it encompasses the coastal jungles and canals of Tortuguero National Park and Barra del Colorado Wildlife Refuge. In the central and southern Caribbean, nearly everything of tourist interest lies along the main artery to Limón (the Guápiles Highway) and the coastal highway south.

Limón, Central Caribbean

**The Northern Caribbean Coast** encompasses the coastal jungles and canals of Tortuguero National Park and Barra del Colorado Wildlife Refuge. Boat and air travel are the only ways to reach this roadless region.

Punta Cocles, South Caribbean

7

**Coastal Talamanca** stretches south from port-of-call Limón to Panama. Towns along the coast have an Afro-Caribbean hippie vibe—some more backpacker-ish than others. Beaches are fringed with forest and waters are rough. Surfers make the trip for Salsa Brava.

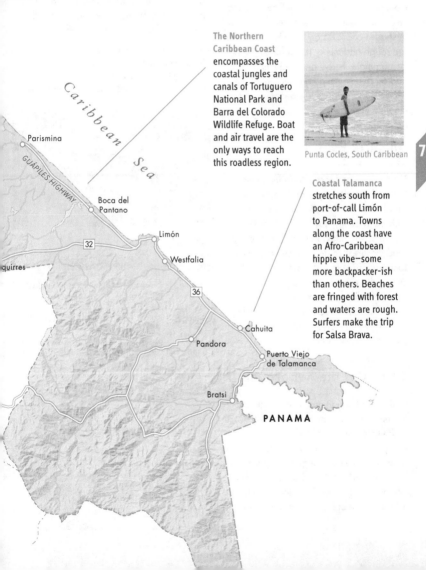

Caribbean Sea

Parismina

GUÁPILES HIGHWAY

Boca del Pantano

Limón

32

Westfalia

quirres

36

Cahuita

Pandora

Puerto Viejo de Talamanca

Bratsi

**PANAMA**

# CARIBBEAN PLANNER

## Not *that* Caribbean

Costa Rica's Caribbean coast is sometimes called its Atlantic coast, so as not to confuse tourists looking for the white sand and clear-blue waters of the Caribbean Islands. This Caribbean is very different, with sands in shades of brown and black, waters that are rough and murky (ideal for surfing), dense jungle, heavy and frequent rain, and an as-yet unsophisticated, laid-back approach to tourism. It is beautiful and fascinating in its own way, but it's definitely not St. Barths.

## When to Go

The Caribbean lacks a true dry season, though February–April and September–October could be called *drier* seasons with many sunny days and intermittent showers. The heaviest rains (and periodic road closures) come in December and January, prime tourist months elsewhere. During the rainiest months prices are lower and tourists fewer. Temperatures remain constant year-round, with daily highs of 29–31°C (84–88°F) and lows of 21–23° C (69–73°F).

## Don't Get the Runaround

Check road conditions before you set out for the Caribbean from points west. Most of the time it is one of the country's most easily reached regions, but occasional closures of the route through Braulio Carrillo National Park north of San José necessitate passing through Turrialba, which can add a couple of hours to your journey.

## Getting There

This historically isolated sector of Costa Rica is today one of the most accessible. The southern coast is a 3- to 4-hour drive from San José, over decent roads (by Costa Rican standards), and public transportation is frequent. The northern Caribbean coast is another story: the total absence of roads means you have to arrive by plane or boat. Most travelers go with a tour or book at one of the large hotels that include transport to and from San José.

DRIVING ALERT: When visiting the Caribbean coast by car, remember that fog often covers the Braulio Carrillo mountains after noon, making driving hazardous. Cross this area in the morning.

## What to Do

| ACTIVITY | WHERE TO DO IT |
|---|---|
| Fishing | Barra del Colorado, San Juan River, Tortuguero |
| Diving | Gandoca-Manzanillo Wildlife Refuge |
| Snorkeling | Gandoca-Manzanillo Wildlife Refuge |
| Surfing | Cahuita, Puerto Viejo de Talamanca |
| Turtle-watching | Gandoca-Manzanillo Wildlife Refuge, Tortuguero |
| White-water rafting | Siquirres |
| Wildlife-viewing | Barra del Colorado, Gandoca-Manzanillo Wildlife Refuge, Tortuguero |

## Choosing a Place to Stay

The glitzy resorts of the Pacific coast are nowhere to be found in the Caribbean, where the norm is small, independent lodgings, usually family owned and operated. Fewer tourists in this region means plenty of decent lodging at affordable prices. And unless you travel during Christmas or Easter weeks you can usually find a place to stay without much advance planning. But tourism *is* growing, so it's risky to show up without reservations. Surprisingly few places here have air-conditioning; but sea breezes and ceiling fans usually provide sufficient ventilation. Smaller places don't take credit cards; those that do may give discounts if you pay with cash.

## How Much Time?

Attractions near Guápiles and Siquirres lend themselves to long day trips from San José. Tour operators also have whirlwind daylong Tortuguero trips from San José. Avoid these—the area really deserves two or three days, which is the length of the classic Tortuguero package that includes transportation, lodging, food, and tours. Choose a single Caribbean destination and stay put if you have just a few days. If you have a week, you can tackle the north and south coasts.

## Package Tours

■ **Horizontes**
(☎ 222–2022
⊕ www.horizontes.com) tours include naturalist guides and transport by 4WD vehicle.

■ **Río Indio Adventure Lodge**
(☎ 296–0095
⊕ www.rioindiolodge.com) has all-inclusive guided trips from San José to a luxury eco-hotel just over the border in Nicaragua.

■ **Talamanca Adventures**
(☎ 224–3570
⊕ www.talamanca-adventures.com) leads off-the-beaten-path tours familiarizing you with everything from Caribbean cooking to rain-forest conservation.

## Prices

| | $$$$ | $$$ | $$ | $ | ¢ |
|---|---|---|---|---|---|
| **Restaurants** | over $25 | $15–$25 | $10–$15 | $5–$10 | under $5 |
| **Hotels** | over $250 | $150–$250 | $75–$150 | $50–$75 | under $50 |

WHAT IT COSTS in Dollars

Restaurant prices are per-person for a main course at dinner. Hotel prices are for two people in a standard double room in high season, excluding service and tax (16.4%).

---

### Rain Check

Packing for wet weather is a necessity. Be sure to bring:

■ a collapsible umbrella

■ a poncho

■ Zip-lock bags for cameras and other things you'll take on hikes and tours

■ waterproof sandals

■ quick-drying clothing

THE COMPLETE PACKAGE

If you don't want to be bothered arranging the logistics of transportation to remote Tortuguero, consider booking a package tour. Many lodges listed in the chapter have similar packages, varying in length from one night to two weeks, that include transport from San José, overnights, meals, and guided tours.

# THE NORTHERN LOWLANDS

By Jeffrey
Van Fleet

That proverbial fork in the road presents you with a choice just beyond the immense Braulio Carrillo National Park north of San José. The highway branches at Santa Clara, having completed its descent onto the Caribbean plain. A left turn takes you north to Puerto Viejo de Sarapiquí and the forest-clad hills of the eastern slope of the Cordillera Central. If you stay on the well-maintained main Guápiles Highway, you head southeast toward Limón and the Caribbean coast. The highway passes through sultry agricultural lowlands, home to large banana and cacao plantations, but bypasses the region's three main communities, burgeoning Guápiles and the smaller towns of Guácimo and Siquirres. You may not see any reason to stop when driving through the region— the Caribbean coast beckons, after all—but a couple of decent lodgings and lesser-known sights might be incentive to take a break.

## Guápiles

**❶** Guápiles is fast becoming the hub of northeastern Costa Rica, and with all the facilities in town, residents of the region find little need to trek to San José anymore. The smaller town of Guácimo lies 12 km (7 mi) east on the Guápiles Highway.

### Exploring

Curious how those tropical houseplants you have at home started out? Ornamental plant farm **Costa Flores** conducts one-and-a-half-hour English-language tours—advance reservations are required—through its gardens and facilities. (Riotously colored heliconias are a specialty here.) The tour ends at the packing house, where you see how plants are prepared for export. Then you get to create your own floral bouquet to take with you as a souvenir. ⊠ *3½ km/2 mi north of Guácimo on road to Río Jiménez* ☎ *716–6457* ⌦ *costaflo@racsa.co.cr* 🖃 *$15* ☉ *Weekdays, 8–4; weekends by reservation.*

### Where to Stay

$ 🏨 **Hotel Río Palmas.** Think of it as a hacienda motel. Proximate to EARTH ( ⇨ *below*), near the town of Guácimo, the Río Palmas has a red-tile-roof open-air restaurant that grabs your eye as you're speeding by on the highway. The restaurant is a popular stop for tour buses or individual travelers en route to and from the Caribbean. Behind an arched, whitewashed entry gate, one-story tile-roof cabinas wrap around a central courtyard with a fountain. Exotic plantings abound, and the staff can arrange hikes, farm and jungle tours, and horseback rides to private waterfalls. ⊠ *Pocora de Guácimo, 15 km/9 mi east of Guápiles on Guápiles Hwy.* ☎ *760–0330 or 760–0305* 🖷 *760–0296* ⊕ *www. hotelriopalmas.com* ↩ *32 rooms* ⌘ *Restaurant, fans, cable TV, pool, horseback riding, laundry service; no a/c in some rooms, no room phones.* 🖃 *AE, MC, V.*

## CLOSE UP

# Rain Forest Aerial Tram

JUST 15 KM (9 MI) BEYOND the eastern boundary of Braulio Carrillo, a 4-square-km (2½-square-mi) preserve houses a privately owned and operated engineering marvel: a series of gondolas strung together in a modified ski-lift pulley system. (To lessen the impact on the jungle, the support pylons were lowered into place by helicopter.) The tram gives you a way of seeing the rain-forest canopy and its spectacular array of epiphyte plant life and birds from just above, a feat you could otherwise accomplish only by climbing the trees yourself. The founder, Dr. Donald Perry, also developed a less elaborate system of canopy touring at nearby Rara Avis; of the two, this is more user-friendly. Though purists might complain that it treats the rain forest like an amusement park, it's an entertaining way to learn the value and beauty of rain-forest ecology. The concept is expanding: in 2003 the company opened similar facilities one hour from the central Pacific town of Jacó and in the Caribbean-island nation of Dominica, and at this writing plans to open another facility in St. Lucia.

The 21 gondolas at the original site hold five people each, plus a bilingual biologist-guide equipped with a walkie-talkie to request brief stops for gaping or snapping pictures. The ride covers 2½ km (1½ mi) in 1½ hours. The price includes a biologist-guided walk through the area for ground-level orientation before or after the tram ride. You can arrange a personal pickup in San José for a fee; alternatively, there are public buses (on the Guápiles line) every half hour from the Gran Terminal del Caribe in San José. Drivers know the tram as the *teleférico*. Many San José tour operators make a daylong tour combining the tram with another half-day option; combos with the Britt Coffee Tour or INBioparque in Santo Domingo, both near Heredia, are especially popular. Ten rustic (no a/c or TV) but cozy cabinas are available on-site for $80 per person. The facility operates the lodging only if at least two cabins are being rented at the same time. Electricity shuts off after 9 PM. Cabin rates include meals and tram tours. A café is open to all for breakfast and lunch. ⊠ *Reservations: Avda. 7 at C. 7 San José* ☎ *257–5961* 🖷 *257–6053* ⊕ *www.rainforestram. com* 🖘 *$49.50; $78.50 includes round-trip transportation from San José hotels* 🚍 *AE, MC, V* 🕙 *Tours Mon. 9–4, Tues.–Sun. 6:30–4. Call for reservations 6 AM–9:30 PM.*

## To & From Guápiles

*60 km/38 mi (1 hour) northeast of San José.*

Guápiles lies just north of Braulio Carrillo National Park and straddles the highway to the Caribbean. It is easily accessible from San José just 60 km (38 mi) to the southwest or Limón 84 km (50 mi) to the east.

### Guápiles Essentials

🏦 Bank/ATM **Banco Nacional** ⊠ 400 m east and 50 m north of hospital. **BAC San José** ⊠ Across from Instituto Nacional de Seguros.

NICARAGUA

San Juan del Norte

Barra del Colorado **5**

BARRA DEL COLORADO NATIONAL WILDLIFE REFUGE

Tortuguero **4**
see map page 391

*San Juan*

*Colorado*

*Suerte*

La Pavona

*Tortuguero*

TORTUGUERO NATIONAL PARK

Puerto Viejo de Sarapiqui

◆ La Selva Biological Station

**4**

◆ Rara Avis

Cariari

*Perismina*

Parismina

San Rafael

*Aguas Zarcas*

Santa Clara

Braulio Carrillo National Park

◆ Volcán Barva

Sacramento

**32**

Guápiles **1**

**2** EARTH

Guácimo

◆ Rain Forest Arial Tram

Costa Flores

*Guápiles Hwy.*

Siquirres **3**

AgriTour/ Pineapple Tour

Matina

*Matina*

Stratford

Bristol

**32**

Liverpool

◆ Zorqui

Cordillera Central

**32**

Heredia

★ San Jose

◆ Volcán Irazú National Park

Pacayas

Cartago

Juan Vlñas

*Reventazón*

**10**

◆ GUAYABO NATIONAL MONUMENT

Tres Equis

*Pacuare*

TAPANTÍ NATIONAL WILDLIFE REFUGE

San Marcos

Santa Maria

**CA 2**

| 0 | | 20 miles |
| 0 | | 20 kilometers |

# The Caribbean Coast

*Caribbean Sea*

**Moín**
**7** **6** **Limón**
✈
*Isla Uvita*

*Banano*

36

Penshurt

**Cahuita**
**8**
see map
page 406

*Punta Vargas*

*Puerto Vargas*

*Playa Cocles*

*Playa Chiquita*

**Cahuita**
**National Park** **9**

*Playa Negra*

*Punta Uva*

HITOY
CERERE
BIOLOGICAL
RESERVE

*strella*

Bribri

Manzanillo **11** **Gandoca-Manzanillo**
**National Wildlife Refuge**

Gandoca

**Puerto Viejo**
**de Talamanca**
**10**
see map
page 415

Sixaola

Daytonia

TO BOCOS
DEL TORO →

Guabito

**PANAMÁ**

▸ Hospital **Hospital de Guápiles** ✉ 90 m south of fire station ☎ 710-6801.
▸ Pharmacy **Farmacia San Martín** ✉ Across from Palí ☎ 710-1115. **Farmacia Santa
Marta** ✉ Across from Banco Nacional ☎ 710-6253.
▸ Post Office **Correos** ✉ North of MUCAP.

## EARTH

❷ The nonprofit institution of higher education EARTH (Escuela de Agri-
cultura de la Región Tropical Húmeda, or Agricultural School of the
Tropical Humid Region) researches the production of less pesticide-
dependent bananas and other forms of sustainable tropical agriculture,
as well as medicinal plants. The university graduates some 100 students
from Latin America and Africa each year. EARTH's elegant stationery,
calendars, and other paper products made from banana stems, tobacco
leaves, and coffee leaves and grounds are sold at the on-site Oropéndola store and in many tourist shops around the country. The property
encompasses a banana plantation and a forest reserve with nature trails.
Half-day tours are $10; full-day, $15–$20, and lunch is $4 for day visitors. Though priority is given to researchers and conference groups, you're
welcome to stay in the school's 50-person lodging facility, with private
bathrooms, hot water, and ceiling fans, for $55 a night, which includes
the use of a swimming pool and exercise equipment. Reservations are
required. ✉ *Pocora de Guácimo, 15 km/9 mi east of Guápiles on
Guápiles Hwy.* ✉ *Apdo. 4442-1000, San José* ☎ *713-0000* 🖶 *713-0001*
🌐 *www.earth.ac.cr.*

### To & From EARTH
The entrance to EARTH lies just east of the town of Guácimo. Stop and
check with the guard at the gate off the highway. If you're taking the
bus, drivers should drop you off at the stop in front of the gate.

## Siquirres

❸ Its name is a corruption of the words "Si quieres" (if you want), fittingly
impassive for this lackluster town. It anchors a fertile banana- and
pineapple-growing region, and marks the transition point between the
agricultural lowlands and the tropical, palm-laden coast. Siquirres has
the unfortunate historical distinction of at one time being the western-
most point to which Afro-Caribbeans could migrate. The law was implemented in the late 1880s—when large numbers of Afro-Caribbeans
immigrated (mainly from Jamaica) to construct the Atlantic Railroad—
but was abolished by the 1949 constitution.

### Exploring
Pineapples don't get the same attention in world circles as Costa Rican
coffee and bananas, but the **AgriTour Pineapple Tour** (✉ On the highway
7 km/4 mi east of Siquirres ☎ 768-8192, 282-1349 in San José 🌐 www.
agritourscr.com), affililiated with the Del Monte company, can acquaint
you with the life and times of the country's lesser-known crop, from cultivation to drying and packing at a farm just east of town. The two-
hour tour is $15, samples included. Call to make a reservation.

## FODOR'S FIRST PERSON

**Suzanna Starcevic**
*Writer*

The road ended southeast of Guápiles. We removed our shoes at the riverbank (a useless measure, since by day's end we would have sunk knee-deep in mud) and waded across to another world. The Costa Rican Hu-

manitarian Foundation brought us to this Cabécar village to teach Spanish and help the women to develop crafts (most indigenous peoples in Costa Rica have lost ties to their traditions), but in the end, we may have learned the most. It was the kind of travel experience that can't fit within the confines of a postcard.

### Outdoor Activities

RAFTING
★
Siquirres's proximity to the put-in sites of several classic rafting excursions makes it an ideal place to begin a trip. Old standby **Ríos Tropicales** (✉ On the highway in Siquirres ☎ 233–6455 ⊕ www.riostropicales.com) has tours on a Class III–IV section of the Pacuare River between Siquirres and San Martín, as well as the section with the same difficulty between Tres Equis and Siquirres. Not quite so wild, but still with Class III rapids, is the nearby Florida section of the Reventazón. Day excursions normally begin in San José, but if you're out in this part of the country, you can kick off your excursion here at the company's operations center in Siquirres.

### To & From Siquirres
*28 km/17 mi east of Guápiles.*

Siquirres lies just off the main highway and is easily accessible from the east, west, or south (if you're arriving from Turrialba).

### Siquirres Essentials
🏦 Bank/ATM **Banco Nacional** ✉ 50 m south of Servicentro. ✉.
🏥 Hospital **Centro de Salud de Siquirres** ✉ East side of soccer field ☎ 768–6138.
💊 Pharmacy **Farmacia Santa Lucia** ✉ 50 m west of fire station ☎ 768–9304.
📮 Post Office **Correos** ✉ Next to Guardia Rural.

# THE NORTHERN CARIBBEAN COAST

Some compare this densely layered greenery highlighted by brilliantly colored flowers, whose impact is doubled by the jungle's reflection in the mirror-smooth canal surfaces, to the Amazon. That might be stretching it, but there's still an Indiana Jones mystique to the journey up here, especially when you get off the main canals and into the narrower lagoons. The region remains one of those Costa Rican anomalies: roadless and remote, it's nevertheless one of the country's most-visited places. The tourism seasons here are defined not by the rains or lack thereof (it's wet here most of the year) but by the months of prime turtle hatching in Toruguero, or by what's biting in sportfishing paradise Barra del Colorado.

In 1970 a system of canals running parallel to the shoreline was constructed to provide safer access to the region than the dangerous journey up the seacoast. You can continue up the canals, natural and man-made, that begin in Moín, near Limón, and run all the way to Tortuguero and beyond to the less visited Barra del Colorado Wildlife Refuge. Or you can embark at various points north of Guápiles and Siquirres, as do public transportation and most of the package tours. (The lodges' minivans bring you from San José to the put-in point, where you continue your journey by boat.)

## Tortuguero

**4** North of the national park, the hamlet of Tortuguero is a pleasant lit-
Fodor'sChoice tle place with 600 inhabitants, two churches, three bars, a handful of
★ souvenir shops, and a growing selection of inexpensive lodges. (And one more plus: there are no motor vehicles here, a refreshing change from the traffic woes that plague the rest of Costa Rica.) You can also take a stroll on the 32-km (20-mi) beach, but swimming is not recommended because of strong riptides and large numbers of bull sharks and barracuda.

The stretch of beach between the Colorado and Matina rivers was first mentioned as a nesting ground for sea turtles in a 1592 Dutch chronicle. Nearly a century earlier, Christopher Columbus compared traversing the north Caribbean coast and its swimming turtles to navigating through rocks. Because the area is so isolated—there's no road here to this day—the turtles nested

> **WORD OF MOUTH**
>
> "My first comment is about Tortuguero. Go! The package deals are not so pricey when you consider that they are all-inclusive. You literally will spend hardly a dime more."
>
> –Lair

undisturbed for centuries. By the mid-1900s, however, the harvesting of eggs and poaching of turtles had reached such a level that these creatures faced extinction. In 1963 an executive decree regulated the hunting of turtles and the gathering of eggs, and in 1970 the government established Tortuguero National Park, and modern Tortuguero bases its economy on tourism.

### Exploring

The **Caribbean Conservation Corporation** (CCC) runs a visitor center and a museum with excellent animal photos, a video narrating local and natural history, and detailed discussions of the latest ecological goings-on and what you can do to help. There's a souvenir shop next door. For the committed ecotourist, the **John H. Phipps Biological Field Station,** affiliated with the CCC, has camping areas and dorm-style quarters with a communal kitchen. If you want to get involved in the life of the turtles, helping researchers to track turtle migration (current research, using satellite technology, has tracked turtles as far as the Florida Keys), or helping to catalog the population of neotropical migrant birds, arrange a stay in advance through the center. ✉ *From beach, walk north along path and watch for sign* ☎ *709–8091, 297–5510 in San José, 352/373–6441 or 800/678–7853 in U.S.* ⊕ *www.cccturtle.org*

CARIBBEAN
SEA

Boca del
Río San Juan

San Juan
del Norte

Laguna
Ciega

NICARAGUA

Río San Juan

Laguna Agua Dulce

Laguna de Atrás

Laguna Penitencia

Las Esperillas

Isla
Machura

Isla Chapudero

Barra del Colorado Norte

Isla Calero

Barra del
Colorado
Sur

Caño Bravo

Isla Maria

Isla Brava

Río Colorado

Puerto
Lindo

Laguna
Danto

Laguna
Nueve

Islas
Buena
Vistas

Cerro
Coronel

BARRA DEL COLORADO
NATIONAL WILDLIFE
REFUGE

Río Zapote

Caño Moreno

Río Penitencia

Caño Palma

Canal

Caño Suerte

Río Suerte

Caño Chiquero

Cerro
Tortuguero
(119m)

CARIBBEAN
SEA

Isla
Chica

Lagunas del Tortuguero

Lagunas Penitencia

**1**

**2** **3**

**4**

**5** **6**

**7**

**Caribbean Conservation
Corporation/ Visitor Center**

**8** **9** Tortuguero
Village

**10** **11**

TO JUNGLE
TARPON LODGE

**Park Entrance** ◆

Caño

Chiquero

Isla Cuatro
Esquinas

**12**

Parque
Nacional
Tortuguero

0          1 mile

0          1 kilometer

TORTUGUERO
NATIONAL PARK

Chiquero

0          5 miles

0          5 kilometers

**Tortuguero**

LIMÓN

Parismina

🕏 *Apdo. 246–2050, San Pedro* 🖃 *$1* 🕙 *Mon.–Sat. 10–noon and 2–5, Sun. 2–5:30.*

## Outdoor Activities

Tortuguero is one of those "everybody's a guide" places. Quality varies, but most guides are quite knowledgeable. If you stay at one of the lodges, guided tours are *usually* included in your package price. (Check when you book.) If you hire a private guide, $5 per person per hour is the going rate, with most excursions lasting three hours.

TOUR GUIDES AND OPERATORS
Call or stop by the visitor center at the **Caribbean Conservation Corporation** (☎ 709–8091, 297–5510 in San José ⊕ www.cccturtle.org) to get a recommendation for good local guides.

★ **Daryl Loth** (☎ 833–0827 or 709–8011 ✍ safari@racsa.co.cr) is a wealth of information about the area and conducts boat excursions on the canals and responsible turtle-watching tours in season with advance notice. In addition to providing transport to and from Tortuguero, **Viajes Clic-Clic** (☎ 709–8155, 844–0463 or 308–2006) conduct tours of the canals. **Victor Barrantes** (☎ 709–8055 or 838–6330 ✍ tortuguero_info@racsa.co.cr) is the local SANSA agent who conducts hiking tours to Cerro Tortuguero and around the area when he's not meeting the early-morning flights.

FISHING
You have your choice of mackerel, tarpon, snook, and snapper if you fish in the ocean; snook and calba if you fish in the canals. If you opt for the latter, the National Parks Service levies a $30 license fee (you are fishing in the confines of Tortuguero National Park), good for one month. Operators add the fee to your price.

Longtime area fishing expert **Eddie Brown** (☎ 710–8016) is based out of Tortuga Lodge and has daylong fishing packages for $500. **Elvin Gutiérrez** (☎ 709–8071 or 709–8072 ✍ jungle@racsa.co.cr), known as "Primo" to everyone in town, takes two passengers out for two hours or more, at $50 per hour, or for a full nine-hour day ($350). Prices include boat, motor, guide, and refreshments.

TURTLE WATCHING
If you want to watch the *deshove* (egg laying), contact your hotel or the parks office to hire a certified local guide, required on turtle-watching excursions. Note that you won't be allowed to use a camera—flash or non-flash—on the beach and only your guide is permitted to use a flashlight (and that must be covered with red plastic), because lights can deter the turtles from nesting. ⚠ A few unscrupulous locals will offer to take you on a turtle-watching tour outside the allowed February-through-November season, disturbing sensitive nesting sites in the process. If it's not the season, don't go on a turtle exursion. As the signs around town admonish: "Don't become another predator."

## Where to Stay & Eat

The big lodges here offer one- or two-night excursion packages. Rates are expensive, but prices include everything from guides, tours, meals, and snacks to minivan and boat transport, and in some cases air transport to and from San José. If you stop and calculate what you get, the price may not be as bad as it first seemed.

**$** ✗ **Budda Café.** "Hip" was never a word that went hand in hand with Tortuguero, but this place is changing the rules. Pizza, crepes, pastas, and fresh fish are on the menu at this small, canal-side café in the center of town. Lattice wood over the windows, a thatched roof, and of course, a Buddha statue make up the furnishings. Jazzy cha-cha or a Dean Martin ballad might be playing in the background. ⊠ *Next to police station, Tortuguero village* ☎ *709–8084* ⊟ *No credit cards* ☺ *Closed Wed.*

**$** ✗ **Miss Junie.** If Tortuguero had royalty, it would be Miss Junie, the village's best known cook, who continues a tradition started by her mother more than a half century ago and serves cheap, filling, tasty food at an open-air restaurant adjoining her home. (Fidel Castro and Che Guevara were among the early diners here.) Selection is limited, and it's best to call ahead, but you can usually count on a chicken, beef, or fish platter with rice and beans simmered in coconut milk. Your meal includes a beverage and dessert. ⊠ *150 m north of Paraíso Tropical, Tortuguero village* ☎ *709–8102* ⊟ *No credit cards.*

**¢–$** ✗ **La Casona.** You dine at long picnic tables here, the floor is sandy, and reggae plays in the background. It's nothing fancy, rather a congenial place where you can grab a table and chat with your fellow diners about the day's sightseeing. Fish and vegetarian dishes are the staples— try the palmito lasagne—and the banana pancakes for breakfast are a great way to fortify yourself before setting out for the day. ⊠ *North side of soccer field, Tortuguero village* ☎ *709–8092 or 834–1538* ⊟ *No credit cards* ☺ *Breakfast served.*

**¢** ✗ **The Vine Bakery.** Pastas, pizzas, and sandwiches are on the menu, but this small bakery and coffee shop is also a great place to stop for breads made with banana, carrot, and *natilla* (cream), for example. ⊠ *25 m north of Catholic church, Tortuguero village* ☎ *709–8132* ⊟ *No credit cards* ☺ *No dinner. Breakfast served.*

**$$$$** 🏠 **Evergreen Lodge.** Owned by the Pachira people, the Evergreen offers

Fodor'sChoice an entirely different (and intimate) concept in Tortuguero lodging: While
★ other lodges have cabins arranged around a clearing, at Evergreen they penetrate deep into the forest. A network of walking trails extends to Canal Chiquerito, the third waterway inland. Cabins are made from deep red almondwood or gypsum wood. All contain one double and one single, as well as venetian blinds for privacy. Honeymooners make up a substantial portion of the clientele here. Watch for the whimsical ANT CROSSING signs as you walk around the grounds. ⊠ *2 km/1½ mi from Tortuguero village on Canal Penitencia* 🕾 *Apdo. 1818–1002, San José* ☎ *222–7476 or 257–2242* 🖶 *221–3252* ⊕ *www.costaricatravelguide.com/evergreen* ⇥ *30 cabins* ⚐ *Restaurant, kayaking, bar, meeting room; no a/c, no room phones, no room TVs* ⊟ *AE, DC, MC, V* ⫶◯⫶ *AI.*

**$$$$** 🏠 **Hotel Ilán-Ilán.** Small place, small staff, small prices: rooms are simple here, but it's a way to get the Tortuguero-lodge experience at a portion of the cost of the bigger places, and the service is exceptionally friendly. Concrete buildings congregate around a garden filled with the yellow flowering ilán-ilán tree, unique to the region. Rooms are basic, some with one double and one single bed, others with three single beds. Meals are served buffet style if visitor numbers are large; otherwise, they're brought to your table. ⊠ *Across river, 2 km/1½ mi north of Tortuguero*

*Continued on page 397*

# TORTUGUERO NATIONAL PARK

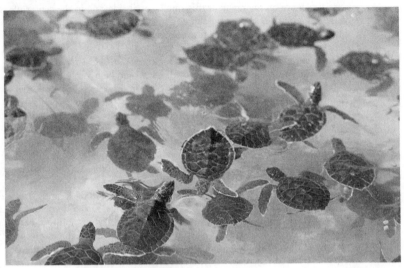

**TORTUGUERO MEANS "TURTLE REGION,"** which is apt, since turtles are the main attraction. Four species of turtles—green, hawksbill, loggerhead, and giant leatherback—lumber up the 35 km (22 mi) of beach at various times of the year and deposit their eggs for safekeeping. The park was, in fact, established to protect the sea turtles' nesting habitat and to protect the turtles themselves. From the time that Europeans set foot on Costa Rican shores in the mid-1500s up until the early 20th century, turtles were aggressively hunted, and their eggs and carapaces exported. Some people still believe the turtle eggs to be a delicacy and some bars (illegally) serve them as snacks.

**FAST FACTS**

**Size:** 189 square km (73 square mi)

**Established:** 1975

**"Dry" Season:** February–April and September–October (But it's never *completely* dry here.)

**Wettest months:** January, June, and July

**What to do:** Turtle tours, canal tours, fishing

**Geography:** Lowland rain forests, swamp forests, beaches, canals, and lagoons

**Number of species catalogued:** 309 birds, 85 freshwater fish, 60 mammals, 7 river turtles, 4 sea turtles

Turtles have the limelight at Tortuguero, but also keep your eyes peeled for **non-turtle species** such as tapirs (in Jolillo groves), jaguars, anteaters, ocelots, howler monkeys, white-faced capuchin monkeys, three-toed sloths, collared and white-lipped peccaries, raccoons, otters, skunks, coatis, and blue morpho butterflies.

The palm-lined **beaches** of Parque Nacional Tortuguero stretch off as far as the eye can see. You can wander the beach independently, but riptides make swimming dangerous, and shark rumors persist.

### Tours

It's virtually impossible to get around Tortuguero on your own. A package tour is the best way to go. Most Tortuguero tours are packaged through local lodges, with one- or two-night stays, and include transportation, meals, and guided tours. ■ TIP➔➔ Opt for at least two nights. The one-night tours give you a scant 18 hours to spend in Tortuguero, with the rest of your time spent coming and going.

Turtle watching is the name of the game most of the year here, and various guides in and around the village of Tortuguero can take you on excursions. For information on package tours, *see* The Caribbean Planner, at the start of this chapter.

### The Turtle-Nesting Ritual

Every two to four years, female turtles come ashore, nesting two to five times in a 12-day period. Each turtle digs a pit with her flippers and scoops out a chamber for depositing about 100 eggs. She fills and conceals the chamber before heading back out to sea. After a 60-day incubation period, the hatchlings emerge. In the ultimate in team effort, they scurry up the sides of the chamber, kicking sand down to the bottom, gradually raising the level of the base of the pit, allowing them to escape, and make a mad dash to the sea. Biologists believe that the nesting site's sand leaves an imprint on the hatchlings—though it's not known exactly how—that draws the females back as adults to the same stretch of beach, to continue the ritual that has taken place for thousands of years. Less than one percent of the hatchlings will make it to adulthood. Most fall victim to birds, dogs, sharks, and humans. That the turtle population survives at all is a remarkable feat of nature.

River and rain forest tour

Tortuguero National Park

## The Endangered Manatee

It is estimated that only about 100 manatees (*vacas marinas*, or "sea cows" in Spanish) remain in Tortuguero even though they were common here prior to 1950. It is thought that numbers have dwindled due to pesticides used on banana plantations, which seep into the water, killing the manatees' food supply and changing the aquatic environment. Also, because the manatees move extremely slowly, they are easy prey and often hit by motorboats.

| SEA-TURTLE SPECIES | NESTING SEASON |
|---|---|
| • Giant Leatherback | February–July |
| • Green | July–October |
| • Hawksbill | March–October |
| • Loggerhead | Infrequently year-round |

The green turtle is the most numerous species, so its nesting season is the most impressive to see.

Hawksbill Turtle

Ironically, efforts to save Tortuguero's turtles have pushed manatees to the margins: Increased boat traffic bringing tourists to help guide turtle hatchlings to sea means more opportunities for manatees to be hit by boats, and scares them deeper into obscure canals. In another bit of irony, manatees provide a service to the very boats that threaten them by eating water hyacinths, which can clog up waterways if they grow unchecked.

Manatees, which are generally 3–3½ meters (10–12 feet) long and weigh 450–800 kilos (1,000–1,800 pounds), are vegetarians, and eat up to 75 kilos (150 pounds) of fresh- and saltwater plants every day. They are the only exclusively herbivorous marine mammals. Their slow digestion makes for lots of gas, so a good way to spot a manatee is to stop and look around for bubbles in the water! Count yourself lucky if you see one of these rare and cute (in a bulldog sort of way) creatures.

### Park Info

**Hours of Operation:** Daily 6–6

**Contacts:** 710–2929 or 710–2939

**Admission:** $7

**Getting There:** The north entrance to the park lies at the southern edge of Tortuguero village. If you come here on a package tour with one of the lodges, your boat trip to and from will take you through the park. Hiking in the park is best accomplished on a guided tour that provides transportation.

☎ *255–2262 or 255–2031* 🖷 *255–1946* ⊕ *www.ilan-ilanlodge.com*
🛏 *24 rooms* ⚘ *Restaurant, fans, whirlpool tub, pool, bar; no a/c, no room phones, no room TVs* ▭ *AE, MC, V* ⊙ *AI.*

**$$$$** 🏨 **Jungle Lodge.** The Jungle Lodge experience begins with your hotel pickup in San José and continues via a minivan trip to the docks north of Siquirres, where you board the lodge's *Miss Caribe* or *Miss America* barges for the last leg of the canal trip. The luxuriously rustic hardwood cabins are well ventilated and have huge bathrooms. Everything is included, save a few small tours. Rates begin at $170 per person. The restaurant serves buffet-style meals. ✉ *1 km/½ mi south of airstrip* ☎ *291–5859 or 291–5868* 🖷 *290–8843* ⊕ *www.grupopapagayo.com* 🛏 *50 rooms* ⚘ *Restaurant, fans, pool, whirlpool tub, 2 bars, laundry service, Internet no a/c, no room phones, no room TVs* ▭ *AE, MC, V* ⊙ *AI.*

**$$$$** 🏨 **Jungle Tarpon Lodge.** On 100 acres, this intimate lodge specializes in sportfishing packages—tarpon, snapper, snook, and barracuda are the catches of the day—but if you don't fish, eco-adventure activities such as turtle-watching and custom tours are arranged as well. Though small, the lodge is a deluxe affair, crafted in fine wood with large rooms, modern tiled bathrooms, and beamed ceilings. Savory local cuisine—heavy on fish—is served in the dining room; some meals are enjoyed on the riverside deck. Transfers to San José, meals, and charters are included in the four- to nine-day packages, which begin at close to $1,500 per person. ✉ *Parsimina River lagoon, southern end of Tortuguero National Park* ☎ *No phone in Costa Rica, 907/262–4515, 360/697–6454, or 800/ 544–2261 in U.S.* 🖷 *907/262–8797 or 360/697–7850* ⌚ *May–mid-Oct.: Great Alaska, 33881 Sterling Hwy., Sterling, AK 99672* ⌚ *Mid-Oct.–Apr.: Great Alaska, Poulsbo, WA 98370* ⊕ *www.jungletarpon.com* 🛏 *6 rooms* ⚘ *Restaurant, dining room, fans, boating, fishing, bar; no a/c, no room phones, no room TVs* ▭ *AE, MC, V* ⊙ *AI.*

**$$$$** 🏨 **Laguna Lodge.** Laguna is the largest of the Tortuguero lodges, and it hums with activity. Jam-packed package tours begin in San José and embark boats at Caño Blanco, north of Siquirres. A mix of concrete and wood buildings spread out over 12 acres of grounds on a thin sliver of land between the ocean and the first canal inland. Rooms have wood paneling and floors, and tiled bathrooms. The property includes a butterfly garden and a small network of trails through secondary forest. Meals are served buffet style at the open-air restaurant that extends out over the canal. The snazzy combo reception–gift shop–meeting room building seems to have sprung straight from the mind of Gaudí. ✉ ☎ *225–3740* 🖷 *283–8031* ⊕ *www.lagunatortuguero.com* 🛏 *95 rooms* ⚘ *2 restaurants, fans, pool, 2 bars, meeting room; no a/c, no room phones, no room TVs* ▭ *AE, DC, MC, V* ⊙ *AI.*

★ **$$$$** 🏨 **Mawamba Lodge.** Nestled between the river and the ocean, Mawamba is the perfect place to kick back and

**WORD OF MOUTH**

"My husband and I were discussing our CR favorites the other day. We both agreed that the bar at the Mawamba Lodge was our favorite bar and the beds were our [least favorite]! Also at Mawamba, we found the food to be very good, with lots of fresh veggies and salads."
                                        –dfarmer

relax. It is also the only jungle lodge within walking distance (about 10 minutes) of town. Packages include transport from San José; when you arrive at the river town of Matina, you're whisked in a 2½-hour launch ride to a 15-acre site with comfortable (hot-water!) rustic cabinas with garden views. Meals are taken in the spacious dining room, and are included in the price, along with transfers and guided tours of the jungle and canals; trips to turtle-heavy beaches cost $10 extra. Packages begin at about $210 per person. ⊠ *½ km/¼ mi north of Tortuguero on ocean side of canal* ✆ *Apdo. 10980–1000, San José* ☎ *293–8181* ⊕ *www. grupomawamba.com* ✆ *Apdo. 10980–1000, San José* 🖷 *239–7657* ⌦ *54 cabinas* ⚒ *Restaurant, dining room, fans, pool, whirlpool tub, beach, bar, shop, laundry service, meeting room; no a/c, no room phones, no room TVs* ⊟ *AE, MC, V* ⦶ *AI.*

**$$$$** 🖼 **Pachira Lodge.** This is the prettiest and most luxurious of Tortuguero's
**Fodor'sChoice** lodges, but not the costliest. Each almond-wood cabina in the lush, well-
★ manicured gardens contains four guest rooms with high ceilings, king-size beds, and bamboo furniture. The stunning pool is shaped like a giant sea turtle: the head is a whirlpool tub, the left paw is a wading pool, and the right paw is equipped for swimmers with disabilities. There is no cross-river transportation into town. Package deals include transport from San José, a jungle tour, and all meals; rates begin at about $260 per person. Pachira is known for being the most competitive marketer of the lodges here, and the place is often full. ⊠ *Across river from Mawamba Lodge* ✆ *Apdo. 1818–1002, San José* ☎ *256–7080 or 257–2242* ⊕ *www.pachiralodge.com* ✆ *Apdo. 1818–1002, San José* 🖷 *223–1119* ⌦ *44 rooms* ⚒ *Restaurant, fans, pool, bar, laundry service; no a/c, no room phones, no room TVs* ⊟ *AE, MC, V* ⦶ *AI.*

**$$$$** 🖼 **Samoa Lodge.** A location on the inland side of the second canal in from the ocean gives this place plenty of room to spread out, and, indeed, a network of hiking trails on the lodge's grounds is one of the attractions here. Buildings are scattered around manicured gardens and contain rooms with vaulted ceilings, all with either one double and one single bed or three single beds. ⊠ *2 km/1½ mi from Tortuguero village on Canal Penitencia* ✆ *Apdo. 10736–1000, San José* ☎ *258–6244* 🖷 *258–5687 or 258–5790* ⊕ *www.samoalodge.com* ⚒ *Restaurant, fans, pool, bar, no-smoking rooms; no a/c, no room phones, no room TVs* ⊟ *AE, DC, MC, V* ⦶ *AI.*

★ **$$$$** 🖼 **Tortuga Lodge.** Lush lawns, orchids, and tropical trees surround this thatched riverside lodge owned by Costa Rica Expeditions and renowned for its nature packages and top-notch, personalized service. Tortuga sets itself apart with its smaller size and markets itself to a higher-budget clientele than do its major competitors here (Laguna, Mawamba, and Pachira). Guest rooms are comfortable, with much-needed mosquito blinds. The chefs do an excellent job of preparing hearty food, which is served family style rather than in a buffet line as at other lodges. Tortuguero National Park is 20 minutes south by boat. ⊠ *Across the river from the airstrip, 2 km/1 mi from Tortuguero* ☎ *710–8016, 257–0766, or 222–0333* 🖷 *257–1665* ⊕ *www.costaricaexpeditions.com* 🖷 *257–1665, 800/886–2609 from U.S.* ⌦ *26 rooms* ⚒ *Dining room,* *fans, pool, fishing, hiking, bar, laundry service; no a/c, no room phones, no room TVs* ⊟ *AE, MC, V* ⏐◯⏐ *FAP.*

**$** ▦ **Casa Marbella.** The best of the in-town hotels is a real find. Cana-
FodorśChoice dian owner and naturalist Daryl Loth is a respected authority on all things
★ Tortuguero, and one of the community's biggest boosters. If he's unable to take you out in his boat himself, he'll find someone who can.
Immaculate rooms have tile floors and varnished wood finishing with
vaulted ceilings and skylights in the bathrooms. Ample breakfasts are
served on the covered back patio facing the lodging's own private canal
dock. The terrace is also a relaxing place for a coffee break on a rainy
afternoon. There's a small kitchenette for your use. ⊠ *Across from
Catholic church, Tortuguero village* ☎ *833–0827 or 709–8011*
⊕ *casamarbella.tripod.com* ⟲ *5 rooms* ⚥ *Fans, travel services; no a/c,
no room phones, no room TVs* ⊟ *No credit cards* ⏐◯⏐ *BP.*

**$** ▦ **El Manatí.** Simple and reasonably priced, El Manatí is popular with
budget travelers and researchers, some of whom study the lodge's namesake—the endangered manatee. The comfortable but slightly run-down
rooms have firm beds and mosquito screens. The contiguous terraces
look across a narrow lawn to the river, where you can kayak and canoe.
Chestnut-beaked toucans, poison dart frogs, and three types of monkeys hang out in the surrounding jungle. ⊠ *Across river, about 1 km/½
mi north of Tortuguero* ☎ *817–8667* ⟲ *11 rooms, 8 cabins* ⚥ *Restaurant, fans, boating, bar; no a/c, no room phones, no room TVs* ⊟ *No
credit cards* ⏐◯⏐ *BP.*

**¢** ▦ **Cabinas Miriam.** Village institution Miss Miriam is gone, but her
daughters continue her long tradtion of fussing over guests in two 2-
story buildings fronting the soccer field, just a short walk from the beach.
Rooms are simple, with tile floors and three beds each. Grab a filling
meal of Caribbean food at the restaurant next door. ⊠ *North and south
side of soccer field, 300 m north of entrance to national park, Tortuguero
Village* ☎ *821–2037, 709–8107, or 709–8002* ⟲ *14 rooms* ⚥ *Restaurant, fans; no a/c, no room phones, no room TVs* ⊟ *No credit cards.*

## Shopping

★ Octagonal **Jungle Shop** (⊠ 25 m north of Catholic church, Tortuguero
village ☎ 709–8072) has the best selection of souvenirs in town. Tiles,
feather paintings, and original-design T-shirts are the standouts, and they
are things you won't find at every other store in Costa Rica. The town's
largest souvenir emporium, **Paraíso Tropical** (⊠ West side of Tortuguero
school, Tortuguero village ☎ 709–8095) has a huge selection of wood
carvings and sandals in addition to the standard T-shirt and postcard
fare. You can't miss it; it's right at the pier where the lodges' boats dock
for their afternoon tours of the village. **Souvenirs Pura Vida** (⊠ Across
from police station, Tortuguero village ☎ 709–8037) is small but has
a nice variety of colorful T-shirts and wood carvings.

## To & From Tortuguero

It's easier than you'd think to get to remote Tortuguero. Flying is the
quickest (and most expensive) option. SANSA and NatureAir provide
early-morning flights to and from San José. SANSA agent **Victor Barrantes**
(☎ 709–8055 or 838–6330) meets both planes—they arrive and depart

within 15 minutes of each other—and offers boat-taxi service to and from town for $2. Call and confirm with him the day before if you need a ride. If you're staying at one of the lodges, its boat will meet you at the airstrip.

The big lodges all have packages that include transportation to and from San José along with lodging, meals, and tours. Guide-staffed minivans pick you up at your San José hotel and drive you to the put-in site, usually somewhere north of Siquirres, where you board a covered boat for the final leg on the canals to Tortuguero. The trip up entails sightseeing and animal viewing. The trip back to San José stops only for a lunch break. This is the classic "leave the driving to them" way to get to Tortuguero.

A boat from the port of Moín, near Limón, is the traditional budget method of getting to Tortuguero if you are already on the Caribbean coast. Arrive at the docks by 9 AM and you should be able to find someone to take you there. The going price is $30 one way; $50 round-trip,

> **CAUTION**
>
> Wear mosquito repellent in low-lying coastal areas, where a few cases of dengue have been reported.

and travel time is about three hours. **Alexis Soto and Sebastián Torres** (☎ 900/296–2626 beeper) partner to provide a reliable boat service between Moín and Tortuguero for about $50 round-trip. Arrange in advance. If you arrive in Moín in your own vehicle, JAPDEVA, Costa Rica's Atlantic port authority, operates a secure, guarded parking facility for your car while you are in Tortuguero.

It's entirely possible to make the trip independently from San José, a good option if you are staying in the village rather than at a lodge. A direct bus departs from San José's Gran Terminal del Caribe to Cariari, north of Guápiles, at 9 AM. At Cariari, disembark and walk five blocks to the local terminal, where you can board a noon bus for the small town of La Pavona. From there, boats leave at 1:30 PM to take you to Tortuguero, arriving around 3 PM. The Cariari–La Pavona–Tortuguero bus–boat service is provided by **Viajes Clic-Clic** (☎ 709–8155, 844–0463 or 308–2006) for $10 one way. La Pavona has secure parking facilities.

⚠ Avoid Rubén Bananero, a company that provides bus–boat transport from Cariari via an inconvenient route through the Geest banana plantation. They begin to hustle you the minute you get off the bus in Cariari, insisting the La Pavona route does not exist. They also require that you buy a round-trip ticket, limiting your return options, and do everything they can to steer you toward hotels that pay them a commission.

Water taxis provide transport from multiple points in the village to the lodges. Expect to pay about $2–$3 per trip.

## Tortuguero Essentials

🖥 Internet **La Casona** ✉ North side of soccer field ☎ 709-8092.

🖥 Visitor Information **Kiosk** ☎ Town center ☞ Information on the town's history, the park, turtles, and other wildlife; no staff. **Tortuguero Information Center** ✉ Across from Catholic church ☎ 709-8011 or 833-0827 ✍ safari@racsa.co.cr

# Barra del Colorado

**5** Up the coast from Tortuguero is the ramshackle hamlet of Barra del Colorado, a popular sportfishing hub characterized by plain stilted wooden houses, dirt paths, and a complete absence of motorized land vehicles (though some locals have added motors to their hand-hewn canoes).

## Exploring

Bordered to the north by the Río San Juan and the frontier with Nicaragua is the vast, 905-square-km (350-square-mi) **Barra del Colorado Wildlife Refuge** (Refugio Nacional de Vida Silvestre Barra del Colorado), really the only local attraction for nonanglers. Most people arrange trips here through their lodge. Transportation once you get here is almost exclusively waterborne, as there are virtually no paths in this swampy terrain. The list of species that you're likely to see from your boat is almost the same as that for Tortuguero; the main difference here is the feeling of being farther off the beaten track. You can realistically get as far as the 640,000-acre **Río Indio-Maiz Biological Reserve** when crossing the border here. The reserve is a continuation of the Barra del Colorado Wildlife Refuge, but in Nicaraguan territory. If you want to venture there, book a room at the Río Indio Adventure Lodge ( ⇨ *below*) in Nicaragua, which takes care of all border-crossing protocol. ⊠ 🕾 *No phone* 🖃 *Free* ⊗ *24 hours.*

## Outdoor Activities

FISHING   Fishing is the name of the game here, and your lodge in Barra del Colorado will handle all the arrangements for you.

## Where to Stay

**$$$$**  **Río Indio Adventure Lodge.** Near the small village of San Juan del Norte, in the midst of the Río Indio-Maiz Biological Reserve ( ⇨ *above*), is Nicaragua's only true ecotourism lodge, which has a rustic luxury. Packages include van transport from San José to Puerto Viejo de Sarapiquí, with continuation by boat another three hours up the Sarapiquí and San Juan rivers to the lodge. Or you can opt for air transport to Barra del Colorado with another hour's boat journey up the Río Colorado to the site. So tied is San Juan del Norte to its southern neighbor that the lodge's information offices and telephone numbers are in Costa Rica rather than Nicaragua. ⊠ *San Juan del Norte, Nicaragua* 🕾 *296–0095, 866/593–3176 in North America* 🖷 *291–0835* ⊕ *www. rioindiolodge.com* 🖙 *34 rooms* ⚹ *Restaurant, fans, in-room safes, pool, laundry service, Internet, bar, tours; no a/c, no room phones, no room TVs* ⊟ *AE, DC, MC, V* 🍽 *AI.*

**$$$$**  🕾 **Río Colorado Lodge.** This long-established lodge caters almost exclusively to sportfishing folk and tours, complete with a modern fleet of 10- and 26-foot sportfishing vessels. (Tarpon and snook are the catch here.) Guest rooms have twin beds, paneled ceilings, white curtains, and basket lamp shades. The all-inclusive packages include airport pickup, all meals, and fishing trips; rates begin at about $1,500 per person. Alternatively, there are some fly-in, boat-out nature-tour packages that include Tortuguero National Park and are considerably cheaper. Given the logistics of getting here, it doesn't pay to stay only one night. ✉ *35-min flight from San José* ☎ *710–6879, 232–4063 San José, 800/243–9777 in U.S.* 🖷 *231–5987, 813/933–3280 in U.S.* ⊕ *www.riocoloradolodge.com* 🛏 *Apdo. 5094–1000, San José* ⚓ *18 rooms* ☁ *Restaurant, a/c, fans, fishing, bar, laundry service; no room phones, no room TVs* ⊟ *AE, MC, V* 🍽 *AI.*

## To & From Barra del Colorado
*25 km/16 mi northwest of Tortuguero.*

SANSA and NatureAir have very early-morning flights from San José. You're likely staying at a fishing lodge if you come this far, and a representative will meet your flight and escort you to your lodge and back.

## Crossing into Nicaragua via the San Juan River

Crossing into Nicaragua here is both difficult and easy. A stay at the Río Indio Lodge offers the easiest (and most expensive) option, with guided transportation included in your package price. The lodge will handle the $10 immigration fee levied by Nicaraguan authorities. Less formally, a 40-km (24-mile) boat trip from Puerto Viejo de Sarapiquí up the Río Sarapiquí takes you to the San Juan and lets you officially enter Nicaragua. Passports are required for the trip, but you won't acquire a Nicaraguan stamp as a souvenir if you remain on the river, as is the case for most excursions. Venturing any farther into Nicaragua on your own is impossible here; you run up against the largely forested eastern half of the country.

> **THE NICARAGUA CANAL?**
>
> Spurred by the 1840s California Gold Rush, the San Juan River became an important crossroads allowing miners and gold to move between New York and San Francisco some 70 years before the Panama Canal opened. Cornelius Vanderbilt financed the dredging of the waterway to allow ships to pass up the river to Lake Nicaragua. From there a rail line connected to the Pacific Ocean. As the Panama Canal ages, there is again talk of resurrecting this "wet-dry" canal. So far, plans remain on the drawing board.

It remains essentially roadless, much like Tortuguero and Barra del Colorado immediately to the south. The western immigration point at Peñas Blancas provides a much easier entry into Nicaragua ( ⇨ *chapter 4*).

# COASTAL TALAMANCA

The landscape along the Guápiles Highway changes from farmland to tropical as you approach the port city of Limón. Place names change too. You'll see signs to towns called Bristol, Stratford, and Liverpool, reflecting the region's British Caribbean heritage.

## Limón

❻ The colorful Afro-Caribbean flavor of Costa Rica's most important port (population 85,000) is the first sign of life for seafaring visitors to Costa Rica's east coast. Christopher Columbus was the first visitor: he dropped anchor here on his final voyage to the New World in 1502. Limón is a lively, if shabby, town with a 24-hour street life. The wooden houses are brightly painted, but the grid-plan streets look rather worn, largely because of the damage caused by a 1991 earthquake. Street crime, including pickpocketing and nighttime mugging, is not uncommon here. Long charged with neglecting the city, the national government has now turned attention to Limón. New businesses are coming in, a positive sign of urban renewal, and the town has beefed up security with a more visible police presence.

## CRUISING INTO LIMÓN

If you arrive in Limón on a cruise ship, a day in the Caribbean is yours for the taking. The Tortuguero canals, the beaches at Puerto Viejo de Talamanca, or the sloth rescue center at Aviarios del Caribe near Cahuita are three popular excursions. A few hardy souls venture as far away as the Rain Forest Aerial Tram or San José. But many remain in Limón to shop and explore. (The terminal is right downtown.) A legion of taxi drivers waits at the terminal exit.

Limón receives thousands of visitors every year, owing in large part to its newest incarnation as a port of call. Carnival, Celebrity, Cunard, Holland America, Norwegian, Princess, and Royal Caribbean cruise ships all dock at the Terminal de Cruceros, downtown, during the October–August season, with December–March seeing one or two boats each day.

NAVIGATING LIMÓN

*Avenidas* (avenues) run east and west, and *calles* (streets) north and south, but Limón's street-numbering system differs from that of other Costa Rican cities. "Number one" of each avenida and calle begins at the water and numbers increase sequentially as you move inland, unlike the evens-on-one-side, odds-on-the-other scheme used in San José. But the scarcity of street signs means everyone uses landmarks anyway. Official red taxis ply the streets, or wait at designated taxi stands near Parque Vargas, the Mercado Municipal, and the cruise-ship terminal.

Across from the east side of the Black Star Line buildings is the city's palm-lined central park, the **Parque Vargas.** From the promenade facing the ocean you can see the raised dead coral left stranded by the 1991 earthquake. Nine or so Hoffman's two-toed sloths live in the trees of Parque Vargas; ask a passerby to point them out, as spotting them requires a trained eye.

West of Parque Vargas is the lively enclosed **Mercado Municipal** (Municipal Market; ⊠ Pedestrian mall, Avda. 2, between Cs. 3 and 4), where you can buy fruit for the road ahead, and experience the sights, sounds, and smells of a Central American market.

On the left side of the highway as you enter Limón is a large **Chinese cemetery,** Chinese workers having made up a large part of the 1880s railroad-construction team that worked here. Thousands died of malaria and yellow fever. Look for the COLONIA CHINA and corresponding sign in Chinese on the hill in the cemetery.

## Outdoor Activities

Limón's growing crop of tour operators serves cruise-ship passengers almost exclusively. **Laura Tropical Tours** (⊠Terminal de Cruceros ☎758–1240) has excursions to banana plantations, Tortuguero, and Cahuita National Park. **Mambo Tours** (⊠ Terminal de Cruceros ☎798–1542) can take you on 3- to 8-hour excursions around the region, and even on an all-day trip to the Rain Forest Aerial Tram or San José.

## Where to Stay & Eat

**$–$$** ✗ **Brisas del Caribe.** Here's a case study in what happens when cruise ships come to town. This old downtown standby, once charmingly as off kilter as the crooked umbrellas on its front tables, got rid of its video poker machines (and the locals who always hoped to get lucky playing them) and tiled the floors and remodeled. The food is still good—seafood and surprisingly decent hamburgers, a real rarity in Costa Rica, are the fare here—but a bit of the local color has faded. ⊠ *North side of Parque Vargas* ☎ *758–0138* ☰ *AE, DC, MC, V.*

**$$** 🏨 **Hotel Maribú Caribe.** Perched on a cliff overlooking the Caribbean Sea between Limón and Portete, these white conical thatched huts have great views but you're a long way from the ocean itself. The lovely grounds have green lawns, shrubs, palm trees, and a large, kidney-shape pool. The poolside bar discourages exertion. The hotel is immensely popular on weekends, but during the week you'll likely have the place to yourself. ⊠ *4 km/2½ mi north on road to Portete, Apdo. 623–7300* ☎ *795–2543* 🖷 *795–3541* ✐ *maribu@racsa.co.cr* ⬮ *52 rooms* ⬩ *Restaurant, a/c, cable TV, bar, laundry service; no phones in some rooms* ☰ *AE, DC, MC, V* ⓘⓄⓘ *BP.*

**$** 🏨 **Hotel Park.** The prices can't be beat here in this pastel-and-pink business-class hotel in central Limón. All rooms have modern furnishings and private balconies, so opt for one fronting the ocean. The air-conditioned dining room is a pleasant respite from the heat of the port city. ⊠ *Avda. 3, between Cs. 2 and 3* ☎ *798–0555* 🖷 *758–4364* ✐ *irlyxie@racsa.co.cr* ⬮ *33 rooms* ⬩ *Restaurant, a/c, cable TV, meeting room* ☰ *AE, MC, V.*

## Shopping

The cruise-ship terminal contains an orderly maze of souvenir stands. Vendors are friendly; there's no pressure to buy. Many shops populate the restored port building across the street. Spelling is not its forte, but the **Caribean Banana** (⊠ 50 m north Terminal de Cruceros, west side of Parque Vargas ☎758–3619) stands out from the other shops in the Black Star Line building with a terrific selection of wood carvings.

## To & From Limón

*100 km/62 mi southeast of Guápiles, 160 km/100 mi (3½ hours) east of San José.*

If you're coming to the Caribbean coast, you'll pass through Limón. The Guápiles Highway that began in San José ends here at the ocean, but bypasses the heart of downtown by a couple of blocks. Just after the sign to SIXAOLA and the coastal highway south to Cahuita and Puerto Viejo de Talamanca is the city center. The main bus terminal lies at Avenida

# Caribbean Carnaval

IF YOU'RE HERE IN EARLY OR mid-October, don't miss Limón's Carnaval, arguably Costa Rica's biggest blowout. The weeklong celebration is held around October 12 (Columbus Day in the U.S.), which is celebrated by the rest of Latin America as the Dí de la Raza (Day of the Race), with "race" referring to the mixed population resulting from the encounter of European and indigenous peoples, a day that tends to have decidedly leftist political overtones. But the holiday is the Día de las Culturas (Day of the Cultures) in Costa Rica, and is a joyous multicultural celebration of the

encounter of New and Old Worlds in the country's most multicultural city. Historians here debate whether or not Carnaval was ever intended to coincide with the holiday. Most agree that it was simply a revitaliztion of the October Sin Kitt harvest celebrations once held on the Caribbean island of St. Kitts, the native home of 19th-century Afro-Caribbeans who immigrated to Costa Rica to work on the Atlantic Railroad. Expect a week's worth of colorful parades and vibrant reggae and calypso music. Book lodging weeks in advance if you plan to be in Limón during that time.

2 and Calle 8, across from the soccer stadium and serves routes from San José, Guápiles, and Siquirres. Buses to Cahuita and Puerto Viejo de Talamanca and all points on the south coast arrive and depart from a stop across from Radio Casino on Avenida 4 between calles 3 and 4.

## Limón Essentials

🏛 Bank/ATM **BAC San José** ✉ Avda. 3, between Cs. 2 and 3. **Banco Nacional** ✉ Avda. 2, between Cs. 3 and 4. **Scotiabank** ✉ Avda. 3 and C. 2

🏛 Hospital **Hospital Dr. Tony Facio** ✉ Highway to Portete ☎ 758-2222.

🏛 Pharmacy **Farmacia Buenos Aires** ✉ 25 m east of Mercado Municipal ☎ 798-4732. **Farmacia Limonense** ✉ First floor, Radio Casino ☎ 758-0654.

🏛 Internet **Café Internet** ✉ Gran Terminal del Caribe, Avda. 2 and C. 8, across from the soccer stadium ☎ 798-0128. **Internet Cinco Estrellas** ✉ 50 m north of Terminal de Cruceros ☎ 758-5752.

🏛 Post Office **Correos** ✉ Avda. 2 and C. 4.

🏛 Visitor Information **JAPDEVA (Atlantic Port Authority)** ✉ Terminal de Cruceros ⌖ Accessible to cruise-ship passengers only.

## Moín

❼ The docks at Moín are a logical next stop after visiting neighboring Limón, especially if you want to take a boat north to explore the Caribbean coast. You'll probably be able to negotiate a waterway and national-park tour with a local guide, and if you call in advance you can arrange a tour with the man considered the best guide on the ★ Caribbean coast: **Modesto Watson** (☎ 226-0986), a local Miskito Indian guide. He's legendary for his bird- and animal-spotting skills as well as his howler monkey imitations.

## To & From Moín
*5 km/3 mi north of Limón.*

Moín is a quick taxi ride from the center of Limón.

## Cahuita

**8** Dusty Cahuita, its main dirt street flanked by wooden-slat cabins, is a backpackers' vacation town—a hippie hangout with a dash of Afro-Caribbean spice tossed in. And after years of negative crime-related publicity, Cahuita has beefed up security—this is one of the few places in the country where you will be conscious of a visible and reassuring, though not oppressive, police presence—and is making a well-deserved comeback on the tourist circuit. Tucked in among the backpackers' digs are a few surprisingly nice get-away-from-it-all lodgings and restaurants with some tasty cuisine at decent prices. No question that nearby Puerto Viejo de Talamanca has overtaken Cahuita and has become the hottest spot on the southern Caribbean coast. But as Puerto Viejo grows exponentially, Cahuita's appeal is that it remains small and manageable.

NAVIGATING Cahuita's tiny center is quite walkable, if dusty in the dry season and
CAHUITA muddy in the wet season. It's about a 30-minute walk to the end of the

Playa Negra road to Hotel La Diosa. Take a taxi if going to or from Playa Negra after dark. Cahuita has no formally licensed red taxis, with transportation provided informally instead by private individuals. To be on the safe side, have your hotel or restaurant call a driver for you.

Bicycles are a popular means of utilitarian transport in Cahuita. Seemingly everyone rents basic touring bikes for $4–$8 per day, but quality varies widely. **Cabinas Brigitte** (⊠ Playa Negra road, 1½ km/1 mi from town ☎ 755–0053) rents good bikes for $8 per day. **Cahuita Tours** (⇨ *below*) also has bike rentals.

### Exploring

★ A lodge in the midst of becoming a full-fledged nature center, **Aviarios del Caribe** has dense gardens that have attracted over 300 bird species. Proceeds go to goodhearted owners Judy and Luis Arroyo's sloth rescue center on the premises. Buttercup, the very first of their charges, holds court in the nature-focused gift shop. ⊠ *9 km/5 mi north of Cahuita, follow signs on Río Estrella delta* ☎ *750–0775* ⊕ *www.ogphoto.com/ aviarios.*

At most butterfly gardens around Costa Rica you get wet during the rainy season. (The mesh enclosures don't offer much protection from ☺ the moisture.) But that's not the case at the **Cahuita Butterfly Garden**, where a bamboo roof covers the perimeter of the 1,100-square-meter facility. The friendly owners conduct tours in English, French, and Spanish. There's a souvenir shop and small café that serves refreshments, as well as a lounge area outfitted with whimsical wooden chairs. (The owner is a sculptor.) ⊠ *Coastal highway at the entrance to Cahuita* ☎ *755–0361* 🎟 *$7* ⊙ *Daily 9–4.*

### Outdoor Activities

Cahuita is small enough that its tour operators don't focus simply on the town and nearby national park but instead line up excursions around the region, even as far away as the Tortuguero canals to the north and Bocas del Toro, Panama, to the south.

**Cahuita Tours** (⊠ Main street, 180 m north of Ricky's Bar ☎ 755–0000 or 755–0101 ✉ cahuitat@racsa.co.cr) is the town's largest and most established tour operator. They can set you up with any of a variety of adventures, including river rafting and kayaking, tours of the Tortuguero canals and mountains, and of indigenous reserves (for a glimpse into traditional life). They can also reconfirm flights and make lodging reservations. We recommend them over their competitors. **Turística Cahuita** (⊠ Main street, across from Supermercado Safari ☎ 755–0071 ✉ dltacb@racsa.co.cr) arranges personalized excursions to nearby rain forests and indigenous reserves and conducts snorkeling tours.

### Where to Stay & Eat

$–$$  ✕**BluSpirit.** The Caribbean-Italian couple that owns this small beach restaurant on Playa Negra has "married" their respective native cuisines. The menu is small and handwritten, but you can opt for spaghetti *al pomodoro* (with tomato sauce), red snapper, or something in between. Try the *fruta del mar* pasta that mixes shrimp, lobster, and crab in a tangy barbecue sauce. There's live entertainment many evenings, and the manager makes amazing piña coladas. ✉ *200 m west of police station on Playa Negra Rd.* ☎ *755–0122* ⊟ *No credit cards* ⊘ *Closed Wed. No lunch.*

**$–$$**   ✕ **Cha Cha Chá.** Québécois owner Bertrand Fleury's sign triumphantly announces CUISINE OF THE WORLD at the entrance to his restaurant on Cahuita's main street. (He counts

Fodor'sChoice
★

> **CAUTION**   ⚠
>
> That man on the street who asks you, "Do you want a smoke?" isn't offering you a Marlboro. A simple "*No, gracias,*" is all you need. The problem is no worse here than anywhere else in Costa Rica, but drugs get more publicity in the Caribbean.

French, Italian, Brazilian, and Canadian heritage in his family tree.) Thai shrimp salad and Tex-Mex fajitas are two of the typically eclectic dishes. The menus is small, but what's done is done impeccably well. A delectable specialty is *langosta cha cha chá*, lobster in a white-wine garlic sauce with fresh basil. Paintings by local artists hang on the walls of the candlelit outdoor dining area, separated from the street by miniature palm trees. The place is (deservedly) popular and has a scant 11 tables. ✉ *Main street, 200 m north of Ricky's Bar* ☎ *394–4153* ⊟ *MC, V* ⚑ *Reservations essential* ⊘ *Closed Mon. No lunch.*

**$–$$**   ✕ **Sobre las Olas.** This is arguably Cahuita's choicest location for a restaurant. The name means "over the waves," and this is one of the few seaside restaurants around at the black-sand beach heading just out of town. Octopus is a specialty, but if you're not that adventurous, a variety of other seafood and pasta dishes awaits. Lunch includes sandwiches and lighter fare. Or stop by for the delicious all-afternoon *bocas* (appetizers) when those 3 PM hunger pangs hit you. ✉ *180 m west of police station on Playa Negra Rd.* ☎ *755–0109* ⊟ *AE, DC, MC, V* ⊘ *Closed Tues.*

**$**   ✕ **Caribbean Roots & Culture.** Miss Edith's daughter Elizabeth learned to cook at her mother's side, and the results show at her new restaurant on Cahuita's main street. Jerk and rondón are on the menu here, but Elizabeth has spiced up her mother's recipes—the veggie curries pack a bit of a punch. The clientele is a bit spicier, too: the largely young backpacking crowd has turned this into a fun, lively place to hang out in the evening. ✉ *Main street, 100 m north of Ricky's Bar* ☎ *755–0248* ⊟ *No credit cards* ⊘ *Closed one day each week. Varies. No lunch.*

**$**   ✕ **Miss Edith.** Miss Edith is revered for her flavorful Caribbean cooking, vegetarian meals, and herbal teas for whatever ails you. Back in the old days she served on her own front porch; she's since moved to more ample surroundings on an easy-to-miss side street at the north end of town. A bit of the mystique disappeared with the move, but her made-to-order dishes—*rondón* (stew of vegetables and beef or fish) and spicy jerk chicken—are good no matter where they are served. ✉ *East of police station* ☎ *755–0248* ⊟ *No credit cards* ⊘ *Closed Sun.*

**$**   ✕ **Restaurante Relax.** From your vantage point at this open-air restaurant above Ricky's Bar you can survey all that goes on in Cahuita's main intersection. Skewers of shrimp and chicken turn on the grill, but the Italian-Mexican owners also toss in pastas and fajitas to give their native cuisines sufficient representation. ⊠ *Above Ricky's Bar* ☎ *755–0322* ▭ *No credit cards* ☽ *Closed Tues. No lunch.*

★ **$–$$**  ✕▥ **Magellan Inn.** Arguably Cahuita's most elegant lodging, this group of bungalows is graced with tile-floor terraces facing a pool and gardens growing on an ancient coral reef. Carpeted rooms have original paintings and custom-made wooden furniture. Feast on intensely flavored French and creole seafood specialties at the Casa Creole ($–$$), open for dinner each evening on the hotel's patio; don't miss the house pâté or the homemade ice cream. The open-air bar rocks to great blues and jazz recordings in the evenings and mellows with classical music at breakfast. ⊠ *2 km/1 mi north of town at end of Playa Negra Rd.* ⌂ *Apdo. 1132–7300, Limón* ☎▤ *755–0035* ⊕ *magellaninn. toposrealestate.org* ⟋ *6 rooms* ⌖ *Restaurant, a/c, fans, pool, bar; no room phones, no room TVs* ▭ *AE, MC, V* ¶◯¶ *CP.*

**$**  ▥ **Atlántida Lodge.** Attractively landscaped grounds, the beach across the road, and a large pool are Atlántida's main assets. You're welcomed to your room by a lovely assortment of fresh and dried flowers; the rooms themselves are a little on the rustic side, but have tile floors and pretty terraces. All the coffee and bananas you can drink and eat are yours as well. ⊠ *Next to soccer field at Playa Negra* ☎ *755–0115* ▤ *755–0213* ⊕ *www.atlantida.co.cr* ⟋ *30 rooms* ⌖ *Restaurant, fans, pool, gym, whirlpool tub, massage, kayaking, bar, laundry service, meeting room; no a/c, no room phones, no room TVs* ▭ *AE, DC, MC, V.*

**$**  ▥ **Bungalows Aché.** Like Alby Lodge next door, Aché scatters wooden bungalows—three octagonal structures in this case—around wooded grounds near the center of town, yet seemingly far away. You get newer buildings here with bed, rocking chair, and porch hammock. The largest bungalow sleeps four. The Swiss owner accepts euros, as well as dollars and colones, for payment. ⊠ *180 m west of national park entrance* ☎ *755–0119* ⊕ *www.bungalowsache.com* ⟋ *3 bungalows* ⌖ *Fans, refrigerators; no a/c, no room phones, no room TVs* ▭ *No credit cards.*

**$**  ▥ **El Encanto Bed & Breakfast.** Zen Buddhist owners have cultivated a
FodorśChoice  serene and beautiful environment here, ideal for physical and spiritual
★  relaxation. Lodgings are in a garden with an extensive bromeliad collection and Buddha figures. Choose between comfortable rooms or bungalows, all decorated with art from all over the globe; some rooms have a double vaulted ceiling with strategically placed screens that keep the place wonderfully ventilated. Amenities include queen-size beds, hot water, and secure parking. Breakfast comes complete with homemade breads and cakes. The beach is across the street, and massage and yoga classes are available on weekends. ⊠ *200 m west of police station on Playa Negra Rd.* ☎ *755–0113* ▤ *755–0432* ⊕ *www.elencantobedandbreakfast.com* ⌂ *Apdo. 7–7302, Cahuita* ⟋ *4 rooms, 3 bungalows* ⌖ *Fans, some kitchenettes; no a/c in some rooms, no room phones, no TV in some rooms* ▭ *AE, MC, V* ¶◯¶ *BP.*

**$**  ▥ **Hotel La Diosa.** The owners' interest in Eastern religions is evidenced in the hotel's name (La Diosa means "goddess") and by the sign depicting a Hindu goddess. They have also opted for little touches such as the rounding of corners and cachá-wood rails to "enhance feminine energy." But that's as New Age as the place gets. Brightly painted stone or wood

CLOSE UP

# The Old Atlantic Railroad

**CHRISTOPHER COLUMBUS** became the Caribbean's (and the country's) first tourist when he landed at Uvita island near Limón during his fourth voyage to the New World in 1502. But the region was already home to thriving, if small, communities of Kekoldi, Bribri, and Cabecar indigenous peoples. If Costa Rica was an isolated backwater, the Caribbean remained even more remote from colonial times through most of the 19th century.

New York industrialist Minor Keith changed all that in 1871 with his plan to launch the British-funded Atlantic Railroad, a mode of transportation that would permit easier export of coffee and bananas to Europe. Such a project required a massive labor force, and thousands of West Indians, Asians, and Italians were brought to Costa Rica to construct the 522 km (335 mi) railroad from Limón to San José. Thousands are reputed to have died of yellow fever, malaria, and snakebite during construction of the project. Those who survived were paid relatively well, however, and by the 1930s many Afro-Caribbean residents owned their own small plots of land.

When the price of cacao rose in the 1950s they emerged as comfortable landowners. Until the Civil War of 1948, black Costa Ricans were forbidden from crossing into the Central Valley lest they upset the country's racial balance, and they were thus prevented from following work when United Fruit abandoned many of its blight-ridden northern Caribbean plantations in the 1930s for green-field sites on the Pacific plain.

Costly upkeep of rail service, construction of the Braulio Carrillo Highway to the coast, declining banana production, and an earthquake that rocked the region in 1991 all sounded the death knell for the railroad. The earthquake was also a wake-up call for many here. The long lag time for aid to reach stricken areas symbolized the historic neglect for the region on the part of the central government. Development has been slower to reach this part of the country. (Telephones and electricity are still newfangled inventions in some smaller communities here.) As elsewhere in the country, communities now look to tourism to put *colones* in the coffers.

cabins—a few have air-conditioning, a rarity here—are scattered around the grounds. All have bright furnishings, and art posters hang on the walls. A bridge leads from the pool to the beach. ⊠ *2 km/1 mi north of town at end of Playa Negra Rd.* ☎ *755–0055* 🖶 *755–0321* ⊕ *www. hotelladiosa.net* ➪ *10 cabins* ⌂ *Restaurant, fans, pool, massage, bar; no a/c in some rooms* ⊟ *AE, DC, MC, V* ⬧ *BP.*

$ ▦ **Kelly Creek Hotel-Restaurante.** Owners from Madrid have created a wonderful budget option in this handsome wooden hotel on the creek bank across a short pedestrian bridge from the park entrance. Each of the four hardwood-finished guest rooms is big enough to sleep a small army and has two double beds. Owner Andrés de Alcalá barbecues meat and fresh fish on an open-air grill and also cooks paella and other Spanish specialties. Caiman come to the creek bank in search of snacks, and the monkeys, parrots, jungles, and beaches of the national park are just yards away, as is the lively center of Cahuita. ✉ *Next to park entrance* ☎ *755–0007* ⊕ *www.kellycreekhotel.com* ➥ *4 rooms* ⟁ *Restaurant, fans; no a/c, no room phones, no room TVs* ⊟ *AE, DC, MC, V.*

¢ 🖳**Alby Lodge.** You're right in town, but you'd never know it at this friendly lodging. Cabins with hardwood floors prop up on stilts and come complete with hot-water baths, log tables, mosquito nets, and a hammock on the front porch. Make use of the shared kitchen facilities and outdoor barbecue. The forested grounds and high thatched roof keep the temperature pleasantly bearable in otherwise balmy Cahuita. It's next to the park, so the howler monkeys are your morning alarm clock. ✉ *180 m west of national park entrance* ☎☎ *755–0031* ⊕ *www.albylodge. com* ➥ *4 cabins* ⟁ *Fans; no a/c, no room phones, no room TVs* ⊟ *No credit cards.*

### Nightlife

Other than two local bars, Cahuita's nightlife centers on restaurants, all pleasant places to linger over dinner for the evening. Lively reggae, soca, and samba blast weekend evenings from the turquoise **Coco's Bar** (✉ Main Rd.). The assemblage of dogs dozing on its veranda illustrates the rhythm of local life. **Ricky's Bar** (✉ Opposite corner from Coco's) is more subdued, quiet, and touristed than Coco's.

### To & From Cahuita
*44 km/26 mi (45 min) southeast of Limón.*

Autotransportes MEPE buses travel from San José four times a day, and hourly throughout the day from Limón and Puerto Viejo de Talamanca. Car travel is straightforward: watch for signs in Limón and head south on the coastal highway. Road conditions wax and wane with the severity of the previous year's rains, and with the speed with which highway crews patch the potholes. Cahuita has three entrances from the highway: the first takes you to the far north end of the Playa Negra road, near the Magellan Inn; the second, to the middle section of Playa Negra, near the Atlántida; and the third, to the tiny downtown.

The proximity of the Panamanian border means added police vigilance on the coastal highway. No matter what your mode of transport, expect a passport inspection and cursory vehicle search at a police checkpoint just north of Cahuita.

### Cahuita Essentials
🗂 Internet **Internet** ✉ 50 m east of Ricky's Bar ☎ 755-0435.
🗂 Post Office **Correos** ✉ East of police station.

## Cahuita National Park

❾ The only Costa Rican park jointly administered by the National Parks Service and a community, Parque Nacional Cahuita starts at the southern edge of the town of Cahuita. The park's rain forest extends right to the edge of its curving, utterly undeveloped 3-km (2-mi) white-sand beach. Roughly parallel to the coastline, a 7-km (4-mi) trail passes through the forest to Cahuita Point, encircled by a 2½-square-km (1½-square-mi) coral reef. The hike takes only a few hours, but you have to ford several rivers on the way, so check conditions beforehand, as they can be prohibitive in the rainy season.

There's good snorkeling off Cahuita Point—watch for blue parrot fish and angelfish as they weave their way among equally colorful species of coral, sponges, and seaweeds. Sadly, the coral reef is slowly being killed by sediment, intensified by deforestation and the erosive effects of a 1991 earthquake. ■ TIP→→ Use a local guide to find the best reefs (or to snorkel independently, swim out from the beach on the Puerto Vargas side), and don't snorkel for a few days after it rains, as the water is sure to be murky. You can take a ride in a glass-bottom boat from Cahuita; visibility is best in September and October. The road to the park headquarters at Puerto Vargas is 5 km (3 mi) south of Cahuita on the left. Here you find the ranger station as well as campsites that have been carved out of the jungle, scattered along the beachfront. ☎ 755–0461 Cahuita entrance, 755–0302 Puerto Vargas entrance ✉ By donation at Cahuita entrance; $7 at Puerto Vargas entrance ☉ Daily 6–5 Cahuita entrance; Daily 7–4 Puerto Vargas entrance.

## Outdoor Activities
Operators in Cahuita or Puerto Viejo de Talamanca can hook you up with excursions to and in the park, or you can go on your own, especially if you use the entrance at the south edge of the village.

BICYCLING  You can bike through Cahuita National Park, but the trail gets pretty muddy at times, and you run into logs, river estuaries, and other obstacles. Nevertheless, mountain bikes are a good way to get around on the dirt roads and trails surrounding Cahuita and Puerto Viejo de Talamanca. (The southern entrance to the park is close enough to Puerto Viejo that you could bike there just as easily as from Cahuita.) Cycling is easiest in the dry season, though many hardy souls are out during the long rainy season. Rent bikes in Cahuita or Puerto Viejo.

HIKING  A serious hiking trail extends as far as Puerto Vargas. If you're coming from Cahuita, you can take a bus or catch a ride into Puerto Vargas and hike back around the point in the course of a day. Be sure to bring plenty of water, food, and sunscreen. Along the trail you might spot howler and white-faced capuchin monkeys, coatis, armadillos, and raccoons.

SNORKELING  Cahuita's reefs are just one of several high-quality snorkeling spots in the region. Rent snorkeling gear in Cahuita or Puerto Viejo de Talamanca or through your hotel; most hotels also organize trips. It's wise to work with a guide, as the number of good snorkeling spots is limited and they're not always easily accessible. Cahuita established a community lifeguard team in 2002, unusual in Costa Rica. ⚠ As elsewhere up and down the Caribbean coast, the undertow poses risks for even experienced swimmers. Use extreme caution and never swim alone.

## To & From Cahuita National Park
*Just south of Cahuita.*

Choose from two park entrances: one is at the southern end of the village of Cahuita; the second is at Puerto Vargas, just off the main road,

## Reefs at Risk

CLOSE UP

**ONE OF THE MOST COMPLEX** organisms in the marine world, a coral reef is an extraordinary and extraordinarily delicate habitat. Coral reefs are the result of the symbiotic relationship between single-cell organisms called zooxanthellae and coral polyps. The zooxanthellae grow inside the cells of the polyps, producing oxygen and nutrients that are released into the coral tissues. Corals secrete calcium carbonate (limestone) that, over time, forms the vast coral reef "superstructure." Zooxanthellae require exposure to sunlight to thrive. The healthiest coral reefs are in clear, clean, tropical seawater at a temperature of 70 to 80°F (20 to 25°C). Healthy coral reefs are biologically rich gardens occupied by a diverse selection of life forms, from microscopic unicellular algae and phytoplankton to a wide range of fish.

Unfortunately, coral reefs in Costa Rica are in danger. Dirt and sediment from banana plantations and logging areas, as well as runoff from pesticide use, are killing them. The dirty runoff literally clogs the pores of the zooxanthellae and smothers them. In Golfo Dulce, 98% of one of the oldest reefs in Costa Rica has been destroyed by this sedimentation. The once-enormous reefs of Cahuita are almost entirely gone.

Human visitors, including careless snorkelers, have also damaged reefs. Just touching a reef damages it. When exploring a coral reef, look but don't touch, and snorkel only on its outer side, preferably in calm weather. Can the reefs be saved? With commitment and time, yes. Coral is resilient, and will grow back–if the Costa Rican government makes it a priority.

5 km (3 mi) south of town. If you don't have a car you can get there easily via bike or taxi.

## Puerto Viejo de Talamanca

⑩ This muddy, colorful little town has become one of the hottest spots on the international budget-travel circuit, and swarms with surfers, New Age hippies, beaded and spangled punks, would-be Rastafarians of all colors and descriptions, and wheelers and dealers—both pleasant and otherwise. Time was when most kids came here with only one thing on their mind: surfing. Today many seem to be looking for a party, with or without the surf.

But if alternative lifestyles aren't your bag, there are plenty of more "grown-up" offerings on the road heading southeast and northwest out of town. At last count, some 44 nationalities were represented in this tiny community, and most are united in concern for the environment and orderly development of tourism. (Few want to see the place become just another Costa Rican resort community.) Some locals bemoan the loss of their town's innocence, as drugs and other evils have surfaced, but only in small doses: this is still a fun town to visit, with a great variety of hotels, cabinas, and restaurants in every price range. Unlike other parts of Costa Rica, no one has been priced out of the market here.

Locals use "Puerto Viejo"—and they always drop the "de Talamanca" part—to refer to the village. You have access to the beach right in town, and the Salsa Brava, famed in surfers' circles for its pounding waves, is here off the coast, too. The best strands of Caribbean sand are outside the village: Playa Cocles, Playa Chiquita (technically a series of beaches), and Punta Uva, all dark sand, line the road heading southeast from town. Playa Negra—not the Playa Negra near Cahuita—is the black-sand beach northwest of town. Punta Uva, with fewer hotels and the farthest from the village, sees fewer crowds and more tranquillity. Playa Negra shares that distinction, too—for now—but developers have eyed the beach as the next area for expansion.

NAVIGATING PUERTO VIEJO DE TALAMANCA
You can manage the town center quite easily on foot, though it is dusty in the dry season and muddy when it rains. Everyone gets around via bike here, and seemingly everyone has one for rent. Quality varies widely. Expect to pay a $4–8 per day for a good bike. **Cabinas Grant** (⊠ 100 m south of bus stop ☎ 750–0292) has the best selection of quality bikes in town. Priority is given to guests at **Cabinas Casa Verde** (⊠ 200 m south and 200 m east of bus stop ☎ 750–0015), but there are usually enough bikes for you to rent one for a half- or full day even if you don't stay here. There are a couple of official red licensed cabs, but most taxi service here is informal, with private individuals providing rides. To be on the safe side, have your hotel or restaurant call one for you.

## Exploring

At the **Finca La Isla Botanical Garden** you can wander around a working tropical fruit, spice, and ornamental plant farm. Sloths abound, and you could see a few poison dart frogs. A $10 guided tour includes admission and a glass of the farm's homemade fruit juice. You get the fruit juice if you wander around on your own, too, and can purchase a $1 self-guide tour book in English, Spanish, French, or German. ⊠ ½ km/¼ mi west of town at Playa Negra ☎ 750–0046 ⊕ www.greencoast.com/garden.htm ☜ $5 ☉ Fri.–Mon. 10–4.

Cacao once ruled the Talamanca region, but few plantations are left these days. One friendly Swiss couple continues the tradition and gives you a **Chocolate Tour** of their working plantation. Follow the life cycle of this little-known crop, from cultivation to processing. There's sampling at the tour's conclusion. Call to reserve a tour (you need a minimum of four people) and to be picked up from the Playa Chiquita School. Since these folks are Swiss, they can tailor the commentary in German, French, or Italian, in addition to English or Spanish. ⊠ 6 km/4 mi southeast of town at Playa Chiquita ☎ 750–0075 ☜ $15/person ☉ Open for tours only.

Unlike most such establishments in Costa Rica, which are for show only, the working **Butterfly Garden** cultivates 60 to 80 species of butterflies, three of which are unique to the area, for shipment to similar facilities around the world. The knowledgeable staff provides guided tours with bilingual commentary. ⊠ 7 km/4½ mi southeast of town at Punta Uva ☎ 750–0086 ☜ $5 ☉ Daily 8–4.

# Puerto Viejo de Talamanca

CARIBBEAN SEA

REEF

REEF

TO
PLAYA COCLES, PLAYA CHIQUITA,
PUNTA UVA, MANZANILLO,
CHOCOLATE TOUR,
BUTTERFLY GARDEN →

Stanford's Disco

Jhonny's
Police
Mot Rocks Café
El Parquecito
Bambú
ATEC/Phones
Bar Maritza
Bus Stop
Post Office
Supermarket
Cabinas Grant

PUERTO VIEJO

Soccer Field

Bank

← TO PLAYA NEGRA,
BRIBRI, CAHUITA, LIMÓN,
FINCA LA ISLA
BOTANICAL GARDEN

TO
KISKADEE →

**KEY**
6 *Restaurants*
1 *Hotels*

0        1/8 mile
0        1/8 kilometer

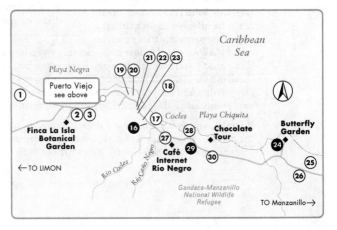

Caribbean Sea

Playa Negra

Puerto Viejo
see above

Finca La Isla
Botanical
Garden

← TO LIMON

Río Cocles

Río Cano Negro

Cocles

Playa Chiquita

Café
Internet
Río Negro

Chocolate
Tour

Butterfly
Garden

Gandaca-Manzanillo
National Wildlife
Refugee

TO Manzanillo →

## Outdoor Activities

As in Cahuita, tour operators and outfitters here can set up tours and activities anywhere on the south Caribbean coast.

Tours with **ATEC** (Association for Ecotourism and Conservation of Talamanca; ⊠ Across from Restaurant Tamara ☎☎ 750–0191 ⊕ www.greencoast.com/atec.htm) have an environmental or cultural bent, such as Afro-Caribbean or indigenous-culture walks—tours to the nearby Kekoldi indigenous reserve are especially popular—rain-forest hikes, coral-reef snorkeling trips, fishing trips, bird-watching tours, night walks, and adventure treks. Local organizations and wildlife refuges receive 15%–20% of ATEC's proceeds. Well-established operator **Terraventuras** (⊠ 100 m south of bus stop ☎ 750–0750 ⊕ www.terraventuras.com) can lead you around Puerto Viejo de Talamanca and Cahuita, or take you on excursions to Tortuguero, the Gandoca-Manzanillo Wildlife Refuge, and Bocas del Toro in Panama. It also rents good-quality surfboards, bicycles, boogie boards, and snorkeling gear.

RAFTING Rafting excursions lie about two hours away, but one San José–based outfitter has an office here. New kid on the block in Costa Rican rafting circles, ★ **Exploradores Outdoors** (⊠ Across from ATEC ☎ 750–0641 or 222–6262 ⊕ www.exploradoresoutdoors.com) is already highly regarded. It has day excursions on the Pacuare and Reventazén rivers, with a pickup point here or in San José, and the option to start in one place and be dropped off at the other.

SURFING Surfing is the name of the game in Puerto Viejo, for everyone from newbies to Kelly Slaters. The best conditions are late December through March, but there's action all year. Longtime surfers compare the south Caribbean to conditions found in Hawaii, but without the "who-do-you-think-you-are?" attitude. There are a number of breaks here, most famously **Salsa Brava**, which breaks fairly far offshore and requires maneuvering past some tricky currents

> **CAUTION**
>
> The conditions that make the Caribbean so popular among surfers spell danger for swimmers. Drownings occur each year. Strong riptides can pull you out to sea, even in waist-deep water, before you realize what's happening. Never swim alone in these parts—good advice anywhere.

and a shallow reef. Hollow and primarily right-breaking, Salsa Brava is one gnarly wave when it gets big. If it gets *too* big, or not big enough, check out the breaks at Punta Uva, Punta Cocles, or Playa Chiquita. Boogie-boarders and bodysurfers can also dig the beach-break waves at various points along this tantalizingly beautiful coast.

If you're, say, over 30, but have always wanted to try surfing, consider the friendly, three-hour $35 surf school at **Aventuras Bravas** (⊠ Across from Stanford's ☎ 849–7600). You start out with a small wave near the bus stop, and get a money-back guarantee that you'll be standing by the end of the lesson. You can also rent equipment here. A youthful surfing crowd staffs the small **Salsa Brava Surf Shop** (⊠ Next to Hotel Puerto Viejo ☎ 750–0668 ✍ salsabravasurfshop@hotmail.com), which rents, sells, and repairs surfboards and boogie boards.

## Where to Stay & Eat

★ **$–$$$** ✕ **Amimodo.** The name translates "my way, " and the exuberant Italian owners really do it their way, combining the cuisine of northern Italy, from where they came, with Caribbean flavors. Your antipasto might be classic bruschetta or *jamón de tiburón* (shark ham with avocado dressing). Or your ravioli might be stuffed with tropical shrimp, pineapple, and curry, with avocado sauce on the side. The tropical veranda with gingerbread trim spills over onto the beach with abundant greenery, and the restaurant is a popular gathering place for Puerto Viejo's Italian community. ⊠ *200 m east of Stanford's* ☎ *750–0257* ☱ *AE, DC, MC, V* ☉ *Closed Wed. No lunch weekdays.*

**$–$$** ✕ **Café Viejo.** This has fast become the hot place to see and be seen on Puerto Viejo's main drag. The owners, four brothers who learned to cook at the knee of their Italian grandmother back in Rimini, have concocted a menu, several pages long, of pizzas and handmade pastas. Recorded reggae and mambo music bops in the background. ⊠ *Across from ATEC* ☎ *750–0817* ☱ *AE, DC, MC, V* ☉ *Closed Tues., no lunch.*

**$–$$** ✕ **La Pecora Nera.** Though the name means "black sheep" in Italian, there's
**Fodor$Choice** nothing shameful about this thatch-roof roadside restaurant. There's al-
★ ways a lot more to choose from than what appears on the sparse-looking menu. Wait for owner/chef Ilario Giannoni to come out of the kitchen and triumphantly announce—with flair worthy of an Italian opera—which additional light Tuscan entrées, appetizers, and desserts they've concocted that day. Be prepared for a long, leisurely dining experience with attentive service. It's worth the wait; this is one of the country's top Italian restaurants. ⊠ *3 km/2 mi southeast of town at Playa Cocles* ☎ *750–0490* ☱ *No credit cards* ☉ *Closed Mon. Apr.–Nov.*

**$–$$** ✕ **Lotus Garden.** Sushi is hard to come by in Costa Rica, period, let alone way out here, and these folks do a good job with it, given the remoteness of the location. The open-air restaurant puts a Caribbean spin on Japanese cuisine, using local ingredients such as sushi-quality marlin whenever possible and, according to the owner, forever experimenting with new dishes. Try the Puerto Viejo roll, much like a California roll, but made with snapper and mango. The all-you-can-eat sushi bar ($14/person) draws crowds. Other Asian dishes, and tropical fruits, miso soup, fried rice, and a good selection of wines and sakes round out the menu. ⊠ *200 m east of Stanford's* ☎ *750–0232* ☱ *AE, DC, MC, V.*

**$** ✕ **Chile Rojo.** There's not a thing about the name or furnishings to reflect its Thai and Middle-Eastern offerings, and you might miss this hole-in-the-wall place driving by on Puerto Viejo's main street. Choose from Thai grilled tuna, falafel, hummus, and somosa. Sushi is available on Saturday. In deference to the town's European tourist trade, the restaurant accepts euros as payment too. ⊠ *Across from ATEC* ☎ *750–0025* ☱ *No credit cards.*

7

## Afro-Caribbean Heritage

COSTA RICA DOESN'T GET MORE diverse than its Caribbean region. Roughly a third of the people here are Afro-Caribbean, descendants of West Indians who arrived in the late 19th century to build the railroad and remained to work on banana and cacao plantations. Although Jamaicans brought some aspects of British colonial culture with them, such as cricket and the maypole dance, these habits have long since given way to reggae, salsa, and soccer, much to the chagrin of the older generation. The substantial East Asian population here also counts railroad workers as its ancestors, and small pockets of indigenous peoples have lived here since pre-Columbian times.

The Atlantic coast's long African-Caribbean heritage makes it the likeliest place in the country to find English-speakers, though residents will speak a Caribbean-accented English that may sound unfamiliar to you. "Okay" is a general all-purpose greeting heard on the coast, and is gradually replacing the older generation's traditional "Wha' happin!" (What's happening?) With Spanish now the language of instruction in all schools, young people here are less likely to speak English than their elders.

---

$ ✕ **El Loco Natural.** El Loco Natural epitomizes Puerto Viejo: lively, or-

Fodor'sChoice ganic, all the rage, but confident enough in itself to not have to be too

★ trendy. Ordering is by sauces: Thai peanut, Indonesian-Caribbean curry, Mexican chipotle, or Malaysian-guayaba curry. Then select vegetables, chicken, shrimp, or fish (marlin or tuna). Bar stools on the balcony face the street and let you survey the goings-on below. You'll be better able to converse with your fellow diners if you sit at the tables inside: live music gets going later on Thursday and Saturday evenings, and sometimes on Sundays, too. It's easy to miss its second-floor location above the Color Caribe souvenir shop. ⊠ *100 m south of bus stop* ☎ *750–0263* ▤ *No credit cards* ☼ *Closed Tues. and Wed. mid-Dec.–Apr. and July–Sept.; Closed Mon.–Wed. May–June and Oct.–mid-Dec.*

¢–$ ✕ **Restaurant Tamara.** Once upon a time, this two-story unpretentious place was the only restaurant in town. The Caribbean food is tasty and authentic: you can't lose with the chicken in Caribbean sauce or virtually any of the fresh fish dishes. In the nondescript indoor seating area you're cooled by a fan and entertained by TV; the outdoor seating area has a palpable Jamaican motif. ⊠ *Across from ATEC* ☎ *750–0148* ▤ *AE, MC, V.*

¢–$ ✕ **Selvin's.** An old standby at Punta Uva, Selvin's keeps limited hours, especially in the off-season, so head out here if you're fortunate enough to be in town when it's open. The owner, known to everyone in town as "Blanca," cooks up a menu of rondón, rice and beans, lobster, shrimp, and chicken with sweet mole sauce. This is one of the few places around that accepts traveler's checks as payment. ⊠ *7 km/4½ mi southeast of town at Punta Uva* ☎ *750–0664* ▤ *No credit cards* ☼ *Closed Mon. and Tues. Dec.–May and Mon.–Thurs. June–Nov.*

★ ¢  ✕ **Bread & Chocolate.** The take-away line for brownies forms at the gate before this place opens at 6:30 AM, but stick around and fortify yourself with a hearty breakfast of cinnamon-oatmeal pancakes, French toast, or creamy scrambled eggs, washed down with a cup of French-press coffee. Lunch gives way to jerk chicken, tomato hummus, and roasted red peppers. Everything is homemade, right down to the mayonnaise. This is the newest of the bakery-slash-breakfast-and-lunch cafés to open in town; the friendly, chatty owners who park their vegetable oil–powered vehicle out in front give this place the edge. ⊠ *50 m south of post office* ☎ *750–0051* ⊟ *No credit cards* ⊙ *Closed Mon. and Tues., No dinner. Breakfast served.*

¢  ✕ **La Casa del Pan.** The young owners at this tiny bakery whip up German-style breads. It's worth a stop if you're on the road between Puerto Viejo and the beaches. ⊠ *5 km/3 mi southeast of town at Playa Chiquita* ☎ *843–4552* ⊟ *No credit cards* ⊙ *Closed. Tues., no dinner. Breakfast served.*

¢  ✕ **Soda Miss Sam.** The front-porch is always full of diners, and Miss Sam has been dishing up hearty Caribbean cuisine for years, though she prefers not to divulge how many. She usually has rice and beans going, or can fix a casado with chicken, beef, pork, or fish and freshly squeezed fruit juices as accompaniment. ⊠ *300 m south, 200 m east of bus stop* ☎ *750–0108* ⊟ *No credit cards* ⊙ *Closed Sun.*

$$$  ▥ **Las Palmas Beach Hotel.** The closest thing the area has to a beach resort, the orange Las Palmas is a bit un–Puerto Viejo in that regard. But if relaxing poolside knowing that the beach lies a few steps away appeals to you, then this is the place. (And that beach is the tranquil Punta Uva.) Rooms, all with ocean views, have tile floors and bright floral-print spreads and drapes and congregate around the pool. Sliding glass doors that allow you to see out but not in afford a measure of privacy and lead onto individual terraces or balconies. ⊠ *9 km/5½ mi southeast of town at Punta Uva* ☎ *759–9090* 🖷 *759–9222* ⊕ *www.laspalmashotel.com* ⇌ *30 rooms, 5 suites* ⌂ *Restaurant, a/c, cable TV, fans, refrigerators, pool, whirlpool tub, horseback riding* ⊟ *AE, DC, MC, V* ▯ *EP.*

$$  ▥ **Cariblue Bungalows.** A youthful Italian who came here to surf years ago stayed on and built a lodging that combines refinement with that hip Puerto Viejo vibe in exactly the right proportions. Cariblue's finely crafted all-wooden bungalows are spaciously arrayed on the edge of the jungle, across the road from the splendid white-sand beaches of Punta Cocles. Cabinas are linked to the main ranch-style building by paths that meander through a gently sloping lawn shaded with enormous trees. Expansive verandas and beautiful bathroom-tile mosaics add an air of refinement; hammocks add an air of relaxation. Breakfasts are huge. ⊠ *2 km/1 mi southeast of town at Playa Cocles* ⌂ *Apdo. 51-7304, Puerto Viejo de Talamanca* ☎ *750–0035 or 750–0518* 🖷 *750–0057* ⊕ *www.cariblue.com* ⇌ *16 bungalows* ⌂ *Restaurant, fans, pool, whirlpool tub, massage, 2 bars, shop, laundry service; no room phones, no room TVs* ⊟ *AE, MC, V* ▯ *BP.*

FodorśChoice ★

★ $$  ▥ **Shawandha Lodge.** The service is personalized and friendly at Shawandha, whose spacious, beautifully designed bungalows are well back from the road at Playa Chiquita. The thatch-roof bungalows have elegant hardwoods, four-poster beds, and verandas with hammocks. Each bathroom has a unique and beautiful tile mosaic. The hearty breakfast starts off with an impressive fruit plate. A white-sand beach lies 180 meters away, across the road. Even if you don't stay here, stop by and enjoy a distinctive French-Caribbean dinner in the open-air restaurant. ⊠ *6 km /4 mi southeast of town at Playa Chiquita* ☎ *750–0018* ⊟ *750–0037* ⊕ *www.shawandhalodge.com* ⇨ *12 bungalows* ⅃ *Restaurant, fans, in-room safes, bar, laundry service; no a/c, no room phones, no room TVs* ⊟ *AE, DC, MC, V* ⅃⊙⅃ *BP.*

$–$$ 🖳 **El Pizote Lodge.** El Pizote observes local architectural mores while offering more than most in the way of amenities. All standard rooms have polished wood paneling, reading lamps, mirrors, and firm beds. Each of the two-room bungalows sleeps six. The restaurant serves breakfast, dinner, and drinks all day. Guanábana and papaya grow on the grounds, and hiking trails lead off into the jungle. Tranquil Playa Negra is just across the road. ⊠ *300 m before entrance to town at Playa Negra* ⅃ *Apdo. 1371–1000, San José* ☎ *750–0088 or 750–0227* ⊟ *750–0226* ⅃ *pizotelg@hotmail.com* ⇨ *24 bungalows* ⅃ *Restaurant, fans, pool, bar, laundry service; no a/c in some rooms, no room phones, no room TVs* ⊟ *V.*

$–$$ 🖳 **Jordan's Jacuzzi Suites.** As befits the name of the place, each of the three suites here—and more are being constructed at this writing—contains its own whirlpool tub. What's atypical of Puerto Viejo is the use of Japanese styling in each large unit, with statuary, fabric, and local woods used throughout, as well a four-poster king-size bed and air-conditioning. The suites bear the names "Shogun," "Samurai," and "Geisha." ⊠ *200 m east of Stanford's* ☎ *750–0232* ⇨ *3 suites* ⅃ *Restaurant, a/c, fans, kitchenettes, whirlpool tubs; no room phones, no room TVs* ⊟ *AE, DC, MC, V.*

$–$$ 🖳 **Villas del Caribe.** Right on the beach north of Punta Uva, these multiroom villas are commodious and comfortable, if somewhat pedestrian in design. Each has a blue-tile kitchen, a small sitting room with low-slung couches, a plant-filled bathroom, and a patio with hammock and excellent views of the beach. Upstairs are one or two spacious bedrooms with a wooden deck. ⊠ *4 km /2½ mi southeast of town at Playa Chiquita* ☎ *750–0202, 233–2200 in San José* ⊟ *750–0203, 221–2801 in San José* ⊕ *www.villascaribe.net* ⇨ *12 villas* ⅃ *Restaurant, fans, kitchenettes, beach; no a/c, no room phones, no room TVs* ⊟ *AE, DC, MC, V* ⅃⊙⅃ *BP.*

$ 🖳 **Azania.** Eight thatch-roof, A-frame bungalows spread around Azania's ample gardens, and sleep four. The first floor contains a queen-size bed, and a ladder leads to the second floor with a pair of single beds. Much-appreciated mosquito netting covers all of them. You'll luxuriate in the semi-open shower in the blue-tile bathrooms. Meals are served in the rancho dining area next to the free-form pool. ⊠ *1.5 km/1 mi southeast of town at Playa Cocles* ☎ *750–0540* ⊟ *750–0371* ⊕ *www.azania-costarica.com* ⇨ *8 bungalows* ⅃ *Restaurant, fans, refrigerators, whirlpool tub, pool, bar; no a/c, no room phones, no room TV* ⊟ *AE, DC, MC, V* ⅃⊙⅃ *BP.*

**$**   **Cabinas Casa Verde.** If you've graduated from your backpacker days
**Fodor'sChoice** and are a bit more flush with cash but still want to be near the action,
★   this old standby on a quiet street a couple of blocks from the center of
town is ideal. The comfortable cabinas are decorated with an interesting variety of touches such as shell mobiles, watercolor frescoes, and
indigenous tapestries. And yet, overall, rooms have a neat-as-a-pin quality. Exotic birds flutter constantly through the lush plantings that screen
the cabinas from the street. The place is immensely popular, since the
price is low and it's clean and well run; reserve well in advance. ⊠ *200
m south and 200 m east of bus stop* ☎ *750–0015* 🖶 *750–0047* ⊕ *www.
cabinascasaverde.com* 🖃 *Apdo. 37–7304, Puerto Viejo de Talamanca*
🛏 *17 rooms, 9 with bath* ☾ *Cafeteria, fans, some refrigerators, massage, bicycles, laundry service; no room phones, no room TVs* ⊟ *AE,
MC, V* ⦿ *EP.*

**$**   **Casa Camarona.** Though half the rooms have air-conditioning at this
secluded lodging, you hardly need it. The abundant shade and sea
breezes keep the rooms delightfully cool. All the spacious, wooden, rustic rooms front the ocean—the second-story rooms have the best view—
and have two double beds. Meals are served at the seaside Caribbean
restaurant. ⊠ *3 km/2 mi south of town at Playa Cocles* 🖃 *Apdo.
2070–1002, San José* ☎ *750–0151 or 283–6711* 🖶 *750–0210 or
222–6184* ⊕ *www.casacamarona.co.cr* 🛏 *18 rooms* ☾ *Restaurant,
fans, bar, laundry facilities, no-smoking rooms; no a/c in some rooms,
no room phones, no room TVs* ⊟ *AE, DC, MC, V* ⦿ *CP.*

**$**   **Escape Caribeño.** Wonderfully friendly Italian owners Gloria and
Mauro Marchiori are what make this place: they treat you like family.
A dozen immaculate hardwood bungalows line a pleasant garden area
amply populated with hummingbirds, just outside of town. All cabins
have hammocks, mosquito nets, double beds, and even a bunk bed or
two for larger groups. Across the road lie two stucco cabins in a wooded
area on the beach, both with kitchenette. Breakfast is served in a thatch-
roof dining area in the center of the garden. ⊠ *400 m southeast of Stanford's* 🖶 *750–0103* ⊕ *www.escapecaribeno.com* 🛏 *14 cabins* ☾ *Fans,
in-room safes, some kitchenettes; no a/c in some rooms, no room phones,
no room TVs* ⊟ *AE, DC, MC, V.*

**$**   **Hotel La Perla Negra.** The owners' previous experience as designers
is evident in the fine construction of this handsome, two-story wooden
structure across a tiny dirt road near the end of Playa Negra. All rooms
have balconies, half with ocean views, half with jungle views. The three-
meal restaurant features grilled meats and fish. Between the building and
the beach is a spacious, inviting pool. ⊠ *Playa Negra, 1 km/½ mi north
of Puerto Viejo* ☎ *750–0111* 🖶 *750–0114* ⊕ *www.perlanegra-
beachresort.com* 🛏 *24 rooms, 1 apartment* ☾ *Restaurant, fans, pool,
kayaking, bar, laundry service; no a/c in some rooms, no room phones,
no room TVs* ⊟ *AE, MC, V* ⦿ *CP.*

**$**   **La Costa de Papito.** Papito's raised cabins are deep in the property's
wooded grounds and furnished with whimsical bright tropical-blue and
zebra-stripe prints. Breakfast is served at the table and chairs on your
porch, which has a hammock or swing chair. ⊠ *2 km/1 mi southeast
of town at Playa Cocles* 🖶 *750–0080* ⊕ *www.lacostadepapito.com*

7

🛏 *10 cabins ⚐ Restaurant, fans, massage, spa, bicycles, kayaking; no room phones, no room TVs* ☰ *AE, DC, MC, V.*

**$** 🏠 **Pachamama.** So cool and shady is this place set within the confines of the Gandoca-Manzanillo Wildlife Refuge that the owners took out the ceiling fans. No one ever needed them. Though still within sight of the Puerto Viejo–Manzanillo road, Pachamama delivers a get-away-from-it-all nature experience at a fraction of the cost of other Costa Rican eco-lodges. Cozy wood cabins are simply furnished with two beds and mosquito netting and colorful spreads and drapes. A house

> ### A BAD RAP
>
> The Caribbean has a reputation among Costa Ricans for being crime-ridden, mainly because of a few high-profile cases here years ago, the nearness of the Panamanian border, and the fact that this is an impoverished region compared to other parts of the country. In actuality, the problem is no better or worse here than elsewhere. Just take the standard precautions you would when you travel anywhere and stick to well-traveled tourist paths.

can be rented by the week or month. Personal touches such as breakfast brought to the porch of your cabin are standard. ✉ *9 km/5½ mi southeast of town at Punta Uva* ☎ *759–9196* ⊕ *www.greencoast.com/pachamama.htm* 🛏 *2 bungalows, 1 house ⚐ Bicycles, kayaking, laundry service; no a/c, no room phones, no room TVs* ☰ *No credit cards* ⫶◯⫶ *BP.*

**$** 🏠 **Totem.** Each of the tropical-blue units contains a living room and bedroom with bamboo furnishings, a queen bed, and bunks. We like the two rooms on the upper balcony with stupendous ocean views, and overlooking the gurgling, fountain-fed pool. The restaurant serves Italian food, but you'll have to be content without wine. (There's no liquor license.) ✉ *1½ km/1 mi southeast of town at Playa Cocles* ☎ *750–0758* 📠 *750–0825* 🛏 *6 cabinas ⚐ Restaurant, fans, cable TV, pool, bar, Internet; no a/c in some rooms,* ☰ *AE, DC, MC, V* ⫶◯⫶ *BP.*

**$** 🏠 **Yaré Hotel.** The sound of the jungle is overpowering, especially at night, as you relax in your brightly pastel-painted Yaré cabina. All rooms have hot water and verandas with hammocks. The restaurant is open for breakfast, lunch, and dinner. ✉ *3½ km/2 mi southeast of town at Playa Cocles* ✒ *Apdo. 117–1007, San José* ☎ *750–0420* 📠 *750–0106* ⊕ *www.hotelyare.com* 🛏 *22 rooms ⚐ Restaurant, fans, some kitchenettes, refrigerators, laundry service; no room phones, no room TVs* ☰ *AE, DC, MC, V* ⫶◯⫶ *CP.*

**¢–$** 🏠 **Agapi.** Agapi means "love" in Greek, and Costa Rican–Greek owners Cecilia and Tasso lovingly watch over their guests with some of the most attentive service around. Seven furnished apartments overlook the beach and come complete with fully equipped kitchen, hot-water bath, hammock, mosquito nets over the beds, and private balcony. An additional six rooms have two full-size beds each, and all have an ocean view. A common area in the back contains a beachside barbecue. ✉ *1 km/½ mi southeast of Stanford's* ☎ *750–0446* 📠 *750–0418* ⊕ *www.agapisite.com* 🛏 *6 rooms, 7 apartments ⚐ Fans, some kitchens; no a/c, no room phones, no TV in some rooms* ☰ *AE, MC, V* ⫶◯⫶ *EP.*

¢–$ 🛏 **Kaya's Place.** Rooms range from the upper-level half-dozen with shared cold-water bath to the sumptuous garden-view rooms at the back at this place at Playa Negra just outside of town. The friendly, environmentally conscious owners also have a meditation room in the back. All rooms make maximum use of ironwood, nispero, and blackwood construction and furnishings. The irregular shapes take advantage of every inch of wood, to keep things in as natural a state as possible. Few of the railings and room corners follow straight lines or 90-degree angles. ⊠ *200 m north of town at Playa Negra* 🕾 *750–0690* 🖷 *750–0713* ⊕ *www.kayasplace.com* 🛏 *20 rooms, 14 with bath* ⌂ *Restaurant, fans, bar, bicycles, massage, laundry service; no a/c, no room phones, no room TVs* ▭ *AE, DC, MC, V.*

¢ 🛏 **Coco Loco Lodge.** The cool, forested grounds here lie close to the center of town but seem so far away. The Austrian owners lavish you with lots of personal attention. The bungalows on stilts are simply furnished but contain hot-water baths, mosquito nets over the beds (you'll need them), and hammocks on the porch. There's also one fully furnished house available for short- or long-term rental. Great coffee is included in the room rate; a huge buffet breakfast is extra. ⊠ *180 m south of bridge at entrance to town* 🕾🕾 *750–0281* ⊕ *www.cocolocolodge.com* 🛏 *5 cabins, 1 house* ⌂ *Fans; no a/c, no room phones, no room TVs* ▭ *MC, V.*

¢ 🛏 **Hotel Pura Vida.** The friendly owners help make this the nicest of the lowest-end budget lodgings in the center of town. Rooms are basic, but clean, bright, and well ventilated and arranged around a center patio. Guests have use of the shared kitchen. ⊠ *270 m south of bus stop* 🕾 *750–0002* 🖷 *750–0296* 🛏 *10 rooms, 3 with bath* ⌂ *Fans; no a/c, no room phones, no room TVs* ▭ *AE, MC, V.*

## Nightlife

The distinction between dining spot and nightspot blurs as the evening progresses, with many restaurants becoming pleasant places to linger over dinner. Bars each have their special nights for live music. The town's main drag between El Loco Natural and Salsa Brava is packed with pedestrians, bicycles, and a few cars most evenings, with the block between Café Viejo and El Parquecito getting the most action. Wander around; something is bound to entice you in. ■ TIP➔➔ When out after dark, ask a staff member at the restaurant, bar, or club to call you a taxi at the end of the night.

BARS  Play billiards, and chow down on pizza or sandwiches at **El Dorado** (⊠ Across from ATEC), a much quieter alternative to the noisier bars. **Maritza Bar** (⊠ 50 m east of bus stop) is frequented by locals, and has live music on Sunday night. **Oasis Tropical** (⊠ Across from Stanford's) is little more than a big green awning under which you'll find a *típico* restaurant with a karaoke machine. Tex-Mex appetizers and all types of cocktails are the draw at **Sunset Tapas Bar** (⊠ On beach near bus stop), a block off the main drag. You can watch U.S. football on television during the season.

DANCE CLUBS  Ticos come from miles around for the Friday and Monday reggae nights at **Bambú** (⊠ Next to Jhonny's), but the place is closed most other

CLOSE UP

## A Province Apart

**THE CAPITAL'S HISTORIC NEGLECT** of this region has given rise to an "us vs. them" outlook among the people here. It extends to the tourism industry as well, with laments that the Instituto Costarricense de Turismo (Costa Rican Tourism Institute, or ICT) would rather promote the sunnier Pacific coast to international markets. Some here charge that subtle racism is at play. (Memories of early-20th-century government racial policies that segregated this region still remain.) The San José press doesn't help matters by splashing stories of crime in the Caribbean on front pages while giving little attention to comparable problems in Jacó, Tamarindo, or the capital. Any racial issues that *do* exist in Costa Rica—and that analysis goes way beyond the scope of this book—pale in comparison to those of many other countries. And the true cause for the Caribbean's lighter tourism may be as non-sociological as the weather: the fact remains that it's rainier here than elsewhere in the country; it's just not the typical fun-in-the-sun mass-tourist destination. And it's exactly that road-less-traveled aspect of the Caribbean and its unique ethnic make-up that makes the region worth visiting.

evenings. **Jhonny's Place** (⊠ 230 m east of bus stop) has nights variously devoted to reggae, jazz, R&B, and hip-hop. The dancing usually gets started after 11 PM. **Stanford's Disco** (⊠ 100 m from the town center on the road to Manzanillo) is the place to merengue or salsa the weekend nights away.

LIVE MUSIC    Caribbean and Italian restaurant **El Parquecito** (⊠ 50 m east of ATEC) pulls live-music duty Tuesday, Friday, and Saturday evenings. You're bound to hear "No, Woman, No Cry" and all the other reggae anthems. Second-floor organic-food restaurant **El Loco Natural** (⊠ 150 m west of ATEC ☎ 750–0263) has live music Thursday and Saturday evenings, and some Sundays.

### Shopping
Vendors set up stands at night on the beach road near El Parquecito, with jewelry being the prime fare. But the town counts a few honest-to-goodness souvenir stores, too.

**Calor Caribe** (⊠ Across from ATEC) is a small, standard souvenir shop with wood carvings, masks, coffee, and banana-paper products.

★   Puerto Viejo's best shop, **Luluberlu** (⊠ 200 m south and 50 m east of bus stop), sells a wonderful selection of local indigenous carvings—balsa and *chonta* wood are especially popular—and jewelry, paintings, and ceramics by 30 artists from the region. And those elaborate lamps really do collapse for easy transport in your carry-on luggage.

### To & From Puerto Viejo de Talamanca
*16 km/10 mi (15 minutes) south of Cahuita.*

The turnoff to Puerto Viejo de Talamanca is 10 km (6 mi) down the coastal highway south of Cahuita. (The highway itself continues south to Bribrí and Sixaola at the Panamanian border.) The village lies another 5 km (3 mi) beyond the turnoff. The paved road passes through town and continues to Playas Cocles and Chiquita and Punta Uva before the pavement peters out at the entrance to the village of Manzanillo. Autotransportes MEPE buses travel from San José four times a day, and hourly throughout the day from Limón and Cahuita. All buses from San José go into Puerto Viejo de Talamanca; most, but not all Limón-originating buses do as well, but a couple drop you off on the highway. Check if you board in Limón.

A scant three buses per day ply the 15-km (9 mi) paved road between Puerto Viejo and Manzanillo, so unless your schedule meshes exactly with theirs, you're better off biking or taking a taxi to and from the far-flung beaches along the way. Taxis charge $5 to Playas Cocles and Chiquita (as well as north to Playa Negra), $6 to Punta Uva, and $10 to Manzanillo.

### Puerto Viejo de Talamanca Essentials

🏧 Bank/ATM **Banco de Costa Rica** ⊠ 50 m south of bridge at entrance to town ☞ Visa only.

🏧 Pharmacy **Farmacia Amiga** ⊠ Next to Banco de Costa Rica ☎ 750-0698.

🏧 Internet **ATEC** ⊠ Across from Restaurant Tamara ☎ 750-0398. **Café Internet Río Negro** ⊠ Playa Cocles, 4 km/2½ mi southeast of town ☎ 750-0801. **El Tesoro** ⊠ Playa Cocles ☎ 750-0128.

🏧 Post Office **Correos** ⊠ 50 m west of ATEC.

🏧 Visitor Information **ATEC** ⊠ Across from Restaurant Tamara ☎☎ 750-0191 ⊕ www.greencoast.com/atec.htm.

## Gandoca-Manzanillo National Wildlife Refuge

⑪ The Refugio Nacional de Vida Silvestre Gandoca-Manzanillo stretches along the southeastern coast from the town of Manzanillo to the Panamanian border. Because of weak laws governing the conservation of refuges and the value of coastal land in this area, Gandoca-Manzanillo is less pristine than Cahuita National Park and continues to be developed. However, the refuge still has plenty of rain forest, *orey* (a dark tropical wood) and Jolillo swamps, 10 km (6 mi) of beach where four species of turtles lay their eggs, and almost 3 square km (1 square mi) of *cativo* (a tropical hardwood) forest and coral reef. The Gandoca estuary is a nursery for tarpon and a wallowing spot for crocodiles and caimans.

The easiest way to explore the refuge is to hike along the coast south of Manzanillo. You can hike back out the way you came in, or arrange (in Puerto Viejo de Talamanca) to have a boat pick you up at Punta Mono (Monkey Point), a three- to four-hour walk from Manzanillo, where you find secluded beaches hidden by tall cliffs of fossilized coral. The mangroves of Gandoca, with abundant caimans, iguanas, and waterfowl, lie six to eight hours away. Park administrators can tell you more and recommend a local guide; inquire when you enter Manzanillo village and the locals will point you toward them. ☎ *750–0398 (ATEC)* ⊕ *Daily 7–4.*

## Outdoor Activities

A guide can help you get the most out of this relatively unexplored corner of the country. The **Association of Naturalist Guides of Manzanillo** (✉ Main Rd. ☎ 759–9064 or 843–9122 ✎ guiasmant@yahoo.com.mx) is consortium of quality, knowledgeable local guides who know the area well and lead a variety of half- and full-day tours. They can take you for a hike in the reserve or out to Monkey Point, with a return trip by boat. They also have horseback riding, bird-, dolphin-, and turtle-watching, and traditional fishing excursions.

DIVING AND SNORKELING

The friendly staff at **Aquamor Adventures** (✉ Main Rd. ☎ 759–9012 ⊕ www.greencoast.com/aquamor2.htm) specializes in land- and ocean-focused tours of the Gandoca-Manzanillo Wildlife Refuge, and can tend to all your water-sporting needs in these parts, with guided kayaking, snorkeling, and scuba-diving tours, as well as equipment rental. They also offer the complete sequence of PADI-certified diving courses. Companies in Puerto Viejo de Talamanca (⇨ *above*) can arrange boat trips to dive spots and beaches in the refuge as well.

DOLPHIN WATCHING

The **Talamanca Dolphin Foundation** (✉ Main road, Manzanillo ☎ 759–9012 ⊕ www.dolphinlink.org) has 2½-hour dolphin observation tours—excellent opportunities to see bottlenose, *tucuxi* (gray), and Atlantic spotted dolphins swimming this section of the coast.

## Where to Stay & Eat

¢–$$ ✕ **Restaurant Maxi's.** Cooled by sea breezes and shaded by tall, stately palms, this two-story, brightly painted wooden building offers weary travelers cold beer, potent cocktails, and great seafood at unbeatable prices after a day's hike in the refuge. Locals and expatriates alike—and even chefs from Puerto Viejo's fancier restaurants—come here for their lobster fix, and the fresh fish is wonderful, too, and now that the road is paved all the way to Manzanillo, the weekend crowds are getting ever larger. Locals tend to congregate in the rowdy but pleasant downstairs bar, where reggae beats into the wee hours. ✉ *Main road, Manzanillo* ☎ *759–9073* ▭ *No credit cards.*

$$$ ▨ **Almonds & Corals Tent Lodge Camp.** Buried in a dark, densely atmospheric beachfront jungle within the Gandoca-Manzanillo Wildlife Refuge, Almonds & Corals takes tent camping to a new level. The "campsites" are freestanding platforms raised on stilts and linked by boardwalks lighted by kerosene lamps. Each safari-style tent is protected by a peaked roof, enclosed in mosquito netting, and has beds, electric lamps, hammocks, and hot water. A fine three-meal restaurant is tucked into the greenery halfway down to the property's exquisite, secluded beach. Rustic camping this is not, but the locale does provide that close-to-nature experience. Your wake-up call is provided by howler monkeys and chatty parrots. ✉ *Near end of road to Manzanillo* ☎ *759–9056 or 272–2024* 🖶 *272–2220* ⊕ *www.almondsandcorals.com* ✉ *Apdo. 681–2300, San José* 🛏 *25 tent-cabins* ⟋ *Restaurant, fans, whirlpool tub, bar, laundry service, airport shuttle; no a/c, no room phones, no room TVs* ▭ *AE, MC, V* ▯ *MAP.*

¢ ▨ **Cabinas Something Different.** On a quiet street, these shiny, spic-and-span motel-style cabinas are the nicest option in the village of Manzanillo.

Each bright tile-floor unit comes with a TV—quite a rarity in these parts—a table, and a small porch. Several sleep up to four people. ✉ *180 m south of Aquamor, Manzanillo* ☎ *759–9014 or 826–9473* 🖨 *759–9097* 🛏 *18 cabins* ⚲ *Fans, refrigerators, cable TV no a/c in some rooms, no room phones* ⊟ *No credit cards* ⬭ *EP.*

## To & From Gandoca-Manzanillo National Wildlife Refuge
*15 km/9 mi (20 minutes) southeast of Puerto Viejo.*

The road from Puerto Viejo de Talamanca ends at the entrance to the village of Manzanillo. Just three buses each day—morning, midday, and late afternoon—connect the two. All taxi drivers in Puerto Viejo charge $10 for the trip here.

## Crossing into Panama via Sixaola

Costa Rica's sleepy border post at Sixaola fronts Guabito, Panama's equally quiet border crossing, 44 km (26 mi) south of the turnoff to Puerto Viejo de Talamanca. Both are merely collections of banana-plantation stilt houses and a few stores and bars; neither has any lodging or dining options, but this a much more low-key crossing into Panama than the busy border post at Paso Canoas on the Inter-American Highway near the Pacific coast. If you've come this far, you're likely headed to **Bocas del Toro,** the real attraction in the northwestern part of Panama. This archipelago of 68 islands continues the Afro-Caribbean and indigenous themes seen on Costa Rica's Atlantic coast, and offers diving, snorkeling, swimming, and wildlife viewing. The larger islands are home to a growing selection of hotels and restaurants, everything from funky to fabulous. Bocas has acquired a cult following among long-term foreign visitors to Costa Rica, who find it a convenient place to travel when their permitted three-month status as a tourist has expired, since a quick 72-hour jaunt out of the country gets you another three months in Costa Rica.

**WORD OF MOUTH**

"There is a place on the Sixaola River where you can have a boatman take you across to Chase, Panama, for a minimal fee—if you are interested in saying you've been to Panama! We thought that was kind of cool."

–shillmac

■ TIP➜➜ Whatever your destination in Panama, come armed with dollars. Panama uses U.S. currency, but refers to the dollar as the *balboa*. (It does mint its own coins, all the same size as their U.S. counterparts.) No one anywhere will accept or exchange your Costa Rican colones.

Costa Rican rental vehicles may not leave the country, so crossing into Panama as a tourist is an option only via public transportation. The bus route from San José to Cahuita and Puerto Viejo de Talamanca terminates here at the border approximately six hours after leaving the capital. Disembark and head for the Costa Rican immigration office down a flight of stairs from the west end of a former railroad bridge. Officials place an exit stamp in your passport, after which you walk across the bridge and present your passport to Panamanian immigration. U.S., U.K., and Canadian visitors must also purchase a $5 tourist card for entry into the country; Australian and New Zealand citizens need only their passports. The **Consulate of Panama** (☎ 281–2103) in San José can provide more information. The border crossings are open 7 AM–5 PM (8 AM–6 PM Panamanian time) daily. Set your watch one hour ahead when you enter Panama.

Taxis wait on the Panamanian side to transport you to the small city of Changuinola, the first community of any size inside the country, from which there are bus and air connections for travel farther into Panama. Taxis can also take you to Almirante, where you'll find boat launches to Bocas del Toro.

# THE CARIBBEAN ESSENTIALS

## Transportation

### BY AIR

ARRIVING & DEPARTING You can fly from San José to the airstrip in either Tortuguero (TTQ) or Barra del Colorado (BCL) via NatureAir or SANSA. At this writing, NatureAir is scheduled to begin landing at the small airport just south of Limón (LIO), with continuing service to Bocas del Toro, Panama. For more information about air travel between the Caribbean and San José, *see* Air Travel *in* Smart Travel Tips A to Z.)

### BY BUS

ARRIVING & DEPARTING The transport companies serving this part of the country provide reliable service. Buses to Limón and Guápiles use London-style double-decker vehicles on many of the runs. Autotransportes MEPE, which has a lock on bus service to the south Caribbean coast, has a reputation for being lackadaisical, but is really quite dependable. Drivers and ticket sellers are accustomed to dealing with foreigners; even if their English is limited, they'll figure out what you want. Bus fares to this region are reasonable. From San José, expect to pay $1.50 to Guápiles, $2.50 to Limón, $5 to Cahuita, $6 to Puerto Viejo de Talamanca, and $7 to Sixaola and the Panamanian border.

All bus service to this part of the country must take alternate routes on those occasions when heavy rains and landslides close the highway through Braulio Carrillo National Park north of San José. The detour passes through Cartago, Paraíso, and Turrialba and rejoins the Caribbean highway at Siquirres. It can add anywhere from one to three hours to your journey. Check before you set out if you travel during the worst of the rainy season.

For more information about bus travel between the Caribbean and San José, *see* Bus Travel *in* Smart Travel Tips A to Z.)

GETTING AROUND Buses from San José stop first in Cahuita, then Puerto Viejo de Talamanca before heading to Sixaola. Many buses originate in Limón, traveling to points south. It's the most cost-efficient way to travel.

### BY CAR

The paved two-lane Guápiles Highway continues from Santa Clara southeast to Guápiles, EARTH, Siquirres, and Limón, a total distance from San José to the coast of about 160 km (100 mi). South of Limón, a paved road covers the roughly 40 km (25 mi) to Cahuita, then passes the Cahuita turnoff and proceeds for roughly 16 km (10 mi) toward Puerto Viejo de Talamanca. It is paved as far as the village of Manzanillo. Four-wheel drive is always preferable, but the major roads in this region are generally passable by any car. Just watch for potholes and unpaved sections—they can appear on any road at any time, without marking or warning. The heavier the previous year's rainy season has been, the deeper the *huecos* (potholes, in Costa Rican vernacular). One-lane bridges appear frequently south of Limón. If the triangular CEDA EL PASO sign faces you, yield first to oncoming traffic.

Road travel to and from this part of the country occasionally becomes more complicated when heavy rains cause landslides blocking the highway near the Zurquí Tunnel in Braulio Carrillo National Park just north of San José. The alternate route is a long, slow journey via Cartago, Paraíso, and Turrialba, rejoining the main route at Siquirres. Check before you set out when traveling during the heaviest of the rainy season.

You cannot drive to Tortuguero or Barra del Colorado; you must fly or take a boat.

■ TIP→→ Several gas stations flank the highway between Guápiles and Limón. South of Limón you'll find just one, Penshurt, north of Cahuita. Fill the tank when you get the chance.

There are no rental agencies in this region. Rent in San José.

### BY SHUTTLE VAN

If you prefer a more private form of travel, consider taking a shuttle. Gray Line Tourist Bus has daily service that departs from many San José hotels at 7 AM for Cahuita and Puerto Viejo de Talamanca. Comfortable air-conditioned Interbus vans depart from San José hotels daily at 10 AM for Guápiles, Siquirres, Limón, Cahuita, and Puerto Viejo de Talamanca. Reserve tickets ($25) a day in advance.

🄵 Shuttle Van Services **Gray Line Tourist Bus** ☎ 232–3681 or 220–2126 ⊕ www.graylinecostarica.com. **Interbus** ☎ 283–5573 ⊕ www.interbusonline.com.

## Contacts & Resources

Banks, internet cafés, post offices, and emergency contacts are listed at the end of each town entry.

### BANKS & EXCHANGING SERVICES

Most larger tourist establishments are prepared to handle credit cards. Banks are sparse in this region. Changing U.S. dollars or traveler's checks is possible at the few offices of Banco Nacional, but lines are long. The Scotiabank and BAC San José in downtown Limón have ATMs that accept Plus- and Cirrus-affiliated cards. The Banco de Costa Rica's

ATM in Puerto Viejo de Talamanca accepts only Plus cards. You're best off taking care of getting cash with your ATM card back in San José before venturing here.

## INTERNET

There are public computers for Internet use in Cahuita, Guápiles, Limón, Puerto Viejo de Talamanca, and Tortuguero. Expect to pay $2–$3 per hour. Connection times are slower in this part of the country than in San José.

## MAIL & SHIPPING

The privatized Correos de Costa Rica provides reasonable postal service from this part of the country, but your best bet is to wait and mail letters and cards from San José. DHL and UPS have offices in Limón for express shipping of packages.

# UNDERSTANDING
# COSTA RICA

Costa Rica at a Glance

A Brief History

Books, Movies & Television

Wildlife & Plant Glossary

Menu Guide

Vocabulary

# COSTA RICA AT A GLANCE

## Fast Facts

**Capital:** San José
**Type of government:** Democratic republic
**Independence:** September 15, 1821 (from Spain)
**Population:** 4,016,173
**Population density:** 79 persons per square km (204 persons per square mi)
**Literacy:** 96%

**Language:** Spanish (official); English spoken by most in the tourism industry
**Ethnic groups:** White (including mestizo) 94%, black 3%, Amerindian 1%, Asian 1%, other 1%
**Religion:** Roman Catholic 76%, Evangelical Protestant 14%, other 6%, none 4%

## Geography & Environment

**Land area:** 52,400 square km (21,000 square mi; approximately the size of the U.S. state of West Virginia)
**Coastline:** 1,290 km (802 mi)
**Terrain:** Rugged central range with 112 volcanic craters that separates the eastern and western coastal plains
**Natural resources:** Hydroelectric power, forest products, fisheries products
**Natural hazards:** Droughts, flash floods, thunderstorms, earthquakes, hurricanes, landslides

**Flora:** 9,000 species, including 1,200 orchid species and 800 fern species; tidal mangrove swamps, tropical rain forest, subalpine forest
**Fauna:** 36,518 species, including 34,000 species of insects and 2,000 species of butterflies
**Environmental issues:** Deforestation, rapid industrialization and urbanization, air and water pollution, soil degradation, plastic waste

## Economy

**Currency:** Colón, (*pl.*) colones
**GDP:** $35.34 billion
**Per capita income:** $4,280
**Unemployment:** 6.7%
**Major industries:** Tourism, microprocessors, food processing, textiles and clothing, construction materials, fertilizer, plastic products
**Agricultural products:** Coffee, pineapples, sugar, bananas, corn, rice, beans, potatoes, beef
**Exports:** $5.1 billion

**Major export products:** Bananas, coffee, electronic components, pineapples, sugar, textiles, electricity
**Export partners:** U.S. 51%, Europe 23%, Central America 11%, Japan 2%
**Imports:** $6.4 billion
**Major import products:** Chemicals, consumer goods, electronic components, machinery, petroleum products, vehicles
**Import partners:** U.S. 56%, Europe 10%, Mexico 5%, Central America 5%, Japan 5%, Venezuela 4%

## Did You Know?

- Tourism earns more foreign exchange than bananas and coffee combined.

- Costa Rica did away with its military in 1949.

- Five percent of the world's plant and animal species are found in this country.

- Costa Rica is the home of five active volcanoes—including Volcán Arenal, the second-largest active volcano in the world.

# A BRIEF HISTORY

## First Encounters

In mid-September 1502, on his fourth and last voyage to the New World, Christopher Columbus was sailing along the Caribbean coast of Central America when his ships were caught in a violent tropical storm. He found sanctuary in a bay protected by a small island; ashore, he encountered native people wearing heavy gold disks who spoke of great amounts of gold in the area. Sailing farther south, Columbus encountered more natives wearing gold. He was convinced that he had discovered a land of great wealth. Some say this is why Columbus named the land Costa Rica, the "Rich Coast." Others believe the name referred to the lush greenery of the land itself.

## The Spanish Colonial Era

The first few attempts by the Spanish to conquer Costa Rica, beginning in 1506, were unsuccessful due to sickness and starvation among the Spanish troops, hearty resistance by the indigenous population, and rivalries between various expeditions. By 1560, almost 60 years after its discovery, no permanent Spanish settlement existed in Costa Rica, and the indigenous peoples had not been subdued. But explorer Juan Vásquez de Coronado—a "good Coronado" as Ticos are fond of saying, to distinguish him from other pillaging conquistadors named Coronado—founded the colonial capital of Cartago in 1563.

Costa Rica remained the smallest and poorest of Spain's Central American colonies, producing little wealth for the empire. Unlike other colonies around it, Costa Rica was largely ignored in terms of conquest. Costa Rican settlers and native peoples endured the difficult living conditions of an agriculture-based existence in exchange for Spain's lack of interest. The population stayed at fewer than 20,000 for centuries and was mainly confined to small, isolated farms in the highland Cen-

tral Valley and the Pacific lowlands. By the end of the 18th century, however, Costa Rica began to emerge from isolation. Some trade with neighboring Spanish colonies was carried out and the population began to expand across the Central Valley.

When Napoléon defeated and removed King Charles IV in 1808 and installed his brother Joseph on the Spanish throne, Costa Rica pledged support for the old regime, even sending troops to Nicaragua in 1811 to help suppress a rebellion against Spain. By 1821, though, sentiment favoring independence from Spain was prevalent throughout Central America, and a declaration of independence for all of Central America was issued by Guatemala on September 15 of that year. Costa Rica then became part of the Mexican empire until 1826, when it became part of the United Provinces of Central America. Costa Rica declared its independence as a sovereign nation in 1838.

The only major threat to that sovereignty took place in 1856, when the mercenary army of U.S. adventurer William Walker invaded the country from Nicaragua, which it had conquered the year before. Walker's plan to turn the Central American nations into slave states was cut short by Costa Rican president Juan Rafael Mora, who raised a volunteer army and repelled the invaders, pursuing them into Nicaragua and joining troops from various Central American nations to defeat the mercenaries. This conflict produced national hero Juan Santamaría, a young drummer boy from a poor family ( ⇨ CloseUp "A National Hero" *in* chapter 2).

## Foundations of Democracy

For the major part of the 19th century the country was ruled by a succession of wealthy families. Coffee was introduced to the country the 1820s and bananas in the 1870s, and these crops became the country's major sources of foreign exchange. The government spent profits from the coffee trade on improving roads and ports, and other projects that included San José's Teatro Nacional.

In 1889 the first free popular election was held, characterized by full freedom of the press, frank debates by rival candidates, an honest tabulation of the vote, and the first peaceful transition of power from a ruling group to the opposition. This provided the foundation of political stability that Costa Rica enjoys to this day.

Booming exports were cut short by the arrival of World War I, followed by the Great Depression and World War II. Poverty soared and a social revolution threatened in the late 1930s, as the popular Communist Party threatened strikes and violence. Costa Rica's version of the New Deal came in 1940, when conservative president Rafael Angel Calderón Guardia allied with the Catholic Church and implemented many of the Communist Party's demands, leading to a system of socialized medicine, minimum wage laws, low-cost housing, and worker-protection laws.

The success of Calderón's social reforms was tainted by accusations of corruption, which resulted in a civil uprising in 1948, led by the still-revered José "Don Pepe" Figueres Ferrer, who had been exiled by Calderón as the political leader of the opposition. After a few months of armed conflict, a compromise was reached—Figueres would respect Calderón's social guarantees and preside over an interim government for 18 months. In 1949 Figueres abolished Costa Rica's military and created a national police force, nationalized the banking system and public utilities, and implemented health and education reforms. He stepped down after 18 months, only to be reelected twice in free elections.

## The Modern Era

During the 1950s and 1960s, insurance, telecommunications, the railroad system (now defunct), ports, and other industries were nationalized. The state-led economic model, although increasingly inefficient, led to a rising standard of living until the early 1970s, when an economic crisis introduced Costa Ricans to hyperinflation. By the mid-1980s Costa Rica had begun pulling out of its economic slump, in part thanks to efforts to diversify the economy. By the mid-1990s, tourism had surpassed bananas as the country's largest earner of foreign exchange, and high-tech companies such as Intel and Motorola opened plants and service centers in Costa Rica, providing good-paying jobs for educated professionals.

Recent years have seen the continued growth of the tourism industry, and the establishment of a thriving but controversial Internet-based gambling industry tied to U.S. sporting events. The economy continues to bedevil Costa Rica: inflation hovers around 9% annually and the country's currency continues to be devalued on a regular basis. Attempts to privatize state-owned industries have been unsuccessful, and the process of negotiating a Central American free-trade agreement with the United States (and its mandated opening of state enterprises to competition) continues to generate heated debate.

Today the challenge facing Costa Rica is how to conserve its natural resources while still permitting modern development. The government has been unable or unwilling to control illegal logging, an industry that threatens to destroy the country's old-growth forests. Urban sprawl in the Central Valley and the development of megaresorts along the Pacific coast threaten forests, wildlife, and the slow pace of life that makes Costa Rica so enjoyable for visitors. Although tourism provides a much-needed injection of foreign exchange into the economy, the government has not fully decided which direction it should take. The buzzwords now are "ecotourism" and "sustainable development," and it is hoped that Costa Rica will find it possible to continue down these roads.

# BOOKS, MOVIES & TELEVISION

## Books

*Inside Costa Rica,* by Tom Barry and Silvia Lara (Interhemispheric Resource Center), is an in-depth factual rundown of the country. For an analysis of Costa Rican culture and society, read *The Ticos: Culture and Social Change in Costa Rica,* by Mavis Hiltunen Biesanz et al. (Lynne Rienner Publishers). David Rains Wallace's *The Quetzal and the Macaw: The Story of Costa Rica's National Parks* (Sierra Club Books) is an entertaining and informative account of Costa Rica's exemplary conservation efforts. *The Costa Rica Reader,* by Marc Edelman and Joanne Kenen (Grove Weidenfeld), is a critical anthology and comparison of traditional and progressive versions of the country's history.

Some of the most popular books on this country feature its rich natural history. *A Guide to the Birds of Costa Rica,* by F. Gary Stiles and the late Alexander F. Skutch (Cornell), is a first-rate field guide. Skutch also wrote some entertaining chronicles combining natural history, philosophy, and anecdotes, among them *A Naturalist in Costa Rica* (University Press of Florida).

The *Costa Rica: Eco-Traveller's Wildlife Guide,* by Les Beletsky (Academic Press), gives an overview of the most common fauna. For an in-depth look at local ecology, read *A Neotropical Companion,* by John Kricher (Princeton University Press); *Tropical Nature,* by Adrian Forsyth and Ken Miyata (Macmillan); or the encyclopedic *Costa Rican Natural History* (University of Chicago Press), compiled by tropical biology expert Daniel Janzen, Ph. D. *Field Guide to the Wildlife of Costa Rica,* by Carrol L. Henderson (University of Texas Press), offers an in-depth look at some 300 species of birds, mammals, reptiles, amphibians, butterflies, moths, and other invertebrates.

Costa Rica has a rich literary tradition, but few of its writers have been translated into English. Those who have can be hard to find in the United States. For insight on local culture, pick up *Costa Rica: A Traveler's Literary Companion,* edited by Barbara Ras (Consortium), a collection of translated short stories by the country's best writers. *Years Like Brief Days* (Dufour Editions) is one of the most popular novels of Fabián Dobles, famous for his humorous depiction of life in rural Costa Rica in the early 20th century. *The Lonely Men's Island* (Editorial Escritores Unidos, Mexico), the first novel of José León Sánchez, recounts the author's years on Isla San Lucas—the Costa Rican version of Alcatraz—where he was sent for stealing the statue of the country's patron saint, La Virgen de Los Angeles.

## Movies & Television

*Jurassic Park* (1993) was set on Costa Rica's isolated Cocos Island, but the film was actually shot in Hawaii. Oddly enough, much of the film version of *Congo* (1995), another Michael Crichton novel, was shot in Costa Rica. Most of Ridley Scott's *1492: Conquest of Paradise* (1992) was filmed on Costa Rica's Pacific coast. If you're more interested in the waves that break off that coast, check out the surf classic *The Endless Summer* (1966); both the original and remake have Costa Rica footage. An excellent documentary on underwater life in Costa Rica (as well as in the Galápagos and Australia) is *Wonders of the Deep* (1998; Madacy Entertainment).

Season two of the reality TV series *Temptation Island* was set in Costa Rica, not an island, of course. Cable TV loves Costa Rica: episodes of The Discovery Channel's *Mythbusters,* Animal Planet's *The Jeff Corwin Experience,* and E!'s *Wild On* have been shot here and cycle through their schedules as reruns.

# WILDLIFE & PLANT GLOSSARY

Here is a rundown of some of the most common and attention-grabbing mammals, birds, reptiles, amphibians, plants, and even a few insects that you might encounter. We give the common Costa Rican names, so you can understand the local lingo, followed by the latest scientific terms.

## Fauna

**Agouti** (*guatusa; Dasyprocta punctata*): A 20-inch tail-less rodent with small ears and a large muzzle, the agouti is reddish brown on the Pacific side, more of a tawny orange on the Caribbean slope. It sits on its haunches to eat large seeds and fruit.

**Anteater** (*oso hormiguero*): Three species of anteater inhabit Costa Rica—the giant (*Myrmecophaga tridactyla*), silky (*Cyclopes didactylus*), and collared, or vested (*Tamandua mexicana*). Only the last is commonly seen, and too often as roadkill. This medium-size anteater, 30 inches long with an 18-inch tail, laps up ants and termites with its long, sticky tongue and has long, sharp claws for ripping into insect nests.

**Armadillo** (*cusuco; Dasypus novemcinctus*): The nine-banded armadillo is widespread in Costa Rica and also found in the southern United States. This nocturnal and solitary edentate roots in soil with a long muzzle for a varied diet of insects, small animals, and plant material.

**Bat** (*murciélogo*): With more than 100 species, Costa Rica's bats can be found eating fruit, insects, fish, small vertebrates, nectar, and even blood, in the case of the infamous vampire bat (*vampiro, Desmodus rotundus*), which far prefers cattle blood to that of any tourist. As a group, bats are extremely important ecologically, and are essential to seed dispersal, pollination, and controlling insect populations.

**Butterfly** (*mariposa*): Estimates of the number of butterfly species in Costa Rica vary, but all range in the thousands. The growing number of butterfly gardens popping up around the country are testament to their popularity among visitors. Three Costa Rican Morpho species—spectacular, large butterflies—have a brilliant-blue upper wing surface. The blue morpho (*Morpho peleides*), arguably the most distinctive, is common in moister areas and has an intense ultraviolet upper surface; one is white above and below; and one is brown and white. Adults feed on rotting fallen fruit; they never visit flowers.

**Caiman** (*caiman*): The spectacled caiman (*Caiman crocodilus*) is a small crocodilian (to 7 feet) inhabiting fresh water, subsisting mainly on fish. Most active at night (it has bright-red eye shine), it basks by day. It is distinguished from the American crocodile by a sloping brow and smooth back scales.

**Coati** (*pizote; Nasua narica*): This is a long-nose relative of the raccoon, its long tail often held straight up. Lone males or groups of females with young are active during the day, on the ground, or in trees. Omnivorous coatis feed on fruit, invertebrates, and small vertebrates.

**Cougar** (*puma; Felis concolor*): Mountain lions are the largest unspotted cats (to 8 feet, including the tail) in Costa Rica. Widespread but rare, they live in essentially all-wild habitats and feed on vertebrates ranging from snakes to deer.

Crocodile (*lagarto*; *Crocodylus acutus*): The American crocodile, up to 16 feet in length, is found in most major river systems, particularly the Tempisque and Tárcoles. It seldom attacks humans, preferring fish and birds. It's distinguished from the caiman by a flat head, narrow snout, and spiky scales.

Ctenosaur (*garrobo*; *Ctenosaura similis*): Also known as the black, or spiny-tailed iguana, this is a large (up to 18 inches long with 18-inch tail) tan lizard with four dark bands on its body and a tail ringed with sharp, curved spines. Terrestrial and arboreal, it sleeps in burrows or tree hollows. It lives along the coast in the dry northwest and in wetter areas farther south. The fastest known reptile (clocked on land), the ctenosaur has been recorded moving at 21.7 mi per hour.

Dolphin (*delfín*): Several species, including bottlenose dolphins (*Tursiops truncatus*), frolic in Costa Rican waters. Often seen off Pacific shores are spotted dolphins (*Stenella attenuata*), which are small (up to 6 feet), with pale spots on the posterior half of the body; they often travel in groups of 20 or more and play around vessels and in bow wakes. Tucuxi dolphins (*Sotalia fluviatilis*) have also been spotted in small groups off the southern Caribbean coast, often with bottlenose dolphins.

Frigatebird (*tijereta del mar*; *Fregata magnificens*): A large, black soaring bird with slender wings and forked tail, this is one of the most effortless and agile flyers in the avian world. More common on the Pacific coast, it doesn't dive or swim but swoops to pluck its food, often from the mouths of other birds.

Frog and Toad (*rana*, frog; *sapo*, toad): Some 120 species of frog exist in Costa Rica; most are nocturnal, except for the strawberry poison dart frog (*Dendrobates pumilio*) and green-and-black poison dart frog. The bright coloration of these two species, either red with blue or green hind legs or charcoal black with fluorescent green markings, warns potential predators of their toxicity. The red-eyed leaf frog (*Agalychnis callidryas*) is among the showiest of nocturnal species. The large, brown marine toad (*Bufo marinus*), also called cane toad or giant toad, comes out at night.

Howler Monkey (*mono congo*; *Alouatta palliata*): These dark, chunky-bodied monkeys (to 22 inches long with 24-inch tail) with black faces travel in troops of up to 20. Lethargic mammals, they eat leaves, fruits, and flowers. The males' deep, resounding howls serve as communication among and between troops.

Hummingbird (*colibrí*): Weighing just a fraction of an ounce, hummingbirds are nonetheless some of the most notable residents of tropical forests. At least 50 varieties can be found in Costa Rica, visiting typically red, tubular flowers in their seemingly endless search for energy-rich nectar. Because of their assortment of iridescent colors and bizarre bills and tail shapes, watching them can be a spectator sport. Best bets are hummingbird feeders and anywhere with great numbers of flowers.

**Iguana** (*iguana*): Mostly arboreal but good at swimming, the iguana is Costa Rica's largest lizard: males can grow to 10 feet, including tail. Only young green iguanas (*Iguana iguana*) are bright green; adults are much duller, females dark grayish, and males olive (with orangish heads in breeding season). All have round cheek scales and smooth tails.

**Jacana** (*gallito de agua*; *Jacana spinosa*): These birds are sometimes called "lily trotters" because their long toes allow them to walk on floating vegetation. Feeding on aquatic organisms and plants, they're found in almost any body of water. They expose yellow wing feathers in flight. Sex roles are reversed; "liberated" females are larger and compete for mates (often more than one), whereas the males tend to the nest and care for the young.

**Jaguar** (*tigre*; *Panthera onca*): The largest New World feline (to 6 feet, with 2-foot tail), this top-of-the-line predator is exceedingly rare but lives in a wide variety of habitats, from dry forest to cloud forest. It's most common in the vast Amistad Biosphere Reserve, but it is almost never seen in the wild.

**Jesus Christ Lizard** (*gallego*): Flaps of skin on long toes enable this spectacular lizard to run across water. Costa Rica has three species of this lizard, which is more properly called the basilisk: lineated (*Basiliscus basiliscus*) on the Pacific side is brown with pale lateral stripes; in the Caribbean, emerald (*Basiliscus plumifrons*) is marked with turquoise and black on a green body; and striped (*Basiliscus vittatus*), also on the Caribbean side, resembling the lineated basilisk. Adult males grow to 3 feet (mostly tail), with crests on the head, back, and base of tail.

**Leaf-Cutter Ant** (*zompopas*; *Atta* spp.): Found in all lowland habitats, these are the most commonly noticed neotropical ants, and one of the country's most fascinating animal phenomena. Columns of ants carrying bits of leaves twice their size sometimes extend for several hundred yards from an underground nest to plants being harvested. The ants don't eat the leaves; their food is a fungus they cultivate on the leaves.

**Macaw** (*lapas*): Costa Rica's two species are the scarlet macaw (*Ara macao*), on the Pacific side (Osa Peninsula and Carara Biological Reserve), and the severely threatened great green macaw (*Ara ambigua*), on the Caribbean side. These are huge, raucous parrots with long tails; their immense bills are used to rip fruit apart to reach the seeds. They nest in hollow trees and are victimized by pet-trade poachers and deforestation.

**Magpie Jay** (*urraca*; *Calocitta formosa*): This southern relative of the blue jay, with a long tail and distinctive topknot (crest of forward-curved feathers), is found in the dry northwest. Bold and inquisitive, with amazingly varied vocalizations, these birds travel in noisy groups of four or more.

**Manatee** (*manatí*; *Trichechus manatus*): Although endangered throughout its range, the West Indian manatee can be spotted in Tortuguero, meandering along in shallow water, browsing on submerged vegetation. The moniker "sea cow" is apt, as they spend nearly all their time resting or feeding. Their large, somewhat amorphous bodies won't win any beauty contests, but they do appear quite graceful.

Margay (*caucel; Felis wiedii*): Fairly small, this spotted nocturnal cat (22 inches long, with 18-inch tail) is similar to the ocelot but has a longer tail and is far more arboreal: mobile ankle joints allow it to climb down trunks head first. It eats small vertebrates.

Motmot (*pájaro bobo*): These handsome birds of the understory have racket-shape tails. Nesting in burrows, they sit patiently while scanning for large insect prey or small vertebrates. Costa Rica has six species.

Ocelot (*manigordo; Felis pardalis*): Mostly terrestrial, this medium-size spotted cat (33 inches long, with 16-inch tail) is active night and day, and feeds on rodents and other vertebrates. Forepaws are rather large in relation to the body, hence the local name, which means "fat hand."

Opossum (*zorro pelón; Didelphis marsupialis*): Like the kangaroo, the common opossum belongs to that rare breed of mammals known as marsupials, distinguished by their brief gestation period and completion of development and nourishment following birth in the mother's pouch. The Costa Rican incarnation does not "play possum," and will bite if cornered rather than pretend to be dead.

Oropendola (*oropéndola; Psarocolius* spp.): This crow-size bird in the oriole family has a bright-yellow tail and nests in colonies, in pendulous nests (up to 6 feet long) built by females in isolated trees. Males make an unmistakable, loud, gurgling liquid call. The bird is far more numerous on the Caribbean side.

Parakeet and Parrot (*pericos,* parakeets; *loros,* parrots): There are 15 species in Costa Rica (plus two macaws), all clad in green, most with a splash of a primary color or two on the head or wings. They travel in boisterous flocks, prey on immature seeds, and nest in cavities.

Peccary: Piglike animals with thin legs and thick necks, peccaries travel in small groups (larger where the population is still numerous); root in soil for fruit, seeds, and small creatures; and have a strong musk odor. Costa Rica has two species: the collared peccary (*saíno, Tayassu tajacu*) and the white-lipped peccary (*chancho de monte, Tayassu pecari*). The latter is now nearly extinct.

Pelican (*pelícano*): Large size, a big bill, and a throat pouch make the brown pelican (*Pelecanus occidentalis*) unmistakable in coastal areas (it's far more abundant on the Pacific side). Pelicans often fly in V formations and dive for fish.

Quetzal One of the world's most exquisite birds, the resplendent quetzal (*Pharomachrus mocinno*) was revered by the Maya. Glittering green plumage and the male's long tail coverts draw thousands of people to highland cloud forests for sightings from February to April.

Roseate Spoonbill (*garza rosada; Ajaja ajaja*): Pink plumage and a spatulate bill set this wader apart from all other wetland birds; it feeds by swishing its bill back and forth in water while using its feet to stir up bottom-dwelling creatures. Spoonbills are most common around Palo Verde and Caño Negro.

Sloth (*perezoso*): Costa Rica is home to the brown-throated three-toed sloth (*Bradypus variegatus*) and Hoffmann's two-toed sloth (*Choloepus hoffmanni*). Both grow to 2 feet, but two-toed (check forelegs) sloths often look bigger because of longer fur and are the only species in the highlands. Sloths are herbivorous, accustomed to a low-energy diet, and well camouflaged.

Snake (*culebra*): Costa Rica's serpents can be found in trees, above and below ground, and even in the sea on the Pacific coast. Nearly all of the more than 125 species are harmless, but are best appreciated from a distance. Notable members of this group include Costa Rica's largest snake, the boa constrictor (*Boa constrictor*), reaching up to 15 feet, and the fer-de-lance (*terciopelo, Bothrops asper*) which is a much smaller (up to 6 feet) but far more dangerous viper.

Spider Monkey (*mono colorado, mono araña*): Lanky and long-tailed, the black-handed spider monkey (*Ateles geoffroyi*) is the largest monkey in Costa Rica (to 24 inches, with 32-inch tail). Moving in groups of two to four, they eat ripe fruit, leaves, and flowers. Incredible aerialists, they can swing effortlessly through branches using long arms and legs and prehensile tails. Caribbean and southern Pacific populations are dark reddish brown; northwesterners are blond.

Squirrel Monkey (*mono titi*): The smallest of four Costa Rican monkeys (11 inches, with 15-inch tail), the red-backed squirrel monkey (*Saimiri oerstedii*) has a distinctive facial pattern (black cap and muzzle, white mask) and gold-orange coloration on its back. It is the only Costa Rican monkey without a prehensile tail. The species travels in noisy, active groups of 20 or more, feeding on fruit and insects. Numbers of this endangered species have been estimated between 2,000 and 4,000 individuals. Almost all squirrel monkeys in Costa Rica are found in Manuel Antonio National Park or in parts of the Osa Peninsula.

Tapir (*danta; Tapirus bairdii*): The largest land mammal in Costa Rica (to 6½ feet), the tapir is something like a small rhinoceros without armor. Adapted to a wide range of habitats, it's nocturnal, seldom seen, but said to defecate and sometimes sleep in water. Tapirs are herbivorous and use their prehensile snouts to harvest vegetation. The best opportunities for viewing wild tapirs are in Corcovado National Park.

Toucan (*tucán, tucancillo*): This bird is familiar to anyone who's seen a box of Froot Loops® cereal. The aracaris is one, a slender toucan with the trademark bill. Keel-billed (*Ramphastos sulfuratus*) and chestnut-mandibled toucans (*Ramphastos swainsonii*) are the largest (18 inches and 22 inches); they are black with bright-yellow "bibs" and multihued bills. The smaller, stouter emerald toucanet (*Aulacorhynchus prasinus*) and yellow-eared toucanet (*Selenidera spectabilis*) are aptly named.

Three-Wattled Bellbird (*pájaro campana; Procnias tricarunculata*): Although endangered, the bellbird can be readily identified in cloud forests where it breeds (around Monteverde, for example) by its extraordinary call, a bold and aggressive "bonk," unlike any other creature in the forest. If you spot a male calling, look for the three pendulous wattles at the base of its beak.

Turtles (*tortuga*): Observing the nesting rituals of the five species of marine turtles here is one of those truly memorable Costa Rican experiences. Each species has its own nesting season and locale. The olive ridley (*lora; Lepidochelys olivacea*) is the smallest of the sea turtles (average carapace, or hardback shell, is 21–29 inches) and the least shy. Thousands engage in nighttime group nesting rituals on the North Pacific's Ostional. At the other extreme, but only slightly farther north on Playa Grande, nests the leatherback (*baula; Dermochelys coriacea*) with its five-foot-long shell. On the north Caribbean coast, Tortuguero hosts four of them: the leatherback, the hawksbill (*carey; Eretmochelys imbricata*), the loggerhead (*caguama; Caretta caretta*), and the green (*tortuga verde; Chelonia mydas*), with its long nesting season (June–October) that draws the most visitors and researchers.

Whales (*ballena*): Humpback whales (*Megaptera novaeanglia*) appear off the Pacific coast between November and February; they migrate from California and as far as Hawaii.

White-Faced Capuchin Monkey (*mono cara blanca; Cebus capuchinus*): Medium-size and omnivorous, this monkey (to 18 inches, with 20-inch tail) has black fur and a pink face surrounded by a whitish bib. Extremely active foragers, they move singly or in groups of up to 20, examining the environment closely and even coming to the ground. It's the most commonly seen monkey in Costa Rica.

White-Tailed Deer (*venado; Odocoileus virginianus*): Bambi would feel at home in Costa Rica, although his counterparts here are slightly smaller. As befits the name, these animals possess the distinctive white underside to their tail (and to their bellies). They are seen in drier parts of the country, especially in the northwest province of Guanacaste.

## Flora

Ant-acacia (*acacia; Acacia* spp.): If you'll be in the tropical dry forest of Guanacaste, learn to avoid this plant. As if its sharp thorns weren't enough, acacias exhibit an intense symbiosis with various ant species (*Pseudomyrmex* spp.) that will attack anything—herbivores, other plants, and unaware human visitors that come in contact with the tree. The ants and the acacias have an intriguing relationship, though, so do look, but don't touch.

Bromeliad (*piña silvestre*): Members of the family Bromeliaceae are *epiphytes,* living on the trunk and branches of trees. They are not parasitic, however, and so have adapted to acquire all the necessary water and nutrients from what falls into the central "tank" formed by the leaf structure. Amphibians and insects also use the water held in bromeliads to reproduce, forming small aquatic communities perched atop tree branches. In especially wet areas, small bromeliads can even be found on power lines.

Heliconia (*helicónia; Heliconia* spp.): It's hard to miss these stunning plants, many of which have huge inflorescences of red, orange, and yellow, and leaves very much the size and shape of a banana plant. With luck, you'll catch a visit by a hummingbird—truly a visual treat.

Mangroves (*manglares*): Taken together, this handful of salt-tolerant trees with tangled, above-ground roots make up their own distinct ecosystem. Buttressing the land against the sea, they serve as nurseries for countless species of fish and other marine animals and provide roosting habitat for marine birds. Mangroves are found on the coast in protected areas such as bays and estuaries.

Naked Indian Tree (*indio desnudo; Bursera simaruba*): This tree can be found in forests throughout Costa Rica, often forming living fences, and is instantly identifiable by its orange bark that continually sloughs off, giving rise to another common name, the tourist tree. One theory suggests that the shedding of its bark aids in removing parasites from the tree's exterior.

Orchid (*orquídea*): The huge Orchidaceae family has more than 1,200 representatives in Costa Rica alone, with nearly 90% percent living as epiphytes on other plants. The great diversity of the group belies not only examples of great beauty, but exquisite adaptations between flowers and their insect pollinators. With a combination of rewards (nectar) and trickery (visual and chemical cues), orchids exhibit myriad ways of enticing insects to cooperate.

Strangler Fig (*Matapalo; Ficus spp.*): Starting as seedlings high in the canopy, these aggressive plants grow both up toward the light, and down to the soil, slowly taking over the host tree. Eventually they encircle and "strangle" the host, killing it, leaving a ring of fig trunk around an empty interior. Figs with ripe fruit are excellent places for wildlife spotting, as they attract monkeys, birds, and an assortment of other creatures.

# MENU GUIDE

Rice and beans are the heart of Costa Rica's *comida típica* (typical food). It's possible to order everything from sushi to crepes in and around San José, but most Ticos have a simple diet built around rice, beans, and the myriad fruits and vegetables that flourish here. Costa Rican food isn't spicy, and many dishes are seasoned with the same five ingredients—onion, salt, garlic, cilantro, and red bell pepper.

| Spanish | English |
| --- | --- |

## General Dining

| Spanish | English |
| --- | --- |
| Almuerzo | Lunch |
| Bocas | Appetizers or snacks (literally "mouthfuls") served with drinks in the tradition of Spanish tapas. |
| Casado | Heaping plate of rice, beans, fried plantains, cabbage salad, tomatoes, *macarrones* (noodles), and fish, chicken, or meat—or any variation thereof; *casado* and *plato del día* are often used interchangeably |
| Cena | Dinner |
| Desayuno | Breakfast |
| Plato del día | Plate of the day |
| Soda | An inexpensive café; casados are always found at sodas |

## Especialidades (Specialties)

| Spanish | English |
| --- | --- |
| Arreglados | Sandwiches or meat and vegetable puff pastry |
| Arroz con mariscos | Fried rice with fish, shrimp, octopus, and clams, or whatever's fresh that day |
| Arroz con pollo | Chicken with rice |
| Camarones | Shrimp |
| Ceviche | Chilled seafood marinated in lime juice, served with chopped onion and garlic |
| Chilaquiles | Meat-stuffed tortillas |
| Chorreados | Corn pancakes, served with *natilla* (sour cream) |
| Corvina | Sea bass |
| Empanadas | Savory or sweet pastry turnover filled with fruit or meat and vegetables |
| Empanaditas | Small empanadas |
| Gallo pinto | Rice sautéed with black beans (literally, "spotted rooster"), often served for breakfast |
| Langosta | Lobster |
| Langostino | Prawns |

| | |
|---|---|
| Olla de carne | Soup of chayote squash, corn, yuca (a tuber), and potatoes |
| Palmitos | Hearts of palm, served in salads or as a side dish |
| Pescado ahumado | Smoked marlin |
| Picadillo | Water squash, potatoes, carrots, or other vegetables chopped into small cubes and combined with onions, garlic, and ground beef |
| Pozol | Corn soup |
| Salsa caribeño | A combination of tomatoes, onions, and spices that accompanies most fish dishes on the Caribbean coast |

## Postres (Desserts) & Dulces (Sweets)

| | |
|---|---|
| Cajeta de coco | Fudge made with coconut and orange peel |
| Cajeta | Molasses-flavored fudge |
| Dulce de leche | Thick syrup of boiled milk and sugar |
| Flan | Caramel-topped egg custard |
| Mazamorra | Cornstarch pudding |
| Melcochas | Candy made from raw sugar |
| Pan de maiz | Sweet corn bread |
| Tres leches cake | "Three milks" cake, made with condensed and evaporated milk and cream |

## Frutas (Fruits)

| | |
|---|---|
| Aguacate | Avocado |
| Anon | Sugar apple; sweet white flesh; resembles an artichoke with a thick rind |
| Banano | Banana |
| Bilimbi | Looks like a miniature cucumber crossed with a star fruit; ground into a savory relish |
| Fresa | Strawberry |
| Cas | A smaller guava |
| Granadilla | Passion fruit |
| Guanábana | Soursop; large, spiky yellow fruit with white flesh and a musky taste |
| Guayaba | Guava |
| Mamon chino | Rambutan; red spiky ball protecting a white fruit similar to a lychee |
| Marañone | Cashew fruit; used in juices |
| Melon | Canteloupe |
| Mora | Blackberry |
| Palmito | Heart of palm |

| | |
|---|---|
| Piña | Pineapple |
| Pipa | Green coconut; sold at roadside stands with ends chopped off and straws stuck inside |
| Sandia | Watermelon |
| Carambola | Star fruit |

## Bebidas (Beverages)

| | |
|---|---|
| Agua dulce | Hot water sweetened with raw sugarcane |
| Batido | Fruit shake made with milk (con leche) or water (con agua) |
| Café con leche | Coffee with hot milk |
| Café negro | Black coffee |
| Fresco natural | Fresh-squeezed juice |
| Guaro | Harsh, clear spirit distilled from fermented sugarcane |
| Horchata | Cinnamon-flavored rice drink |
| Refrescos | Tropical fruit smoothie with ice and sugar |

# VOCABULARY

| | English | Spanish | Pronunciation |
|---|---|---|---|
| **Basics** | | | |
| | Yes/no | Sí/no | see/no |
| | OK | De acuerdo | de a-**kwer**-doe |
| | Please | Por favor | pore fah-**vore** |
| | May I? | ¿Me permite? | may pair-**mee**-tay |
| | Thank you (very much) | (Muchas) gracias | (**moo**-chas) **grah**-see-as |
| | You're welcome | Con mucho gusto | con **moo**-cho **goose**-toe |
| | Excuse me | Con permiso | con pair-**mee**-so |
| | Pardon me | ¿Perdón? | pair-**dohn** |
| | Could you tell me? | ¿Podría decirme? | po-dree-ah deh-**seer**-meh |
| | I'm sorry | Disculpe | Dee-**skool**-peh |
| | Good morning! | ¡Buenos días! | **bway**-nohs **dee**-ahs |
| | Good afternoon! | ¡Buenas tardes! | **bway**-nahs **tar**-dess |
| | Good evening! | ¡Buenas noches! | **bway**-nahs **no**-chess |
| | Goodbye! | ¡Adiós!/¡Hasta luego! | ah-dee-**ohss**/**ah**-stah-**lwe**-go |
| | Mr./Mrs. | Señor/Señora | sen-**yor**/sen-**yohr**-ah |
| | Miss | Señorita | sen-yo-**ree**-tah |
| | Pleased to meet you | Mucho gusto | **moo**-cho **goose**-toe |
| | How are you? | ¿Cómo está usted? | **ko**-mo es-**tah** oo-**sted** |
| | Very well, thank you. | Muy bien, gracias. | **moo**-ee bee-**en**, **grah**-see-as |
| | And you? | ¿Y usted? | ee oos-**ted** |
| **Days of the Week** | | | |
| | Sunday | domingo | doe-**meen**-goh |
| | Monday | lunes | **loo**-ness |
| | Tuesday | martes | **mahr**-tess |
| | Wednesday | miércoles | me-**air**-koh-less |
| | Thursday | jueves | hoo-**ev**-ess |
| | Friday | viernes | vee-**air**-ness |
| | Saturday | sábado | **sah**-bah-doh |

## Months

| January | enero | eh-**neh**-roh |
|---------|-------|----------------|
| February | febrero | feh-**breh**-roh |
| March | marzo | **mahr**-soh |
| April | abril | ah-**breel** |
| May | mayo | **my**-oh |
| June | junio | **hoo**-nee-oh |
| July | julio | **hoo**-lee-yoh |
| August | agosto | ah-**ghost**-toh |
| September | septiembre | sep-tee-**em**-breh |
| October | octubre | oak-**too**-breh |
| November | noviembre | no-vee-**em**-breh |
| December | diciembre | dee-see-**em**-breh |

## Useful Phrases

| Do you speak English? | ¿Habla usted inglés? | **ah**-blah oos-**ted** in-**glehs** |
|------------------------|----------------------|--------------------------------------|
| I don't speak Spanish | No hablo español | no **ah**-bloh es-pahn-**yol** |
| I don't understand (you) | No entiendo | no en-tee-**en**-doh |
| I understand (you) | Entiendo | en-tee-**en**-doh |
| I don't know | No sé | no seh |
| I am American/ British | Soy americano (americana)/ inglés(a) | soy ah-meh-ree-**kah**-no (ah-meh-ree-**kah**-nah)/ in-**glehs** (**ah**) |
| What's your name? | ¿Cómo se llama usted? | koh-mo seh **yah**-mah oos-**ted** |
| My name is . . . | Me llamo . . . | may **yah**-moh |
| What time is it? | ¿Qué hora es? | keh **o**-rah es |
| It is one, two, three . . . o'clock. | Es la una. . . . Son las dos, tres | es la **oo**-nah/sohn lahs dohs, tress |
| How? | ¿Cómo? | **koh**-mo |
| When? | ¿Cuándo? | **kwahn**-doh |
| This/Next week | Esta semana/ la semana que entra | **es**-teh seh-**mah**-nah/lah seh-**mah**-nah keh **en**-trah |
| This/Next month | Este mes/el próximo mes | **es**-teh mehs/el **proke**-see-mo mehs |

| This/Next year | Este año/el año que viene | es-teh **ahn**-yo/el **ahn**-yo keh vee-**yen**-ay |
|---|---|---|
| Yesterday/today/ tomorrow | Ayer/hoy/mañana | ah-**yehr**/oy/mahn-**yah**-nah |
| This morning/ afternoon | Esta mañana/ tarde | es-tah mahn-**yah**-nah/**tar**-deh |
| Tonight | Esta noche | es-tah **no**-cheh |
| What? | ¿Qué? | keh |
| What is it? | ¿Qué es esto? | keh es **es**-toh |
| Why? | ¿Por qué? | pore **keh** |
| Who? | ¿Quién? | kee-**yen** |
| Where is . . . ? | ¿Dónde está . . . ? | **dohn**-deh es-**tah** |
| the bus stop? | la parada del autobus? | la pah-**rah**-dah del oh-toh-**boos** |
| the post office? | la oficina de correos? | la oh-fee-**see**-nah deh koh-**reh**-os |
| the museum? | el museo? | el moo-**seh**-oh |
| the hospital? | el hospital? | el ohss-pee-**tal** |
| the bathroom? | el baño? | el **bahn**-yoh |
| Here/there | Aquí/allá | ah-**key**/ah-**yah** |
| Open/closed | Abierto/cerrado | ah-bee-**er**-toh/ ser-**ah**-doh |
| Left/right | Izquierda/derecha | iss-key-**er**-dah/ dare-**eh**-chah |
| Straight ahead | Derecho | dare-**eh**-choh |
| Is it near/far? | ¿Está cerca/lejos? | es-**tah sehr**-kah/ **leh**-hoss |
| I'd like . . . | Quisiera . . . | kee-see-ehr-ah |
| a room | un cuarto/una habitación | oon **kwahr**-toh/ **oo**-nah ah-bee-tah-see-**on** |
| the key | la llave | lah **yah**-veh |
| a newspaper | un periódico | oon pehr-ee-**oh**-dee-koh |
| a stamp | la estampilla | lah es-stahm-**pee**-yah |
| I'd like to buy . . . | Quisiera comprar . . . | kee-see-**ehr**-ah kohm-**prahr** |
| a dictionary | un diccionario | oon deek-see-oh-**nah**-ree-oh |
| soap | jabón | hah-**bohn** |
| suntan lotion | loción bronceadora | loh-see-**ohn** brohn-seh-ah-**do**-rah |
| a map | un mapa | oon **mah**-pah |

| | | |
|---|---|---|
| a magazine | una revista | **oon**-ah reh-**veess**-tah |
| a postcard | una tarjeta postal | **oon**-ah tar-**het**-ah post-**ahl** |
| How much is it? | ¿Cuánto cuesta? | **kwahn**-toh **kwes**-tah |
| Telephone | Teléfono | tel-**ef**-oh-no |
| Help! | ¡Auxilio! ¡Ayuda! ¡Socorro! | owk-**see**-lee-oh/ ah-**yoo**-dah/ soh-**kohr**-roh |
| Fire! | ¡Incendio! | en-**sen**-dee-oo |
| Caution!/Look out! | ¡Cuidado! | kwee-**dah**-doh |

## Salud (Health)

| | | |
|---|---|---|
| I am ill | Estoy enfermo(a) | es-**toy** en-**fehr**-moh(mah) |
| Please call a doctor | Por favor llame a un médico | pohr fah-**vor ya**-meh ah oon **med**-ee-koh |
| acetaminophen | acetaminofen | a-say-ta-**mee**-no-fen |
| ambulance | ambulancia | ahm-boo-**lahn**-see-a |
| antibiotic | antibiótico | ahn-tee-bee-**oh**-tee-co |
| aspirin | aspirina | ah-spi-**ree**-na |
| capsule | cápsula | **cahp**-soo-la |
| clinic | clínica | **clee**-nee-ca |
| cold | resfriado | rays-free-**ah**-do |
| cough | tos | toess |
| diarrhea | diarrea | dee-ah-**ray**-a |
| fever | fiebre | fee-**ay**-bray |
| flu | Gripe | **gree**-pay |
| headache | dolor de cabeza | doh-**lor** day cah-**bay**-sa |
| hospital | hospital | oh-spee-**tahl** |
| medication | medicamento | meh-dee-cah-**men**-to |
| pain | dolor | doh-**lor** |
| pharmacy | farmacia | fahr-**mah**-see-a |
| physician | médico | **meh**-dee-co |
| prescription | receta | ray-**say**-ta |
| stomach ache | dolor de estómago | doh-**lor** day eh-**sto**-mah-go |

# INDEX

# LODGING DIRECTORY

## PHOTO CREDITS

**Cover Photo** (red-eyed tree frog): Turco. F8, *Michael Javorka/viestiphoto.com*. F9 (left), *Jenny K. Frost*. F9 (right), *Juan Amighetti/Costa Rica Tourist Board (ICT)*. F12, *Ken Ross/viestiphoto.com*. F13, *Ken Ross/ viestiphoto.com*. F14, *Philip Coblentz/Brand X Pictures*. F16, *Jenny K. Frost*. F17, *Ken Ross/viestiphoto.com*. F18 (left), *Ken Welsh/age fotostock*. F18 (right), *Jenny K. Frost*. **Chapter 1: San José:** 1, *Costa Rica Tourist Board (ICT)*. 2 (top), *Ken Ross/viestiphoto.com*. 2 (bottom left), *Ken Ross/viestiphoto.com*. 2 (bottom right), *José Fuste Raga/age fotostock*. 3, *CostaRicaPhotos.com*. 4, *Ken Ross/viestiphoto.com*. 5 (left), *Ken Ross/viestiphoto.com*. 5 (right), *Dan Peha/viestiphoto.com*. **Chapter 2: Central Valley:** 51, *Juan Amighetti/Costa Rica Tourist Board (ICT)*. 52 (top), *Ken Ross/viestiphoto.com*. 52 (bottom left), *Costa Rica Consulate*. 52 (bottom right), *Costa Rica Tourist Board (ICT)*. 53 (left), *G. Cozzi /age fotostock*. 53 (right), *Rios Tropicales*. 55 (top), *Rancho Naturalista*. 55 (bottom), *Dan Peha/viestiphoto.com*. 81 (top), *Ken Ross/viestiphoto.com*. 81 (bottom), *Philip Coblentz/Brand X Pictures*. 83, *Costa Rica Tourist Board (ICT)*. 84, *Kevin Schafer/age fotostock*. 85, *Ken Ross/viestiphoto.com*. **Chapter 3: The Northern Plains:** 95, *Ken Ross/viestiphoto.com*. 96 (top), *Ken Ross/viestiphoto.com*. 96 (bottom left), *Ken Ross/ viestiphoto.com*. 96 (bottom right), *Costa Rica Tourist Board (ICT)*. 97 (top), *Ken Ross/viestiphoto.com*. 97 (bottom left), *Ken Ross/viestiphoto.com*. 97 (bottom right), *Ken Ross/viestiphoto.com*. 98, *Ken Ross/viestiphoto.com*. 126 (top), *Ken Ross/viestiphoto.com*. 126 (bottom), *Sky Walk, Monteverde*. 127 (top), *Sky Walk, Monteverde*. 127 (bottom), *Jenny K. Frost*. 128, *Ken Ross/viestiphoto.com*. **Chapter 4: The North Pacific:** 155, *Costa Rica Tourist Board (ICT)*. 156 (top), *CostaRicaPhotos.com*. 156 (bottom), *Juan Amighetti/Costa Rica Tourist Board (ICT)*. 157 (top), *Costa Rica Tourist Board (ICT)*. 157 (center), *Alvaro Leiva/age fotostock*. 157 (bottom), *Ken Ross/viestiphoto.com*. 159, *Ken Ross/ viestiphoto.com*. 175 (top), *Ken Ross/viestiphoto.com*. 175 (bottom), *Joe Viesti/viestiphoto.com*. 176 (top), *Ken Ross/viestiphoto.com*. 176 (bottom), *Ken Ross/viestiphoto.com*. 177 (top), *©age fotostock*. 177 (center), *Hotel Luna Azul*. 177 (bottom), *Punta Islita Ocean Resort*. 178 (top), *Ken Ross/viestiphoto.com*. 178 (bottom), *Ken Ross/viestiphoto.com*. **Chapter 5: The Central Pacific:** 241, *Scott West/viestiphoto.com*. 242 (top), *CostaRicaPhotos.com*. 242 (bottom), *Ken Ross/viestiphoto.com*. 243 (top), *Juan Amighetti/Costa Rica Tourist Board (ICT)*. 243 (center), *Ken Ross/viestiphoto.com*. 243 (bottom), *Jenny K. Frost*. 245, *Ken Ross/viestiphoto.com*. 293, *Philip Coblentz/Brand X Pictures*. 294, *Alvaro Leiva/age fotostock*. 295, *SuperStock/age fotostock*. 296, *Alison Skrabek*. 297, *Ken Ross/viestiphoto.com*. **Chapter 6: South Pacific:** 311, *Ken Ross/viestiphoto.com*. 312 (top), *Ken Ross/viestiphoto.com*. 312 (bottom left), *Ken Ross/ viestiphoto.com*. 312 (bottom right), *Ken Ross/viestiphoto.com*. 313 (top), *Costa Rica Tourist Board (ICT)*. 313 (bottom), *Ken Ross/viestiphoto.com*. 314, *Ken Ross/viestiphoto.com*. 315 (top), *Costa Rica Consulate*. 315 (bottom), *Ken Ross/viestiphoto.com*. 367, *Ken Ross/viestiphoto.com*. 369 (first row left), *Ken Ross/ viestiphoto.com*. 369 (first row center), *Philip Coblentz/Brand X Pictures*. 369 (first row right), *SuperStock/age fotostock*. 369 (second row left), *Robert Winslow/viestiphoto.com*. 368 (second row center), *Bill Terry/viestiphoto.com*. 368 (second row right), *Bill Terry/viestiphoto.com*. 368 (third row left), *Ken Ross/viestiphoto.com*. 368 (third row center), *Mary Clay/viestiphoto.com*. 368 (third row right), *Bill Terry/viestiphoto.com*. 368 (fourth row left), *Eric Horan/age fotostock*. 368 (fourth row center), *Kevin Schafer/age fotostock*. 368 (fourth row right), *Morales/age fotostock*. 368 (bottom), *Kevin Schafer/age fotostock*. **Chapter 7: The Caribbean Coast:** 379, *Alfredo Maiquez/age fotostock*. 380 (top), *Costa Rica Tourist Board (ICT)*. 380 (bottom left), *Ken Ross/viestiphoto.com*. 380 (bottom right), *Alison Skrabek*. 381 (top), *Costa Rica Tourist Board (ICT)*. 381 (bottom), *Costa Rica Tourist Board (ICT)*. 382, *Ken Ross/viestiphoto.com*. 383, *Robert Winslow/viestiphoto.com*. 394, *Joe Viesti/viestiphoto.com*. 395, *Ken Ross/viestiphoto.com*. 396 (top), *Ken Ross/viestiphoto.com*. 396 (bottom), *Caribbean Conservation Corporation*.

# FODOR'S KEY TO THE GUIDES

AMERICA'S **GUIDEBOOK LEADER** PUBLISHES GUIDES FOR **EVERY KIND OF TRAVELER**. CHECK OUT OUR MANY SERIES AND FIND YOUR **PERFECT MATCH**.

### FODOR'S GOLD GUIDES
America's favorite travel-guide series offers the most detailed insider reviews of hotels, restaurants, and attractions in all price ranges, plus great background information, smart tips, and useful maps.

### COMPASS AMERICAN GUIDES
Stunning guides from top local writers and photographers, with gorgeous photos, literary excerpts, and colorful anecdotes. A must-have for culture mavens, history buffs, and new residents.

### FODOR'S 25 BEST / CITYPACKS
Concise city coverage in a guide plus a foldout map. The right choice for urban travelers who want everything under one cover.

### FODOR'S AROUND THE CITY WITH KIDS
Up to 68 great ideas for family days, recommended by resident parents. Perfect for exploring in your own backyard or on the road.

### SEE IT GUIDES
Illustrated guidebooks that include the practical information travelers need, in gorgeous full color. Perfect for travelers who want the best value packed in a fresh, easy-to-use, colorful layout.

### FODOR'S FLASHMAPS
Every resident's map guide, with 60 easy-to-follow maps of public transit, parks, museums, zip codes, and more.

### FODOR'S LANGUAGES FOR TRAVELERS
Practice the local language before you hit the road. Available in phrase books, cassette sets, and CD sets.

### THE COLLECTED TRAVELER
These collections of the best published essays and articles on various European destinations will give you a feel for the culture, cuisine, and way of life.

---

At bookstores everywhere.                     www.fodors.com/books

# ABOUT OUR WRITERS

Yolanda Hernandez, our Central Pacific writer, arrived in Costa Rica in 2002 to write for a non-profit housing organization. Based in the San José area, she's now a freelance writer, editor, and translator, and a theater student. She travels throughout Latin America and the Caribbean.

Seasoned traveler and journalist Dorothy MacKinnon arrived in Costa Rica in 1999, promptly fell in love with the country, and took up a post in San José to contribute stories to *The Tico Times* on ecotourism—and to write the North Pacific and South Pacific chapters of this guide. Along the way, she has learned Spanish and become a passionate birder and enthusiastic nature lover. In her past life, she was a newspaper editor for *The Washington Post*.

Joy Rothke is a freelance journalist who lived in the northern lowlands of Costa Rica for three years, where she learned to love birds and ignore insects. Joy has been published in many print and on-line newspapers and journals, including the *Chicago Tribune, San Francisco Chronicle, The New York Times* syndicate, *The Tico Times, Diablo* magazine, *San Francisco Focus* magazine (where she also served as an editor), Salon.com, Women.com, and MSN Sidewalk.com.

Biologist and naturalist Ryan Sarsfield travels extensively in Central and South America, but considers Costa Rica his first home away from home. He has studied insect dung in Guanacaste, Costa Rica; birds in Pohnpei, Micronesia; and rattlesnakes in Sonora, Mexico. He has also taught Spanish on a Japanese cruise ship and English in Brazil; and led tours in Brazil and Venezuela. Ryan revised the Central Valley chapter and wrote the wildlife glossary.

Suzanna Starcevic came to Costa Rica in 2000 on a whim, and is mildly surprised (but very pleased) to find herself still there. A journalist by trade, she has worked her way across Canada as a writer and editor, and spent three years as weekend editor at *The Tico Times*. She currently works as a translator and freelance writer. Suzanna revised the Smart Travel Tips A to Z chapter.

San José–based freelance writer and pharmacist Jeffrey Van Fleet has spent the last decade enjoying Costa Rica's long rainy seasons and Wisconsin's cold winters. (Most people would try to do it the other way around.) He saw his first resplendent quetzal, that bird-watcher's Holy Grail, while researching this guide. Jeff is a regular contributor to Costa Rica's English-language newspaper, *The Tico Times,* and has written for Fodor's guides to Chile, Argentina, Peru, and Central and South America. Jeff wrote the San José, Caribbean, and Welcome to Costa Rica chapters, and updated the Understanding Costa Rica chapter.